Krause · Jäger (Eds.)
High Performance Computing in Science and Engineering '98

Springer

Berlin
Heidelberg
New York
Barcelona
Hong Kong
London
Milan
Paris
Singapore
Tokyo

E. Krause   W. Jäger (Eds.)

High Performance Computing in Science and Engineering '98

Transactions of the High Performance Computing
Center Stuttgart (HLRS) 1998

With 234 Figures, 40 in Color

 Springer

Egon Krause
Aerodynamisches Institut der RWTH Aachen
Wuellnerstraße zw. 5 u. 7
52062 Aachen
Germany
e-mail: ek@aia.rwth-aachen.de

Willi Jäger
Interdisziplinäres Zentrum für Wissenschaftliches Rechnen
Universität Heidelberg
Im Neuenheimer Feld 368
69120 Heidelberg
Germany
e-mail: jaeger@iwr. uni-heidelberg.de

Front cover figure: "Flow in Axial Turbines" – Institute of Thermal Turbomachinery and Machinery Laboratory, University of Stuttgart

Library of Congress Cataloging-in-Publication Data applied for

Die Deutsche Bibliothek – CIP-Einheitsaufnahme

High performance computing in science and engineering: transactions of the High Performance Computing Center Stuttgart (HLRS) 1998 / E. Krause; W. Jäger (ed.). – Berlin; Heidelberg; New York; Barcelona; Hong Kong; London; Milan; Paris; Singapore; Tokyo; Springer, 1999
    ISBN 3-540-65030-X

Mathematics Subject Classification (1991): 65Cxx, 65C99, 68U20

ISBN 3-540-65030-X Springer-Verlag Berlin Heidelberg New York

Cover design: E. Kirchner, Heidelberg

Typeset by the Authors and Goldener Schnitt, Sinzheim

SPIN: 10678318   46/3143 – 5 4 3 2 1 0 – Printed on acid-free paper

Preface

Prof. Dr. Egon Krause
Aerodynamisches Institut, RWTH Aachen
Wüllnerstr. 5 u. 7, D-52062 Aachen

Prof. Dr. Willi Jäger
Interdisziplinäres Zentrum für Wissenschaftliches Rechnen
Universität Heidelberg
Im Neuenheimer Feld 368, D-69120 Heidelberg

Computers have caused a revolution in science and technology. The fascinating development of hard- and software is continuing at an amazing speed and is having an impact on culture and society. Latest research results combined with modern, high-power hard- and software make it possible to tackle and solve problems of a magnitude previously too formidable to deal with. Computational Sciences and Engineering using mathematical modeling, software technology and modern computer systems are growing areas of research with an important impact on scientific and technological progress. Scientists and engineers have become used to PCs and workstations as a daily tool of their investigations; networks of workstations and graphic systems are part of the basic equipment of every research institute. Despite the fact that in these localized systems the available potential is constantly increasing, there is an urgent demand for especially powerful computers to solve complex and challenging problems. These tools can only be provided through special centers and have to be shared globally. High-performance computing has to be considered a basic requirement for the future development. This needs a well-structured system of computer equipment ranging from small to very large scales and a network of competence in modeling, algorithms and software.
The High-Performance Computing Center (HLRS) in Stuttgart is an institution specialized in problems demanding the use of supercomputers. It was founded by the Land Baden-Württemberg in 1996 upon the recommendations of the Deutsche Forschungsgemeinschaft (German Research Association) and of the Wissenschaftsrat (German Science Council).
The aim of the Center is to provide the computer facilities necessary to solve crucial scientific and technological problems which can be addressed only with the help of most powerful hardware and efficient software. Scientists from universities and research institutions throughout the Federal Republic as well as research teams from industry have access to all facilities of the Center, in particular to the high-performance computers installed. This is an open-minded approach which is rather unique in the Federal Republic. The Center is the first of its kind, jointly operated by the Ministry for Science, Research, and Art of the Land Baden-Württemberg, and two local companies, "debis Systemhaus" and "Porsche AG". The Center is supervised by a scientific steering committee representing the Länder of the Federal Republic and the Land Baden

Württemberg. It is assisted by the competence center "WiR", a regional research network in Computational Science.

This volume contains the contributions to the First Workshop on High-Performance Computing in Science and Engineering, organized by HLRS in Stuttgart, June 22-24, 1998. After two years of operation of the Center, a first review was scheduled in order to obtain an overview of the work carried out and to get a first evaluation of the impact of the HRLS. At the same time, the workshop presented first hand information on the state of the art in High-Performance Computing and Computational Sciences and Engineering.

Altogether some 80 projects were computed on the massively-parallel system CRAY T3E/512 installed in the Center, and about 90 projects on the vector-parallel system NEC SX4/32.

The scientific projects on the massively-parallel system dealt with numerical simulations of problems in theoretical physics (45%), fluid mechanics (20%), chemistry (13%), solid-state physics (about 10%), and climate studies (about 9%). Further problems originated from bio-informatics, structural mechanics, electrical engineering, informatics, and combustion processes.

The vector-parallel system was used mainly for the simulation of problems in fluid mechanics (66%), solid-state physics (20%), chemistry (7%), theoretical physics (4%), prediction of flames (3%), and electrical engineering.

All projects were evaluated by external reviewers and by the members of the scientific steering committee representing the various disciplines. Only those projects were admitted which necessarily had to be implemented on a high-performance computer to make a solution possible. The papers contained in this volume are a selection of 37 contributions describing various solutions to problems in fluid mechanics, reactive flows, in engineering and computer sciences, theoretical physics, solid-state physics, and chemistry. The primary aim is to demonstrate the vast field of applicatio of high-performance computing in science and engineering ranging, for example, from numerical simulations of complex flow phenomena to modeling of earthquakes or the dynamics of amorphous silica.

The projects accepted had to justify the use of high-performance computers and to prove computing expertise. The resulting computation times were large in many instances. The Monte-Carlo Simulation of Hubbard Models, a problem in theoretical physics for example, needed over 20% of the available total capacity of the massively-parallel system, the simulation of earthquakes about the same percentage, and the simulation of the regional climate in Southern Germany more than 10%. Similar data were obtained for the vector-parallel machine. The three largest projects were characterized by relatively large usage of machine capacity: Over 35% of the available capacity were required for simulating turbulent flows, about 20% for simulating the transition from laminar to turbulent flows, and about the same amount for simulating high-temperature superconductors. The demand for computing on high-performance systems is still increasing, more projects are expected to be initiated. According to the reviewers of the various disciplines, the results obtained justify continuation of the work. Furthermore, it has become obvious that there should be stronger support by mathematics, computer sciences and informatics for the applied sciences.

More attention should be paid to the fact that sufficient high-performance computer capacity for future investigations has to be provided. Simulations of combustion processes or turbulent flows, climate models, electro-magnetic compatibility, molecular dynamics, and material sciences will require a substantial increase in high-performance computing power. With this first proceedings volume we gratefully acknowledge the far-sighted and continuous financial support by the Land Baden-Württemberg and the Deutsche Forschungsgemeinschaft necessary for establishing the Center in Stuttgart, and also for supporting the various projects during the past years. The recommendations of the Wissenschaftsrat were very much appreciated in particular when initiating the Center. We are grateful to Springer-Verlag for helping to inform a larger community about the activities in high-performance computing by publishing this volume.

Stuttgart, July 1998

W. Jäger   E. Krause

Contents

Physics

Prof. Dr. Hanns Ruder
Institut für Theoretische Astrophysik, Universität Tübingen
Auf der Morgenstelle 10, 72076 Tübingen

In particular in mathematics and natural sciences, the use of supercomputers has made possible the treatment of formerly completely intractable problems. It also provides the possibility of analyzing complex systems by the aid of simulation. This procedure is now becoming as important as theoretical investigations and closely interacts with the latter. A visionary formulation of the scientific potential arising from an optimal use of the supercomputers at the HLRS can be found in the "Report of the High Performance Computing and Networking (HPCN) Advisory Committee" already published in 1992:

More than a simple computational tool, HPCN is a new paradigm of investigation. Bringing closely together simulation (a simplified abstraction of reality) and modelling (a conceptual artifical representation of the real world) it offers the triple power of explanation, prediction and optimisation. HPCN can provide insight to exceptionally complex problems concerning physical, engineering, chemical and biological, economic and social systems in a manner analogous to the use of telescopes and microscopes to make new discoveries and inventions.

In almost all fields of physics, such as atomic and molecular physics, solid state physics, plasma physics, hydrodynamics, electrodynamics, quantum mechanics, quantum chromodynamics, high-energy physics, astro- and geophysics, fundamental new results were achieved by means of HPCN. During the past years, HPCN has been growing to an autonomous discipline for which the German designation "Wissenschaftliches Rechnen" has been adopted. This generally means supercomputer-aided numerical simulation of processes which are investigated in engineering, natural sciences and most recently economic and social sciences. In this context, numerical simulation is more and more becoming a pillar equivalent to the two classical pillars of gaining knowledge, namely the theoretical investigation and the experiment. Corresponding to the problems involved and the methods and tools used, "Wissenschaftliches Rechnen" has a strongly interdisciplinary character by integrating contributions from different fields of natural sciences, applied and numerical mathematics as well as informatics.

In the following, eight out of numerous projects in the field of physics currently running at the HLRS have been selected to illustrate with examples from electrodynamics, quantum mechanics, quantum chromodynamics, hydrodynamics, solid state and geophysics the scientific progress which can be achieved with the supercomputer resources of the HLRS.

Universal Fluctuations of Dirac Spectra [*]

M.E.Berbenni-Bitsch and S. Meyer

Fachbereich Physik - Theoretische Physik, Universität Kaiserslautern,
D-67663 Kaiserslautern, Germany

Abstract. A new link between Quantum Chromodynamics (QCD), the theory of strongly interacting elementary particles and mesoscopic systems in condensed matter physics is established through random matrix methods. Ensembles of complete eigenvalue spectra of the QCD Dirac operator are calculated for the first time for different lattice volumes ranging from lattice size 4^4 to 16^4. This amounts among other things to diagonalize sparse hermitean matrices of size 40 000 times 40 000 with very high precision for typical several thousand different matrices. The computation is only feasible on a massive paralell processing system like the CRAY T3E The remarkable agreement with the predictions of chiral random matrix models establishes the notion of universal fluctuations in systems with disorder and offers new insights into fundamental questions like spontaneous chiral symmetry breaking and the quark mass puzzle.

1 Introduction

Spontaneous chiral symmetry breaking is an important nonperturbative aspect of QCD responsible among many other things for the observed meson masses. As a consequence the character of the eigenvalue spectrum of the euclidean Dirac operator near zero follows from symmetries alone in the zero quark mass limit. By the Banks-Casher relation [1] and the Leutwyler-Smilga sum rule [2] for the quark density of states and its moments the eigenvalue spectrum is directly related to the quark condensate, which is the order parameter for chiral symmetry breaking. The chiral phase transition is therefore manifest in the critical behaviour of the quark density of states and is reminiscent to the Mott transition in a metal.

Chiral symmetry breaking has been studied in lattice QCD for more than two decades [3]. A serious difficulty ever since then is the finite euclidean box of the numerical simulation where strictly speaking spontaneously breakdown of a continuous symmetry cannot take place. To overcome this limitation of Lattice QCD and to unravel the structure of the spectral density of the Dirac operator near zero, chiral random matrix models have been used to model the spectrum of the massless Dirac operator in QCD [4]. An important assertion of this work is the universal behaviour of the spectral density very close to

---

[*] Based on the talk of the second author at the Workshop on High Performance Computing in Science and Engineering, University of Stuttgart, June 22-24, 1998. This work was supported by DFG under grant Me 567/5-3.

the origin with the startling consequence to obtain it for QCD from much simpler random matrix models.

2   The Dirac Operator Spectrum

At infinite volume the quark density of states is directly related to the quark condensate [1]. This can be seen as follows.

The spectral representation of the quark Green's function is given by

$$S(x,y) = \sum_n \frac{\phi_n(x)\phi_n^+(y)}{m - i\lambda_n}$$

where $\phi_n(x)$ and λ_n are eigenfunctions and eigenvalues of massless Euclidean Dirac operator in a background gauge field

$$i\slashed{D}\phi_n(x) = \lambda_n\phi_n(x).$$

Except for zero modes, the eigenvalues occur in pairs $\pm\lambda_n$. Integration of $S(x,y)$ gives

$$\frac{1}{V}\int dx S(x,x) = -\frac{2m}{V}\sum_{\lambda_n>0}\frac{1}{m^2 + \lambda_n^2}$$

where zero modes have been dropped. The level spectrum in the $V \to \infty$

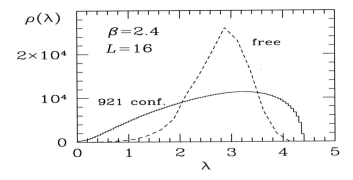

Fig. 1. Free Dirac spectral density (dashed curve) and spectral density with $\beta = 2.40$ (histogram) for $SU(2)$, quenched on a 16^4 lattice

limit becomes dense, one can introduce the average eigenvalue density

$$\rho(\lambda) = \langle \sum_n \delta(\lambda - \lambda_n) \rangle$$

and the average $<>$ is over gauge fields weighted with S_{QCD}. After proper renormalization the infrared part of the spectrum is related to the chiral order parameter

$$< \bar{\psi}\psi > = - \lim_{V \to \infty} \frac{\pi}{V}\rho(0)$$

where the limit $V \to \infty$ is taken before the chiral limit. It follows,that eigenvalues near zero are spaced as $\Delta\lambda \sim \frac{1}{V\rho(0)}$, whereas the non-interacting Dirac operator has spacing $\Delta\lambda \sim \frac{1}{V^{1/4}}$. An exampel for the free spectral density and the interacting spectral density is shown in Fig.1.

It was discovered in [2], that the analysis goes through also at finite volume,provided only that the quark mass m is not too small. The spontaneous formation of the chiral condensate occurs, if the quark mass m is large compared to the level spacing, e.g. $V m | < \bar{\psi}\psi > | \gg 1$. The spectral density close to zero is rescaled by introducing the microscopic spectral density

$$\rho_s(z) = \lim_{V \to \infty} \frac{1}{V\Sigma}\rho(\frac{z}{V\Sigma})$$

with $\Sigma = | < \bar{\psi}\psi > |$, $z = \lambda V \Sigma$, and the region around $\lambda = 0$ is magnified by a factor V .

3   Finite Volume Sum Rules

Different scales for the QCD partition function occur in a finite volume. When the box size L is much larger than the Compton wave length of the Goldstone particles $\sim 1/m_\phi \sim 1/\sqrt{m \cdot \Lambda_{QCD}}$, then Leutwyler and Smilga [2] have argued, that there is an intermediate range

$$\frac{1}{\Lambda_{QCD}} \ll L \ll \frac{1}{\sqrt{m\Lambda_{QCD}}}$$

where the mass dependence of the QCD partition function is given by the effective partition function

$$Z_{eff}(m,V) = \int_{U \in G/H} dU e^{Re\, V\Sigma tr\, MU e^{i\Theta/n_f}}$$

here $\Sigma = | < \bar{\phi}\phi > |$, M is the mass matrix, Θ is the vacuum angle. The Integration is over the Goldstone manifold, which is determined by the chiral symmetry breaking. Then the Leutwyler-Smilga sum rule follows from chiral symmetry breaking alone, it reads with quarks in the fundamental representation and with n_f flavours :

$$\frac{1}{V^2} \sum_{\lambda_n > 0} \langle \frac{1}{\lambda_n^2} \rangle = \frac{\Sigma^2}{4 n_f}$$

This sum rule is a nontrivial check of any lattice calculation, it has been tested for the first time recently [5]. For small eigenvalues $\lambda \sim \frac{1}{\Sigma \cdot V}$ much more detailed predictions from random matrix models have been obtained.

It has been shown by Shuryak and Verbaarshot [6], that chiral random matrix models can be related to the effective partition function. Chiral random matrix models have the global symmetries of the QCD Dirac operator, but otherwise independently Gaussian distributed random matrix elements,

$$Z = \int dT \prod_{f=1}^{n_F} \det \begin{pmatrix} im_f & T \\ T^+ & im_f \end{pmatrix} e^{-N\Sigma^2 tr(T^+ T)}$$

where T is a random NxN complex matrix, with N identified with the Volume V and Σ is the chiral condensate. Depending on the anti-unitary symmetries of the Dirac operator the matrix elements of T can be real, complex or real quaternions. For SU(2) with staggered fermions the matrix elements are real quaternions. The chiral random matrix model partition function has the following properties

- chiral symmetry is spontaneously broken
- the chiral order parameter satisfies the Banks-Casher relation

$$\Sigma = \frac{\partial}{\partial m_f} \log Z(m_f) = \lim_{N \to \infty} \frac{\pi \rho(0)}{N}$$

- the Leutwyler-Smilga sum rule, which follows from the chiral symmetry breaking holds:

$$\frac{1}{N^2} \sum_{\lambda_n > 0} \langle \frac{1}{\lambda_n^2} \rangle = \frac{\Sigma^2}{4 n_f}$$

4   Complete Spectra from the CRAY T3E

The computational demands of our study let us move to the massively parallel processing CRAY T3E with 512 nodes and a peak rate of 600 MFlops in 64 bit arithmetic per node. In our implementation the physical four-dimensional lattice is divided into non-overlapping sublattices of equal size, these are distributed among the different processors as shown in Fig. 2.

To calculate the product between Dirac operator and fermion fields

$$\not{D} \cdot \psi = \frac{1}{2} \sum_\mu \alpha_{i,\mu} \left(U_{i,\mu} \psi_{i+\mu} - U_{i-\mu,\mu}^\dagger \psi_{i-\mu} \right)$$

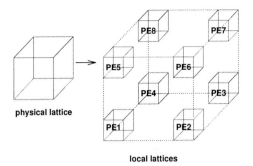

Fig. 2. Distribution of the physical lattice onto 8 processors in three dimensions.

one boundary layer of gauge and fermionic fields of all neighbouring sub-lattices must be copied into the local memory of each processor. To perform the communication among the CPUs CRAY supports basically three libraries: Parallel Virtual Machine (PVM), Message Passing Interface (MPI) and shmem-lib. Whereas PVM and MPI allow for writing portable code, the CRAY-specific shmem-lib delivers the highest throughput and shortest latency times. For this reason and because of the simple applicability of the shmem-lib, we decided to employ it for our implementation of the HMC QCD code.

The calculation of the spectrum of the Dirac operator $-D\!\!\!\!/^2$ is done in three steps: First, we tridiagonalize $-D\!\!\!\!/^2$ *locally* (i.e. on each processor) using the Lanczos procedure. Then we determine the eigenvalues of the tridiagonal matrix using the ScaLapack routine PSSTEBZ based on bisection, which distributes the work among the processors. As a last step, the spurious eigenvalues, which are caused by rounding errors are found using the method proposed by Cullum and Willoughby. This last step is done on a single processor.

We performed two sets of speed and scalability measurements of our code on a 16^4 lattice: one in the quenched approximation and one with dynamical fermions at $m = 0.05$. The former showed a communicational loss of about 6% using 256 PEs, whereas the second 12%, showing both a good scalability of the code (see Fig.3) The performance per processor is about 115 MFlops with dynamical fermions.

In a basis of eigenvectors which diagonalize $D\!\!\!\!/$ with eigenvalues $i\lambda_n$ the chiral condensate is given by

$$< \bar{\psi}\psi >= \frac{2m}{V/2} \sum_{n=1}^{V/2} \frac{1}{\lambda_n^2 + 4m^2}$$

As a consistency check for our spectrum calculation we compared the chiral condensate which results from (4) with that obtained with the stochastic

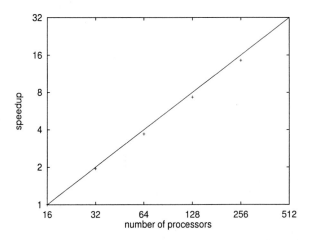

Fig. 3. Relative gain in real time using different numbers of processors on the T3E normalized over the time with 16 processors. The lattice volume is 16^4.

estimator. In Fig.(4) one can see the good agreement of the time evolutions of the both.

From the eigenvalue spectrum we obtain for the chiral condensate $< \bar{\psi}\psi >= 0.2557(2)$, while from the stochastic estimator $< \bar{\psi}\psi >= 0.2556(2)$. Our implementation demonstrates that the CRAY T3E is a very suitable system for calculations in lattice QCD.

5   Direct Comparison with Random Matrix Models

In the staggered fermion scheme with n_f flavours degree and gauge group SU(2) the gauge covariant Dirac operator is a NxN sparse antihermitian matrix and every eigenvalue of $i\not{D}$ is twofold degenerate due to a global charge conjugation symmetry. The squared Dirac operator $-\not{D}^2$ couples only even to even and odd to odd lattice sites, respectively. Thus, $-\not{D}^2$ has $V/2$ distinct eigenvalues.

We use the Cullum-Willoughby version of the Lanczos algorithm [7] to compute the complete eigenvalue spectrum of the sparse hermitian matrix $-\not{D}^2$ in order to avoid numerical uncertainties for the low-lying eigenvalues. There exists an analytical sum rule, $tr(-\not{D}^2) = 4V$, for the distinct eigenvalues of $-\not{D}^2$. We have checked that this sum rule is satisfied by our data, the largest relative deviation was $\sim 10^{-8}$.

The sum of the eigenvalues of $-\not{D}^2$ are given by $\frac{1}{4}tr(-\not{D}^2) = V$ for the hypercubic lattice volume V with periodic or antiperiodic boundary conditions and there are $\frac{V}{2}$ different eigenvalues [8].

We use a hybrid Monte Carlo algorithm to simulate the SU(2) Wilson gauge action coupled to $n_f = 4$ flavours of staggered fermions [9]. The cou-

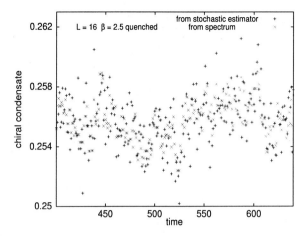

Fig. 4. Time evolution of the chiral condensate calculated by means of Eq. (4) and of that obtained with the stochastic estimator.

pling of the Wilson action $\beta = \frac{4}{g^2}$ has been varied from $\beta = 1.8$ to $\beta = 2.5$ in our quenched spectrum calculations.

The lattice parameters, the number of complete spectra and the statistical analysis of the lowest eigenvalue λ_{min} is summarized in Table 1. Also given are the integrated autocorrelation times τ_{int} of the lowest eigenvalue λ_{min}. Without these numbers any further statistical analysis of the eigenvalue spectrum would be very difficult.

– test of the Leutwyler-Smilga sum rule with $n_f = 0$ $\langle \sum_n \lambda_n^{-2} \rangle / V^2 = \langle \bar{\psi}\psi \rangle^2 / 2$

β	L	statistics	λ_{min}	τ_{int}
1.8	8	1999	0.00295(3)	0.69(7)
2.0	4	9979	0.0699(5)	1.3(1)
	6	4981	0.0127(1)	0.69(5)
	8	3896	0.00401(3)	0.71(6)
	10	1416	0.00164(2)	0.7(1)
2.2	6	5542	0.0293(3)	1.7(2)
	8	2979	0.0089(1)	1.2(2)
2.5	8	576	0.194(9)	8(3)
	16	543	0.016(2)	12(7)

Table 1. Lattice parameters and statistical analysis of the complete spectra of the Dirac operator.

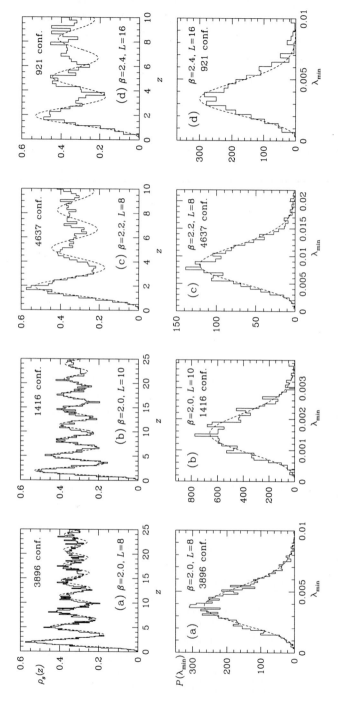

Fig. 5. Lattice data and RMT prediction : Finite size effects, $SU(2)$, quenched, $\beta = 2.0$, microscopic spectral density and smallest eigenvalue lattice sizes are 4^4, 6^4, 8^4 and 10^4

The data in the first column of Table 2 have an error from the statistical fluctuations of the eigenvalues, whereas the error in the prediction is the uncertainty of the zero mass extrapolation for the chiral condensate.

L	data	prediction	deviation
4	7.76(10)	6.40(21)	19.2%
6	8.61(61)	7.31(19)	16.3%
8	8.20(20)	7.54(31)	8.4%
10	7.97(30)	7.78(27)	2.4%

Table 2. Comparison of lattice data and analytical predictions for the Leutwyler-Smilga sum rule for λ_n^{-2}. The numbers are in units of 10^{-3}.

6   Conclusions

In summary, we have performed a high-statistics study of the eigenvalue spectrum of the lattice QCD Dirac operator with particular emphasis on the low-lying eigenvalues. In the absence of a formal proof, our results provide very strong and direct evidence for the universality of ρ_s. In the strong coupling domain, the agreement with analytical predictions from random matrix theory is very good. On the scale of the smallest eigenvalues, agreement is found

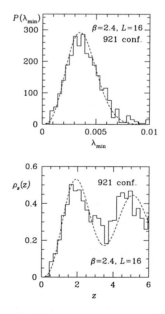

Fig. 6. Lattice data and RMT prediction : Lattice 16^4, $SU(2)$, quenched, $\beta = 2.4$ distribution of the smallest eigenvalue and microscopic spectral density

even in the weak-coupling regime. Furthermore, we found that the Leutwyler-Smilga sum rule for λ_n^{-2} is satisfied more accurately with increasing physical volume. We predict that corresponding lattice data for SU(2) with Wilson fermions and for SU(3) with staggered and Wilson fermions will be described by random matrix results for the GOE, chGUE, and GUE, respectively . (The $U_A(1)$ symmetry is absent for the Hermitean Wilson Dirac operator.) The identification of universal features in lattice data is both of conceptual interest and of practical use. In particular, the availability of analytical results allows for reliable extrapolations to the chiral and thermodynamic limits. In future work we hope to analyze the fate of the fermionic zero modes in the approach to the continuum limit, and we expect random-matrix results to be a useful tool in the analysis.

7   Acknowledgement

It is a pleasure to thank A.Schäfer, J.J.Verbaarschot and Tilo Wettig for their productive collaboration on this project. We would also like to thank T.Guhr and H.A.Weidenmüller for stimulating discussions. One of us (S.M) enjoyed the kind hospitallity of SCRI, Florida State University and of IWR , University of Heidelberg while the work described has been performed. It is a great pleasure to thank Tony Kennedy for discussions and comments. This work was supported in part by DFG . The numerical simulations were performed on a CRAY T3E at the HLRS, University of Stuttgart.

References

1. T. Banks and A. Casher, Nucl. Phys. **B169**, 103 (1980)
2. H. Leutwyler and A.V. Smilga, Phys. Rev. **D46**, 560 (1992)
3. for a recent update see e.g. LATTICE '96, Proceeding of the XIVth International Symposium on Lattice Fields Theory, Washington University, St. Louis, USA, 4-8 June, 1996, Nuclear Physics B (Proc. Suppl.) **53** (1997)
4. for a recent review see J.J.M. Verbaarschot, Random matrix model approach to chiral symmetry, Nucl. Phys. B (Proc. Suppl.) **53**, 88 (1997).
5. M.E.Berbenni-Bitsch, S. Meyer, A.Schäfer, J.J.M. Verbaarschot, and T. Wettig, Phys. Rev. Lett.**80**, 1146 (1998) .
6. E.V. Shuryak and J.J.M. Verbaarschot, Nucl. Phys. A **560**, 306 (1993).
7. J. Stoer and R. Bulirsch, *Introduction to Numerical Analysis*, Springer (New York) 1993, § 6.5.3.
8. T. Kalkreuter, Phys. Rev. D **51**, 1305 (1995).
9. S. Duane, A.D. Kennedy, B.J. Pendleton, and D. Roweth, Phys. Lett. B **195**, 216 (1987); S. Meyer and B. Pendleton, Phys. Lett. B **241**, 397 (1990).
10. M.E.Berbenni-Bitsch, A.D. Jackson, S. Meyer, A.Schäfer, J.J.M. Verbaarschot and T. Wettig, Nuclear Physics B (Proc. Suppl.) **63** , 820 (1998)
11. M.E.Berbenni-Bitsch and S. Meyer Nuclear Physics B (Proc. Suppl.) **63** , 814 (1998)

Computations of Convection Driven Spherical Dynamos

by E. Grote, F.H. Busse and A. Tilgner

Institute of Physics, University of Bayreuth, 95440 Bayreuth

1 Introduction

The geodynamo, i.e. the process by which the Earth's magnetic field is generated in the liquid outer core of the Earth, is generally regarded as one of the fundamental problems of geophysics. It is the prevailing opinion among geophysicists that thermal and chemical buoyancy originating in connection with the solidification of the inner core and the general cooling of the Earth cause convection flows in the outer core which consists of liquid iron together with some lighter elements. The mechanical energy of the convection flow provides the energy for the sustenance of the magnetic field against Ohmic losses. The mechanism by which this transfer of energy is accomplished is called a homogeneous dynamo in order to distinguish it from the common inhomogeneous dynamos used in technical applications.

The possibility of a dynamo operating in a singly connected domain of an electrically conducting fluid with an essentially homogeneous distribution of conductivity has been in doubt for a long time. In fact, Cowling [1] has proved in 1934 that axially symmetric magnetic fields can not be generated in this way. But later authors [2,3] have shown that the generation of non-axisymmetric fields is indeed possible by the homogeneous dynamo process.

A similar development has occured in the problem of thermal convection in rotating spherical fluid shells. Early attempts have tried to solve this problem on the basis of the assumption of axisymmetry [4]. But it became evident from the analysis of Roberts [5] that non-axisymmetric modes lead to lower critical values of the Rayleigh number for the onset of convection. The correct asymptotic solution of the linear problem describing convection in the form of azimuthally traveling convection rolls was derived by Busse [6]. Since then numerous papers on nonlinear convection in rotating spheres have appeared. For a review see [7].

The necessity of representing a time dependent three-dimensional velocity field together with an equally complex magnetic field has made the problem of the convection driven dynamo in rotating spherical fluid shells a formidable challenge for computational analysis. Early attempts to solve the full magnetohydrodynamic dynamo problem in rotating spherical shells were made in the eighties. Gilman and Miller [8] and Glatzmaier [9,10,11] developed computer codes and applied them to astrophysical problems. Zhang and Busse [12,13,14] used the bifurcation approach to follow dynamo solution branches departing from branches of non-magnetic convection. This approach has later been extended in [15,16]. With the rapid increase of computer capacity it has become feasible to approach parameters relevant for the Earth's core. In a series of papers Glatzmaier and Roberts [17,18,19] have demonstrated that chaotic dynamos exhibiting features similar to those of the geomagnetic field can be simulated on supercomputers. The use of hyper-diffusivities by Glatzmaier and Roberts and also by other more recent authors [20,21] has been criticized, however, because of its potential for changing the physics of the problem [22]. Moreover, the magnetic Prandtl number Pm which is defined as the ratio between viscous and magnetic diffusivities is still large compared to unity in the numerical simulations while it is assumed to be of the order of 10^{-6} in the Earth's core [23]. It thus appears that realistic planetary dynamos have not yet been reached in the numerical simulations.

In this article we first outline the numerical problem to be solved and then discuss the steps that have been taken in the computer development in order to achieve an efficient use of the resources provided by supercomputers. In a fourth section we discuss some recent, not yet published results for convection driven dynamos in rapidly rotating spherical shells. Further results can be seen in a soon to be published paper that is appended to this article.

2   Formulation of the Mathematical Problem

Since the density within the liquid iron core of the Earth does not change by more than 30% it is generally accepted that effects of compressibility can play only a minor role in the dynamics of the core and that the Boussinesq approximation of the equation of motion provides a good approximation. A solenoidal velocity field can thus be assumed and the dependence of density on pressure can be neglected. We shall assume the dependences on temperature T and the concentration S of light elements of the density ϱ in the form

$$\varrho = \varrho_0(1 - \alpha(T - T_0 + \hat{\Theta}) - \delta(S - S_0 + \Sigma)) \tag{1}$$

where T and S refer to the temperature and concentration distribution in the static solution of the problem which depends on the distance $\hat{r}$ from the center of the sphere only. In the heat equation for the deviation $\hat{\Theta}$ of temperature from the basic static solution of the problem only the difference between the actual temperature gradient and the adiabatic temperature gradient enters. The equations of motion for the velocity vector $\hat{u}$, the heat equation for $\hat{\Theta}$, the diffusion equation for the deviation Σ from the basic static solution S, and the equation of induction for the magnetic flux density $\hat{B}$ can thus be written in the form

$$\nabla \cdot \hat{u} = 0 \tag{2a}$$

$$\left(\frac{\partial}{\partial t} + \hat{u} \cdot \nabla\right)\hat{u} + 2\boldsymbol{\Omega} \times \hat{u} = -\nabla\pi - g(\gamma\Theta + \delta\Sigma) + \nu\nabla^2\hat{u} + \frac{1}{\varrho\mu}(\nabla \times \hat{B}) \times \hat{B} \tag{2b}$$

$$\left(\frac{\partial}{\partial t} + \hat{\boldsymbol{u}} \cdot \nabla\right) \hat{\Theta} = -\hat{\boldsymbol{u}} \cdot \nabla(T - T_{is}) + \kappa_\tau \nabla^2 \hat{\Theta} \tag{2c}$$

$$\left(\frac{\partial}{\partial t} + \hat{\boldsymbol{u}} \cdot \nabla\right) \Sigma = -\boldsymbol{u} \cdot \nabla S + \kappa_S \nabla^2 \Sigma \tag{2d}$$

$$\left(\frac{\partial}{\partial t} + \hat{\boldsymbol{u}} \cdot \nabla\right) \hat{\boldsymbol{B}} = \hat{\boldsymbol{B}} \cdot \nabla \hat{\boldsymbol{u}} + \lambda \nabla^2 \hat{\boldsymbol{B}} \tag{2e}$$

where the material properties such as the kinematic viscosity ν, the thermal diffusivity κ_τ, the diffusivity of light elements κ_S, and the magnetic diffusivity λ have been assumed as constants. Here λ is given by the inverse of the product of the electrical conductivity and the magnetic permeability μ.

Since the equations of motion are considered in the reference frame rotating with the mean rotation rate Ω of the core, the Coriolis force plays an important role in the equations of motion. But the centrifugal force has been neglected since it is regarded small in comparison with the gravity vector $\boldsymbol{g}$. The dependence of the latter on $\hat{r}$ will be assumed in the form

$$\boldsymbol{g} = -\gamma \hat{\boldsymbol{r}} \tag{3}$$

where $\hat{r}$ is the position vector with respect to the center of the sphere. For the difference $T - T_{is}$ between the temperature of the static solution and the corresponding adiabatic or isentropic temperature distribution T_{is} we shall assume for simplicity

$$T - T_{is} = -\beta \hat{r}^2 / 2. \tag{4}$$

It is convenient to introduce dimensionless variables through the use of the thickness d of the fluid shell as length scale, d^2/ν as time scale, $\beta d^2 \nu / \kappa_\tau$ as scale of the temperature and $\nu(\mu \varrho_0)^{\frac{1}{2}}/d$ as scale for the magnetic flux density. For the dimensionless variables we shall drop the symbol $\hat{\ }$. Because the physical role of $\hat{\Theta}$ and Σ is analogous if both, thermal and chemical buoyancy, drive convection motions, we shall drop the concentration Σ from further consideration and interprete Θ as representing both variables. Only when the two sources of buoyancy are counteracting each other, i.e. one exerts a stabilizing influence, must new physical effects be expected.

Since $\boldsymbol{u}$ and $\boldsymbol{B}$ are solenoidal vector fields the general representation in terms of poloidal and toroidal components can be used,

$$\boldsymbol{u} = \nabla \times (\nabla \times \boldsymbol{r}v) + \nabla \times \boldsymbol{r}w \tag{5a}$$

$$\boldsymbol{B} = \nabla \times (\nabla \times \boldsymbol{r}h) + \nabla \times \boldsymbol{r}g \tag{5b}$$

The equations for the scalar functions v and w are obtained through multiplication with $\boldsymbol{r}$ of the curl curl and of the curl of equation (2b)

$$[(\nabla^2 - \frac{\partial}{\partial t})L_2 + \tau \frac{\partial}{\partial \varphi}]\nabla^2 v + \tau Q w - R L_2 \Theta = -\boldsymbol{r} \cdot \nabla \times [\nabla \times (\boldsymbol{u} \cdot \nabla \boldsymbol{u} - \boldsymbol{B} \cdot \nabla \boldsymbol{B})] \tag{6a}$$

$$[(\nabla^2 - \frac{\partial}{\partial t})L_2 + \tau\frac{\partial}{\partial\varphi}]w - \tau Qv = \mathbf{r} \cdot \nabla \times (\mathbf{u} \cdot \nabla\mathbf{u} - \mathbf{B} \cdot \nabla\mathbf{B}) \qquad (6b)$$

The heat equation (2c) assumes the form

$$\nabla^2\Theta + L_2v = P(\frac{\partial}{\partial t} + \mathbf{u} \cdot \nabla)\Theta \qquad (6c)$$

Multiplication of the equation of induction and of its curl by $\mathbf{r}$ yields

$$\nabla^2 L_2h = Pm[\frac{\partial}{\partial t}L_2h - \mathbf{r} \cdot \nabla \times (\mathbf{u} \times \mathbf{B})] \qquad (6d)$$

$$\nabla^2 L_2g = Pm[\frac{\partial}{\partial t}L_2g - \mathbf{r} \cdot \nabla \times (\nabla \times (\mathbf{u} \times \mathbf{B}))] \qquad (6e)$$

In writing the above equation we have introduced a spherical system of co-ordinates r, θ, φ and have used the definitions

$$L_2 \equiv -r^2\nabla^2 + \frac{\partial}{\partial r}r^2\frac{\partial}{\partial r} \qquad (7a)$$

$$Q \equiv r\cos\theta\nabla^2 - (L_2 + r\frac{\partial}{\partial r})(\cos\theta\frac{\partial}{\partial r} - \frac{\sin\theta}{r}\frac{\partial}{\partial\theta}) \qquad (7b)$$

To avoid long expressions we have retained the vector notation for some terms on the right hand side of equation (2). The external conditions and material properties enter the equations through the Rayleigh number R, the rotation parameter τ, the Prandtl number P and its magnetic counterpart Pm which are defined by

$$R = \frac{\alpha\gamma\beta d^5}{\nu\kappa}, \quad \tau = \frac{2\Omega d^2}{\nu}, \quad P = \frac{\nu}{\kappa}, \quad Pm = \frac{\nu}{\lambda} \qquad (8)$$

where α is the thermal expansivity.

Assuming stress-free boundaries with fixed temperatures we obtain the conditions

$$v = \frac{\partial^2}{\partial r^2}v = \frac{\partial}{\partial r}\frac{w}{r} = \Theta = 0 \quad \text{at} \quad r = r_i \equiv \frac{\eta}{1-\eta} \quad \text{and at} \quad r = r_o \equiv \frac{1}{1-\eta} \qquad (9a)$$

where η is the radius ratio of the spherical boundaries. $\eta = 0.4$ will be assumed in this paper. For the magnetic field electrically insulating boundaries are used, i.e. the poloidal field h must be matched with potential fields h^e in the insulating regions,

$$g = h - h^e = \frac{\partial}{\partial r}(h - h^e) = 0 \quad \text{at} \quad r = r_i \quad \text{and at} \quad r = r_o \qquad (9b)$$

3   Numerical Methods and Implementation

For the numerical solution an expansion in spherical harmonics and in Chebychev polynomials is used. We use the magnetic variables h and g as examples. Θ, v, w are treated analogously

$$h(r, \theta, \varphi, t) = \sum_{l=1}^{\infty} \sum_{m=-l}^{l} \frac{1}{r} H_l^m(r, t) P_l^m(\cos \theta) e^{im\varphi} \tag{10a}$$

$$g(r, \theta, \varphi, t) = \sum_{l=1}^{\infty} \sum_{m=-l}^{l} \frac{1}{r} G_l^m(r, t) P_l^m(\cos \theta) e^{im\varphi} \tag{10b}$$

In actual computations the sums over l are truncated at some finite L. The boundary conditions (5b) require

$$G_l^m = \left(\frac{\partial}{\partial r} - \frac{l+1}{r_i} \right) H_l^m = 0 \quad \text{at} \quad r = r_i \tag{11a}$$

$$G_l^m = \left(\frac{\partial}{\partial r} + \frac{l}{r_0} \right) H_l^m = 0 \quad \text{at} \quad r = r_0 \tag{11b}$$

To complete the spatial discretization, H_l^m and G_l^m are decomposed into N Chebychev polynomials T_n:

$$G_l^m(r, t) = \sum_{n=0}^{N-1} g_{l,n}^m(t) T_n(x) \tag{12a}$$

$$H_l^m(r, t) = \sum_{n=0}^{N-1} h_{l,n}^m(t) T_n(x) \tag{12b}$$

where x is defined by $x \equiv 2(r - r_i) - 1$. In order to allow fast transforms, N collocation points are chosen to lie at $x_n = \cos(\pi \frac{n-1}{N-1})$, $n = 1, \ldots, N$. The dynamic equations are converted into a system of ODEs in time by enforcing the full equations at every collocation point. The decomposition into Chebychev polynomials is thus merely used to compute radial derivatives.

The temporal discretization is performed through the combination of a Crank-Nicolson step for the diffusion term with a second order Adams-Bashforth step for the nonlinear terms. At the beginning of each time step all fields and their first and second derivatives are given in r, l, m-space. At this stage the spectral coefficients of v, w, θ, g, h are stored such that coefficients with identical m are stored at the same processor. The computation of the nonlinear terms in spectral space would involve time consuming convolutions. In the "pseudo-spectral" method on the other hand, $\boldsymbol{u}$, $\boldsymbol{B}$ and Θ are computed in r, θ, φ-space where the nonlinear products can be rapidly evaluated.

The calculation of u and B requires adding associated Legendre functions and performing a Fourier transform (equations 5 and 10). The summation over l in (10) is implemented as matrix vector multiplications and obviously parallelizes over m. The summation over m is the Fourier transform which requires interprocessor communication. Before the actual FFT, data is redistributed such that individual processors contain all data with a given index l. The fast Fourier transform algorithm can then be executed locally and in parallel for separate l and r. The nonlinear terms are now easily obtained since they only involve multiplications of local data. The transformation back into r, l, m-space is performed with a FFT followed by a Gauss quadrature. These are technically the same operations as for the first transformation. At the end of the FFT the original data distribution is restored, i.e. all variables at a given m are collected in the storage of individual processors. The Gauss quadrature is again expressed as matrix vector multiplications which run independently on all processors for different m.

Once the nonlinear terms have been obtained, they can be combined as required by the Adams-Bashforth scheme and added to the terms of the implicit time step involving the variables at the present moment in time only. To complete the time step, a set of N linear equations needs to be solved for every l, m. Boundary conditions are also included in this set of equations. The coefficients in these equations are independent of m and are collected in separate matrices which are inverted during initialization and multiplied with vectors containing the spectral coefficients of v, w, θ, g, h during the actual time step. These multiplications separate again in m and involve only local data for each processor. The discretized equations are formulated such that the updated fields are obtained in n, l, m-space where the radial derivatives can be conveniently computed. A fast cosine transform brings the variables back into r, l, m-space ready for use in the next time step. For further details we refer to the analogous numerical treatment of the problem of nonmagnetic convection in [7].

N_p	2	4	8	16	32
t_p	9.5	10.4	11.1	12.5	20.9

Table 1: Total CPU time per time step t_p in seconds used by N_p processors for a resolution of 33 Chebychev polynomials and 64×65 real coefficients in the angular decomposition. Ideally, t_p is independent of N_p.

In summary, the computational burden lies mostly in matrix-vector multiplications, followed by fast cosine and Fourier transforms. The matrix vector multiplications carried out at each processor are of course readily vectorized. However, with the resolutions used so far, each vector is relatively short (64 elements). Only the FFT needs to shuffle data between processors. Interprocessor communication contributes little to the CPU time expenditure. Table 1 shows the accumulated CPU time per time step for a calculation running on different numbers of processors. The speed-up is limited by load balancing. For instance, the number of matrix vector multiplications to be performed is not always a multiple of the number of processors in use. However, the performance of the spectral method evidenced in table 1 compares well with speed-ups commonly achieved with grid methods, e.g. finite elements.

4   Some Recent Results

Most of the dynamo solutions that are obtained through the integration of equations (6) in time exhibit a chaotic time dependence. Although planetary dynamos are undoubtedly turbulent and considerable similarity between solutions of equations and observations can be found, a deeper understanding of the dynamical processes can best be obtained when stationary or time periodic dynamos are studied.

In figure 1 a typical stationary dynamo at the relatively high value of $\tau = 10^4$ is shown. The non-axisymmetric components of the fields are drifting with respect to the rotating frame of reference in the prograde azimuthal direction. The $m = 8$ mode is realized in both, the magnetic and the velocity fields. In addition an amplitude vacillation with the wavenumber $m = 2$ can be noticed which propagates in the retrograde direction. It should be noted that only even values of m have been admitted for the calculations to be reported in this section. It must be expected that vacillations with $m = 1$ will become predominant when all integer values m are taken into account. The amplitude of the vacillation amounts to about 10% for the velocity field but is somewhat higher in case of the magnetic field. The magnetic energy exceeds by a factor 2 the kinetic energy. In contrast to the latter the magnetic energy is dominated by the axisymmetric components of the poloidal as well as the toroidal fields.

As the magnetic Reynolds number is increased through an increase in the magnetic Prandtl number, the stationary dynamo of the form shown in figure 1 becomes unstable and is replaced by a chaotic dynamo. This transition is evident from the evolution in time of kinetic and magnetic energies shown in figure 2. In this figure we have used the property that the kinetic energy as well as the magnetic energy can be written as the sum of the poloidal energy depending only on the function v or h and the toroidal energy depending only on w or g in expressions (5). A further decomposition is possible into energies of the axisymmetric and of the non-axisymmetric components. In the initial stages of the transition the vacillation of the magnetic field increases strongly in amplitude and the contribution of the $m = 10$ mode becomes comparable to that of the $m = 8$ mode as shown in figure 3. At a later stage the dynamo has become chaotic. But the velocity still remains rather regular in the form of the familiar columns aligned with the axis of rotation, while the magnetic field has become rather irregular as shown in figure 4. At the same time the non-axisymmetric components of the magnetic field have increased while the

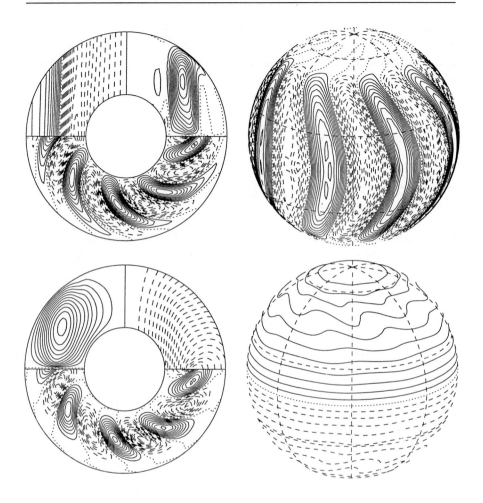

Fig. 1 Velocity field and magnetic field in the case $\tau = 10^4, R = 2.5 \cdot 10^5, P = 1, Pm = 40$. Solid (dashed) lines indicate positive (negative) values, the dotted line corresponds to zero. The upper left plot shows lines of constant $\overline{u}_\varphi$ in the upper left quarter and meridional streamlines in the upper right quarter, while in the lower half lines of constant $r\frac{\partial}{\partial\varphi}v$ are shown in the equatorial plane. The upper right plot shows lines of constant L_2v in the spherical surface $r = (r_i + r_0)/2$. The lower left plot shows lines of constant $\overline{B}_\varphi$ in the upper left quarter and meridional field lines in the upper right quarter, while in the lower half lines of constant $\frac{r}{\sin\vartheta}\frac{\partial}{\partial\varphi}h$ are shown on the conical surface $\theta = 70°$. (Since the magnetic field is nearly dipolar, only weak field lines exist in the equatorial plane.) The lower right plot shows lines of constant radial magnetic field, $L_2h = $ const., at the surface of the sphere.

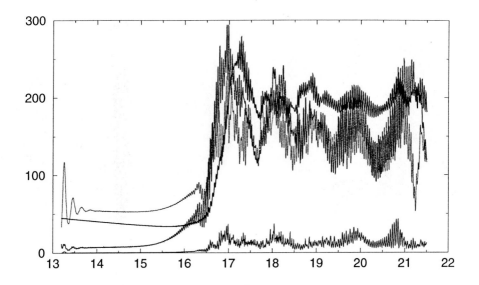

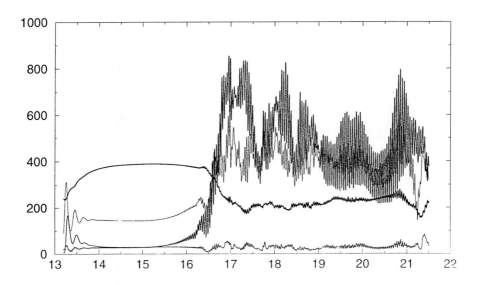

Fig. 2 Magnetic energies (thick lines) and kinetic energies of convection (thin lines) as a function of time in the case $P = 1, \tau = 10^4, R = 2.5 \cdot 10^5, Pm = 50$. Upper (lower) plot displays poloidal (toroidal) energies. Energies of axisymmetric components are indicated by solid lines while energies of non-axisymmetric components are given by dotted lines. The energy of the axisymmetric poloidal component of flow in the upper plot has been multiplied by the factor 10^3; the energy of the axisymmetric toroidal component of flow in the lower plot has been multiplied by 5.

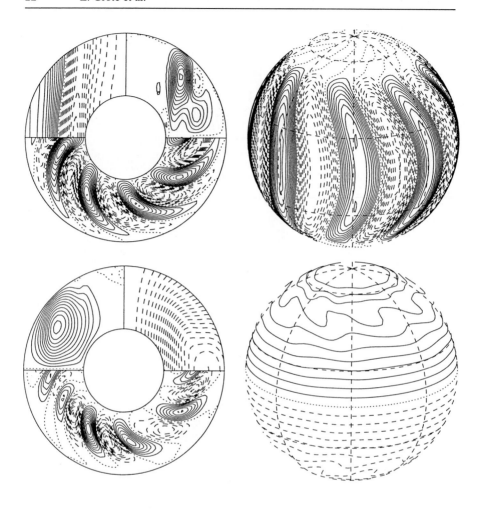

Fig. 3 Same as figure 1, but for the case of figure 2 plotted at the time $t = 15.9$.

previously dominating mean toroidal component of the magnetic field has decreased. We thus have found that two rather different types of dynamos can be realized with only small changes in the external parameters. It is even possible that both types of dynamos can be realized in a stable fashion for the same set of external parameters such that initial conditions will determine which dynamo is actually realized. But this problem will be the subject of future research.

Fig. 4 Same as figure 1, but for the case of figure 2, plotted at the time $t = 21.5$.

References

[1] Cowling, T.G., 1934: The magnetic field of sunspots, *Monthly Not. Roy. Astr. Soc.* **94**, 39-48

[2] Backus, G.E., 1958: A class of self sustaining dissipative spherical dynamos, *Ann. Phys.* **4**, 372-447

[3] Herzenberg, A., 1958: Geomagnetic dynamos, *Phil. Trans. Roy. Soc. London, Ser. A* **250**, 543-585

[4] Chandrasekhar, S., 1961: "Hydrodynamic and Hydromagnetic Stability", Oxford: Clarendon Press

[5] Roberts, P.H., 1968: On the thermal instability of a rotating-fluid sphere containing heat sources, *Phil. Trans. Roy. Soc. London A* **263**, 93-117

[6] Busse, F.H., 1970: Thermal instabilities in rapidly rotating systems, *J. Fluid Mech.* **44**, 441-460

[7] Tilgner, A., Ardes, M., and Busse, F.H., 1997: Convection in Rotating Spherical Fluid Shells, *Acta Astron. Geophys. Univ. Comeniae* **19**, 337-358

[8] Gilman, P.A., and Miller, J., 1981: Dynamically consistent nonlinear dynamos driven by convection in a rotating spherical shell, *Astrophys. J. Suppl* **46**, 211-237

[9] Glatzmaier, G.A., 1984: Numerical Simulations of Stellar Convective Dynamos. I. The Model and Method, *J. Comput. Phys.* **55**, 461-484

[10] Glatzmaier, G.A., 1985: Numerical Simulations of Stellar Convective Dynamos. II. Field propagation in the convection zone, *Astrophys. J.* **291**, 300-307

[11] Glatzmaier, G.A., 1985: Numerical Simulations of Stellar Convective Dynamos. III. At the base of the convection zone, *Geophys. Astrophys. Fluid Dyn.* **31**, 137-150

[12] Zhang, K.-K., and Busse, F.H., 1988: Finite amplitude convection and magnetic field generation in a rotating spherical shell, *Geophys. Astrophys. Fluid Dyn.* **44**, 33-53

[13] Zhang, K.-K., and Busse, F.H., 1989: Convection driven magnetohydrodynamic dynamos in rotating spherical shells, *Geophys. Astrophys. Fluid Dyn.* **49**, 97-116

[14] Zhang, K.-K., and Busse, F.H., 1990: Generation of Magnetic Fields by Convection in a Rotating Spherical Fluid Shell of Infinite Prandtl Number, *Phys. Earth Planet. Int.* **59**, 208-222

[15] Hirsching, W., and Busse, F.H., 1995: Stationary and chaotic dynamos in rotating spherical shells, *Phys. Earth Planet. Int.* **90**, 243-254

[16] Wicht, J., and Busse, F.H., 1997: Magnetohydrodynamic dynamos in rotating spherical shells, *Geophys. Astrophys. Fluid Dyn.* **86**, 103-129

[17] Glatzmaier, G.A., and Roberts, P.H., 1995a: A three-dimensional self-consistent computer simulation of a geomagnetic field reversal, *NATURE* **377**, 203-209

[18] Glatzmaier, G.A., and Roberts, P.H., 1995b: A three-dimensional convective dynamo solution with rotating and finitely conducting inner core and mantle, *Phys. Earth Plan. Int.* **91**, 63-75

[19] Glatzmaier, G.A., and Roberts, P.H., 1996: An anelastic evolutionary geodynamo simulation driven by compositional and thermal convection, *Physica D* **97**, 81-94

[20] Kuang, W., and Bloxham, J., 1997a: Numerical Modelling of Magneto-hydrodynamic Convection in a Rapidly Rotating Spherical Shell I: Weak and Strong Field Dynamo Action, *J. Comp. Phys.*

[21] Kuang, W., and Bloxham, J., 1997b: An Earth-like numerical dynamo model, *NATURE* **389**, 371-374

[22] Zhang, K., and Jones, C.A., 1997: The effect of hyperviscosity on geo-dynamo models, *Geophys. Res. Lett.* **24**, 2869-2872

[23] Braginsky, S.I., and Roberts, P.H., 1995: Equations Governing Convec-tion in the Earth's Core and the Geodynamo, *Geophys. Astrophys. Fluid Dyn.* **79**, 1-97

Dynamical Behavior of Persistent Spins in the Triangular Potts Model

A Large-Scale Monte Carlo Study

Michael Hennecke

Computing Center, University of Karlsruhe, D–76128 Karlsruhe, Germany*
Institute for Theoretical Physics, Cologne University, D–50923 Köln, Germany

Abstract. This article summarizes the results of a series of Monte Carlo simulations of persistent spins or "survivors" in the triangular Q-state Potts model. It is shown that the fraction $F(t)$ of survivors decays algebraically in time t, with nontrivial exponents θ depending on Q but not on temperature T. At zero temperature, asymptotic exponents θ have been calculated for the whole range of $Q = 3$ to ∞. In accordance with exact results in one dimension and early Monte Carlo studies in two dimensions, θ increases from 0.31 to unity as Q increases from 3 to ∞. For small Q, it has also been shown that θ approaches the same *universal* value for both zero and non-zero temperatures (below the critical temperature T_C).

1   Introduction

The Q-state Potts model[1] is a simple model of statistical physics in which each lattice site can take one of Q "colors," and an energy is associated with the boundary between two interacting sites if they have different colors. It has originally been proposed to study phase transitions in spin systems (with the case $Q = 2$ corresponding to the Ising model), but has also been utilized to model the coarsening processes of various cellular structures[2,3] including grain growth of polycrystalline films[4] and the evolution of thin films of soap froth[5–7].

At zero temperature, evolving a random initial configuration under a single spin-flip dynamics induces a coarsening process because the system tries to minimize its energy by aligning neighboring spins. At nonzero temperatures (below the critical temperature T_C), the behavior is similar except for the existence of thermal fluctuations which may increase the energy and roughen the interfaces between domains of different colors.

It is a well-established fact that in such systems, quantities like the average domain area $A(t)$ increase linearly with time. However, in recent years Derrida et al.[8–10] have observed non-trivial dynamical behavior of the fraction $F(t)$ of persistent spins in Ising and Potts models. At zero temperature, this quantity is simply the number of spins which have not flipped until time t. Exact results in one dimension[8,9] showed that $F(t)$ decays algebraically

---

* Permanent address. E-mail: `Hennecke@RZ.UNI-KARLSRUHE.DE`

with an exponent θ varying continuously between zero and one as Q increases from 1 to ∞. In two dimensions, early Monte Carlo simulations by Derrida et al.[10] confirmed the Q-dependence of the exponent θ. But results for high Q were inaccurate due to curvature in the log-log plots, and some of the simulations on a square lattice showed that the dynamics stopped due to the existence of blocking configurations.

Derrida[11] extended the concept of persistent spins to non-zero temperatures and proposed a way of measuring $F(t)$ by comparing an initially ordered system with an initially random system, both evolving under the same thermal noise. His simulations showed a weak temperature dependence of θ for both the Ising and $Q = 7$ Potts model. Simulations on a 256-processor Cray T3E by Stauffer[12] revealed that in the Ising case, this apparent temperature dependence was due to limited statistical accuracy and that θ asymptotically approaches the zero temperature result $\theta = 0.22$ for all $T < T_C$.

In this article, we present the results of three extensive Monte Carlo simulations[13–15] which have been performed on the University of Karlsruhe's IBM RS/6000 SP. This work addresses many of the open questions about the dynamics of persistent spins in the 2D Potts model, and allowed an accurate calculation of the exponents θ. Section 2 presents the main results of two simulation projects at zero temperature, and the extension of these simulations to nonzero temperatures is discussed in Sect. 3. A more detailed discussion of these results can be found in Ref. [13–15]. Section 4 points out some of the computational details of the simulations and the operational environment of the IBM RS/6000 SP.

2   The Zero Temperature Case

For $Q \geq d + 1$ where d is the dimensionality of the lattice, the Potts model exhibits vertices which may significantly influence the dynamics. Additionally, it is known that at $T = 0$ finite energy barriers cannot be overcome by a single spin-flip dynamics, and that microscopic "blocking" configurations may even completely stop the dynamical evolution of the system[16,17].

Therefore, the first series of simulations[13] concentrated on the choice of the lattice and the dynamics of the Monte Carlo method. After selecting the triangular lattice (which does not show blocking like the square lattice), a random selection of lattice sites during the simulation (instead of a loop over all lattice sites), and a mayority rule for the selection of a site's new color, extensive simulations for $Q = \infty$ have been performed. These simulations revealed that both $A(t)$ and $F(t)$ show significant deviations from algebraic behavior for a very large range of times and system sizes. Figure 1 shows the fraction $F(t)$ of persistent spins, where measurement of $F(t)$ has been started once at $t_0 = 0$ and once at $t_0 = 500$ MCS when macroscopically large domains have already been formed. The latter case corresponds to experiments on soap froth, in which measurements have to be done with macroscopic bubble sizes.

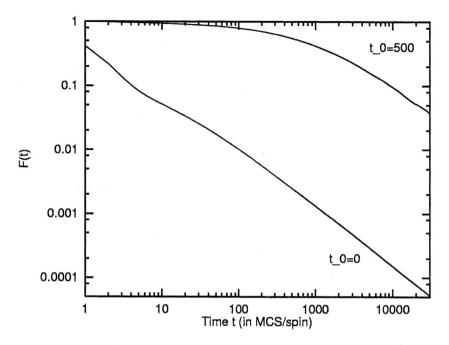

Fig. 1. Fraction of never flipped spins $F(t)$ as a function of time (in MCS/spin), for $t_0 = 0$ (bottom) and $t_0 = 500$ MCS (top). From Ref. [13].

It agrees qualitatively with Fig. 2 of Tam et al.[7]. However, for analyzing Monte Carlo simulations only the case $t_0 = 0$ is used.

By simulating 128 lattices of sizes 500×500 up to 4000×4000 in parallel, it could be confirmed that asymptotically both $A(t)$ and $F(t)$ change linearly with time for $Q = \infty$. For finite Q, figures 3 and 2 show the pronounced finite time effects and the resulting effective exponents for small times as a function of Q. These results have been obtained from a second series of simulations [14] with 128 lattices of size 2000×2000. They clearly demonstrate that deviations of the dynamics of the average domain area $A(t)$ from linear behavior are *only* a finite time effect and that the exponent α of algebraic growth is independent of Q. In contrast, $F(t)$ shows both finite time effects and a *real* Q-dependence of the asymptotic value of θ. Table 1 lists the resulting exponents.

Table 1. Asymptotic exponents θ as a function of Q. Error estimates are of the order of 0.01. From Ref. [14].

Q	3	4	5	7	9	12	24	64	128	256	∞
θ	0.31	0.37	0.41	0.47	0.51	0.56	0.65	0.75	0.81	0.85	0.99

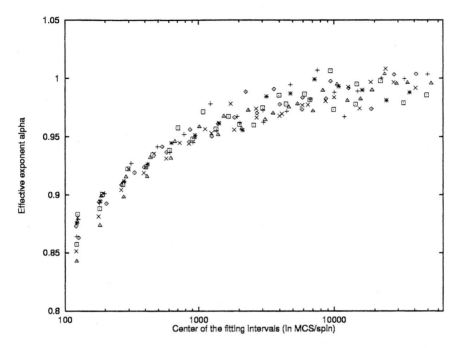

Fig. 2. Effective exponents α versus the center of the fitting intervals (in MCS/spin). $Q = 3, 4, 5, 7, 9, 12, 24, 64, 128, 256, \infty$, same symbols as in Fig. 3. From Ref. [14].

3   Dynamics in the Low-Temperature Phase

At nonzero temperatures, one cannot measure the fraction of persistent spins by the number of spins which never flipped until time t because in the presence of thermal fluctuations, this quantity decays exponentially fast. Derrida[11] has extended the concept of persistent spins to nonzero temperatures below T_C by comparing a system A where coarsening takes place when starting from a random initial configuration to a system B which starts with all spins having the same color 1.

When submitting both systems to the same thermal noise, it is possible to distinguish thermal fluctuations from motions of interfaces in the coarsening process, since the spin flips in system B can be attributed to thermal fluctuations. The fraction $r(t)$ of spins which stay in color 1 can then be determined by measuring the fraction of spins which have been identical in system A and B until time t. Derrida[11] observed a weak temperature dependence of the exponents θ for the Ising and 7-state Potts model but asked for more simulations to clarify this point. Stauffer[12] was able to show that for the two-dimensional Ising model the exponent θ is indeed independent of temperature.

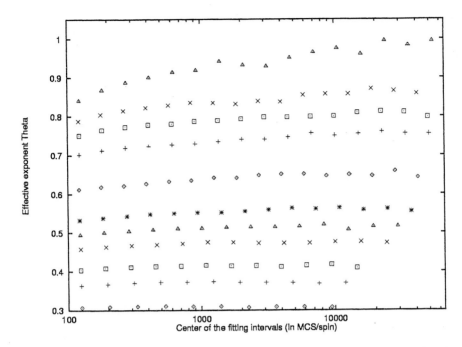

Fig. 3. Effective exponents θ versus the center of the fitting intervals (in MCS/spin). $Q = 3, 4, 5, 7, 9, 12, 24, 64, 128, 256, \infty$ from bottom to top. From Ref. [14].

Our third series of Monte Carlo simulations (project POTTS-T) addressed this question for the Potts model, by simulating 144 samples of size 1000×1000 for $Q = 3$ and 7. Initial simulations showed that the time series for $r(t)$ vary considerably from sample to sample, and effective exponents for θ showed very irregular behavior. Different lattice sizes, random number generators, and initial configurations have been employed to confirm that this behavior is not an artifact of the RNG or a finite size effect. Vizualization of checkpoints of the simulations and a separate measurement of $r(t)$ for all Q colors finally revealed that these effects are due to an asymmetry in the growth of domains of different colors. The fraction of some colors grows while others shrink, and the exponent θ depends on which behavior the color of system B exhibits for the sample run at hand.

Unfortunately, this unexpected result implied that a large amount of simulation results could not be fully utilized and the program has been extended to simulate not only two systems (system A and system B in color 1), but $Q + 1$ systems where system A was simultaneously compared with all Q different colors. This technique increased the required memory and computing time by a factor of two to four, but by measuring the corresponding Q different fractions $r_q(t)$, the total fraction $F(t)$ of persistent spins could then be

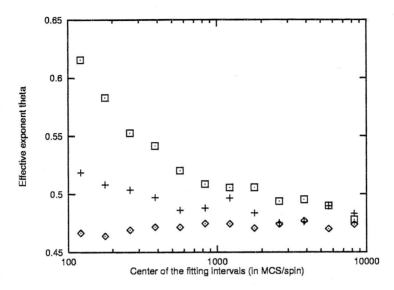

Fig. 4. Effective exponents θ for the $Q = 7$ Potts model at $T = \frac{1}{3}T_C$ (diamonds), $T = \frac{2}{3}T_C$ (crosses) and $T = \frac{5}{6}T_C$ (boxes). From Ref. [15].

calculated as

$$F(t) = \sum_{q=1}^{Q} r_q(t) \sim t^{-\theta}. \tag{1}$$

and behaved very regularly. Figure 4 shows the results for $Q = 7$. They confirm that the exponent θ is *universal* (independent of temperature) not only in the Ising model[12] but also in the Potts model.

4 Computational Details

The above simulations have been very time-consuming, and could only be completed by using large amounts of computing resources of the IBM RS/6000 SP at the University of Karlsruhe. Since the author is permanently working in the team which operates the SP, they have at the same time provided an extensive test bed for identifying and resolving various operational problems with the machine and so have been very useful in improving the overall availability and stability of the system after its upgrade to 256 nodes.

Since each of the nodes has been capable to hold even the $Q + 1$ lattices for the simulations described in Sect. 3 and a large number of independent samples is required to obtain sufficiently accurate statistics, almost all of the runs have been "trivially" parallelized by simulating independent runs in parallel. So nothing special can be reported about the parallelization of the code. The total resource consumption of projects conducted by the author on the Karlsruhe SP is summarized in Tab. 2.

Table 2. Approximate resource utilization on the Karlsruhe SP. Programs normally executed on 64, 128 and 144 nodes. Data for user **rz48** also includes various jobs from other projects, data for user **svg1** is exclusively for project POTTS-T.

Timeframe	account	jobs	CPU-hours
2Q1997	rz48	667	33.500
3Q1997	rz48	204	39.908
4Q1997	rz48	238	45.486
1Q1998	rz48	131	20.579
1Q1998	svg1	31	9.883

Each Monte Carlo step for the current study has been very expensive, this is mainly caused by

- the conservative approach of random site selection instead of a loop through the lattice;
- the use of a triangular lattice with 6 instead of 4 nearest neighbors for a square lattice;
- the more complex logic to implement the mayority rule on that lattice, and for general Q.

It has therefore been necessary to regularly write checkpointing information to disk in order to be able to simulate the long times required to reach the asymptotic regime. Since visual inspection of intermediate steps of the simulations has proven very useful, a Fortran 90 module has been developed[18] to write the lattice configuration as well as the information about persistent spins to disk in standard PPM and PBM graphics file formats. Each processor writes its own checkpointing information into a private directory, and a restart job reads the latest complete checkpoint as its starting configuration. Apart from this restart functionality, each checkpoint could be easily inspected visually by standard graphics packages like **xv** to get an impression about the current lattice configuration.

Since a compete checkpoint of a job simulating 128 lattices of size 2000 × 2000 requires more than 1.5GB of disk space and checkpoints were written every two hours, the simulations produced a significant amount of output. All these files have been written to the IBM Parallel I/O File System[19] PIOFS which provides global working filespace ($WORK) with a lifetime of at least 3 days to all SP users. This filesystem has been designed to provide high-bandwith I/O to parallel applications by distributing I/O requests not only to several disks (as in I/O disk striping) but by also distributing the load to several file server nodes to circumvent bottlenecks that arise when a single (NFS or DFS) file server is accessed in parallel by a large number of clients. Directory operations are still processed serially by one dedicated metadata server node. Two important problems with this file system have been discovered:

- It is very ineffective to redirect **stdout** output to a PIOFS file by standard shell redirection mechanisms. This is common practice in many applications, but causes enormous performance losses when many nodes write such redirected I/O to PIOFS. The reason is that while normal file I/O is buffered at each client node with buffer sizes of at least 64KB, redirected I/O is written line by line without buffering. PIOFS is designed to handle few large I/O requests and not a lot of very small ones, and so cannot handle this situation effectively.
- After several weeks of operation with frequent I/O errors and file system corruptions in PIOFS, an internal design problem in the PIOFS server software has been detected: The problem is that data I/O requests and control requests (like directory lookups) have been processed in one queue within in the PIOFS servers. This had the consequence that large data I/O requests caused timeouts for control requests (like directory operations) which were blocked behind the data request. Conversely, a large number of directory operation requests causes a huge number of tokens circulating among all the PIOFS servers, this in turn causes data I/O errors due to timeouts.

The PIOFS users have been educated by computing center staff that output data should always be written to an explicitly opened file rather than redirecting it to a file, and the second problem has been fixed by IBM by modifications of the internal PIOFS server token handling. Additionally, LVM mirroring of the PIOFS disks has been activated to protect against disk failiures which would cause a loss of the complete filesystem, and the original large PIOFS system with 16 servers has been split into two separate PIOFS systems with 8 servers each to reduce the overhead associated with too many PIOFS servers. After these actions in July 1997, the PIOFS file system is running very stable even with the very diverse job mixture which is characteristic for the Karlsruhe SP.

Acknowledgements

The author would like to thank D. Stauffer for proposing these projects and for stimulating discussions, and B. Derrida for helpful correspondence.

Computations have been performed on 64 to 144 nodes of the University of Karlsruhe's IBM RS/6000 SP parallel computer, often as part of system stress testing during or after hardware and software upgrades. The author would like to thank F. Bösert, K. Geers, H. Gernert, K. Gottschalk, C. Howar, R. Laifer, and W. Preuss for good cooperation and for their engagement in managing and running the SP.

Continuous support of the IBM POWERparallel Systems Laboratory, Poughkeepsie, has been very helpful in resolving some problems with the Parallel I/O File System and the LoadLeveler batch system.

References

1. F.Y. Wu. The Potts model. *Reviews of Modern Physics 54*, pages 235–268, 1982.
2. J. Stavans. The evolution of cellular structures. *Reports on Progress in Physics 56*, pages 733–789, 1993.
3. A.J. Bray. Theory of phase-ordering kinetics. *Advances in Physics 43*, pages 357–459, 1994.
4. M.P. Anderson, G.S. Grest, and D.J. Srolovitz. Computer simulation of normal grain growth in three dimensions. *Philosophical Magazine B 59*, pages 293–329, 1989.
5. J.A. Glazier, S.P. Gross, and J. Stavans. Dynamics of two-dimensional soap froth. *Physical Review A 36*, pages 306–312, 1987.
6. J.A. Glazier. Coarsening in the two-dimensional soap froth and the large-Q Potts model: a detailed comparison. *Philosophical Magazine 62*, pages 615–645, 1990.
7. W.Y. Tam, R. Zeitak, K.Y. Szeto, and J. Stavans. First-Passage Exponent in Two-Dimensional Soap Froth. *Physical Review Letters 78*, pages 1588–1591, 1997.
8. B. Derrida, A.J. Bray, and C. Godreche. Non-trivial exponents in the zero temperature dynamics of the 1D Ising and Potts models. *Journal of Physics A 27*, pages L357–L361, 1994.
9. B. Derrida, V. Hakim, and V. Pasquier. Exact First-Passage Exponents of 1D Domain Growth: Relation to a Reaction-Diffusion Model. *Physical Review Letters 75*, pages 751–754, 1995.
10. B. Derrida, P.M.C. de Oliveira, and D. Stauffer. Stable spins in the zero temperature spinodal decomposition of 2D Potts models. *Physica A 244*, pages 604–612, 1996.
11. B. Derrida. How to extract information from simulations of coarsening at finite temperatures. *Physical Review E 55*, pages 3705–3707, 1997.
12. D. Stauffer. Universality of Derrida coarsening in Ising models. *International Journal of Modern Physics C 8*, pages 361–364, 1997.
13. M. Hennecke. Survivors in the two-dimensional Potts model: Zero temperature dynamics for $Q = \infty$. *Physica A 246*, pages 519–528, 1997.
14. M. Hennecke. Survivors in the two-dimensional Potts model: Zero temperature dynamics for finite Q. *Physica A 252*, pages 173–178, 1998.
15. M. Hennecke. Universality of Derrida coarsening in the triangular Potts model. *International Journal of Modern Physics C 9*, pages 325–330, 1998.
16. P.S. Sahni, D.J. Srolovitz, G.S. Grest, M.P. Anderson, and S.A. Safran. Kinetics of ordering in two dimensions. II. Quenched systems. *Physical Review B 28*, pages 2705–2716, 1983.
17. E.A. Holm, J.A. Glazier, D.J. Srolovitz, and G.S. Grest. Effects of lattice anisotropy and temperature on domain growth in the two-dimensional Potts model. *Physical Review A 43*, pages 2662–2668, 1991.
18. M. Hennecke. portable_anymap - A Fortran 90 module to handle PBM, PGM and PPM files. In preparation.
19. *IBM AIX Parallel I/O File System: Installation, Administration, and Use*, August 1996. IBM Document SH34-6065-03.

Dynamical localization in the Paul trap — the influence of the internal structure of the atom

Karl Riedel, Päivi Törmä, Vladimir Savichev, and Wolfgang P. Schleich

Abteilung für Quantenphysik, Universität Ulm, 89069 Ulm, Germany

Abstract. We show that quantum localization occurs in the center-of-mass motion of a two-level ion stored in a Paul trap and interacting with a standing laser field. The variable showing localization is identified to be the vibrational quantum number of a reference Floquet oscillator. The quantum localization length is shown to oscillate as a function of the atom-field detuning with a period given by the secular frequency of the trap. Furthermore, we simulate the effect of spontaneous emission on the system and show that in the limit of far detuning the phenomenon of dynamical localization is not destroyed by decoherence.

1 Introduction

Dynamical localization is one of the most striking finger prints of quantum chaos [1,2]. It is related to Anderson localization [3] of electronic waves in one-dimensional disordered solids, where randomness of the lattice-site energies leads to classical diffusion. The quantum suppression of this diffusion is manifested in the localization of eigenstates. In systems capable of showing dynamical localization no real randomness is present; the dynamics is deterministic but chaotic due to the time periodicity and nonlinearity of the potential. Quantum localization is associated with the Floquet states of the system since there are no stationary eigenstates.

The periodically kicked rotator [1], described by the dimensionless Hamiltonian

$$H = \frac{p^2}{2} + \lambda \cos(\theta) \sum_n \delta(t - nT), \tag{1}$$

where T is the period of kicking, is the paradigm of dynamical localization. Delta-type kicks whose strength depends on the angle variable θ and on the control parameter λ cause classical diffusion in the action variable p. When the motion of the rotator is quantized one observes localization in the momentum p. Even when the motion of the rotator is quantized, the kicks are still 'classical'. In other systems closely related to the kicked rotator, such as atoms interacting with a phase-modulated standing wave [4] and the recently considered [5] problem of an ion stored in a Paul trap [6] and interacting with a standing wave, this means that the internal quantum structure of the atom has been adiabatically eliminated in the atom-light interaction. Now one can ask what happens when the kicks too have a quantum character. This is investigated in this paper by considering explicitely the internal stucture in the two-level approximation of the ion stored in a Paul trap and interacting with a laser field. We observe localization also in this case, but in addition to that another quantum effect is found: oscillations in the localization length as a function of the atom-laser detuning. These oscillations do not appear in the classical diffusion rate, unlike in the case of atoms in a phase modulated standing wave, where there is a correspondence between oscillations in the quantum and classical momentum distribution [7–9].

In our previous work [5] we already brought up the importance of the micro-motion in the Paul trap for the phenomenon of dynamical localization. For the qualitative description of the localization the reference frequency [10] of the time-dependent oscillator was essential. The reference frequency carries information about the micro-motion. Now we show that also the secular frequency, which describes the time-averaged motion in the trap, plays a role in localization: the oscillations in the localization length as a function of the detuning are determined by the secular frequency.

Dynamical localization has been experimentally observed only in two types of systems, namely in the suppression of ionization of Rydberg atoms in microwave fields [11] and the localization in the momentum distribution of an atom moving in a phase modulated standing wave [4]. We have proposed [5] that dynamical localization could be observed in the center-of-mass motion of an ion stored in a Paul trap. Nowadays ions in traps can be cooled down to the quantum regime, their dynamics can be controlled using laser fields and the quantum state can be reconstructed from the resonance fluorescence [12–14]. Dynamical localization is a coherence effect and thus its experimental verification requires the system not to be too sensitive to noise [9,15,16]. In this paper we have simulated the effect of spontaneous emission on the dynamical localization in the Paul trap, and show that indeed the drastic difference between the classical and quantum behaviour is preserved in the limit of far-detuning.

In section II we describe the system. In section III we consider the localization for finite detunings and discuss the oscillations found in the localization length. The effect of decoherence is considered in section IV, and the conclusions are drawn in section V.

2   The System

2.1   Hamiltonian

We consider the standard Paul trap set-up realized experimentally in many labs [12–14]: a standing electromagnetic wave of frequency ω_L and wave k aligned along the x-axis couples the internal states of a single two-level ion of mass m to the center-of-mass motion. The resulting dynamics of the ion follows from the time-dependent Schrödinger equation with the Hamiltonian

$$\hat{\tilde{H}} = \frac{\hat{\tilde{p}}^2}{2m} + \frac{1}{2}\frac{m\omega^2}{4}\left[a + 2q\cos\left(\omega\tilde{t}\right)\right]\hat{\tilde{x}}^2 + \frac{1}{2}\hbar\omega_0\hat{\sigma}_z$$
$$+ \hbar\tilde{\Omega}_0\hat{\sigma}_x\cos(k\hat{\tilde{x}} + \phi)\cos(\omega_L\tilde{t}). \tag{2}$$

Here the parameters a and q denote [6] the DC and AC voltages applied to the trap and the frequencies ω, ω_0 and $\tilde{\Omega}_0$ correspond to the frequency of the AC field, the atomic transition frequency and the Rabi-frequency, respectively, and ϕ is the phase of the standing wave. We describe the internal structure of the ion by the Pauli matrices $\hat{\sigma}_x$ and $\hat{\sigma}_z$.

In rotating wave approximation and dimensionless variables of position $\hat{x} \equiv k\hat{\tilde{x}}$, time $t \equiv \omega\tilde{t}/2$, momentum $\hat{p} \equiv \frac{2k}{m\omega}\hat{\tilde{p}}$, coupling $\Omega_0 \equiv \tilde{\Omega}_0/\omega$ and detuning $\Delta = (\omega_a - \omega_L)/\omega$ the dimensionless Hamiltonian reads

$$\hat{H} \equiv \frac{4k^2}{m\omega^2}\hat{\tilde{H}} = \frac{1}{2}\hat{p}^2 + \frac{1}{2}(a + 2q\cos 2t)\hat{x}^2 - k\Delta\hat{\sigma}_z + k\Omega_0\cos(\hat{x} + \phi)\hat{\sigma}_x. \tag{3}$$

The dynamics of the ion is described by the time–dependent Schrödinger equation

$$ik\frac{\partial}{\partial t}\begin{pmatrix}\psi_e(x,t)\\\psi_g(x,t)\end{pmatrix} = \hat{H}\begin{pmatrix}\psi_e(x,t)\\\psi_g(x,t)\end{pmatrix}. \tag{4}$$

The indices e and g refer to excited and ground states, respectively. Here the effective Planck constant $k = \frac{2k^2\hbar}{m\omega}$ follows from the commutation relation $[\hat{x}, \hat{p}] = \frac{2k^2}{m\omega}[\hat{\tilde{x}}, \hat{\tilde{p}}] = \frac{2k^2}{m\omega}i\hbar = ik$.

2.2   Density matrix and Bloch equations

The general description of the quantum systems interacting with the enviroment is given in terms of the density matrix:

$$\frac{d\hat{\rho}(t)}{dt} = \frac{1}{ik}[\hat{H}, \hat{\rho}(t)], \tag{5}$$

where $\hat{\rho}(t)$ is the density matrix operator and $\hat{H}$ is the Hamiltonian (3).

To get a "classical" analog of the fully quantum dynamics we have to consider time evolution of the averaged values. In our case, important physical characteristics are the center of mass position and momentum of the ion in the trap and evolution of the populations of the excited and ground states:

$$x(t) = \text{Tr}\hat{x}\hat{\rho}(t)$$
$$p(t) = \text{Tr}\hat{x}\hat{\rho}(t)$$
$$r_1(t) = \text{Tr}\hat{\sigma}_x\hat{\rho}(t) = 2\text{Re}\int dx\rho_{eg}(x, x)$$
$$r_2(t) = \text{Tr}\hat{\sigma}_y\hat{\rho}(t) = 2\text{Im}\int dx\rho_{eg}(x, x)$$
$$r_3(t) = \text{Tr}\hat{\sigma}_z\hat{\rho}(t) = \int dx\rho_{ee}(x, x) - \rho_{gg}(x, x).$$

Dynamical equations for the averaged values can be obtained using density matrix evolution equation, Heisenberg represenation for the operators $\hat{x}, \hat{p}$ and conventional commutation relations:

$$\dot{x}(t) = p(t)$$

$$\dot{p}(t) = -(a + 2q\cos(2t))x(t) + k\Omega_0 \int dx' \sin(x' + \phi) 2\mathrm{Re}\rho_{eg}(x', x')$$

$$\dot{r}_1(t) = -2\Delta r_2(t)$$

$$\dot{r}_2(t) = 2\Delta r_1(t) + 2\Omega_0 \int dx' \cos(x' + \phi)(\rho_{ee}(x', x') - \rho_{gg}(x', x'))$$

$$\dot{r}_3(t) = -2\Omega_0 \int dx' \cos(x' + \phi) 2\mathrm{Im}\rho_{eg}(x', x').$$

In the classical approximation we consider that quantum x -distribution is a very narrow one and localized near the averaged classical trajectory $x(t)$. Using this we can take smoothly changing potentials out of the integrals. Finally, we get the folowing set of the classical evolution equations:

$$\dot{x} = p \tag{6}$$

$$\dot{p} = -(a + 2q\cos(2t))x + k\Omega_0 \sin(x + \phi)r_1 \tag{7}$$

$$\dot{r}_1 = -2\Delta r_2 \tag{8}$$

$$\dot{r}_2 = 2\Delta r_1 + 2\Omega_0 \cos(x + \phi)r_3 \tag{9}$$

$$\dot{r}_3 = -2\Omega_0 \cos(x + \phi)r_2. \tag{10}$$

2.3   Diabatic and adiabatic potentials

The system has two limiting cases when the equations for the dynamics of the excited and ground states can be decoupled, namely when the detuning Δ is zero or very high compared to the coupling Ω_0 [17]. In the on-resonance situation the decoupled states are the so-called diabatic states

$$|v_\pm\rangle = \frac{1}{\sqrt{2}}(|e\rangle \pm |g\rangle), \tag{11}$$

and they are influenced by the potentials

$$V_\pm = \pm k\Omega_0 \cos(x + \phi). \tag{12}$$

The solutions of the problem for finite detuning are the adiabatic states, which in the limit of far detuning are just the ground and the excited states. The x-dependent part of the potentials which they see is

$$U_\pm \simeq U_{g/e} = \pm \frac{k\Omega_0^2 \cos^2(x + \phi)}{2\Delta}. \tag{13}$$

If we start with an equal superposition of the excited and ground states when $\Delta = 0$, we get formally the same potential affecting the center-of-mass motion as when the upper state is adiabatically eliminated, only the coupling Ω_0 and the scaling of x have to be chosen differently in both cases. This allows us to compare the results for $\Delta = 0$ to those presented in [5], where the adiabatic elimination was utilized.

2.4   Classical dynamics and Poincaré surface of section

Dynamical localization arises from the properties of the quantum evolution in the domain of classically chaotic dynamics. Choosing the maximum of the cosine potential to be located at the center of the trap potential, i.e. $\phi = 0$ the dynamics become chaotic. This is shown in Fig.1, where we plot the Poincaré surface of section describing the classical center-of-mass motion. This is an adequate description when the laser is chosen on resonance with or far detuned

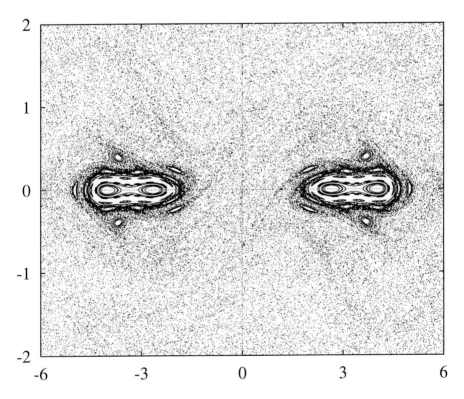

Fig. 1. Poincaré surface of section for an ion moving under the influence of a time-dependent trap potential and a standing wave laser field. The laser is tuned on resonance with the atomic transition, so the internal degrees of freedom decouple. The parameters are $a = 0.0$, $q = 0.4$, $\Omega_0 = 2.24$; these values are used in all the figures. The dynamics is chaotic except the stable islands around the phase space points $(\pm \pi, 0)$.

from the atomic transition and the equations of motion can be decoupled in the adiabatic and diabatic states, respectively [18]; for finite detuning the system has more than one degree of freedom and a two–dimensional Poincaré surface of section looses its unique meaning. We observe a chaotic sea with two stable islands in the neighbourhood of the minima of the standing laser field at $x = \pm\pi$. These regular structures are remnants of the two integrable limits: $\Omega_0 = 0$ corresponding to the Mathieu equation and $\Omega_0 \gg 1$ corresponding to the pendulum. We use the trap parameters $a = 0$, $q = 0.4$ selected from the stable region of the Mathieu equation and the coupling constant $\Omega_0 = 2.24$. The choice of the parameters a, q, Ω_0 and the effective Planck constant $\hbar = 0.29$ is motivated by present experimental conditions (c.f. the discussion in [5]).

2.5   Quantum Monte Carlo simulations, the effect of the spontaneous decay, numerical procedures

In order to investigate localization we calculate the time-evolution of a Gaussian wave-packet centered initially at the stochastic region near the origin using the split-operator method [19] with a grid of 8192 points. We control numerical errors using an adaptive time step–size algorithm: The wave–packet is propagated in the interval $[t, t + \Delta t]$ by one time–step of length Δt and by two time–steps of length $\frac{\Delta t}{2}$. According to the properties of the split–operator–method this gives an error caused in this interval of e.g. the impuls of order $O(\Delta t^3)$ and $2O\left(\left(\frac{\Delta t}{2}\right)^3\right) = \frac{1}{4}O(\Delta t^3)$, respectively. Therefore the difference of both results is an approximation for the numerical error ϵ_{num} of the first procedure with one time–step in the interval $[t, t + \Delta t]$. Observe, that the error of the second procedure is only $\frac{\epsilon_{num}}{4}$. Assuming that the numerical error increases linearly in time, we can calculate the allowed error $\epsilon_{allowed}$ due to an interval of length Δt, decide wether $\frac{\epsilon_{num}}{4}$ is small enough for the actual time–step and get an approximation for the length of the next time–step Δt_{new}

$$\Delta t_{new} \approx \sqrt{3.2 \frac{\epsilon_{allowed}}{\epsilon_{num}}} \Delta t. \tag{14}$$

With this choice of Δt_{new} the numerical error of the next time–step is approximately 0.8 times the allowed error for this step.

To make a comparison to the classical case we calculate 4096 trajectories starting from a classical Gaussian ensemble centered initally at the origin and having the same widths in the position and momentum as the quantum wavepacket. The effect of spontaneous emission is simulated by the quantum Monte Carlo method [20] using the effective non–hermitian Hamiltonian

$$\hat{H}_{eff} = \hat{H} - i\hbar\frac{\gamma}{2}\hat{\sigma}_+\hat{\sigma}_-,$$

where γ is the spontaneous decay rate scaled by ω. The moments of time when a spontaneous emission takes place are chosen at random. Then the wave–function is projected on the ground–state and renormalized

$$|\Psi\rangle \to \frac{\hat{\sigma}_-|\Psi\rangle}{\langle\Psi|\Psi\rangle}.$$

Also the recoil $p \in [-k, k]$ has to be taken into account, which is also chosen randomly according to the probability distribution [21]

$$N(p) = \frac{3}{8k}\left(1 + \left(\frac{p}{k}\right)^2\right).$$

When the results given by single runs are averaged, one obtains the same result as given by a master equation [22].

3 Dynamical localization

Dynamical localization in our system happens both in position and momentum, as indicated in Fig.2. Here we show for a detuning $\Delta = 0.29$ that is identical to the secular frequency ω_s the variances of position and momentum both in the classical and quantum cases, as well as probability distributions averaged over the time interval $[450\pi, 500\pi]$. We start from an equal superposition of the ground and excited states. The classical position and momentum widths show diffusion, whereas in the quantum case Δx and Δp are stabilized around an average value. The classical probability distributions are broad, but the quantum ones show a narrow peak on top of a more exponential-like background. The position distribution has two sidepeaks at the positions of the stable islands at $x = \pm\pi$ in Fig.1.

The Floquet theory of the Paul trap [10] provides us with a self-consistent explanation of the phenomena we observe. The motion in a time-periodic harmonic oscillator is described by the solution $\epsilon(t)$ of the classical Mathieu equation

$$\ddot{\epsilon}(t) + [a + 2q\cos 2t]\,\epsilon(t) = 0 \qquad (15)$$
$$\epsilon(0) = 1 \quad \dot{\epsilon}(0) = i\omega_r. \qquad (16)$$

The solution becomes the Floquet solution, i.e. a periodic function multiplied by a time-dependent phase,

$$\epsilon(t) = e^{i\omega_s t}\sum_{n=-\infty}^{\infty} c_n e^{i2nt}, \qquad (17)$$

when the initial condition is chosen to be

$$\omega_r = \omega_s + \sum_{n=-\infty}^{\infty} 2nc_n. \qquad (18)$$

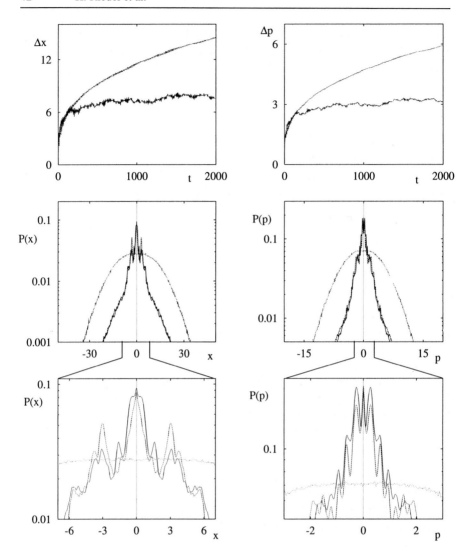

Fig. 2. Classical and quantum dynamics of a two–level ion in a Paul trap interacting with a standing light wave. Here we do not account for spontaneous emission.
Above: The widths of the quantum and classical position and momentum distributions as a function of time. The classical ones (upper curves) show diffusion, which
in the quantum case (lower curve) is suppressed by dynamical localization. Middle: The corresponding position and momentum probability distributions averaged
over the time interval $[450\pi, 500\pi]$. The dashed and solid curve correspond to the
position and momentum distribution of the ion in the excited and ground state,
respectively. The classical ones are broad polynomial curves whereas the quantum
dynamics produces sharp, exponential-like distributions. Bottom: Amplification of
the region around the origin. The distributions corresponding to the ion in the
ground state or the excited state follow each other rather closely. However, in the
position distribution there is a qualitative difference at the origin. The probability

Here ω_s is the so-called secular frequency describing the time-averaged motion in the trap. In the explanation of dynamical localization the reference frequency plays the main role, since it contains information about the micromotion and time-periodicity of the potential, which are essential for classical chaos and dynamical localization. The secular frequency, being related to a time-independent device, is insufficient to describe the dynamical phenomena.

The classical diffusion becomes apparent if we transform the Hamiltonian of the system utilizing the Floquet solution (17)–(18) of the Mathieu equation. The time, position, and momentum are scaled with $|\epsilon(t)|$ as follows

$$\tau(t) = \int_0^t \frac{dt'}{|\epsilon(t')|^2} \tag{19}$$

$$\chi(\tau) = \frac{x(t)}{|\epsilon(t)|} \tag{20}$$

$$\Pi(\tau) = \frac{d\chi(\tau)}{d\tau}. \tag{21}$$

The equations of motion for the center-of-mass motion described by the new position χ and momentum Π, and for the Bloch vector then become

$$\dot{\chi} = \Pi \tag{22}$$
$$\dot{\Pi} = -\omega_r^2 \chi + k\,\Omega_0 |\epsilon(t)|^3 \sin(|\epsilon(t)|\chi)r_1 \tag{23}$$
$$\dot{r}_1 = 2\Delta|\epsilon(t)|^2 r_2 \tag{24}$$
$$\dot{r}_2 = -2\Delta|\epsilon(t)|^2 r_2 - 2\Omega_0|\epsilon(t)|^2 \cos(|\epsilon(t)|\chi)r_3 \tag{25}$$
$$\dot{r}_3 = 2\Omega_0|\epsilon(t)|^2 \cos(|\epsilon(t)|\chi)r_2. \tag{26}$$

Here the dot means derivation with respect to the new time τ. From Eq.(23) we see that the time evolution of the new position variable is governed by the static harmonic oscillator term $-\omega_r^2\chi$, but perturbed by a potential which is a function of time and the position χ. This structure becomes even more apparent when we use the action-angle variables I and θ of the harmonic oscillator with frequency ω_r,

$$\chi = \sqrt{\frac{2I}{\omega_r}}\sin\theta \tag{27}$$

$$\Pi = \sqrt{2I\omega_r}\cos\theta, \tag{28}$$

---

distribution of the ion in the ground state is rectangular with a sharp peak on top. Here we have used the coupling–strength $\Omega = 2.24$ of the standing wave and the detuning $\Delta = 0.29 = \omega_s$. The effective Planck constant is $k = 0.29$ here and in the following figures.

to reformulate the equations of motion:

$$\dot{I} = k\,\Omega_0 \sqrt{\frac{2I}{\omega_r}} \cos\theta |\epsilon(t)|^3 \sin\left(|\epsilon(t)|\sqrt{\frac{2I}{\omega_r}} \sin\theta\right) r_1 \tag{29}$$

$$\dot{\theta} = \omega_r - \frac{k\,\Omega_0 \sin\theta}{\sqrt{2I\omega_r}} |\epsilon(t)|^3 \sin\left(|\epsilon(t)|\sqrt{\frac{2I}{\omega_r}} \sin\theta\right) r_1 \tag{30}$$

$$\dot{r}_1 = 2\Delta|\epsilon(t)|^2 r_2 \tag{31}$$

$$\dot{r}_2 = -2\Delta|\epsilon(t)|^2 r_2 - 2\Omega_0 |\epsilon(t)|^2 \cos\left(|\epsilon(t)|\sqrt{\frac{2I}{\omega_r}} \sin\theta\right) r_3 \tag{32}$$

$$\dot{r}_3 = 2\Omega_0 |\epsilon(t)|^2 \cos\left(|\epsilon(t)|\sqrt{\frac{2I}{\omega_r}} \sin\theta\right) r_2. \tag{33}$$

The dynamics described by these equations leads to fast diffusion of the angle variable θ and slow diffusion of the action variable I [23,24]. This in turn causes diffusion in both position and momentum, which is visible in our numerical results. Furthermore, if diffusion in I is approximately linear in time and proportional to a diffusion constant D, we have

$$\Delta\chi_{classical} = D_\chi \tau^{\alpha_\chi} = \sqrt{D}/\omega_r \tau^\alpha \tag{34}$$

$$\Delta\Pi_{classical} = D_\Pi \tau^{\alpha_\Pi} = \sqrt{D}\omega_r \tau^\alpha, \tag{35}$$

where $\alpha = 1/4$. This leads to

$$\frac{\Delta\Pi_{classical}}{\Delta\chi_{classical}} = \omega_r. \tag{36}$$

Quantum mechanically the action variable corresponds to the vibrational quantum number of the reference oscillator, which should be the variable showing dynamical localization — this leads to localization in both position and momentum, which we observed. The widths of the localized distributions should consequently be related to the localization length l via the simple relations

$$\Delta\chi^2 = \frac{k}{\omega_r}\left(l + \frac{1}{2}\right) \tag{37}$$

$$\Delta\Pi^2 = k\omega_r \left(l + \frac{1}{2}\right). \tag{38}$$

which implies

$$\frac{\Delta\Pi}{\Delta\chi} = \omega_r. \tag{39}$$

We have confirmed the relations (36) and (39) for the unscaled variables (x,p) numerically by observing that we have constant values of the ratios $D_p/D_x \simeq 0.475$ and $\Delta p/\Delta x \simeq 0.415$ when the detuning Δ is varied from zero to ten and $\Omega = 2.24$. Moreover, these ratios are indeed close to the reference frequency $\omega_r = 0.436$ and not to the secular frequency $\omega_s = 0.293$. For detunings in the range $\Delta \in \{0.1, 2.0\}$ we found that $\alpha_x = 0.26$ and $\alpha_p = 0.23$ with the standard deviation of 0.01.

3.1   Quantum oscillations in the localization length

The quantum widths in position and momentum, i.e. the localization length, show characteristic oscillations as a function of the detuning Δ. These oscillations do not appear in the classical widths. In Fig.3 we show the classical and quantum widths Δx averaged from $t = 200\pi$ to 500π. The width of the classical distribution at a certain time is determined by the classical diffusion constant, which is proportional to the perturbing potential caused by the laser field. The classical width decreases monotoneously with Δ as shown in Fig.3. This is easily understood by considering the limiting case of large de-

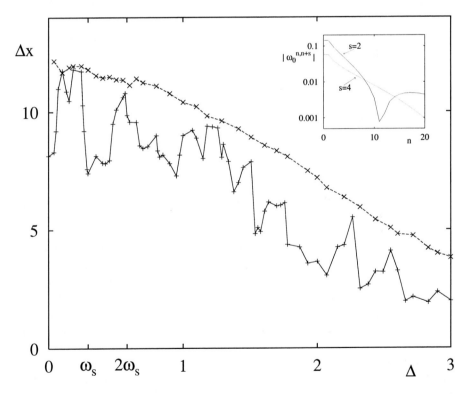

Fig. 3. The quantum and classical position spreads as a function of the detuning Δ averaged from 200π to 500π.
The quantum curve always lies below the classical one. Hence the quantum mechanical position distribution is always narrower than the corresponding classical one. The classical curve decays monotonously as a function of detuning. In contrast the quantum one displays a lot of structure reflecting.

tuning, when the effective potential becomes [17] proportional to the effective coupling constant Ω_0^2/Δ. As Δ increases, the perturbation is simply smaller and the diffusion slower.

The quantum widths show a distinctly different behaviour. It shows a lot of structure and in particular two sharp minima and maxima for $\Delta < 1$. The minimum around $\Delta = 0$ is related to the separable quantum dynamics in two diabatic potentials. As the detuning starts to be nonzero, quantum jumps between the diabatic states add up to the additional mixing transitions. The quantum diffusion rate quickly rises to the maximal classical one; that corresponds to the formation of the first maximum. As it turns out, the next minimum fits the condition $\Delta \approx w_s$, where $w_s = 0.29$ is the secular frequency. The origin of this resonance becomes more clear, when we consider the quantum equations and write the initial Hamiltonian in the interaction picture where the dynamics of the trap as well as the internal state energy are transformed away by unitary transformations (c.f. [25]). The interaction Hamiltonian describing transitions between the trap states becomes

$$H_{int}(t) = \sum_{n=0}^{\infty} \left[\sum_{s=-n}^{\infty} \right]_{s=even} \sum_{l=-\infty}^{\infty} kw_l^{n,n+s} e^{2i\left(l - \frac{sw_s}{2} + \Delta\right)t} \sigma_+ |n\rangle \langle n+s| + H.c.$$

(40)

with

$$\eta = \left(\frac{k}{2\omega_r} \right)^{1/2}$$

(41)

and

$$w_l^{n,n+s} = \Omega_0 \sqrt{\frac{n!}{(n+s)!}} [i\eta]^s \frac{1}{\pi} \int_{-\pi/2}^{\pi/2} dt [\phi^*(t)]^s e^{-\frac{1}{2}\eta^2 [\phi(t)]^2} e^{-2ilt},$$

(42)

Here $|n\rangle$ denotes the n'th energy eigenstate of the time independent reference oscillator. We utilize the Floquet solution $\epsilon(t) = \exp(iw_s t)\phi(t)$, where $\phi(t) = \phi(t + \pi)$ is a periodic function. From the term $e^{2i\left(l - \frac{sw_s}{2} + \Delta\right)t}$ we can expect resonance effects, when Δ obeys the condition $l - \frac{sw_s}{2} + \Delta = 0$. For $l = 0, s = 2$ we have $\Delta = w_s$, which corresponds to the two phonon resonance transitions. One could expect enhancement of the quantum diffusion rate on resonance. Instead we have a deep minimum. In order to understand this we have calculated the characteristic frequencies $w_l^{n,n+s}$ for $l = 0$ and $s = 2, 4$ at different vibrational quantum numbers n. From the inset we note, that $|w_0^{n,n+2}|$ has a deep minimum around $n = 10$, which explains suppression of the diffusion over the vibrational states. For $|w_0^{n,n+4}|$ we have a normal behaviour. This causes the quantum diffusion turning back to its maximum near the classical value, which explains the formation of the second maximum.

Oscillations in the momentum width appear also in another example of a system showing classical chaos and quantum localization, namely that of atoms in phase-modulated standing wave [7,8]. There the oscillations, how-ever, are of classical origin and appear both in the classical and quantum widths. The oscillations we see here are a quantum effect. This has remark-able consequences. It has been shown for the kicked rotator, the paradigm of dynamical localization, that the localization length is related to the classical diffusion constant D and Planck constant by $l \sim D/\hbar^2$. Thus any oscillations in the rate of the classical diffusion should be reflected in the quantum lo-calization length as well. In Fig.4 we show the localization lengths obtained from the quantum widths as well as the estimate based on Eqs.(34)–(38) and the assumption $l \sim t_*$, where t_* is the quantum break time when the classical and quantum results start to differ. The estimate gives from the position diffusion $l \sim (D_x \omega_r / k)^{1/(1-\alpha_x)}$ or from the momentum diffusion $l \sim (D_p/(k\omega_r))^{1/(1-\alpha_x)}$. In our case these estimates based on classical diffu-sion are not able to completely describe the quantum localization; they give

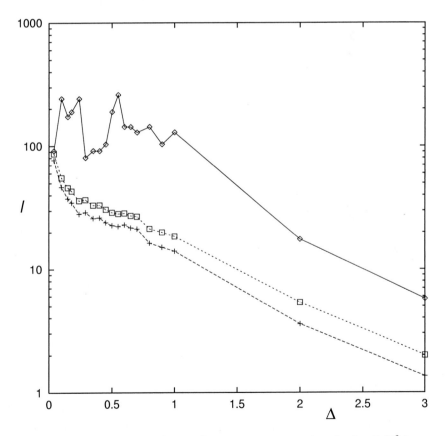

Fig. 4. The localization length (full line) and the estimates given by $l \sim D/k^2$ from the position and momentum distributions (dashed and dotted lines, respectively) as a function of the detuning Δ.

some order of magnitude estimate, but do not explain the prominent oscillations in the quantum localization length. Unlike in the previous examples of dynamical localization with only one quantum degree of freedom, we have now in addition to that another one, the two-level structure, which leaves its traces to the quantum localization length but not the classical diffusion rate.

The non-trivial effect of the detuning is visible also in the shape of the position and momentum distributions. In Fig.5 we show for $\Delta = 0.18$, $\Delta = 0.40$

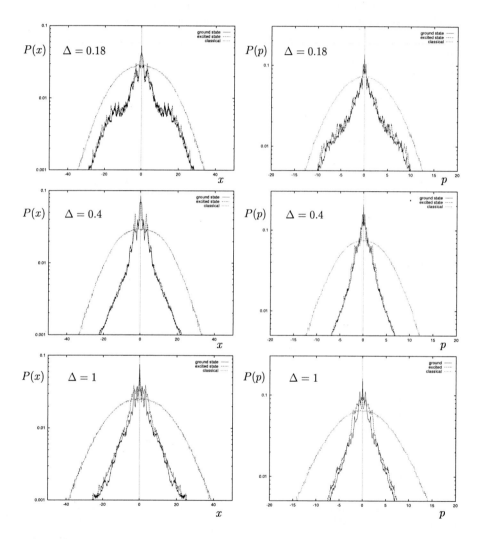

Fig. 5. The position and momentum probability distributions for three different values of the detuning Δ, averaged over the time interval $[450\pi, 500\pi]$. The shapes of the quantum distributions are modified by Δ, whereas the classical ones are of the same type for all the chosen detunings.

and $\Delta = 1.0$ the probability distributions averaged over the time interval $[450\pi, 500\pi]$. (The case $\Delta = 0.29$ is shown in Fig.2.) With growing detuning the position and momentum distributions tend to become more clearly exponentially localized, instead of consisting of a background plus an exponential peak as for $\Delta = 0.18$.

4   The effect of decoherence

In this chapter we consider the effect of noise on our system by simulating spontaneous emission using the quantum Monte Carlo technique [20]. The purpose of our investigations is twofold. First, we want to show that indeed the phenomenon we see is a quantum interference effect, i.e. it is destroyed by decoherence. This we see clearly in the situation when the laser is tuned on resonance with the atomic transition. Second, we want to show that in the far-detuned limit the effect of noise is negligible and the phenomenon of dynamical localization could be experimentally observed.

In Fig.6 we show the results of the simulations with a realistic rate of spontaneous emission $\gamma = 2$ corresponding to the decoherence rate of the $S \to P$ transition at 19.4 MHz in $^9Be^+$ [26], and compare them to the classical result and to the quantum result without noise. The breaking of the coherence destroys localization. The position and momentum widths in this case are larger than the classical ones. This is the extra diffusion caused by the random recoil kicks following each spontaneous emission event. Namely, if we neglect the recoil — which of course is not realistic — the result follows the classical curve. The position and momentum distributions are classical–type, polynomial curves on the logarithmic scale. Note that the pattern of the standing wave appears on top of the distributions.

In Fig.7 we show the results for $\Delta = 1000$, corresponding to a detuning of 10 GHz, a value which was mentioned in [5]. The small oscillations in the localized Δx and Δp are destroyed, but the main phenomenon, the substantial quantum suppression of classical diffusion is still visible. Note that although in a single realization of the dynamics the coherence of the two–level superposition is completely destroyed in one single spontaneous emission, it affects only slightly the motional coherence because the population of the excited state is very low. Furthermore the small difference between the results with and without spontaneous emission in Fig.7 is of the same order of magnitude that was found for the experiments on localization of atomic momentum transfer from a phase modulated standing wave [16].

From the position and momentum distributions in Fig.7 we see again that the standing wave pattern is very clearly reflected in the excited state position distribution. It follows exactly the potential by which the excited state is affected in the adiabatic approximation, see Eq.(13). In the ground state position distribution, there is more probability in the classical-like background than in the case of no spontaneous emission. We found that this background is very slowly growing; it seems that a real steady state cannot be reached any more. However, if we increase the detuning, the real steady state can be asymptotically approached. Since dynamical localization appears for a large range of parameters [5], there is a lot of room for optimizing the parameters. Thus the phenomenon of dynamical localization in a Paul trap could be experimentally observed—also a comparison to the results in [16] suggests this.

5   Conclusions

It has been known that there are basically two ways of controlling dynamical localization, namely through the classical diffusion and through the quantized nature of the variable showing localization. This is expressed in the estimate

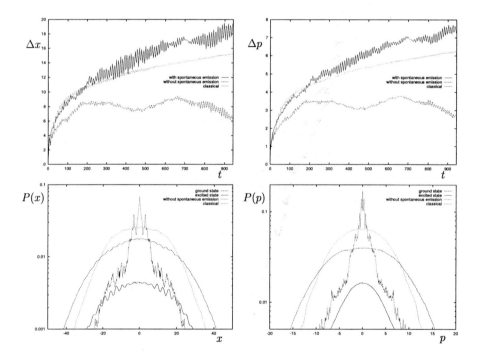

Fig. 6. The position and momentum spreads and the corresponding probability distributions (averaged over the time interval $[200\pi, 250\pi]$) in the presence of spontaneous emission (full line) and without spontaneous emission (dashed) compared to the classical case (dotted). The laser is on resonance with the atomic transition, $\Delta = 0$, and the rate of spontaneous emission $\gamma = 2$ here and in the following figures. The results in the case of spontaneous emission have been obtained by averaging over a sufficient number of runs, in this case 79 runs. We note that localization is destroyed and the distributions become even broader than the classical ones. The pattern of the standing wave appears on the top of the distributions.

for the localization length, $l \sim D/k^2$. There D is the classical diffusion coefficient, which is determined by the perturbing potential; the coupling to this potential is called the control parameter, since it is a direct way to control the localization length. The scaled Planck constant k describes how important the quantization of the system is with respect to the perturbation. We have shown in this paper that, when the perturbing potential has a quantum character as well, the relation $l \sim D/k^2$ is not exactly true any more; we observe oscillations in the localization length which do not appear in the

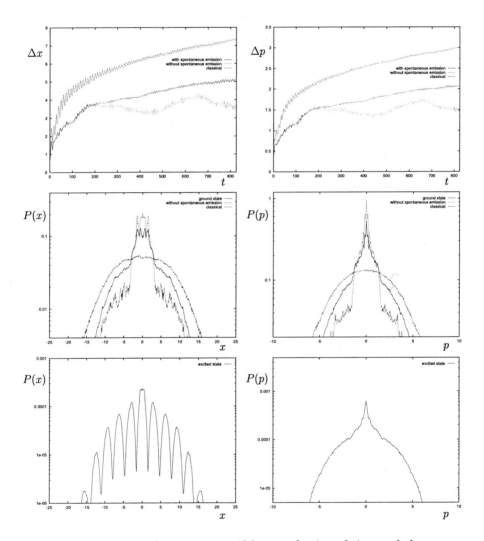

Fig. 7. The position and momentum widths as a funtion of time and the corresponding probability distributions averaged over the time interval $[200\pi, 250\pi]$ in the case of far detuning $\Delta = 1000$. Spontaneous emission does not destroy the localization. An average over 49 runs has been made.

classical diffusion rate. The parameter determining the oscillations could be called the quantum control parameter.

We considered a two-level ion stored in a Paul trap and interacting with a standing wave. The explicite time dependence can be transformed away from the center-of-mass motion using Floquet theory, after which the system can be viewed as a static Floquet reference oscillator affected by an explicitely time-dependent perturbing potential. We observed classical diffusion and quantum localization in the reference oscillator action variable, leading to localization in both position and momentum. When the atom-field detuning Δ was varied, we found oscillations in the quantum position and momentum widths, which are not present in the classical ones. These resonances appear when the quantum control parameter Δ is a multiple of the secular frequency describing the time-averaged motion in the trap.

We simulated the effect of spontaneous emission on the system and showed, that for large enough detunings it becomes negligible and the quantum interference effect of dynamical localization is preserved.

Acknowledgements

We thank B. Kneer and M. El Ghafar for many discussions and useful comments. P. T. and V. S. acknowledge the support of the Deutsche Forschungsgemeinschaft. We thank the Rechenzentrum Ulm and the Rechenzentrum Karlsruhe for their technical support.

References

1. F. Haake, *Quantum Signatures of Chaos* (Springer-Verlag, Berlin 1992).
2. *Quantum Chaos*, Eds. G. Casati and B. Chirikov (Cambridge University Press, 1995).
3. P. W. Anderson, Phys. Rev. **109**, 1492 (1958).
4. F. L. Moore, J. C. Robinson, C. Bharucha, P. E. Williams and M. G. Raizen, Phys. Rev. Lett. **73**, 2974 (1994); theoretical proposal in R. Graham, M. Schlautmann, and P. Zoller, Phys. Rev. A **45**, R19 (1992).
5. M. El Ghafar, P. Törmä, V. Savichev, E. Mayr, A. Zeiler, and W. P. Schleich, Phys. Rev. Lett. **78**, 4181 (1997).
6. W. Paul, Rev. Mod. Phys. **62**, 531 (1990).
7. J. C. Robinson, C. Bharucha, F. L. Moore, R. Jahnke, G. A. Georgaki, M. G. Raizen and B. Sundaram, Phys. Rev. Lett. **74**, 3963 (1995).
8. P. J. Bardroff, I. Bialynicki-Birula, D. S. Krähmer, G. Kurizki, E. Mayr, P. Stifter, and W. P. Schleich, Phys. Rev. Lett. **74**, 3959 (1995).
9. In [R. Graham and S. Miyazaki, Phys. Rev. A **53**, 2683 (1996)] the problem of atoms in phase modulated standing wave was considered without the adiabatic elimination of the upper state. The emphasis of that paper was, however, on the study of spontaneous emission, not on the effect of the extra quantum degree of freedom as such.

10. R. J. Glauber, *Laser manipulation of Atoms and Ions*, Proc. Int. School of Physics 'Enrico Fermi' Course 118, Eds. E. Arimondo et al. (North Holland, Amsterdam 1992); see also G. Schrade, P. J. Bardroff, R. J. Glauber, C. Leichtle, V. Yakovlev and W. P. Schleich, Appl. Phys. B **64**, 181 (1997).

11. For a review see for example P. M. Koch and K. A. H. van Leeuwen, Phys. Rep. **255**, 289 (1995); G. Casati, Phys. Rev. A **45**, 7670 (1992).

12. D. M. Meekhof, C. Monroe, B. E. King, W. M. Itano and D. J. Wineland, Phys. Rev. Lett. **76**, 1796 (1996); C. Monroe, D. M. Meekhof, B. E. King and D. J. Wineland, Science **272**, 1131 (1996); D. Leibfried, D. M. Meekhof, B. E. King, C. Monroe, W. M. Itano, and D. J. Wineland, Phys. Rev. Lett. **77**, 4281 (1996).

13. G. Birkl, J. A. Yeazell, R. Rückerl, and H. Walther, Europhys. Lett. **27**, 197 (1994); H. Katori, S. Schlipf, and H. Walther, Phys. Rev. Lett. **79**, 2221 (1997).

14. B. Appasamy, Y. Stalgies, J. Eschner, W. Neuhauser, and P. E. Toschek, IQEC'96 Technical Digest (Optical Society of America, Washington DC 1996).

15. M. Arndt, A. Buchleitner, R. N. Mantegna and H. Walther, Phys. Rev. Lett. **67**, 2435 (1991); F. L. Moore, J. C. Robinson, C. Bharucha, B. Sundaram and M. G. Raizen, Phys. Rev. Lett. **75**, 4598 (1995); R. Blümel, A. Buchleitner, R. Graham, L. Sirko, U. Smilansky, and H. Walther, Phys. Rev. A **44**, 4521 (1991).

16. P. Goetsch and R. Graham, Phys. Rev. A **54**, 5345 (1996).

17. A. P. Kazantsev, G. I. Surdutovich and V. P. Yakovlev, *Mechanical Action of Light on Atoms* (World Scientific, Singapore 1990).

18. For more information about the classical dynamics of this system see R. Chacón and J. I. Cirac, Phys. Rev. A **51**, 4900 (1994); M. El Ghafar, E. Mayr, V. Savichev, P. Törmä, A. Zeiler, and W. P. Schleich, J. Mod. Opt. to appear (1997).

19. M. D. Feit, J. A. Fleck, JR and A. Steiger, J. of Comput. Phys. **47,** 412 (1982).

20. R. Dum, A. S. Parkins, P. Zoller, and C. W. Gardiner, Phs. Rev. A **46**, 4382 (1992); K. Mœlmer, Y. Castin, and J. Dalibard, J. Opt. Soc. Am. B **10**, 523 (1993).

21. J. Javanainen and S. Stenholm, *Broad Band Resonant Light Pressure*, Appl. Phys. **21**, 35 (1980)

22. H. Carmichael, *An Open System Approach to Quantum Optics* (Springer–Verlag, Berlin 1991)

23. G. M. Zaslavsky, *Chaos in Dynamic Systems* (Harwood Academic Publishers, Chur 1985).

24. Of course, not any potential is able to cause classical diffusion; for instance for a running wave we found neither classical nor quantum diffusion, because we can define a frame where the ion does not see the potential caused by the running wave.

25. P. J. Bardroff, C. Leichtle, G. Schrade, and W. P. Schleich, Phys. Rev. Lett. **77**, 2198 (1996).

26. S. R. Jefferts, C. Monroe, E. W. Bell, and D. J. Wineland, Phys. Rev. A **51**, 3112 (1995).

Interacting Particle-Liquid Systems

Kai Höfler, Matthias Müller, Stefan Schwarzer, and Bernd Wachmann

Institut für Computeranwendungen I
Pfaffenwaldring 27,
70569 Stuttgart, Germany

Abstract. We present two Euler-Lagrangian simulation methods for particles immersed in fluids described by the Navier-Stokes equation. These implement the coupling between particle and fluid phase by (i) direct integration of the stress tensor on the particle surface discretized according to the grid topology and (ii) by a tracer particle method, which employs the volume force term in the Navier-Stokes equation to emulate "rigid" body motion. Both methods have been parallelized and applied to bulk sedimentation of about 65 000 particles (in one simulation 10^6 particles have been simulated). We also report results for the rheology of shear-thinning suspensions, modelled by hydrodynamically interacting particles in shear flows. Aggregation occurs due to attractive, short range forces between the particles. We also address a deficiency of the MPI communication library on the CRAY T3E which had to be resolved to improve the performance of our algorithm.

1 Introduction

Many applications in chemical engineering [1,2], fluid mechanics [3], geology [4], and biology involve systems of rigid or elastic particles immersed in a liquid or gas flow. Examples of such systems arise in the context of sedimentation processes, gas-solid or liquid-solid fluidized beds, suspension rheology like the behavior of blood, pastes, etc., mixing processes when sediment-laden rivers enter lakes or the sea, pneumatic conveying, ticking hour glasses, flocculation in suspensions and many more. In these systems the long-ranged hydrodynamic interactions mediated by the fluid in the interstitial voids of the particulate, granular system greatly change the physical behavior of the particle assembly as compared to the "dry" state which is characterized by the short-ranged, viscoelastic forces governing the grain-grain contacts. The influence of an interstitial medium can never be neglected, when its density is of the same order as that of the grains themselves. As we will demonstrate, despite the complexity of the problem, the simulation of particle-fluid systems is feasible on modern parallel computers.

Our paper is organized as follows. We first describe our simulation techniques for particle-suspension flows in detail. Then we will show and discuss the obtained results on bulk sedimentation under gravity and aggregation in shear flows and the required computational effort. In the appendix we present information concerning the implementation of the parallel cartesian grid communication in the MPI library of the CRAY-T3E gathered for optimizing our algorithms.

2 Modeling

2.1 Fluid Modeling

The fluid motion is in many cases well represented by the incompressible Navier-Stokes equations,

$$\frac{\partial \mathbf{v}}{\partial t} + (\mathbf{v} \cdot \nabla)\mathbf{v} = -\nabla p + \frac{1}{Re}\nabla^2 \mathbf{v} + \mathbf{f}^l, \tag{1}$$

$$\nabla \cdot \mathbf{v} = 0, \tag{2}$$

where $\mathbf{v}$ is the fluid velocity measured in units of some typical velocity U; $Re = aU/\nu$ is the particle Reynolds number, a the radius of the cylindrical or spherical particles considered, and ν the dynamic viscosity of the fluid. The pressure p is measured in units of $\rho^l U^2$, where ρ^l is the fluid density. The point force $\mathbf{f}^l$ usually represents body forces like gravity, but local force distributions may be used to model boundary conditions as well, as we will see below. It is convenient to eliminate gravity from the equations since it cancels the induced constant hydrostatic pressure gradient; we then have to take care to add buoyancy when we consider the forces acting on particles.

In order to solve the fluid equations (2), we use a regular, fixed grid—a staggered marker and cell mesh—for a second order spatial discretization [5], employ a simple explicit Euler time stepping, but an implicit determination of the pressure in an operator splitting approach to satisfy the incompressibility constraint at all times. The resulting pressure Poisson equation is solved by multi-grid techniques. For more details, please see [5,6].

2.2 Particle Forces and Motion

During the sedimentation process the particles may collide. To avoid a large overlap we introduce a central, repulsive and dissipative force acting if and only if particles are in contact. We write for this contact force acting on particle i,

$$\begin{aligned}
\mathbf{F}_i^{\text{el}} = &-K_n(a_i + a_j - (\mathbf{x}_j - \mathbf{x}_i) \cdot \hat{\mathbf{n}}_{ji})\,\hat{\mathbf{n}}_{ji} \\
&-2\gamma m_{red}(\mathbf{v}_{ij} \cdot \hat{\mathbf{n}}_{ij})\,\hat{\mathbf{n}}_{ij},
\end{aligned} \tag{3}$$

where K_n denotes the stiffness of the spring, $\mathbf{x}_i$ denotes the position vector of the center of particle i, and $\hat{\mathbf{n}}_{ji}$ is the unit vector pointing from the center of particle i to the center of j, $\mathbf{v}_{ij}$ is the relative velocity of the colliding spheres, γ is a damping constant, $m_{ij} = m_i m_j/(m_i + m_j)$ the reduced mass and a_i the radius of particle i.

The resulting equations of the translational motions are solved by a leap-frog Verlet algorithm, the equations of the rotational motions are analogously solved by a similar leap-frog Verlet algorithm using quaternions instead of Eulerian angles [7].

2.3   Interaction models

The major advantages of fixed grid techniques for liquid simulations as the one outlined above compared to, e.g., finite element techniques, is (i) their speed owing to the simplicity of the data structures and (ii) that no grid remapping is required due contortion of the deformation of the computational domain in adaptive techniques. However, computational accuracy usually suffers in fixed-grid methods, because the boundaries cannot easily be represented. In one approach [8,9], we have used analytic expansions to represent the flow in the vicinity of the particle surface, but found the computational costs too large to be able to simulate systems large enough to study collective phenomena over sufficiently long time intervals.

Here we present results from two alternative methods. In the first one, we use (A) a rather fine grid and a first order discretization of the particle boundary. In the second, we use (B) the volume force term in Eq. (2) to model the boundary.

(A) Grid adapted boundary geometry. The hydrodynamic force and torque acting on an arbitrarily shaped body suspended in a fluid can be described by a surface integral of the stress tensor $\overleftrightarrow{\sigma} = -p\mathbb{I} + \frac{1}{Re}\left(\nabla v + (\nabla v)^t\right)$, where p denotes the fluid pressure, v the velocity of the fluid and $\mathbb{I}$ the second rank unit tensor. The resulting force F and torque T acting on the particle are written as follows:

$$F = \int_\Omega \overleftrightarrow{\sigma} \cdot dA, \quad T = \int_\Omega r_{CM} \times \overleftrightarrow{\sigma} \cdot dA \qquad (4)$$

Here r_{CM} refers to the vector connecting the center of mass of the particle and the surface point where the force $\overleftrightarrow{\sigma} \cdot dA$ acts and Ω refers to the surface of the particle.

Numerically, we compute the force and torque acting on the particles by decomposing the particle surface into square patches perpendicular to the coordinate axes. As visualized in Fig. 1, the expression for $\overleftrightarrow{\sigma}$ is calculated on each patch, multiplied by the normal $\hat{n}$ and the area h^2 of each patch and then summed over all surface patches.

(B) Marker technique. As announced in the introduction, we now show how to make use of the volume force term in the Navier-Stokes equation to model the boundary conditions between particles and liquid[10]. To this end, we imagine that the physical particles in the fluid are decomposed as follows: We need (i) a rigid particle template endowed with a certain mass m_i^t and moment of inertia I_i^t, which complements (ii) mass and moment of inertia of the volume V_i of liquid covered—but not replaced—by the template. We must require $m_i^t + \rho_f V_i = m_i$, and $I_i^t + I_f = I_i$, i.e., that template plus liquid

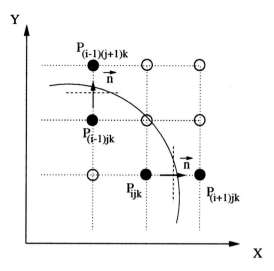

Fig. 1. Calculation of the pressure on the particle surface. The curved line indicates the particle surface. We calculate the mean value of the pressure from two corresponding points separated by the particle surface. The dashed line symbolizes a "surface patch" and the corresponding surface vector $\boldsymbol{n}$. We evaluate the gradients of the velocity components Δv_{ijk}^{mn} analogously by calculating, e.g., $\Delta v_{ijk}^{xy} = v_{ijk}^{x} - v_{i(j-1)k}^{x}$, from two velocity points separated by the surface of the particle. The discretization shown here is coarser than in the actual simulations.

volume elements together yield the correct mass m_i and moment of inertia I_i of the physical particle.

In order to achieve the coupling, we distribute reference points j with coordinates $\mathbf{r}_{ij}$ over the particle templates with respect to the center of particle i at $\mathbf{x}_i$. These reference points move due to the translation and rotation of the particle template and follow trajectories $\mathbf{x}_{ij}^r(t)$,

$$\mathbf{x}_{ij}^r(t) = \mathbf{x}_i(t) + \mathbf{O}_i(t)\mathbf{r}_{ij}, \tag{5}$$

where $\mathbf{O}_i(t)$ is a matrix describing the orientation of the template. Each reference point is associated with one tracer particle (superscript m) at $\mathbf{x}_{ij}^m$ which is passively advected by the flow field, $\dot{\mathbf{x}}_{ij}^m = \mathbf{v}(\mathbf{x}_{ij}^m)$. Whenever reference point and tracer are not at the same position forces shall arise (see below) to make the tracer follow the reference point, i.e., the liquid motion coincides with the particle motion.

Between a tracer and its reference point we introduce a damped spring which gives rise to a force density in the liquid:

$$\mathbf{f}_{ij}^l(\mathbf{x}_{ij}^m) = h^{-d}(-k\boldsymbol{\xi}_{ij} - 2\gamma\dot{\boldsymbol{\xi}}_{ij})\delta(\mathbf{x}_{ij}^m). \tag{6}$$

In this equation, $\boldsymbol{\xi}_{ij} = \mathbf{x}_{ij}^m - \mathbf{x}_{ij}^r$ denotes the distance of tracer and reference point, k is the spring constant, γ is the damping constant, $\delta(\mathbf{x})$ the Dirac distribution, and h^d the volume of liquid associated with one marker particle. It should be clear that this force law is largely arbitrary. We have verified that its choice does not have significant influence on the motion of the physical particle as a whole, provided that k is chosen sufficiently large to ensure that ξ_{ij} remains always small and the density of markers is about $1/h^d$ [11].

2.4   Simulations of bulk sedimentation

Experimentally observed sedimentation velocities of monodisperse suspensions are well described by the *Richardson-Zaki* relation [12]:

$$v(\varPhi) = v_s (1 - \varPhi)^\tau , \qquad (7)$$

where v_s refers to the Stokes velocity of a single sphere in an infinite medium ($\varPhi \to 0$). The exponent τ is a function of Re and is ≈ 5 in the viscous regime ($Re < 0.5$) [7,13].

In our periodic system we measure the sedimentation velocity as the time average velocity of the particles in the frame where the total volume flux across a horizontal cut through the system vanishes,

$$v(\varPhi) = \langle \frac{1}{N} \sum_{i=1}^{N} v_z^i \rangle_t. \qquad (8)$$

To interpret our data for different $\varPhi$ and system sizes L, we assume that the dependence on L/a expresses itself only through the prefactor of (8), i.e., we assume $v_s = v_s(L/a)$ and that the functional dependence on $\varPhi$ remains the same. Thus, in order to normalize our data, we first calculate $v_s(L/a)$ for each value of L/a as the sedimentation speed of a single particle. Then we calculate the settling velocity as a function of volume fraction for the same ratio L/a and divide by $v_s(a/L)$. The results are displayed in Fig. 2. We also show data for the distribution of particle velocities perpendicular and parallel to the direction of gravity. We observe that the tails of the velocity distribution decay slower than in Gaussian fashion, reflecting the fact that we deal with a interacting system not in thermodynamic equilibrium.

2.5   Resource consumption

Typical runs for the results in section 2.3 have been performed on $4 \times 4 \times 4$ nodes and require about 10 hours per CPU to sample data for one initial configuration. For example, at system size $L/a = 97.2$, 64 processing nodes supplied about $16.8 \times 10^6 \approx (4 \times 64)^3$ grid points to resolve the fluid motion and about 65 000 particles (at $\varPhi = 0.30$) were simulated. In this configuration, in 3D about $4\mu s$ were needed typically for the update of one of the fluid grid points. The update time per particle depends very strongly on the coupling between particles and liquid. The boundary technique requires about $900\mu s$

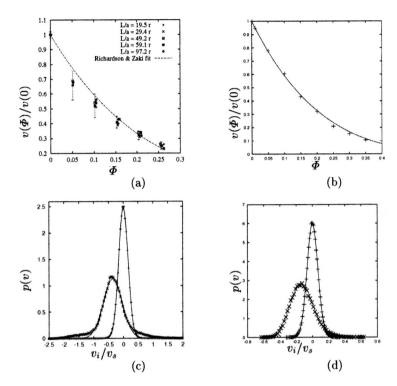

Fig. 2. (a,b) Mean speed as a function of volume fraction and velocity distributions (c,d) of sedimenting particles. In (a) we display data from runs for periodic cubic systems of size ranging from 19.5 to 97.2 L/a, comprising from 530 to 65 770 particles. Velocities are normalized with respect to the velocity of one single particle in the simulation volume. The data in (b) is obtained using the "marker" method. In (c) and (d) velocity distributions are plotted measured at of size $L/a = 29.4$, $\Phi = 0.15$ (c), $L/a = 20$, $\Phi = 0.30$ (d) for boundary (c) and marker method (d). Here, symbols refer to simulation data averaged over runs for 4 different initial configurations and lines indicate fits to Gaussian distributions.

per particle, whereas the marker algorithm needs roughly $7\mu s$ per marker and about 100 markers are needed to represent one physical particle [11]. In short runs on up to 512 processors we have verified that the CPU time and memory consumption of the used algorithms scale linear in the number of grid points and particles (up to 10^6). In separate runs, the employed particle tracking (short-range molecular dynamics) algorithm has shown linear behavior for up to 1.7×10^9 particles simulated concurrently on two supercomputers [14].

Thus, it is clear that the resource consumption of the particle-liquid algorithms is dominated by the domain decomposed fluid solver. Efficiency issues related to the layout of the partitioning are described in the appendix.

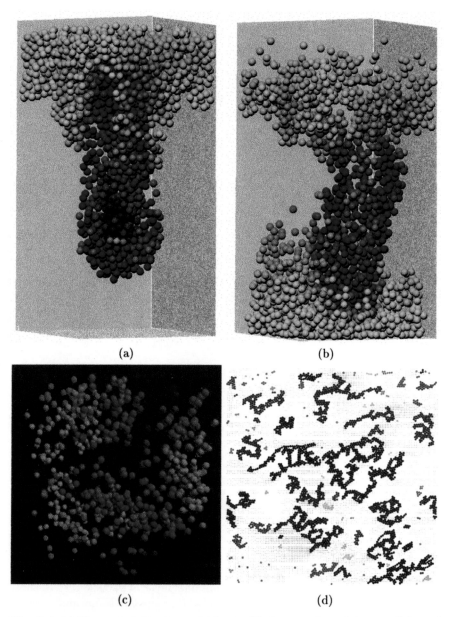

(a)   (b)

(c)   (d)

Fig. 3. (a,b) Finger evolution in unstably stratified suspension of clear particle and particle laden liquid in an elongated container with aspect ratio 1:1:2. Red denotes upward, blue downward moving particles.   (c) Steady state in a batch sedimentation simulation with cubic periodic cells. Color as above.   (d) Cluster formation in 2D shear-flows after total strain 50 starting from a random homogeneous situation. Interior voids are filled by pockets of incompressible liquid.

In our algorithm, typically four "layers" of fluid grid information must be exchanged between processors in order to compute the forces on the particles of radius a=4h correctly. It is essentially this communication on the finest grid level which caused the parallel efficiency to assume a value of about 0.8 for the largest feasible domains per processor, still decreasing with domain size. In comparison we could neglect the contribution of the multigrid fluid solver, which requires frequent communication on the coarsest grid levels, where the ratio of bulk-computation to surface-communication is lowest.

2.6   Aggregation

Whereas the geometrical aspects of the particles control the rheological behavior of suspensions with large particles, inter-particle forces other than the hydrodynamic forces discussed above give rise to very interesting phenomena for smaller particles. Since electrostatic interactions are often screened due to residual ions, the remaining forces are often due to polarization effects, like hydrogen bonding or van-der-Waals interaction. Their attractive nature can lead to clustering phenomena between the particles which can dramatically change the rheological behavior of the suspensions from Newtonian behavior to shear thinning or shear thickening behavior [15–17].

We introduce an attractive model force which lets particles stick on contact and allows the contact to break when the tension exceeds a certain threshold. We study the suspension behavior in two-dimensional shear flows where the shear induces pronounced aggregation of particles [18]. The equilibrium of cluster creation due to the formation of contacts and cluster destruction, due to the breaking of contacts due to the shear forces, which increase as the cluster grows, leads to an typical cluster size which decreases as a function of shear rate $\dot{\gamma}$. Consequently, as we show in Fig. 4, we find shear-thinning behavior of the suspension which in restricted parameter ranges can be described by a power-law dependence of the excess suspension viscosity $\Delta\eta \sim \dot{\gamma}^{-x}$, $x \approx 0.4\ldots0.5$.

The effect of the hydrodynamic interactions is to lower the values of the exponent x in comparison to similar models that do not fully incorporate the hydrodynamics [15].

3   Conclusion

We have presented several ways to efficiently compute the behavior of particles immersed in a liquid in 2D and 3D. In particular in 3D, the simulation of systems sizes that allow extrapolation to realistic systems requires the computational power of large parallel computers.

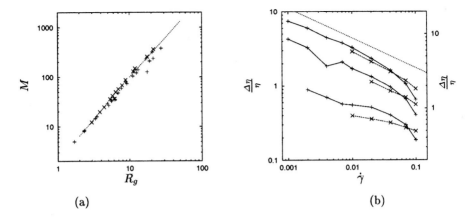

Fig. 4. (a) Average cluster mass M as function of the mean radius of gyration R_g. The lines are guides to the eye and indicate slopes of 1.7 for small and of 1.6 for "large" clusters. Each data point corresponds to one simulation run with total strain $\dot{\gamma} t_{total} = 100$. Shear rates vary from $\dot{\gamma}/\dot{\gamma}_c = 0.001 \ldots 0.1$, volume fractions in the range $\phi = 0.1 \ldots 0.3$ and system sizes are $L/a = 128\,(\times)$ and $L/a = 64\,(+)$.
(b) Cluster stress contribution to the steady state excess viscosity $\Delta \eta / \eta$ as a function of shear rate $\dot{\gamma}/\dot{\gamma}_c$ for different particle volume fractions $\Phi = 0.10$, 0.20 and 0.30 (bottom to top). Different symbols refer to different system size, the larger system $(128a)^2$ leading to larger viscosities (right hand side scale, $\times$) than the small system of $(64a)^2$ (left hand side scale, $+$).

4   Acknowledgments

We would like to acknowledge the contributions from students and colleagues at the ICA at large who contributed to the software development and the scientific ideas entering our projects. Without financial support of the University of Stuttgart and the cooperation of its computing center RUS and the HLRS, our projects would not have been possible. K. H., M. M., and B. W. thank Deutsche Forschungsgemeinschaft for financial support through SFB 404 and SFB 382.

A   Communication on the T3E

In order to distribute the work between several processing elements (PEs), our applications use a domain decomposition into cuboids. The topology in this case is a three dimensional cartesian grid. The communication between neighboring domains is split in successive steps, one for each spatial dimension. The topology is created with a call to `MPI_Cart_create`. This function is not only used for convenience but also to allow the MPI implementation to optimize by *reordering* the processing elements (PEs).

We define the bandwidth to be the amount of data per unit time that one PE can send. Because two simultaneous sends in different directions take place, the theoretical peak bandwidth of the network is in this case 600MB/s. The memory bandwidth of the T3E-900 with stream buffers enabled limits this to 300MB/s.

We observe always a bandwidth below 200MB/s (see Fig. 5a). Thus, only one send request seems to be active at a time. The bandwidth decreases further to 124MB/s when the number of PEs is increased. This effect is called contention: messages sent at the same time interfere with each other because the communication network cannot handle them simultaneously. However, in principle there is no reason for such a contention, since the layout of the T3E is a bidirectional, three dimensional torus. Two neighbors in a cartesian grid should have a direct connection. From the operating system's point of view

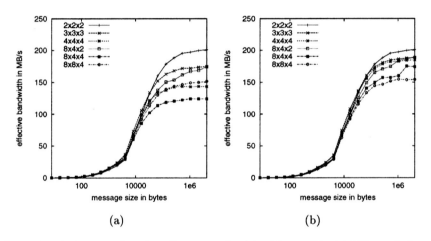

Fig. 5. Bandwidth as a function of message size (a) without, (b) with PE reordering.

there is now way to decide whether a request for 64 PEs will be mapped to a $4 \times 4 \times 4$ or a $8 \times 8 \times 1$ grid. However, contention occurs even if the layout of the physical PEs corresponds to the requested grid topology which implies that `MPI_Cart_create` does not reorder the PE ranks to optimize the mapping.

Therefore, we have implemented an own version of this call to perform reordering. The result is shown in Fig. 5b. The bandwidth drops only to 154MB/s. We checked the quality of a mapping by looking at the average number of hops a message has to travel. The hop count of the grids created by our mapping was between 1 and 1.8 compared to between 1.3 and 2.8 of CRAY's implementation of `MPI_Cart_create`. Whenever the layout of the physical PEs corresponds to the requested grid topology the hop count was one. The performance is between 2 and 40 percent faster than the unoptimized mapping for PE numbers larger than 8. Contention only occurs when the operating system provides an irregular PE cluster. In the case of 8x8x4 PEs the domain was practically separated into two partitions with 128 PEs each.

References

1. S. L. Soo. *Particles and Continuum: Multiphase Fluid Dynamics.* Hemisphere Publishing Corporation, New York, Washington, Philadelphia, London, 1989.
2. Dimitri Gidaspow. *Multiphase Flow and Fluidization.* Academic Press, San Diego, 1994.
3. Elisabeth Guazelli and Luc Oger, editors. *Mobile Particulate Systems,* Dordrecht, 1995. Kluwer Academic. Proc. NATO ASI, Cargèse, July 4-15, 1994.
4. K. Pye and H. Tsoar. *Aeolian Sand and Sand Dunes.* Unwin Hyman, London, 1990.
5. Roger Peyret and Thomas D. Taylor. *Computational Methods for Fluid Flow.* Springer Series in Computational Physics. Springer, New York, Berlin, Heidelberg, 1983.
6. Wolfgang Kalthoff, Stefan Schwarzer, and Hans Herrmann. An algorithm for the simulation of particulate suspensions with inertia effects. *Phys. Rev. E,* 56(2):2234-2242, 1997.
7. M. P. Allen and D. J. Tildesley. *Computer Simulations of Liquids.* Clarendon Press, Oxford, 1987.
8. Wolfgang Kalthoff. *Dynamische Eigenschaften von Zweiphasenströmen: Ein Simulationsansatz für Partikel in Flüssigkeiten.* PhD thesis, Universität Stuttgart, 1997.
9. B. Wachmann, W. Kalthoff, S. Schwarzer, and H. J. Herrmann. Collective drag and sedimentation: Comparison of simulation and experiment in two and three dimensions. submitted to Granular Matter, 1997.
10. Stefan Schwarzer. Simulation of particles in liquids. In J.-P. Hovi, S. Luding, and H. Herrmann, editors, *Physics of Dry Granular Media.* Kluwer Academic, Dordrecht, 1998. [Proc. NATO ASI Cargèse, 1997].
11. Kai Höfler. *Räumliche Simulation von Zweiphasenflüssen.* Master's thesis, Universität Stuttgart, 1997.
12. J. F. Richardson and W. N. Zaki. Sedimentation and fluidisation: Part 1. *Trans. Instn Chem. Engrs.,* 32:35-53, 1954.
13. H. Nicolai, B. Herzhaft, E. J. Hinch, L. Oger, and E. Guazzelli. Particle velocity fluctuations and hydrodynamic self-diffusion of sedimenting non-brownian spheres. *Phys. Fluids,* 7(1):12-23, 1995.
14. Matthias Müller. Weltrekorde durch Metacomputing. *BI, Rechenzentrum Universität Stuttgart,* 11/12 1997.
15. M. Doi and D. Chen. Simulation of aggregationg colloids in shear flow. *J. Chem. Phys.,* 90(10):5271-5279, 1989.
16. M. Doi and D. Chen. Simulation of aggregationg colloids in shear flow. II. *J. Chem. Phys.,* 91(4):2656, 1989.
17. R. Wessel and R. C. Ball. Fractal aggregates and gels in shear flow. *Phys. Rev. A,* 46(6):R3008-R3011, 1992.
18. Stefan Schwarzer and Sitangshu B. Santra. Fluid dynamical simulation of monomer aggregation in shear flow. in preparation, 1997.

Finite Difference Modeling of Earthquakes

Martin Karrenbach[1]

Geophysical Institute, Karlsruhe University, 76187 Karlsruhe, Germany

Abstract. Understanding of strong earthquake motions includes the knowledge of wave propagation from source to receiver. Seismic elastic wave propagation is modelled on a large scale from the earthquake source through a heterogeneous earth to the receiver placed close to the infrastructure. Finite Difference techniques in two and three dimensions compute the full wave form solution to the wave propagation problem. The model size used in this example is 400kmx400kmx200km and source frequencies up to 2 Hz. The Finite Difference modeling software is written in High Performance Fortran and relies on on the SEPLIB processing package for Input/Ouput and parameter retrieval. A Large scale parallel machine proved to be necessary to be able to run realistic models and achieve acceptable turn-around time of modeling sequences for research purposes. The small modeling scenario in this paper demonstrates the practicality of modeling earthquake wave propagation realistically and shows that in the future it can be used in more elaborate modeling scenarios as they are planned for the Collaborative Research Project SFB 461 and other international collaborative research projects at Karlsruhe University.

1 Numerical Modeling Technique

The elastic wave equation describes a physical system and thus, is based on a set of conservation principles and constitutive relations. A typical choice of variables is the particle displacement velocity $\dot{\underline{u}}(\underline{x}, t)$, the deformation tensor $\underline{\underline{\epsilon}}(\underline{x}, t)$, the momentum density, which is the product $\rho(\underline{x}, t)\dot{\underline{u}}(\underline{x}, t)$ and the stress $\underline{\underline{\sigma}}(\underline{x}, t)$. In elastic media certain conservation principles must hold. The total momentum must be preserved throughout the entire volume. The temporal change in momentum has to equal the total force operating on the surface S of the volume plus the contribution of external forces within the volume V. The particle movement on the surface leads to a temporal change in the deformation of the volume V, where $\underline{\underline{h}}$ is the external deformation applied at locations within the volume (for explicit derivations see Aki, 1980 and Karrenbach, 1998).

So far we have considered the geometry and distribution of physical variables within the medium. We still have to characterize material properties. This is often done by explicitly giving a stress-strain relationship. The stress could be an complicated function of the strain and other variables, but a linear relationship simplifies to

$$\underline{\underline{\sigma}} = \underline{\underline{\underline{\underline{c}}}}\,\underline{\underline{\epsilon}}. \tag{1}$$

where the stress tensor $\underset{\sim}{\sigma}$ and the strain tensor $\underset{\sim}{\epsilon}$ are linearly related via a fourth order tensor $\underset{\approx}{c}$. To get the equivalent differential description of the problem, we demand that the equations that are given as integrals, must hold true also at each arbitrary point in the medium. Therefore, we consider small subvolumes and subsurfaces in the domain. Requiring conservation laws and stress strain relationships to hold at each point in the medium leads then to a set of partial differential equation

$$\frac{d}{dt}(\rho\dot{\underline{u}}) = \nabla\underset{\sim}{\sigma} + \underline{f} \tag{2}$$

and

$$\frac{d}{dt}(\underset{\approx}{c}^{-1}\underset{\sim}{\sigma}) = \nabla^t\dot{\underline{u}} + \underline{h} \tag{3}$$

For the anisotropic elastic case the differential operator ∇, defined by

$$\nabla^t = \frac{1}{2}\left(\frac{\partial}{\partial x_l} + \frac{\partial}{\partial x_k}\right) \qquad \text{with} \qquad k, l = 1, 2, 3 \tag{4}$$

operates on the displacement field $\underline{u}$ and results in the symmetric strain tensor $\underset{\sim}{\epsilon}$. The indices k and l, and in the following the indices i and j, range over the number of space axes and the number of vector components.

Thus we have a set of partial differential equations plus the associated boundary and initial conditions. A few simplifications can be made for some special types of media, such as density and the parameter $\underset{\sim}{c}$ being time-invariants, as we would assume for elastic media. Above equations can be written in several different ways. As they stand, they use a particular set of variables, namely velocity and stress as state variables, another is the formulation that uses primarily displacements to characterize the state of the physical system. The choice of variables has some practical implications and in the following sections we deal with the displacement formulations, since it can be cast as a set of first order equations and boundary conditions which can be applied at each single intermediate step. To solve the above continuous equations numerically I proceed to discretize the medium and partial differential operators.

2   Finite Difference Parallel Implementation

Above sets of partial differential operators are approximated on a regular grid topology by convolutional operators. For spatial derivatives high-order optimized Finite Difference stencils are used. Temporal derivatives are accurate up to second order. An explicit time stepping scheme on a staggered spatial grid is used, with temporal and spatial sampling intervals adjusted to guarantee numerical stability and accuracy.

The method is implemented in High Performance Fortran and is described in detail in Karrenbach (1998). The program is suitable for solving a variety of seismic forward modeling problems, in exploration and production settings as well as realistic earthquake modeling. In the Diploma Thesis of Aursch-Schmidt (1998) a series of basic two-dimensional modeling tests as well as earthquake modeling has been carried out with this implementation on single workstations. These tests have been limited to two dimensions due to run-time and memory limits. For realistic three-dimensional seismic modeling of earthquake scenarios large-scale parallel computers need to be used, such as the Cray T3-E. We use the original portable High Performance version of the code. On the parallel machine data distribution directives are recognized and parallel language constructs automatically distribute array subsets and computations among processing nodes.

Benchmarking of optimal layouts and choice of language constructs has been tested and is described in detail in a companion paper Karrenbach et al. (1998). The HPF data distribution directive, allows to indicate to the compiler how multi dimensional arrays should be distributed onto various processors. The basic template of the computational floating point arrays consists of a five-dimensional array. The following list shows the actual distributions used for a five-dimensional array (`wave[nz,nx,ny,ncomp,ntau]`) of seismic data.

HPF compiler directives for data distribution `!HPF$ DISTRIBUTE`

- `(BLOCK,BLOCK,BLOCK,*,*)`
- `(BLOCK,BLOCK,*,*,*)`
- `(*,BLOCK,*,*,*)`
- `(BLOCK,*,*,*,*)`
- `(*,BLOCK,BLOCK,*,*)`

are used depending on the modeling grid topology.

All data objects used in the code have the first three indices in common, which describe the spatial dimensions. All data objects that contain these spatial dimensions are distributed on various processors with identical topology, such that in those subsets dimensions are aligned for optimal storage and cache access. The remaining dimensions describe internal indices of the physical quantity and are usually stored locally in the individual processor's memory.

The computationally most intensive part is the computation of one- dimensional spatial derivatives for each spatial direction (eqn. 4), that have to be carried out for each timestep. These derivatives are implemented as parallel highorder convolutional operators. HPF with proper array distribution has no problem in performing efficiently for this computational kernel. The chosen block-layout guarantees that large portions of the data objects, remain in one single processor, such that when the convolution is performed, data communication is only necessary for the block boundary values.

In this paper the validity of the modeling is demonstrated for a small 3D earth model, which corresponds to a computational grid of 200x200x100 grid points per spatial object subset. Since access is required to all field variables at any time, such a model size corresponds to a total memory requirement of ca 1.4 GB. The runtime will depend on the maximum source frequency of the earthquake and the recording time limit.

3   Earthquake Modeling In A Realistic 3D Setting

In this project we bring the previously introduced numerical techniques to bear on modeling earthquakes realistically. The underlying earth model is one of the necessary ingredients.

The generation of a subsurface model often is a cumbersome task involving members of various geoscience disciplines, such as geologists and geophysicists. In this particular case the 3D earth model was derived from seismic earthquake recordings by tomographic travel time inversion techniques (Lorenz, 1997). The model area is located in Rumania and encompasses a 400 km by 400 km surface area and extends up to 200 km in depth. The X axis in the Figure 1 represents geographically the East-West direction and similarly the Y axis represents the North-South direction. In the frontal view of the snapshot the outlines of material variations are visible. The colors represent various levels of compressional wave speed. We can recognize manifestations of material which shows slightly higher and lower velocity than the surrounding background material. Contrasts are typically smaller than 1 km/s. The side view represents another depth section and the top view is a slice through the volume at constant depth. We can easily recognize that the earth model is complex and cannot be realistically approximated by simple shapes or analytical functions.

3.1   Wave Field Snapshots

In this model an earthquake source can be activated. Its characteristics are derived from inversion results of real earthquake recordings. The fault plane is obliquely oriented in space. Along the fault plane a material displacement takes place. Such a material disturbance radiates elastic energy and the resulting waves are displayed in Figure 2. It shows a snapshot of a vertical displacement component. The front side and top view, show planes that cut the wave field volume fairly close to the location of the earthquake. At fixed time steps we see the amplitude distribution. We clearly distinguish compressional and shear wavefronts. Figure 3 shows the same wave field again, but the top surface views the displacement right on the top of the earth's surface. Already, one can recognize preferred energy radiation directions. This is caused by the spatial orientation of the extended areal source and by the heterogeneities in the material. We observe the snapshots on three perpendicular planes cut through the wave field volume at locations that pass through the earthquake hypocenter.

3.2   Snapshot at the Surface

The observation plane is moved up in the vertical direction to the surface in order to see what is registered at the surface. The elastic waves propagate in the subsurface and it takes some time until the first wave front reaches the earth's surface. At the surface they are reflected and generate additionally surface waves. We can see that in some directions the energy density is larger than in other directions. Thus we can have a varying impact of those waves at the surface.

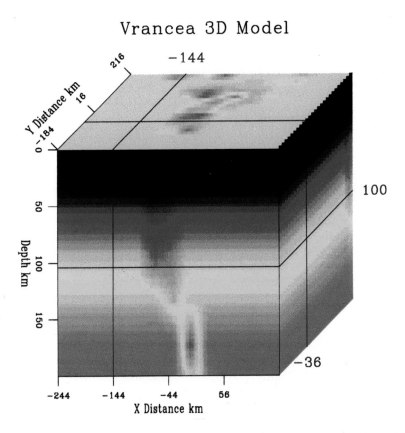

Fig. 1. Vrancea model derived from Tomography. [Movie slices through model]

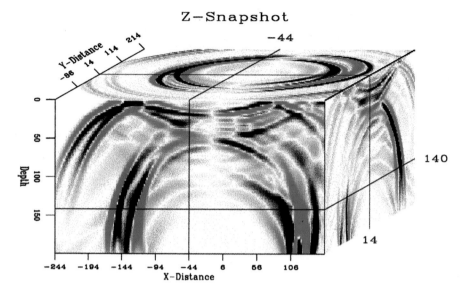

Fig. 2. Vrancea 3D snapshot vertical displacement component. Display planes through the earthquake location. [Movie steps through time evolution]

3.3 Recording Locations

In Figure 4 a simulated areal photograph of the modeled wave field is depicted. The symbols denote the locations where actual seismographs are deployed in the field in Rumania. These locations are superimposed on the wave field at a certain point in time. In contrast to the numerical modeling, where we have the entire wave field at small grid distances available, those real-world recording locations are very sparse. Such sparse localities make it difficult to invert real recordings with great accuracy and reliability.

3.4 Seismograms

In numerical simulations one is able to place recording devices at each point on the numerical model. The seismograms of those hypothetical recording stations are shown in Figure 5. Those seismograms represent the vertical ground motion at each of the surface locations in our model. This enables one to generate artificial data which can be compared with recorded data and which can tell how well the model is in agreement with the real world, thus leading to a improved inversion method.

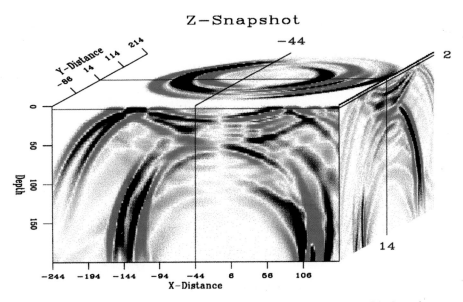

Fig. 3. Vrancea 3D snapshots of vertical displacement component. Display planes through the earthquake location and the surface. [Movie steps through time evolution]

Fig. 4. Bird's eye view of a surface snapshot in the modeled area, with real recording stations superimposed.

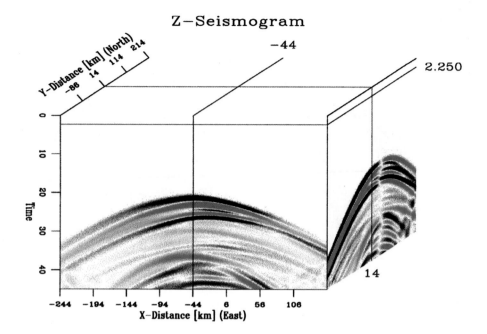

Fig. 5. 3D seismograms of vertical displacement component. [Movie slices through seismogram volume]

4   Conclusion

A portable Finite Difference modeling software written in High Performance Fortran and I/O based on the SEPLIB processing package allows to model earthquake wave propagation in 3D earth models. This small modeling scenario demonstrates the practicality of modeling earthquake wave propagation realistically and shows that in the future it can be used for more elaborate modeling scenarios as they are planned for the Collaborative Research Project SFB 461 and other international collaborative projects at Karlsruhe University.

References

1. Karrenbach, M.: Elastic Tensor Wave Fields, 1995, Ph.D. Thesis, Stanford University.
2. Karrenbach, M.: Modeling Physical Systems, 1998, Karlsruhe University.
3. Aursch-Schmidt, M.: Seismische Modellierung mit Finite Differenzen in 2D, 1998, Diploma Thesis, Karlsruhe University.
4. Lorenz, F. and Pohl, M.: A Tomography model of the Vrancea Region, personal communication, 1997.
5. Karrenbach, M. and Knopf P.: Parallel Seismic Processing, 1998, this issue.
6. Koelbel, J.: High Performance Fortran Handbook, 1992.

Parallel Seismic Data Processing

Martin Karrenbach[1], Petra Knopf[2], and Matthias Jacob[3]

Geophysical Institute, Karlsruhe University, 76187 Karlsruhe, Germany

Abstract. In Geophysics measured seismic data sets need to be analyzed using numerical operators. Such operators consist of Fourier Transforms, integral transforms, convolutions and other mathematical concepts. The result of such inversion methods is a realistic description of the subsurface of the earth. In this project we port a seismic processing package, called SEPLIB, which has been developed at Stanford University, to a parallel environment such as the Cray T3E. This package is a cornerstone of current software development for seismic algorithms in the Geophysical Institute at the University of Karlsruhe and as such is used as a basis for other computationally intensive seismic projects. We concentrate in this article on the end user aspect of utilizing High Performance Fortran to implement geophysical seismic algorithms. We compare strategies in which the computational domain is distributed over various processors with ensembles of computational grids aligned using the HPF standard language.

1 Seismic Data Processing

The memory and time requirements of seismic calculations suggest parallel implementations. Geophysical experiments usually produce large data sets (Gigabytes and Terabytes), when structure and material properties are to be analyzed in 3 dimensions. Analysis of those data applies sequences of mathematical operations. Often these operations can be described by linear and non-linear operators, such as Fourier Transforms, convolutions and other integral or differential transforms. In the end, the seismic data inversion produces a detailed description of the earth' interior. Figure 2 shows the result of a two-dimensional acquisition geometry for a real experiment (Courtesy of Mobil Oil Co., USA). The three faces of the three-dimensional data volume are projected on to two dimensions. The gray-scale amplitudes depict the signal strengths of reflected and recorded signals from the subsurface. The color black signifies maximum negative amplitude, the color white signifies maximum positive ampltidues and gray colors signify grades in between those to extremes. Several high contrast layers give rise to strong reflection amplitudes.

1.1 Seismic Data Topology

When carrying out a typical seismic experiment (Fig. 1), the subsurface is probed by elastic waves that emanate from a source point and illuminate a particular part of the subsurface. At material discontinuities part of the waves are reflected back to the surface and the remaining part is transmitted further and possibly reflected again later.

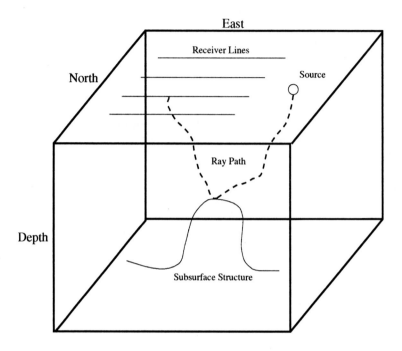

Fig. 1. Example of a common acquisition geometry for marine seismic data.

Historically, there exist a number of seismic processing packages, both commercial and public. SEPLIB is such a publically available processing package, that has been developed at Stanford University over the years. Within this package conventional processing operators can be applied to seismic data. Development of novel operators is relatively easy, since Input/Output, Parameter retrieval etc. are standardized and data are stored in a network transparent format. Currently the processing system is ported to a multitude of UNIX platforms (HP, Convex, Intel, IBM AIX, SP-2, SGI Origin, DEC, SUN, etc.).

Within this project SEPLIB has been ported to the Cray T3E. Numerical seismic methods have different practical requirements such that it is ideal to have the package installed on various different platforms. To leverage the strength of the Cray T3E, fast computation and large amount of physical memory, we ported it to this distributed memory machine. Typically, we aim at developing initial modules on workstations and migrate to larger machines as necessary. This smooth migration path is only possible if we choose programming and software standards wisely. In an innovative truely object-oriented approach we used Java as a high performance computing lan-

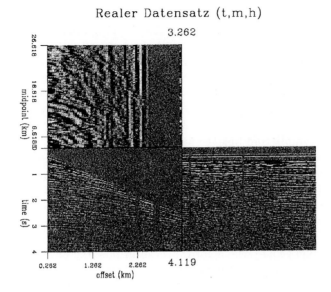

Fig. 2. Mobil AVO data set 2D acquisition geometry.

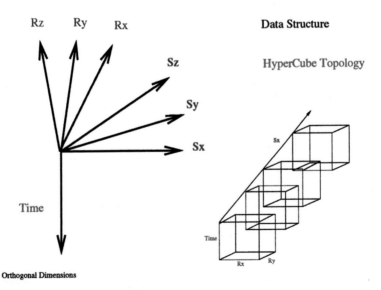

Fig. 3. A seismic data set topology exhibits a quasi regular, N-dimensional hyper-cube topology. The arrangement of subcubes on the right shows a particular simple case.

guage (Jacob, 1998). However, in the conventional implementation the core libraries in SEPLIB are mostly written entirely in the "C" programming language, with a numerical user libraries mostly implemented in Fortran. The binding of object code originating from different languages has long since been a problem, when porting packages onto different platforms or when using different compilers, since no rigorous standard exists. The size of floating point or integer numbers and the object symbol name generation have to be taken into account carefully. On the Cray T3E we used the native C and Fortran 90 compiler to compile and link the basic package.

The software package is composed of several libraries, data processing routines, and modular programs. Individual modules can be combined via socket communication (Unix pipes) to achieve a sequence of processes. Simple tools, called **Sepzilla and Pipe**, have been designed and implemented as **perl, csh** or **ksh** scripts to run the originally serial modules in parallel, without any change to the existing SEPLIB software system. Some classes of particularly simple parallel geophysical algorithms can in this way be run in parallel without the need for reprogramming. The use of these tools is thus very limited, yet nevertheless extremely useful for seismic data processing. Both tools use remote shells directly to coarsely parallelize the operations and distribute the load.

Several projects of the Geophysical Institute at Karlsruhe University depend on the availability of this software package on the Cray T3E. Users can write their own application code and link with SEPLIB libraries to get their basic functionality. Usually those people program their algorithm in the Fortran language. This language is still widely used in the seismic industry.

2   Expressing Parallelism Efficiently

In seismic data processing many numerical operations are inherently parallel. The same type of operation is applied to subsets of the original data set. Standard processing sequences that pertain to a certain experimental configuration, such as common source or common midpoint processing, fall automatically in this category. This kind of parallelism is obvious and can be easily utilized by first adequately dividing up the input data set, distributing it on different processing nodes and finally collecting the processed subsets and combining them into the complete output data set. This kind of macro task level parallelism is implemented using remote shell invocations and socket communication. The high-level perl script **Sepzilla** achieves data and process management in a portable manner on distributed memory machines. The only requirement is that the usual non-parallel SEPLIB environment is installed. While Sepzilla is a reasonable way to parallelize some specific simple parallel seismic processing flows, it is not possible to program novel parallel algorithms in it, as could be done easily in HPF or other parallel languages.

This is a convenient way to operate in parallel the already existing serial SEPLIB programs and processing sequences. The end user only has to learn the **Sepzilla** interface and is then ready to utilize the parallel processing power of the parallel distributed memory machine. In such a mode, parallelism within the macro task is not leveraged, but there is also no need to program the macro operation explicitly in a parallel fashion. The user can write up the algorithm in a traditional serial fashion.

In some instances parallelism is not easily achieved by simply sub diving the input and output data ensembles. In this case the geophysical algorithm has to be programmed in some language explicitly parallel. Often a programming language, such as Fortran or C is used and messages are passed explicitly by obeying some standard (MPI,PVM). While the programmer does not need to learn a parallel language syntax, he has to insert subroutine calls and programming logic to utilize the capabilities of the parallel machine. While this technique can lead to very efficient code, the programmer carries the burden of debugging not just the numerical behavior of the algorithm, but also the message passing logic of the program, which can lead to time consuming tracking of dead locks and communication bottlenecks. This task does not pertain to the geophysical numerical method itself on which we would like to focus.

Another alternative is to use High Performance Fortran (HPF). In this new Fortran language parallelism can be expressed by language constructs as well as by using standard compiler directives. The task of inserting explicit message passing is taken over by the compiler. The user then relies on the compiler to take the necessary action to parallelize and distribute data objects efficiently.

We concentrate on the geophysicist as an end user who (re)writes frequently high level numerical algorithms and needs a flexible, portable, efficient and easily debugable way to implement methods. He should not be bogged down by tracking deadlocks or other programming bugs, that have nothing to do with the inherent geophysical problem to be solved. HPF is simpler to use under these circumstances, but in reality might show some communication bottlenecks.

Since most of the actual message passing and parallel data access is hidden by the compiler and the run time system, it is important to investigate, how parallelism can be expressed efficiently on a high level, yet stay platform and compiler independent. In this paper we investigate this practical issue by implementing several benchmarks on top of the SEPLIB environment.

HPF provides several language constructs to express parallelism explicitly. Most of them act on the elements of multi-dimensional arrays. We decided on testing the following combinations.

HPF parallel language constructs:

- explicit **do**-loop
- **array** notation

- **forall** statement
- **forall** construct

In addition to language constructs we can use special comments that will be recognized by HPF compilers. We use the data distribution directive, which allows to indicate to the compiler how multi-dimensional arrays should be stored in various processors. The following list shows the actual distributions used for a 5-dimensional array of seismic data.

HPF compiler directives for data distribution **!HPF$ DISTRIBUTE**

- default (no directive)
- **(BLOCK,BLOCK,BLOCK,*,*)**
- **(BLOCK,BLOCK,*,*,*)**
- **(*,BLOCK,*,*,*)**
- **(BLOCK,*,*,*,*)**
- **(*,BLOCK,BLOCK,*,*)**

Distribution in blocks keeps junks of the original array locally in processors. A * forces entire dimensions to be located in each single processing element. Thereby one can easily determine data locality and array access patterns for a given algorithm. The two rightmost indices are always forced to stay in a processor, while the three leftmost indices can take on a variety of distribution types. We vary the distributions only for the dimensions connected to spatial physical dimensions of the entier array, since those likely to produce the largest difference in algorithm behaviour in reality.

3   Benchmarking Array Distribution in HPF

The benchmarking times are measured with the intrinsic HPF time measurement function: **system_clock**. It is a standard timer function available within the language. The time measured is the user time that elapsed for all the statements between read-outs of the timer.

The data object consists of a 5-dimensional floating point array presenting the hypercube topology in Figure 3:
field(1:nz,1:nx,1:ny,1:ncomp,1:ntau)
A small scale array object for modeling purposes might have the following dimensions:
nz=100, nx=100, ny=100, ncomp=3, ntau=3, --- 10^7 **elements**
A more small scale object for processing purposes might have the dimensions:
nz=1000, nx=60, ny=1800, ncomp=3, ntau=1, --- 3.2410^8 **elements**

The **ncomp** and **ntau** axes typically (depending on the processing flow) can be independent of other axes. The main computational effort for modeling seismic wave fields lie in the **nz,nx,ny** sub-space. Operations can range from independent 1D operators along individual axes to 2D and 3D local and global numerical operations, such as 3D Finite Difference stencils or multi-dimensional Fourier Transforms.

In this particular example we test computational kernels for time-stepping a seismic wave field, thus testing mainly floating point performance and memory access.

In Figure 4 and 5 we investigate the runtime behaviour of the different parallel language constructs for a fixed size floating point array of dimensions (100,100,100,3,3). The problem is distributed onto 8 processors. The x-axis in Figure 4 and 5 represents the data mapping of the data object via HPF compiler directives. The directives are abbreviated as: **default:** no direc-

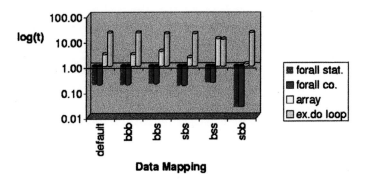

Fig. 4. Runtime comparison of computational kernels for Cray T3E. Runtime is plottet logarithmically due to large differences. Shortest runtime is produced by sbb = (*,BLOCK,BLOCK,*,*) distribution with forall statements and constructs.

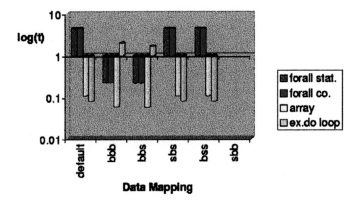

Fig. 5. Runtime comparison of computational kernels for IBM SP-2 using the xlhpf compiler. Shortest runtime is produced by bbs = (BLOCK,BLOCK,*,*,*) distribution with array notation.

tive , **bbb**: (BLOCK,BLOCK,BLOCK,*,*) , **bbs**: (BLOCK,BLOCK,*,*,*) , **sbs**: (*,BLOCK,*,*,*), **bbs**: (BLOCK,*,*,*,*), and **sbb**: (*,BLOCK,BLOCK,*,*) . The y-axis represents the elapsed user time in minutes on a logarithmic scale. Color bars indicate the timing for different parallel constructs operating on the object, i.e.: `explicit do-loop`, `array`, `forall statement`, and `forall construct`. Bars below the baseline indicate that computation take less time than for bars above the baseline. The longer the bar extends below the baseline, the shorter is the actual runtime in this case.

On Cray T3E, Figure 4, the `forall construct` language construct produced the best performance results for all cases of data mapping. A slight improvement is visible compared against the `forall statement`. The compiler can optimze the statements in the construct and place synchronization barriers at beginning and end of the construct, instead of having to synchronize each `forall statement`, as the lanugage standard requires. The shortest computation time is achieved by the `forall construct` with a **sbb** data layout. The first array axis is placed in memory in each node, thus avoiding inter-node communication, when computation proceeds along this axis. However, depending on the computational array size, this mapping cannot always be used. On the **IBM-SP**, Figure 5, the `array` notation achieved for **bbb** and **bbs** data distributions the best performance results. Significant longer computation times were needed by `forall constructs` and `forall statements` with **sbs,bss** data layouts. It seems that particular compiler optimzations and particular physical memory and cache access mechanisms on those two different platforms give rise to the necessity of using different data distributions and language constructs, when solving otherwise identical problems.

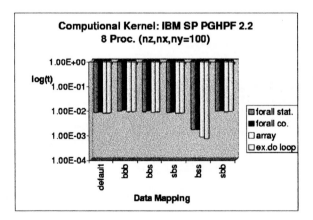

Fig. 6. Runtime comparison of computational kernels for IBM SP-2 using the `pghpf` compiler. The implementation of parallel parallel constructs is balanced. Due to the problem topology a speedup of the **bss** = (BLOCK,*,*,*,*) array distribution is visible.

Above benchmarks tested the runtime behaviour of a fixed processor topology. In order to obtain information about scalability behaviour we repeated the same test with varying number of processors used to solve the problem.

Due to the size of most large-scale seismic computations, the **bbb** layout is a likely data mapping candidate to be used in practice. Figure 7 demonstrates the scalability of the **bbb** data distribution on a CrayT3E. The test was con-

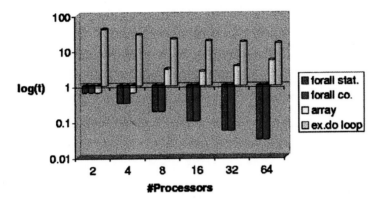

Fig. 7. Scalability of a bbb distribution for computational kernels on Cray T3E. For `forall` statements and constructs the speedup is nearly linear.

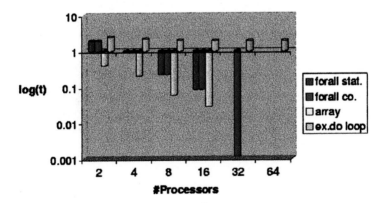

Fig. 8. Scalability of a bbb distribution for computational kernels on IBM SP-2 using the XLHPF compiler. For `forall` statements and constructs and `array` notation the speedup is nearly linear up to 16 processors. At 32 processors the computational subsets are so small, that they fit in the processors' cache and thus achieve superlinear speedup. Some measurements at high processor numbers timing measurements that were to small to be measured accurately by the `system_clock` function.

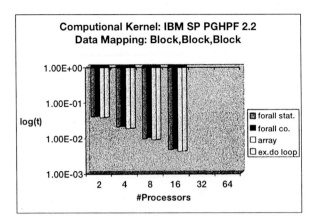

Fig. 9. Scalability of a bbb distribution for computational kernels on IBM SP-2using the PGI HPF compiler. For `forall` statements and constructs and `array` notation the speedup is nearly linear up to 16 processors. Above 20 processors measurement are unavailable due to a current number of process limitation on the available SP-2.

ducted with 2, 4, 8, 16, 32 and 64 processors. Using **forall construct** and **forall statement** we observe a nearly linear scaling, whereas the performance for the **array** notation is decreasing. On the IBM-SP, Figure 8, we determined a linear performance improvement for **array notation, forall constructs** and **forall statements** for the **xlhpf** compiler. Superlinear speedup occured, when the number of processors was large enough, such that indivual array subsets fittet within the cache of the processors. On some tests timing measurements were not reliable (resulting in null timings) with the current **xlhpf** implementation and are thus omitted from the Figure 8. The **pghpf** compiler shows in Figure 6 similar behaviour for all parallel constructs on the IBM SP-2 in its performance. One array distribution fits particularly well to the computational kernel, leading to a substantial speed up. A nearly linear speedup of the **bbb** data distribution can be achieved on this benchmark using any of the parallel constructs, as shown in Figure 9.

4   Conclusion

The optimal layout of n-dimensional arrays is platform dependent as well as problem topology dependent. Different data topologies require different layouts of the seismic arrays. If we can keep sub-sets of the seismic array locally on a processor or even in cache, we can save in data communication cost. We found that **array notation** is fastest on IBM SP-2 using the **xlhpf** compiler, while on the Cray T3E **forall** constructs with the **pghpf** compiler proved fastest. On the SP-2 **pghpf** indicates that no particular parallel construct is preferred and thus all lead to similar computation times. Unfortunately we were only able to use programs that were compiled with the **pghpf** compiler for less than 20 nodes due to particular machine limits. Since **xlhpf** does not exhibit this limitaiton, we consider it as well in all our comparisons. Efficient implementation of parallel constructs can differ from platform to platform and from compiler to compiler.

Our optimistic hope, that we could write entirely platform independent source code, was dampened. Yet it is easy enough to produce differently layed-out executable versions of the program that can adjust to the problem topolgoy at hand. Small benchmark runs are then necessary to determine which layout suits the problem best. HPF is not the panacea in portability (HPF compiler implementations definitely differ in performance), but goes a long way. Only a minimum of platform dependent adjustments are necessary.

References

1. Programming linear operators in C++, Stanford Exploration Project, http://sepwww.stanford.edu/clop
2. Jacob, M., Philippsen, M. and Karrenbach, M.: Large-Scale Parallel Algorithms in Java: A Feasibility Study, to appear in: Concurrency: Theory & Practice, Volume 10, 1998
3. Koelbel, J.: High Performance Fortran Handbook, 1992.
4. PGI HPF compiler User Guide: http://www.pgroup.com/hpf_docs/pghpf_ug/hpfug.html
5. PGI HPF compiler Reference Guide: http://www.pgroup.com/hpf_docs/pghpf_ref/hpfwsr.html
6. xlHPF compiler Reference Guide: http://www.uni.karlsruhe.de/ÃIX/XLHPF
7. Apprentice, Manual Page Craytools
8. SEPLIB: Processing Package, Stanford Exploration Project, http://sepwww.stanford.edu/
9. Yilmaz, O.: Seismic Data Processing, Society of Exploration Geophysicists, 1986 http://www.seg.org/.

Parallel computing on Near-field Scanning Optical Microscopy (NSOM)

Characterisation of the Depolarization NSOM

G. von Freymann, Th. Schimmel, and M. Wegener

Institut für Angewandte Physik, Universität Karlsruhe (TH), Kaiserstraße 12, D - 76128 Karlsruhe

Abstract. The contrast mechanism in the Depolarization Near-field Scanning Optical Microscope is studied numerically. We solve the complete set of the vectorial Maxwell equations with the Green-dyade-formalism. The mathematical method and its numerical implementation are discussed in detail. First results like the polarization dependence of the image contrast are presented.

1 Introduction

Small apertures in close proximity of a sample allow for spatial resolution in an optical experiment which is essentially only limited by the aperture size [Pohl84]. Thus subwavelength resolution can be obtained. Different variations of this general idea have recently attracted considerable attention, see e. g. [Goed97]. The aperture is often considered to be the essential point of near-field scanning optical microscopy, and can be realized by metal coating of an optical fiber tip. Recent experiments claim, however, that subwavelength resolution can also be achived with uncoated optical fiber tips [Lang98] while others come to a negative conclusion [Sand97]. To clear this discussion, we solve the complete set of the vector maxwell equations for a model geometry, working in internal reflection with cross polarized detection. Image contrast is obtained due to the depolarization of the incident light in the tip-sample region. Thus we call this apparatus the depolarization near-field scanning optical microscope (DP-NSOM) [Adel98].

2 Model

The DP-NSOM works as follows: a laser beam (here a helium-neon laser with wavelength $\lambda = 633\,\text{nm}$) is sent through a polarizer to obtain a linearly polarized beam. Coupled into the fiber, it propagates downwards (negative z-direction) and is reflected due to the interaction with tip and sample. An essential element in this setup is a fiber optical polarization manipulator, which allows to control the polarization at the tip. The reflected beam is then sent through an analyser orthogonal to the incident polarization, so that only depolarized components are detected. Due to the numerical exact

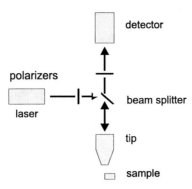

Fig. 1. The simulated experimental setup: A linearly polarized laser beam is sent down the optical fiber. The cross polarized components of the backreflected light are detected.

controllable polarization, the polarization manipulator can be neglected in the computer simulations, see Fig. 1. Due to the huge numerical effort required it is currently impossible to simulate a whole macroscopic fiber. However, there is no need to simulate such extended geometries. We are interested in the optical near-field in the tip-sample region and a small part of the tip outside this region. This allows us to determine the intensity propagating in the fiber towards the detector. To calculate this intensity, a knowledge of the total field inside the tip is necessary.

The tip and the sample are embedded in a homogenous reference medium (here: vacuum), described by the dielectric constant $\epsilon_{\text{ref}}(\omega)$. Then the dielectric constant of the whole system can be written as

$$\epsilon(\mathbf{r}, \omega) = \epsilon_{\text{ref}}(\omega) + \triangle\epsilon_S(\mathbf{r}, \omega). \tag{1}$$

where $\triangle\epsilon_S(\mathbf{r}, \omega)$ vanishes outside the objects. The solution of the resulting wave equation

$$-\nabla \times \nabla \times \mathbf{E}(\mathbf{r}) + k^2\epsilon_{\text{ref}}(\omega)\mathbf{E}(\mathbf{r}) = -k^2\triangle\epsilon_S(\mathbf{r}, \omega)\mathbf{E}(\mathbf{r}). \tag{2}$$

can be written as

$$\mathbf{E}(\mathbf{r}) = \mathbf{E}_0(\mathbf{r}) + \int_S \hat{G}_0(\mathbf{r}, \mathbf{r}', \omega) \cdot V(\mathbf{r}', \omega)\mathbf{E}(\mathbf{r}')\,\mathrm{d}\mathbf{r}'. \tag{3}$$

where $\mathbf{E}_0(\mathbf{r})$ is the solution of the homogenous differential equation, $\hat{G}_0(\mathbf{r}, \mathbf{r}', \omega)$ is the Green-dyade of the reference medium and $V(\mathbf{r}', \omega) = -k^2\triangle\epsilon_S(\mathbf{r}', \omega)$. Equation (3) is known as the *Lippmann-Schwinger-equation*.

The Lippmann-Schwinger-equation gives a solution $\mathbf{E}(\mathbf{r})$ for the whole system, if the incident field $\mathbf{E}_0(\mathbf{r})$, the Green-dyade $\hat{G}_0(\mathbf{r}, \mathbf{r}', \omega)$, and the field inside the objects $E(r')$ are known. Olivier Martin developed an algorithm to solve exactly the Lippmann-Schwinger-equation (3) [Mart94]. This algorithm is based on computing the Green-dyade for the whole system using the Dyson-equation.

The Dyson-equation is the Lippmann-Schwinger-equation for operators:

$$\hat{G}(r,r',\omega) = \hat{G}_0(r,r',\omega) + \int_S \hat{G}_0(r,r'',\omega) \cdot V(r'',\omega)\hat{G}(r'',r',\omega)\,dr''$$

(4)

Knowing the Green-dyade belonging to the whole system, it is possible to calculate the total field inside the objects using the following equation:

$$E(r) = E_0(r) + \int_S \hat{G}(r,r',\omega) \cdot V(r',\omega)E_0(r')\,dr'$$

(5)

Look at the incident field $E_0(r')$ that replaces the field inside the detector, while $\hat{G}(r,r',\omega)$ is the Green-dyade of the whole system. To solve the equations shown above, we discretize our model geometry using cubic meshes with different volumes, assuming that the field variations are small over a mesh.

3   Numerical Implementation

Using N meshes to discretize the geometry, the discretized Lippmann-Schwinger- and Dyson-equation are written as follows (w^k = volume of the mesh k):

$$E^i = E_0^i + \sum_{k=1}^{N} \hat{G}_0^{i,k} V^k w^k E^k \qquad i = 1 \ldots N.$$

(6)

$$\hat{G}^{i,j} = \hat{G}_0^{i,j} + \sum_{k=1}^{N} \hat{G}_0^{i,k} V^k w^k \hat{G}^{k,j} \qquad i,j = 1 \ldots N.$$

(7)

Adding only one mesh ($k = 1$) to the reference system, the sums vanish:

$$E_1^i = E_0^i + \hat{G}_0^{i,1} V^1 w^1 E_1^1$$

(8)

$$\hat{G}_1^{i,j} = \hat{G}_0^{i,j} + \hat{G}_0^{i,1} V^1 w^1 \hat{G}_1^{1,j} \qquad \begin{cases} i = 1 \ldots N \\ j = i+1 \ldots N \end{cases} .$$

(9)

Solving this equations in a first step for the added mesh

$$E_1^1 = E_0^1 + \hat{G}_0^{1,1} V^1 w^1 E_1^1$$

(10)

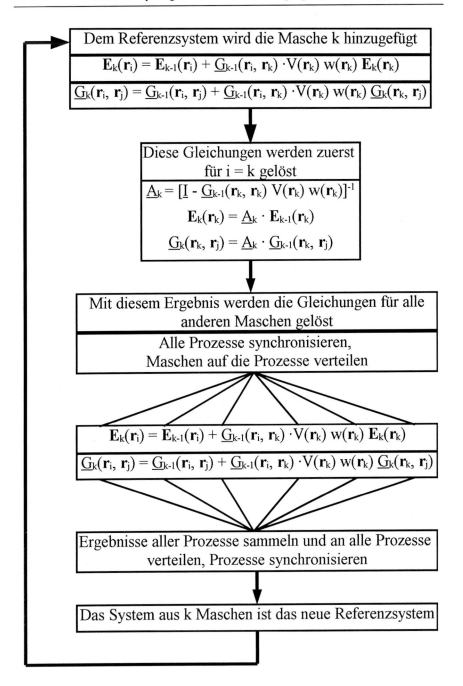

Fig. 2. Schematical representation of the algorithm. $\underline{I}$ is the unit matrix, all underlined symbols are matrizes, bold quantities are vectors. Solving the Dyson-equation j is running from 0 to N.

$$\hat{G}_1^{1,j} = \hat{G}_0^{1,j} + \hat{G}_0^{1,1} V^1 w^1 \hat{G}_1^{1,j} \qquad j = i+1\ldots N \qquad (11)$$

and calculating the influence of this mesh to the meshes at all other places

$$\boldsymbol{E}_1^i = \boldsymbol{E}_0^i + \hat{G}_0^{i,1} V^1 w^1 \boldsymbol{E}_1^1 \qquad (12)$$

$$\hat{G}_1^{i,j} = \hat{G}_0^{i,j} + \hat{G}_0^{i,1} V^1 w^1 \hat{G}_1^{1,j}. \qquad (13)$$

deliver the Green-dyade and the electromagnetic field for the system with one mesh, the new reference system. To obtain the solution for the whole problem, each mesh will be added in a similar manner until all meshes are calculated. The equations can be written iteratively as

$$\boldsymbol{E}_n^i = \boldsymbol{E}_{n-1}^i + \hat{G}_{n-1}^{i,k} V^k w^k \boldsymbol{E}_n^k \qquad (14)$$

$$\hat{G}_n^{i,j} = \hat{G}_{n-1}^{i,j} + \hat{G}_{n-1}^{i,k} V^k w^k \hat{G}_n^{k,j} \qquad (15)$$

where n means the number of the actual added mesh. A visualization of this algorithm [Gira95] expanded with our parallel addition shows Fig. 2. The calculation of the Green-dyade is done in parallel to speed up the calculation. The index j is of essential role to the calculation time. Starting with $j = i+1$ then only such elements of the Green-dyade are calculated, which have to be known for the solution. Beginning with $j = 1$, then it is possible to obtain the whole field distribution inside the objects for any incident field with the same wavelength at once, using equation (5). For one polarization this doubles the calculation time, but if one is interested in other polarizations, no further calculation of the green-dyade is necessary. This can speed up the simulation and minimize the numerical effort.

The Green-dyade of the homogenous medium can be found in [Yagh80].

3.1 Performance

For each mesh there are twelve equations to solve. Three for the electromagnetic field and nine for the Green-dyade. Due to the connection of each mesh with all other meshes over the Green-dyade, this number grows in the second power of the mesh number. For each mesh the interactions with all other meshes have to be calculated. This needs, using N meshes, at all $3N + 9N^2$ equations to solve. With complex numbers this ends up at $2N(3N + 9N^2)$ equations. For a small geometry discretized with 500 meshes this are 2,251,500,000 real equations.

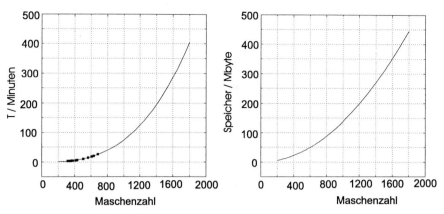

Fig. 3. Calculation time and need of memory using 10 processes in parallel.

4   Numerical results

The object under investigation is a small glass bar ($n=1.5$, 60 nm x 120 nm x 40 nm) centered at the origin. The tip is formed like an experimental used one, see Fig. 4. To studie the influence of depolarization on the image contrast we perform the following linescans: a) linescan along the x-axis over an edge, polarization parallel to the x-axis, b) linescan along the x-axis over a corner, polarization parallel to the x-axis, and c) linescan along the x-axis over an edge, polarization orthogonal to the x-axis. Tip height above the sample is parameter.

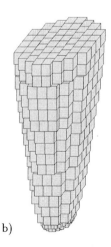

Fig. 4. a) A scanning electron micrograph of a fiber tip used in the experiments. b) The model tip used in the simulations.

To calculate the total field intensity at the detector's position, we have to elongate the small discretized tip with fiber optic assumptions. Only light propagating within the angle of total internal reflection is guided by the fiber. Integrating over an area belonging to such an opening angle delivers the total field intensity at the detector's position.

a) linescan along the x-axis over an edge, polarization parallel to the x-axis:

We use the following two detection modes: the IP-mode for detection in the incident polarization, and the OP-mode for detection in the orthogonal polarization. The tip scans in constant height above the glass bar. In Fig. 5 it can be seen that the OP-mode shows subwavelength structures (with a full width at half maximum of 71 nm, corresponding to $\lambda/9$), which disappear when the tip-sample separation is successively increased. This behaviour indicates near-field resolution and is contrasted by the IP-mode which exhibits much weaker subwavelength structures.

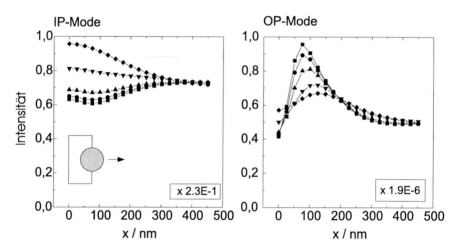

Fig. 5. Linescans over a glass bar in constant height (5 nm, 10 nm, 20 nm, 50 nm, and 100 nm).

The different tip heights are indicated with the following symbols:

—■— 5 nm,   —●— 10 nm,   —▲— 20 nm,   —▼— 50 nm,   —◆— 100 nm

We interpret the physics of the imaging process as follows: objects much smaller than the wavelength of light depolarize a linearly polarized electromagnetic wave. Thus both, tip and the spatially separated sample lead to a depolarized component which introduces a certain constant background in the OP-mode. If tip and sample are in close proximity, the combined depolarization of the tip-sample region is larger, thus more signal is detected in the OP-mode. This depolarization leads to the image in the OP-mode. Therefore not the object itself but rather the edges which are perpendicular to the incident electric field vector are imaged.

b) linescan along the x-axis over a corner, polarization parallel to the x-axis

If this assumptions hold, then the depolarization must be even stronger, when scanning over a corner rather than an edge. Fig. 6 shows the results for exactly the same parameter as in Fig. 5, except for the scanning position (see inset). All details in the signal can be reproduced, but the signal intensity is much stronger.

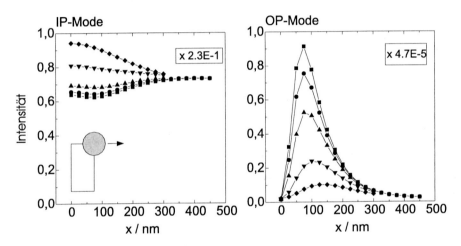

Fig. 6. Linescans over a corner of the glass bar.

c) linescan along the x-axis over an edge, polarization orthogonal to the x-axis

As assumed, the depolarization contrast vanish, while scanning with polarization parallel to the edges. No discontinuity in the material distribution exists for the electric field in this configuration, thus no depolarization occurs (see Fig. 7).

5   Conclusions

We have presented the numerical algorithm used to solve the complete set of the vectorial maxwell equations. For a model geometry we have shown that subwavelength resolution can be obtained by scanning an uncoated optical fiber tip in the near-field of a sample and detecting the orthogonal linear polarization of the internally reflected light.

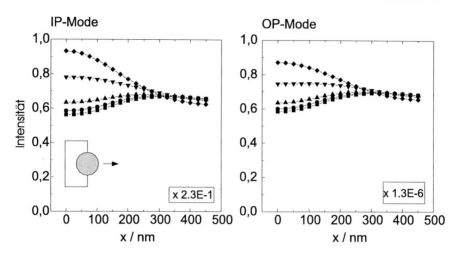

Fig. 7. Linescans over the edge of the glass bar. The incident polarization is parallel to the edge, therfore no contrast is shown.

6   Acknowledgement

We acknowledge support through the DFG Sonderforschungsbereichs 195.

References

[Adel98]   Ch. Adelmann, J. Hetzler, Th. Schimmel, M. Wegener, H. Weber, and H. v. Löhneysen *Appl. Phys. Lett.*. submitted (1998).

[Gira95]   Christian Girard, Alain Dereux, and Olivier J. F. Martin. *NATO ASI Series E* **300**, 1–20, 1995.

[Gira94]   Christian Girard, Alain Dereux, and Olivier J. F. Martin. *Physical Review B* **49**(19), 13872–13881, 1994.

[Goed97]   W. Göhde, J. Tittel, T. Basch, C. Bäuchle, U. C. Fischer, and H. Fuchs. *Rev. Sci. Instrum.* **68**, 2466, 1994.

[Lang98]   W. Langbein, J. M. Hvam, S. Madsen, M. Hetterich, and C. Klingshirn. *Phys. Stat. Sol. A* **164**, 541, 1997. S. Madsen, S. I. Bozhevolnyi, and J. M. Hvam. *Optics Commun.*,, in press (1998).

[Mart94]   Olivier J. F. Martin, Alain Dereux, and Christian Girard. *J. Opt. Soc. Am. A* **11**(3), 1073–1079, 1994.

[Pohl84]   D. W. Pohl, W. Denk, and M. Lanz. *Appl. Phys. Lett.* **44**, 1984.

[Sand97]   V. Sandoghdar, S. Wegscheider, G. Krausch, and J. Mlynek. *J.Appl. Phys.* **81**(6), 2499–2503, 1997.

[Yagh80]   Arthur D. Yaghjian. *Proceedings of the IEEE* **68**(2), 248–263, 1980.

Solid State Physics

Prof. Dr. Werner Hanke
Physikalisches Institut, Universität Würzburg
Am Hubland, D-97074 Würzburg,

Before the year 1937 the only known concept of classifying metals, insulators and semiconductors was based on the filling of electronic bands [?,?]. On the famous Bristol conference in 1937 though de Boer and Verway [?] reported that many transition metal oxides with partially filled d-electron bands do not fit into this picture. Experiments revealed that they are either poor conductors or even insulators in spite of their partially filled bands. Soon later Peierls [?] discovered that in some special cases the electron-electron correlations arising from strong coulomb repulsion can prevent the electrons from moving thus yielding an insulator. This article founded the field of strongly correlated electrons.

In the following decades much progress on the theoretical side came from Sir Neville Mott [?,?,?]. He introduced the intuitive picture that the partially filled band is split by the strong coulomb repulsion of electrons sitting on the same site. This leads to a completely filled valence band well separated by a gap from the empty conduction band. Nowadays we call this phenomenon a *Mott Insulator*.

The activity in the field of strongly correlated electrons exploded after the discovery of High-Temperature Superconductors by Bednorz and Müller in the year 1986 [?]. These Materials become superconducting upon doping and are antiferromagnetic insulators at half filling. The proximity of these two phases is another hint for the importance of strong electron-electron correlations in these materials. Because of the strong interactions all standard theoretical approaches (weak coupling) have so far failed. A detailed microscopic understanding is highly desirable because these materials offer a wider range of technical applications than the classical *low temperature* superconductors described by the *Bardeen-Cooper-Schrieffer* theory [?]. This is due to the high transition temperatures that are already reached by cooling with the (relatively cheap) liquid nitrogen.

In the last decade a whole zoo of new and exciting materials with great potential for technical applications was discovered: heavy fermion superconductors (UBe_{13}, UPt_3), magnetic heavy fermion systems ($NpBe_{13}$, U_2Zn_{17}, UCd_{11}), Manganites with colossal magneto-resistance ($La_{0.8}Ca_{0.2}MnO_3$, $La_{1-x}Pb_xMnO_3$) and Kondo-insulators ($FeSi$) to name a few. The effect of colossal magneto-resistance has possible future applications in computer storage media.

So far a detailed microscopic understanding for all the strongly correlated electron systems came mostly from numerical calculations like Quantum-Monte-Carlo [?,?] and exact diagonalizations [?] of small clusters whereas analytical perturbation-theory-like approaches mainly failed due to the strong electron-electron interactions. As mentioned above, weak coupling perturbation-theory predicts metals instead of insulators; the results of density-functional theory are often by a factor of two off compared to experiments.

For this reason the computer-oriented condensed-matter physics community is very grateful for the immense resources that have been made available for solving these exciting problems numerically. The in this book presented articles are excellent examples for the success of numerical work in this new field generated from the interaction between material science and many-particle physics.

References

1. A. Sommerfeld, Z. Phys. **47**, 1 (1928).
2. F. Bloch, Z. Phys. **57**, 545 (1929).
3. J. H. de Boer, E. J. W. Verway, Proc. Phys. Soc. A **49**, 59 (1937).
4. R. Peierls, Proc. Phys. Soc. A **49** (1937).
5. N. F. Mott, Proc. Phys. Soc. A **62**, 416 (1949).
6. N. F. Mott, Can. J. Phys. A **34**, 1356 (1956).
7. N. F. Mott, Phil. Mag. A **6**, 287 (1961).
8. G. Bednorz, K. A. Müller, Z. Phys. B **64**, 189 (1986).
9. J. Bardeen, L. M. Cooper, J. R. Schrieffer, Phys. Rev. **108**, 1175 (1957).
10. R. Preuss, A. Muramatsu, P. Dieterich, W. von der Linden, F.F. Assaad and W. Hanke, Phys. Rev. Lett. **73** S. 732 (1994).
11. R. Preuss, W. Hanke und W. von der Linden, Phys. Rev. Lett. **75**, 1344 (1995).
12. R. Eder, W. Hanke, S. C. Zhang, Phys. Rev. B **57**, 13781 (1998).

Quantum Monte Carlo simulations of one hole in the t-J model

M. Brunner and A. Muramatsu

Institut für Theoretische Physik III,
Universität Stuttgart, Pfaffenwaldring 57, D-70550 Stuttgart, Germany.

Abstract. Numerical simulations of the two-dimensional t-J model with one hole in the limit $J/t \ll 1$ are performed for rather large systems ($N \sim 10 \times 10$) using a world-line loop-algorithm. It is shown that in the one-hole case with $J = 0$, very low temperatures ($\beta t \sim 3000$) are necessary in order to reach Nagaoka's state. Full polarization becomes unstable for $J \sim 10^{-4}t$ towards partial polarization up to $J/t \lesssim 0.01$. $J/t \gtrsim 0.05$ leads to minimal spin. The two-hole case shows enhanced total spin up to the lowest attainable temperatures ($\beta t = 150$), well below those reached by other finite-temperature methods.

1 Introduction

Since the discovery of high-T_c superconductors (HTS), a great deal of interest was focused on strongly correlated systems like the Hubbard and t-J models. Especially the latter system attracts a lot of attention since it can be viewed as a model on its own right for HTS [1] and not only as the strong coupling limit of the Hubbard model. A key method for their understanding is provided by numerical simulations. For the Hubbard model, quantum Monte Carlo (QMC) simulations [2] can be performed for not too large values of the interaction U ($\lesssim 12$ in units of the hopping matrix element t) and also not too large inverse temperatures β ($\lesssim 10/t$), except for the half-filled case, where the so-called minus-sign problem is absent, thus limiting our understanding of the doped phase at low temperatures in the strong coupling limit. On the other hand, exact diagonalizations of the t-J model [3] provide information on precisely that limit but confined to rather small sizes N ($\lesssim 30$). QMC simulations for the t-J model were successfully performed in one-dimension [4], whereas previous simulations in higher dimensions suffered under metastability problems [5] or were restricted to the computation of energies in the ground state [6]. Further numerical studies were carried out using high-temperature expansions (HTE) [7,8] and density-matrix renormalization-group (DMRG) [9,10].

2   The loop algorithm for the t-J model

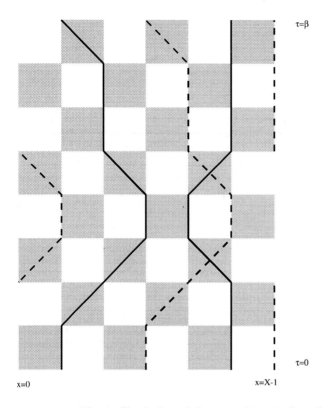

$\tau=\beta$

$\tau=0$

x=0   x=X-1

Fig. 1. Checkerboard-decomposition in $(1+1)$ dimensions

The loop algorithm used to simulate the t-J model is based on world-line algorithms that was successfully used for solving different one dimensional lattice problems [11,12]. The word-line algorithm is based on splitting up the Hamilton operator into several parts $\mathcal{H} = \mathcal{H}_1 + \mathcal{H}_2 + \ldots \mathcal{H}_p$, where each term consists of commuting two site interactions (*checkerboard breakup*). Furthermore one uses the Trotter formula [13] to approximate the partition function $\mathbf{Z} = tr\left[\left(e^{-\Delta\tau\mathcal{H}_1}e^{-\Delta\tau\mathcal{H}_2}\ldots e^{-\Delta\tau\mathcal{H}_p}\right)^n\right]$, where n is a large integer and $\Delta\tau = \beta/n$. The systematic error one acquires is $\mathcal{O}(\Delta\tau^2)$. Then one inserts a full set of states at all interstitial sites to obtain

$$\mathbf{Z} = \sum_{i_1,i_2,\ldots,i_{np}} <i_1|e^{-\Delta\tau\mathcal{H}_1}|i_2> \ldots < i_{np}|\mathcal{H}_p|i_1> . \qquad (1)$$

This corresponds to a $(d+1)$-dimensional classical lattice in space time instead of a d-dimensional quantum lattice. The simulation is performed by summing statistically over all possible states on the interstitial sites. In our case these states are in occupation number representation, so they can be visualized as world-lines in real space and time (see figure). The easiest way to sum over the configurations is by changing one state locally (i.e upgrading a word-line) and then accepting or rejecting the new state with the help of a heat bath or Metropolis algorithm. This method only works well for rather small correlation lengths (i.e high temperature) in one dimension. For large correlation lengths ξ the method suffers from long autocorrelation times $\tau \sim \xi^2$ [14]. In two dimensions this method breaks down completely for fermions, because one cannot change the topology of the world-lines with local upgrading. The newly developed cluster algorithms [15] are able to solve both problems for many systems. Instead of changing the world-lines locally, a cluster algorithm can change the configuration globally in a single step. This is done by statistically assigning graphs to the local configurations in a consistent way and then connecting those graphs to closed loops. The length of these loops can vary from connecting four points of the configuration (in (1+1) dimensions) to connecting all points of the configuration. Then, the loops are flipped (i.e. each state on the loop is inverted) with a certain probability.

For some systems like the Heisenberg antiferromagnet the autocorrelation time is dramatically reduced by using a cluster algorithm. Although the cluster algorithm is in principal an algorithm that works best for systems with only two possible states per site, it may be extended to systems with more possible states per site, such as the Hubbard model [16] or the t-J model [17,18].

3 Implementation of the algorithm on massive parallel computers

The general implementation of the above algorithm is as follows: Each point of the (2+1)-dimensional lattice is assigned to a single element of a one dimensional array of integers. As the code is completely in C the points in the array are generally addressed by pointers. One can now store the information of the local configuration and of the local graphs into this single integer. In that way it is possible to handle very large lattices (i.e. $12 \times 12 \times 20000$) without memory problems. All operations on the lattice can be done by bit manipulations (AND, OR, XOR).

The implementation on a massive parallel computer can be done in a rather simple way as most of the time no communication between the nodes is needed. Generally the code of a Quantum Monte Carlo algorithm can be split up into three parts:
The first part consists of input routines for the parameters. Then follows a warmup period.
In the second part of the program the updates and measurements are performed.

In the final section we gather the measurements of the different nodes and calculate the averages and statistical errors.

Whereas the first and third part have a lot of communication between the nodes, there is no communication at all in the second part. As this is the part of the code where most of the CPU-time is consumed, we have a nearly linear scaling of the statistical quality of our results with the number of nodes (see figure) The communication between the different nodes is made

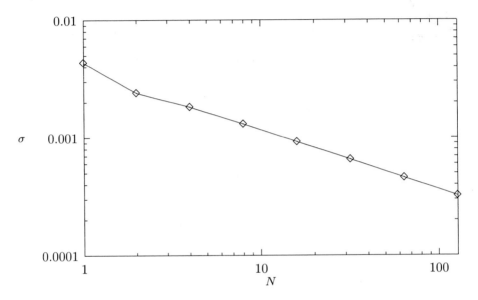

Fig. 2. The statistical error σ is plotted against the number of nodes N, where the CPU-time per node is fixed. The relationship $\sigma \sim \frac{1}{\sqrt{N}}$ is what one expects for a optimal Monte Carlo code.

with the library **M**essage **P**assing **I**nterface. In the first part of the program we mainly use MPI_broadcasts to distribute the values of used parameters like e.g size of the system or temperature. The last part of the program uses MPI_gather to gather the measurements of the simulations on the different nodes.

4 Results

We use a representation of the t-J model where it is obvious that it has no minus sign problem in the case of one hole and $J = 0$ [19,20]. As shown below, this enables us to reach very low temperatures, $(\beta t \sim 3000)$ that are necessary to converge to Nagaoka's ferromagnetic ground state. Such a slow convergence suggests that a high density of low lying excitations is present. We interpret them in the frame of a spin-wave theory, such that an effective ferromagnetic exchange interaction J_{eff} can be assigned for each lattice size. Finite-size scaling shows, that $J_{eff} \to 0$ in the thermodynamic limit as is expected. Hence, Nagaoka's ferromagnetic state has zero spin-stiffness in that limit. A frequently addressed question is the stability of Nagaoka's state for $J \neq 0$ or more than one hole [21–23]. Our simulations show that for $N = 10 \times 10$, $J \gtrsim 5 \times 10^{-4}$ suffices to bring the system to a ground-state without maximal spin. Simulations for more than one-hole could be performed up to temperatures as low as $\beta t \sim 150$, where an increase in total spin is observed due to the additional hole. Although the ground-state could not be reached, the limitation being the minus-sign problem, it should be remarked that such temperatures are by far lower than those attained previously by either QMC ($\beta t \lesssim 2$) [5] or HTE ($\beta t \lesssim 5$) [8]. On increasing J, we show that the system goes to minimal spin at $J/t \gtrsim 0.05$, whereas for $J/t \lesssim 0.01$ the system is partially polarized.

We first describe shortly the representation of the t-J model used in the simulations. Exact operator identities lead to a decomposition of the standard creation ($c^\dagger_{i,s}$) and annihilation ($c_{i,s}$) operators for fermions with spin $s = \uparrow, \downarrow$ [19,20]

$$c^\dagger_{i,\uparrow} = \gamma_{i,+} f_i - \gamma_{i,-} f^\dagger_i, \quad c^\dagger_{i,\downarrow} = \sigma_{i,-}(f_i + f^\dagger_i), \tag{2}$$

where $\gamma_{i,\pm} = (1 \pm \sigma_{i,z})/2$, $\sigma_{i,\pm} = (\sigma_{i,x} \pm i\sigma_{i,y})/2$, the spinless fermion operators fulfill the canonical anticommutation relations $\{f^\dagger_i, f_j\} = \delta_{ij}$, and $\sigma_{i,\alpha}$, $\alpha = x, y$, or z are the Pauli matrices. The constraint to avoid doubly occupied states reduces in this case to $\sum_i \gamma_{i,-} f^\dagger_i f_i = 0$ which is a holonomic constraint in contrast to the one normally used with the standard representation. Moreover, this constraint commutes with the Hamiltonian (3), such that once the simulation is prepared in that subspace, it remains there in the course of the evolution in imaginary time. The t-J Hamiltonian in this new representation has the following form

$$H_{t-J} = t \sum_{<i,j>} \left(P_{ij} f^\dagger_i f_j + \frac{J}{2} \Delta_{ij}(P_{ij} - 1) \right), \tag{3}$$

where $P_{ij} = (1 + \boldsymbol{\sigma}_i \cdot \boldsymbol{\sigma}_j)/2$, $\Delta_{ij} = (1 - n_i - n_j)$, and $n_i = f^\dagger_i f_i$. The constant added in (3) ensures that H_{t-J} reduces to the standard t-J model. In the case of one hole with $J = 0$, there is only one fermion present and the simulation has no minus-sign problem due to the exchange of fermions. For $J > 0$ a minus sign can occur because the exchange of two spins in space time generates them.

In the following we describe the results for the limit $J \to 0$ and mainly with one hole. Figure 3 shows the structure form factor

$$S(\boldsymbol{q}) = \frac{1}{N} \sum_{\boldsymbol{x}_i} \left(\exp\left(\imath \boldsymbol{x}_i \cdot \boldsymbol{q}\right) \sum_j S_j^z S_{j+\boldsymbol{x}_i}^z \right) \tag{4}$$

at $\boldsymbol{q} = 0$, i.e. $< S_{Tot}^z{}^2 >$ for $N = 8 \times 8$ and $N = 10 \times 10$ sites, as a function of βt. As can be clearly seen, very low temperatures ($\beta t \sim 1000 - 3000$) are needed in order to reach the fully saturated ferromagnet as predicted by Nagaoka's theorem. This suggests that a high density of low energy excitations is present as would be expected in the case of a Heisenberg ferromagnet. As a simple test of this hypothesis, we compare the temperature dependence of $S(\boldsymbol{q} = 0)$ from the QMC simulation with a spin-wave result, where the ferromagnetic exchange coupling J_{eff} of the hypothetical Heisenberg ferromagnet is chosen such as to fit the results of the simulation in Fig. 3. It is seen that the agreement is rather good in the low temperature sector, where the spin-wave approximation is expected to work. The inset of Fig. 3 shows that $J_{eff} \propto 1/N$, such that in the thermodynamic limit the spin-stiffness vanishes.

Figure 4 shows that ferromagnetic correlations are enhanced by adding a second hole to the system ($N = 12 \times 12$), suggesting a picture of a ferromagnetic polaron surrounding each hole, with a size limited by thermal fluctuations. Our result is consistent with a stability analysis by Barbieri et al. [24], where the Nagaoka state is stable for two holes and $N \gtrsim 12 \times 12$. However, such a comparison should be taken with care since the results of Ref. [24] are strictly valid in the limit $N_h \ll \ln N$, where N_h is the number of holes. Also DMRG studies [10] support a Nagaoka state for such a low doping ($\delta \sim 1.4\%$), although the geometry used in that case is quite different from ours, and boundary effects on stripe geometries can be more important than in our case, with periodic boundary conditions on a square lattice. Although the minus-sign problem precludes simulations at lower temperatures, $\beta t \sim 150$ is the lowest temperature reached so-far by numerical methods (in fact a factor 50 - 100 lower), extending thus significantly the region of validity for a ferromagnetic state for more than one-hole.

Exact diagonalization studies have shown, that the Nagaoka state breaks down for $J > J_1 \sim 0.075t$ in a 4×4 system [25]. Further they show, that the system goes to minimal spin for $J > J_2 \sim 0.088$. Between J_1 and J_2 the system is partially polarized. In the following we show, that whereas J_1 changes by orders of magnitude with system-size, J_2 is barely affected. In fact, for $N = 10 \times 10$ J_1 and J_2 are of different order of magnitude. Fig. 5 shows that the system is partially polarized for $J = 0.0005t$, this being the smallest value at which fully polarization does not set in, such that $J_1 \lesssim 0.0005$. Fig. 6 shows a comparison of $S(\boldsymbol{q})$ for $\boldsymbol{q} = (\pi, \pi)$ and $\boldsymbol{q} = (0, 0)$ between a system with one hole ($J = 0.01t$ and $0.05t$), on the one side, and a Heisenberg antiferromagnet (full line) on the other side. Although antiferromagnetic

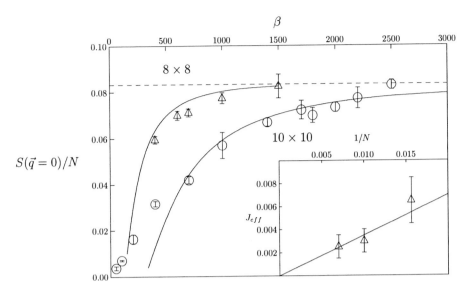

Fig. 3. $S(q = 0)/N$ for $N = 8 \times 8$ ($\triangle$) and 10×10 ($\circ$), with one hole at $J = 0$. The dotted line represents the fully saturated ground state. The full lines correspond to $S(q = 0)$ of a Heisenberg ferromagnet in spin wave theory with $J_{eff} = 0.0065t$ and $J_{eff} = 0.0030t$, respectively. The inset shows J_{eff} vs. $1/N$

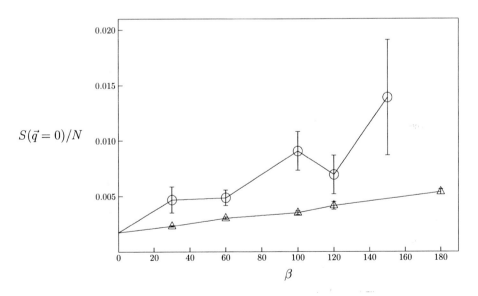

Fig. 4. Comparison of $S(q = 0)/N$ for one ($\triangle$) and two holes ($\circ$) in a 12×12 lattice. Total spin is enhanced by the additional hole.

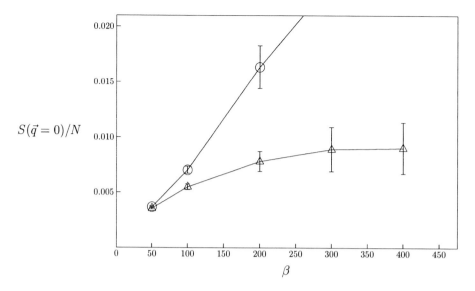

Fig. 5. Full polarization is unstable for $J = 5 \cdot 10^{-4} t$ ($\triangle$) in a $N = 10 \times 10$ system. For comparison the data for $J = 0$ is shown ($\circ$).

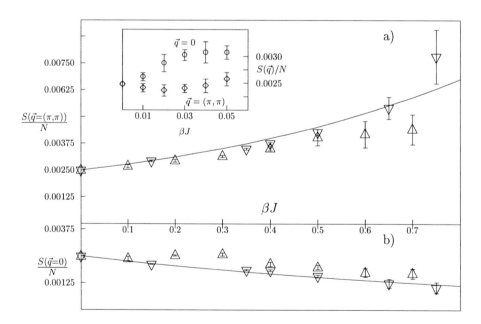

Fig. 6. a) $S(\boldsymbol{q} = (\pi,\pi))/N$ for $J = 0.01t$ ($\triangle$) and $0.05t$ ($\triangledown$) vs. βJ. b) The same for $S(\boldsymbol{q} = (0,0))/N$. The solid lines correspond to the AF-Heisenberg model calculated with the same algorithm. Inset: $S(\boldsymbol{q})$ for $J = 0.001t$.

fluctuations dominate at low temperatures both for $J = 0.01t$ and $0.05t$, and ferromagnetic fluctuations decrease with β, $S(\boldsymbol{q} = 0)$ saturates for $\beta t > 60$ in the case $J = 0.01t$, indicating that the system will stay partially polarized. This situation corresponds to a ferromagnetic polaron smaller than the system size. In fact, the spin-spin correlations around a hole are for $J = 0.01t$ of ferromagnetic character for the first two neighbours of the hole, the rest being antiferromagnetically correlated [26]. For $J = 0.05$, the t-J model with one hole can hardly be distinguished from the Heisenberg antiferromagnet, so we conclude, that the system goes to a state with minimal total spin. Furthermore, the collapse of the data on the curve for the Heisenberg antiferromagnet shows, that independent of the actual value of J/t, J is always the relevant energy scale for the states with dominant antiferromagnetic fluctuations. A quite different behaviour is observed at $J = 0.001t$ (see inset Fig. 6), where ferromagnetic fluctuations start to dominate, as shown by $S(\boldsymbol{q})$ increasing with β for $\boldsymbol{q} = (0,0)$, whereas it decreases for $\boldsymbol{q} = (\pi, \pi)$. Such a scale is of the order of J_{eff}, and hence will drop to zero in the thermodynamic limit. In contrast to this, the scale at which the system goes to a minimal spin state, barely depends on system size ($J_2 \sim 0.08t$ for 4×4 and $J_2 \sim 0.05t$ for 10×10), indicating that at this energy, the ferromagnetic polaron responsible for the partial polarization becomes unstable.

Summarizing, we have performed QMC simulations of fermions in the limit of infinitely strong correlations. The world-line loop-algorithm allows simulations of rather large systems ($N \lesssim 12 \times 12$) and very low temperatures (up to $\beta t \sim 3000$). Such temperatures are necessary in order to reach the fully polarized state in the case of one-hole and $J = 0$. Several regions can be distinguished for finite J. For $J \lesssim J_1 = 5 \times 10^{-4}t$ fully polarization is found, whereas for $J_1 < J < 10^{-3}t$, partial polarization with dominant ferromagnetic fluctuations are found. For $10^{-3}t \lesssim J \lesssim 0.01t$, dominant antiferromagnetic fluctuations are observed but the system is still partially polarized. This corresponds to a ferromagnetic polaron with finite extension. Finally, $J/t \gtrsim 0.05$ corresponds to minimal spin. The two-hole case shows enhanced total spin up to the lowest attainable temperatures ($\beta t = 150$) that are by far lower than the ones reached by any other finite-temperature numerical method.

We are very gratefull to Antimo Angelucci for instructive discussions on the initial stages of the project. The calculations were performed at LRZ München and HLRS Stuttgart. We thank the above institutions for their support.

References

1. F. Zhang and T. M. Rice, Phys. Rev. B **37**, 3759 (1988).
2. D. J. Scalapino, J. Low Temp. **95**, 169 (1994).
3. E. Dagotto, Review of Modern Physics **66**, 763 (1994).
4. F. F. Assaad and D. Würtz, Phys. Rev. B **50**, 136 (1991).

5. X. Y. Zhang, E. Abrahams, and G. Kotliar, Phys. Rev. Lett. **66**, 1236 (1991).
6. M. Boninsegni and E. Manousakis, Phys. Rev. B **46**, 560 (1992).
7. W. Puttika, M. Luchini, and T. Rice, Phys. Rev. Lett. **68**, 538 (1992).
8. W. Puttika, M. Luchini, and M. Ogata, Phys. Rev. Lett. **69**, 2288 (1992).
9. S. White and D. Scalapino, preprint **cond-mat/9605143**, (1996).
10. S. Liang and H. Pang, Europhysics Letters **32**, 173 (1995).
11. J. E. Hirsch, R. L. Sugar, D. J. Scalapino, and R. Blankenbecler, Phys. Rev. B **26**, 5033 (1982).
12. F. F. Assaad, W. Hanke, and D. J. Scalapino, Phys. Rev. B **49**, 4327 (1994).
13. H. F. Trotter, Proc. Am. Math. Soc. **10**, 545 (1959).
14. H. G. Evertz and M. Marcu, in *Quantum Monte Carlo Methods In Condensed Matter Physics*, edited by M. Suzuki (World Scientific Publishing Co. Pte. Ltd., Singapore, 1993).
15. H. G. Evertz, M. Marcu, and G. Lana, Phys. Rev. Lett **70**, 875 (1993).
16. N. Kawashima, J. E. Gubernatis, and H. G. Evertz, Phys. Rev. B **50**, 136 (1994).
17. M. Brunner, Quanten-Monte-Carlo-Simulationen des t-J-Modells, 1996.
18. B. Ammon *et al.*, cond-mat/9711022 .
19. G. Khaliullin, JETP Lett. **52**, 389 (1990).
20. A. Angelucci, Phys. Rev. B **51**, 11580 (1995).
21. B. Doucot and X. G. Wen, Phys. Rev. B **40**, 2719 (1989).
22. Y. Fang, A. E. Ruckenstein, E. Dagotto, and S. Schmitt-Rink, Phys. Rev. B **40**, 7406 (1989).
23. P. Wurth, G. Uhrig, and E. Müller-Hartmann, Annalen der Physik **4**, 144 (1995).
24. A. Barbieri, J. Tiera, and A. Young, Phys. Rev. B **41**, 11697 (1990).
25. J. Bonča, P. Prelovšek, and I. Sega, Phys. Rev. B **39**, 7074 (1989).
26. M. Brunner and A. Muramatsu, unpublished .

$SU(2)$-spin Invariant Auxiliary Field Quantum Monte-Carlo Algorithm for Hubbard models

F.F. Assaad

Institut für Theoretische Physik III,
Universität Stuttgart, Pfaffenwaldring 57, D-70550 Stuttgart, Germany.

Abstract. Auxiliary field quantum Monte Carlo methods for Hubbard models are generally based on a Hubbard-Stratonovitch transformation where the field couples to the z-component of the spin. This transformation breaks $SU(2)$ spin invariance. The symmetry is restored only after summation over the auxiliary fields. Here, we analyze an alternative decomposition, which conserves $SU(2)$ spin invariance, but requires the use of complex numbers. We show that this algorithm gets rid of the very large fluctuations observed in imaginary time displaced correlation functions of quantities which do not commute with the z-component of the total spin. The algorithm prooves to be efficient for the study of spin dynamics.

Auxiliary field quantum Monte Carlo Algorithms for Hubbard models are usually based on the discrete Hubbard-Stratonovtich decomposition [1]:

$$\exp\left(-\Delta\tau U \sum_i \left(n_{i,\uparrow} - \frac{1}{2}\right)\left(n_{i,\downarrow} - \frac{1}{2}\right)\right) \tag{1}$$

$$= \tilde{C} \sum_{s_1,\ldots,s_N = \pm 1} \exp\left(\tilde{\alpha} \sum_i s_i \left(n_{i,\uparrow} - n_{i,\downarrow}\right)\right).$$

Here, $n_{i,\sigma} = c_{i,\sigma}^\dagger c_{i,\sigma}$ where $c_{i,\sigma}^\dagger$ ($c_{i,\sigma}$) creates (annihilates) an electron on site i with z-component of spin σ, $\cosh(\tilde{\alpha}) = \exp\left(\Delta\tau U/2\right)$ On an N-site lattice, the constant $\tilde{C} = \exp\left(\Delta\tau U N/4\right)/2^N$ and $\Delta\tau$ corresponds to an imaginary time step. As apparent from the above equation, for a fixed set of Hubbard- Stratonovitch (HS) fields, $s_1 \ldots s_N$, $SU(2)$-spin symmetry is broken. (i.e. the expression is not invariant under the transformation $c_{j,\sigma} \to \left[\exp\left(i\phi e\sigma/2\right)\right]_{\sigma,s'} c_{j,s'}$. Here, e is a unit vector and σ is a vector consisting of the Pauli-spin matrices.) Clearly $SU(2)$ spin symmetry is restored after summation over the HS fields.

Alternatively, one may consider [1]

$$\exp\left(-\Delta\tau U \sum_i \left(n_{i,\uparrow} - \frac{1}{2}\right)\left(n_{i,\downarrow} - \frac{1}{2}\right)\right) \tag{2}$$

$$= C \sum_{s_1,\ldots,s_N = \pm 1} \exp\left(i\alpha \sum_i s_i \left(n_{i,\uparrow} + n_{i,\downarrow} - 1\right)\right).$$

where $\cos(\alpha) = \exp\left(-\Delta\tau U/2\right)$ and $C = \exp\left(\Delta\tau U N/4\right)/2^N$. With this choice of the HS transformation $SU(2)$ spin invariance is retained for any given HS configuration.

The aim of this note, is to address the question: will we obtain a more efficient and/or reliable quantum Monte Carlo algorithm if we enhance the number of symmetries conserved by the HS transformation. We consider the extended Hubbard model:

$$H = -\frac{t}{2}\sum_i K_i - W\sum_i K_i^2 + U\sum_i (n_{i,\uparrow} - \frac{1}{2})(n_{i,\downarrow} - \frac{1}{2}) \qquad (3)$$

with the hopping kinetic energy

$$K_i = \sum_{\sigma,\delta}\left(c_{i,\sigma}^\dagger c_{i+\delta,\sigma} + c_{i+\delta,\sigma}^\dagger c_{i,\sigma}\right). \qquad (4)$$

Here $W \geq 0$, $\delta = \pm a_x, \pm a_y$ where a_x, a_y are the lattice constants. We impose twisted boundary conditions:

$$c_{i+La_x,\sigma} = \exp\left(2\pi i\Phi/\Phi_0\right)c_{i,\sigma}, \quad c_{i+La_y,\sigma} = c_{i,\sigma}, \qquad (5)$$

with $\Phi_0 = hc/e$ the flux quanta and L the linear length of the square lattice. The boundary conditions given by Eq. (5) account for a magnetic flux threading a torus on which the lattice is wrapped. At half-filling, and constant value of U/t the W-term drives the ground state from a antiferromagnetic Mott insulator to a $d_{x^2-y^2}$ superconductor [2]. At $U/t = 4$, this quantum transition occurs at $W_c/t \sim 0.3$. At finite values of $W < W_c$, numerical simulations are consistent with the occurrence of a $d_{x^2-y^2}$ superconductor upon doping of the Mott insulating state [3].

To decompose the W-term, we use the approximate relation

$$e^{\Delta\tau W K_i^2} = \frac{1}{4}\sum_{l=-2,-1,1,2}\gamma(l)\exp\left(\sqrt{\Delta\tau W}\eta(l)K_i\right) + O(\Delta\tau^4), \qquad (6)$$

where the fields η and γ take the values:

$$\gamma(\pm 1) = 1 + \sqrt{6}/3, \quad \gamma(\pm 2) = 1 - \sqrt{6}/3$$
$$\eta(\pm 1) = \pm\sqrt{2\left(3 - \sqrt{6}\right)}, \quad \eta(\pm 2) = \pm\sqrt{2\left(3 + \sqrt{6}\right)}$$

$$(7)$$

Since K_i is invariant under a rotation in spin space, the above Hubbard-Stratonovitch decomposition conserves $SU(2)$-spin symmetry. Thus, the choice of the HS transformation for the Hubbard term will determine whether the algorithm is $SU(2)$-spin invariant or not.

We have carried out our simulations with the Projector QMC algorithm [4,5]. Within this approach, the ground state expectation value of an observable O is obtained with:

$$\frac{\langle\Psi_0|O|\Psi_0\rangle}{\langle\Psi_0|\Psi_0\rangle} = \lim_{\Theta\to\infty}\frac{\langle\Psi_T|e^{-\Theta H}Oe^{-\Theta H}|\Psi_T\rangle}{\langle\Psi_T|e^{-2\Theta H}|\Psi_T\rangle}. \tag{8}$$

The ground state $|\Psi_0\rangle$ is filtered out of a trial wave function, $|\Psi_T\rangle$, provided that $\langle\Psi_0|\Psi_T\rangle \neq 0$. We choose the trial wave function to be a spin singlet solution of the non interacting Hamiltonian (U=W=0). An explicit construction of such trial wave functions may be found in reference [2].

After Trotter decomposition of the imaginary time propagation and HS transformation of the two-body terms, one obtains:

$$\frac{\langle\Psi_T|e^{-\Theta H}Oe^{-\Theta H}|\Psi_T\rangle}{\langle\Psi_T|e^{-2\Theta H}|\Psi_T\rangle} = \sum_x \Pr(\Theta, x)\langle O\rangle(\Theta, x) + O(\Delta\tau^2), \tag{9}$$

where x denotes a configuration of HS fields, and $\langle O\rangle(\Theta, x)$, corresponds to the value of the observable O the the HS fields x. At half-band filling particle-hole symmetry leads to positive values of $\Pr(\Theta, x)$ which may thus be interpreted as a probability distribution and sampled with Monte Carlo methods. This statement is valid for both choices of the HS transformation of the Hubbard term $(1, 2)$.

We now compare the $SU(2)$ spin invariant algorithm based on Eq. (2) to the $SU(2)$ spin non-invariant algorithm based on Eq. (1). The $SU(2)$ spin-invariant algorithm forces us to work with complex numbers. On the other hand, for many applications real numbers may be used for the $SU(2)$ non-invariant code. For the comparison discussed below, and to keep the CPU time approximately constant, we have carried out twice as many sweeps for the $SU(2)$ non-invariant code than for the $SU(2)$ invariant code. We consider various observables at half-band filling.

a) **Magnetization.** In the case of the $SU(2)$-invariant algorithm, and the above mentioned choices of the trial wave function one has:

$$\langle c_{i,\uparrow}^\dagger c_{j,\uparrow}\rangle(\Theta, x) = \langle c_{i,\downarrow}^\dagger c_{j,\downarrow}\rangle(\Theta, x). \tag{10}$$

Thus, the total magnetization, $m_z(q) = \sum_j e^{iqj}(n_{i,\uparrow} - n_{i,\downarrow})$ is identical to zero for all values of the HS fields:

$$\langle m_z(q)\rangle(\Theta, x) \equiv 0. \tag{11}$$

On the other hand, the $SU(2)$ non-invariant algorithm, equation (10) is not valid, and one obtains zero magnetization, only after summation over the HS fields. At $q = (\pi, \pi) \equiv Q$, $L = 6$, $\langle n\rangle = 1$, $U/t = 4$ and $W/t = 0$ one obtains after 2×10^5 sweeps, $\langle m_z(Q)\rangle = -0.16 \pm 0.31$. Thus for this trivial case, the advantage of the $SU(2)$ invariant algorithm over the $SU(2)$ non-invariant algorithm is infinite.

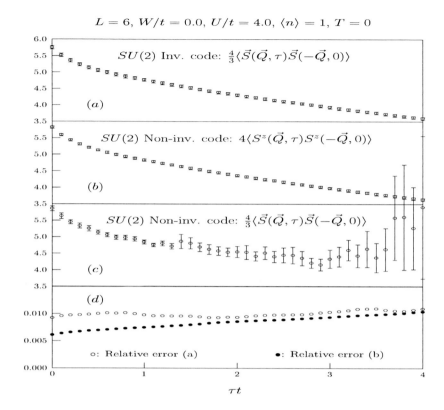

$L = 6$, $W/t = 0.0$, $U/t = 4.0$, $\langle n \rangle = 1$, $T = 0$

Fig. 1. Imaginary time displaced spin-spin correlations, at $\boldsymbol{Q} = (\pi, \pi)$. The $SU(2)$ invariant code is based on the HS transformation of Eq. (2) and $SU(2)$ non-invariant on Eq. (1). To keep the CPU time approximately constant between the two simulations, we have carried out twice as many sweeps for the $SU(2)$ non-invariant code as for the $SU(2)$ invariant code. Here, we have used periodic boundary conditions, $\Phi = 0$ in Eqn. (5).

b) **Imaginary time displaced spin-spin correlations**. Here we consider the quantity: $S^\alpha(\boldsymbol{q}, \tau)S^\alpha(-\boldsymbol{q}, 0)$ where $S^\alpha(\boldsymbol{q}, \tau) = \sum_{\boldsymbol{j}} e^{i\boldsymbol{q}\boldsymbol{j}} e^{\tau H} S_{\boldsymbol{j}}^\alpha e^{-\tau H}$, $S_{\boldsymbol{j}}^\alpha$ being the α-component of the spin operator on site $\boldsymbol{j}$. The numerically stable computation of imaginary time displaced correlation functions within the Projector QMC algorithm is described in Ref. [6]. In the SU(2)-invariant algorithm one obtains with the above mentioned trial wave function:

$$\langle S^\alpha(\boldsymbol{q}, \tau)S^\alpha(-\boldsymbol{q}, 0)\rangle(\Theta, x) \equiv \langle S^\gamma(\boldsymbol{q}, \tau)S^\gamma(-\boldsymbol{q}, 0)\rangle(\Theta, x). \quad (12)$$

Here, α, γ run over the three components of the spin. In the case of the SU(2) non-invariant the above equation is valid only after summation over the HS fields, x. Fig. 1 plots the spin-spin correlations for $\langle n \rangle = 1$, $U/t = 4$ and $W/t = 0$ on a 6×6 lattice. The half-filled Hubbard model is expected to show long-range antiferromagnetic order in the thermodynamic limit. Thus, $\frac{1}{N}\langle \boldsymbol{S}(\boldsymbol{Q},\tau)\boldsymbol{S}(-\boldsymbol{Q},0)\rangle$ is should saturate to a finite value in the *large L* and τ limits. Here, L is the linear size of the square lattice and N the number of sites. On a finite size lattice, a spin gap is expected, thus leading to an exponential decay in τ of the considered quantity. If one compares the quantity $\langle \boldsymbol{S}(\boldsymbol{Q},\tau)\boldsymbol{S}(-\boldsymbol{Q},0)\rangle$ for both codes, (Fig. 1a and Fig. 1c) it is clear that the $SU(2)$ invariant code does much better. The large fluctuations in the case of the $SU(2)$ non-invariant code may be traced back to the x and y-components of the spin-spin correlation function. In fact, considering only the z-component of the correlation function (Fig. 1b) yields good results. The HS transformation of equation (1) conserves the z-component of the total spin, but not the other components. We now consider the z-component of the spin-spin correlations and compare both algorithms. We have plotted in Fig. 1d the relative errors for both codes. Overall, the SU(2) spin-invariant

$L = 8$, $W/t = 0.35$, $U/t = 2.0$, $\langle n \rangle = 1$, $T = 0$, $\Phi = \Phi_0/2$

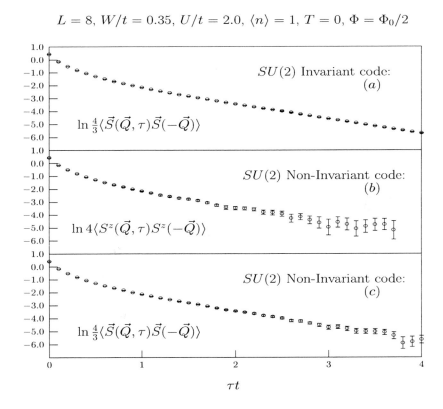

Fig. 2. Same as Fig. 1 for the parameter set: $W/t = 0.35$, $U/t = 2$ and at half-band filling. Here we use antiperiodic boundary conditions set $\Phi = \Phi_0/2$. It is clear that the $SU(2)$-invariant code does substantially better at *large* values of τ.

code produces larger errors within the considered τ-range. However, for the $SU(2)$-invariant code the relative error, is to a first approximation independent of τ. In contrast, the relative error for the $SU(2)$ non-invariant code grows as a function of τ. At large values of τ we expect the the $SU(2)$ invariant code to be more efficient. To confirm this statement, we consider the parameter set: $\langle n \rangle = 1$, $U/t = 2$, $W/t = 0.35$, $\Phi = \Phi_0/2$ on a 8×8 lattice. The data is shown in Fig.2. It is clear that the $SU(2)$-invariant code does much better at $large$ values of τt. In Fig. 2, the z-component of the spin-spin correlations (Fig. 2b) shows larger fluctuations than $\langle S(Q, \tau)S(-Q, 0) \rangle$ (Fig. 2c). Exactly the opposite is seen in Figs. 1b and 1c.

c) Π-modes. The Π modes introduced in the $SO(5)$ theory of the unification of antiferromagnetism and superconductivity are defined by: $\Pi^\alpha = \sum_{p,s,s'} g(p)c_{p+Q,s} (\sigma^\alpha \sigma^y)_{s,s'} c_{p,s'}$ [7]. Here, σ^α corresponds to the Pauli spin matrix and for the case of d-wave superconductivity, we consider $g(p) = \cos(p_x) - cos(p_y)$. The $SU(2)$-spin invariant code satisfies

$$\langle \Pi^\alpha(\tau)\Pi^{\alpha,\dagger}(0) \rangle(\Theta, x) \equiv \langle \Pi^\gamma(\tau)\Pi^{\gamma,\dagger}(0) \rangle(\Theta, x). \tag{13}$$

In the case of the $SU(2)$ non-invariant code, the above equation is valid for all values of γ and α only after summation over the HS fields x. In the table, imaginary time Π correlations are considered for both algorithms. For the $SU(2)$ non-invariant code, substantial fluctuations in $\langle \Pi^z(\tau)\Pi^{z,\dagger}(0) \rangle$ are observed at $large$ values of τ. On the other hand, the error-bars in $\langle \Pi^x(\tau)\Pi^{x,\dagger}(0) \rangle$ are smaller. We again attribute the large fluctuations in the z component of the Π mode correlations to fact that Π^z does not commute with the z-component of the total spin. In contrast, Π^x does commute with the z-component of the total spin. The $SU(2)$-invariant code shows good convergence, and the results agree with those obtained for the x-component of the Π-mode within the $SU(2)$ non-invariant algorithm.

d) **Single particle Green functions.** We have not found any significant improvements in the fluctuations of the imaginary time single particle Green functions between the two algorithms. To be more precise, the fluctuation of $\frac{1}{N} \sum_{\sigma,i} \langle c_{i,\sigma}(\tau)c_{i,\sigma}^\dagger \rangle$ are to a first approximation independent of the choice of HS transformation. Thus for both considered codes, the error-bars scale as $C/\sqrt{N_{sweeps}}$ where C is a constant independent on the choice of the algorithm, and N_{sweeps} denotes the number of sweeps carried out.

In conclusion, we have considered an alternative HS transformation for Hubbard type models which conserves $SU(2)$ spin symmetry. This algorithm requires the use of complex numbers and does not introduce a sign problem at half-band filling. In the case of $SU(2)$ non-invariant algorithms based on Eq. (1), very large fluctuations can occur in the calculation of imaginary time displaced quantities of the form $\langle A(\tau)A^\dagger \rangle$ when A does not commute with the z-component of the total spin. In the $SU(2)$ invariant formulation, this pathology does not occur. We have compared the two algorithms in the worst case scenario where real numbers can be used for the $SU(2)$ non-invariant algorithm. By keeping the CPU time constant for both codes we have shown

τt	SU(2) invariant code $\langle \Pi^z(\tau)\Pi^{z,\dagger}(0)\rangle$	SU(2) non-invariant code $\langle \Pi^x(\tau)\Pi^{x,\dagger}(0)\rangle$	SU(2) non-invariant code $\langle \Pi^z(\tau)\Pi^{z,\dagger}(0)\rangle$
0	0.15055 ± 0.00080	0.15097 ± 0.00073	0.13837 ± 0.01506
0.2	0.05902 ± 0.00058	0.05920 ± 0.00051	0.05845 ± 0.00387
0.4	0.02915 ± 0.00055	0.02941 ± 0.00040	0.02846 ± 0.00215
0.6	0.01474 ± 0.00046	0.01547 ± 0.00032	0.01373 ± 0.00254
0.8	0.00728 ± 0.00046	0.00859 ± 0.00039	0.00841 ± 0.00105
1	0.00397 ± 0.00038	0.00480 ± 0.00053	0.00394 ± 0.00104
1.2	0.00240 ± 0.00033	0.00251 ± 0.00033	0.00086 ± 0.00080

Table 1. Π-mode correlation functions at half-filling for $U/t = 4$, $W/t = 0.35$ on a 6×6 lattice. Data in the last two columns were obtained with the SU(2) non-invariant code. Within this algorithm, the x and y components of the Π-mode correlation function are identical. For the SU(2) spin-invariant algorithm, the results are independent on the considered components of the correlation function. To keep the CPU time approximately constant between the two simulations, we have carried out twice as many sweeps for the SU(2) non-invariant code as for the SU(2) invariant code.

that the long imaginary time behavior of the spin-spin correlations are obtained more efficiently with the SU(2) invariant code than with the SU(2) non-invariant code. Thus, the SU(2) invariant code is more efficient for the measure of spin gaps which may be extracted from the long imaginary time decay of the spin-spin correlations. More generally, it is an efficient code for the study of spin dynamics. The fluctuations of other quantities such as single particle green function, were invariant under the choice of the HS transformation.

Acknowledgments

M. Muramatsu is thanked for many instructive conversations. The computations were carried out on the T3E of the HLRS,Stuttgart, as well as on the T90 and T3E of the HLRZ, Jülich.

References

1. J.E.Hirsch, Phys. Rev. B **28** 4059 (1983).
2. F.F. Assaad, M. Imada and D.J. Scalapino, Phys. Rev. Lett. **77**, 4592, (1996). Phys. Rev. **B 56**, 15001, (1997).
3. F.F. Assaad and M. Imada Phys. Rev. B. **58**, (1998).
4. G. Sugiyama and S.E. Koonin, Annals of Phys.**168** 1, (1986).
5. S. Sorella, S. Baroni, R. Car, And M. Parrinello, Europhys. Lett. **8**, 663, (1989). S. Sorella, E. Tosatti, S. Baroni, R. Car, and M. Parinello, Int. J. Mod. Phys. B**1** (1989) 993.
6. F.F. Assaad and M. Imada, J. Phys. Soc. Jpn. **65**,189, (1996).
7. S.C. Zhang, Science, **275**, 1089, (1997).

Temperature dependent band structure of the Kondo insulator

C. Gröber and R. Eder

Institut für Theoretische Physik, Universität Würzburg, Am Hubland, 97074 Würzburg, Germany

Abstract. We present a Qantum Monte Carlo (QMC) study of the temperature dependent dynamics of the Kondo insulator. Working at the so-called symmetrical point allows to perform minus-sign free QMC simulations and thus reach temperatures of less than 1% of the conduction electron bandwidth. Study of the temperature dependence of the single particle Green's function and dynamical spin correlation function shows a surprisingly intricate low temperature band structure and gives evidence for two characteristic temperatures, which we identify with the Kondo and coherence temperature, respectively. In particular, the data show a temperature induced metal-insulator transition at the coherence temperature.

The theoretical description of the Kondo lattice remains an outstanding problem of solid state physics. This model, or variations of it, may be viewed as the appropriate one for understanding such intensively investigated classes of materials as the heavy electron metals[1,2] and the Kondo insulators[3]. Experimental results indicate that the electronic structures of Kondo lattice compounds undergo quite dramatic changes with temperature[4]. It is the purpose of the present manuscript to report a QMC study of the electronic structure of the so-called Kondo insulator, which shows that this model indeed undergoes a quite profound change of its unexpectedly intricate band structure as temperature increases. We are using a one dimensional (1D) 'tight-binding version' of the model with L unit cells and 2 orbitals/unit cell:

$$H = -t \sum_{i,\sigma} (c_{i+1,\sigma}^\dagger c_{i,\sigma} + H.c.) - V \sum_{i,\sigma} (c_{i,\sigma}^\dagger f_{i,\sigma} + H.c.)$$
$$- \epsilon_f \sum_{i,\sigma} n_{i,\sigma} + U \sum_i f_{i,\uparrow}^\dagger f_{i,\uparrow} f_{i,\downarrow}^\dagger f_{i,\downarrow}. \tag{1}$$

Here $c_{i,\sigma}^\dagger$ ($f_{i,\sigma}^\dagger$) creates a conduction electron (f-electron) in cell i, $n_{i,\sigma} = f_{i,\sigma}^\dagger f_{i,\sigma}$. Throughout we consider the case of 'half-filling' i.e. two electrons/unit cell and, as an important technical point, we restrict ourselves to the symmetric case, $\epsilon_f = U/2$. The latter choice, while probably not leading to any qualitative change as compared to other ratios of ϵ_f/U, has the crucial advantage that at half-filling the model acquires particle-hole symmetry, i.e. the Hamiltonian becomes invariant under the transformation $\alpha_{i,\sigma} \to exp(i\mathbf{Q} \cdot \mathbf{R}_i)\alpha_{i,\sigma}^\dagger$, where $\alpha = c, f$ and $\mathbf{Q} = (\pi, \pi, ...)$ (this holds for bipartite lattices with only nearest neighbor hopping). Particle-hole symmetry in turn implies that the QMC-procedure does not suffer from the notorious 'minus-sign problem' anymore, so that reliable simulations for temperatures as low as $\beta t=30$, corresponding to $\approx 0.8\%$ of the conduction electron bandwidth, can be performed without problems. This allows to scan the dynamical correlation functions of the system over a wide temperature range. Previously a QMC study for the 2 dimensional model at half-filling was performed by Vekic *at al.*[5], more recently a study of the temperature dependence of *static* susceptibilities for the strong coupling version of the model has been reported by Shibata *et al.*[6]. It is widely believed that the Kondo lattice has two distinct characteristic temperatures. At the Kondo temperature, T_K, the f-electrons start to form loosely bound singlets with the conduction electrons. This manifests itself in a deviation of the spin susceptibility from the high-temperature Curie form due to the 'quenching' of the f-electron magnetic moment and an increase of the dc-resistivity due to resonant scattering from the newly formed low energy bound states[1]. The second (and lower) characteristic temperature is the coherence temperature, T_{coh}, where the local singlets establish long range coherence amongst themselves so as to participate in the quasiparticle bands of a Fermi-liquid like electronic state. Experimentally the coherence temperature is signaled by the onset of a decrease of the dc resistivity with temperature[1], and the formation of the 'heavy bands' which (judging by the volume of the Fermi surface) incorporate the f-electrons[7]. While there is as yet no experimental proof, one might expect on the basis of these considerations, that at temperatures above T_{coh} the f-electrons do not participate in the Fermi surface volume, whereas they do so below.

Turning to the Kondo insulator we note that the electron count for these systems is such that the 'Fermi surface' comprising both, conduction and f-electrons, would precisely fill the Brillouin zone so that the system is a 'nominal' band insulator. If increasing temperature causes the f-electrons to 'drop out' of the Fermi surface volume, this should manifest itself as an insulator-to-metal transition because the volume of the collapsed Fermi surface is no longer sufficient to cover the entire Brillouin zone. Tranferring the above scenario for heavy Fermion metals to the Kondo insulator one would therefore expect that the system remains a metal above T_{coh}, with a Fermi surface that excludes the f-electrons, and becomes insulating below T_{coh}, when the f-electrons participate in the Fermi surface volume to turn the system into a 'nominal' band insulator. In fact insulator-to-metal transitions which are induced by temperature[4], or hydrostatic pressure[8] have been observed experimentally. As will be seen below, our data for the Kondo insulator are remarkably consistent with such an interpretation.

To begin with, we consider the T-dependence of the single particle spectral function. This is defined as ($\alpha=c,f$)

$$A_\alpha(k,\omega) = \frac{1}{Z} \sum_{\nu,\mu} e^{\beta\omega_{\nu\mu}} |\langle\nu|\alpha_{k,\sigma}|\mu\rangle|^2 \delta(\omega - \omega_{\nu\mu}), \qquad (2)$$

where the sum is over all eigenstates $|\nu\rangle$ of $H - \mu N$ in the grand canonical ensemble, Z denotes the partition function and $\omega_{\nu\mu}$ the difference of the energies of the states ν and μ. Figure 1 shows the angle-integrated spectral density, $D_\alpha(\omega)=(1/L)\sum_k A_\alpha(k,\omega)$. At the lowest temperature, $\beta t=30$,

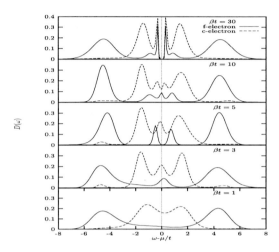

Fig. 1. Angle integrated spectral density $D(\omega)$ for an $L=16$ Kondo lattice for different temperatures. Parameter values are $U/t=8$, $V/t=1$.

$D_\alpha(\omega)$ shows the behaviour expected for a Kondo insulator: the c-electron density is roughly consistent with the standard $1D$ tight-binding density of states, with indications of the two van-Hove singularities at $\pm 2t$. Around μ, however, the spectral density shows a small but unambiguous gap, which demonstrates the insulating nature of the ground state. The f-like spectral density shows very sharp low energy peaks at the edges of this gap, as well as high-intensity 'Hubbard bands' at approximately $\pm U/2$. There are also two weak 'side bands' at approximately $\pm 0.8t$. With the exception of these, all features are consistent with exact diagonalization[9] and $d \to \infty$ results[10] at $T=0$. This suggests that the sidebands are already an effect of the finite temperature and the further development with T confirms this. Inspection of the series $\beta t=30, 10$ shows that with increasing T a transfer of spectral weight from the low energy peaks at the gap-edges into the sidebands is taking place. This is accompanied by a narrowing of the gap, and at $\beta t=10$ the gap practically closes; in the spectrum for this temperature the two low-energy peaks seem to have collapsed into a single one right at μ - we believe that these are in fact still two peaks, which however are too closely spaced to be resolved. Increasing T even further ($\beta t=5$), the low energy peaks disappear completely. The c-electron spectral density no longer shows any indication of a gap, whereas the f-like sidebands stay at a relatively high energy away from μ. The extreme low energy states thus have pure c-character (within the resolution of the QMC procedure) and the system is a metal with a c-like Fermi surface. We therefore interpret the temperature where the gap closes as the analogue of the coherence temperature. With increasing T the energy of the sidebands is lowered and at $\beta t=3$ they collapse into a single peak right at μ. This probably indicates a second transition and at the relatively large value of $\beta t=1$ another reconstruction of the band structure has taken place, namely the disappearance of the f-like sidebands. The upper and lower Hubbard band for the f-electrons are now quite broad, and actually the possibility that there are very low-intensity f-like features near μ cannot be completely ruled out. However, the overall trend is quite obviously a strong decrease of the sidebands. Interpreting the latter as the lattice-analogue of the Kondo-resonance in the impurity case[11], the temperature of the second transition should correspond to the Kondo temperature T_K. In the present case T_K is very high because of the relatively large value of the c-f hybridization, $V=t$. We also note that the closing of a gap in the f-like density of states in 2 dimensions was previously found by Vekic $et\ al.$[5].

To get a more detailed picture, we consider the k-resolved single particle spectral function, shown in Figure 2 for some temperatures in between the two transitions. For $\beta t=30$ the c-electrons show a standard $\cos(k)$ band, albeit with a clear gap at $k_F^0=\pi/2$, the Fermi momentum of nonhybridized conduction electrons. At this momentum the band changes its spectral character and 'bends over' into a practically dispersionless f-like band, which can be followed up to $k=\pi$. This kind of band structure is familiar from various studies[9,10,12]. The weak and practically dispersionless f-like sidebands are at somewhat higher energy and, at very high energies, the f-like Hubbard bands. The width of the Hubbard bands seems to depend strongly on momentum - this is a deficiency of the QMC and maximum entropy method, which is most accurate near μ. As seen in the k-integrated spectra, raising the temperature leads to a transfer of spectral weight from the 'flat band' forming the single-particle gap into the Kondo resonance-like sidebands. At $\beta t=5$, where the gap has closed, the c-electron spectrum shows a very conventional $\cos(k)$-band with no more indication of any gap. At k_F^0 there is now one symmetric and unsplit peak right at μ - as it is required by particle-hole symmetry for a metallic system. The system thus has a Fermi surface as expected for un-hybridized c-electrons, i.e. the f-electrons indeed have 'dropped out' of the Fermi surface volume. The dispersionless f-like sidebands are at a relatively high energy. The tiny low energy 'foot' seen in some of the c-like spectra may indicate a very weak mixing of the c-electrons into the Kondo-resonance but apparently this no longer leads to a gap. Rather, the Kondo resonance is now essentially decoupled from the Fermi surface physics. Finally, for $\beta t=1$, even these Kondo resonance-like sidebands have disappeared and the only f-like peaks in the spectral function are the upper and lower Hubbard bands. At this high temperature the f-electrons do not participate in the low energy

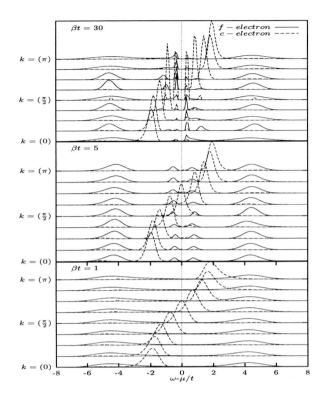

Fig. 2. Momentum resolved single-particle spectral function $A(k,\omega)$ at different temperatures. Parameters as in Figure 1, the momentum k increases in steps of $2\pi/L = \pi/8$ from the bottom of each panel.

physics at all. The expectation value of $-V\sum_{i,\sigma}(c_{i,\sigma}^{\dagger}f_{i,\sigma}+H.c.)$ decreases by $\approx 30\%$ between $\beta t = 30$ and $\beta t = 1$ - while there is appreciable mixing even at high temperature, this does obviously not lead to coherent band formation any more.

We proceed to the dynamical spin correlation function (SCF), defined as

$$S(k,\omega) = \frac{1}{Z}\sum_{\nu,\mu}e^{-\beta E_{\mu}}|\langle\nu|S_{\alpha}^{z}(k)|\mu\rangle|^{2}\delta(\omega - \omega_{\nu\mu}), \qquad (3)$$

where $S_{\alpha}^{z}(k)$ is (the Fourier transform of) the z-component of the spin-operator for α-electrons. This is shown in Figure 3. At $\beta t = 30$, the f-like SCF shows an intense branch of low energy excitations with a tiny but clearly resolved spin wave-like dispersion. The spectral weight of this branch is sharply

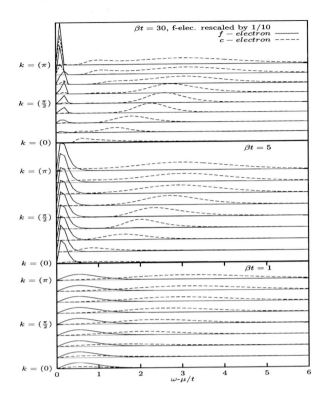

Fig. 3. Dynamical spin correlation function $S(k, \omega)$ for different temperatures. Parameters are as in Figure 1.

peaked at $k=\pi$, indicating relatively long ranged and strong antiferromagnetic spin correlations. Fitting the equal (imaginary) time f-like spin correlation function in real space to the expression $S(r)=A(e^{-r/\zeta}+e^{-(L-r)/\zeta})$ we obtain the values $\zeta=4.61, 4.67$ and 2.18 for $\beta t=30, 20$ and 10. The dominant feature in the c-like SCF on the other hand, is a free electron-like particle-hole continuum. Interestingly enough, there is also a replica of the f-electron spin wave branch in the c-like SCF. This shows that at low excitation energies c and f electrons behave as a single 'all-electron fluid', whose excitations have composite f-c character. The free electron continuum itself does have a gap of $\approx 0.6t$ at $k=\pi$ - this corresponds to approximately twice the single particle-gap in $A(k, \omega)$[13]. We proceed to $\beta t=5$, where the single-particle gap has closed. The f-like SCF still shows a low-energy peak with finite excitation energy, which however is practically dispersionless, both with respect to its energy and with respect to its spectral weight. In other words, the magnetic f-excitation becomes practically immobile. The metal-insulator transition thus is related to a drastic change of the spin correlation function[5] - the question whether the longer ranged spin correlations below the transition are the driving force behind the gap formation[13] or whether the change of the spin correlations is merely a 'byproduct' of the collapse of the single-particle gap, remains to be clarified. In any way, the almost completely localized spin dynamics of the f-electrons naturally should lead to a Curie-law for the static spin susceptibility at temperatures above T_{coh}. A crossover from an activation-gap dominated susceptibility at low temperatures and a Curie law at high temperatures has indeed been observed by Shibata *et al.*[6]. In the c-like SCF the particle-hole continuum persists and the gap near $k=\pi$ is now very small or zero (the absence of the gap in the single particle spectrum suggests it to be zero). There is no more distinguishable peak in the c-like SCF which would correspond to the dispersionless f-like spin resonance - this suggests that the f-electrons now are largely decoupled from the c-like band, as indicated by their non-participation in the Fermi surface. At the very high $\beta t=1$, there is still some (very weak) indication of the low energy f-electron spin resonance, but the intensity is low and the resonance is now relatively broad. It should be noted that the relative change of the f-like magnetic moment is less than 2% over the entire temperature range we studied - temperature thus affects only the coupling of these moments to the conduction electrons.

For the relatively large value of $V=1$ the higher of the two crossover temperatures (i.e. the Kondo temperature) is already rather high, $\beta t \geq 1$. Based on the impurity results[14] one might expect that for smaller V the Kondo temperature is lower, and to check this, we have performed simulations at fixed $\beta t=5$, but with variable hybridization. Figure 4 shows the results for the single particle spectral density. The weight of the Kondo resonance-like sidebands for fixed temperature decreases with V, and for $V/t=0.25$ they have disappeared completely. In the k-resolved c-electron spectrum (not shown) there is now only a very sharp nearest neighbor-hopping band with a clear Fermi level crossing at k_F^0 and the f-like spin correlation function shows no more indication of the low energy resonance - the overall picture is completely the same as for $V/t=1$ and $\beta t=1$, with the sole exception that all features are much sharper due to the lower temperature. Here we do not pursue the issue of the detailed parameter dependence of the characteristsic temperatures - it is quite obvious, however, that lower values of V shift the characteristic temperatures of the system towards lower values, but otherwise leave the physics unchanged.

In summary, we have studied the temperature evolution of various dynamical correlation functions of the Kondo insulator and found indications for two distinct electronic crossovers. At the low temperature crossover the single-particle gap closes so that the system becomes a metal, the magnetic cor-

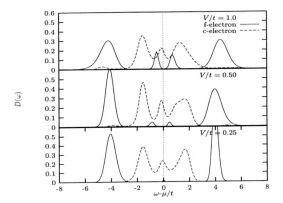

Fig. 4. Single particle spectral density $D(\omega)$ at $\beta t=5$ for different V/t. All other parameters are as in Figure 1.

relations on the f-sites become localized, and the 'spin gap' closes due to c-like spin excitations. While c and f electrons seem to form a coherent 'all-electron fluid' below the crossover temperature, the c and f-like features in the correlation functions above this temperature are decoupled. We therefore interpret this temperature as the analogue of the coherence temperature in heavy-Fermion metals. At the high-temperature crossover both, the dispersionless f-like Kondo-resonance in the single-particle spectrum and the f-like low-energy spin excitation disappear. The only remaining f-like feature in the single particle spectrum are the high-energy 'Hubbard bands', corresponding to the 'undressed' transitions $f^1 \to f^0$ and $f^1 \to f^2$. We therefore interpret this second temperature as the Kondo temperature of the system.

The calculations were carried out on the Cray-T3E supercomputer at the HLRS Stuttgart. The QMC algorithm ran on 64 processors with different initial configurations of the ising field [15]. Communication was used to gather the results from each processor in order to perform the statistical analysis. With this scheme a total performance of 8 Gigaflops has been achieved.

References

1. G. R. Stewart, Rev. Mod. Phys. **56**, 755 (1984).
2. P. Fulde, J. Keller, and G. Zwicknagl, Solid State Phys. **41**, 1 (1988).
3. G. Aeppli and Z. Fisk, Comments Condens. Matter Phys., **16** 155 (1992).
4. Z. Schlesinger et al., Phys. Rev. Lett. **71**, 1748 (1993).
5. M. Vekic et al., Phys. Rev. Lett. **74**, 2367 (1994).
6. N. Shibata et al., cond-mat/9712315.

7. L. Tailefer *et al.*, J. Magn. Magn. Mater. **63& 64** 372 (1987).

8. J. Cooley *et al.*, Phys. Rev. Lett. **74**, 1629 (1995).

9. K. Tsutsui *et al.*, Phys. Rev. Lett. **76**, 279 (1996).

10. A. M. Tahvildar-Zadeh, M. Jarrel, and J. K. Freericks, e-print cond-mat/9710136.

11. O. Gunnarson and K. Schönhammer, Phys. Rev. B. **28**, 4315 (1983).

12. R. Eder, O. Stoica, and G. A. Sawatzky, Phys. Rev. B. **55**, 6109 (1997); see also cond-mat/9711248.

13. H. Tsunetsugu, M. Sigrist, and K. Ueda, Rev. Mod. Phys. **69**, 809 (1997).

14. K. G. Wilson, Rev. Mod. Phys. **47**, 773 (1975).

15. J. E. Hirsch, Phys. Rev. B **28**, 4059 (1983).

Numerical study of spin-charge separation in one dimension

M. G. Zacher[1], E. Arrigoni[1], W. Hanke[1], and J. R. Schrieffer[2]

[1] Institut für Theoretische Physik, Universität Würzburg, D-97074 Würzburg, Germany
[2] NHMFL and Department of Physics, Florida State University, Tallahassee, Florida 32310

Abstract. The problem of spin-charge separation is analyzed numerically in the metallic phase of the one-band Hubbard model in one dimension by studying the behavior of the single-particle Green's function and of the spin and charge susceptibilities. We first analyze the Quantum-Monte Carlo data for the imaginary-time Green's function within the Maximum Entropy method in order to obtain the spectral function at real frequencies. For some values of the momentum sufficiently away from the Fermi surface two separate peaks are found, which can be identified as charge and spin excitations.

In order to improve our accuracy and to be able to extend our study to a larger portion of the Brillouin zone, we also fit our data with the imaginary-time Green's function obtained from the Luttinger-model solution with two different velocities as fitting parameters. The excitation energies associated with these velocities turn out to agree, in a broad range of momenta, with the ones calculated from the charge and spin susceptibilities. This allows us to identify these single-particle excitations as due to a separation of spin and charge. Remarkably, the range of momenta where spin-charge separation is seen extends well beyond the region of linear dispersion about the Fermi surface. We finally discuss a possible extension of our method to detect spin-charge separation numerically in two dimensions.

1 INTRODUCTION

One-dimensional (1D) interacting fermion systems show a number of anomalous properties which cannot be understood in the framework of the Fermi-liquid theory of normal metals. In particular, their momentum distribution and density of states are in sharp contrast with Fermi-liquid theory for energies and momenta close to the Fermi surface. In general, 1D systems can be described by an effective low-energy theory based on the exactly solvable Luttinger model with suitably renormalized parameters and are thus referred to as Luttinger liquids (LL).[1–3] One of the most striking features of the Luttinger model is the complete separation of spin and charge degrees of freedom which manifests itself in the splitting of the single-particle spectral function in two peaks corresponding to spin and charge excitations propagating independently .[4–6,3] Another important characteristic of the Luttinger model is the presence of power-law behavior with interaction-dependent exponents for various correlation functions.

Beside its application to 1-D systems, LL theory has received particular attention in the past years in the framework of the theory of high-T_c superconductors. The normal phase of the high-T_c CuO_2 planes shows in fact a number of anomalous properties which can be possibly understood, if one assumes that the CuO_2 planes are in a kind of two-dimensional LL state.[7–11] In particular, it has been suggested that spin-charge separation could be present also in the CuO_2 planes and that it plays an essential role in the way particles are allowed to tunnel between the planes.[12]

Numerical methods have been proven to be crucial for the theoretical understanding of models describing the CuO_2 planes, since electron correlation is rather strong in these systems and perturbative methods are necessarily limited. Spin-charge separation is predicted exactly for the Luttinger model : an *ideal* exactly-solvable model. It is thus important to test numerically to what extent spin-charge separation can occur in a one-dimensional *physical model*. Moreover, in order to prove the theories mentioned above, it would be important to check whether some two-dimensional models exist, which display spin-charge separation.

In this work, we present a systematic Quantum-Monte-Carlo study of spin-charge separation *away* from half filling, where Luttinger-liquid theory is expected to hold, in the *whole* Brillouin zone (BZ). The nontrivial prediction of Luttinger-liquid theory is, in fact, that spin-charge separation occurs in the *metallic* phase, where the band dispersion is *linear*.

For *some* values of the momentum k we are able to see two peaks in the single-particle spectral function which correspond to the spin and charge excitations. However, due to the limited resolution of the Maximum Entropy method , it is not possible to resolve the two peaks in most of the BZ.[17] For this reason, in the rest of the BZ we work with the imaginary-time Green's function $\mathcal{G}(k, \tau)$ which is obtained directly from Quantum-Monte-Carlo data without the need of analytic continuation. This has the advantage that one does not need to introduce a further source of error produced by the analytic continuation to real frequencies. Specifically, we perform a nonlinear χ^2 fit of $\mathcal{G}(k, \tau)$ by using the solution of the Luttinger model $\mathcal{G}^{(LM)}_{v_1, v_2, K_\rho}(k, \tau)$[1] with two velocities v_1, v_2, and a normalization constant c as fitting parameters.[18] Our fit yields a finite value of the difference $v_2 - v_1$ larger than the statistical error in a large portion of the Brillouin zone. Moreover, the fitted values of the corresponding excitation energies $v_1(k - k_F)$ and $v_2(k - k_F)$ *coincide*, within the statistical error, with the spin and charge excitations, respectively, calculated independently via the associated susceptibilities. It is remarkable that this behavior extends well beyond the region of linear dispersion around k_F where Luttinger liquid behavior is expected.

Our paper is organized as follows. In Sec. 2, we introduce the model, and we show the results of the Quantum-Monte-Carlo simulation and analytic continuation to real frequencies by means of the Maximum Entropy method. In Sec. 3, we discuss and show the results of our fit of the imaginary-time

Green's function with the result from the Luttinger model. Finally we draw our conclusions in Sec. 4.

2   QUANTUM-MONTE-CARLO SIMULATION

We consider the 1D-Hubbard model with periodic boundary conditions described by the following Hamiltonian:

$$H = -t \sum_{i,\sigma} \left(c^{\dagger}_{i+1,\sigma} c_{i,\sigma} + \text{h.c.} \right) + U \sum_i n_{i\downarrow} n_{i\uparrow} - \mu \sum_i (n_{i\downarrow} + n_{i\uparrow}) , \quad (1)$$

where $c^{(\dagger)}_{i,\sigma}$ are annihilation (creation) operators for an electron at site i with spin σ and $n_{i\sigma} = c^{\dagger}_{i,\sigma} c_{i,\sigma}$. The energy scale t of the model will be set to unity in the rest of the paper.

The interaction term can be separated from the kinetic term by introducing L discrete timeslices $(\beta = L\Delta\tau)$ [13–15]:

$$Z = \text{Tr} e^{-\beta H} = \text{Tr} \prod_{l=1}^{L} e^{-\Delta\tau H_{kin}} e^{-\Delta\tau H_{int}} + O(\Delta\tau^2) . \quad (2)$$

Applying a Hubbard-Stratonovich transformation

$$e^{-\Delta\tau U n_{i\uparrow} n_{i\downarrow}} = c \sum_{\sigma_i(l)=\pm 1} e^{\lambda_1 \sigma_i(l)(n_{i\uparrow} - n_{i\downarrow}) - \lambda_2 (n_{i\uparrow} + n_{i\downarrow})} \quad (3)$$

with interaction dependent constants $\lambda_{1/2}$ [16] brings the interaction part into bilinear form. The fermionic part in the partition function can now be integrated out:

$$Z = \text{Tr}_\sigma \prod_{\alpha=\pm 1} \det \left[1 + \mathbf{B}_L(\alpha) \mathbf{B}_{L-1}(\alpha) \ldots \mathbf{B}_1(\alpha) \right] \quad (4)$$

with

$$\mathbf{B}_l(\alpha) = e^{-\Delta\tau \mathbf{K}} e^{\mathbf{V}(\alpha,l)} \quad (5)$$

$$K_{ij} = \{-t \text{ if } i \text{ and } j \text{ are neighbors}, 0 \text{ otherwise}\} \quad (6)$$

$$V_{ij}(\alpha,l) = \delta_{ij} (\lambda_1 \alpha \sigma_i(l) + \Delta\tau\mu - \lambda_2) \quad (7)$$

The trace over the bosonic field $\sigma_i(l)$ can now be evaluated by Monte-Carlo methods [16,19].

The simulations were carried out on a 64-site lattice with inverse temperature $\frac{1}{k_B T} = \beta = 20$, Hubbard repulsion $U = 4$ and an electron density of $\langle n \rangle \approx 0.75$. We used a discretization of the imaginary-time axis $\Delta\tau = 0.0625$

In order to achieve the for this project necessary accuracy, 64 processors on the Cray-T3E supercomputer were running parallel Monte-Carlo jobs. Each processor started with a different random field configuration $\sigma_i(l)$. During the run the calculated mean values for physical observables on each processor were gathered to make a statistical analysis. In addition to that the raw mean values of each processor were written on disc to be able to perform a more complex analysis after the end of the calculation. With this scheme a total performance of 8 Gigaflops was achieved.

The simulations yield the one- and two-particle Green's functions at discrete imaginary times τ with $0 \leq \tau \leq \beta$. The spectra (one-particle photoemission spectrum, charge- and spin-susceptibilities) were then obtained by analytically continuing the imaginary-time results to real frequencies by means of the Maximum-Entropy method [20,21,17].

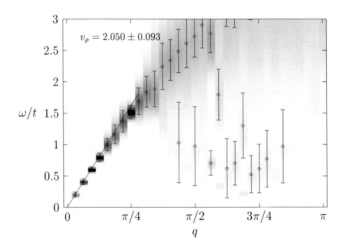

Fig. 1. Density plot of the charge susceptibility $\chi_\rho(q,\omega)$ as obtained by the analytic continuation of the Quantum-Monte-Carlo charge-charge correlation function with the Maximum-Entropy method. The grayscale corresponds to the value of $\chi_\rho(q,\omega)$ (darker regions correspond to larger values of $\chi_\rho(q,\omega)$) and the dots with errorbars show the peak position with their uncertainty. The linear fit (straight line) for small q yields the charge velocity v_ρ as indicated in the upper left corner.

Figures 1 and 2 show a density plot of the charge- and spin susceptibilities χ_ρ and χ_σ, respectively. The grayscale gives a measure for the value of $\chi_{\rho/\sigma}(q,\omega)$ as a function of momentum transfer q and excitation energy ω. The dispersion relation for spin- and charge-excitations is defined by the maxima of $\chi_{\rho/\sigma}$ which are indicated by dots with errorbars in the figure. A linear fit of these maxima near $q = 0$ yields the spin- and charge-velocities $v_\sigma = 1.170 \pm 0.074$ and $v_\rho = 2.050 \pm 0.093$ which agree very well (within the statistical error) with Bethe-Ansatz results [22] for the infinite lattice and zero temperature.

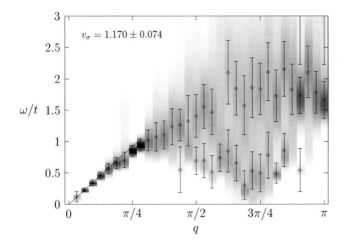

Fig. 2. Density plot of the spin susceptibility $\chi_\sigma(q,\omega)$ with the same conventions as Fig. 1 The linear fit (straight line) yields the spin velocity v_σ.

However, it is not sufficient to have two different velocities (or, equivalently, energy dispersions) for the two-particle spin and charge modes in order to conclude that the system shows spin-charge separation. In fact, in a Fermi liquid there are spin and charge excitations that originate from collective modes and do not destroy the quasiparticle [23]. The quasiparticles thus remain well-defined and do not split into a charge and a spin excitation as it occurs in a Luttinger liquid. On the other hand, in a Luttinger liquid (or in spin-charge separated system in general) a particle injected at a certain point x decays into a spinon and a holon propagating with different velocities. The separation of the two excitations could then be detected by means of a "diagnostic operator" measuring the time dependence of spin and charge at a given point y far away from x. In the case of spin-charge separation, this diagnostic operator would then measure two different passing times for the charge and spin perturbations of the injected particle. True spin-charge separation in the sense of the Luttinger model should be thus identified with different energy dispersions in the spin and charge susceptibilities *associated with* corresponding low-lying excitations in the single-particle spectrum.

In Fig. 3 we plot this single-particle spectrum $A(k,\omega)$[17] in the whole Brillouin zone. Close to the Fermi momentum the band dispersion is approximately linear, which justifies the mapping to the Luttinger model. However, the spectrum becomes broader when going away from the Fermi surface. This phenomenon has two reasons: First, the resolution of the maximum-entropy method gets worse at higher energies, due to the exponential kernel in the spectral theorem, and second, according to Luttinger liquid theory, the single peak starts to split into two peaks representing the spin- and charge-excitations propagating with different velocities. However, for k very close to

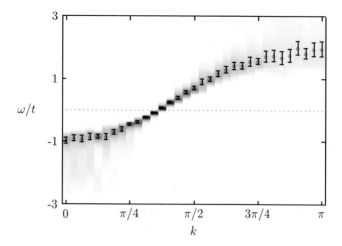

Fig. 3. Density plot of the single-particle photoemission spectrum $A(k,\omega)$ with the same conventions as Fig. 1. It is seen that the dispersion around the Fermi energy (dotted line) is linear over a broad momentum range thus justifying our *Luttinger-liquid* ansatz for the single-particle Green's function.

k_F these two peaks, which should be separated by an energy $(v_2-v_1)(k-k_F)$, are still too close together for the Maximum Entropy method to distinguish them. On the other hand, at larger values of $(k-k_F)$ the excitation energies are too high and the maximum entropy method becomes less reliable as explained above. In both these cases the two peaks merge into a single broader peak and spin-charge separation is not detectable. There are, however, some favorable intermediate k-points where spin-charge separation is directly detectable in the single-particle spectral function. In figure 4 we show the spectral function for one of these favorable points. Here k is neither too close nor too far from the Fermi surface and the maximum-entropy method (without using any *prior knowledge*) yields two well-separated peaks. Their positions are consistent with the spin and charge excitation energies (indicated by two dots with horizontal errorbars) calculated independently from the spin- and charge- velocities ($\omega_{\rho/\sigma} = \Delta k\, v_{\rho/\sigma}$). Previously, it was not possible to resolve spin-charge separation in the one-particle spectrum[17]. This is partly due to the fact that the calculations were carried out in a low doping regime ($\langle n \rangle$ close to 1) where the difference of spin- and charge-velocities is relatively small .[22] A very important reason for this success was also the high computing power that was available for this project.

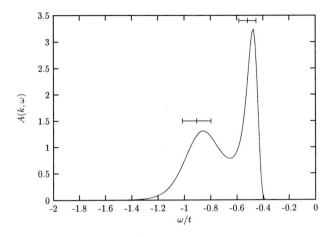

Fig. 4. Single-particle photoemission spectrum $A(k,\omega)$ (in arbitrary units) for $k - k_F = -4.5\,\frac{\pi}{32}$. The dots with horizontal errorbars indicate the position of spin- and charge-excitations calculated by $\omega_{\rho/\sigma} = (k - k_F)\,v_{\rho/\sigma}$ with $v_{\rho/\sigma}$ obtained from Figs. 1 and 2. For this k-point close to the Fermi momentum the Maximum-Entropy method is able to resolve two separate peaks in the spectral function which can be identified as the spinon and holon excitation, respectively.

3   FIT OF THE IMAGINARY-TIME GREEN'S FUNCTION

In order to carry out a *systematic* study of spin-charge separation it is important to detect spin and charge excitations over the whole BZ, or at least in an extended region around the Fermi surface. However, due to the additional rather large error introduced by the Maximum Entropy analytic continuation method to the Quantum-Monte-Carlo data, this turns out to be very difficult for many k points, as we have discussed above. For this reason, we work directly with the data for the *imaginary-time* Green's function $\mathcal{G}(k,\tau)$. In the asymptotic limit ($\tau > 1$) and close to the Fermi surface ($+k_F$) this function should approach the Green's function of the Luttinger model for right-moving fermions, i. e.

$$\mathcal{G}^{(LM)}_{v_1,v_2,K_\rho}(k,\tau) \equiv \int dx\ e^{-ikx}\tilde{\mathcal{G}}^{(LM)}_{v_1,v_2,K_\rho}(x,\tau)\,, \tag{8}$$

with

$$\tilde{\mathcal{G}}^{(LM)}_{v_1,v_2,K_\rho}(x,\tau) \tag{9}$$

$$= \frac{e^{ik_F x}c}{\sqrt{v_1\tau + ix}\sqrt{v_2\tau + ix}(x^2 + v_2^2\tau^2)^{-(K_\rho+1/K_\rho-2)/8}}\,,$$

where c is a normalization constant[24] and k_F the Fermi momentum. Therefore, in order to identify the spin and charge excitations *directly* in the

Green's function, we carry out a nonlinear χ^2 fit of our data for $\mathcal{G}(k,\tau)$ to $\mathcal{G}^{(LM)}_{v_1,v_2,K_\rho}(k,\tau)$. The fit parameters are the two velocities v_1 and v_2, and the normalization constant c .[18] Due to the statistical error in the Quantum-Monte-Carlo data, we get statistical errors Δv_1, Δv_2, and Δc for the parameters v_1, v_2, and c, respectively. The splitting of the single-particle mode into two excitations is thus detected when the difference between the two velocities is larger than the statistical error. Furthermore, in order to make sure that the two excitations coincide with the spin and the charge modes one has to compare v_1 and v_2 with the velocities v_ρ and v_σ calculated independently via the susceptibilities.

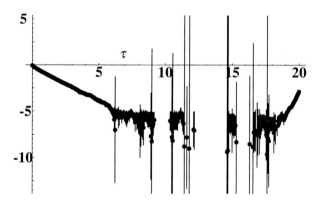

Fig. 5. Logarithmic plot of the imaginary-time Green's function $\mathcal{G}(k,\tau)$ vs τ with $k = k_F + \pi 9/64$, as obtained from Quantum-Monte-Carlo data.

However, in order to carry out this fit one should not use the data from the whole interval $0.0 \leq \tau \leq \beta$ for the following reasons. First of all the Hubbard model and the Luttinger model Green's function should coincide only asymptotically. For this reason, we choose $\tau \geq 1.0$. Moreover, the interval $\beta/2 \leq \tau \leq \beta$ is equivalent to the one $-\beta/2 \leq \tau \leq 0$ so that we can omit the former. In addition, as can be seen in Fig. 5 the log of the imaginary-time Green's is quite sharply defined up to $\tau \approx 5.0$. For $\tau > 5.0$, large (relative) errors start to develop due to the small value of the Green's function in these points. For this reason, we choose to carry out our fit only for the data in the interval $1.0 \leq \tau \leq 5.0$ in order to select the less "noisy" data. In order to check that our results do not depend on this choice, we also carry out the fit for the data in the interval $1.0 \leq \tau \leq \beta/2 = 10.0$. This turns out to be quite similar to the first one and is reported elsewhere [27]. In Fig. 6 we show the result of our fit with the $T = 0$ Green's function [(8) with (9)] for several values of $q = (k - k_F)$. The vertical black lines show the value of the spinon and holon excitation energies $\varepsilon_1(q) \equiv v_1(q)\, q$ and $\varepsilon_2(q) \equiv v_2(q)\, q$, respectively, obtained from the fit with the single-particle Green's function.[25] As one can see, we obtain a clear separation of the two modes for almost all the q points. In addition, the velocities are slightly q-dependent as expected from a curved band. To check that these modes correspond to spin and charge degrees of freedom, we plot in the same figure the dispersions calculated from the peaks of the corresponding susceptibilities. The width of the gray regions indicate the peak positions within their uncertainty. As one can see, the dispersions obtained in the two ways coincide within the statistical error. We find it remarkable that, even at k-points far from k_F, the fit with the Luttinger-liquid Green's function is in agreement with the two-particle response, although the dispersion is no longer linear. It thus seems that spin and charge separation survives even at higher energies.

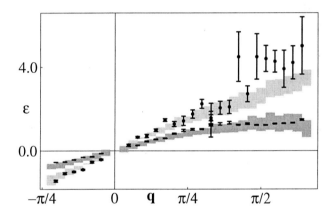

Fig. 6. Spin and charge dispersions ε_1 and ε_2 vs $q = k - k_F$ (errorbars without and with central dot, respectively) as obtained from the χ^2 fit of the Quantum-Monte-Carlo data for the imaginary-time Green's function with the Luttinger liquid Green's function [(8) with (9)]. The Luttinger liquid Green's function is taken at zero temperature and with correlation exponent $K_\rho = 1$. The fit is carried out for the data in the time interval $1.0 \leq \tau \leq 5.0$. For comparison, we also show the dispersions obtained from the peak positions (with corresponding uncertainty) of the spin (dark gray) and of the charge (light gray) dispersions (Cfr. Figs. 2 and 1).

In Fig. 6 we used the simplest form of (9), namely, the one with $K_\rho = 1.0$. This is not, in principle, the correct value of the correlation exponent K_ρ when $U \neq 0$. Actually, one could use K_ρ as a further parameter to fit the data or, alternatively, use the result from the Bethe-Ansatz solution[26]. It turns out, however, that an attempt to fit K_ρ yields an error of the order of 0.5, which means that K_ρ cannot be determined by our fit. It also turned out that the *result* of the fit does not depend crucially on the value of K_ρ we are using [27]. For this reason, the non-interacting value $K_\rho = 1.0$ can be safely used. This is important, because in this way it is possible to test the occurrence of spin-charge separation even *without* knowing whether the system has anomalous scaling ($K_\rho \neq 1$) or not. This could be useful in cases where the anomalous exponent may be not known a priori and may be difficult to evaluate. In this case, one can assume a form of the fitting function without spectral anomaly (i. e., $K_\rho = 1$), but simply with a branch cut due to spin-charge separation. This could be useful, for example, to test spin-charge separation in 2-D as we shall discuss below.

Since the Quantum-Monte-Carlo simulations are carried out at finite temperature we also performed our fit with a Luttinger model Green's function for finite temperatures. It turns out that the results are not appreciably different and we can safely use the $T = 0$ *ansatz* (the details are published elsewhere [27]).

Finally, to check that the two different velocities v_1 and v_2 obtained are not an artifact of our fit, we carry out a fit of the *non-interacting* Green's function $\tilde{G}^{(0)}(k, \tau; \beta)$ with the function (8) assuming artificially the same statistical errors as the ones obtained in the Quantum-Monte-Carlo simulation. As one can see in Fig. 7, in this case the spin and charge velocities obtained are equal within the statistical error, as it should be.

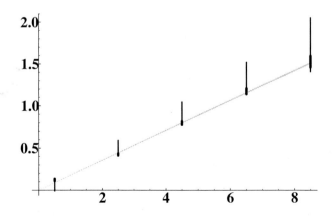

Fig. 7. Fit of the $U = 0$ imaginary-time Green's function with Eq. (8). The straight line shows $\omega = v_F q$ where v_F is the Fermi velocity of the $U = 0$ system.

Another motivation of this work was to test a "diagnostic operator" that can be applied to detect numerically the occurrence of spin and charge separation in a many-body system from Quantum-Monte-Carlo data. If one uses exact diagonalization, where the spectral function of the system can be evaluated directly, it is of course not necessary to fit the imaginary-time Green's function. However, we believe that the systems that can be studied by exact diagonalization (10-16 sites) are too small to allow for a systematic study of spin-charge separation. The Fourier transform (in momentum and imaginary-frequency space) of the spin-charge separated Green's function Eq. (9) with $K_\rho = 1$ reads

$$\hat{\mathcal{G}}^{(LM)}_{v_1,v_2,K_\rho}(k,\omega) \propto \frac{1}{\sqrt{i\omega - \varepsilon_1(k)}\sqrt{i\omega - \varepsilon_2(k)}} \, , \qquad (10)$$

where $\varepsilon_1(k) = v_1(k - k_F)$ and $\varepsilon_2(k) = v_2(k - k_F)$ represent the spin and charge excitations (measured from the chemical potential) in which the single-particle excitation is split. The same form of $\hat{\mathcal{G}}^{(LM)}_{v_1,v_2,K_\rho}(k,\omega)$ could be expected to hold asymptotically, i.e. for small frequencies and close to the Fermi surface, in higher dimensions. Close to the Fermi surface, one will have a direction-dependent dispersion $\varepsilon_i(\boldsymbol{k}) = (\boldsymbol{k} - \boldsymbol{k}_F) \cdot \boldsymbol{v}(\boldsymbol{k}_F)$ where $\boldsymbol{v}(\boldsymbol{k}_F)$ is the Fermi velocity of the point at the Fermi surface $\boldsymbol{k}_F$ closest to $\boldsymbol{k}$. Spin-charge separation would be signaled by two different, direction-dependent $\varepsilon_1(\boldsymbol{k})$ and $\varepsilon_2(\boldsymbol{k})$ for a given $\boldsymbol{k}$.

4   CONCLUSIONS

To summarize, we carried out a test of spin-charge separation in the 1-D Hubbard model at finite doping. It is in general difficult to resolve the peaks corresponding to the spin and charge excitations in the single-particle spectral function due to the loss of accuracy which occurs when analytically continuing the imaginary-time Quantum-Monte-Carlo results to real frequencies. For some values of the momentum close to the Fermi surface, however, we were able to resolve two peaks whose energies correspond to the peaks at the same $q = k - k_F$ in the spin and charge susceptibilities, respectively.

By fitting the Quantum-Monte-Carlo data for the imaginary-time Green's function with the exact solution from the Luttinger model with the spin and charge velocities as fitting parameters, we have been able to resolve the two excitations over the whole Brillouin zone. The two excitation energies found in the fit agree, within statistical error, with the spin and charge excitations, respectively, identified with the peaks of the spin and charge susceptibilities. Remarkably, this occurs also away from the region where the band dispersion is linear. We also suggested a possible extension of this "diagnostic operator" to test a possible occurrence of spin-charge separation in two dimensions.

The calculations were carried out on the Cray-T3E supercomputer at the HLRS Stuttgart and at the CRAY-T90 at the HLRS Jülich. On the parallel CRAY-T3E the QMC algorithm ran on 64 processors with different initial configurations of the ising field. Communication was used to gather the results from each processor in order to perform the statistical analysis. With this scheme a total performance of 8 Gigaflops has been achieved.

References

1. V. J. Emery, in *Highly-Conducting One-Dimensional Solids*, edited by J. T. Devreese, R. E. Evrard, and V. van Doren (Plenum Press, New York, 1979).
2. F. D. M. Haldane, J. Phys. C **14**, 2585 (1981).
3. J. Voit, Reports on Progress in Physics **58**, 977 (1995).
4. E. H. Lieb and F. Y. Wu, Phys. Rev. Lett. **20**, 1445 (1968).
5. V. Meden and K. Schönhammer, Phys. Rev. B **46**, 15753 (1992).
6. J. Voit, J. Phys. Cond. Matt. **5**, 8305 (1993).
7. P. W. Anderson, Phys. Rev. B **42**, 2624 (1990).
8. P. W. Anderson, Phys. Rev. Lett. **64**, 1839 (1990).
9. P. W. Anderson, Science **258**, 672 (1992).
10. D. Clarke, S. Strong, and P. Anderson, Phys. Rev. Lett. **74**, 4499 (1995).
11. P. W. Anderson, Phys. Rev. B **55**, 11785 (1997).
12. D. G. Clarke, S. P. Strong, and P. W. Anderson, Phys. Rev. Lett. **72**, 3218 (1994).
13. M. Suzuki, Prog. Theor. Phys. **56**, 1454 (1976).
14. M. Suzuki, Comm. Math. Phys. **51**, 183 (1976).
15. H. Trotter, Prog. Am. Math. Soc. **10**, 544 (1959).
16. J. E. Hirsch, Phys. Rev. B **28**, 4059 (1983).
17. R. Preuss, A. Muramatsu, W. von der Linden, P. Dieterich, F. F. Assaad, W. Hanke, Phys. Rev. Lett. **73**, 732 (1994).
18. The results of the fit turns out to depend very weakly on the value of K_ρ used (cf. Sec. 3).
19. S. R. White *et al.*, Phys. Rev. B **40**, 506 (1989).
20. R. N. Silver *et al.*, Phys. Rev. Lett. **65**, 496 (1990).
21. J. E. Gubernatis *et al.*, Phys. Rev. B **44**, 6011 (1991).
22. H. J. Schulz, Int. J. Mod. Phys. B **5**, 57 (1991).
23. D. Pines and P. Nozières, *The Theory of Quantum Liquids* (W. A. Benjamin, inc., New York, 1966), Vol. I.
24. It is not possible to fix the constant c through sum rules, since the two Green's functions coincide only asymptotically.
25. The q-dependence of the velocities is due to the fact that we fit independently $\mathcal{G}(k_F + q, \tau)$ for each q.
26. H. J. Schulz, Int. J. Mod. Phys. **5**, 57 (1991).
27. M. G. Zacher, E. Arrigoni, W. Hanke and J. R. Schrieffer, Phys. Rev. B **57**, 6370 (1998).

The interplay between *d*-wave superconductivity and antiferromagnetic fluctuations: a quantum Monte Carlo study

F.F. Assaad

Institut für Theoretische Physik III,
Universität Stuttgart, Pfaffenwaldring 57, D-70550 Stuttgart, Germany.

Abstract. We consider the repulsive Hubbard model on a square lattice with an additional term, W, which depends upon the square of a single-particle nearest-neighbor hopping. At half-band filling, constant W, we show that enhancing U/t drives the system from a *d*-wave superconductor to an antiferromagnetic Mott insulator. At zero temperature in the superconducting phase, spin-spin correlations follow a powerlaw: $e^{-i\mathbf{r}\cdot\mathbf{Q}}|\mathbf{r}|^{-\alpha}$. Here $\mathbf{Q} = (\pi, \pi)$ and α is in the range $1 < \alpha < 2$ and depends upon the coupling constants W and U. This results is reached on the basis of large scale quantum Monte-Carlo simulations on lattices up to 24×24, and is shown to be independent on the choice of the boundary conditions. We define a pairing (magnetic) scale by the temperature below which *short range d*-wave pairing correlations (antiferromagnetic fluctuations) start growing. With finite temperature quantum Monte Carlo simulations, we demonstrate that both scales are identical over a large energy range. Those results show the extreme compatibility and close interplay of antiferromagnetic fluctuations and *d*-wave superconductivity.

The understanding of the interplay between *d*-wave superconductivity and antiferromagnetism is a central issue for the understanding of the phase diagram of High-T_c superconductors [1]. The aim of this work is to further study a model which shows a quantum transition between a *d*-wave superconductor and an antiferromagnetic Mott insulator. It thus enables us to address the above question. The model we consider, has been introduced in Ref. [2]. It is defined by:

$$H = -\frac{t}{2}\sum_i K_i - W \sum_i K_i^2 + U \sum_i (n_{i,\uparrow} - \frac{1}{2})(n_{i,\downarrow} - \frac{1}{2}) \qquad (1)$$

with the hopping kinetic energy

$$K_i = \sum_{\sigma,\boldsymbol{\delta}} \left(c_{i,\sigma}^\dagger c_{i+\boldsymbol{\delta},\sigma} + c_{i+\boldsymbol{\delta},\sigma}^\dagger c_{i,\sigma} \right). \qquad (2)$$

Here, $W \geq 0$, $\boldsymbol{\delta} = \pm \boldsymbol{a}_x, \pm \boldsymbol{a}_y$, and $n_{i,\sigma} = c_{i,\sigma}^\dagger c_{i,\sigma}$ where $c_{i,\sigma}^\dagger$ ($c_{i,\sigma}$) creates (annihilates) an electron on site i with z-component of spin σ. We impose twisted boundary conditions:

$$c_{i+L\boldsymbol{a}_x,\sigma} = \exp\left(2\pi i \Phi/\Phi_0\right) c_{i,\sigma}, \quad c_{i+L\boldsymbol{a}_y,\sigma} = c_{i,\sigma}, \qquad (3)$$

with $\Phi_0 = hc/e$ the flux quanta and L the linear length of the square lattice. The boundary conditions given by Eq. (3) account for a magnetic flux threading a torus on which the lattice is wrapped. One major advantage of the above model consists in the fact that at half-band filling, the sign problem in the quantum Monte-Carlo (QMC) method may be avoided. This statement is valid even for the above boundary conditions. Hereafter, we will only consider the half-filled case.

Previously we have considered the model of Eq. (1) at fixed values of U and as a function of W. At $U/t = 4$ we have shown that the quantum transition between the Mott insulator and d-wave superconductor occurs at $W_c/t \sim 0.3$ [2]. We have equally considered the model at finite doping and given numerical evidence of the occurrence of a doping induced quantum transition between the Mott insulator and d-wave superconductor [3]. Here, we fix $W/t = 0.35$ and vary U/t for the half-filled case. The advantage of this choice of parameters is that it provides us with a *large* parameter range in the superconducting phase where QMC simulations are extremely precise, thus allowing us to reach large lattices. This allows us to reliably study the nature of the spin degrees of freedom in the superconducting state. We have used two QMC algorithms. i) The Projector QMC algorithm which produces zero temperature results in a canonical ensemble [4,5] and ii) the finite temperature grand canonical QMC method [6,7]. The application of those algorithms for the above model has been discussed in reference [2]. Both algorithms, generate a systematic error proportional to $(\Delta\tau)^2$ where $\Delta\tau$ denotes the imaginary time step. To determine the exponent of the spin-spin correlations we have extrapolated $\Delta\tau$ to zero.

We first concentrate of the charge degrees of freedom at zero temperature. To distinguish between a superconductor and insulator, we compute the ground state energy as a function of the twist in the boundary condition: $E_0(\Phi)$. For an insulator, the wave function is localized and hence, an exponential decay of $\Delta E_0(\Phi) \equiv E_0(\Phi) - E_0(\Phi_0/2)$ as a function of lattice size is expected [8]. In the Hartree-Fock spin density wave (SDW) approximation for the half-filled Hubbard model, one obtains $\Delta E_0(\Phi) = \alpha(\Phi)L \exp(-L/\xi)$ where ξ is the localization length of the wave function. On the other hand, for a superconductor, $\Delta E_0(\Phi)$ shows anomalous flux quantization: $\Delta E_0(\Phi)$ is a periodic function of Φ with period $\Phi_0/2$ and a non vanishing energy barrier is to be found between the flux minima [9–11] so that $\Delta E_0(\Phi_0/4)$ remains finite as $L \to \infty$. Fig. (1) plots $\Delta E_0(\Phi/4)$ versus $1/L$ at $W/t = 0.35$ and for various values of U/t. At values of $U/t \leq 4$, the data is consistent with a $1/L$ form and scales to a finite value. At $U/t = 5$, the data may be fitted to the above SDW form. Thus, for values of $W/t = 0.35$, the data is consistent with the occurrence of a quantum transition between a superconductor and a Mott insulator at $4 < U_c/t < 5$.

In order to determine the symmetry of the superconducting state, we have computed equal time pairing correlations in the extended s-wave and $d_{x^2-y^2}$

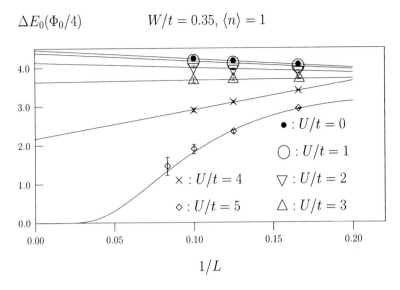

$\Delta E_0(\Phi_0/4)$ $W/t = 0.35,\ \langle n \rangle = 1$

$1/L$

Fig. 1. $\Delta E_0(\Phi_0/4) \equiv E_0(\Phi_0/4) - E_0(\Phi_0/2)$ as a function of inverse linear size L. For $U/t \leq 4$ the data is a consistent with a $1/L$ form which extrapolates to a non-vanishing value in the thermodynamic limit. At $U/t = 5$ the data may be fitted the SDW from $L\exp(-L/\xi)$ thus signaling an insulating state.

channels:

$$P_{d,s}(r) = \langle \Delta^{\dagger}_{d,s}(r)\Delta_{d,s}(0)\rangle \tag{4}$$

with

$$\Delta^{\dagger}_{d,s}(r) = \sum_{\sigma,\delta} f_{d,s}(\delta)\sigma c^{\dagger}_{r,\sigma} c^{\dagger}_{r+\delta,-\sigma}. \tag{5}$$

Here, $f_s(\delta) = 1$ and $f_d(\delta) = 1(-1)$ for $\delta = \pm a_x\ (\pm a_y)$. The vertex contribution to the above quantity is given by:

$$P^{v}_{d,s}(r) = P_{d,s}(r) - \sum_{\sigma,\delta,\delta'} f_{d,s}(\delta)f_{d,s}(\delta') \tag{6}$$

$$\left(\langle c^{\dagger}_{r,\sigma}c_{\delta',\sigma}\rangle\langle c^{\dagger}_{r+\delta,-\sigma}c_{0,-\sigma}\rangle + \langle c^{\dagger}_{r,\sigma}c_{0,\sigma}\rangle\langle c^{\dagger}_{r+\delta,-\sigma}c_{\delta',-\sigma}\rangle \right).$$

Per definition, $P^{v}_{d,s}(r) \equiv 0$ in the absence of interactions. Fig. 2 plots $P^{v}_{d}(r)$ along the diagonal of the lattice. We consider lattices ranging up to $L = 24$. For a fixed lattice size, one notices a plateau structure as a function of distance. The extrapolation of this plateau value to the thermodynamic limit is hard and the above criterion of flux quantization, proves to be a more efficient method to conclude superconductivity [12]. In comparison to the d-wave signal, the extended s-wave signal at *large* distances (data not shown)

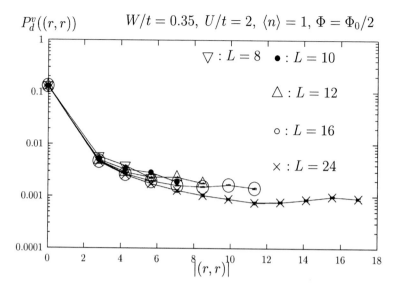

Fig. 2. Vertex contribution to the d-wave pair field correlations. Here, the temperature is set to $T = 0$.

r	$P_s^v(r)$	$P_d^v(r)$
$(0,0)$	0.2950 ± 0.0018	0.1304 ± 0.0011
$(0,1)$	0.0932 ± 0.0009	0.0238 ± 0.0006
$(0,2)$	0.0076 ± 0.0002	0.0252 ± 0.0003

Table 1. Short range vertex contribution of pair-field correlations in the extended s- and d-wave channels. Here we consider an $L = 24$ lattice at $W/t = 0.35$, $U/t = 2$ and $\langle n \rangle = 1$. The boundary conditions are set by $\Phi = \Phi_0/2$. The distance r is in units of the lattice constant.

may not be distinguished from zero within our accuracy. The extended s-wave pair-field correlation dominate at short distances. The data confirming this statement may be found in the table.

The added W-term, contains no processes which explicitly favor d-wave superconductivity. On the contrary, one would expect the W-term to favor extended s-wave symmetry, and this shows up on short length scales. The fact that d-wave symmetry dominates at long-range is a result of the underlying magnetic structure.

To study the spin degrees of freedom, we have computed equal time spin-spin correlations

$$S(r) = \frac{4}{3}\langle S(r)S(0)\rangle \tag{7}$$

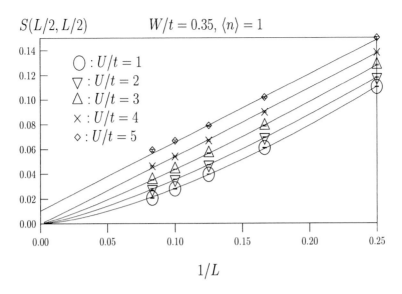

Fig. 3. $S(L/2, L/2)$ versus $1/L$. The simulations were carried out at $\Phi/\Phi_0 = 0$. Here the $\Delta\tau$ systematic error is extrapolated to zero and the temperature is set to $T = 0$. The solid lines are least square fits to the form: $L^{-\alpha}$. The result of the fit is summarized in Eq. (8).

where $\boldsymbol{S}(\boldsymbol{r})$ denotes the spin operator on site $\boldsymbol{r}$. Fig. 3, plots $S(L/2, L/2)$ versus $1/L$ where L corresponds to the linear size of the lattice. We consider periodic boundary conditions, and various values of U/t. W/t is constant and set to $W/t = 0.35$. For values of $U/t \leq 4$ the data is consistent with a powerlaw decay:

$$S(L/2, L/2) \sim L^{-1.49} \text{ for } U/t = 1$$
$$S(L/2, L/2) \sim L^{-1.32} \text{ for } U/t = 2$$
$$S(L/2, L/2) \sim L^{-1.17} \text{ for } U/t = 3$$
$$S(L/2, L/2) \sim L^{-1.01} \text{ for } U/t = 4. \tag{8}$$

At $U/t = 5$ extrapolation of the data leads to a finite staggered moment, and thus the presence of antiferromagnetic long-range order. The statement in Eq. (8) is surprising and deserves confirmation. To cross-check the validity of the above equation, we demonstrate numerically that it is independent on the choice of the boundary condition. Fig. 4 plots $S(L/2, L/2)$ at $U/t = 1$ and $U/t = 2$ for $W/t = 0.35$. At $\Phi = 0$, the solid lines corresponds to least square fits to the form $cL^{-\alpha}$. We thus determine the exponent α. The data at $\Phi = \Phi_0/2$ is consistent at large distances with the form $\tilde{c}L^{-\alpha}$ thus showing that the exponent α is independent on the choice of the boundary. For the

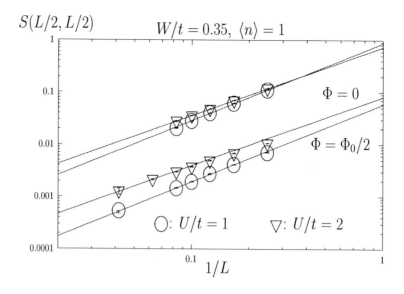

Fig. 4. $S(L/2, L/2)$ versus $1/L$ for different boundary conditions. The solid line for the $\Phi = 0$ data is obtained from least square fit to the form $L^{-\alpha}$. The same value of the exponent α was used to fit the data at $\Phi = \Phi_0/2$. Here the $\Delta\tau$ systematic error is extrapolated to zero, and $T = 0$.

$\Phi = \Phi_0/2$ simulations we were able to reach lattices up to 24×24. At $U/t = 2$ and for the boundary conditions set by $\Phi = \Phi_0/2$, $P_d^v(L/2, L/2)$ (see Fig. 2) decays slower than $S(L/2, L/2)$ (see Fig. 4) thus confirming that the pairing correlations are dominant [13].

Having put Eq. (8) on a numerically firm basis, we now argue why it is a surprising result. In two dimensions, correlation functions which decay slower than $1/r^2$ lead to divergences in Fourier space. The Fourier transform of the spin-spin correlations at $U/t = 2$ is plotted in Fig. 5. One sees a systematic increase of $S(\mathbf{Q} = (\pi, \pi))$ as a function of system size [14]. In contrast, a mean field d-wave BCS calculation, yields spin-spin correlations which decays as a powerlaw with $\alpha_{BCS} = 3.5$. This mean-field result leads to a finite $S(\mathbf{Q})$ in the thermodynamic limit. Another surprise comes from the dependence of the exponent α on the coupling constants, U and W. This is a feature which occurs in one dimensional quantum systems such as the $t - J$ or Hubbard models.

We now consider the model at finite temperatures with the use of the grand-canonical QMC algorithm. In Fig. 6 (a) we plot S(Q) for values of U/t ranging from $U/t = 0$ to $U/t = 8$. We define the magnetic scale, T_J, as the temperature scale where $S(Q)$ starts growing. In Figs. 6 (b) and (c) we consider the vertex contribution to the d-wave paring correlations at distance

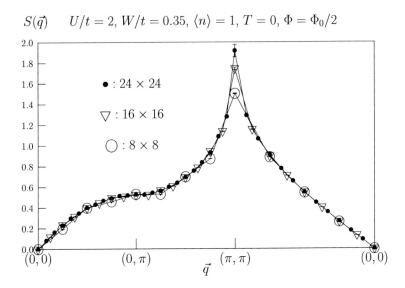

Fig. 5. Fourier transform of the equal time spin-spin correlations.

$\mathbf{R} = (L/2, L/2)$: $P_d^v(L/2, L/2)$. Here, we consider an $L = 10$ lattice. At this distance the s-wave pairing correlations are negligible. We define the d-wave pairing scale, T_p^d, by the temperature scale at which $P_d^v(L/2, L/2)$ starts growing. From the data, we conclude that

$$T_p^d \equiv T_J \tag{9}$$

That is, antiferromagnetic fluctuations as well as d-wave pairing fluctuations occur hand in hand at the same energy scale. If $U/t > U_c/t$ ($U/t < U_c/t$) antiferromagnetic correlations (d-wave pair-field correlations) will dominate at low temperatures. We note that in the large U/t limit, T_J should scale as t^2/U. That up to $U/t = 8$ we still do not see this behavior, may be traced back to the fact that the W-term enhances the band-width [15]. $T_p^d \equiv T_J$ is a natural consequence of the assumption of $SO(5)$ symmetry which unifies antiferromagnetism with d-wave superconductivity [16]. The data, however, does not demonstrate the presence of this symmetry in this model and further work is required.

In conclusion, we have considered aspects of the $t - U - W$ model defined in Eq.(1). The model, at half-band filling, shows rich physics and allows us to study the interplay between magnetism and d-wave superconductivity. We have pointed out the surprising nature of the spin-spin correlations in the superconducting state: $S(r) \sim e^{-ir \cdot Q}|r|^{-\alpha}$, where $Q = (\pi, \pi)$, α is in the range $1 < \alpha < 2$ and depends on the coupling constants W and U. Those conclusions are based on large scale calculations for system sizes up to 24×24.

$L = 10,\ W/t = 0.35,\ \langle n \rangle = 1$

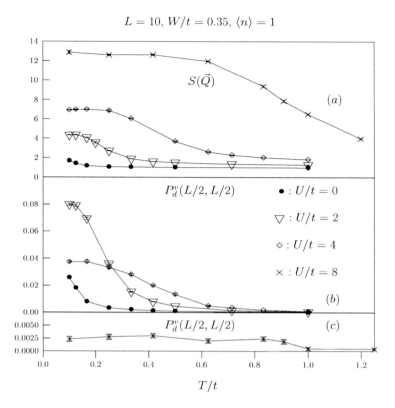

T/t

Fig. 6. (a) $S(Q = (\pi, \pi))$ as a function of temperature, for different values of U/t. (b)-(c): $P_d^v(L/2, L/2)$ versus temperature. The calculations presented in the figure were carried out at $\Phi = 0$.

We have equally shown that the energy scales at which d-wave pairing and antiferromagnetic fluctuations occur are identical. The further understanding of spin and charge dynamics, as well as the doping of the model remains for further studies.

Acknowledgments

M. Imada, D.J. Scalapino and M. Muramatsu are thanked for many instructive conversations. The computations were carried out on the T3E of the HLRS, Stuttgart, as well as on the T90 and T3E of the HLRZ, Jülich.

References

1. J.G. Bednorz and K.A. Müller, Z. Phys. B **64**, 189, (1986).

2. F.F. Assaad, M. Imada and D.J. Scalapino, Phys. Rev. Lett. **77**, 4592, (1996). Phys. Rev. B, Phys. Rev. **B 56**, 15001, (1997).
3. F.F. Assaad and M. Imada Phys. Rev. B. **58**, (1998).
4. G. Sugiyama and S.E. Koonin, Annals of Phys.**168** (1986) 1.
5. S. Sorella, S. Baroni, R. Car, And M. Parrinello, Europhys. Lett. **8** (1989) 663. S. Sorella, E. Tosatti, S. Baroni, R. Car, and M. Parinello, Int. J. Mod. Phys. **B1** (1989) 993.
6. J.E.Hirsch, Phys. Rev. B **31**, 4403, (1985).
7. S.R. White et al. Phys. Rev. B**40**, 506, (1989).
8. W. Kohn, Phys. Rev. **133A**, 171, (1964).
9. N. Byers and C.N. Yang, Phys Rev. Let.**7**, 46, (1961).
10. C.N. Yang, Reviews of Mod. Phys. **34**, 694 (1962).
11. F.F. Assaad, W. Hanke and D.J. Scalapino, Phys. Rev. Lett. **71**, 1915 (1993), Phys. Rev. B **49**, 4327 (1994).
12. Flux quantization, measures directly the superfluid density which does not require the knowledge of the symmetry of pairing correlations, the *form factor* of the Cooper pair, or the nature of the *quasiparticle* which constitute the Cooper pair. We note however that we not yet established firmly the occurrence of a flux minima at $\Phi/\Phi_0 = 0$ [2].
13. At $U/t = 2$ and $U/t = 1$, one may show numerically that the vertex contribution to the d-wave pairing susceptibility grows quicker than the vertex contribution to the staggered spin susceptibility as a function of system size [15].
14. We note that obtaining the exponent α from the size scaling of $S(\mathbf{Q})$ requires larger lattice sizes than the ones considered here. Short range spin-spin correlations included in $S(\mathbf{Q})$ are still important for the considered lattice sizes.
15. F. F. Assaad et al. unpublished.
16. S.C. Zhang, Science, **275**, 1089, (1997).

Towards a Time-Dependent Density-Functional Description of Multiple Multiphoton-Ionization of Helium in Strong Laser Fields

M. Petersilka and E.K.U. Gross

Institut für Theoretische Physik, Universität Würzburg, Am Hubland, 97074 Würzburg, Germany

Abstract. In this work we address the problem of multiple ionization of atoms in strong laser fields (in the infrared and visible range). To this end we numerically solve the full, three-dimensional time-dependent Kohn-Sham equations for a Helium atom in a strong (780nm) laser field. Explicit density functionals for the calculation of ionization probabilities are developed. From the results, we will draw conclusions about the role of electronic correlation in the ionization dynamics and about the validity of present-day exchange-correlation potentials.

1 Introduction

Owing to the rapid experimental progress in the field of laser physics, ultra-short laser pulses of very high intensities have become available in recent years. The electric field produced in such pulses can reach or even exceed the strength of the static nuclear Coulomb field experienced by an electron on the first Bohr orbit. In the hydrogen atom, this electric field is of the order of $5.1 \times 10^9 \mathrm{V/m}$, which corresponds to the electric field amplitude of an electromagnetic plane wave of an intensity of $3.51 \times 10^{16} \mathrm{W/cm^2}$. If an atom is placed in the focus of such a laser pulse one observes a wealth of novel phenomena [1–3] which cannot be explained by ordinary perturbation theory.

The advent of short laser pulse experiments has revealed evidence of a significantly enhanced production of doubly charged noble gas atoms [4]. Recently, in high precision measurements covering a wide dynamical range of intensity dependent ionization [5,6], a "knee" structure in the double ionization yields of Helium has been observed. Up to an intensity of roughly $3 \times 10^{15} \mathrm{W/cm^2}$, the double-ionization yields are *orders of magnitude* above the signal that one would expect from a "sequential" mechanism, in which the second electron only comes from the ionization of He^+. The He^+ and the He^{2+} curves saturate at the same intensity, indicating that the ionization does proceed nonsequentially.

The salient feature of enhanced double ionization suggests the existence of a "direct" process where the amount of energy absorbed from the radiation field is shared among the two electrons. Needless to say, that the so-called "single-active electron approximation" [7,8], which is based on the assumption that just one electron at a time is being active in the interaction with the external laser field, is not capable of describing these effects. Perturbative methods [9] and the solution of theoretical models based on a simplified dielectronic interaction [10] underline the importance of time-dependent electron-electron correlation during the process. Further evidence of the fact that electron correlation leads to qualitative effects in intense laser-atom interactions was gained from the recent solution of the time-dependent Schrödinger equation of a one-dimensional model atom [11].

The double-ionization measurements constitute the most distinct manifestation of electron correlation in the physics of intense laser-atom interactions, making indispensable a non-perturbative quantum mechanical description of interacting electrons in strong, time-dependent external fields. In principle, this requires the full solution of the three-dimensional time-dependent Schrödinger equation for interacting many-particle systems. Work along these lines for the helium atom has already begun [12–14], but the problem is, even with the use of modern massively parallel computers, barely numerically tractable. Clearly, in view of its computational advantages, time-dependent density functional theory [15,16] opens up a viable route towards the exploration of the physics of time-dependent many-particle systems. It provides an in principle exact alternative to account for the fully correlated character of the problem by virtue of the time-dependent exchange-correlation potential. The solution of the time-dependent Kohn-Sham equations brings within reach a fully nonlinear time-dependent *all electron* treatment of atoms in strong laser fields.

2   Integration of the time-dependent Kohn-Sham Equations, Numerical Method

By virtue of the theorem of Runge and Gross [15], every observable can, in principle, be calculated from the time-dependent density. In the framework of time-dependent density functional theory, this density can be obtained from

$$n(\mathbf{r}, t) = \sum_{j=1}^{N} |\varphi_j(\mathbf{r}, t)|^2 \tag{1}$$

(N being the number of electrons) with orbitals $\varphi_{j\sigma}(\mathbf{r}, t)$ satisfying the time-dependent Kohn-Sham equation

$$i\frac{\partial}{\partial t}\varphi_j(\mathbf{r}, t) = \left(-\frac{\nabla^2}{2} + v(\mathbf{r}, t) + \int d^3r' \frac{n(\mathbf{r}', t)}{|\mathbf{r} - \mathbf{r}'|} + v_{\text{xc}}[n](\mathbf{r}, t)\right)\varphi_j(\mathbf{r}, t) \tag{2}$$

(atomic units are used throughout). In practice, the time-dependent exchange-correlation potential v_{xc} has to be approximated. The total *external* potential experienced by the electrons in the helium atom (in dipole approximation and length gauge) is given by

$$v(\mathbf{r}, t) = E_0 \, f(t) \, z \, \sin(\omega t) - \frac{2}{r}. \tag{3}$$

The electric field of the laser with frequency ω and peak strength E_0 is assumed to be polarized along the z-direction, and can be further characterized by the envelope function $f(t)$.

During the propagation, a 6-cycle duration laser pulse with a trapezoidal temporal shape was taken: the envelope function in (3) was linearly ramped from zero to one over the first two cycles, held constant for the following two laser cycles and finally ramped down linearly over the last two cycles of the pulse. For each run, the equidistant time-steps were chosen according to $\Delta t \leq (4U_{p0})^{-1}$, with $U_{p0} = E_0^2/(4\omega^2)$ being the ponderomotive potential at the peak of the pulse.

From about half of the pulse duration, the time-dependent probability density reaches the grid boundary. To avoid spurious reflections, the grid is surrounded by an absorbing boundary: After each time step, the orbitals are multiplied by a function which is unity on the interior of the grid and then falls to zero like $\cos^{1/4}$ over a width of roughly ten percent of the respective total grid size.

Due to axial symmetry, discretization in cylindrical coordinates leads to a nonuniform rectangular grid in the (ρ, z)-plane. In the z-direction, the dimension of the grid is governed by the classical amplitude $\alpha_{\mathrm{class}} = E_0/\omega^2$ of the quiver motion of an electron in the electric field E_0 at the peak of the pulse. The grid was chosen to include the classical amplitude α_{class} at least 4 times, i.e. $|z| < z_{\mathrm{max}}$ with $z_{\mathrm{max}} > 2\alpha_{\mathrm{class}}$. At the same time, the stepsize Δz cannot be too large, in order to permit propagation of sufficiently large momentum components of the wavefuntion.

The integration of the single-particle equations is performed using the standard finite-difference representation of the kinetic-energy operator. This discretization leads to a pentadiagonal matrix representation of the Kohn-Sham Hamiltonian (2). To obtain the ground state density, diagonalization of the Hamilton matrix without external field is performed using an implementation [17] of the block Lanczos algorithm [18].

The time-dependent orbitals are labelled by the indices characterizing their initial state: the orbital $\varphi_{1s}(\mathbf{r}, t)$ describes an electron which initially occupied a 1s orbital.

Owing to the occurrence of density-dependent terms in the Kohn-Sham Hamiltonian (2), the numerical time propagation has to be carried out using a two-step predictor-corrector approach, with the laser potential evaluated midway between two time steps. Employing the Crank-Nicholson technique in each step, this requires the solution of highly dimensional linear equations *twice* for each time step [19].

The large sets of linear equations arising within this implicit propagation scheme (for a typical grid, on the order of 200000 complex-valued unknowns have to be determined at each time step) can be effectively solved by using a Generalized Minimal Residual (GMRES) method [20]. The required matrix-vector products are well suited to be carried out on a vector-supercomputer.

3   Density Functional Approach to Ionization Yields

A possible way to define ionization probabilities is by means of a geometrical concept. By dividing the space $\mathbb{R}^3$ into two regions, the analyzing volume A (which has to be appropriately chosen), and its complement $B = \mathbb{R}^3 \setminus A$, the norm of the correlated two-particle wavefunction can be written as

$$1 = \int_A d^3r_1 \int_A d^3r_2 \, |\Psi(\mathbf{r_1},\mathbf{r_2},t)|^2 +$$
$$+ 2 \int_A d^3r_1 \int_B d^3r_2 \, |\Psi(\mathbf{r_1},\mathbf{r_2},t)|^2 + \int_B d^3r_1 \int_B d^3r_2 \, |\Psi(\mathbf{r_1},\mathbf{r_2},t)|^2. \quad (4)$$

The second term (AB) in equation (4) is equal to the probability of finding one electron inside the volume A and simultaneously finding a second electron outside the volume A. This is interpreted as single ionization. In analogy, the third term (BB) in equation (4) is given the interpretation of double ionization. The above interpretation rests on the assumption that (i) those components of the time-dependent wave function, which belong to the continuum at the end of the pulse, have propagated away from the nucleus so that their contribution to the norm inside the analyzing volume can be neglected and (ii) that the analyzing volume is large enough so that the bound-state population is well represented by the norm inside A.

Even with the most powerful supercomputers to date, the calculation of the time-dependent, three-dimensional, fully correlated wavefunction remains to be an computationally extremely demanding task [14].

In the framework of time-dependent density functional theory on the other hand, much of the numerical load can be circumvented by the solution of the time-dependent Kohn-Sham equations (1,2). The basic variable within this scheme, however, is the time dependent *density* $n(\mathbf{r}, t)$ rather than the time-dependent wave function. The Kohn-Sham determinant, built from the orbitals satisfying equations (1,2) is solely designed to reproduce the physical density. Besides that, the Kohn-Sham determinant has no rigorous physical meaning. Moreover, due to the nonlinear character of the time-dependent Kohn-Sham equations, the Kohn-Sham determinant lacks the principle of superposition: It is well known from the solution of the time-dependent Hartree-Fock (TDHF) equations, which, in the case of Helium, can be regarded a special case of the the time-dependent Kohn-Sham equations, that stable transition probabilities cannot be calculated from TDHF wave functions. The projection of a TDHF wave function on stationary states gives probabilities oscillating in time even in the absence of an external field.

By virtue of the Runge-Gross theorem, every observable can be expressed as a functional of the density. The key problem is how to construct these functionals in explicit terms. In the special case of two-electron systems, the diagonal of the time-dependent two-particle density matrix is

$$\Gamma(\mathbf{r_1}, \mathbf{r_2}, t) = 2\,|\Psi(\mathbf{r_1}, \mathbf{r_2}, t)|^2\,. \tag{5}$$

The two-particle density matrix in turn is related to the density via the pair-correlation function

$$g(\mathbf{r_1}, \mathbf{r_2}, t) := \frac{\Gamma(\mathbf{r_1}, \mathbf{r_2}, t)}{n(\mathbf{r_1}, t)\,n(\mathbf{r_2}, t)} \tag{6}$$

which satisfies the important sum rule

$$\int d^3 r_2 n(\mathbf{r_2}, t)\,(g(\mathbf{r_1}, \mathbf{r_2}, t) - 1) = -1\,. \tag{7}$$

Physically, the product $n(\mathbf{r_2}, t)\,g(\mathbf{r_1}, \mathbf{r_2}, t)$ is the (conditional) probability to find an electron at $(\mathbf{r_2}, t)$, if we know that there is an electron at $(\mathbf{r_1}, t)$. The crucial point is that the pair-correlation function can, in principle exactly, be expressed as a functional of the density: $g[n](\mathbf{r_1}, \mathbf{r_2}, t)$.

With the pair-correlation function being a functional of the time-dependent density, the expressions for single- and double ionization probabilities of helium read

$$P^0(t) = \frac{1}{2} \int_A d^3 r_1 \int_A d^3 r_2\, n(\mathbf{r_1}, t)\, n(\mathbf{r_2}, t) g[n](\mathbf{r_1}, \mathbf{r_2}, t) \tag{8}$$

$$P^{+1}(t) = \int_A d^3 r\, n(\mathbf{r}, t) - \int_A d^3 r_1 \int_A d^3 r_2\, n(\mathbf{r_1}, t)\, n(\mathbf{r_2}, t) g[n](\mathbf{r_1}, \mathbf{r_2}, t) \tag{9}$$

$$P^{+2}(t) = 1 - \int_A d^3 r\, n(\mathbf{r}, t) + \frac{1}{2} \int_A d^3 r_1 \int_A d^3 r_2\, n(\mathbf{r_1}, t)\, n(\mathbf{r_2}, t) g[n](\mathbf{r_1}, \mathbf{r_2}, t). \tag{10}$$

In practice, the density functional approach towards the calculation of ionization involves two basic approximations:

1. The time-dependent density is calculated using some approximate exchange-correlation potential.
2. The functional dependence of the pair-correlation function g on the density n in equations (8) – (10) is only approximately known.

3.1   Exact Exchange-Only Limit, Mean-Field Approach

In a "Hartree-Fock world", the exact wave functions of many-particle systems would be Slater-determinants. For Helium, the exact pair-correlation function in this exchange-only limit is simply a constant:

$$g_x[n](\mathbf{r_1}, \mathbf{r_2}, t) = \frac{1}{2}\,. \tag{11}$$

Substituting the x-only pair-correlation function into equations (8) – (10), the ionization probabilities of helium are given by

$$P^0(t) = N_{1s}(t)^2 \tag{12}$$

$$P^{+1}(t) = 2N_{1s}(t)(1 - N_{1s}(t)) \tag{13}$$

$$P^{+2}(t) = (1 - N_{1s}(t))^2 \tag{14}$$

where we have defined

$$N_{1s}(t) := \frac{1}{2} \int_A d^3r \, n(\mathbf{r}, t) = \int_A d^3r \, |\phi_{1s}(\mathbf{r}, t)|^2 . \tag{15}$$

The formulas (12) - (14) could have been obtained directly from Eq. (4) by substituting any determinantal wavefunction for the exact wave function Ψ. In particular, approximating the true wave function in a *mean-field* sense by the Kohn-Sham determinant, equations (12) - (14) represent the most straightforward way to extract information about ionization probabilities from a time-dependent Kohn-Sham calculation. However, this notion sacrifices the joint probability character of the two-particle density matrix, and one is left with just an uncorrelated product of single-particle densities.

3.2   Correlation Contributions

The definition of the x-only limit for the pair-correlation function suggests to distinguish between exchange and correlation contributions to the pair-correlation function. Combining the exact exchange expression (11) with the correlation contribution g_c in the density functional approach (8) – (10), exactifies the mean-field expressions (12) - (14) by adding correlation corrections

$$P^0(t) = N_{1s}(t)^2 + \frac{1}{2} \int_A d^3r_1 \int_A d^3r_2 \, n(\mathbf{r_1}, t) \, n(\mathbf{r_2}, t) g_c[n](\mathbf{r_1}, \mathbf{r_2}, t) \tag{16}$$

$$P^{+1}(t) = 2N_{1s}(t)(1 - N_{1s}(t)) - \int_A d^3r_1 \int_A d^3r_2 \, n(\mathbf{r_1}, t) \, n(\mathbf{r_2}, t) g_c[n](\mathbf{r_1}, \mathbf{r_2}, t) \tag{17}$$

$$P^{+2}(t) = (1 - N_{1s}(t))^2 + \frac{1}{2} \int_A d^3r_1 \int_A d^3r_2 \, n(\mathbf{r_1}, t) \, n(\mathbf{r_2}, t) g_c[n](\mathbf{r_1}, \mathbf{r_2}, t) . \tag{18}$$

In the literature, a variety of approximate functionals for the pair correlation function g have been put forward [21–24] which allow for quite accurate calculations of ground-sate properties of many-particle systems [25]. At present, the properties of an explicitly *time-dependent* pair-correlation function are a rather unexplored topic. For the time being, we will thus use existing functionals, developed for stationary systems, in the spirit of an adiabatic approximation. The time-dependence of the pair-correlation function is modelled by evaluating the stationary functional with the density at a certain instant of time t:

$$g[n](\mathbf{r_1}, \mathbf{r_2}, t) \approx g^{\text{stat}}[\rho](\mathbf{r_1}, \mathbf{r_2})\big|_{\rho = n(t)} . \tag{19}$$

Since, for two-electron systems, the exact time-dependent pair-correlation function in the x-only limit is given by equation (11), spatial and temporal nonlocality can be viewed as pure electron correlation effects in these systems.

A pair-correlation function suitable for our calculations can be deduced within the self-interaction correction (SIC) scheme of Perdew and Zunger [26]. For two electrons, only "self-exchange" is present which, in the SIC scheme, is treated exactly. For the correlation contributions, the parametrization of Perdew and Wang [24] was employed.

As a second functional, we tested a coordinate space model for g_c, developed by A.D. Becke [23]:

$$g_c^{\text{Model}}[n](\mathbf{r_1}, \mathbf{r_2}) = \frac{\lambda\left(|\mathbf{r_1} - \mathbf{r_2}| - z_{\uparrow\downarrow}(\mathbf{r_1})\right) n(\mathbf{r_1})}{2(1 + z_{\uparrow\downarrow}(\mathbf{r_1}))n(\mathbf{r_2})} F(\gamma|\mathbf{r_1} - \mathbf{r_2}|), \qquad (20)$$

where γ is determined by the sum rule (7). For the damping factor F, analytic approximations like $F_2(x) = (1 + x)e^{-x}$ or $F_3(x) = e^{-x^2}$ can be chosen. In extension to the original work of Becke, we propose to use a "correlation length" which is inversely proportional to the Hartree potential v_{H}:

$$z_{\uparrow\downarrow} = \frac{4C_{\uparrow\downarrow}}{v_{\text{H}}}, \quad \text{with} \quad C_{\uparrow\downarrow} = 0.62. \qquad (21)$$

3.3   Approximations to the time-dependent Exchange-Correlation Potential in Helium

For the time-dependent exchange-correlation potential occurring in the time-dependent Kohn-Sham equations (1,2), we have employed the following functionals:

The Time-Dependent Hartree-Fock (TDHF) Potential. For two-electron systems, the exchange potential

$$v_x^{\text{TDHF}}[n](\mathbf{r}, t) = -\frac{1}{2} \int d^3r' \frac{n(\mathbf{r'}, t)}{|\mathbf{r} - \mathbf{r'}|} \qquad (22)$$

of the restricted Hartree-Fock equations is identical with the *exact* exchange-only potential in a time-dependent Kohn-Sham treatment of helium.

The Adiabatic Local Density Approximation. The easiest way to go beyond the exchange-only approximation, is to use the so-called "adiabatic" local density approximation (**ALDA**). It employs the functional form of the static LDA with a time-dependent density:

$$v_{\text{xc}}^{\text{ALDA}}[n](\mathbf{r}, t) = -\left(\frac{3}{\pi}n(\mathbf{r}, t)\right)^{1/3} + v_c^{\text{LDA}}(\rho)\big|_{\rho=n(\mathbf{r},t)} \qquad (23)$$

In the actual calculations, the parametrization of Perdew and Wang [27] was used for the correlation part.

The Time-Dependent SIC-Potential. For the Helium atom, the expression for the time-dependent SIC (**TDSIC**) exchange-correlation potential reads:

$$v_{\text{xc}}^{\text{TDSIC}}[n](\mathbf{r}, t) = -\frac{1}{2} \int d^3r' \frac{n(\mathbf{r}', t)}{|\mathbf{r} - \mathbf{r}'|} +$$
$$+ \left(v_c^{\text{LDA}}(\rho, \zeta = 0) - v_c^{\text{LDA}}(\tfrac{1}{2}\rho, \zeta = 1) \right)\big|_{\rho = n(\mathbf{r}, t)} \tag{24}$$

(where $\zeta = (n_\uparrow - n_\downarrow)/n$ is the relative spin polarization). Like in TDHF, the exchange part is treated exactly. In the time-dependent calculations, the correlation potential was evaluated using the parametrization of Perdew and Wang [27].

A Model Potential. To obtain a correlation potential with a nonlocal functional dependence of the density, we start out from the (λ-averaged) expression of the correlation energy which results from the model correlation hole of equation (20) [23]:

$$E_c^{\text{Model}} = -0.8 \int d^3r \, n(\mathbf{r})^2 z_{\uparrow\downarrow}^2 \left[1 - \frac{\ln(1 + z_{\uparrow\downarrow}^2)}{z_{\uparrow\downarrow}} \right]. \tag{25}$$

With the presently proposed expression (21), the resulting correlation potential

$$v_c^{\text{Model}}[n](\mathbf{r}) = -0.4n(\mathbf{r})z_{\uparrow\downarrow}^2 \left[1 - \frac{\ln(1 + z_{\uparrow\downarrow}^2)}{z_{\uparrow\downarrow}} \right] +$$
$$+ 0.8C_{\uparrow\downarrow} \int d^3r' \frac{\frac{z_{\uparrow\downarrow}(1 + 2z_{\uparrow\downarrow})}{1 + z_{\uparrow\downarrow}} - \ln(z_{\uparrow\downarrow})}{v_H(\mathbf{r}')^2 |\mathbf{r} - \mathbf{r}'|} \tag{26}$$

exhibits a truly nonlocal functional dependence on the density. In combination with exact exchange (22), this forms a self-interaction free exchange-correlation potential $v_{\text{xc}}^{\text{Model}}$ for the helium atom. The only extra effort in using this potential consists in an additional evaluation of a Coulomb-type integral in (26). For the ground state of helium, this functional yields an eigenvalue and a correlation energy which are very close to the exact DFT values [28]. In the time-dependent case, $v_{\text{xc}}^{\text{Model}}$ is evaluated for the density at time t.

4   Results: Ionization of Helium in a 780nm Field

We have calculated the ionization probabilities for Helium using a 6-cycle trapezoidal laser pulse (see section 2) of frequency $\omega = 0.0584$ a.u. (1.6 eV) with peak intensities between $2 \times 10^{14} \text{W/cm}^2$ and $1.14 \times 10^{16} \text{W/cm}^2$.

Due to the high ponderomotive energy of the electron, a resolution of up to 11000 time steps per optical cycle is needed. For all runs, the boundaries of the cylindrical analyzing volume A were fixed at $-z_A = z_A = \rho_A = 20$ a.u.[1]

The intensity-dependent probability for single ionization of helium obtained from the mean-field expressions (12) – (14) at the end of the pulse is displayed in figure 1. For all four approximations to the exchange-correlation potential $v_{xc}(\mathbf{r}, t)$, the probability for singly ionized helium reaches its maximum of 0.5 around an intensity of $4 \times 10^{15} \text{W}/\text{cm}^2$. The subsequent decrease in probability is typical of the single-atom response. Then the He$^+$ population is depleted in favor of the doubly charged ion production. In current experiments, this behaviour is not resolved owing to the spatial intensity profile of the laser focus [29], which gives rise to a monotonic increase of the ion yield due to the expansion of the focal volume.

In our calculations, the saturation intensity tends to be shifted towards higher intensities for two reasons: First, the pulse lengths employed are roughly a factor of 10 shorter than the pulses in experiment. A lower saturation intensity occurs when the pulse is longer. Second, the binding energy of the initial finite-difference orbital is elevated by 4% compared to that of the true helium ground state.

Below the saturation intensity, the single-ionization probabilities from figure 1 comply with the eigenvalues of the initial orbitals. Due to the local approximation of the exchange contribution, the LDA ground-state orbital is much more weakly bound than in the remaining approximations. Hence, the ionization probabilities in ALDA (23) are significantly larger than the probabilities obtained in TDHF (22), TDSIC (24) and from the model potential (26).

The intensity-dependent *double* ionization probabilities, calculated from the mean-field equation (14) at the end of the pulse are given in figure 2. Compared to the calculated ionization probability from the ground-state of the He$^+$ ion (SEQ), we observe an enhanced probability for the production of doubly charged ions from the ground state of the neutral He atom. For high intensities, the double ionization curve has to merge with the single-ionization from the ground state of He$^+$, since, in the saturation region of the He$^+$ yield (i.e. after an almost complete depletion of neutral helium in the focus) the He$^+$ ion becomes the dominating source for the production of doubly ionized species. In the literature, this notion has been termed a "sequential" process (SEQ). Strictly speaking, no clear definition of a "sequential" or "nonsequential" process is possible due to the indistinguishability of electrons. Both electrons are active at the same time. Experimentally, on the other hand, one

---

[1] This choice is arbitrary, but the results are not very sensitive to this choice. For a choice of $-z_{A\,\text{min}} = z_{A\,\text{max}} = \rho_A = 10$ a.u. the results differ only slightly, due to the small percentage of the population in the range between 10 a.u. to 20 a.u.

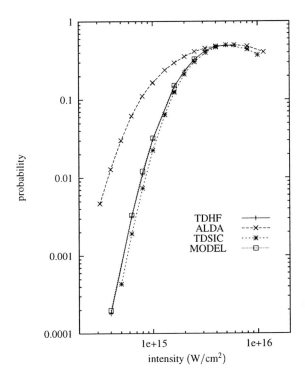

Fig. 1. Calculated He$^+$ ion probabilities from the ground state of the Helium atom irradiated by a 6-cycle (16 fs), 780nm laser pulse, using equation (13) and for different exchange-correlation potentials (see text).

only observes a final degree of ionization after the laser-atom interaction has died off.

However, independent of the choice of the exchange-correlation potential, the calculated probabilities are too high for the intensities beyond the maximum of the single ionization probability. Hence, the calculations do not reproduce the famous "knee" structure which is observed in the double ionization yield of helium in the experiment of Walker et al. [6]. Below the intensity of 4×10^{15}W/cm^2, the double ionization probabilities are again highest in ALDA, followed by quite some interval by the results of the model-potential, which are again close to the TDHF results. At higher intensities, both the TDHF and the MODEL curve merge with the TDSIC curve. Interestingly, around $I = 4 \times 10^{15}$W/cm^2 – at the maximum of the single-ionization probabilities – the ALDA-results cross the results from the other, self-interaction free potentials, resulting in a *lower* ionization probability than obtained with the remaining three potentials. But, despite this somewhat lower probability

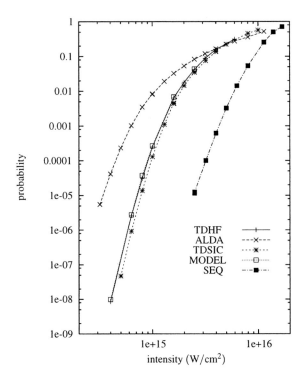

Fig. 2. Calculated double ionization probabilities from the ground state of the Helium atom irradiated by a 6-cycle (16 fs), 780nm laser pulse, using equation (14) and for different exchange-correlation potentials (see text).

in that intensity region, the ALDA results are still far from reproducing a "knee"-structure.

A decisive measure for the ionization dynamics is provided by the ratio of double-ionization yields to single-ionization yields. The He^{2+}/He^+ ratio of the experimental data [6] varies by about a factor of 10 and exhibits a distinctly marked plateau (with an experimental value of about 0.002) which extends up to the onset of "sequential" He^{2+} production. In figure 3 we have compiled the ratios of the double-ionization probabilities to single ionization probabilities calculated for the different exchange-correlation potentials employed. In contrast to experiment, the ratios show a variation of about 4 orders of magnitude, and a complete lack of any plateau structure. Hence, compared to experiment, the calculated double ionization probabilities are too small for low intensities, but too large for higher intensities. The situation is a bit less severe in ALDA. The ratios calculated in ALDA intersect with those obtained in the remaining approximations at the intensity where the single ionization yields have their maximum $(4 \times 10^{15} \text{W/cm}^2)$. Evidently, the functionals employed are not able to reproduce the features present in the strong-field double ionization of helium.

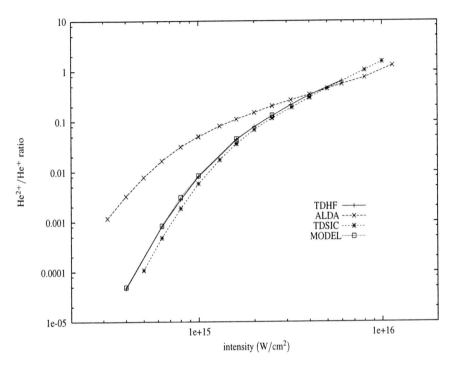

Fig. 3. Comparison of the ratios of double ionization probability to single ionization probability calculated from equations (13) and (14) for helium in a 780nm laser field using the TDHF, ALDA, TDSIC and the Model potential.

So far, our analysis was entirely based on the mean-field expressions (13) – (14) for the ionization probabilities. To go beyond this limit, we use the concept of the pair-correlation function of section 3.

The SIC pair-correlation function [26] as well as the coordinate space model (20) treat the exchange hole of helium exactly, thus conserving the bulk of information already contained in the uncorrelated equations (12) – (14), leading to corrections around the mean-field description. The resulting ionization probabilities are then given by the expressions (17) and (18). To this end, we examine the correlation correction

$$\int_A d^3 r_1 \int_A d^3 r_2 \, n(\mathbf{r_1}, t) \, n(\mathbf{r_2}, t) g_c[n](\mathbf{r_1}, \mathbf{r_2}) \qquad (27)$$

evaluated at the densities obtained from a TDSIC calculation for various peak intensities at the end of the 6 cycle, 780nm pulse. The evaluation of (27) involves a full 5-dimensional numerical quadrature, which is ideally suited to be carried out on a parallel computer.

If the system is only weakly ionized, the density is still concentrated around the nucleus, and, owing to the sum rule (7) a rather small value of the integral (27) is expected. At higher intensities, the highly excited density becomes more diffuse and, due to the finite volume effects, the contribution from (27) increases in magnitude. A countercurrent effect is the decrease of the norm inside A. Hence, as a function of intensity, we expect the correlation contribution (27) to possess an extremum.

From figure 4, all three approximations to the correlation correction agree within an order of magnitude. The two model correlation holes give an almost vanishing correction for low intensities. The correction obtained from the SIC pair-correlation function exhibits a marked change in sign. This is in accordance with our anticipation from the plot of the He^{2+}/He^+ ratio. However, although the resulting corrections point in the right direction, they are still too small to account for a visible correction in the ionization spectra. Moreover, we do not observe the expected extremum.

To provide a rationale, we note:

1. The modelling of a correlation factor, being at the heart of the quantum many-body problem, is a formidable task even for the ground state of many electron systems. Arbitrarily accurate and, at the same time, universal correlation factors are not available to date.

2. Most approximations to the correlation factors explicitly require the evaluation of the sum rule (7) during the calculation. However, such a prescription is barely numerically tractable in the case of ionization studies, since it involves numerical integrations over very large grids.

3. Approximations which circumvent this problem, are mostly based on the homogeneous electron gas and are geared to a good representation of the *spherical average* of the exchange-correlation hole. In particular, this applies to the LDA. Nevertheless, also improved functionals like the SIC [26] and the real-space model of equation (20) only provide an approximation to the angular average of the hole function around some reference point.

4. The application of even the best available *ground-state* functional to such highly excited systems like an atom in a strong laser pulse has its obvious limitations.

5. Strictly speaking, one has to use explicitly time-dependent correlation factors $g_c[n](\mathbf{r}, \mathbf{r}', t)$, which are capable of dealing with highly excited states also in a nonperturbative situation. Moreover, explicitly time dependent correlation factors should account for memory effects, i.e. the correlation factor $g_c(t)$ at time t is determined not only by the density $n(t)$ at the same point in time but depends on the density values $n(t')$ at all previous times $t' \leq t$. Such memory effects are completely neglected in the present adiabatic treatment.

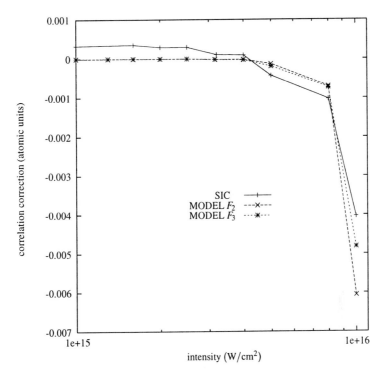

Fig. 4. Correlation corrections (27) to the mean-field equations (12) – (14), evaluated for final densities at various intensities, using three different approximations to the correlation hole (see text). The densities were obtained from a TDSIC calculation.

Another quantity which has to be approximated in a density functional approach is the exchange-correlation potential v_{xc}. The comparison between the (mean-field) ionization probabilities in ALDA with the ionization probabilities calculated from the other functionals reveals that the time-dependent density – and hence the whole dynamics of the system – can be strongly influenced by the choice of the exchange-correlation potential. After all, it is the density which determines the ionization probability.

For a one-dimensional model atom with a softened Coulomb interaction, Lappas and van Leeuwen have solved the full time-dependent Schrödinger equation including an external 780nm laser field [11]. From the two-particle wavefunction, they were able to reproduce the "knee" structure in the double ionization probability of helium. Even if the corresponding exact densities of the one-dimensional model system are inserted in the mean-field equations (13) and (14), a distinct, although shifted "knee" structure is still visible in the intensity dependent ionization probability. This suggests that an improved approximation of the exchange-correlation potential alone will account for the essence of the "knee" feature.

5   Summary and Conclusion

The results of our simulations have confirmed that the time-dependent Hartree-Fock approximation, which neglects electron correlation, fails to reproduce the correct ionization dynamics of helium. In principle, time-dependent density functional theory offers a possibility to include these correlation effects in a numerically tractable way. In this work, we presented the first density functional study of multiple multiphoton-ionization of helium in strong laser fields. Functionals are constructed which allow the calculation of ionization probabilities from the time-dependent density alone. To this end two basic approximations are involved: (i) the time-dependent exchange-correlation potential and (ii) the time-dependent pair correlation function need to be approximated. As a matter of fact, it turned out that the established *stationary* correlation functionals, which were employed in the spirit of an adiabatic approximation, are not sufficient to correct the defects of the TDHF approximation. Most of the correlation error (at optical frequencies) is already contained in the time-dependent densities. Hence, the (time-dependent) exchange-correlation potential needs to be improved in the first place. The fact that even a correlation potential which depends nonlocally on the density, and which reproduces the ground-state properties of helium almost exactly, leads only to a marginal improvement over the Hartree-Fock results in the time-dependent case, shows that the adiabatic approximation can lead to substantial errors at optical frequencies. Hence, explicitly time-dependent correlation functionals with memory are required to correctly describe strong field multiple ionization in the optical region. Work along these lines is in progress.

Many helpful discussions with T. Kreibich, D.G. Lappas, R. van Leeuwen and C.A. Ullrich are greatfully acknowledged. This work was supported by the Deutsche Forschungsgemeinschaft.

References

1. in *Super Intense Laser-Atom Physics IV*, Vol. 13 of *NATO ASI Series*, edited by H.G. Muller and M.V. Fedorov (Kluwer, Dordrecht, 1996).
2. in *Multiphoton Processes 1996*, No. 154 in *Institute of Physics Conference Series*, Institute of Physics, edited by P. Lambropoulos and H. Walther (Institute of Physics Publishing, Bristol, 1997).
3. M. Protopapas, C.H. Keitel, and P.L. Knight, Rep. Prog. Phys. **60**, 389 (1997).
4. A. L'Huillier, L.A. Lompré, G. Mainfray, and C. Manus, J. Physique **44**, 1247 (1983).
5. D.N. Fittinghoff, P.R. Bolton, B. Chang, and K.C. Kulander, Phys. Rev. Lett. **69**, 2642 (1992).

6. B. Walker, B. Sheehy, L.F. DiMauro, P. Agostini, K.J. Schafer, and K.C. Kulander, Phys. Rev. Lett. **73**, 1227 (1994).

7. J.L. Krause, K.J. Schafer, and K.C. Kulander, Phys. Rev. Lett. **68**, 3535 (1992).

8. J.L. Krause, K.J. Schafer, and K.C. Kulander, Phys. Rev. A **45**, 4998 (1992).

9. A. Becker and F.H.M. Faisal, J. Phys. B: At. Mol. Opt. Phys. **29**, L197 (1996).

10. J.B. Watson, A. Sanpera, D.G. Lappas, P.L. Knight, and K. Burnett, Phys. Rev. Lett. **78**, 1884 (1997).

11. D. G. Lappas and R. van Leeuwen, J. Phys. B: At. Mol. Opt. Phys. **31**, L249 (1998).

12. P. Lambropoulos and X. Tang, in *Atoms in Intense Laser Fields*, edited by M. Gavrila (Academic Press, Boston, 1992).

13. J. Parker, K.T. Taylor, C.W. Clark, and S. Blodgett-Ford, J. Phys. B: At. Mol. Opt. Phys. **29**, L33 (1996).

14. K.T. Taylor, J.S. Parker, D. Dundas, and S. Vivito, in *Multiphoton Processes 1996*, No. 154 in *Institute of Physics Conference Series*, Institute of Physics, edited by P. Lambropoulos and H. Walther (Institute of Physics Publishing, Bristol, 1997), p. 56.

15. E. Runge and E.K.U. Gross, Phys. Rev. Lett. **52**, 997 (1984).

16. E.K.U. Gross, J.F. Dobson, and M. Petersilka, in *Density Funcional Theory II*, Vol. 181 of *Topics in Current Chemistry*, edited by R.F. Nalewajski (Springer, Berlin, 1996), p. 81.

17. O.A. Marques, Technical report, CERFACS (unpublished).

18. C. Lanczos, J. Res. Nat. Bur. Stand. **45**, 255 (1950).

19. C.A. Ullrich, Ph.D. thesis, Universität Würzburg, 1995.

20. R. Barrett, M. Berry, T. F. Chan, J. Demmel, J. Donato, J. Dongarra, V. Eijkhout, R. Pozo, C. Romine, and H. Van der Vorst, *Templates for the Solution of Linear Systems: Building Blocks for Iterative Methods, 2nd Edition* (SIAM, Philadelphia, PA, 1994).

21. R. McWeeny, *Methods of Molecular Quantum Mechanics* (Academic Press, London, 1989).

22. R.M. Dreizler and E.K.U. Gross, *Density Functional Theory, An Approach to the Quantum Many-Body Problem* (Springer, Berlin Heidelberg, 1990).

23. A.D. Becke, J. Chem. Phys. **88**, 1053 (1988).

24. J.P. Perdew and Y. Wang, Phys. Rev. B **46**, 12947 (1992).

25. Tobias Grabo and E.K.U. Gross, Chem. Phys. Lett. **240**, 141 (1995).

26. J.P. Perdew and A. Zunger, Phys. Rev. B **23**, 5048 (1981).

27. J.P. Perdew and Y. Wang, Phys. Rev. B **45**, 13244 (1992).

28. M. Petersilka, Ph.D. thesis, Universität Würzburg, 1998.

29. A. L'Huillier, L.A. Lompré, G. Mainfray, and C. Manus, Phys. Rev. A **27**, 2503 (1983).

Chemistry and High-Performance Computing

Bernd Artur Hess
Physikalische und Theoretische Chemie, Universität Bonn
Wegelerstrasse 12, D 53115 Bonn, Germany

Theoretical and Computational Chemistry are relatively recent subfields of chemistry, being developped in the last few decades. Their importance is witnessed by the fact that an ever increasing fraction of papers in top chemistry journals like the Journal ofthe American Chemical Society reports results obtained from computational methods.

This success in supporting experimental investigations of molecular systems and even larger aggregates of atoms --- clusters, solids and surfaces --- is largely based on the availability of large computational resources enabling the solution of the dynamic equations governing the motion of the constituent particles. The solution of these equations enables us to study structural and electronic properties of the systems and materials under investigation. Depending on the questions that were asked, these equations derive from classical mechanics or quantum mechanics. The paradigm for such equations is the multi-particle Schrödinger equation, which is a high-dimensional (non-separable) partial differential equation (in $3N$ variables, if the systems contains N particles) modeling the quantum-mechanical dynamics of the system. As a rule, it must be solved to high accuracy, of the order of ten digits, because the interesting quantities are usually differences between the eigenvalues of the Hamiltonian operator, the key quantity in the Schrödinger equation. The number of particles involved in the solution of the Schrödinger equation is typically the number of electrons in the system, and quantum chemists have managed to diminish the expense for the solution of this equation from a factorial dependence on the number of system variables to a polynomial one.

Thus, the development of algorithms for the solution of the quantum - chemical equations has had a most important impact on the development of the field, and it still has. Nevertheless, it would be impossible to tackle the calculations of realistic chemical systems without the rapid development of computational resources in
the last two decades. Imagine that a limited number of eigenvalues and eigenvectors of (real symmetric, diagonal-dominant) matrices of sizes of the order of one billion (10^9) can nowadays be determined without too much effort. This means that of the order of 10^{18} matrix elements would have to be handled, if all matrix elements were different from zero. Fortunately they are not --- the Hamiltonian matrix is sparse in typical applications, but not in a regular fashion which would enable the use of well-known methods for, say, band matrices. Obviously, it is difficult to store even the remaining number of matrix elements on any storage device. So, the modern approach is to refrain from storage of the

matrix elements and calculate them 'on the fly', when they are needed in the diagonalization process.

The advent of high-performance computing has literally added a new dimension to Theoretical and Computational Chemistry. This refers to the time dimension in the dynamical simulations reported in this volume, or the complication of an additional magnetic field in the Hamiltonian. It is obvious that the large number of time steps required in a realistic dynamical simulation --- be it classical or quantum mechanical --- is a main bottleneck in simulations which require resolution (time steps) of femtoseconds or picoseconds at best, and for which run times of microseconds or even milliseconds would be desirable to obtain solutions for realistic materials. This goal is not yet achieved today, but fortunately there are problems for which meaningful answers can be obtained already in much shorter simulation times.

Many approaches benefit from the methods of vectorization and parallelization, which are inherent in the modern high-performance computing approach: many problems in quantum chemistry are mapped to matrix problems, for which parallel algorithms are well known, and many even admit 'natural' (coarse-grain) parallelization. Although often considered trivial, this parallelism may be decisive for practical applications. For instance, it is often of importance to calculate a large number of points on a potential hypersurface, and the availability of high-performance computers, making use of coarse-grain parallelization, enables us to tackle problems which were otherwise simply not feasible.

Thus, the availability of high-performance computing resources enables us to extend the realm of applications of quantum chemical and classical simulations to new classes of chemical problems. It is now possible to tackle calculations involving large molecules, solve realistic problems by computer simulation of materials and study homogeneous and heterogeneous catalysis at the microscopic scale. Theoretical and Computational Chemistry are thus proceeding to practical applications of ever increasing importance also for industrial development.

Hydrogen Molecule in a Magnetic Field: The Global Ground State of the Parallel Configuration

Thomas Detmer, Peter Schmelcher, and Lorenz S. Cederbaum

Theoretische Chemie, Physikalisch–Chemisches Institut,
Universität Heidelberg, INF 253, D–69120 Heidelberg,
Federal Republic of Germany

Abstract. The electronic structure of the hydrogen molecule in a magnetic field is investigated for parallel internuclear and magnetic field axes. The lowest states with $^1\Sigma_g$, $^3\Sigma_u$ and $^3\Pi_u$ symmetry are studied for a broad range of field strengths $0 \le B \le 100$ a.u. As a major result we determine the transition field strengths for the crossings among these states: The global ground state for $B \lesssim 0.18$ a.u. is the strongly bound $^1\Sigma_g$ state. The crossing of the $^1\Sigma_g$ with the $^3\Sigma_u$ state occurs at $B \approx 0.18$ a.u. while the crossing between the $^3\Sigma_u$ and $^3\Pi_u$ state occurs at $B \approx 12.3$ a.u. Therefore, the *global ground state* of the hydrogen molecule for the parallel configuration is the *unbound* $^3\Sigma_u$ state for $0.18 \lesssim B \lesssim 12.3$ a.u. The ground state for $B \gtrsim 12.3$ a.u. is the strongly bound $^3\Pi_u$ state. This result is of great relevance to the chemistry in the atmospheres of magnetic white dwarfs and neutron stars.

1 Introduction

The electronic structure of the hydrogen molecule in field-free space has been extensively studied, both theoretically and experimentally. Very accurate theoretical potential energy curves (PECs) have been calculated not only within the scheme of the Born-Oppenheimer approximation, but also including nonadiabatic and relativistic corrections. Contrary to these large number of investigations little is known concerning the electronic structure of the hydrogen molecule in the presence of a strong magnetic field. Highly excited states of H_2 were studied for a field strength of 4.7 T in Ref. [1]. For intermediate field strengths two studies of almost qualitative character investigate the PEC of the lowest $^1\Sigma_g$ state [2,3]. A few investigations were performed in the high field limit [4–7], where the magnetic forces dominate over the Coulomb forces and therefore several approximations can be performed. Very recently a communication has been published which reports on Hartree-Fock calculations of the hydrogen molecule in strong magnetic fields [8].

Many interesting phenomena can be observed concerning the electronic structure and behavior of a hydrogen molecule in the presence of a magnetic field. The work of Turbiner [3] indicates a decrease of the internuclear equilibrium distance and a simultaneous increase of the dissociation energy with increasing magnetic field strength for the $^1\Sigma_g$ state. Ortiz and coworkers [6] showed that in sufficiently strong fields (B $\gtrsim 3 \times 10^3$ a.u.) the $^3\Pi_u$ state is the global ground state for a H$_2$ molecule oriented parallel to the magnetic field.

The behavior and structure of molecular systems in the presence of strong external magnetic fields are of great importance for different branches of physics like astrophysics, atomic and molecular physics of Rydberg states and certain areas of solid state physics like excitons and/or quantum nano structures. A detailed knowledge of the electronic structure of the hydrogen molecule is of particular relevance in astrophysics since it might lead to a better understanding of the spectra of white dwarfs and neutron stars. Hereby not only the ground state but also excited states are of interest. Recently a controversial discussion arose concerning the electronic structure of a hydrogen molecule in a superstrong magnetic field (see Refs. [4,6,9,10] and references therein). It was conjectured that in superstrong magnetic fields the $^3\Sigma_u$ state would be the ground state of H$_2$ [4]. This state possesses a very shallow van der Waals minimum in field-free space at R ≈ 8 a.u. Due to the spin-Zeeman shift the $^3\Sigma_u$ state monotonously decreases in energy with increasing magnetic-field strength. Therefore a crossing exists between the $^1\Sigma_g$ and the $^3\Sigma_u$ state at some magnetic-field strength B$_c$. For that reason the authors expected the weakly bound $^3\Sigma_u$ state to be the ground state of the hydrogen molecule in superstrong fields. For such magnetic-field strengths, hydrogen might then be able to form a Bose-Einstein condensate and become superfluid. However it has been proved that the $^3\Pi_u$ state is the true ground state for magnetic-field strengths B $\gtrsim 3 \times 10^3$ a.u. [6]. For magnetic-field strengths smaller than B $= 3 \times 10^3$ a.u. the ground state of the hydrogen molecule was not known.

From the above it is evident that accurate investigations of the electronic structure of the hydrogen molecule are very desirable. In the present investigation we perform a first step to elucidate the electronic properties of the hydrogen molecule in a strong magnetic-field. Particular emphasis is placed on the intermediate regime which is of relevance to the physics of white dwarfs. We investigate the electronic structure of the lowest $^1\Sigma_g$, $^3\Sigma_u$ and $^3\Pi_u$ states. We hereby focus on the case of the parallel internuclear and magnetic-field axes. This configuration is distinct by its higher symmetry compared to the case of an arbitrary angle θ between the internuclear and magnetic-field axis. It has been shown [11] that the diabatic energy curves exhibit extrema at $\theta = 0°$, and it can therefore be expected that the parallel configuration plays an important role.

In the present investigation we focus on the hydrogen molecule with negligible value of the pseudomomentum, i.e., negligible motional Stark term and collective motion perpendicular to the magnetic field. For instance, in the atmosphere of white dwarfs this corresponds to the situation of not too high temperatures. The results of our calculations include accurate adiabatic PECs for the complete range of field strengths $0 \leq$ B ≤ 100 a.u. Moreover we provide a discussion of the global ground state of the parallel configuration and give the transition field strengths for the crossings between the $^1\Sigma_g$ state and the lowest triplet states of the Σ and Π manifold.

2   Theoretical Framework

Our starting point is the fixed nuclei Hamiltonian within the scheme of the Born-Oppenheimer approximation in the presence of a magnetic field [12,13]. The origin of our coordinate system coincides with the midpoint of the internuclear axis of the hydrogen molecule and the protons are located on the z axis. The magnetic field is chosen parallel to the z axis of our coordinate system and the symmetric gauge is adopted for the vector potential. The gyromagnetic factor of the electron is chosen to be equal to two. The Hamiltonian, therefore, takes on the following appearance:

$$H = \sum_{i=1}^{2} \left\{ \frac{1}{2}\mathbf{p}_i^2 + \frac{1}{8}\left(\mathbf{B}\times\mathbf{r}_i\right)^2 + \frac{1}{2}\mathbf{L}_i\mathbf{B} - \frac{1}{|\mathbf{r}_i - \mathbf{R}/2|} - \frac{1}{|\mathbf{r}_i + \mathbf{R}/2|} \right\}$$
$$+ \frac{1}{|\mathbf{r}_1 - \mathbf{r}_2|} + \frac{1}{R} + \mathbf{S}\mathbf{B} \tag{1}$$

The symbols $\mathbf{r}_i$, $\mathbf{p}_i$ and $\mathbf{L}_i$ denote the position vectors, the canonical conjugated momenta and the angular momenta of the two electrons, respectively. $\mathbf{B}$ and $\mathbf{R}$ are the vectors of the magnetic field and internuclear distance, respectively and R denotes the magnitude of $\mathbf{R}$. With $\mathbf{S}$ we denote the vector of the total electronic spin. Throughout the paper we will use atomic units.

The Hamiltonian (1) commutes with the following operators:

- the parity operator P
- the projection L_z of the electronic angular momentum on the internuclear axis
- the square S^2 of the total electronic spin
- the projection S_z of the total electronic spin on the internuclear axis

In the case of field free space we encounter an additional independent symmetry namely the reflections of the electronic coordinates at the xz (Σ_v) plane. The eigenfunctions possess the corresponding eigenvalues ± 1. This symmetry does not hold in the presence of a magnetic field. Therefore, the resulting symmetry groups for the hydrogen molecule are $D_{\infty h}$ in the case of field free space and $C_{\infty h}$ in the presence of a magnetic field [11].

In order to solve the fixed-nuclei electronic Schrödinger equation belonging to the Hamiltonian (1) we expand the electronic eigenfunction in terms of molecular configurations. In a first step the total electronic eigenfunction Ψ_{tot} of the Hamiltonian (1) is written as a product of its spatial part Ψ and its spin part χ, i.e. we have $\Psi_{\text{tot}} = \Psi\chi$. For the spatial part Ψ of the wave function we use the LCAO-MO-ansatz, i.e. we decompose Ψ with respect to molecular orbital configurations ψ of H_2, which respect the corresponding symmetries (see above) and the Pauli principle:

$$\Psi = \sum_{i,j} c_{ij} \left[\psi_{ij} \left(\mathbf{r_1}, \mathbf{r_2} \right) \pm \psi_{ij} \left(\mathbf{r_2}, \mathbf{r_1} \right) \right]$$

$$= \sum_{i,j} c_{ij} \left[\Phi_i \left(\mathbf{r_1} \right) \Phi_j \left(\mathbf{r_2} \right) \pm \Phi_i \left(\mathbf{r_2} \right) \Phi_j \left(\mathbf{r_1} \right) \right] \tag{2}$$

The molecular orbital configurations ψ_{ij} of H_2 are products of the corresponding one-electron H_2^+ molecular orbitals Φ_i and Φ_j. The H_2^+ molecular orbitals are built from atomic orbitals centered at each nucleus. A key ingredient of this procedure is a basis set of nonorthogonal optimized nonspherical Gaussian atomic orbitals which has been established previously [14, 15]. For the case of a H_2−molecule parallel to the magnetic field these basis functions read as follows:

$$\phi_{kl}^m \left(\rho, z, \alpha, \beta, \pm R/2 \right) =$$
$$\rho^{|m|+2k} \left(z \mp R/2 \right)^l \exp \left\{ -\alpha \rho^2 - \beta \left(z \mp R/2 \right)^2 \right\} \exp \left\{ im\phi \right\} \tag{3}$$

$\rho = \sqrt{x^2 + y^2}$ and z denote the electronic coordinates perpendicular and parallel to the magnetic field, respectively. m, k and l are parameters depending on the subspace of the H-atom for which the basis functions have been optimized and α and β are variational parameters. For a more detailed description of the construction of the molecular electronic wave function we refer the reader to Ref. [13].

In order to determine the molecular electronic wave function of H_2 we use the variational principle which means that we minimize the variational integral $\frac{\int \Psi^* H \Psi}{\int \Psi^* \Psi}$ by varying the coefficients c_i. The resulting generalized eigenvalue problem reads as follows:

$$\left(\underline{H} - \epsilon \underline{S} \right) \mathbf{c} = 0 \tag{4}$$

where the Hamiltonian matrix $\underline{H}$ is real and symmetric and the overlap matrix is real, symmetric and positive definite. The vector $\mathbf{c}$ contains the expansion coefficients. The matrix elements of the Hamiltonian matrix and the overlap matrix are certain combinations of matrix elements with respect to the optimized nonspherical Gaussian atomic orbitals (3).

3   Computational Aspects

With the abbreviation $\phi_i \left(\mathbf{r_1} \right) := \phi_{i,kl}^m \left(\rho, z, \alpha, \beta, \pm R/2 \right)$, the following matrix elements have to be evaluated:

$$\int d\mathbf{r_1} \phi_i \left(\mathbf{r_1} \right) \phi_k \left(\mathbf{r_1} \right) \tag{5a}$$

$$\int d\mathbf{r}_1 \phi_i(\mathbf{r}_1) \left\{ \mathbf{p}_1 - \frac{1}{2}(\mathbf{B} \times \mathbf{r}_1) \right\}^2 \phi_k(\mathbf{r}_1) \tag{5b}$$

$$\int d\mathbf{r}_1 \phi_i(\mathbf{r}_1) \frac{1}{|\mathbf{r}_1 \pm R/2|} \phi_k(\mathbf{r}_1) \tag{5c}$$

$$\int d\mathbf{r}_1 d\mathbf{r}_2 \phi_i(\mathbf{r}_1) \phi_j(\mathbf{r}_2) \frac{1}{|\mathbf{r}_1 - \mathbf{r}_2|} \phi_k(\mathbf{r}_1) \phi_l(\mathbf{r}_2) \tag{5d}$$

All these integrals are evaluated in Cartesian coordinates. For details of the transformation of these integrals from cylindrical to Cartesian coordinates we refer the reader to Ref. [13]. For the simple overlap matrix elements in Eq.(5a) a closed-form analytical expression can be given which has been implemented. The matrix elements for the kinetic, paramagnetic, and diamagnetic operator in Eq. (5b) can be reduced to simple overlap matrix elements Eq.(5a).

The evaluation of the electron-nucleus (Eq. 5c) and electron-electron (Eq. 5d) integrals is much more complicated. First, one has to regularize the singularities. This is done by the following transformation at the expense of an additional integration [16]:

$$\frac{1}{f(\mathbf{r})} = \pi^{-1/2} \int_{-\infty}^{+\infty} exp\left[-u^2 f^2(\mathbf{r})\right] du$$

$$= \frac{2}{\pi^{1/2}} \int_0^1 exp\left[-f^2(\mathbf{r}) \frac{v^2}{1-v^2}\right] \frac{dv}{(1-v^2)^{3/2}} \tag{6}$$

In our case, $f(\mathbf{r})$ equals $|\mathbf{r}_1 \pm R/2|$ for the electron-nucleus integral or $|\mathbf{r}_1 - \mathbf{r}_2|$ for the electron-electron integral, respectively.

In the case of the electron-nucleus integral, we first perform the integration over the electronic coordinates. This integration is done by a special kind of exact quadrature, the so-called Rys quadrature which has been proved to be very useful for the fast calculation of two electron integrals, in particular for higher angular momenta of the involved orbitals [17]. We emphasize that this quadrature technique yields the exact result for the integration. Only one integration over the u coordinate remains to be done. This last integration is performed by a numerical algorithm. We herefore used a modified Clenshaw-Curtis quadrature described in Ref. [18]. In order to enhance the performance of our calculations, the algorithm of this quadrature was rewritten in the following way: Normally the routine is intended to perform one integration at each step. The molecular orbitals ϕ_i in Eqs. (5a), (5b), (5c), (5d) are constructed by means of different atomic orbitals ϕ_n in Cartesian coordinates. Within these integrals, only the powers of the polynomials in the electronic x and y coordinates change but the power of the z coordinate remains the same. It is therefore useful to perform all integrals over Cartesian coordinates belonging to a molecular orbital ϕ_i in one step. We hereby avoid the repeated numerical integration of identical integrals. For the special case of sufficiently small powers of the z-coordinate we implemented explicitly the analytical solutions of the integration over the z coordinate, i.e., we implemented 60 different functions for different z-integrations. For a matrix with a dimension of 4000 we are able to evaluate all integrals of the forms Eqs. (5a),(5b), (5c) within six seconds at a 120 MHz node on the IBM/SP2 at the Scientific Supercomputing Center (SSC) in Karlsruhe.

The electron-electron integrals are the most difficult ones to solve. Again we first remove the singularity of the integrand by transformation (6). Subsequently six integrations over the electronic coordinates are performed with the Rys quadrature technique. In total this corresponds to a rather lengthy calculation. Finally the last integration is again done with a modified Clenshaw-Curtis quadrature. Following these steps for the evaluation of the electron-electron integrals leads to serious trouble. Integrals centered at different nuclei turn out to possess very similar values. In fact, many numerically evaluated integrals are identical within the accuracy of our numerical integration. Therefore, if we simply add the results of different integrals, the desirable accuracy is easily lost. To avoid this problem the corresponding integrands have been combined in a suitable manner: Instead of adding the results of different integrals we added the integrands and then numerically performed the integration. We hereby got rid of this kind of accuracy problems. Due to the new kind of integrands the termination condition of the standard Clenshaw-Curtis quadrature proved to be no longer valid. We therefore implemented a new criterion to ensure the convergence of our numerical integration. Similar to the electron-nucleus integrals we used a variety of different functions for the special cases of the second z integration. The size of the program package for the evaluation of the electron-electron and electron-nucleus integrals (programming language C) amounts to 12000 lines.

For the numerical solution of the eigenvalue problem (4) we used the standard NAG library. The typical dimension of the Hamiltonian matrix for each Σ or Π subspace varies between approximately $N = 2000$ and $N = 4500$ depending on the magnetic field strength. For the reason of finite computer precision the dimension of the space spanned by the N different functions may be - from a numerical point of view - less than N. Therefore, for some particular internuclear distances and sets of basis functions, a direct attempt to solve Eq. (4) fails as a conseqence of numerical instabilities. In that cases a different policy was adopted. We used the whole space spanned by the N basis functions, determined its dimension and consecutively solved the eigenvalue problem in an orthonormal basis by means of a singular value decomposition of the overlap matrix (see, e.g., Ref. [19]). Depending on the dimension of the Hamiltonian matrix and the internuclear distance, it takes between 100 and 1000 minutes for a calculation at one fixed internuclear distance at a 120 MHz node of the IBM/SP2 at the SSC. As a result we obtained data for the lowest six states at this internuclear distance for each subspace (singlet/triplet resp. gerade/ungerade parity) within the Σ or Π manifold. That means within one calculation we are able to obtain data for 24 electronic states.

The overall accuracy of our results with respect to the total energy is estimated to be typically of the order of magnitude of 10^{-4} and for some cases of the order of magnitude of 10^{-3}. It should be noted that this estimate is rather conservative; in some ranges of the magnetic field strength and internuclear distance, e.g., close to the separated atom limit, the accuracy is 10^{-5} or even better. The positions, i.e. internuclear distances, of the maxima and the minima in the PECs were determined with an accuracy of 10^{-2} a.u. Herefore about 350 points were calculated on an average for each PEC. It was not necessary to further improve this accuracy since a change in the internuclear distance about 1×10^{-2} a.u. results in a change in the energy which is typically of the order of magnitude of 10^{-4} or smaller.

In order to perform our calculations at the parallel supercomputer IBM/SP2 at the SSC in Karlsruhe we used the Message Passing Interface (MPI). At the starting point of each job we selected a number of different internuclear distances (which normally coincided with the number of nodes) at which the calculations should be performed and a number of parameters independent of the internuclear distance. The number of nodes which had been typically used in our calculations varies between 30 and 50. In the next step we delivered these data with the help of MPI to the different nodes which takes less than one second. Afterwards we independently performed the calculations at one (ore more) fixed internuclear distances at each of the processors which was done in the following manner: First, we simultaneously calculated four Hamiltonian matrices for each of the subspaces (singlet/triplet resp. gerade/ungerade parity) within the manifold. Afterwards, in order to keep the amount of main memory bounded, we stored these matrices at the local disk and freed the main memory space which had been needed for the calculation of the Hamiltonian matrices. Now we consecutively solved the corresponding eigenvalue problems for each of the subspaces. With the procedured described above we gained a maximum advantage from the resources of a parallel computer since the interprocess comunication is reduced to the possible minimum and the data is stored at the local disks of the nodes.

4   The PECs of the $^1\Sigma_g$, $^3\Sigma_u$ and $^3\Pi_u$ State

4.1   The $^1\Sigma_g$ State

Let us begin our investigation by considering the lowest $^1\Sigma_g$ state of the hydrogen molecule, which is the ground state in field-free space. In field-free space the energy curve of the $^1\Sigma_g^+$ state shows only one minimum at the equilibrium distance of 1.4011 a.u. with a total energy of -1.1744757 a.u. In the dissociation limit we have two H atoms in their ground states, i.e., $H_2 \rightarrow H(1s) + H(1s)$. Therefore, in the separated atom limit the total energy approaches -1.0 a.u. which corresponds to the energy of two H atoms in the ground state.

For the total energy at the equilibrium distance in field-free space we obtained a total energy of -1.174195 a.u. which yields a dissociation energy of 0.174195 a.u. This corresponds to a relative accuracy in the total energy of about 2.4×10^{-4} compared to the benchmark result in Ref. [20]. This accuracy in the total energy can be improved if one concentrates on a single calculation at the fixed equilibrium distance of the ground state. By use of optimized parameters for that point we obtained a total energy of 1.174429 a.u. which reduces the relative error in the total energy to 4×10^{-5}

In contrast to the numerous investigations concerning the behavior and structure of the hydrogen molecule in field-free space only a few studies deal with the hydrogen molecule in strong magnetic fields [1–7, 21]. Most of these deal with the hydrogen molecule in superstrong magnetic fields as large 10^{11} or even 10^{12} G (in atomic units this corresponds to $B = 42.54414$ a.u. and $B = 425.4414$ a.u., respectively).

First of all we mention that our computational method is by no means restricted to a special range of the magnetic-field strength. We were therefore able to study the development of the total energy with respect to the field strength ranging from field-free space up to a very strong field.

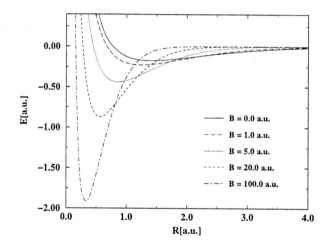

Fig. 1. PECs for $B = 0.0$, 1.0, 5.0, 20.0 and 100.0 $a.u.$ for the lowest $^1\Sigma_g$ state ; the energy is shown with respect to the dissociation limit i.e., $E(R) = E_t(R) - \lim\limits_{R \to \infty} E_t(R)$

Figure 1 shows the energy curves of the $^1\Sigma_g$ state of the hydrogen molecule for different field strengths. In order to display electronic energies for varying magnetic field strengths in the same viewgraph the total energy is substracted by the energy in the dissociation limit, i.e. we show the quantity

$E(R) = E_t(R) - \lim\limits_{R\to\infty} E_t(R)$. For the $^1\Sigma_g$ state the dissociation channel is $H_2 \to H(0^+) + H(0^+)$ which means that the energy in the dissociation limit corresponds to the energy of two hydrogen atoms in the lowest electronic state with positive z-parity. The overall behavior we observe is a monotonously increasing total energy as well as dissociation energy and a monotonously decreasing equilibrium internuclear distance. The decrease in the equilibrium internuclear distance originates from the simoultaneous decrease of the electron cloud perpendicular and parallel to the magnetic field. Figure 1 illustrates the particularly drastical growth in the dissociation energy for magnetic field strengths $B \gtrsim 1$ au. As an example we mention the field strength $B = 100$ a.u. where the dissociation energy amounts to 1.913369 a.u. at an internuclear equilibrium distance of 0.33 a.u. At the same time the potential well becomes more and more pronounced, i.e. its width decreases strongly. Furthermore the asymptotic behavior of the PEC for large values of R changes with the magnetic field strength. With increasing value of B the dissociation limit is reached at much smaller values of the internuclear distance, i.e the onset of the asymptotic behavior can be observed for much smaller internuclear distances. Furthermore transition states appear in the PEC for magnetic field strengths $B \gtrsim 1$ au.

Finally we investigated the question whether vibrational levels exist in the PEC discussed above which is of great importance to the existence of bound states. In the presence of a magnetic field the determination of vibrational levels is a much more complicated task than in field free space. For details describing the determination of vibrational levels within an external magnetic field we refer the reader to Ref. [12, 13, 22]. For the PEC of the $^1\Sigma_g$ state we obtained many, i.e. of the order of magnitude of a few dozens, of vibrational levels for the entire regime $B = 0 - 100$ a.u. of field strengths. This means that the $^1\Sigma_g$ state is a bound state with respect to the internuclear distance R for this wide range of field strengths.

4.2   The $^3\Sigma_u$ State

In field-free space the electronic PEC of the $^3\Sigma_u^+$ state is repulsive, i.e., does not exhibit a well-pronounced potential well. The united atom limit of this state is the ^3S 1s2p helium state, and the dissociation channel is $H_2 \to H(1s) + H(1s)$. For $R \leq 4$ a.u. we obtained an overall relative accuracy of 6×10^{-4} compared to the results in Ref. [23]. For larger values of the internuclear distance this accuracy further increases, and we obtained a relative accuracy of at least 3×10^{-6}. The best conventional CI calculations for this state with a basis set of spherical Gaussian-type orbitals were performed in Ref. [24]. Comparing our results with the data given in Ref. [24] it can be seen that our values of the total energy are lower by 1.0% and 0.4% for $R \leq 2.0$ and $R \geq 2.0$, respectively. The PEC for the $^3\Sigma_u^+$ state for different magnetic-field strengths is presented in Fig. 2.

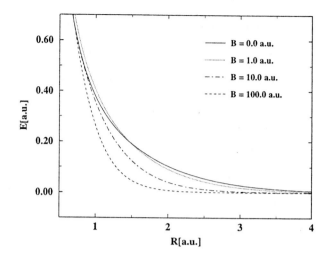

Fig. 2. PECs for $B = 0.0, 1.0, 10.0$ and 100.0 $a.u.$ for the lowest $^3\Sigma_u$ state; the energy is shown with respect to the dissociation limit i.e., $E(R) = E_t(R) - \lim_{R \to \infty} E_t(R)$

Despite the fact that the PEC of the $^3\Sigma_u^+$ state is predominantly repulsive it exhibits a very shallow van der Waals minimum around R $\sim$ 8 a.u.. Due to the dissociation of the $^3\Sigma_u^+$ state into H (1s) + H (1s), we encounter a dipole-dipole interaction of induced dipole moments for large internuclear distances which is proportional to $\frac{-1}{R^6}$. For the van der Waals minimum we obtained a dissociation energy of 1.9×10^{-5} a.u. at an internuclear distance of 7.9 a.u..

In the following we discuss the development of the PEC for the $^3\Sigma_u^+$ state depending on the magnetic-field strength. First, we focus on the global structure which is shown in Fig. 2. In the presence of a magnetic field the separated atom limit is given by $H_2 \to H(0^+) + H(0^+)$, i.e., the molecule dissociates into two hydrogen atoms in their ground states with positive z parity. The corresponding united atom state in the presence of a magnetic field is the $^30^-$ helium state. A closer look at the total energies of the $^1\Sigma_g$ and $^3\Sigma_u$ states reveals that for magnetic-field strengths larger than 0.2 a.u. the $^3\Sigma_u$ state is lower in energy than the $^1\Sigma_g$ state. Therefore, the crossing between these two states happens between the two field strengths 0.1 and 0.2 a.u. A more detailed discussion of the transition between these two states is given in Sect. 5.

The development of the van-der-Waals minimum with increasing magnetic field strength is as follows. In field-free space the van der Waals potential is given by a law proportional $\frac{1}{R^6}$ due to the dipole-dipole interaction of induced dipoles in first order perturbation theory. In the presence of a magnetic field we have to pay attention to another interaction between atoms in s states.

In first-order perturbation theory two atoms in a magnetic field interact like two permanent quadrupoles. Therefore the leading expression in first-order perturbation theory is proportional to $\frac{1}{R^5}$. For dissociation energy E_d remains approximately constant up to field strengths $B \lesssim 0.2$ a.u. while the position of the minimum slightly decreases from 7.89 to 7.73 a.u. With further increasing field strength E_d decreases very rapidly and for $B \gtrsim 2.0$ a.u. no minimum has been found. No vibrational levels were found for any field strength.

4.3   The $^3\Pi_u$ State

The PEC of the $^3\Pi_u$ state exhibits a deep potential well in field free space which is located at an internuclear distance of 1.96 a.u. with a total energy of -0.737521 a.u. This result corresponds to a relative error of 6.3×10^{-5} compared to the very accurate results given in Ref. [25]. The accuracy for larger internuclear distances is of the order of magnitude of 10^{-6}. In the presence of a magnetic field the equilibrium internuclear distance R_{eq} remains approximately constant for $0 \leq B \leq 0.01$ a.u. At the same time the dissociation energy E_d varies only slightly, i.e. increases from 0.115522 to 0.112559 a.u. for $B = 0$ and $B = 0.01$ a.u., respectively. For larger field strengths we observe a strong increase in the dissociation energy and a simultaneous decrease in the corresponding equilibrium internuclear distance. The dissociation energy for $B = 100$ a.u. amounts to 1.811759 a.u. which documents the enormous increase in E_d to be clearly seen also in Fig. 3.

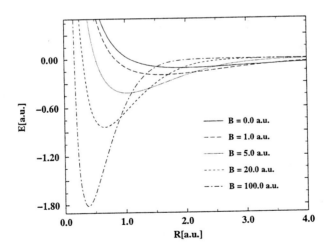

Fig. 3. PECs for $B = 0.0$, 1.0, 5.0, 20.0 and 100.0 $a.u.$ for the lowest $^3\Sigma_u$ state; the energy is shown with respect to the dissociation limit i.e., $E(R) = E_t(R) - \lim\limits_{R \to \infty} E_t(R)$

An interesting phenomenon can be observed around a field strength of $B = 100$ a.u. For that field strength regime the PEC of the $^3\Pi_u$ state exibits a shallow hump with a maximum located at $R_{max} = 3.11$ a.u. and a second minimum at $R_{eq2} = 4.51$ a.u. However, this additional minimum is very shallow and the dissociation energy amounts to only 4.604×10^{-5} a.u. Therefore, both the second minimum and the maximum cannot be seen in Fig. 3.

In the high field regime, i.e. for field strengths larger than 1×10^7 T, the $^3\Pi_u$ state has been investigated by Ortiz and coworkers [6] and Lai [5]. The equilibrium internuclear distance R_{eq} for the $^3\Pi_u$ state at a field strength of 1×10^7 T was determined to be 0.51 a.u. with a total ground state energy of 163.03 eV at the equilibrium internuclear distance R_{eq} [6]. In the present investigation we performed a calculation for the same field strength 1×10^7 T (42.54414 a.u.) and obtained a slightly different equilibrium internuclear distance of 0.50 a.u. with a somewhat lower total energy of 163.54409 eV. The difference in the total energy at $R = 0.50$ and 0.51 a.u. within our calculations amounts to only 3.57×10^{-4} eV. The total energy in the separated atom limit within our calculations was determined to be -4.798851 a.u. Compared with the best available data in the literature (see Ref. [6]) our result shows an improvement of approximately 0.31% in the total energy and of 1.19% in the corresponding dissociation energy.

The number of vibrational levels for the first well, which is about 20 in field free space, remains of the same order of magnitude for arbitrary field strengths $0 \le B \le 100$ a.u. For the second minimum occuring at a field strength of 100 a.u., the lower estimate of the vibrational energy is located inside the well while the upper estimate lies above and we therefore cannot decide whether it accomodates a vibrationally bound state.

5   The Ground State of the Hydrogen Molecule in a Magnetic Field

The ground state of the hydrogen molecule in field free space is the $^1\Sigma_g^+$ singlet state. In the presence of a magnetic field, the diamagnetic term in the Hamiltonian (1) causes an increase in the total energy with increasing field strength. At the same time, due to the interaction of the total electronic spin with the magnetic field, the spin-Zeeman shift occuring for triplet states with ($M_s = -1$) lowers the total energy. As a result the $^1\Sigma_g$ singlet state is not expected to remain the global ground state of the parallel configuration for sufficiently strong fields.

In the following we determine the crossings among the $^1\Sigma_g$ singlet state and the four lowest triplet states of the Σ and Π manifold and discuss the global ground state of the parallel configuration. Detailed data concerning dissociation energies, equilibrium internuclear distances and dissociation channels of these states are provided in Refs. [13, 26].

In Figs. 4a and 4b we show the total energies at the corresponding equilibrium internuclear distances of the $^1\Sigma_g$, $^3\Sigma_g$ and $^3\Pi_u$ state as well as the total energy in the dissociation limit of the $^3\Sigma_u$ state as a function of the field strength. For the $^3\Pi_g$ state, which is a bound state only for field strengths $B \lesssim 0.1$ a.u., we show the total energy at R_{eq} for $B \leq 0.1$ a.u. and the total energy in the dissociation limit for $B \geq 0.2$ a.u. First we focus on crossings occuring in the regime of no too large magnetic field strengths ($B \leq 0.7$ a.u.) which are illustrated in Fig. 4a.

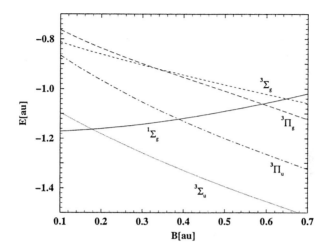

Fig. 4a. Transitions between the lowest $^1\Sigma_g$ and the lowest Σ and Π triplet states showing the total energy of the $^1\Sigma_g$, $^3\Sigma_g$ and $^3\Pi_u$ state (bound) at the corresponding equilibrium internuclear distance, the total energy in the dissociation limit of the $^3\Sigma_u$ state (unbound). For the $^3\Pi_g$ state we show the total energy at R_{eq} for $B \leq 0.1$ *a.u.* and the total energy in the dissociation limit for $B \geq 0.2$ *a.u.*

The transitions between the $^1\Sigma_g$ and the four triplet states occur at field strengths of approximately 0.18 a.u. ($^3\Sigma_u$), 0.39 a.u. ($^3\Pi_u$), 0.59 a.u. ($^3\Pi_g$) and 0.65 a.u. ($^3\Sigma_g$). Furthermore, a crossing at a field strength of 0.33 a.u. exists between the $^3\Pi_g$ and the $^3\Sigma_g$ state. With further increasing magnetic field strength the total energy of the $^1\Sigma_g$ state increases strongly and in particular the total energy of the $^3\Pi_u$ state decreases more rapidly than that of the $^3\Sigma_u$ state. Therefore, a transition occurs between the two latter states which is illustrated in Fig. 4b. As can be seen from Fig. 4b, the transition field strength occurs at $B \approx 12.3$ a.u.

We therefore encounter the following situation for the H_2 molecule oriented parallel to a magnetic field: For $B \lesssim 0.18$ a.u. the ground state is the strongly bound $^1\Sigma_g$ state. For an intermediate range of field strengths, i.e. for $0.18 \lesssim B \lesssim 12.3$ a.u., the ground state is the $^3\Sigma_u$ state. The PEC of the $^3\Sigma_u$ state is, apart from a very shallow van der Waals minimum, a purely

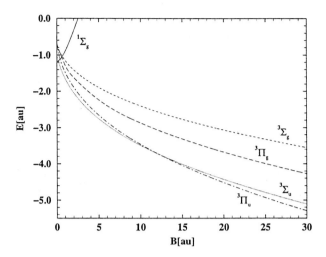

Fig. 4b. Transition between the lowest $^3\Sigma_u$ and $^3\Pi_u$ state showing the total energy of the $^1\Sigma_g$, $^3\Sigma_g$ and $^3\Pi_u$ state (bound) at the corresponding equilibrium internuclear distance, the total energy in the dissociation limit of the $^3\Sigma_u$ state (unbound). For the $^3\Pi_g$ state we show the total energy at R_{eq} for $B \leq 0.1$ $a.u.$ and the total energy in the dissociation limit for $B \geq 0.2$ $a.u.$

repulsive curve [13] and therefore the hydrogen molecule is unstable (unbound) in the corresponding regime of field strengths $0.18 \lesssim B \lesssim 12.3$ a.u. This result is of great importance for astrophysics in order to decide whether hydrogen molecules exist in the vicinity of white dwarfs. For magnetic fields $B \gtrsim 12.3$ a.u. the ground state is again a strongly bound, namely the $^3\Pi_u$ state and molecular hydrogen may exist in the vicinity of astrophysical objects which exhibit such huge magnetic field strengths.

6   Outlook

In the present article we investigated the electronic structure of the low-lying $^1\Sigma_g$, $^3\Sigma_u$ and $^3\Pi_u$ states depending on the magnetic field strength and determined the global ground state of the parallel configuration. The most important result is, that the ground state of molecular hydrogen is unbound for a certain range of field strengths. This is of great importance for the chemistry in the atmosphere of certain degenerate astrophysical objects: it may help to decide whether molecular hydrogen can exist in the vicinity of white dwarfs. At present we are working on the analysis and interpretation of data obtained for several excited electronic states of the hydrogen molecule of the parallel configuration.

A very challenging task is to clarify whether the above results are valid for any angle of the internuclear axis with respect to the magnetic-field axis.

In principle it is possible that a potential well might develop if the internuclear and magnetic-field axes do not coincide. The investigation of such configurations is an important task in the future.

Finally we emphasize that both, the present calculations concerning the case of parallel internuclear and magnetic field axes as well as investigation concerning the electronic structure at arbitrary angles $\neq 0$ are very expensive from a numerical point of view. As an example we mention that our calculations needed a total amount of CPU time of approximately 120000 hours at an 120 MHz node of the IBM/SP2 in Karlsruhe.

References

1. T. S. Monteiro and K. T. Taylor, J. Phys. B **23**, 427 (1990).
2. S. Basile, F. Trombetta, and G. Ferrante, Nuovo Cimento **9**, 457 (1987).
3. A. V. Turbiner, Pis'ma Zh. Eksp. Teor. Fiz. **38**, 510 (1983), [JETP Lett. **38**, 618 (1983)].
4. A. V. Korolev and M. A. Liberman, Phys. Rev. A **45**, 1762 (1992).
5. D. Lai, E. E. Salpeter, and S. L. Shapiro, Phys. Rev. A **45**, 4832 (1992).
6. G. Ortiz, M. D. Jones, and D. M. Ceperley, Phys. Rev. A **52**, R3405 (1995).
7. D. Lai and E. E. Salpeter, Phys. Rev. A **53**, 152 (1996).
8. Y. P. Kravchenko and M. A. Liberman, Phys. Rev. A **56**, R2510 (1997).
9. A. V. Korolev and M. A. Liberman, Phys. Rev. Lett. **74**, 4096 (1995).
10. D. Lai, Phys. Rev. Lett. **74**, 4095 (1995).
11. P. Schmelcher and L. S. Cederbaum, Phys. Rev. A **41**, 4936 (1990).
12. P. Schmelcher, L. S. Cederbaum, and U. Kappes, *in "Conceptual Trends in Quantum Chemistry", edited by Eugene S. Kryachko* (Kluwer Academic Publishers, Dordrecht, 1994).
13. T. Detmer, P. Schmelcher, F. K. Diakonos, and L. S. Cederbaum, Phys. Rev. A **56**, 1825 (1997).
14. P. Schmelcher and L. S. Cederbaum, Phys. Rev. A **37**, 672 (1988).
15. U. Kappes and P. Schmelcher, J. Chem. Phys. **100**, 2878 (1994).
16. K. Singer, Proc. R. Soc. London, Ser. A **402**, 412 (1960).
17. M. Dupuis, J. Rys, and H. F. King, QCPE **338**, HONDO (1976).
18. T. Håvie, CERN **71-26**, 6 (1971).
19. W. H. Press, S. A. Teukolsky, W. T. Vetterling, and B. P. Flannery, *Numerical Recipes in C* (University Press, Cambridge, 1996).
20. L. Wolniewicz, J. Chem. Phys. **103**, 1792 (1995).
21. M. Demeur, P. H. Heenen, and M. Godefroid, Phys. Rev. A **49**, 176 (1994).
22. T. Detmer, P. Schmelcher, and L. S. Cederbaum, J. Phys. B **28**, 2903 (1995).
23. J. W. Liu and S. Hagstrom, J. Phys. B **27**, L729 (1994).
24. F. Borondo, F. Martin, and M. .Yanez, J. Chem. Phys. **86**, 4982 (1986).
25. W. Kolos and J. Rychlewski, J. Mol. Spectros. **66**, 428 (1977).
26. T. Detmer, P. Schmelcher, and L. S. Cederbaum, Phys. Rev. A **57**, 1767 (1998).

Interfaces in immiscible polymer blends: A Monte Carlo simulation approach on the CRAY T3E

A. Werner, F. Schmid, M. Müller, and K. Binder

Institut für Physik
Johannes Gutenberg Universität
D55099 Mainz, Germany

Abstract. Polymeric materials pose a challenge for Monte Carlo simulations because of the widely spread length and time scales involved. Using large scale computer simulations we investigate the interfacial structure in a partially compatible polymer mixture. The problem is studied in the framework of a coarse grained lattice model – the bond fluctuation model on the simple cubic lattice, choosing $N = 32$ and lattice linear dimensions $L \times L \times D$ up to $512 \times 512 \times 64$. We employ a two dimensional geometric decomposition scheme to implement this algorithm on the CRAY T3E. The algorithm scales very well with the number of processors. The structure of polymer coils near interfaces between coexisting phases of symmetrical polymer mixtures (AB) is discussed, as well as the structure of symmetric diblock copolymers of the same chain length N adsorbed at the interface. Distribution functions for monomers at the chain ends, in the center of the copolymer chain, and in the center of the individual blocks are obtained. These are compared to the predictions of the self consistent field theory. For low copolymer concentration ("mushroom regime") the copolymer extends its blocks into the appropriate bulk phases; individual blocks are only mildly perturbed ("dumb-bell"-like). At higher copolymer concentration, the copolymer displaces the homopolymer from the interface ("dry brush").

1 Introduction

Blending chemically different polymers is a cheap and straightforward way of creating new materials, and polymeric "alloys" are therefore industrially and technologically omnipresent[1,2]. Prominent examples are rubber toughened plastics. However, most pairs (A,B) of chemically different homopolymers do not mix: any unfavorable enthalpy per monomer, multiplied by the large number of monomers in a chain ("chain length" N_A, N_B; for simplicity only "symmetric mixtures", $N_A = N_B = N$ are treated here), will exceed the entropy of mixing (which is of order $k_B T$, T being the absolute temperature). Therefore the widely used polymer blends are not homogeneous on mesoscopic scales, but rather fine dispersion of one polymer in another[4]. Correlations between interfacial and bulk properties are present on various length scales. In practice one often uses block copolymers [5,6] as polymeric surfactants that control the size of the minority droplets in the dispersion.

The classical explanation[1,2] for the usefulness of the block copolymer to produce fine enough dispersion is based on the fact that the adsorption of block copolymers at the AB interface lowers the interfacial tension[7,8]. However, this mechanism was recently questioned[4,9,10], and it was argued that the primary effect of the adsorbed block copolymer is a kinetic one, *i.e.*, they prevent the small droplets to a large extent from coagulation. Moreover, the local structure of the polymer interface and macroscopic properties are intimately coupled. *E.g.* the width of the interface between the coexisting phases determined the number of entanglements of the extended macromolecules across the interface. The entanglement density at the interface, in turn, correlates with the mechanical properties (*e.g.* fracture toughness) of the material[3].

Also from the point of view of basic science, interfaces in polymeric systems pose exciting questions. Even for such basic and important quantities like the interfacial width, a comparison between experimental results and theoretical predictions is difficult: While theories – like the self-consistent field theory[11] – calculate an intrinsic interfacial profile, experiments measure profiles which are broadened by capillary waves (cf. Fig.1). The investigation of these smooth, long wavelength variation of the local interfacial position is one of the goals pursued in the Monte Carlo simulations on the CRAY T3E at the HLR Stuttgart.

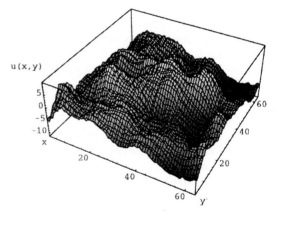

Fig. 1. A typical snapshot of the local interfacial position $u(x,y)$ in a binary homopolymer blend (system size $L = 64$, inverse temperature $\epsilon = 0.03$ and chain length $N = 32$). The local interfacial position was coarse grained on a length scale $B = 8$, which corresponds roughly to the chain's radius of gyration. Long wavelength fluctuation of the local interfacial position are clearly visible.

A quantitative comparison between experiments and simulations with analytical theories has to take due account of capillary waves. While the broadening of capillary waves is a universal interfacial phenomenon, the study of interfacial fluctuations in polymer blends is particularly rewarding. One the one hand, the typical length scale in polymer blends is much larger than in their monoatomic counterparts; a fact which facilitates the application of several experimental techniques[12,13]. One the other hand, there exist sophisticated analytical approaches[11] which, apart from interfacial fluctuations, are believed to provide a detailed description of interfaces in high molecular weight blends. Hence, the effects of interfacial fluctuations in polymer blends can be nicely isolated and a comparison to experiments is possible.

For a more complete understanding one clearly needs detailed knowledge of interfacial properties, both with and without adsorbed copolymers, including the detailed configurations of the chains at the interface. While numerous elegant experiments have provided already interesting information[12,13], computer simulations[14–17] are a tool that can "look" at many static and dynamical properties simultaneously and in great detail. Moreover, parameters which are input in corresponding analytical theories can be estimated from such simulations and, hence, simulations can provide a stringent test of the necessary assumptions and approximations. Unfortunately, simulations of polymer blends and interfaces are considerably more exacting in computational terms than those of small molecular fluids or magnetic systems. The difficulties stem from the widely spread time and length scales caused by the extended structure of the macromolecules.

2   Model and the simulation technique

2.1   The bond fluctuation model and computational requirements

The accurate determination of the macroscopic behavior of polymer composites is not feasible even with state-of-the-art supercomputers. Yet there is ample evidence[6] that by a careful choice of simulation and analysis techniques, coarse grained model of flexible polymers – like the bond fluctuation model[18] – provide useful insights. In the framework of the bond fluctuation model each effective monomer blocks a cube of 8 neighboring sites from further occupancy on a simple cubic lattice in three dimensions. Effective monomers are connected by effective bond vectors of length $2, \sqrt{5}, \sqrt{6}, 3,$ or $\sqrt{10}$ in units of the lattice spacing $a_0 \equiv 1$. Each effective bond represents a group of $n \approx 3 - 5$ subsequent $C - C$-bonds along the backbone of the chain[6,19]. Hence, the chain length $N = 32$ employed in the present simulations corresponds to a degree of polymerization of $100 - 160$ in a real polymer. For a number fraction $\Phi = 1/16$ of occupied sites, properties of a concentrated solution or dense melt are well reproduced[20]. Binary interactions between monomers are catered for by a short ranged square well potential $-\epsilon_{AA} = -\epsilon_{BB} = \epsilon_{AB} = 1/k_BT$ which is extended up to a distance $\sqrt{6}$[21]. This interaction range comprises 54 sites which contribute to the first peak of the monomer-monomer density pair correlation function. The statistical segment length b in the relation for the radius of gyration $R_g = b\sqrt{N/6}$ is $b = 3.05$ ($R_g \approx 7$ for $N = 32$). The Flory-Huggins parameter is $\chi = 2z_{\text{eff}}\epsilon$ where $z_{\text{eff}} \approx 2.65$ denotes the effective coordination number in the bulk[14,22]. The normalized compressibility is $k_B T \kappa a_0^{-3} = 4.1$. The bulk phase diagram of the binary[21,22] and ternary blend[17], the correlation length of concentration fluctuations[23,26], etc. have been determined in previous work.

Interfaces are studied in a $L \times L \times D$ geometry[14,16] where the lattice linear dimensions L parallel to the interface are $L = 512$, and perpendicular $D = 64$. The dimension D perpendicular to the interface is set by the requirement that each "bulk"-like region has to be much larger than the coil extension $R_g(N = 32) \approx 7$. The larger the lateral dimension L the stronger the effect of capillary waves on the apparent interfacial profiles. Choosing boundary conditions periodic in x, y directions and "antiperiodic" in z direction ($i.e.$, an A-chain part leaving the box at $z = -D/2$ reenters at $z = +D/2 + 1$ as a B-chain, etc.), one maintains a system with a single interface around $z = 0$. The system is initialized (for homopolymer interfaces) by choosing chains that have their center of gravity in the lower part of the box ($z < 0$) as B-chains, and in the upper part as A-chains. This corresponds to complete segregation between A and B in the bulk. Very long runs to equilibrate the model system are required in order to allow for a build-up of long range capillary wave fluctuations of the interface. Note that the interfacial position itself can fluctuate and therefore the origin of the z-axis is always fixed at the center of the (instantaneous) interfacial profile for all "measurements".

For simulating interfaces with adsorbed copolymers[16], we initialize the system using an equilibrated homopolymer interface. Then, by choosing 1024 chains (out of 32768) whose center of mass is in the interval $[-\delta, +\delta]$ with $\delta = 3$ or 9, we "transform" them into copolymers. The configurations are equilibrated with $2.5 \cdot 10^5$ attempted local displacements per monomer. For $\epsilon = 0.1$ (where the concentration of the copolymer in the bulk is 0.04%[17]) no effect of varying δ was found. We average over 86 configurations, taken every 10^4 attempted moves per monomer. We estimate that under the chosen conditions about 60% of the interfacial area is covered by copolymers, $i.e.$, we study the dilute case ("mushroom regime"). For higher copolymer concentrations we proceed similarly.

2.2   Implementation on the CRAY T3E

Within the framework of the Monte Carlo simulation the thermodynamical average is approximated by the average over a large number of statistically independent system configurations[6,19]. The Monte Carlo algorithm lets the polymer conformations evolve via random monomer displacements[18,20]. Since each movement displaces the center of mass of a polymeric coil only by a distance of the order $1/N$, one needs large number of attempted movements between two statistically independent configurations. By virtue of the absence of long range interactions, we decided to exploit the geometrically parallelism of the problem[24]. The system size with geometry $L \times L \times D$ is partitioned into $n \times m$ columns of size $(L/n) \times (L/m) \times D$. Each column is placed into

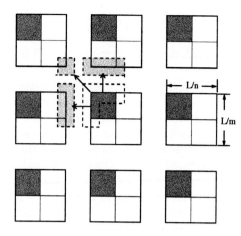

Fig. 2. Two dimensional geometric decomposition of the simulation box. Subcolumns, in which monomers are simultaneously moved are darkly shaded, whereas the boundary regions are denoted by dashed lines.

the local memory of a PE. PEs work locally on their respective column, but require additional information about 3 lattice slices in the x and y direction. The width of this boundary region, which is presented by the shaded area in Fig. 2 is set by the interference range of a trial movement. Note, that the boundary region is *not* small compared to the column size. Each column is split further into 4 subcolumns, in order to prevent the overlap of interference ranges between monomers that are being moved simultaneously. Monomers of the same subcolumn on each PE are moved at the same time in a random order. After each monomer has been attempted to be moved at most once, changes in the boundary region are communicated to the three neighbors, as indicated in Fig. 2. Then each PE generates random numbers for the moves of the next subcolumn and updates its boundary in turn. The general features of geometric decomposition are well known and in the following we briefly comment on aspects pertinent to our polymer model.

- The degrees of dynamical freedom are related to the monomers and hence dilutely distributed with an average density of $\Phi = 1/16$. Only about 15% of the attempted monomer movements are accepted due to various constraints (*e.g.* excluded volume).
- The CPU time required for an attempted monomer displacement may vary substantially from attempt to attempt since the constraints are checked sequentially. Hence proposed moves can be quickly rejected because of the excluded volume or bond length constraints, whereas the time consuming calculation of the interaction energy will be performed only if all other constraints are fulfilled.
- In addition, the monomers can cross the logical PE boundaries in course of their motion. This results in a slight fluctuation of the number of particles on each PE. However, the system exhibits the behavior of a dense polymer melt, hence local density fluctuations are not too large.

The program code is implemented in ANSI-C. The first PE reads the starting configurations in binary format and broadcasts the data to the other PEs along a binary tree. This reduces the startup times of the program significantly. A bit coding technique is used to store all information about a monomer (*e.g.* its type A or B, the location of its neighbors along the chain) into a single integer. This reduces the memory requirements by a factor 4 compared to the vectorizing Y-MP code. Moreover, most of the operations can be performed on the whole integer without referring to specific bits. Only the *changes* in the boundary regions are communicated to the neighbors, this reduces the average message size by a factor 30 in comparison to sending the whole boundary portion of the lattice to the neighbors. Communications are performed via shared memory routines, which are advantageous for rather short messages due to their low startup times. The PEs are only locally synchronized by handshaking between their logical neighbors. It was found that this leads to a substantial reduction of the communication time because slight load imbalances average out. The program scales very well with the number of PEs up to 256 processors[24] and 2 T3E PE achieve more attempted monomer movements than a vectorizing program code on the CRAY Y-MP[21]. This allows us to investigate extremely large system size which comprise more than 1 million monomers. Typically we have employed 64 processors in parallel and the typical CPU time for an individual program run amounts to 1 hour per PE.

3   Results

In the present paper, we focus on the configurational properties of the chains in the interfacial region of a strongly segregated mixture, considering adsorbed diblock copolymers of the same chemical nature AB, symmetric composition ($\bar{f} = 1/2$)[5,6], and the same chain length as the homopolymers.

3.1   Density profiles of monomers and single segments

Due to the capillary wave broadening we have averaged the interfacial profiles only over a small fraction of the lateral system extension. We have chosen a lateral block size $B = 8$ to obtain a width of the composition profile which agrees nicely with the results of the self-consistent field calculations[15]. Fig. 3 presents detailed density profiles in a system with a low concentration of copolymers at the interface. In this limit, the adsorbed copolymers do not overlap. The composition profiles p_A and p_B are hardly influenced by the adsorption of the copolymers and coincide with the corresponding profiles p_A^0 and p_B^0 in a binary blend. Therefore one can model the behavior of the copolymer adsorbed at the interface as a single copolymer at a homopolymer interface. The total density of copolymers p_c, however, is enriched at

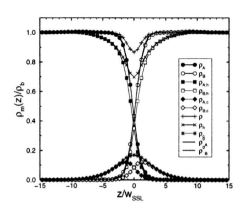

Fig. 3. Monomer density normalized by the bulk density $p_m(y)/p_{bulk}$ plotted vs. z/w_{SSL} where the interfacial width in the strong segregation limit (SSL) is $w_{SSL} = b/(6\chi)^{1/2} \approx 1.71$ at $\epsilon = 0.1$. Shown are the total density p, A and B monomers separately (p_A, p_B), homopolymers irrespective of their nature (p_h), and A and B monomers belonging to a copolymer $(p_{A,c}, p_{B,c})$. The monomer profiles for a pure homopolymer system are denoted by p_A^0, p_B^0.

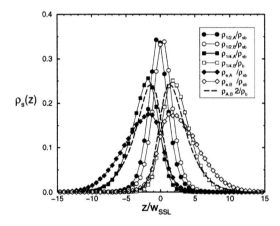

Fig. 4. Profiles of the individual copolymer segments in units of the appropriate bulk densities at low copolymer concentration. The areal density is $n_c \pi R_g^2 / L^2 = 0.65$ where n_c denotes the number of copolymers. See text for a description of the symbols.

the interface and the densities of the individual copolymer blocks $p_{A,c}$ and $p_{B,c}$ exhibit the expected behavior[7,8]: the copolymer adsorbs at the interface where the different blocks can extend in the appropriate bulk phases. It is instructive to investigate the various segment profiles of the copolymers (Fig. 4). While the chain ends of the homopolymers are enriched at the interface (not shown) we find the opposite behavior for the ends of the copolymer $p_{e,A}$ and $p_{e,B}$, which are extended into the bulk. The total monomer density profile p_A and p_B is similar to the spatial distribution of the middle segments of the individual blocks $p_{1/4,A}$ and $p_{1/4,B}$. The monomer in the middle of the copolymer $p_{1/2,A}$ and $p_{1/2,B}$, where the two blocks are joint together, are located closest to the interface. However, the width of the distribution is still larger than the width of the total composition profile.

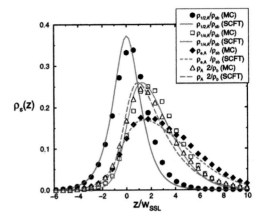

Fig. 5. Comparison between the results of the Monte Carlo simulation (symbols) and the self-consistent field theory. See text for a description of the symbols

Using independently measured values for the statistical segment length b and the Flory-Huggins parameter χ, one can compare the Monte Carlo results to self-consistent field calculations[16] without any adjustable parameter. Having fixed the lateral block size B as to achieve agreement between the total monomer composition profile extracted from the simulations and the self-consistent field calculations, we obtain almost quantitative agreement for other profiles. These include not only the profiles of the individual segments presented in Fig. 5 but also profiles for the orientations of the whole copolymer chains and the individual blocks (not shown). While homopolymers align parallel to the interface[14], the copolymer as a whole orients perpendicular. The conformation of individual blocks, however, hardly differs from the behavior of the homopolymers. Hence, the conformation of the adsorbed diblock at low copolymer concentration resembles a "dumb-bell". A similar behavior was found for pure diblocks in the disordered state[25].

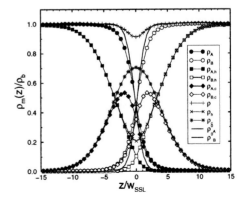

Fig. 6. Monomer densities analogous to Fig.3 for a higher concentration of copolymers at the same temperature. The areal density is $n_c \pi R_g^2 / L^2 = 3.8$. Hence, the copolymers strongly overlap. Symbols as in Fig. 3.

At higher copolymer concentration there are pronounced changes in the behavior: In order to accommodate a greater areal density at the interface the copolymers are expected to displace the homopolymers from the interface, to stretch perpendicular to the interface and, hence, form a "dry brush". The corresponding density profiles are presented in Fig. 6. Indeed, the copolymers constitute the majority at the interface, but the homopolymers are not completely expelled from the center of the interface. The width of the total A monomer density profile increases by 40% upon adsorption. Moreover, a careful analysis of the dependence of the interfacial width on the block size B reveals a significant reduction of the interfacial tension. Both effects would improve the application properties of the polymeric composite.

4 Summary and Discussion

Using an efficient implementation of a coarse grained lattice model for flexible polymers, we have investigated interfacial properties in polymer blends[26–29] and their modification due to the adsorption of copolymers[16,30] via large scale Monte Carlo simulations. The simulations provide convincing evidence for a broadening of interfacial profiles due to capillary waves[26] and yield a detailed picture of the structure of the interface and the molecular conformations of the adsorbed copolymers. Taking account of this capillary broadening in the analysis of the Monte Carlo data, they compare almost quantitatively with self-consistent field calculations[16,27] without adjustable parameters. As far as corresponding experimental results are available, e.g. from the work of Russell and coworkers[13], experiment and simulation also agree qualitatively. On the other hand, by obtaining simultaneous information on both density profiles of various monomers along the chains and on bond orientations we clearly can go beyond experiment, resulting in a very detailed "picture" of homopolymer and block copolymer configurations at the interface. But obviously the present work, restricting attention to a single chain length (chosen also the same for both homopolymers and copolymers) is a first step only. The influence of various asymmetries (different chain length of the blocks, different chain stiffnesses[27], etc.) can be investigated and the chain length behavior[31–33] deserves our attention.

Acknowledgments

We acknowledge support from the Deutsche Forschungsgemeinschaft (DFG) grants No Bi 314/3 and Bi 314/12, and by the Bundesministerium für Bildung, Wissenschaft, Forschung und Technologie (BMBF grant No 03N8008C). Generous access to the CRAY-T3E at the HLR Stuttgart is acknowledged. It is a great pleasure to thank W. Oed and H. Weber for helpful programming advice.

References

1. D.S. Walsh, J.S. Higgins, A. Maconnachie (eds.) *Polymer Blends and Mixtures*, (Martinus Nijhoff, Dordrecht, 1985).
2. L.A. Kleintjens, P.J. Lemstra (eds.) *Integration of Fundamental Polymer Science and Technology* (Elsevier, Amsterdam 1986).
3. S.T. Milner, MRS Bulletin 22 (1997) 38.
4. F.S. Bates, G.H. Fredrickson, Annu. Rev. Phys. Chem. 41 (1990) 525.
5. K. Binder, Adv. Polymer Sci. 112 (1994) 181.
6. L. Leibler, Makromol. Chem., Macromol. Symp. 16 (1988) 1.
7. A.N. Semenov, Macromolecules 25 (1992) 4967.
8. N.C. Beck, S.-K. Tai, R.M. Briber, Polymer 37 (1996) 3509.
9. S.T. Milner, H. Xi, J. Rheol. 40 (1996) 663.
10. R. Schnell, M. Stamm, C. Creton, Macromolecules 31 (1998) 2284.
11. E. Helfand, Y. Tagami, J. Chem. Phys. 56 (1971) 3592; ibid 57 (1972) 1812. J. Noolandi, K.M. Hong, Macromolecules 15 (1982) 482; ibid 17 (1984) 1531. K.R. Shull, Macromolecules 26 (1993) 2346.
12. M. Stamm, D.W. Schubert, Annu. Rev. Mat. Sci 25 (1995) 326. B. Löwenhaupt, G.P. Hellmann, Colloid & Polymer Sci. 268 (1990) 885. K.R. Shull, E.J. Kramer, T. Hadziioannou, W. Tang, Macromolecules 23 (1990) 4780. D.G. Bucknall, J.S. Higgins, J. Penfold, Physica B 180, 181 (1992) 468. K.H. Dai, L.J. Norton, E.J. Kramer, Macromolecules 27 (1994) 1949.
13. P.F. Green, T.P. Russell, Macromolecules 24 (1991) 2931; K.R. Shull, A.M. Mayes, T.P. Russell, Macromolecules 26 (1993) 3929.
14. M. Müller, K. Binder, W. Oed, Faraday Trans. 91 (1995) 2369.
15. F. Schmid, M. Müller, Macromolecules 28 (1995) 1825.
16. A. Werner, F. Schmid, K. Binder, M. Müller, Macromolecules 29 (1996) 8241.
17. M. Müller, M. Schick, J. Chem. Phys. 105 (1996) 8885.
18. I. Carmesin, K. Kremer, Macromolecules 21 (1988) 2819. H.-P. Deutsch, K. Binder, J. Chem. Phys. 94 (1991) 2294;
19. K. Binder (ed.) *Monte Carlo and Molecular Dynamics Simulations in Polymer Science* (Oxford University Press, New York 1995).
20. W. Paul, K. Binder, D.W. Herrmann, K. Kremer, J.Phys. II (France) 1 (1991) 37.
21. H.-P. Deutsch, K. Binder, J.Phys. II (France) 3 (1993) 1049.
22. M. Müller, K. Binder, Macromolecules 28 (1995) 1825.
23. M. Müller, K. Binder, J.Phys. II (France) 6 (1996) 187.
24. M. Müller, EPFL Supercomputer Review 7 (1995) 21.
25. H. Fried, K. Binder, J. Chem. Phys. 94 (1991) 8349; K. Binder, H. Fried, Macromolecules 26 (1993) 2860.
26. A. Werner, F. Schmid, M. Müller, K. Binder, J.Chem.Phys. 107 (1997) 8175.
27. M. Müller, A. Werner, J.Chem.Phys. 107 (1997) 10764.
28. K. Binder, M. Müller, F. Schmid, A. Werner, Physica A 249 (1998) 293.
29. M. Müller, F. Schmid, Annual Reviews in Computational Physics, D. Stauffer (edt). (1998, in press).
30. K. Binder, M. Müller, F. Schmid, A. Werner, Macromolecular Symposia (1998, in press).
31. A. Werner, *Dissertation*, Universität Mainz (1998).
32. F. Schmid, J.Phys.Cond.Matt. (in preparation).
33. A. Werner *et al.* (in preparation).

Computer Simulations of the Dynamics of Amorphous Silica

Jürgen Horbach, Walter Kob, and Kurt Binder

Institute of Physics, Johannes Gutenberg-University,
Staudinger Weg 7, D-55099 Mainz, Germany

Abstract. We present the results of a large scale computer simulation we performed to investigate the dynamical properties of supercooled silica. We show that parallel supercomputers such as the CRAY-T3E are very well suited to solve these type of problems. We find that at low temperatures the transport properties such as the diffusion constants and the viscosity agree well with the experimental data. At high temperatures this simulation predicts that in the transport quantities significant deviations from the Arrhenius law should be observed. Finally we show that such types of simulations can be used to investigate also complex dynamical quantities, such as the dynamical structure factor, and that the wave-vector and frequency range accessible is significantly larger than the one of real experiments.

Introduction

By now it is well established that computer simulations are an excellent method to gain insight into the structure and the dynamics of supercooled liquids and glasses [1–4]. The main advantage of such simulations is that they allow to investigate these systems in full microscopic detail on length and time scales that range from the microscopic to the mesoscopic scale. Hence such simulations permit to study these materials to a level of detail which is not possible in real experiments.

Most of the recent large scale simulations of supercooled liquids and glasses were performed for systems in which the interaction is *short ranged*. The main reason for this is the fact that the simulation of materials in which the interaction is long-ranged, such as, e.g., the Coulombic interaction in ionic glasses, were considered to be too demanding from a computational point of view, i.e. it would not have been possible to simulate such systems over a mesoscopic time range (several nano seconds). However, with the recent advancement of powerful parallel computers this situation has changed and today it is possible to simulate also materials which have long ranged interaction over a mesoscopic time range. In this paper we therefore present some of the results of a large scale simulation in which we investigated the dynamics of SiO_2 in its supercooled state. The reason for choosing silica are twofold: On the one hand silica is a very important material in different fields, such as in physics and chemistry (since silica is the prototype of a so-called network forming glass), geosciences (since many geologically relevant materials contain a large amount of silica) and technology (windows,containers and optical fibers). On the other hand there exist since a few years microscopic potentials that can be used to do *realistic* simulations of silica, such as the potential proposed by van Beest *et al.* [5]. As it will be shown below, the combination of a reliable potential and a large simulational effort allow to investigate the properties of silica to an extent which is not possible in real experiments.

Model and details of the simulations

In molecular dynamics computer simulations one integrates numerically the Newtonian equations of motion of the individual particles [3,6]. Thus these equations depend on the interaction potential between the different particles and the quality and reliability of the results of the simulation depends crucially on the quality of this interaction potential. A few years ago van Beest *et al.* have proposed an interaction potential for SiO_2 [5] which has been shown to be remarkably reliable to predict the static properties of amorphous silica [7]. The functional form of this pair-potential is given by

$$\phi(r_{ij}) = \frac{q_i q_j e^2}{r_{ij}} + A_{ij} e^{-B_{ij} r_{ij}} - \frac{C_{ij}}{r_{ij}^6} \quad . \tag{1}$$

Here r_{ij} is the distance between ions i and j, and the values of the constants q_i, A_{ij}, B_{ij} and C_{ij} can be found in Ref. [5]. The system consists of 8016 ions and the density was fixed to the experimental value of 2.37 g/cm^3. This corresponds to a box size of 48.4Å. The reason for choosing a system size that is significantly larger than the one usually used in this field [2] is that strong finite size effects are present in smaller systems [8] which have of course to be avoided. The temperatures investigated were 6100 K, 5200 K, 4700 K, 4300 K, 4000 K, 3760 K, 3580 K, 3400 K, 3250 K, 3100 K, 3000 K, 2900 K and 2750 K. The temperature of the system was controlled by coupling it to a stochastic heat bath, i.e. by substituting periodically the velocities of the particles with the ones from a Maxwell-Boltzmann distribution with the correct temperature. After the system was equilibrated at the target temperature, we continued the run in the microcanonical ensemble, i.e. the heat bath was switched off.

As can be seen from Eq. (1), the interaction potential contains a long-ranged Coulombic term. As already mentioned in the introduction, it is precisely this part of the interaction which is the most time consuming in the calculation of the forces on the individual particles and therefore great care has to be taken that this part of the computer code is programmed in an

efficient way. To do this we made use of the so-called Ewald summation technique [6], a method whose computational effort scales, in the ideal case, with
$N^{3/2}$, where N is the number of particles. That we were indeed able to reach
this ideal case is demonstrated in Fig. 1, where we show for two different
system sizes the number of seconds needed to make one time step. For the
calculation of the total forces on the particles we used a computational technique called force-parallelization, i.e. every processor unit was given a specific
(fixed) number of particles to take care of. Such an approach is appropriate if
the calculation of the forces is very time consuming, as it is the case with long-
range potentials, and is preferred to the so called geometric parallelization,
which is more appropriate if the interactions are short ranged.

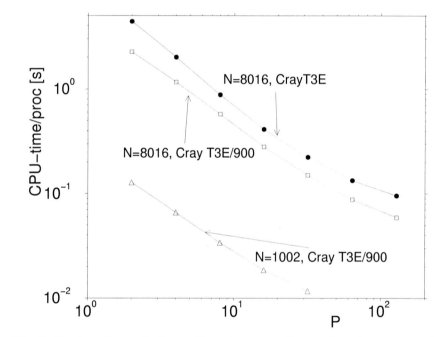

Fig. 1. Number of seconds for one time step versus the number of processor units
for two different system sizes N and two different models of a CRAY-T3E.

In order to speed up the calculations of the forces we expressed them as
a series of *even* polynomials in r_{ij} (with an even polynomial the calculation
of square roots is avoided) and this led to a speedup of about 1.5. At the
end the overall performance of the code was 55 MFLOPS on 64 processors
of a CRAY-T3E. All the parallelization was done by using MPI subroutines
and the rest of the code was written in FORTRAN. In Fig. 1 we show the
number of seconds needed for one time step as a function of P, the number of
processors, in a double logarithmic plot. As can be seen from this figure, the
scaling of this time with P is almost perfect for up to 64 processors and even

quite good for 128 processors. Also included is a curve with the older model of the CRAY-T3E (filled symbols) and we recognize that this model is about 30% slower than the newer model, the CRAY-T3E/900 (open symbols).

As we will see below, the relaxation times of the system increases rapidly with decreasing temperature. Therefore the number of time steps needed to equilibrate the system and to measure the various dynamical quantities increases with decreasing temperature. At the lowest temperature the runs had a length of 12 million time steps and they lasted about 20 days when 64 processors were used, thus giving a total time for such a run of about 1280 days of (single) processor time. In order to improve the statistics of the results we made at each temperature at least two independent runs.

Results

One of the simplest quantities to describe the dynamics of liquids is the so-called mean squared displacement (MSD), i.e. the average distance a tagged particle has moved in a time t. The MSD $\langle r^2(t) \rangle$ is thus given by:

$$\langle r^2(t) \rangle = \frac{1}{N_\alpha} \sum_{i=1}^{N_\alpha} \langle |r_i(t) - r_i(0)|^2 \rangle \quad . \tag{2}$$

Here $r_i(t)$ is the location of particle i at time t, N_α is the number of ions of type $\alpha \in \{\text{Si,O}\}$ and $\langle . \rangle$ is the thermal average. The time dependence of the MSD for the Si-atoms is shown in Fig. 2. From this figure we recognize that for short times the MSD shows a quadratic dependence on t. This dependence comes from the ballistic motion of the particles at very short times, i.e. $r_i(t) \approx r_i(0) + v_i t$. At high temperatures (top curves) this dependence crosses over, at long times, to a diffusive behavior, i.e. $\langle r^2(t) \rangle \propto t$. The similar behavior is seen at low temperatures (bottom curves). However, we see that at these temperatures a third type of time dependence occurs, in that, after the ballistic motion at short times and before the diffusive motion at long times, there is a time regime in which the MSD is essentially flat. The microscopic origin for this third regime is that in this time regime the particles are trapped in the cage formed by their neighbors and thus can move around only in this cage. Only for much larger times this cage starts to break up, the particles can start to move further and thus the MSD shows the linear (diffusive) time dependence.

Using the Einstein relation, it is possible to calculate from the MSD the diffusion constant D, i.e.

$$D = \lim_{t \to \infty} \frac{\langle r^2(t) \rangle}{6t} \quad . \tag{3}$$

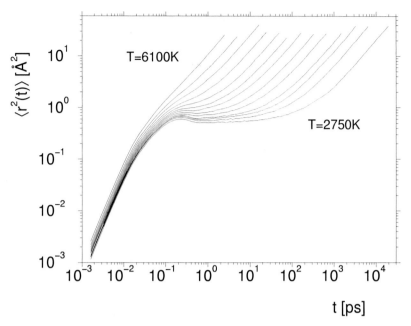

Fig. 2. Time dependence of the mean squared displacement for the Si atoms for different temperatures. Adapted from Ref. [9].

The temperature dependence of the diffusion constant for the Si and O atoms are shown in Fig. 3 where we plot D_α versus the inverse temperature. Experimentally it is found that in amorphous silica the diffusion constant show an Arrhenius dependence [10], i.e. $D \propto \exp(E_A/k_B T)$, where E_A is the activation energy. We find that at low temperatures our data shows indeed such a temperature dependence (solid straight lines) and that the activation energies (slopes) are in very good agreement with the experimental values of Mikkelsen and Brébec [11,12] (given in the figure). Such an excellent agreement between simulation data and experimental data have, to the best of our knowledge, not been obtained so far for this system and only the combination of a good potential and very good computer hardware and codes have made it possible to obtain this agreement.

From Fig. 3 we recognize that for higher temperatures there is a clear deviation from the Arrhenius behavior observed at low temperatures. Such a deviation is well known for simple supercooled liquids [2] but has never been experimentally observed in real silica. It has to be noted, however, that the observed deviations occur only at temperatures above 3000 K, temperatures at which it is extremely difficult to measure a diffusion constant in the laboratory. Nevertheless, the non-Arrhenius dependence found in our simulations might be quite important for geophysical applications since they occur in the temperature range relevant for the interior of the earth.

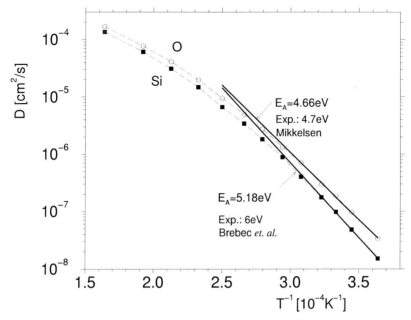

Fig. 3. The diffusion constants for the Si and O atoms versus the inverse temperature. The straight lines are fits with an Arrhenius law. Also included are the values for the activation energies as obtained from our simulation and the experiment (Refs. [11,12]). Adapted from Ref. [9].

A further quantity which is very useful to characterize the dynamics of liquids is the viscosity η, which can also be measured in real experiments. For technical reasons the calculation of η from a simulation is significantly more involved that the one for the diffusion constant [13]. This is the explanation why there hardly exist any simulations in which this quantity has been determined.

In Fig. 4 we show the temperature dependence of η in an Arrhenius plot (open squares). We recognize that in the temperature range investigated this quantity does not show an Arrhenius behavior. Only at the lowest temperatures we have an indication that the temperature dependence crosses over to an Arrhenius dependence. Also included in the figure are experimental values for η [14]. We see that an extrapolation of our data to lower temperatures is compatible with the activation energy as determined from the experiment but that the prefactor is likely to be too small. However, the prefactor of the experimental data is not very reliable [10] and thus it is hard to tell how large the real discrepancy between the simulation and the experimental data really is.

In geosciences it is often customary to use viscosity data in order to compute diffusion constants [15]. For this use is made of the so-called Eyring

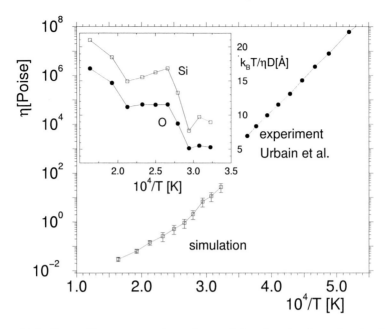

Fig. 4. Main figure: Temperature dependence of the viscosity from the simulation (open squares) and from the experiments of Urbain *et al.* [14] (filled circles). Inset: Test of the validity of the Eyring equation [Eq. (4)]. See text for details.

equation (which is essentially identical to the Stokes-Einstein equation), i.e.

$$D = k_B T / \eta \lambda. \tag{4}$$

Here k_B is Boltzmann's constant and the constant λ (having the dimension of length) is related to the size of an elementary diffusion step and is usually determined from measurements at lower temperatures. Having measured both, D and η, we can now check whether the combination $k_B T / \eta D$ is indeed constant. In the inset of Fig. 4 we plot this ratio and we find that it shows a significant temperature dependence. Thus we conclude that in the temperature range covered by our simulations the Eyring equation is not valid.

One of the most important quantities to describe the dynamics of a liquid *on the microscopic level* is the intermediate scattering function $F(q,t)$, which measures how density fluctuations $\rho(q,t)$ for a given wave-vector q decay as a function of time t [16]. This time autocorrelation function is defined as

$$F(q,t) = \langle \rho(q,t)\rho^*(q,0)\rangle \quad \text{with} \quad \rho(q,t) = \sum_j \exp(i\boldsymbol{q}\cdot\boldsymbol{r}_j(t)) \quad . \tag{5}$$

Its importance stems from the fact that $F(q,t)$, and its time Fourier transform, the dynamical structure factor $S(q,\nu)$, can be measured in neutron and light scattering experiments. Furthermore $F(q,t)$ is also the central quantity for a theoretical description of the dynamics of a liquid [16]. In Fig. 5 we show the wave-vector dependence of $S(q,\nu)$ at a frequency $\nu = 1.64$ THz. This frequency is of particular interest since it corresponds to the one at which the so-called boson peak is observed. The nature of this boson peak is a matter of strong controversy and therefore this dynamical feature has attracted in recent time a lot of attention [18,19]. Also included in the figure are the experimental data from a state of the art neutron time of flight measurement by Wischnewski and Buchenau [17]. In the wave vector range where the experimental data are reliable, i.e. $1.0\text{Å}^{-1} \leq q \leq 3.0\text{Å}^{-1}$, the agreement between the experiment and the simulation is very good. (Note that no fit parameter of any sort enters in the calculation of any of these curves. Therefore we conclude that the present simulation is able to reproduce also very complex quantities such as the dynamical structure factor $S(q,\nu)$ very reliably.

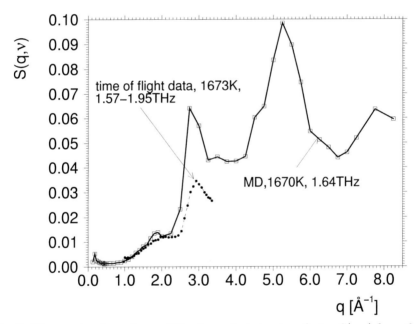

Fig. 5. Wave-vector dependence of the dynamical structure factor $S(q,\nu)$ from the simulation (open symbols). Also included are the time of flight measurements of Wischnewski and Buchenau [17] (filled symbols).

From the figure we also immediately recognize that the q-range accessible to the simulation is significantly larger than the one in which experiments can be performed. For example, in the simulation it is possible to investigate values of q which are so small that the Brillouin line becomes visible (small peak at $q \approx 0.2\text{Å}^{-1}$) a wave-vector range which is hardly accessible in neutron scattering experiments at this frequency. In addition the simulations also have the advantage that the resolution in frequency is significantly higher than the one of the experiment in that in the latter case an average over a frequency range has to be taken in order to get reliable results.

Summary

Using the pair potential proposed by van Beest *et al.* for SiO_2 [5] we have performed a large scale computer simulation of supercooled silica in order to investigate its dynamical properties. At low temperatures the relaxation times of the system become so large that these kind of simulations can be performed only on a large parallel computer, such as the CRAY-T3E. We show that these types of calculations are very well suited to be done on such types of computers. We find that at low temperatures the transport quantities, such as the diffusion constants or the viscosity, compare well with the experimental data. From our simulation we predict that in silica the temperature dependence of the diffusion constants should show a non-Arrhenius behavior at high temperatures.

We demonstrate that such simulations are also able to predict reliably the wave-vector dependence of such complex quantities as the dynamical structure factor $S(q, \nu)$ and that they allow to investigate these quantities in a wave-vector and frequency range which is beyond the present experimental techniques. Therefore such large scale simulations are an effective tool to gain valuable insight into the properties of materials in a way which is presently not feasible in real experiments.

Acknowledgements: We thank U. Buchenau and A. Wischnewski for providing us with their neutron scattering data shown in Fig. 5. We thank the Höchstleistungsrechenzentrum in Stuttgart for a generous grant of computer time on the CRAY-T3E, the Deutsche Forschungsgemeinschaft (DFG, grant No. SFB 262/D1) and the Bundesministerium für Bildung, Forschung, Wissenschaft und Technologie (BMBF, grant No. 03N8008C) for financial support for this research.

References

1. C. A. Angell, J. H. R. Clarke and L. V. Woodcock, Adv. Chem. Phys. **48**, 397 (1981).
2. W. Kob, p.1 in Vol. III *Annual Reviews of Computational Physics*, Ed. D. Stauffer, (World Scientific, Singapore, 1995).
3. K. Binder and W. Kob, to appear in *Analysis of Composition and Structure of Glass, and Glass Ceramics* Eds.: H. Bach and D. Krause (Springer, Berlin, 1998).

4. W. Kob and K. Binder, to appear in *Analysis of Composition and Structure of Glass, and Glass Ceramics* Eds.: H. Bach and D. Krause (Springer, Berlin, 1998).

5. B. W. van Beest, G. J. Kramer, and R. A. van Santen, Phys. Rev. Lett. **64** 1955 (1990).

6. D. Frenkel and B. Smit: *Understanding Molecular Simulation - From Algorithms to Applications* (Academic Press, San Diego, 1996)

7. K. Vollmayr, W. Kob and K. Binder, Phys. Rev. B **54**, 15808 (1996).

8. J. Horbach, W. Kob, K. Binder and C.A. Angell, Phys. Rev. E. **54**, R5897 (1996).

9. J. Horbach, W. Kob and K. Binder, Phil. Mag. B **77**, 297 (1998).

10. O. V. Mazurin, M. V. Streltsina, T. P. Shvaikoskaya: *Handbook of Glass Data* (Elsevier, Amsterdam, 1983) Part A.

11. J. C. Mikkelsen, Appl. Phys. Lett. **45**, 1187 (1984).

12. G. Brébec, R. Seguin, C. Sella, J. Bevenot, J. C. Martin, Acta Metall. **28**, 327 (1980).

13. J. Horbach, Ph.D Thesis (Mainz University, 1998).

14. G. Urbain, Y. Bottinga, and P. Richet, Geochim. et Cosmochim. Acta **46**, 1061 (1982).

15. B. T. Poe, P.F. McMillan, D.C. Rubie, S. Chakraborty, J. Yarger, J. Diefenbacher, Science **276**, 1245 (1997).

16. J.-P. Hansen, I. R. McDonald: *Theory of Simple Liquids* (Academic, London, 1986)

17. A. Wischnewski and U. Buchenau (unpublished).

18. See, e.g., P. Benassi, M. Krisch, C. Masciovecchio, V. Mazzacurati, G. Monaco, G. Ruocco, F. Sette, and R. Verbeni, Phys. Rev. Lett. **77**, 3835 (1996); M. Foret, E. Courtens, R. Vacher, and J.-B. Suck, Phys. Rev. Lett. **77**, 3831 (1996); see also papers in "Proceedings of 6th International Workshop on Disordered Systems, Andalo, March 3rd-6th, 1997", Phil. Mag. B **77** (1998).

19. J. Horbach, W. Kob and K. Binder, J. Non-Crystal. Solids (in press).

Computational Fluid Dynamics

S. Wagner

Institut für Aero- und Gasdynamik, Universität Stuttgart
70550 Stuttgart

CFD applications require the highest percentage of computational time on NEC SX-4 as well as on CRAY T3E within HLRS. Because of the space available only 10 project reviews could be accepted for publication in the proceedings, six of which were presented orally and four in a poster session.

The progress of several projects could not be provided for publication in the proceedings since they were already published in journals. Among these were computations of complex turbulent flows including flows in a Rushton turbine or parallel computation of unsteady separated flows using unstructured, locally refined grids. Large-eddy simulations of turbulent flows around blunt bodies were conducted as well as parallel Direct Numerical Simulations (DNS) with local grid refinement. The investigations included 3-D simulations of turbulent lifting flows in a crystal melt (Czochralski Plant).

The solution of flow problems that are presented in the following CFD section require high performance computers, careful implementation of highly efficient algorithms and sophisticated numerical solution methods. External and internal complex flow problems are treated. The internal flow problems of the first paper include the calculation of the breakdown of a slender vortex in a pipe flow and of the flow in a piston engine during the intake and compression stroke. In addition, large-eddy simulations of turbulent flow through pipe bends and of turbulent jet flows are presented. A single processor performance of 800 MFlops was achieved. Up to one million grid points were necessary to simulate for instance the fuel-air mixing in pistons of Diesel engines. The CPU time amounts to 120 hours. Investigations of this kind have a major impact on the emission values and the breathing capacity of the engine and thus on the maximum available power.

Three contributions regard Direct Numerical Simulation (DNS) i.e. the numerical solution of the three-dimensional unsteady Navier-Stokes equations for turbulent flows without using any turbulence models. In the paper of DNS of point-source induced transition in an airfoil boundary-layer flow the downstream development of a harmonic point-source disturbance in an adverse pressure-gradient boundary-layer was investigated up to late stages of breakdown of the laminar flow around the airfoil. Using the NEC SX-4 (or CRAY T3E) and 15(38) Mega grid points a computing performance of 8(2.6) GFlops was achieved using 11(94) processors with a parallelization scaling factor of 0.82(0.94). Using these high performance computers with fine grid resolution and algorithms of 6th order in space and 4th order in time it could be shown for the first time that the breakdown is not of the fundamental (K-type). Rather, a form of multiple oblique breakdown is observed.

The second contribution of DNS deals with simulations of turbulent boundary-layers using a CRAY T3E-900 of HLRS in Stuttgart and a FUJITSU VPP 700 of Leibniz Computing Center Munich. For the first time a DNS with a locally refined grid near the wall was used for spatially developing flows. This approach led to considerable savings of computation time compared to a complete fine grid.

The goal of a further paper is the development of a parallel software platform to solve partial differential equation problems. State-of-the-art numerical methods are used for the efficient and comfortable solution of partial different equations. Hereby emphasis is put on distributed unstructured grids, adaptive grid refinement, derefinement, coarsening, robust parallel multigrid methods, various finite element (FE) and finite volume (FV) discretizations, dynamic load balancing, mapping and grid partitioning. The layered, hierarchical software (UG package) can be used on a wide range of platforms with a minimal effort for parallelization.

An additional paper presents an efficient algorithm for solving the unsteady incompressible Navier-Stokes equations using multilevel preconditioners or full multigrid to solve the system of linear equations. As a result, the parallel full multigrid algorithm has nearly the same convergence properties as the sequential one.

The next paper presents the parallelization of a multiblock finite-volume CFD code using a static computational and communicational load balancing algorithm. Measurements on an IBM RS/6000 SP system using up to 128 processors show very good performance for various applications and compare very well to a performance model.

An interesting application is the unsteady flow simulation in an axial flow turbine using a parallel implicit Navier-Stokes solver. Tip clearance and blade row interactions as well as typical passage vortices are simulated and show many interesting features of secondary flows. These new findings can help to develop methods for designing more efficient blades.

Navier-Stokes (NS) calculations of the flow around a helicopter fuselage aim at the evaluation and improvement of state-at-the-art NS solvers for the prediction of helicopter fuselage drags. It is shown that the effect of the computational grid on the numerical results is significant and makes the applicability of the code for relatively coarse grids questionable !

In a further project the fluid flow and the separation behaviour between conical rotating discs in a disc stack centrifuge are studied numerically using CFD. The simulations are in good agreement with experimental data.

In a final paper high performance computing of turbulent flow in complex pipe geometries is treated using DNS. The origin of secondary flow motions with two recirculation cells due to curvature effects and the appearance of pressure distribution in a cross section are shown in an impressive manner.

Direct Numerical Simulations of Turbulent Boundary Layers on High Performance Computers

Michael Manhart[1]

Technische Universität, München , Germany

Abstract. Direct Numerical Simulations (DNS) of turbulent zero pressure gradient boundary layers have been performed on two high performance computers with different architectures. The one, a Cray T3E-900, is a massively parallel computer (HLRS computing center, Stuttgart/Germany). The other, a Fujitsu VPP700, is a Vector-parallel computer (Leibniz Computing Center, Munich/Germany). Both computers are well suited for large-scale flow computations. For the first time a DNS with a locally refined grid near the wall has been applied for spatially developing flows. This approach leads to considerable savings of computational time compared to a full grid simulation.

1 Introduction

The correct prediction of separated turbulent flows with engineering methods (e.g. Reynolds averaged Navier Stokes, RANS) is still an unresolved problem in fluid mechanics. A further improvement of existing turbulence models can only be achieved by a deeper insight into the spatial and temporal structure of turbulent flows that can be provided by direct numerical simulation (DNS) or large eddy simulation (LES). In a DNS all relevant turbulent length and time scales have to be resolved. Because of limited computational power up to now only low or moderate Reynolds numbers and simple geometries could have been investigated by DNS. In a LES higher Reynolds numbers can be simulated by resolving only the large scales of the turbulent flow and modelling the small scales by a socalled subgrid scale (SGS) model. However, in regions of high turbulence production (wall layers, mixing layers) problems arise by the use of presently available SGS models (Härtel [3] and Domaradzki *et al.* [1]) At the moment it seems, that these problems can only be overcome and solved by DNS. Although computational power has been continuously increasing during the last years a DNS of a moderately complex flow, like a separated turbulent boundary layer, at a moderate Reynolds number requires the use of the fastest available computers and the most efficient algorithms currently available. For high performance computing currently only parallel machines are suited, like the CRAY T3E-900 or the Fujitsu VPP700, that are considered in this paper. A promising way to save computer resources in a DNS is using a locally refined computational grid in critical regions of the flow and a coarse grid in less critical regions of the flow.

The use of locally refined (zonal) grids in LES and DNS is a relatively new approach. Kravchenko *et al.* [4] performed a zonal grid DNS of turbulent plane channel flow using a combined B-spline/spectral method. Sullivan *et al.* [9] used zonal grids to perform a LES of a planetary boundary layer. Like Kravchenko *et al.* [4] they used spectral interpolation at the boundary between coarse and fine grid. Spectral interpolation delivers highly accurate results but has the disadvantage of being restricted to relatively simple geometries with periodic boundaries. A first step to overcome this drawback has been done by Manhart [6] in a zonal grid DNS of turbulent plane channel flow using a finite volume code.

The purpose of the current research is to extend the zonal grid approach to the direct numerical simulation of turbulent boundary layers with pressure gradients and separation. The zonal grid approach has been implemented in MGLET, a well-tested finite volume code for LES and DNS of turbulent flows in complex geometries (Werner and Wengle [10,11] and Manhart and Wengle [7]). It has already been tested for a turbulent plane channel flow which is a simple geometry (Manhart [6]). The problems that have to be solved in order to apply this approach to a separated boundary layer at moderate Reynolds numbers are concerning the treatment of the boundary conditions and the parallelisation of the code for the efficient use of high performance computers.

The organization of the paper is as follows. In the next section the numerical method is described. Then benchmarks on the two platforms are presented. Finally, some results of the current project are discussed.

2   Numerical Methodology

2.1   The code MGLET

MGLET, is based on a finite volume formulation of the Navier-Stokes equations on a staggered Cartesian non-equidistant grid. The spatial discretization is of second order (central) for the convective and diffusive terms. For the time advancement of the momentum equations an explicit second-order time step (leapfrog with time-lagged diffusion term) is used, i.e.:

$$u^{n+1} = u^{n-1} + 2\Delta t \left[C\left(u^n\right) + D\left(u^{n-1}\right) - G\left(p^{n+1}\right) \right] \tag{1}$$

where C, D and G represent the discrete convection, diffusion and gradient operators, respectively.

The pressure at the new time level p^{n+1} is evaluated by solving the Poisson equation

$$Div\left[G\left(p^{n+1}\right) \right] = \frac{1}{2\Delta t} Div\left(u^*\right) \tag{2}$$

where u^* is an intermediate velocity field, calculated by omitting the pressure term in equation 1. By applying the velocity correction

$$u^{n+1} = u^* - 2\Delta tG\left(p^{n+1}\right) \qquad (3)$$

we arrive at the divergence-free velocity field u^{n+1} at the new time level.

The solution of the Poisson equation is done either in a direct way or iteratively. The iterative solver, which has been used for the calculations presented in this paper, is a point-wise velocity-pressure iteration like that described in Hirt et al. [2]. It is used as a single-grid iteration or, alternatively, as a smoother in a multigrid cycle. When using the iterative solver the remaining divergence depends on the computational time spent. We choose the number of iterations on each refinement level so that the maximal divergence is below a tolerance. The tolerance is chosen in a way that using the relation

$$div_{max} = \Delta u_{max}/\Delta x_{min} \cdot l/U_\infty \qquad (4)$$

leads to a maximal velocity error of $\Delta u_{max} \leq 10^{-5}U_\infty$. Δx_{min} is the minimal grid spacing in the interesting region of the flow, and U_∞ and l are characteristic velocity and length scales, respectively.

2.2   Grid refinement strategy

The refinement for the local grids is done by dividing one coarse grid cell into 8 fine grid cells (figure 1). The coarse and the fine grid are arranged in an overlapping way, so that the coarse grid is defined globally (global grid) and the fine grid is defined only locally (zonal grid). Each second cell-face of the local fine grid lies exactly on a coarse grid cell-face.

The overlapping of the grids allows for flexible handling of grid refinement. One can start the simulation on a coarse grid and later, if in some region of the computation the resolution is not sufficient, a locally refined grid can easily be inserted.

2.3   Solution algorithm of zonal grid calculations

In our approach the coarse-grid and the fine-grid solutions are fully coupled. The coupling is achieved by transferring the fine-grid solution in the overlap region to the coarse grid. This so-called restriction is done at certain steps within the solution algorithm. We use averaging over four cell faces for the velocities and averaging over 8 grid cells for the pressure restriction.

The solution on the coarse-grid level in the non-overlapping region serves as a boundary condition for the fine grid. For solving the Poisson equation on both levels, we use the pressure correction on the coarse grid as a new pressure estimate for the fine grid in a multigrid cycle. This prolongation can be done by first-order or by second order interpolation. The second order

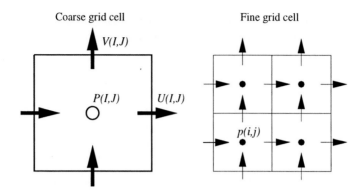

Fig. 1. Refinement strategy of the grid with staggered variable arrangement.

prolongation of the pressure correction delivers a better convergence of the multigrid cycle.

The advancement from time-level n to time-level $n + 1$ is done by the following steps (see also figure 2):

1. explicit time step on both grid-levels independently (convection + diffusion terms)
2. restriction of the fine-grid solution to the coarse grid in the overlapping region
3. solving (or smoothing) the Poisson equation for the pressure on the coarse grid
4. prolongation of the pressure correction from coarse grid to fine grid
5. setting velocity boundary conditions for the fine grid on the intergrid boundary
6. solving (or smoothing) the Poisson equation for the pressure on the fine grid
7. restriction of the fine-grid solution to the coarse grid in the overlapping region

The steps 2 to 6 in the algorithm are part of the multigrid cycle for solving the Poisson equation on both grid levels. Depending on the pressure boundary condition for the zonal grid and on the smoother for the Poisson equation, the multigrid cycle has to be performed iteratively.

2.4   Parallelisation

For running the code on parallel computers we employed the following strategy. The original single-grid code has been extended to a block-structured code in order to manage the multiple grids that arise from the local grid

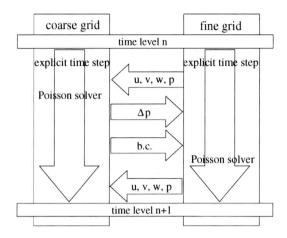

Fig. 2. Coupling algorithm between global coarse grid and local fine grid.

refinement, the multigrid algorithm and parallelisation. In this framework parallelisation is done over the grid blocks using the original subroutines of the single-grid code. A domain decomposition technique has been employed over the second and third direction (in the Fortran arrays) to divide each of the grids into an arbitrary number of subgrids that are treated as independent grid blocks. The communication of neighbouring grids is done using the MPI library. In order to keep the data consistent we employ a red-black algorithm in the velocity-pressure iteration. Therefore the convergence of the iterations is not dependent on the number of PE's used. The boundary conditions for the fine grid on a fine/coarse interface are stored in twodimensional buffer arrays that are updated only at two steps in the algorithm, before step one and in step five. That minimizes the communication between the local fine grid and the underlying global coarse grid that need not necessarily reside on the same processor.

2.5   Configuration and boundary conditions

The geometry of the flow considered, a fully turbulent boundary layer, is sketched in figure 3. The streamwise, spanwise and wall normal directions are denoted by x, y and z, respectively. The Reynolds numbers of the performed simulations based on the inlet momentum thickness are $Re_\theta = 300$ and $Re_\theta = 670$, respectively.

At the inlet plane a time dependent boundary condition is used to trigger turbulent fluctuations in the boundary layer downstream. It is generated by taking fluctuations from a position 10 inlet boundary layer thicknesses δ_0 downstream and superposing them onto a time mean velocity profile corresponding to the Reynolds number considered. As time mean velocity profiles

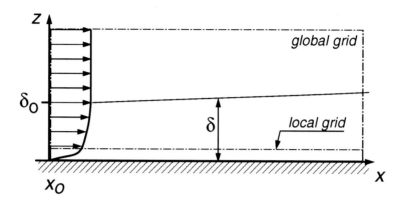

Fig. 3. Geometry of the boundary layer simulations (not to scale).

we have taken the profiles from the simulations of Spalart [8]. The fluctuations are exponentially damped at a wall distance higher than δ_0 in order to prevent the boundary layer from growing in time.

On the exit plane and the top surface the velocity derivatives normal to the boundary are set to zero and for the pressure we use a Dirichlet boundary condition $p = 0$. At the lower boundary (the wall) a noslip boundary condition is applied, and the spanwise direction is assumed to be periodic.

3   Computational efficiency

3.1   Description of the benchmarks

The efficiency of the code on the two high performance computers T3E-900 and VPP700 has been tested by running the code with four different numbers of grid points corresponding to realistic actual problems (see table 1). Considerable efforts have been done to optimize the single-processor performance of MGLET on scalar as well as on vector computers in order to achieve a fair comparison of the two platforms.

The performance of the vector computer VPP700 is extremely sensible on the vector length. We therefore changed the internal organization of the arrays in our Fortran77 code from (z, y, x) to (x, y, z) on the VPP in order to get the largest dimensions on consecutive memory addresses and to achieve a long vector length on the innermost loops. The domain decomposition has then been done over the y- and the z-directions, respectively. On a massively parallel computer, however, it is best to parallelize over the directions with the largest number of grid points, so we left the original organization (z, y, x) and we parallelized over y and x. It turned out that in the current version of the code the communication is partially serial if an even number of subgrids

Table 1. Number of grid points used for performance tests.

Case	#1	#2	#3	#4
N_X	256	576	1156	1156
N_Y	144	320	320	320
N_Z	96	96	96	192
N_{TOT}	$3.5 \cdot 10^6$	$17.7 \cdot 10^6$	$35.4 \cdot 10^6$	$70.8 \cdot 10^6$

is used in the y-direction. This has to be checked and fixed in the future. In our tests we always used the optimal partitioning for the given number of PE's.

3.2   Memory requirements

The code MGLET allows for a flexible handling of blockstructured grids at different refinement levels. The subgrids that arise from domain decomposition are treated as independent grid blocks and a full "administration" is provided for them. This "administration" currently comprises a number of 1D-arrays for each grid. This is a drawback since the required memory on one PE rises with the number of PE's used. The memory requirement of the parallel version for the given numbers of PE's are added in the tables 2-5. One can see that on the vector-parallel computer ($2.0GByte/PE$) there is still room for bigger problems than those considered. On the massively parallel platform ($128MByte/PE$) serious memory problems arise with the current version of our code when really big problems are to be treated.

3.3   Performance

Each of the different cases has been run on the two platforms for 10 time steps. The resulting CPU-times spent in one time step are given in tables 2-5. Some observations can be made: (a) the maximal single processor performance on the VPP700 rises from 540 Mflop/s to 1021 Mflop/s with a vector length of 256 to 1156, (b) the maximal single processor performance on the T3E-900 is at about 70 Mflop/s, (c) a strong degradation of the single processor performance can be found for the smallest problem on both machines with increasing parallelisation. The single processor performance ratio between the VPP700 and the T3E-900 varies between 10 for small problems and 15 for large problems (i.e. long vector lengths). In figure 4 the achieved performance is plotted versus the number of PE's for the different benchmark problems. It seems that on both machines the performance scales with the problem size and number of PE's. If one consideres the actually installed platforms (T3E-900: 512 PE's, VPP700: 32 PE's usable for parallel jobs) one

Table 2. CPU-times per time step, performance and memory requirements for the problem #1 ($256 \cdot 144 \cdot 96$ grid points).

	T3E-900						VPP700			
NPE	16	32	48	64	96	144	2	4	8	16
$sec/\Delta t$	6.2	3.7	2.5	2.4	1.7	1.3	5.9	3.2	1.9	1.2
Mflops	1027	1745	2548	2654	3747	4900	1080	1990	3443	5308
MFlops/PE	64	54	53	42	39	34	540	498	430	331
Mwords/PE	6.0	4.0	2.5	3.5	2.0	2.0	28.0	17.0	11.5	8.5

Table 3. CPU-times per time step, performance and memory requirements for the problem #2 ($576 \cdot 320 \cdot 96$ grid points).

	T3E-900					VPP700			
NPE	40	60	120	160	240	2	4	8	16
$sec/\Delta t$	11.3	7.9	4.5	3.6	3.0	18.2	9.4	4.9	2.8
Mflops	2818	4057	7077	8847	10617	1750	3406	6500	11375
MFlops/PE	70	68	59	55	44	875	852	812	710
Mwords/PE	8.1	6.2	4.4	3.9	3.6	125	65	37	23

Table 4. CPU-times per time step, performance and memory requirements for the problem #3 ($1156 \cdot 320 \cdot 96$ grid points).

	T3E-900			VPP700		
NPE	120	160	240	4	8	16
$sec/\Delta t$	8.5	6.5	4.9	15.6	8.2	4.6
Mflops	7494	9800	13000	4083	7768	13848
MFlops/PE	63	61	54	1021	971	865
Mwords/PE	8.3	7.3	6.7	131	75	47

Table 5. CPU-times per time step, performance and memory requirements for the problem #4 ($1156 \cdot 320 \cdot 192$ grid points).

	T3E-900	VPP700	
NPE	240	8	16
$sec/\Delta t$	9.4	16.2	9.0
Mflops	13626	7913	14155
MFlops/PE	57	989	885
Mwords/PE	10.0	145	90

can conclude that both machines are well suited for the treatment of big problems concerning the performance.

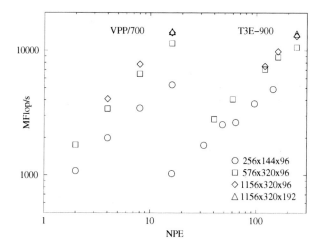

Fig. 4. Mflop-rate achieved by the different test problems on the T3E-900 and VPP700.

4   Results

4.1   Low Reynolds number case

During the course of the project some preparatory test runs have been performed to find an optimal treatment of the turbulent inflow condition for the spatially developing flow of a boundary layer with a pressure gradient and separation. The inflow condition has to fulfill several requirements, (a) turbulent fluctuations have to be triggered during the downstream evolution, (b) a realistic time-averaged velocity profile has to be provided and (c) it should be numerically efficient and parallelizable. A more profound discussion of these aspects can be found in Lund *et al.* [5]. An investigation of various inflow conditions has been done at a low Reynolds number $Re_\theta = 300$ based on the momentum thickness at the inlet. The tests have been done with $N_X = 256$, $N_Y = 144$ and $N_Z = 96$ grid points in streamwise, spanwise and wall normal directions, respectively (see benchmark case #1). The number of time steps required for the statistics is in the range of $N_T = 200000$. In the treatment described above we have varied the streamwise position at which the fluctuations have been extracted from $x/\delta_0 = 5$ ("gdns_04_ad") to $x/\delta_0 = 10$

("gdns_04_ae") and compared it with the approach proposed by Lund *et al.*
[5] ("gdns_04_ag"). The skin friction coefficients c_f of all the three runs shows
a smooth streamwise development after the inlet (figure 5) with the exception
that the run "gdns_04_ae" immediately after the inlet jumps to a somewhat
higher value than that prescribed at the inlet plane. This behaviour is desired
because the prescribed value is somewhat too low as can be seen in figure 6.
In this figure c_f is plotted versus the momentum thickness Reynolds number
Re_θ and compared with some results from the literature. We can see that
the run "gdns_04_ae" shows the most realistic behaviour over the complete
streamwise development that is directly linked to the development of Re_θ
through the streamwise growth of the boundary layer.

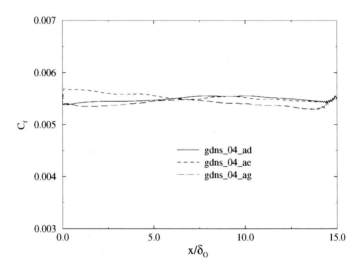

Fig. 5. Skin-friction coefficient c_f versus streamwise distance x/δ_0 .

4.2 Moderate Reynolds number case

In the next section we present a test of the preformance of the zonal grid
approach in a direct numerical simulation of a zero pressure gradient boundary layer. The tests have been performed at the target Reynolds number of
$Re_\theta = 670$ at which the DNS of the separated boundary layer flow shall
be done. The dimensions of the computational box have been chosen to
$(L_X/\delta_0 = 40.96,\ L_Y/\delta_0 = 3.2,\ L_Z/\delta_0 = 3.8)$. We have run three different grid resolutions. Starting from a coarse grid ("apg2") two refined runs
have been done, one with a locally refined grid near the wall up to $z^+ = 60$

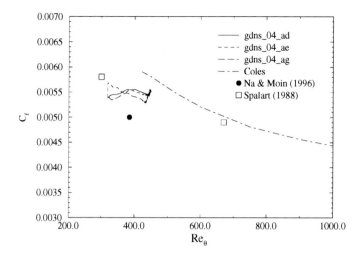

Fig. 6. Skin-friction coefficient c_f versus Reynods number based on momentum thickness Re_θ.

("apg3") and one with a fully refined grid over the total domain ("apg4", see table 6). Again, over $N_T = 200000$ time steps have been done in order to achieve correct second order statistics. The computational requirements are listed in table 7. We see that the local grid refinement leads to considerable savings of computational resources compared with a full grid refinement. The achieved accuracy improvement over the coarse grid run can be seen in the time averaged velocity profile shown in figure 7 in inner coordinates. Up to a wall distance of about $z^+ = 100$ a remarkable accordance of the locally refined and the full fine grid runs can be observed. Only with the higher near-wall resolution the "law of the wall" $U^+ = log(z^+)/0.41 + 5.0$ can be reproduced. The reason for the deviation of the locally refined grid from the fully refined grid above $z^+ = 100$ is not yet be understood. We suspect that there are still problems of the combination of locally refined grids with the inlet boundary condition in conjunction with the parallelisation of the code. Note that in the locally refined grid case parallelisation has been done in y-direction because of performance reasons.

In order to get an impression of what is going on in the near wall region, we plotted isosurfaces of the streamwise fluctuations in figure 8. One clearly can see the elongated "streaky" structures with a streamwise coherence up to 10 boundary layer thicknesses, which corresponds to about 3000 wall units. These structures are considered to play a crucial role in the cycle of turbulence production. Unique in this simulation is the large streamwise extent (35 boundary layer thicknesses) of the computational domain posing no upper

Table 6. Parameter of the grids used for evaluation of the local grid approach.

Case	"apg2"	"apg3"		"apg4"
		local	global	
N_X	512	1024	512	1024
N_Y	80	160	80	160
N_Z	96	32	96	192
N_{TOT}	$3.9 \cdot 10^6$	$3.9 \cdot 10^6$	$5.2 \cdot 10^6$	$31.4 \cdot 10^6$
Δx^+	26	26	13	13
Δy^+	13	13	6.5	6.5
Δz^+_{min}	3.2	3.2	1.6	1.6

Table 7. Computational requirements of the moderate Reynolds number runs on a VPP700, 8 PE's.

Case	"apg2"	"apg3"	"apg4"
memory [words]	$52 \cdot 10^6$	$125 \cdot 10^6$	$396 \cdot 10^6$
$sec/\Delta t$	1.5	2.5	8.0

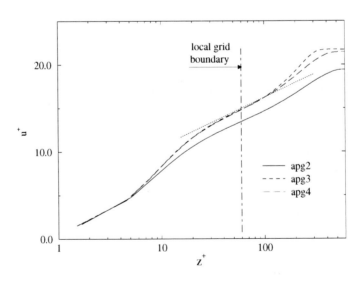

Fig. 7. Time averaged velocity profile in inner coordinates. Dotted line: log law $U^+ = log(z^+)/0.41 + 5.0$.

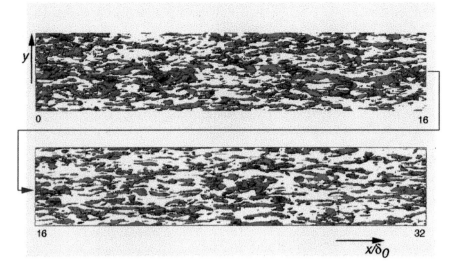

Fig. 8. Top view of isosurfaces of $u'/U_\infty = \pm 0.15$. The streamwise extent is $32 \cdot \delta_0$.

bound for the streamwise evolution of these streaky structures. That allows for detailed studies of their spatio-temporal evolution.

5   Conclusions

In the present paper we have presented some direct numerical simulations performed on the CRAY T3E-900 at the HLRS in Stuttgart and on the VPP700 at the LRZ in Munich. A comparison of the two machines with large scale real-life benchmark problems shows that both machines are well suited for these problems. In order to achieve a maximal performance a considerable amount of numerical work was necessary to adapt the code MGLET on both platforms.

The test runs of a zero pressure gradient boundary layer have shown that an inflow condition has been found that minimizes the transient region necessary to obtain an equilibrium state of the flow. By the use of a locally refined grid in a zero pressure gradient boundary layer the computational requirements of the simulation can be drastically reduced. This can be achieved nearly without loss of accuracy compared to the full refined grid. The large streamwise extent of the simulations, possible on the platforms considered, will provide us with new insights into the dynamics of turbulent wall-bounded flows.

Notes and Comments. We gratefully acknowledge the support of the HLRS in Stuttgart and the LRZ in Munich. The work has been supported by the DFG under grant no. FR 478/15.

References

1. J.A. Domaradzki, W. Liu, C. Härtel, and L. Kleiser. Energy transfer in numerically simulated wall-bounded turbulent flows. *Phys. Fluids A*, 6(4):1583–1599, April 1994.

2. C.W. Hirt, B.D. Nichols, and N.C. Romero. Sola – a numerical solution algorithm for transient fluid flows. In *Los Alamos Sci. Lab.*, Los Alamos, 1975.

3. C.J. Jiménez-Härtel. *Analyse und Modellierung der Feinstruktur im wandnahen Bereich turbulenter Scherströmungen.* PhD thesis, Technische Universität München, DLR-Forschungsbericht 94-22, München, 1994.

4. A.G. Kravchenko, P. Moin, and R. Moser. Zonal embedded grids for numerical simulations of wall-bounded turbulent flows. *J. Comp. Phys.*, 127:412–423, 1996.

5. T.S. Lund, X. Wu, and K.D. Squires. On the generation of turbulent inflow conditions for boundary layer simulations. In *Annual Research Briefs - 1996*, pages 281–295. Center for turbulence research, Stanford, 1996.

6. M. Manhart. Zonal direct numerical simulation of turbulent plane channel flow. In R. Friedrich and P. Bontoux, editors, *Computation and visualization of three-dimensional vortical and turbulent flows. Proceedings of the Fifth CNRS/DFG Workshop on Numerical Flow Simulation*, volume 64 of *Notes on Numerical Fluid Mechanics*. Vieweg Verlag, 1998.

7. M. Manhart and H. Wengle. Large-eddy simulation of turbulent boundary layer flow over a hemisphere. In Voke P.R., L. Kleiser, and J-P. Chollet, editors, *Direct and Large-Eddy Simulation I*, pages 299–310, Dordrecht, March 27-30 1994. ERCOFTAC, Kluwer Academic Publishers.

8. P.R. Spalart. Direct simulation of a turbulent boundary layer up to $R_\theta = 1410$. *J. Fluid Mech.*, 187:61–98, 1988.

9. P.P. Sullivan, J.C. McWilliams, and C.-H. Moeng. A grid nesting method for large-eddy simulation of planetary boundary-layer flows. *Boundary-Layer Meteorology*, 80:167–202, 1996.

10. H. Werner and H. Wengle. Large-eddy simulation of turbulent flow over a square rib in a channel. In H.H. Fernholz and H.E. Fiedler, editors, *Advances in Turbulence*, volume 2, pages 418–423. Springer-Verlag, Berlin, 1989.

11. H. Werner and H. Wengle. Large-eddy simulation of turbulent flow over and around a cube in a plate channel. In F. Durst et al., editors, *Turbulent Shear Flows 8*, Berlin, 1993. Springer.

DNS of Point-Source Induced Transition in an Airfoil Boundary-Layer Flow

C. Stemmer, M. Kloker, U. Rist, and S. Wagner

Institut für Aerodynamik und Gasdynamik, Universität Stuttgart
70550 Stuttgart, Germany

Abstract. Laminar-turbulent transition induced by a harmonic point source disturbance in a flat-plate boundary layer with adverse pressure gradient is investigated by spatial Direct Numerical Simulation (DNS) based on the complete three-dimensional Navier–Stokes equations for incompressible flow. A local disturbance is introduced into the two-dimensional (2-D) base flow at the wall by a harmonic point source. Thus Tollmien–Schlichting waves of a single frequency and a large number of obliqueness angles are stimulated and propagate downstream simultaneously, undergoing amplification by primary and subsequent instabilities, and eventually lead to breakdown of the laminar flow. The development of the wave train in the boundary layer is investigated by the spectral amplitude evolution and the vorticity/shear-layer dynamics. The computational aspects of this LAMTUR project are discussed in detail for runs on the NEC SX-4 and the CRAY T3E supercomputers.

1 Introduction

The investigation of laminar-turbulent transition has engaged many researchers for more than one century. During the last decades, DNS has become an increasingly reliable and powerful tool in transition research to supplement theory and experiment. This could be achieved by increased computer power and using advanced high-order numerics (for a basic review see [1]). To reduce the number of parameters, transition research has focused on so-called controlled transition with the excitation of only a few instability waves in the laminar boundary layer.

A step further towards the understanding of more complex transition mechanisms is the involvement of numerous oblique waves of, at first, a single frequency. The harmonic point source generates by its spatial localization a full spectrum of oblique disturbance waves with well-defined initial phase relations. Moreover, it can be considered as a model for the generation of disturbances by a localized surface roughness and a sound wave.

The present study deals with a 2-D boundary layer present on an airfoil at considerable angle of attack including an extended region of adverse pressure gradient (APG). Studies on a Falkner-Skan boundary layer near separation (β_h=-0.18) by Kloker [2] have shown that, by exciting a 2-D and a pair of 3-D waves of identical frequency (so called K-type scenario), the instability waves periodically cause local separation cells in the boundary layer, precipitating ultimate breakdown of the APG laminar flow.

The DNS results discussed in this paper were also compared with in-flight experiments carried out by four other German univeristary groups (RWTH Aachen, TU Berlin, TH Darmstadt and University Erlangen) using wing gloves for a research motorglider [4]. For any details or results not reported in this paper see [3,4].

2   Governing Equations

The complete Navier-Stokes equations for incompressible, 3-D unsteady flow in the vorticity-velocity formulation are used (see [5,6,2]). The equations are solved in the so-called disturbance formulation. For this purpose, the system is split in a 2-D steady base flow (denoted by the index B) and the 3-D unsteady disturbance flow (denoted by a prime). Thus, all variables $f=f_B+f'$ are nondimensionalized using the reference values $\tilde{L} = 0.065$m, $\tilde{U}_\infty=38.9$m/s; in y-direction, a streching with $\sqrt{Re_L}=384.7$ is performed.

3   Numerical Method

The simulation is based on the *spatial model* with non-periodic inflow-outflow conditions in a rectangular integration domain (Figure 1) which includes a disturbance strip for the disturbance introduction. First, the steady 2-D base

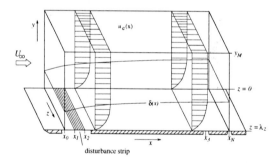

Fig. 1. Integration domain with disturbance strip

flow is calculated using the Navier-Stokes equations with a prescribed streamwise velocity distribution at the upper boundary. Secondly, the disturbances are introduced and the 3-D disturbance flow is calculated.

3.1   Base Flow

One steady transport equation for the spanwise vorticity component has to be solved together with two Poisson-type equations for the velocity components v_B and u_B (for more details see [3]). Fig. 2 summarizes the relevant properties of the calculated base flow.

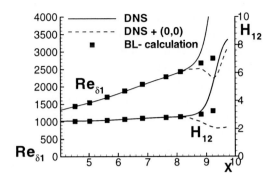

Fig. 2. Integral boundary-layer values Re_{δ_1} (based on displacement thickness) and shape parameter H_{12}; symbols: boundary layer calculation; solid: steady 2-D DNS (base flow); dashed: unsteady 3-D DNS

3.2   Calculation of the Disturbance Flow

For the solution of the unsteady Navier-Stokes equations, the set of three disturbance-vorticity transport equations

$$\frac{\partial \omega_x'}{\partial t} + \frac{\partial}{\partial y}(v'\omega_x' - u'\omega_y' + v_B\omega_x' - u_B\omega_y')$$

$$- \frac{\partial}{\partial z}(u'\omega_z' - w'\omega_x' + u_B\omega_z' + u'\omega_{z_B}) = \tilde{\Delta}\omega_x' \tag{1}$$

$$\frac{\partial \omega_y'}{\partial t} - \frac{\partial}{\partial x}(v'\omega_x' - u'\omega_y' + v_B\omega_x' - u_B\omega_y')$$

$$+ \frac{\partial}{\partial z}(w'\omega_y' - v'\omega_z' - v_B\omega_z' - v'\omega_{z_B}) = \tilde{\Delta}\omega_y' \tag{2}$$

$$\frac{\partial \omega_z'}{\partial t} + \frac{\partial}{\partial x}(u'\omega_z' - w'\omega_x' + u_B\omega_z' + u'\omega_{z_B})$$

$$- \frac{\partial}{\partial y}(w'\omega_y' - v'\omega_z' - v_B\omega_z' - v'\omega_{z_B}) = \tilde{\Delta}\omega_z' \tag{3}$$

have to be solved.

For the disturbance velocities u', v', w' three Poisson-type equations are used:

$$\frac{\partial^2 u'}{\partial x^2} + \frac{\partial^2 u'}{\partial z^2} = -\frac{\partial \omega_y'}{\partial z} - \frac{\partial^2 v'}{\partial x \partial y} \tag{4}$$

$$\tilde{\Delta} v' = \frac{\partial \omega_x'}{\partial z} - \frac{\partial \omega_z'}{\partial x} \tag{5}$$

$$\frac{\partial^2 w'}{\partial x^2} + \frac{\partial^2 w'}{\partial z^2} = \frac{\partial \omega_y'}{\partial x} - \frac{\partial^2 v'}{\partial y \partial z} , \tag{6}$$

where the Laplacian $\tilde{\Delta}$ is defined as

$$\tilde{\Delta} = \frac{1}{Re}\frac{\partial^2}{\partial x^2} + \frac{\partial^2}{\partial y^2} + \frac{1}{Re}\frac{\partial^2}{\partial z^2}. \tag{7}$$

Boundary Conditions. At the *upper boundary* $(y=y_M)$ in the potential flow, the disturbance vorticities vanish. For the disturbance velocity v' exponential decay at the upper boundary is prescribed.

The no-slip condition for u' and w' is satisfied *at the wall* $(y=y_0)$; v' is also zero except for the disturbance strip (Figure 3), where the disturbance function for the harmonic point source is prescribed. The function is designed such that, at any time step of the excitation cycle, no net mass flow is introduced, see Figure 3.

The disturbances are introduced well downstream of the *inflow boundary* of the rectangular integration domain which permits to harmlessly force all disturbance variables to be zero at this boundary.

As for the *outflow boundary* conditions, the implementation of the well-tested method of "artificial relaminarization" [5] is applied, where basically the three disturbance vorticity components are slowly forced to a zero value in a damping domain ($x_3 \le x \le x_4$, $x_4 \le x_N$ in Figure 1).

3.3   Computational Aspects

In streamwise and wall-normal direction, fourth-order finite differences are employed (alternating upwind/downwind/central for the streamwise convective terms), and the periodic spanwise spatial dimension z is discretized using a Fourier spectral ansatz with a number of $(K+1)$ modes. The basic spanwise wavenumber γ for the fundamental Fourier mode $(k=1)$ is related to the spanwise width λ_z of the integration domain through $\gamma=2\pi/\lambda_z$, yielding $\gamma=3.3$ in the considered case. For saving computational effort, the symmetric initial/boundary conditions are exploited by calculating a symmetric flow field with respect to $z=0$. For the time integration, a fourth-order Runge-Kutta scheme is used (see, e.g. [2]).

The spanwise Fourier ansatz principally reduces the 3-D problem in physical space to a set of $(K+1)$ 2-D problems in Fourier space thus enabling a largely parallel computation in Fourier space. However, the modes are coupled by the nonlinear convective terms of the vorticity transport equations

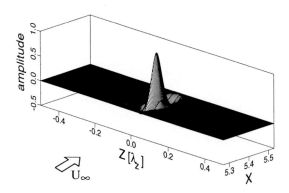

Fig. 3. Normal velocity v' distribution across the disturbance strip over one spanwise wavelength λ_z

and are transformed to physical space ("pseudospectral method" with de-aliasing procedure) for the calculation of the nonlinear vorticity terms, which in turn are parallelized in streamwise direction.

The uniform equidistant grid for the point source problem contains about $2354 \times 161 \times 40$-$186$ ($K=20$-93) points in (x, y, z)-directions (NX, NY, $2K$). The problem has been run on the supercomputers of the hww GmbH, Stuttgart, the NEC SX-4/32 (PVP-type, 32 processors, 8 GB RAM) and the CRAY T3E-512 (MPP-type, 512 processors with 128 MB RAM each) for a high-resolution simulation with $K+1=94$ Fourier modes in spanwise direction. The code performance on a single processor on the NEC SX-4/32 is about 3.5 μs per gridpoint and time step; on the CRAY T3E it is about 107 μs. Hence, 30 processors of the MPP-machine have to make up for the vectorization advantage of the NEC SX-4/32 to reach the same computation speed. Here, the average vector length was 163.

As for the $K=20$ problem on the NEC SX-4 (1.75 GB memory requirement), the serial code reached ≈ 900 MFLOPS (of 2 GFLOPS theoretical peak performance) at a vector operation ratio of 98.9% after adapting the code to the specific features of the NEC SX-4. The NEC SX-4 parallel version reached a speed-up of over 9 (8236 concurrent MFLOPS) when computing on 11 processors parallel in everyday operation. The performance, however, depends heavily on the load of the computer. About 90% of the overall time was spent in parallel execution and only 10% of the total computation time for I/O, system-calls and serial program parts.

An optimal adaptation of the code to the distributed-memory architecture of the CRAY T3E enforces modulo (NX, $K+1$)=0 and a maximum x-y-domain size requiring less memory than the RAM available on one processor (128 MB at present). Finally, a $1410 \times 145 \times 186$ grid has been used for the high-resolution simulation, corresponding to a total used memory of 7.5 GB. We remark here that the memory overhead to match the distributed-memory architecture roughly is 80% in our case, i.e., 1.8 times the memory size is required compared to a shared-memory machine. The speed-up of the parallel code on the CRAY T3E was 88.5 for the concurrent use of 94 Processors (including I/O, etc.).

It is noted that the x-discretisation is the crucial point in resolution requirements. In the high-resolution case, the grid spacing was $\Delta x=0.00164$, $\Delta y=0.1858$ and $\Delta z=0.0105$. The time step in this computation had to be reduced compared to the first case due to a finer resolution in x. The number of time steps per fundamental disturbance period was 1000 in the final simulation stages, and 700 for the standard case (the inflow boundary for the high-resolution simulation has been shifted downstream compared to a first run, using unsteady boundary conditions in the second run at the inflow boundary extracted from the first computation within the domain; thus the number of grid points in x-direction is smaller despite the finer resolution).

4   Numerical Results

The discrete waves will be presented in the frequency-spanwise wave number spectrum (h, k), where the first index gives multiples of the fundamental frequency β, and the second of the fundamental spanwise wave number γ. Mode (1,0) corresponds to a 2-D wave, mode (1,6) has an obliqueness angle of approx. $\pm 45°$ and (1,20) represents a 3-D wave with an approximate angle of $\pm 77°$. The downstream amplitude development (u'-max over y) of the different modes for the basic frequency is shown in Figure 4 in a logarithmic scale.

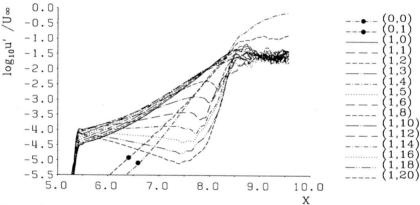

Fig. 4. Amplitude development of different modes in the frequency – spanwise wavenumber spectrum

4.1   DNS Data Analysis

The behaviour of the wave train can be studied by means of Figure 5 which shows lines of corresponding phases of fluctuations ω'_z for a single (disturbance) frequency at the wall. The time signal was Fourier analysed over one disturbance cycle to obtain the Fourier phases of the fluctuations. The left margin of the picture marks the downstream end of the disturbance strip. The boomerang-shaped phase distribution just after the introduction of the disturbances has qualitatively been observed, for instance, by Gilyov et al., Seifert & Wygnanski, both experimentally, and Mack & Herbert theoretically for ZPG flow (see [3]). Curved wave fronts with a straightened middle part are formed. 3-D waves with high wavenumbers are responsible for the regular pattern in spanwise direction beside the point source. These waves decline in amplitude due to the stability properties of the base flow (see [3]). Downstream of $x = 6.5$, the typical wave train has fully developed and exhibits an half opening angle with respect to the centerline of 12°, which is similar to the value observed in Blasius flow and is found in the joint experiments as well. The center region of the wave train straightens downstream of $x \approx 7.5$.

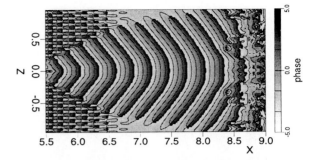

Fig. 5. Phaselines for the disturbance frequency $\beta = 9.45$ of ω_z' at the wall

As the development becomes increasingly non-linear, this shape deformation becomes more pronounced ($x > 8.0$). The sharply defined wave front shape dissolves for $x > 8.5$ where the region of rapid final breakdown begins (recall the increasing APG, Figure 2). The saturation of the amplitudes of the disturbance waves (Figure 4) can be observed at the same downstream location.

To investigate the spanwise development of the disturbance intensity, the u'-rms amplitudes are shown in Figure 6. The development of u'-rms on the centerline ($z=0$) is surpassed by that at $z=0.095$ and $z=0.19$. The centerline u' fluctuations are not the most intensive fluctuations in the area of transition ($x > 8.0$).

The transitional regime (non-linear wave development), where disturbance waves of large obliqueness angles reach amplitudes beyond $1\% \, u'/U_\infty$ and detailed structures can be visualized experimentally, is limited to about one or two TS wavelengths. For the comparison with the experimental results, patterns of the instantaneous wall vorticity ω_z distribution from the high resolution simulation with $K=93$ (which can be compared to hot-film data from the measurements) are evaluated, delivering footprints of the structures in the boundary-layer flow (Figure 7). Very early ($x \approx 8.0$), regions with negative vorticity (white areas) at and close to the wall appear indicating downstream traveling local separation zones. The areas of local separation periodically alternate with areas of very high vorticity (black areas) at the wall. The flat center-part of the wave front deforms in the transition region (Figure 7a) and two areas of high shear *off* centerline ($x=8.1$, $z=\pm0.25$) accelerate compared to the surrounding structures at the wall ($x=8.35$ in Figure 7b). These high-shear areas divide the negative shear area into a centerpart (the remainders

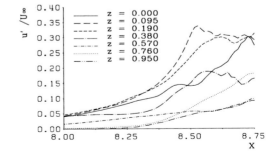

Fig. 6. u'-rms (max. over y) for different spanwise positions ($z = 0.95 \, \widehat{=} \, \lambda_z/2$)

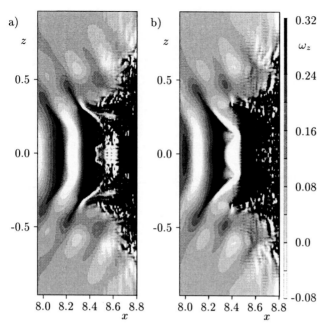

Fig. 7. Vorticity ω_z at the wall ($\sim$ wall shear) a) at $t = t_0$ and b) at $t = t_0 + T/2$

of which can be found one time period later at $x = 8.6$ in Figure 7a, however, largely disintegrated) and two "legs" (white "streaks", $x=8.4$ and $z=\pm0.25$). These streaks can be associated with structures inside the boundary layer to be described below. They fall back compared to the faster centerpart and persist for a surprisingly long time embedded in high-shear areas. The outer ends of the streaks ($x=8.4$ and $z=\pm0.35$, Figure 7b) remain visible in the flow pattern for one time period longer than the aforementioned structures.

The rapid breakdown of the wave train leads to periodically generated turbulent spots rather than to an instant "broad" breakdown region in z. The high-shear area expands in spanwise direction downstream of $x = 8.5$ but the flanks align with the streamwise direction for $x \geq 8.8$ and do not extend across the entire width of the integration domain. In conclusion, the harmonic point source can be regarded as a turbulent spot generator with well-defined initial disturbance conditions.

A streamwise cut at the centerline reveals no distinctive structures associated with breakdown (mind the stretching of the y-coordinate by a factor of 8). Two shear layers are observed at $x=8.4$ and $x=8.5$ in Figure 8a. These layers (dark areas at an inclination of $\approx 45°$) intensify on their way downstream, get ejected towards outer regions of the flow and rapid breakdown occurs (compare Figure 9a half a fundamental time-period later at $x = 8.5$-8.6). The development off-center at $z=0.19$ ($z/\lambda_z=0.1$) reveals further details (Figure 9b). At this spanwise location, a high-shear layer develops much earlier and can be clearly distinguished at $x=8.4$ above an area of high-shear at the wall, the latter induced by flow reversal (early development can be seen as soon as $x=8.25$ in Figure 8b). It extends towards outer regions of the

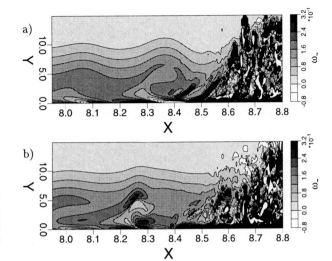

Fig. 8. Instantaneous ω_z contours at $t = t_0$ in the x-y plane a) at $z = 0$ and b) off-center $z = 0.19$

boundary layer (y=6.5) and influences nearby spanwise locations as can be seen in Figure 9a at x=8.4. The virulent breakdown of this high-shear layer (Figure 8b, x=8.6) triggers the breakdown to a turbulent-spot train.

5   Conclusions

The downstream development of a harmonic point-source disturbance in an adverse pressure-gradient boundary-layer has been investigated up to late stages of the breakdown by direct numerical simulations. Using the NEC SX-4 (or CRAY T3E) and 15 (38) Mega grid points, a computing performance of 8 (2.6) GFLOPS has been achieved using 11 (94) processors with a paral-

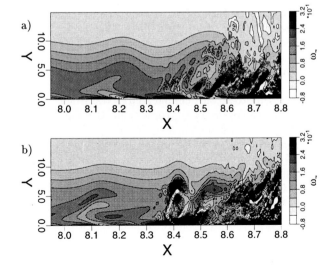

Fig. 9. Instantaneous ω_z contours at t=$t_0 + T/2$ in the x-y plane a) at z=0 and b) off-center z=0.19

lelization scaling factor of 0.82 (0.94). The memory requirement amounted to 1.75 (7.5) GB, with 80% overhead for the run on the CRAY T3E.

The amplitude development of the disturbance waves composing the wave train and the detailed investigation of the vorticity structures indicate that the breakdown is not of the fundamental type (K-type). Rather, a form of *multiple oblique breakdown* is observed that shows a kind of peak/valley splitting with the valley plane at the centerline of the wave train. Velocity fluctuations are larger for spanwise positions just off-center than in the centerline.

The major development of vorticity structures takes place off the centerline. Maxima and minima (local flow reversal) of the spanwise vorticity ω_z appear at the wall. A clear-cut M-shaped coherent structure can be observed in final stages related to ω_z at the wall. Inside the boundary layer close to the boundary layer edge, areas of high shear develop where the shear at the wall is at a maximum. The final stage is rapid due to the strong adverse pressure gradient.

Acknowledgments The authors wish to express their deepest gratitude to Dr. Horst Bestek who initiated this work and gave many helpful suggestions along its path of development. He was Head of the Transition and Turbulence Research Group at the IAG up to his death in September 1997.

This research has been financially supported by the German Research Council (DFG) under contract number Be 1192/7-4.

References

1. L. Kleiser, T. Zang, Numerical simulation of transition in wall-bounded shear flows. *Ann. Rev. Fluid Mechanics*, **23**, 495–537, 1991.
2. M. Kloker and H. Fasel, Direct numerical simulation of boundary-layer transition with strong adverse pressure gradient. In R. Kobayashi (ed.), *Laminar-Turbulent Transition*, IUTAM-Symposium, Sendai, Japan, pp. 481–488. Springer, Berlin, Heidelberg, 1995.
3. C. Stemmer, M. Kloker and S. Wagner, DNS of harmonic point source disturbances in an airfoil boundary-layer flow. *AIAA-98-2436* , 29th AIAA Fluid Dynamics Conference, Albuquerque, New Mexico.
4. J. Suttan, M. Baumann, S. Fühling, P. Erb, S. Becker and C. Stemmer, In-flight research on boundary layer transition – works of the DFG-University Research Group. In H. Körner and R. Hilbig (eds.), *Notes on Numerical Fluid Mechanics*, vol. 60, pp. 343–350. Vieweg Verlag, 1997, 10th Stab Symposium 96, Braunschweig.
5. M. Kloker, U. Konzelmann and H. Fasel, Outflow boundary conditions for Spatial Navier-Stokes Simulations of Transition Boundary Layers. *AIAA J.*, **31**, 620–628, 1993.
6. U. Rist and H. Fasel, Direct numerical simulation of controlled transition in a flat-plate boundary layer. *J. Fluid Mech.*, **298**, 211–248, 1995.

CFD-Applications on NEC SX-4

Egon Krause and Matthias Meinke

Aerodynamisches Institut der RWTH Aachen
52062 Aachen
E-Mail: ek@aia.RWTH-Aachen.de

Abstract Recent applications in the field of computational fluid dynamics are presented, which were run on the NEC SX-4 of the High-Performance Computing Center of Stuttgart. External and internal flow problems were simulated. The internal flow problems include the breakdown of a slender vortex in a pipe flow and the flow in a piston engine during the intake and compression stroke. In addition, large-eddy simulations of turbulent flow through pipe bends and of turbulent jet flows are presented. All results are obtained with explicit or implicit solution schemes on block structured curvilinear grids. The number of grid points varies from 300,000 in the case of a turbulent jet to approx. 2 million in the case of the piston engine flow. All algorithms are vectorized and parallelized. Characteristic computing times and memory requirements are reported for the different applications.

1 Introduction

The numerical simulation of three-dimensional, and especially unsteady flow problems requires extensive computer resources in terms of storage capacities and computational speed, so that efficient numerical methods and an appropriate implementation on high-performance computers are necessary. In the last decades the progress of both computer hardware and numerical methods was considerable. Parallel computers have the largest potential to further increase the computer power substantially in the near future. The combination of the present hardware of supercomputers, like vector-parallel processors, with fast numerical methods, however, is in general not straightforward.

At the Aerodynamisches Institut of the RWTH Aachen a modular program library was developed, which contains several algorithms for the solution of the Navier-Stokes equations. Currently, compressible and incompressible, steady and unsteady, two- and three-dimensional flows can be computed on block structured curvilinear grids. The various algorithms are implemented as modules in a common software environment. It is constructed in such a way that program maintenance is simplified. In addition, functions not related to a specific numerical method, like parallelized multi-block exchange or streak-line integration, are at once available for all algorithms.

This program library has been ported on several vector, parallel, and vector-parallel machines. Computational speed was already reported for selected algorithms, [8]. In this paper recent applications are presented, which were mainly run on the vector-parallel machine NEC SX-4 installed in the

High-Performance Computing Center of Stuttgart. The performance achieved on a single processor is dependent on the algorithm applied and the size of the problem. For the applications presented the overall performance was about 800 MFlops. Further details of the computational resources together with a short description of the physical problems are given in the sections with the different applications.

2　Method of Solution

2.1　Governing Equations

The motion of a viscous fluid is governed by the conservation equations of mass, momentum and energy, the Navier-Stokes equations. In dimensionless form these equations transformed in general, curvilinear coordinates ξ, η and ζ read:

$$\bar{A} \cdot \frac{\partial Q}{\partial t} + \frac{\partial E}{\partial \xi} + \frac{\partial F}{\partial \eta} + \frac{\partial G}{\partial \zeta} = 0 \quad . \tag{1}$$

For a gaseous compressible fluid, $\bar{A}$ is the identity matrix. The vector of the conservative variables multiplied by the Jacobian of the coordinate transformation J is given by:

$$Q = J \left(\rho, \rho u, \rho e \right)^T \quad .$$

Here, ρ denotes the fluids density, $u = (u, v, w)^T$ the velocity vector, and e is the internal energy. The flux vectors E, F, and G are splitted in a convective and a viscous part, e. g.: $E = E_C - E_V$, with

$$E_C = J \begin{pmatrix} \rho U \\ \rho U u + \xi_x p \\ \rho U v + \xi_y p \\ \rho U w + \xi_z p \\ U(\rho e + p) \end{pmatrix} \quad , \text{ and } \quad E_V = \frac{J}{Re} \begin{pmatrix} 0 \\ \xi_x \sigma_{xx} + \xi_y \sigma_{xy} + \xi_z \sigma_{xz} \\ \xi_x \sigma_{xy} + \xi_y \sigma_{yy} + \xi_z \sigma_{yz} \\ \xi_x \sigma_{xz} + \xi_y \sigma_{yz} + \xi_z \sigma_{zz} \\ \xi_x E_{V_5} + \xi_y E_{V_5} + \xi_z E_{V_5} \end{pmatrix} \quad .$$

Herein, ξ_x, ξ_y, ξ_z are the metric terms of the coordinate transformation, U the contravariant velocity, Re the Reynolds-number and $\bar{\bar{\sigma}}$ the stress tensor. E_{V_5} is the dissipative part of the energy flux containing contributions of the stress tensor and the heat flux.

For incompressible flows with constant viscosity, the Navier-Stokes equations simplify significantly. The equation for energy conservation can then be decoupled from the conservation equations for mass and momentum. The energy equation can be omitted, if the distribution of the fluids temperature is not of interest. The vector of the conservative variables in Eq. (1) is then reduced to:

$$Q = J \left(p, u \right)^T \quad .$$

For incompressible flows the matrix $\bar{A}$ becomes singular, which renders the integration of the governing equations more difficult. For fluids with constant density, the vectors of the convective and diffusive fluxes reduce to, e. g.:

$$
\boldsymbol{E}_C = J \begin{pmatrix} U \\ Uu + \xi_x p \\ Uv + \xi_y p \\ Uw + \xi_z p \end{pmatrix} \quad , \text{and} \quad \boldsymbol{E}_V = \frac{J}{Re} \begin{pmatrix} 0 \\ g_1 u_\xi + g_2 u_\eta + g_3 u_\zeta \\ g_1 v_\xi + g_2 v_\eta + g_3 v_\zeta \\ g_1 w_\xi + g_2 w_\eta + g_3 w_\zeta \end{pmatrix} \quad ,
$$

with:

$$
g_1 = \xi_x^2 + \xi_y^2 + \xi_z^2 \ , \quad g_2 = \xi_x \eta_x + \xi_y \eta_y + \xi_z \eta_z \ , \quad g_3 = \xi_x \zeta_x + \xi_y \zeta_y + \xi_z \zeta_z \quad .
$$

2.2 Temporal Discretization

To advance the solution in time for the simulation of compressible flows a commonly used explicit Runge-Kutta multistep method [5] is applied. Alternatively an implicit dual time stepping scheme can be used for problems, for which an explicit scheme becomes inefficient.

For the simulation of incompressible flows Chorin [2] proposed to introduce an artificial equation of state which couples the pressure- to an arbitrary density distribution in order to eliminate the singularity of the matrix $\bar{A}$. Hence, the continuity equation contains a time derivative for the pressure which vanishes for steady-state solutions and $\bar{A}$ in (1) is regular. In [1] this method was extended to unsteady flows by introducing an artificial time τ and adding a pseudo-time derivative $\tilde{A} \cdot \partial \boldsymbol{Q}/\partial \tau$ to (1) such that $diag\{\tilde{A}\} = (1/\beta^2, 1, 1, 1)$, where β^2 controls the artificial compressibility. Thus, the pressure field is coupled to the velocity distribution and the governing equations can be integrated in a similar way as for compressible flows. Since a steady solution is computed within the pseudo time τ, the additional terms vanish, and the unsteady solution of (1) at the physical time t is obtained.

In the following the dual time stepping scheme is briefly described. The convective and viscous fluxes are expanded in Taylor series in order to obtain a linear system of equations of the form:

$$
LHS \cdot \Delta \boldsymbol{Q}^{(\nu)} = RHS \quad , \tag{2}
$$

which has to be solved in each artificial time-step. Here, $\Delta \boldsymbol{Q}^{(\nu)}$ is the change of the primitive or conservative variables within one time-step, LHS contains the discrete spatial derivatives of the Jacobian matrices which result from the linearization, and RHS contains the discrete derivatives in space of equation (1) and a second-, or even higher-order approximation of the physical time-derivative. Details of the linearization and discretization of LHS are given in [1] and [10]. The resulting linear system of equation is here solved with an alternating line Gauß-Seidel relaxation scheme.

2.3   Spatial Discretization

To preserve the conservative properties in the discretized space, Eq. (1) is formulated for a finite control volume. A corresponding difference operator, e. g. δ_ξ for the determination of the flux derivatives for a control volume in a node-centered scheme at a point (i, j, k) reads:

$$(\delta_\xi \boldsymbol{E})_{i,j,k} \;=\; \frac{\boldsymbol{E}_{i+\frac{1}{2},j,k} - \boldsymbol{E}_{i-\frac{1}{2},j,k}}{\Delta \xi} \quad .$$

The formulation of the flux at the half points $i \pm \frac{1}{2}$ determines the properties of the discretization scheme. For the compressible flow problems presented in this paper different formulations are applied. A cell-vertex scheme with artificial damping is used for the subsonic flow in a piston engine, a modified upwind discretization based on the AUSM, [7], is used for the LES of turbulent flows.

For incompressible flows, the projection of the variables to the cell interfaces is carried out with the QUICK-scheme, proposed by Leonard [6]. To avoid high-frequency oscillations in case of flows at high Reynolds-numbers, a fourth-order damping term is added to the continuity equation, which is discretized with central differences, [1].

For both, compressible and incompressible flows, the Stokes stresses are discretized with central differences of second-order accuracy.

2.4   Parallelisation

Parallelisation of the above described algorithms is achieved by assigning the different grid blocks to the processors of a parallel computer. The only difference between the parallel and sequential code is, that the exchange of boundary data between neighbouring blocks is replaced by sending and receiving data with the help of a message passing library. The communication mode is asynchronous blocking. For global communication a binary tree topology is used in order to minimize the time for the exchange of data. In case the different grid blocks differ in size, a perfect load balancing would not be achieved on a parallel machine dedicated for one job. On the NEC SX-4, however, a perfect load balancing is not crucial, since several jobs can be executed in share mode on the same processor.

The computation of streaklines for the purpose of flow visualization has also been parallelized. In order to minimize the communication time all data to be sent to a neighbouring block is packed into a single array and then communicated. A perfect load balancing is very difficult to achieve for the particle tracing, since the number of particles can change rapidly within each block and is unknown before the flow simulation. Again this does not cause efficiency losses on machines which share several jobs on one processor. With the message passing library MPI, efficiency values of about 80% were measured on the shared memory system NEC SX-4 for a load balanced application, almost the same values were measured with PVM on the distributed memory system SNI/Fujitsu VPP300.

3   Applications

3.1   Large-Eddy Simulations of Turbulent Flows

The modelling of turbulence, especially in separated and swirling flows, is still one of the most difficult tasks in CFD. Large-eddy simulations (LES) seems to be most promising for an accurate prediction of such flow problems. In contrast to one-point closure models, which are based on time averaging of the Navier-Stokes equations, LES is based on the solution of the spatially filtered equations, see e. g. [3]. A subgrid scale model is then used to model the filtered turbulent scales. Here, LES of a internal flows in pipe bends and in free turbulent jets including the mixing of different species are presented. Results of validation test cases and details of the algorithm applied have been reported in [9].

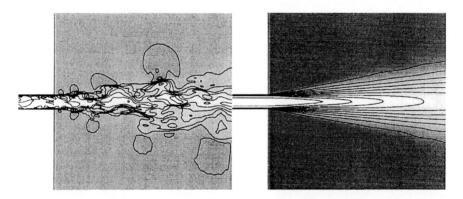

Figure1. Instantaneous (left) and time averaged velocity (right) in streamwise direction for a turbulent plane jet flow

The modelling of turbulence is still one of the most difficult tasks in CFD. In contrast to statistical turbulence models, which are based on time averaging, large-eddy simulations are based on the solution of the spatially filtered Navier-Stokes equations. A simple subgrid scale model is then used to model the filtered turbulent scales. Here, LES of a turbulent jet spreading in a gas at rest are presented. Since the solution of the spatially filtered equations results in an unsteady flow field, a time averaging must be carried out in order to obtain statistical data.

A careful formulation of approximate in- and outflow boundary conditions is important in order to avoid unphysical results. For the inflow boundary

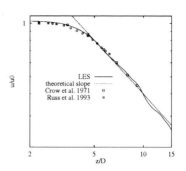

Figure2. Instantaneous flow field of a turbulent round jet of air evolving into stagnant argon. Concentration of Argon.

Figure3. Time averaged centerline velocity of a round air-in-air jet, LES at $Re = 20000$ in comparison to experimental results

within the jet, a solution is extracted from a simulation of a turbulent channel flow for the plane jet and a turbulent pipe flow for the round jet. These simulations are conducted in parallel, so that physical meaningful instantaneous values of the mass flow can be provided at the inflow boundary. At the outflow plane different boundary conditions were tested. Non-reflecting boundary conditions were found to produce the least disturbances but also to be numerically unstable for long term computations, so that an additional filtering of the flow variables was applied at the outflow section.

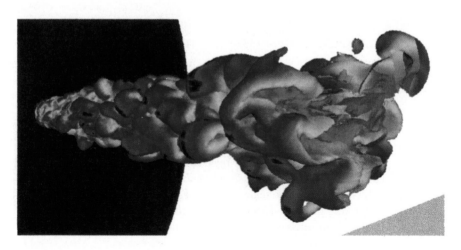

Figure4. Instantaneous flow field of a turbulent round jet. Surface of constant vorticity.

A computation of the plane turbulent jet flow was performed with a second-order modified AUSM scheme applied for the spatial discretization. Time integration is performed by an explicit Runge-Kutta method. The Reynolds-number based on the outlet diameter is $Re = 7600$ and the Mach-number $Ma = 0.1$. The computation was performed on 4 processors of the NEC SX-4. In order to achieve time averaged flow fields on a grid with 300.000 grid points a CPU-time of 400 hours was required. In Fig. 1 the instantaneous solution of the velocity in the streamwise direction is shown together with its time averaged value.

The mixing of gases is an important technical problem. Here it is investigated with a general algorithm which solves additional conservation equations for the partial densities of an arbitrary number of species. A LES of an round air jet evolving into stagnant Argon has been carried out with a similar algorithm as was described for the plane jet. In Fig. 2 the concentration of Argon is shown for a Reynolds-number of $Re = 20000$ based on the diameter and the mean velocity of the jet at the inflow boundary. The instantaneous surface of constant vorticity (Fig. 4) shows the large scale structures of the jet. The time averaging is carried out for the statistical evaluation of first and second moments for a very long time. Approx. 1000 CPU hours CPU-time was required to achieve the velocity profile shown in Fig. 3. It shows good agreement with experimental data.

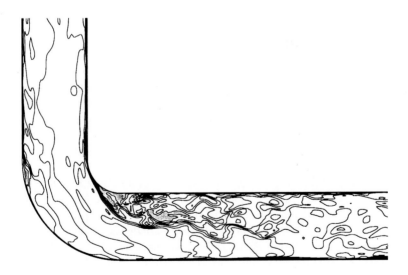

Figure5. Instantaneous flow field in a axial section of a turbulent flow in a 90° bend. Gray scales and lines of constant Mach number for a Reynolds number of 10000 and a Dean number of 3500.

Laminar flow through pipe bends is characterized by a symmetrical two–vortex pattern, which is well–known. However, turbulent flow through pipe bends is much less understood and, here, investigated by extended numerical simulations to get a close insight into the physical conditions of turbulent bend flows. LES are conducted for 90° pipe bends at different Reynolds numbers and different radius ratios of the bend. Double bends are considered as well. For comparison, turbulent bend flows are also investigated experimentally at the Aerodynamisches Institut of the RWTH Aachen.

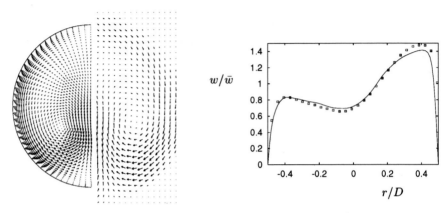

Figure6. Time averaged velocity of a turbulent flow in a radial and axial cross section 1.5 diameters downstream of the curved section of a 90° bend. Comparison of numerical (left, —) and experimental (right, □) solution for a Reynolds number of 5000 and a Dean number of 1800.

Computational results for a Reynolds number of 10000 based on the mean velocity and the pipe diameter, a Dean number of 3500 and a Mach number of 0.1 is shown in Fig. 5. The calculations predict the flow separation expected at the inner side and also on the opposite side near the beginning of the curved section. The comparison of the time averaged results with experimental data shows good agreement in radial cross sections and in the plane of symmetry (Fig. 6). The symmetrical two–vortex flow pattern can be observed only in time averaged flow. The instantaneous flow structure is more complicated and highly unsteady (Fig. 7). Neither the vortices nor the area of separated flow are symmetric. At some points in time three or even four vortices instead of the two Dean–vortices are present. A Fourier analysis of the forces (Fig. 8) onto the structure shows two distinct peaks at Strouhal numbers of 0.3 and 1.7. Possibly the vortex shedding at the inner side of the bend and an oscillation of the Dean vortices, that was found both in the numerical and experimental data, are responsible for these peaks. Currently, further investigations into this subject are carried out.

The relevant time scales of these simulations are determined by the smallest eddies to be resolved on the one hand and on the periodic time of the low

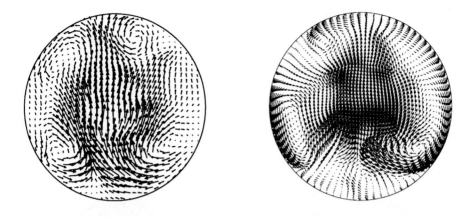

Figure7. Instantaneous velocity vectors of a turbulent flow in a radial cross section at the end of a 90° bend. Comparison of numerical (left) with experimental date (right) for a Reynolds number of 5000 and a Dean number of 1800.

frequency oscillations on the other hand. The ratio of these two time scales determines the required CPU-times. This ratio is rather high for the considered bend flows, resulting in required CPU-times after convergence of solution from 300 h up to 1000 h, depending on the geometric and hydromechanical parameters. For a statistical evaluation of the solution the storing of a large number of intermediate solutions is necessary, so that a total temporary disk space of 0.5 TeraByte is required.

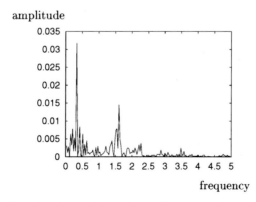

Figure8. Turbulent flow in a 90° pipe bend. Fourier analysis of the forces onto the structure for a Reynolds number of 22000 and a Dean number of 8800.

3.2   Simulation of a Piston Engine Flow

Understanding of the unsteady, three-dimensional, compressible flow field structure in piston engines during the intake and compression stroke is crucial for the development of new engine designs with high performance and low emission values. The flow field determines the flame propagation rate in homogeneous charge spark-ignition engines and the fuel-air mixing and burning rates in Diesel engines, [4]. It has a major impact on the emission values and the breathing capacity of the engine and therefore also on the maximum available power.

Figure9. Flow field during the intake (70° ATDC, left) and compression stroke (300° ATDC, right), surface of constant velocity and streamlines.

Separation of the flow can occur at the valve seat and valve head depending on the seat angle, the rounding of the seat corners, the seat width and the swirl generated in the intake port. An investigation of the above mentioned phenomena with a numerical solution of the Navier-Stokes equations requires the resolution of all important details of the intake and cylinder head geometry. Here this is achieved with a boundary-fitted block structured moving grid system. The grid is refined and coarsened during the opening and closing of the valve and the piston up- and downward motion. In addition to the conservation equations for mass, momentum and energy, a conservation equation for the cell volume [11] is solved. No subgrid scale model is used, with the intention to resolve at least the large scales of the in-cylinder flow field. An explicit finite-volume method of second-order accuracy in time and space was used to discretize all equations. The CPU-time amounts to 120 hours with a computational grid with approx. one million grid points. Fig. 9 shows the flow field during the intake and the compression stroke for a 4V-engine with a pentroof combustion chamber. In the intake process the flow field is dominated by two ring-like vortices generated by the intake jets. These vortices merge during the compression process into a single stretched vortex whose opposite filaments are connected with a high pressure bridge. The streamlines reveal a spiral fluid motion towards this structure.

3.3   Vortex Breakdown

The breakdown of a slender vortex in a slightly diverging circular pipe is simulated using the Navier-Stokes equations for incompressible laminar time-dependent flows. The numerical method is based upon the concept of artificial compressibility combined with a dual-time-stepping technique. Block-structured grids are employed to avoid the singularity on the tube axis. An implicit relaxation scheme is used for the integration in each physical time step.

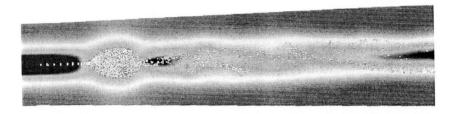

Figure10. Vortex breakdown in a circular pipe. Streaklines and velocity in streamwise direction.

Figure11. Vortex breakdown in a circular pipe: Streaklines and surface of constant velocity.

At the tube-walls no-slip condition and zero pressure gradient normal to the wall are imposed. The velocity distribution in the inflow section of the domain of integration is prescribed by experimental data and the pressure is extrapolated from the interior. Since the vortex flow does not allow to prescribe a constant pressure in the outflow section, the pressure distribution in this plane is computed by solving Poisson's equation. The velocity components are extrapolated from the interior.

Fig. 10 shows the absolute value of the velocity vector in grey scales together with streaklines at a dimensionless time of $T = 108$. In Fig 11 streaklines are shown with a surface of constant value of the velocity vector at the same time level. The Reynolds-number is 3220 based on the pipe diameter and mean velocity at the inflow section. A free stagnation point forms at a dimensionless time of 55. The breakdown-region moves upstream and grows in time. At $T = 108$ bubble-type vortex breakdown is fully developed. Approximately one bubble diameter downstream a smaller spiral-type region can be seen. Shape and position of the breakdown region agree well with experimental flow visualization.

The number of grid points for simulating this flow extends from $180,000$ up to $700,000$. For the finest grid 260 MB of computer memory is required with the present solution algorithm. Using $400,000$ grid points the necessary memory amounts to 208 MB, while the simulation of $\Delta T = 100$ takes 150 CPU-hours. The nonlinear increase of necessary memory results from the fact, that intermediate results are stored only once for all grid-blocks.

4   Conclusion

Several fluid dynamical applications have been presented, which were successfully investigated with the vector-parallel computer NEC SX-4. The solution of these flow problems require considerable computer resources, which can be obtained only if the applied algorithms are carefully implemented. The vectorization rate of the CFD-application is 99%. An average vector unit busy ratio of 95...97% was achieved and a single processor performance of about 800 MFlops. Parallelization of the algorithms had been carried out with efficiency values of about 80%. The total temporary disk requirement is about 0.5 TeraByte.

LES of different internal and free turbulent flows have demonstrated that accurate results can be obtained, which are not achievable with algebraic or two-equation models. The computational resources for the solution of such problems is still very large, since the determination of the turbulence statistics requires a long averaging time for cases in which there are few homogeneous directions.

The flow in a piston engine was simulated on a moving grid with a block structured mesh showing qualitative agreement with experimental data. The solution was used to analyse the vortex topology of the flow field. It could be shown, that starting during the intake stroke two ring-like vortices are generated, which later merge with other secondary vortices to a single vortex structure. This solution will be further developed with the aim to carry out a LES with a resolution of the larger turbulent scales.

The problem of vortex breakdown was successfully simulated in a circular divergent pipe. A steady bubble type breakdown could be predicted with close agreement to experimental data.

Acknowledgements

The work reviewed here was sponsored by the German Research Association (DFG). The authors acknowledge contributions of A. Abdellfattah, Th. Rister, F. Rütten, C. Schulz, and M. Weimer for the different applications presented.

References

1. M. Breuer and D. Hänel. A dual time-stepping method for 3-d, viscous, incompressible vortex flows. *Computers Fluids*, 22(4/5):467–484, 1993.
2. A.J. Chorin. A Numerical Method for Solving Incompressible Viscous Flow. *Journal of Computational Physics*, 2:12–26, 1967.
3. G. Erlebacher, M. Y. Hussaini, C. G. Speziale, and T. A. Zang. Toward the Large-Eddy Simulation of compressible turbulent flows. *Journal of Fluid Mechanics*, 238:155–185, 1992.
4. J. B. Heywood. *Combustion Engine Fundamentals*. McGraw-Hill, 1988.
5. A. Jameson, W. Schmidt, and E. Turkel. Numerical Solution of the Euler equations by finite volume methods using Runge-Kutta time stepping schemes. *AIAA Paper*, No. 81-1259, 1981.
6. B. P. Leonard. A stable and accurate convective modelling procedure based on quadratic upstream interpolation. *Computer Methods in Applied Mechanics and Engineering*, 19:59, 1979.
7. M. Meinke, A. Abdellfattah, and E. Krause. Simulation of Piston Engine Flows in Realistic Geometries. In J.-J. Chattot P. Kutler, J. Flores, editor, *15th International Conference on Numerical Methods in Fluid Dynamics*, pages 195–200. Springer, June 1996.
8. M. Meinke and J. Hofhaus. Parallel Solution Schemes for the Navier-Stokes Equations. In H. W. Meurer, editor, *Supercomputer '93, Anwendungen, Architekturen, Trends*, pages 142–161. Springer Verlag, 1993.
9. M. Meinke, C. Schulz, and Th. Rister. LES of Spatially Developing Jets. In *Notes on Numerical Fluid Mechanics: Computation and Visualization of three-dimensional vortical and turbulent flows*. Vieweg Verlag, to be published, 1997.
10. J. L. Shinn, H. C. Yee, and K. Uenishi. Extension of a Semi-Implicit Shock-Capturing Algorithm for 3-d Fully Coupled, Chemically Reacting Flows in Generalized Coordinates. *AIAA Paper*, No. 87-1577, June 1987.
11. P. D. Thomas and C. K. Lombard. Geometric Conservation Law and Its Application to Flow Computations on Moving Grids. *AIAA Journal*, 17(10):1030–1037, October 1979.

High Performance Computing of Turbulent Flow in Complex Pipe Geometries

Thomas J. Hüttl and Rainer Friedrich

Lehrstuhl für Fluidmechanik
Technische Universität München
Boltzmannstr. 15, 85748 Garching, Germany

Abstract. The numerical study of turbulent flow in pipes is important for fundamental research and allows to solve engineering problems, too. By the use of modern supercomputers the flow through complex pipe geometries can be predicted by the Direct Numerical Simulation method, where the Navier Stokes equations are solved directly and no modelling of turbulence is required. The flow in straight, toroidal and helically coiled pipes has been investigated for the same Reynolds number $Re_\tau = u_\tau R/\nu = 230$. The curvature κ ranges from 0 to 0.1 and the torsion τ ranges from 0 to 0.165. The influence of curvature and torsion on turbulent pipe flow is shown by surface profiles of the axial velocity, the pressure and the intensity of the velocity components perpendicular to the axial velocity.

1 Introduction

Turbulence is a very complex flow phenomenon. Its mechanisms, attitudes and effects have even with the most modern techniques not yet been fully understood. Expensive experiments and extensive numerical simulations inspire each other when the physical secrets of turbulence are investigated and new physical effects are discovered. The most accurate way to study turbulence numerically is solving the flow equations directly without using any model or simplification. This method, which is called Direct Numerical Simulation (DNS) requires big amounts of computing memory, CPU-time and disk or archive memory and has therefore been restricted to simple geometries. Due to the speedy increase of computing power modern high performance computers allow us to study turbulent flow in more complex geometries. Besides the simulation of a special flow configuration, direct numerical simulations allow us to study the physical mechanisms in detail, see fig. 1. The computed data sets can also be used to create, improve and test turbulence models because they are equivalent to fully three-dimensional time dependent experimental measurements.

The turbulent flow in pipes is of great importance in industrial applications in many branches of engineering. Heat exchangers, chemical reactors, exhaust gas ducts of engines, or any kind of pipelines, tubes and conduits transporting gases and liquids consist of straight, curved and coiled pipes.

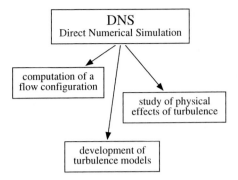

Fig. 1. Benefit of Direct Numerical Simulations

Due to the simple geometry, the turbulent flow in straight pipes has often been investigated in detail by means of direct numerical simulation, see [21,9,10,22]. Curved or helically coiled pipes are used in industrial applications due to the possibility to satisfy space and/or geometric requirements and due to the characteristics of the induced secondary flow, which influences the heat and mass transfer.

The direct numerical simulation of fully developed turbulent flow of an incompressible, newtonian fluid in several pipes with circular cross section, constant curvature κ and torsion τ is the subject of the present investigation. Although the theoretical and experimental investigation of flow in pipes with curvature and torsion in a systematical way is just of recent origin, this flow configuration has always been classified as even more complex than the flow through straight ducts. Williams et al. [24] notice, that the position of maximum axial velocity is moved towards the outer wall of a curved pipe because of centrifugal forces. Later Eustice [11,12] demonstrated the existence of a secondary flow by injecting ink into water, flowing through a coiled pipe.

Due to the lack of supercomputers some decades ago the investigators were unable to solve the Navier-Stokes equations numerically. Besides experiments, only analytical solutions of simplified equations were used to investigate the laminar flow in curved and coiled pipes. Dean [7,8] derived a solution of the laminar flow in loosely coiled ($\kappa << 1$) pipes and showed the typical secondary flow pattern with two recirculation zones. Besides the Reynolds number Re, a new parameter, that is characterizing the magnitude and shape of the secondary motion through a torus, was found. Later this parameter was defined as the Dean number De $= \kappa^{1/2}$Re. For three differently curved pipes Adler [1] presented experimental results of laminar and turbulent flow. Since then a few investigations were reported of laminar toroidal flows without considering torsion effects. A good survey of the voluminous research activities in this area and related topics is given by Berger et al. [2] and additional aspects can be found in Ito [19].

Wang [23] solved laminar helical flow problems with small curvature and small torsion using a perturbation method based on a non-orthogonal helical coordinate system. By extending the Dean equations to a helical pipe flow, Germano [13,14] studied the same problem by introducing an orthogonal coordinate system. In order to describe the torsion effect on the flow a third dimensionless parameter has been defined: the torsion number or the later on called Germano number $Tn = Gn = \tau Re$. Liu and Masliyah [20] used a separation method for their extensive study of laminar flow in helically coiled pipes. Recent studies on laminar flow in curved and helically coiled pipes have been done by Hüttl et al. [17,18] in order to test their finite volume Navier-Stokes code for DNS.

Until now only few investigations have been done to predict the turbulent flow in curved or coiled pipes. Boersma and Nieuwstadt performed a DNS of fully developed turbulent flow in a toroidal pipe for $Re_\tau = Ru_\tau/\nu = 230, \kappa = 0.1$, see [5,6], and Large-Eddy simulations (LES) for higher Reynolds numbers, [3,4].

For the present investigation a finite volume method on a three-dimensional staggered grid with a semi-implicit time integration scheme is used to study the turbulent flow in straight, curved and helically coiled pipes. Our study concentrates on fully developed pipe flow with periodic in- and outflow boundary conditions. We will present surface profiles of the axial velocity. Size and strength of turbulent structures superposed on the mean axial velocity are visualized. For curved and helically coiled pipe flow the induced secondary flow is demonstrated by surface profiles of the intensity of the velocity components perpendicular to the axial velocity. Furthermore the formation of a pressure distribution in a cross section of toroidal and helical pipes is shown, too.

2   Geometry and governing equations

The geometry of a helical pipe can be viewed as a pipe of radius R wound around a cylinder of constant radius $(r_a - R)$ (see fig. 2). With the pitch p_s, defined by the increase in elevation per revolution of coils $2\pi p_s$, the curvature κ and the torsion τ of the helical pipe axis can be calculated from

$$\kappa = \frac{r_a}{(r_a^2 + p_s^2)} \qquad \text{and} \qquad \tau = \frac{p_s}{(r_a^2 + p_s^2)}. \qquad (1)$$

As introduced by Germano [13,14], a helical coordinate system can be established in reference to the master Cartesian coordinate system. By using

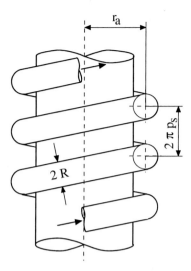

Fig. 2. Helically coiled pipe

the helical coordinates s for axial direction, r for radial direction and θ for circumferential direction, the position of any given point X inside the helical pipe can be described by the vector $\boldsymbol{x}$

$$\boldsymbol{x} = \boldsymbol{P}(s) - r\sin(\theta - \tau s)\,\boldsymbol{N}(s) + r\cos(\theta - \tau s)\,\boldsymbol{B}(s). \tag{2}$$

Here $\boldsymbol{T}$, $\boldsymbol{N}$ and $\boldsymbol{B}$ are the tangential, normal and binormal directions to the generic curve of the pipe axis at the point of consideration (see fig. 3). The metric of the orthogonal helical coordinate system is given by

$$d\boldsymbol{x} \cdot d\boldsymbol{x} = \left(1 + \kappa r\sin(\theta - \tau s)\right)^2 ds^2 + dr^2 + r^2 d\theta^2, \tag{3}$$

where ds, dr and $d\theta$ are the infinitesimal increments in the axial, radial and circumferential directions. With this metric one obtains the scale factors h_s, h_r and h_θ, that are used to express the Navier-Stokes equations in helical coordinates:

$$h_s = 1 + \kappa r\sin(\theta - \tau s), \qquad h_r = 1, \qquad h_\theta = r. \tag{4}$$

The Navier-Stokes equations read in an orthogonal helical coordinate system [16]:

continuity equation:

$$\frac{\partial}{\partial s}(r u_s) + \frac{\partial}{\partial r}(h_s r u_r) + \frac{\partial}{\partial \theta}(h_s u_\theta) = 0 \tag{5}$$

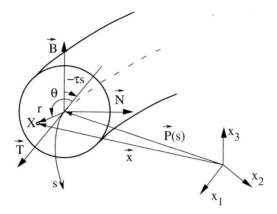

Fig. 3. Description of the orthogonal helical (s, r, θ)-coordinate system, as introduced by Germano [13,14].

_s_-momentum:

$$\frac{\partial u_s}{\partial t} + \frac{1}{h_s}\frac{\partial}{\partial s}(u_s u_s) + \frac{1}{h_s r}\frac{\partial}{\partial r}(h_s r u_s u_r) + \frac{1}{h_s r}\frac{\partial}{\partial \theta}(h_s u_s u_\theta)$$

$$+\frac{\kappa \sin(\theta - \tau s)}{h_s}u_s u_r + \frac{\kappa \cos(\theta - \tau s)}{h_s}u_s u_\theta = -\frac{1}{h_s}\frac{\partial p}{\partial s}$$

$$+\frac{1}{\mathrm{Re}_\tau}\left[\frac{2}{h_s}\frac{\partial}{\partial s}\left(\frac{1}{h_s}\left(\frac{\partial u_s}{\partial s} + \kappa \sin(\theta - \tau s)u_r + \kappa \cos(\theta - \tau s)u_\theta\right)\right)\right.$$

$$+\frac{1}{h_s r}\frac{\partial}{\partial r}\left(h_s h_s r\frac{\partial}{\partial r}\left(\frac{u_s}{h_s}\right) + r\frac{\partial u_r}{\partial s}\right)$$

$$+\frac{1}{h_s r}\frac{\partial}{\partial \theta}\left(\frac{h_s h_s}{r}\frac{\partial}{\partial \theta}\left(\frac{u_s}{h_s}\right) + \frac{\partial u_\theta}{\partial s}\right)$$

$$+\kappa \sin(\theta - \tau s)\left(\frac{\partial}{\partial r}\left(\frac{u_s}{h_s}\right) + \frac{1}{h_s h_s}\frac{\partial u_r}{\partial s}\right)$$

$$\left.+\kappa \cos(\theta - \tau s)\left(\frac{1}{r}\frac{\partial}{\partial \theta}\left(\frac{u_s}{h_s}\right) + \frac{1}{h_s h_s}\frac{\partial u_\theta}{\partial s}\right)\right] \tag{6}$$

_r_-momentum:

$$\frac{\partial u_r}{\partial t} + \frac{1}{h_s}\frac{\partial}{\partial s}(u_s u_r) + \frac{1}{h_s r}\frac{\partial}{\partial r}(h_s r u_r u_r) + \frac{1}{h_s r}\frac{\partial}{\partial \theta}(h_s u_r u_\theta)$$

$$-\frac{\kappa \sin(\theta - \tau s)}{h_s}u_s u_s - \frac{u_\theta u_\theta}{r} = -\frac{\partial p}{\partial r}$$

$$+\frac{1}{\mathrm{Re}_\tau}\left[\frac{1}{h_s}\frac{\partial}{\partial s}\left(h_s\frac{\partial}{\partial r}\left(\frac{u_s}{h_s}\right) + \frac{1}{h_s}\frac{\partial u_r}{\partial s}\right)\right.$$

$$+\frac{2}{h_s r}\frac{\partial}{\partial r}\left(h_s r\frac{\partial u_r}{\partial r}\right) + \frac{1}{h_s}\frac{\partial}{\partial \theta}\left(h_s\left(\frac{1}{rr}\frac{\partial u_r}{\partial \theta} + \frac{\partial}{\partial r}\left(\frac{u_\theta}{r}\right)\right)\right)$$

$$-\frac{2\kappa \sin(\theta - \tau s)}{h_s h_s}\left(\frac{\partial u_s}{\partial s} + \kappa \sin(\theta - \tau s)u_r + \kappa \cos(\theta - \tau s)u_\theta\right)$$

$$\left.-\frac{2}{rr}\left(\frac{\partial u_\theta}{\partial \theta} + u_r\right)\right] \tag{7}$$

θ-momentum:

$$
\frac{\partial u_\theta}{\partial t} + \frac{1}{h_s} \frac{\partial}{\partial s} (u_s u_\theta) + \frac{1}{h_s r} \frac{\partial}{\partial r} (h_s r u_r u_\theta) + \frac{1}{h_s r} \frac{\partial}{\partial \theta} (h_s u_\theta u_\theta)
$$

$$
- \frac{\kappa \cos(\theta - \tau s)}{h_s} u_s u_s + \frac{1}{r} u_r u_\theta = -\frac{1}{r} \frac{\partial p}{\partial \theta}
$$

$$
+ \frac{1}{\mathrm{Re}_\tau} \left[\frac{1}{h_s} \frac{\partial}{\partial s} \left(\frac{h_s}{r} \frac{\partial}{\partial \theta} \left(\frac{u_s}{h_s} \right) + \frac{1}{h_s} \frac{\partial u_\theta}{\partial s} \right) \right.
$$

$$
+ \frac{1}{h_s r} \frac{\partial}{\partial r} \left(h_s \left(\frac{\partial u_r}{\partial \theta} + rr \frac{\partial}{\partial r} \left(\frac{u_\theta}{r} \right) \right) \right)
$$

$$
+ \frac{2}{h_s r r} \frac{\partial}{\partial \theta} \left(h_s \left(\frac{\partial u_\theta}{\partial \theta} + u_r \right) \right)
$$

$$
- \frac{2\kappa \cos(\theta - \tau s)}{h_s h_s} \left(\frac{\partial u_s}{\partial s} + \kappa \sin(\theta - \tau s) u_r + \kappa \cos(\theta - \tau s) u_\theta \right)
$$

$$
\left. + \left(\frac{1}{rr} \frac{\partial u_r}{\partial \theta} + \frac{\partial}{\partial r} \left(\frac{u_\theta}{r} \right) \right) \right] \tag{8}
$$

They are written in dimensionless form. The pipe radius R, the mean friction velocity u_τ and the time $t_{ref} = R/u_\tau$ are used as scaling variables. The dimensionless mass density is set to 1. The mean friction velocity is defined as the square root of the mean wall shear stress as follows:

$$
u_\tau = \sqrt{\frac{\tau_{w,m}}{\rho}}, \qquad \tau_{w,m} = \frac{1}{2\pi} \int_{\theta=0}^{2\pi} \tau_w(\theta) \, d\theta \tag{9}
$$

The dimensionless curvature $\kappa = R\kappa'$ and torsion $\tau = R\tau'$ are nondimensionalized by the pipe radius R. The Reynolds, Dean and Germano numbers based on these scaling quantities are:

$$
\mathrm{Re}_\tau = \frac{R u_\tau}{\nu}, \qquad \mathrm{De}_\tau = \sqrt{\kappa} \mathrm{Re}_\tau, \qquad \mathrm{Gn}_\tau = \tau \mathrm{Re}_\tau \tag{10}
$$

3 Numerical method and boundary conditions

A finite volume method on staggered grids is used to discretize the spatial derivatives and source terms in the governing equations. It leads to central differences of second order accuracy for the mass and momentum fluxes across the cell faces. A semi-implicit time-integration scheme treats all those convection and diffusion terms implicitly which contain derivatives in θ-direction. The remaining convection terms are integrated in time with a second order accurate leapfrog-step. An averaging step all the 50 time steps avoids possible $2\Delta t$-oscillations. Diffusive terms with derivatives in s- and r-directions are treated with a first-order Euler backward step. The size of the time step is selected according to a linear stability argument. The use of a projection step leads to a 3D Poisson problem for the pressure correction, which is solved by a Conjugate Gradient method for unsymmetric matrices.

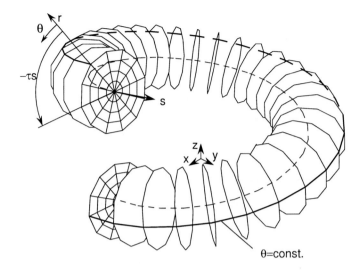

Fig. 4. Visualisation of the rotation of the (θ,r)-coordinate system along the axis.

Boundary conditions are required for all boundaries of the computational domain. At the walls impermeability and no-slip boundary conditions are realized. Velocity components which are needed on the pipe axis, are obtained by interpolation across the axis. In the circumferential direction all variables are periodic by definition. In axial direction periodic boundary conditions are used, too. For helically coiled pipes the rotation of the coordinate system along the pipe axis must be taken into account and the perfect matching of the cells at the in- and out-flow boundaries must be ensured by choosing a suitable combination of axial length and number of grid points in θ-direction (see fig. 4).

The flow is driven in the axial direction by means of a pressure gradient $\Delta P/\Delta s$, which must balance the viscous friction along the pipe wall.

4   Computational details

4.1   Configuration

On order to analyse the influence of curvature κ and torsion τ on turbulence several pipe configurations are computed for the same Reynolds numbers: one straight pipe DP, two toroidal pipes DT, $DTSC$ and five helically coiled pipes DH, $DHSC$, DKH, $DXXH$. The toroidal case DT has also been computed by Boersma and Nieuwstadt [5,6]. It is planned to take their results for comparison.

Table 1. Geometrical parameters of the pipe configurations:

key word	κ	τ	r_a	p_s	h_g	n_{ovl}
DP	0.0	0.0	0.0	0.0	0.0	0
DT	0.1	0.0	10.0	0.0	0.0	0
DTSC	0.01	0.0	100.0	0.0	0.0	0
DH	0.1	0.055	7.678	4.223	26.53	24
DHSC	0.01	0.006875	67.90	46.68	293.3	3
DKH	0.1	0.0275	9.297	2.557	16.06	12
DXH	0.1	0.11	4.525	4.977	31.27	48
DXXH	0.1	0.165	2.686	4.433	27.85	72

The Reynolds number Re_τ based on friction velocity and pipe radius has been taken as 230 for all cases. Therefore the Reynolds number $Re_b = 2u_b R/\nu$, based on bulk velocity u_b and pipe diameter $2R$, varies between 5588 and 6891, see table 2.

Table 2. Flow parameters of the flow simulations:

key word	Re_τ	Re_b	De_τ	De_b	Gn_τ	Gn_b
DP	230.0	6820	0.0	0.0	0.0	0.0
DT	230.0	5632	72.73	1780	0.0	0.0
DTSC	230.0	6931	23.00	693	0.0	0.0
DH	230.0	5625	72.73	1779	12.65	309.0
DHSC	230.0	6891	23.00	689	1.58	47.4
DKH	230.0	5601	72.73	1771	6.325	154.0
DXH	230.0	5613	72.73	1775	25.3	617.0
DXXH	230.0	5588	72.73	1767	37.95	922.0

The Dean number De_b and Germano number Gn_b built with this Reynolds number Re_b are

$$\mathrm{De}_b = \sqrt{\kappa}\mathrm{Re}_b, \tag{11}$$

$$\mathrm{Gn}_b = \tau\mathrm{Re}_b. \tag{12}$$

For each flow case the Dean numbers and Germano numbers can be seen in table 2. For helical pipe flow the length of the computational domain Δl_s along the axial coordinate s has to satisfy the condition

$$\Delta l_s = n_{ovl} \cdot \frac{2\pi}{n_\theta \tau} \quad , \qquad n_{ovl} = 1, 2, 3, \ldots \tag{13}$$

in order to fulfil the cell matching. When using periodical boundary conditions in axial direction, the computational domain Δl_s must be long enough to ensure correct two-point correlations and has therefore been taken to be 15.23, normalized with the pipe radius. The number of overlapping meshes n_{ovl} for the calculated cases can be seen in table 1. For all simulations the same length of the computational domain and the same number of grid points have been taken. The grid has $n_s = 256$, $n_\theta = 180$ and $n_r = 70$ points in axial, circumferential and radial direction, respectively. The grid is equidistant in s- and θ-directions. In the wall-normal radial direction, close to the wall a clustering of grid points is achieved according to

$$\frac{r_k}{R} = \frac{\tanh(\gamma k)}{\tanh(\gamma n_r)}, \quad k = 1, 2, 3, \ldots, n_r \quad , \quad \gamma = 0.0210604 \qquad (14)$$

The distribution ensures that 5 points are below $z^+ = (R - r)^+ = 5$ and that the first point is located below $z^+ = (R - r)^+ = 1$. Further parameters of the numerical grid can be seen in table 3.

Table 3. Parameters of the numerical grids used (for $\kappa = \tau = 0$):

i	Δl_i	n_i	Δi^+_{min}	Δi^+_{max}
s	15.23196	256	13.7	13.7
θ	2π	180	0.094	8.01
r	1.0	70	1.038	5.38

The simulation were started from a turbulent 3D data set for straight pipe flow of $\mathrm{Re}_\tau = 180$.

4.2   Computational costs

Due to the physics of turbulence, a big number of grid points is needed in the whole computational domain to resolve the smallest spatial scales which are at the order of the Kolmogoroff micro scale:

$$l_K = \left(\frac{\nu^3}{\epsilon}\right)^{\frac{1}{4}} \qquad (15)$$

Here, ϵ and ν is the dissipation rate and the kinematic viscosity, respectively. This leads to high requirements of computing memory, computational time and disk and archive space. A DNS with $3.4 \cdot 10^6$ grid points and the minimal number of 7 words per grid point for the pressure and two time levels of the velocity vector needs 24 MWords memory (CPU) and 110 MByte for each in- and output data file. For the statistical evaluation without homogeneous direction about 1000 output files have to be stored on disk or archive and 110 GByte space is needed there. In order to get 1000 statistical independent samples, about 210 dimensionless time units have to be calculated and when using a direct Poisson solver about 125 000 seconds (35 h) of CPU-time (at 900 MFlop/s) are necessary.

For helical pipe flow, a direct solver can not be used and a iterative solver is needed. The simulation code HELIX uses a conjugate gradient method (CGS or BICGSTAB) where auxiliary arrays are needed and therefore more memory is required. (21 words per grid point; 600 MByte for $3.4 \cdot 10^6$ grid points). The iterative solver needs about 50-500 times more CPU-time depending on the accuracy of the pressure solution. Fortunately the axial direction is a homogeneous direction and can be used for building the statistics and a lower number of samples is needed then. The simulation code HELIX is not parallelized but it is well vectorized with 900 MFlop/s on a VPP700.

A high performance vector computer is necessary for the computations. After the development of the code, HELIX was tested, vectorized and optimized on the Fujitsu VPP500 at HRZ, Darmstadt, on the Cray-YMP8 at the Leibniz Rechenzentrum, München (LRZ), (see [15]), and on the Cray T94 (only 4 processors) which was installed in summer 1996 at the LRZ. Right after successfully testing the code with laminar flow simulations [17,18] a new Fujitsu VPP700 was installed at LRZ in spring 1997. The 52 powerful processors with up to 1800 MByte memory and the big amount of disc space, due to the use of cheaper disc-technology than on the Cray T94, made it possible to start all the simulations there. At LRZ the archive and backup system ADSM is big enough to store all the samples for statistical evaluation.

One alternative computer to perform the direct numerical simulations is the NEC SX-4/32 installed at HLRS, Stuttgart. In 1997 when the simulations of helical pipe flow started, the use of CPU-time and disc space was already restricted on the NEC and unrestricted on the Fujitsu VPP700. As the data files are needed in Munich for post-processing, it would have been necessary to transfer the files from Stuttgart to Munich. The low capacity of the data net and the low transfer rate due to a firewall technique at HLRS, Stuttgart, made the decision easy to use the VPP700 firstly. In 1998 it is intended to transfer the code to the NEC in order to test the performance of the code. It is also intended to test the data net between Munich (Garching) and Stuttgart in order to help to improve the network technology. Then it will be easier to perform direct numerical simulations at HLRS, Stuttgart and transfer the data to Munich. At the moment, the discretized and programmed flow equations of toroidal pipe flow are implemented in the parallelized DNS-code MGLET which performs DNS at the Cray T3E at HLRS. In future it will also be possible to use this kind of high performance computers to predict turbulent flow in curved pipes or pipe systems with straight and curved pipes.

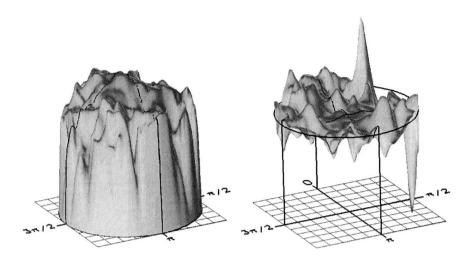

Fig. 5. Surface profiles of the axial velocity components u_s (left) and the pressure (right) for straight pipe flow (case DP).

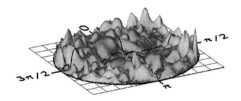

Fig. 6. Surface profile of $u_p = \sqrt{u_\theta^2 + u_r^2}$ for straight pipe flow (case DP).

5 Numerical Results

Although the evaluation of turbulent data sets obtained by Direct Numerical Simulations is mostly done by means of statistical methods, it can also be very instructive to examine the turbulent data fields itself. In order to visualize the flow, surface profiles of the axial velocity u_s, the pressure p and the intensity of the flow perpendicular to the axial velocity $u_p = \sqrt{u_\theta^2 + u_r^2}$ are shown over a cross section of a straight pipe (case DP), a curved pipe (case DT) and a helically coiled pipe (case DH). For the straight pipe, the circumferential position is unimportant, but for the toroidal or helical pipe it is necessary to know that $\theta = 0$, $\pi/2$, π and $3\pi/2$ are the upper, outer, lower and inner position of the cross section respectively.

The axial velocity profile of the straight pipe flow shows that over a mean profile geometrical small structures of high intensity are superposed, see fig. 5. The structures have different sizes and they are distributed over the whole

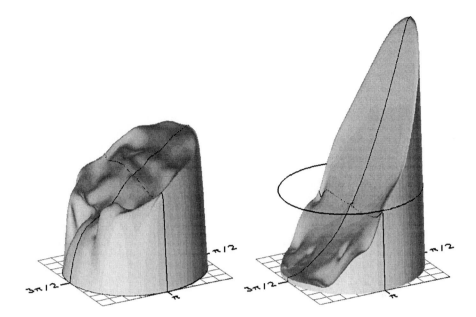

Fig. 7. Surface profiles of the axial velocity components u_s (left) and the pressure (right) for curved pipe flow (case DT).

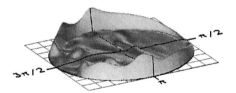

Fig. 8. Surface profile of $u_p = \sqrt{u_\theta^2 + u_r^2}$ for curved pipe flow (case DT).

cross section. The pressure distribution also shows peaks of different size distributed over the whole cross section. There some extremely high peaks can appear. The circle around the pressure distribution denotes the local pressure niveau of the cross section. Its absolute value is unimportant for incompressible flow, but it can be seen that positive peaks look like negative peaks. The flow perpendicular to the axial velocity is visualized in figure 6 for straight pipe flow. The same scale was used for all surface plots of velocities. It can easily be seen that the axial velocity is much higher than both velocity components in a cross section. The fluctuations in axial direction are higher, too, and it seems that the geometrical size of the structures are smaller in figure 6.

The flow in a toroidal pipe is completely different to that in straight pipes. As it is known for laminar flow, the maximum axial velocity is driven out-

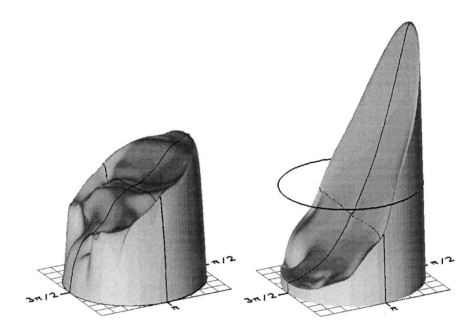

Fig. 9. Surface profiles of the axial velocity components u_s (left) and the pressure (right) for helical pipe flow (case DH).

Fig. 10. Surface profile of $u_p = \sqrt{u_\theta^2 + u_r^2}$ for helical pipe flow (case DH).

wards to the outer wall due to centrifugal effects, see fig. 7. The big peaks and structures can not be seen any more. Only some smaller hills with relatively big geometrical diameter are superposed. Like for laminar flow, a pressure distribution in a cross section occurs with higher pressure at the outer and lower pressure at the inner side of the cross section. The big peaks of the straight pipe flow do not appear any more. At the inner wall two pressure minima can be seen. They are at the center of the recirculation cells. The intensity of the cross section flow u_p is very low and only near the upper and lower wall the secondary motion has a remarkable effect, see fig. 8. There the fluid is driven backwards to the inner side of the pipe, while in the core region of the pipe the flow is driven outwards. This effect can also be seen in the axial velocity profile, where fluid with a higher axial velocity component is near the upper and lower wall convected to the inner side of the pipe. Then it reaches the two recirculation cells where it is driven back to the core region. The flow near the inner wall has a very low axial velocity component and its movement to the outer wall due to the lower secondary motion in this region is very slow. The comparison of the straight pipe flow with the toroidal pipe flow shows that turbulence is extremely damped and the flow almost relaminarizes, although the same Reynolds number Re_τ has been taken for all cases.

In the case of laminar flow, the flow patterns show big torsion effects if the parameters curvature and torsion are of the same order. In opposite to the laminar flow case turbulent flow through helically coiled pipes does not show significant differences to the turbulent curved pipe flow, as far as it can be seen from instantaneous flow fields, see fig. 9, 10. Nevertheless the symmetry of the flow patterns of curved pipe flow is slightly destroyed and it is assumed that further differences will be found if the statistical evaluation has been done.

6   Conclusions

In order to predict the turbulent flow in straight, curved and helically coiled pipes a finite volume code was developed that integrates the incompressible Navier-Stokes equations in an orthogonal helical coordinate system. Several flow configurations were simulated and compared. The movement of the position of maximum axial velocity to the outer wall due to centrifugal forces and the only small influence of torsion was shown by surface profiles of instantaneous velocity fields. The origin of secondary flow motions with two recirculation cells due to curvature effects and the appearance of a pressure distribution in a cross section is shown, too.

As a next step statistical evaluation is envisaged with the aim of studying the statistical moments and the correlations and spetral functions.

References

1. ADLER, M. - Strömung in gekrümmten Rohren, Zeitschrift für angewandte Mathematik und Mechanik, 14: 257-275 (1934).
2. BERGER, S.A., TALBOT, L. and YAO, L.-S. - Flow in curved pipes, Annual Review of Fluid Mechanics, 15, 461-512 (1983).
3. BOERSMA, B.J. and NIEUWSTADT, F.T.M. - Large Eddy simulation of turbulent flow in a curved pipe, In: Tenth symposium on turbulent shear flows, The Pennsylvania State University, 1, Poster Session 1, P1-19 - P1-24 (1995).
4. BOERSMA, B.J. and NIEUWSTADT, F.T.M. - Large-Eddy Simulation of Turbulent Flow in a Curved Pipe, Transaction of the ASME, Journal of Fluids Engineering, vol. 118, pp. 248 - 254 (1996).

5. BOERSMA, B.J. and NIEUWSTADT, F.T.M. - Non-Unique Solutions in Turbulent Curved Pipe Flow, In: J.-P. Chollet et al. (eds.), Direct and Large-Eddy Simulation II, Kluwer Academic Publishers, pp. 257-266, (1997).

6. BOERSMA, B.J. - Electromagnetic effects in cylindrical pipe flow, phd-thesis, Delft University Press, (1997).

7. DEAN, W. R. - Note on the Motion of Fluid in a Curved Pipe, Philosophical Magazine, Series 7, 4 (20) 208-223 (1927).

8. DEAN, W. R. - The Stream-line Motion of Fluid in a Curved Pipe, Philosophical Magazine, Series 7, 5 (30) 673-695 (1928).

9. EGGELS, J.G.M. - Direct and Large Eddy Simulation of Turbulent flow in a Cylindrical pipe geometry, PhD Thesis Delft University of Technology, Delft, The Netherlands (1994).

10. EGGELS, J.G.M., UNGER, F., WEISS, M.H., WESTERWEEL, J., ADRIAN, R.J., FRIEDRICH, R. and NIEUWSTADT, F.T.M. - Fully developed turbulent pipe flow: a comparison between direct numerical simulation and experiment. J. Fluid Mech. 268, 175-209 (1994).

11. EUSTICE, J. - Flow of Water in Curved Pipes, Proc. R. Soc. London Ser. A, 84: 107-118 (1910).

12. EUSTICE, J. - Experiments on Stream-line Motion in Curved Pipes, Proc. R. Soc. London Ser. A, 85: 119-131 (1911).

13. GERMANO, M. - On the effect of torsion on a helical pipe flow., J. Fluid Mech., vol. 125, pp. 1-8 (1982).

14. GERMANO, M. - The Dean equations extended to a helical pipe flow., J. Fluid Mech., vol. 203, pp. 289-305 (1989).

15. HÜTTL, T.J. and FRIEDRICH, R. - Numerische Simulation laminarer und turbulenter Strömungen in gekrümmten und tordierten Rohren - In: Overview of Research Projects on the Cray Y-MP at the Leibniz-Rechenzentrum München, LRZ-Bericht Nr. 9601, pp. 195-200.

16. HÜTTL, T.J. - Simulationsprogramm HELIX: Ein Finite-Volumen Verfahren zur Lösung der inkompressiblen 3D-Navier-Stokes Gleichungen für Rohrgeometrien mit Krümmung und Torsion, Lehrstuhl für Fluidmechanik, TU München, Bericht TUM-FLM-96/29 (1996).

17. HÜTTL, T.J. and FRIEDRICH, R. - Fully Developed Laminar Flow in Curved or Helically Coiled Pipes. -In: Jahrbuch 1997 der Deutschen Gesellschaft für Luft- und Raumfahrt - Lilientahl - Oberth e.V. (DGLR), Tagungsband "Deutscher Luft- u. Raumfahrtkongress 1997, DGLR-Jahrestagung, 14. - 17. Okt. in München", Band 2, DGLR-JT97-181, pp. 1203-1210 (1997).

18. HÜTTL, T.J., WAGNER, C. and FRIEDRICH, R. - Navier Stokes Solutions of Laminar Flows Based on Orthogonal Helical Coordinates -In: Numerical methods in laminar and turbulent flow, C. Taylor, J. Cross (eds.), Pineridge Press, Swansea UK, Vol. 10, pp. 191-202 (1997).

19. ITO, H. - Flow in Curved Pipes, JSME International Journal, 30 (262) 543-552 (1987).

20. LIU, S. and MASLIYAH, J.H. - Axially invariant laminar flow in helical pipes with a finite pitch, J. Fluid Mech., 251: 315-353 (1993).

21. UNGER, F. - Numerische Simulation turbulenter Rohrströmungen, phd-thesis, Technische Univerität München (1994).

22. WAGNER, C. - Direkte numerische Simulation turbulenter Strömungen in einer Rohrerweiterung, PhD Thesis, Technische Univerität München (1995).

23. WANG, C.Y. - On the low-Reynolds-number flow in a helical pipe, J. Fluid Mech., vol. 108, pp. 185-194 (1981).

24. WILLIAMS, G. S., HUBBELL, C. W. and FENKELL, G. H. - Experiments at Detroit, Mich., on the effect of curvature upon the flow of water in pipes, Trans. ASCE, 47:1-196 (1902).

Parallelization of the CFD Code KAPPA for Distributed Memory Computers

Dieke Hafermann

Institute for Fluid Mechanics, University of Karlsruhe, Kaiserstr. 12, 76128 Karlsruhe, Germany

Abstract. This paper presents the parallelization of a multi-block finite-volume CFD code. A simple static computational and communicational load balancing algorithm is proposed and implemented. Measurements on an IBM RS/6000 SP System using up to 128 processors are presented for different application examples and compared to a performance model.

1   Introduction

The code considered here is a 3-D block structured finite-volume cell-centered scheme with an explicit Runge-Kutta type integration in time, developed at the University of Karlsruhe, named KAPPA [4]. The convergence to steady state calculations is accelerated by a full multigrid method and an implicit residual averaging technique [3]. The original artificial dissipation scheme as well as the SLIP and USLIP schemes and the AUSM-scheme are implemented in the code[2]. Several turbulence models ranging from the simple mixing length model of Baldwin/Lomax to linear eddy viscosity two-equation models and non-linear eddy viscosity models are implemented. The application areas of the code are aerospace, automotive, chemical engineering and other industrial research areas.

2   Parallelization Approach

The parallelization approach presented here aims at parallel computers with ten up to some hundred processors with shared and distributed memory. Therefore Message Passage was chosen as the programming model for good performance and portability on both architectures. MPI was used as parallelization interface. The parallelization was realized using the Single Program Multiple Data (SPMD) approach. The serial version of the program results by setting the number of processes to one.

The idea of the parallelization is to make use of the block structure of the computational domain: the parallel processes behave like the original serial version working on a smaller subset of blocks. This approach requires a minimal change to the original design of the code and saves the invested development time. The number of parallel tasks scales with the problem size since more blocks are to be expected for bigger problems. To increase the number of blocks a block splitting algorithm is implemented.

The parallelization affects the program in three areas: input and output, update of the data at the block interfaces and the calculation of global values e.g. body forces

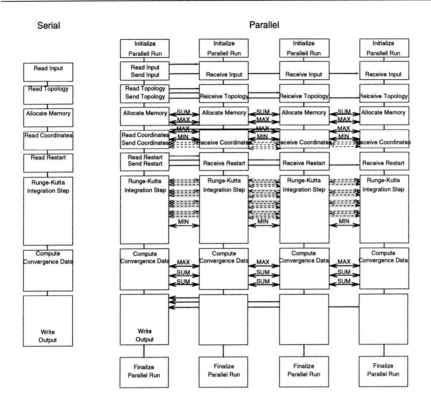

Fig. 1. Comparison between the serial and parallel Version of the Code

and residual values. The update of the block interfaces is the most crucial part for the parallel performance of the program.

Figure 1 shows the differences between the serial and parallel version: at the beginning of the computation every block is assigned to one process. The strategy for input and output must fulfill the requirement that the files are independent of the distribution of blocks onto the processes. Only part of the data contained in the files is needed on the respective processes. One of the processes is selected as master process which reads the input and distributes the relevant data to the other processes and collects and writes the output to disk.

One iteration step consists of several Runge-Kutta stages. During each iteration step data has to be exchanged at the block interfaces after each update of the solution vector. In the serial version and in the case of blocks on the same process a copy operation is performed. This copy procedure has to be replaced by an exchange by message passing for the parallel case if adjacent blocks do not belong to the same process. This operation is marked in the diagram by the dashed arrows on grey background.

At the end of an iteration step the convergence data and the resulting forces are calculated. For this calculation global reduction operations (sum and maximum) have to be performed.

To produce the output files the master process receives the data for all blocks from the respective processes and writes them to disk.

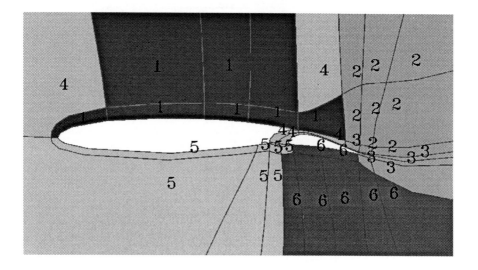

Fig. 2. Example of block distribution onto processes

For a good parallel performance the computational as well as the communicational load must be balanced. For the optimization only the data exchange of the block interfaces is taken into account. The size of the data exchange is proportional to the number of computational cells at the block interface.

The balancing step is divided into two parts. The first part is devoted to distribute the load and to minimize the overall communication between the processes. The aim of the second part is to achieve a maximum of concurrency in the communication between the distributed blocks.

The distribution phase makes use of the topology of the blocks which are considered as nodes connected by graphs. The distance between the nodes denotes the inverse of the amount of data to be transmitted between the blocks. Using a shortest path algorithm which can also be easily parallelized [1], the "distances" between all blocks can be calculated and stored in a communication matrix.

The optimum computational load per process is calculated by dividing the total load by the number of processes. This value is taken as the initial value for the maximum allowed computational load in the distribution procedure.

Examining the communication matrix, one of the two most "distant" blocks is chosen and assigned to one process. All remaining blocks are taken in the order

of their "proximity" to this block and are added to this process if the new load
of the process does not exceed the maximum allowed computational load. This
procedure is repeated for the other processes and the remaining blocks. If all blocks
are distributed the first part is finished otherwise the whole distribution procedure
is repeated with an increased allowed computational load. An example of the block
distribution for six processes resulting from this this procedure is shown for the
region around an airfoil with a flap in figure 2. The distribution achieved by this
rather simple approach is fairly satisfactory.

After the block assignment the resulting communication requirements between
the processes are determined. To save message startup times, all block interface
exchanges between two processes are collected into one message. The data exchange
is organized in substeps, in which every processor either communicates with one of
the other processes or copies data of internal boundaries or pauses.

To achieve a good concurrency in communication the messages are sorted by
size. The internal copying is treated as a message with a smaller weight. Starting
with the largest message, the messages are distributed to the subtasks in a way which
ensures that every process sends and receives data only to or from one process per
substep. Care is taken to minimize the number of substeps. The communication
order is stored for further reference. The data exchange itself is implemented by
executing one simultaneous MPI_SENDRECEIVE-operation per substep.

3   Performance Results

Performance measurements with the parallelized code were executed on the IBM
RS/6000 SP system at the Scientific Supercomputing Center (SSC) Karlsruhe. Up to
128 thin P2SC nodes were employed using the MPI implementation of the parallel
operating environment (POE). Two different 3D test cases are considered. The first

No	case	cells	blocks	$N_{P,min}$	$N_{P,max}$	$t_{ex,min}$	$t_{ex,max}$
1	ONERA M6	92160	30	1	30	2060 s	80 s
2	DNS coarse grid	265000	64	1	64	2108 s	45 s
3	DNS fine grid	2090000	64	4	64	3547 s	255 s
4	DNS fine grid	2090000	512	8	128	2110 s	173 s

Table 1. Test cases for the performance measurements

test case is a steady state calculation of the flow around an ONERA M6 wing with
an irregular block topology, the second is a direct numerical simulation (DNS) of a
mixing layer with a regular block connectivity. The direct numerical simulation was
performed on a coarser and a finer grid level and using different numbers of blocks to
enable the calculation on a greater number of processors. For each case the blocks are
of the same size. For memory allocation reasons the minimum number of processors

were 4 and 8 for the 64 and 512 block DNS fine grid case, respectively. In this cases the calculations with the minimum number were used for the normalization. The precise specifications of the test cases can be found in table 1. The time used for 100 iteration steps is measured. Typically, several thousands iterations are necessary.

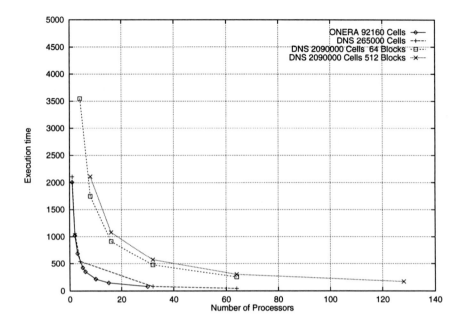

Fig. 3. Execution time as function of processor number

Figure 3 shows the execution time as a function of the number of processors. For all test cases a considerable decrease in the execution time can be observed. The minimum and maximum execution times are given in table 1. The penalty for the additional overhead for smaller block sizes can be seen by comparing the results of the 64 and 512 block cases for an identical number of processes. The increase in execution time by approximately 15 percent results from the additional computation and communication load. Comparing the result for the 64 processor run with 64 blocks and the 128 processor run with 512 blocks a speedup of 1.47 it still achievable.

Figure 4 presents the parallel efficiency of the calculations. For a small number of processes, nearly ideal efficiencies close to one are achieved. The measurements show an 85 percent efficiency for the 30 processor ONERA and the 64 processor fine mesh DNS calculations. The slightly smaller efficiency of the coarse mesh DNS simulation compared to the ONERA test case is again a result of the relatively smaller block sizes. The 512 block DNS case running on 128 processors gives an efficiency

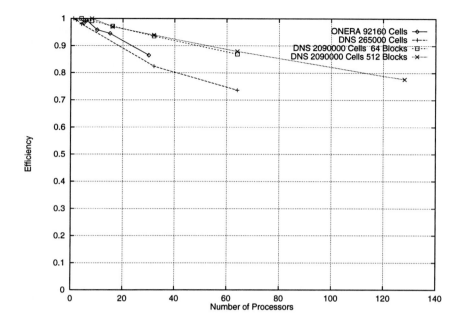

Fig. 4. Parallel efficiency as function of the processor number

of 78 percent normalized by the 8 processor run. Taking into account an efficiency loss between a hypothetical serial run and the 8 processor run, an efficiency of 70 to 75 percent would be realistic.

The speedup in figure 5 presents another view of the same behavior: up to about 10 to 20 processors nearly ideal parallelization results for the ONERA and the fine mesh DNS test case are achieved. A speedup of 100 for the 128 processor DNS calculation demonstrates the high potential of the code for large problems.

4   Performance Analysis

To analyze the run time behavior of the message-passing program and to develop a performance model, the tool Vampir[5] was used to analyze post-mortem trace-files. Using the communication statistics tool of the program a data transmission rate ranging from 3 MB/s to 40 MB/s for the send-receive operations with message sizes varying from 112 KB to 160 KB is found. For comparison: the transfer rate measured for a ping-pong data exchange using MPI_SENDRECEIVE is about 80 MB/s for this message sizes. The timeline view reveals that part of the smaller transmission rate is caused by data-copying in and out of the message buffer. During the copy operation the send-receive is not able to complete. This points to a further potential for the optimization by accessing the data directly with the derived data types and and the nonblocking communication operations of MPI. The global chartview tool of

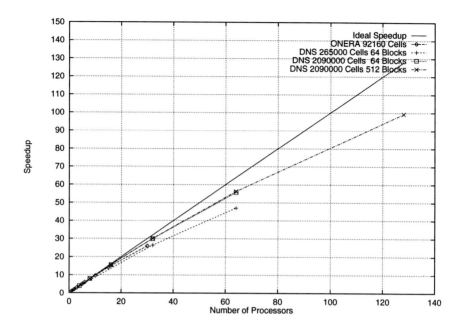

Fig. 5. Speedup as function of processor number

Vampir shows an parallel utilization of 95 to 97 percent for one iteration step, which corresponds to the measurements mentioned above.

This data is used to model the execution time t_s as a function of the number of processors N_P for the DNS calculation.

The serial computation time per iteration t_{cpu} is taken from the serial measurements. It is $21s$ for the coarse grid, $132s$ and $147s$ for the 64 and 512 block fine grid case, respectively. The communication time t_{comm} is assumed to be

$$t_{comm} = t_s + t_w \cdot L. \tag{1}$$

The startup time t_s is assumed to be $40\mu s$, the transfer time t_w for one byte is estimated on the basis of the analysis to be $0.1\mu s$. The message length L can be calculated from the topological information for the different number of processors.

During one iteration step with four (N_{stage}) Runge-Kutta stages, four exchanges and three global reduction operations are necessary. The time for three global reduction operations is

$$t_{gl} = 3 \log_2(N_P)(t_s + 20t_w), \tag{2}$$

the time for exchanging two ghost cell layers with five double precision field values is

$$t_{exch} = N_{stage}(t_s + 2 \cdot 5 \cdot 8Lt_w). \tag{3}$$

The parallel execution time is the sum of the time for the computation, the block exchange and the global reduction multiplied by the number of iterations N_{it}:

$$t_{ex} = N_{it}\left(\frac{t_{cpu}}{N_P} + t_{exch} + t_{gl}\right).$$ (4)

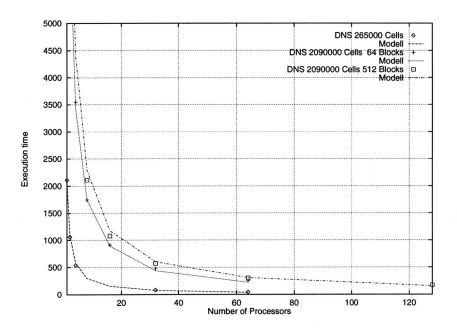

Fig. 6. Comparison of predicted and measured execution time

Figure 6 illustrates the model applied to the DNS test cases. The symbols denote the measured results, the modeled values are represented by lines. The predicted values compare well with the observed performance. The extrapolation of the model for up to 512 processors shows a slight increase in efficiency to 70 percent due to the smaller number and size of the messages to be exchanged: in the 512 processor case, every process handles one block and exchanges six faces with six neighboring processes. Keeping in mind that the performance model presented here is rather simple and the nonlinear communication behavior is not taken into account, the results, however, demonstrate that it is possible to calculate problems of the size of the DNS calculation efficiently with several hundred processors on todays parallel computers. The scalability for a fixed problem size is very good, provided that the size is big enough. The observations are encouraging the use of the parallelized code for solving larger problems on large parallel computers.

5   Conclusion and Outlook

The performance measurements presented in this article show encouraging results. Good performance is achieved for processor numbers up to 128 processors for realistic applications. The analysis results suggest a certain potential for the improvement of the block exchange performance by replacing the send-receive operations with the nonblocking communication and the use of derived data types of the MPI standard.

Further improvement of the code will be done by implementing the parallel input and output of the MPI-2 standard, when available. This will lead to a full SPMD-code and reduce the I/O-requirements which are of particular interest for the visualization of transient processes and larger grid sizes.

References

1. Foster I.: Designing and Building Parallel Programs. Addison-Wesley, New-York 1995.
2. Jameson, A., Schmidt W., Turkel E.: Numerical Solution of the Euler equations by finite volume methods using Runge-Kutta time-stepping schemes. AIAA-paper 81-1259, 1981
3. Jameson, A.: Multigrid Algorithms for Compressible Flow Calculations. Technical Report 1743, MAE-Report, 1985
4. Magagnato, F.: KAPPA-Kompressibel 2.0. Technical Report 97/4 , Institut für Strömungslehre, 1997
5. Pallas GmbH: Vampir Homepage www.pallas.de/pages/vampir.htm

Numerical simulation of the fluid flow and the separation behaviour in a disc stack centrifuge

Uwe Janoske and Manfred Piesche[1]

University of Stuttgart, Institute for Mechanical Process Engineering,
Böblinger Straße 72, D-70199 Stuttgart, Germany

Abstract. The fluid flow and separation behaviour between conical rotating discs in a disc stack centrifuge is studied numerically using computational fluid dynamics. The fluid flow on the one hand is calculated by a Finite-Volume-Method while the separation behaviour is obtained with a Euler-Lagrange-Method. The results of the simulation are in good agreement with experimental data.

1 Introduction

Disc stack centrifuges are used for the separation of phases with different densitites, e. g. water and particles from marine fuel oil or cream from milk. Fig. 1 shows a centrifuge used for industrial purposes.

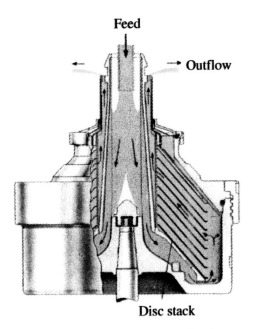

Fig. 1. Disc stack centrifuge [He1].

The suspension flows through the distributor into the rotating cylinder and the adjacent disc stack. The disc stack consists of 50-250 closely spaced corotating discs. The separation takes place due to the centrifugal forces and the difference in the densities. The lighter phase reaches the outlet while the heavier particles assemble at the inner wall of the cylinder. The fluid flow and the separation behaviour in one gap of the disc stack without caulks was examined by Janoske and Piesche [JP1]. A stability criterion was found to predict the transition from laminar to turbulent flow. The separation efficiency could be described by dimensionless parameters. These investigations are going to be extended to gaps with 6 and 18 caulks respectively. The present paper presents the fluid flow and the separation behaviour for laminar flow.

2   Mathematical Model

The geometrical configuration of the examined device is shown in Fig. 2. The suspension with volume flow $\dot{V}$ enters the computational domain at a radius r_a. The gap (width b) is inclined to the axis of rotation at an angle α. At a radius r_i the fluid exits the computational domain. In azimuthal direction the domain covers an angle β. A conical coordinate system (x, y, z) rotating with the discs at angular velocity ω is used for the mathematical modelling. The corresponding velocity components for the fluid and the particles are (u, v, w) and (u_p, v_p, w_p). The x-axis is inclined to the axis of rotation at an angle α. The z-axis is perpendicular to the x-axis. The distance from the axis of rotation is given by $r = x \sin \alpha + z \cos \alpha$.

The following assumptions and postulates were made to develop a well structured model and to limit the mathematical expenditure.

- Suspension flow with Newtonian properties and constant dynamic viscosity μ_f and density ρ_f of the fluid
- Stationary, laminar flow
- Spherical particles with diameter d_p and constant density ρ_p
- Mass concentration of particles $\ll 1$
- Negligible influence of gravity

Dimensionless parameters were obtained by dividing all variables with appropriate scaling quantities. The problem can be described by the following parameters:

- Reynolds number $Re = \dfrac{\rho_f\, b^2\, \omega}{\mu_f}$
- Dimensionless volume flow $Q = \dfrac{\dot{V}}{2\,\pi\,\omega\,b^3}$
- Stokes number $Sto = \dfrac{\rho_p\, d_p^2\, \omega}{\mu_f}$

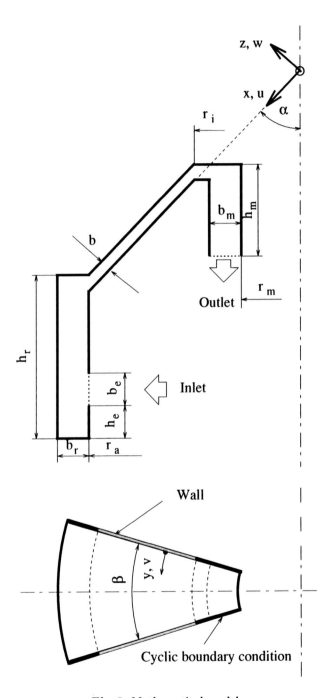

Fig. 2. Mathematical model.

– Ratio of densities $\Delta = \dfrac{\rho_p - \rho_f}{\rho_p}$

– Dimensionless outer radius $\Lambda = \dfrac{r_a}{b}$

– Angle of inclination α

– Angle in azimuthal direction β

– Further geometrical parameters which are kept constant during the calculations

The fluid velocities $\underline{V}$ and the pressure P are described by a mass balance (1) and a momentum balance (2). The trajectories of the particles $\underline{X}_p$ and the particle velocities $\underline{V}_p$ are predicted by integrating the force balance (3) on the particle, which is written in a Lagrangian reference frame.

mass balance

$$\underline{\nabla} \cdot \underline{V} = 0 \tag{1}$$

momentum balance

$$\frac{\partial \underline{V}}{\partial T} + Re\, \underline{\nabla} \cdot (\underline{V}\,\underline{V}) = -\underline{\nabla} P + \underline{\nabla} \cdot \left[(\underline{\nabla}\underline{V}) + (\underline{\nabla}\underline{V})^T \right]$$
$$+ Re\, \underline{\Omega} \times (\underline{\Omega} \times \underline{X}) + 2\,Re\,(\underline{\Omega} \times \underline{V}) \tag{2}$$

force balance on the particle

$$\left(\frac{d\underline{V}_p}{dT} \right)_{abs} = 18 \frac{Re}{Sto}\, (\underline{V}_f - \underline{V}_p) + \frac{1}{2}\,(1 - \Delta) \left(\frac{d\underline{V}_f}{dT} - \frac{d\underline{V}_p}{dT} \right)$$
$$- (1 - \Delta)\, \underline{\nabla} P \tag{3}$$

trajectory of the particle

$$\left(\frac{d\underline{X}_p}{dT} \right)_{abs} = Re\, \left(\underline{V}_p \right)_{abs} \tag{4}$$

The Equations (1)-(4) are solved with the CFD-Code FLUENT using a Finite-Volume-Method. The trajectory equations are solved by step-wise integration over discrete time steps.

Table 1 shows the boundary conditions which were used for the numerical simulation.

The separation efficiency gives the ratio of the particle mass in the effluent and the feed for a certain particle diameter d_p. After the calculation of the particle trajectories, the number of particles in the effluent z_f and the number of particles in the feed z_a is known for every particle diameter. The separation efficiency for a particle diameter d_p is given by:

	fluid phase	dispersed Phase
inlet	constant velocities $U_0 = Q\, B_e^{-1}\, \Lambda^{-2}$, $V_0 = 0,\ W_0 = 0$	particles homogeneously dispersed, no slip between particles and fluid
outlet	zero diffusion flux for $U,\ V,\ W$ overall mass balance	particles escape at outlet
wall	$U = 0,\ V = 0,\ W = 0$	reflection via elastic collision
side	cyclic boundary condition	cyclic boundary condition

Table 1. Boundary conditions for the numerical simulation.

$$T(d_p) = 1 - \frac{\overbrace{\dfrac{\pi}{6}\, \rho_p z_f d_p^3}^{m_f}}{\underbrace{\dfrac{\pi}{6}\, \rho_p z_a d_p^3}_{m_a}} = 1 - \frac{z_f}{z_a} \tag{5}$$

angle in azimuthal direction	$\beta = 20°$
heigth annulus	$H_m = \dfrac{h_m}{b}\dfrac{1}{\Lambda} = 0.15$
heigth cylinder	$H_r = \dfrac{h_r}{b}\dfrac{1}{\Lambda} = 0.5 + \dfrac{1}{\Lambda \sin \alpha}$
heigth inlet	$H_e = \dfrac{h_e}{b}\dfrac{1}{\Lambda} = 0.07$
width annulus	$B_m = \dfrac{b_m}{b}\dfrac{1}{\Lambda} = 0.04$
width cylinder	$B_r = \dfrac{b_r}{b}\dfrac{1}{\Lambda} = 0.04$
width inlet	$B_e = \dfrac{b_e}{b}\dfrac{1}{\Lambda} = 0.06$
radius annulus	$R_m = \dfrac{r_m}{b}\dfrac{1}{\Lambda} = 0.2$
inner radius	$R_i = \dfrac{r_i}{b}\dfrac{1}{\Lambda} = 0.3$

Table 2. Geometrical parameters for the numerical calculations.

3   Numerical Results

Figure 3 shows the dimensionless velocities U,V,W and the Pressure P for one slice of the gap at $X = 31.2$ as a function of the coordinates Y and Z. The calculations are performed for a Reynolds number $Re = 100$, volume flow $Q = 5$, $\Lambda = 25$ and inclination angle $\alpha = 30°$. The velocity V in

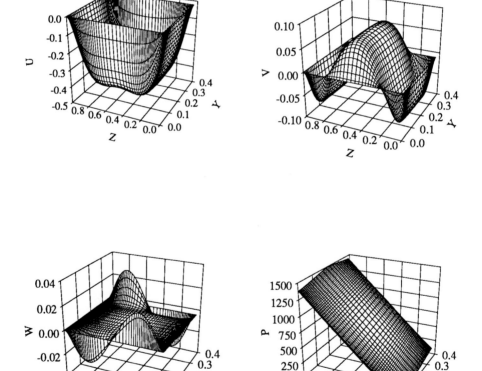

Fig. 3. Velocity and pressure profiles for $Re = 100$, $Q = -5$, $\alpha = 30°$, $\Lambda = 25$, $X = 31.2$, 18 caulks

azimuthal direction differs in many ways from the velocity in a gap without caulks [Br1,Go1]. In the region of the walls ($Z = 0$ and $Z = 1$) the azimuthal velocity is smaller than the velocity of the discs ($V < 0$). In the middle of a gap with caulks, the velocity of the fluid is higher than the velocity of the rotatings discs compared to like a gap without caulks. The negative velocity is caused by the coriolis force between two caulks. The radial velocity U causes a coriolis force in positive Y-direction. As a result, the pressure becomes higher for higher Y to balance the coriolis forces. The radial velocity W becomes smaller at the walls (no-slip condition) and the pressure forces are greater than the coriolis forces. This causes a secondary flow from the pressure to the suction side as shown in Fig. 4. The caulks also reduce the value of the velocity V compared to the velocity V in a gap without caulks. Therefore the influence of the azimuthal velocity on the radial velocity is smaller. The velocity in axial direction W is much lower than the radial velocity U. The

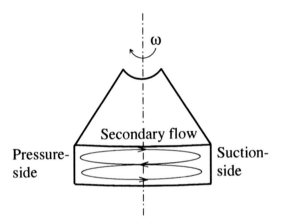

Fig. 4. Secondary flow in the gap.

effect of the Reynolds number on the velocity profiles also depends on the presence of the caulks. For a gap with caulks the influence of the Re-number is smaller than for a gap without caulks. Fig. 5 shows the separation efficiency T as a function of the dimensionless parameters $\Delta Sto \Lambda^3 / Q$. The combination of parameters can be interpreted as a dimensionless particle diameter. The comparison between experiment and calculation shows a good agreement for $T \approx 0.5$. The difference between the two curves can be explained by the experimental determination of the particle size.

4   Conclusion

The fluid flow and the separation behaviour between conical rotating discs in a disc stack centrifuge was studied numerically using computational fluid

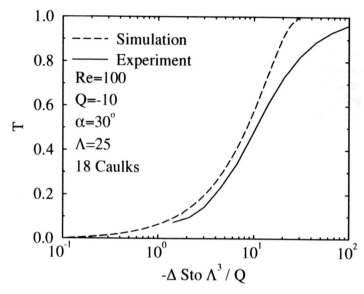

Fig. 5. Separation efficency for 18 caulks.

dynamics. The results of the simulation are in good agreement with experimental data.

References

[He1]   Hemfort, H.: Separatoren-Zentrifugen für Klärung, Trennung, Extraktion. Westfalia Separator AG (1983)

[JP1]   Janoske, U., Piesche, M.: Numerische Simulation der Strömungszustände und des Trennverhaltens von Suspensionen im freien Einzelspalt eines Tellerseparators. Chem.-Ing.-Tech. (to appear)

[Go1]   Gol'din, E. M.: Hydrodynamic flow between separator plates. IZV.AN SSSR., OTN **7**(1957) 80–88

[Br1]   Brunner, A.: Über das Reinigen von Schweröl mittels der Zentrifuge. Dissertation Eidgenössische Technische Hochschule Zürich

Unsteady Flow Simulation in an Axial Flow Turbine Using a Parallel Implicit Navier-Stokes Method

Alexander R. Jung, Jürgen F. Mayer, and Heinz Stetter

Institut für Thermische Strömungsmaschinen und Maschinenlaboratorium, Universität Stuttgart, D-70550 Stuttgart, Germany

Abstract The unsteady flow in an axial flow turbine stage with a second stator blade row is investigated by means of a Navier-Stokes code especially developed for turbomachinery applications. Due to the low aspect ratio of the blades of the test machine a highly three-dimensional flow dominated by secondary flow structures is observed. Simulations that include all blade rows are carried out. The present investigation focuses on the stator/rotor/stator interaction effects. Secondary flow structures and their origins are identified and tracked on their way through the passage. The time-dependent secondary velocity vectors and total pressure distributions as well as flow angles and Mach number distributions as perturbation from the time-mean flow field are shown in cross-flow sections and azimuthal cuts throughout the turbine. Simulations and measurements show a good overall agreement in the time-dependent flow behaviour as well as in the secondary flow structures.

1 Introduction

Present analysis and design methods for turbomachinery are based on steady aerodynamics. However, unsteady flow associated with blade row interaction causes highly three-dimensional flow fields that change periodically with time. The influence of the periodic unsteadiness on loss generation has to be studied for a further improvement of turbomachinery performance.

The most important cause of unsteadiness is the relative motion of blade rows. Turbine rotor flow is influenced by the non-uniform exit flow of the first stator and the periodically incoming wakes induced by the upstream stator blades. In addition passage vortices and the tip clearance vortex develop as the flow passes the rotor. The unsteady three-dimensional rotor exit flow now enters the passage of the second stator and rotor wakes and vortices are cut off by the vanes of the second stator. The already unsteady flow has to follow blade curvature thereby inducing the stator passage vortices. All these effects lead to a strongly disturbed, three-dimensional and highly unsteady second stator exit flow. To understand, describe and model these complex phenomena comprehensive studies of the flow not only in isolated cascades but in the multi-blade row environment of turbomachines are necessary.

Since the beginning of the nineties, several computational studies of flow associated with blade row interaction have been carried out e.g. by Hah et al. [6], Valkov and Tan [13], Gallus et al. [3], Dawes [1], Eulitz et al. [2], He [8], and Hall [7]. Looking at the complex pattern of the flow in multi-blade row machines it becomes obvious that a numerical method to accurately predict the time-dependent secondary flow in a multi-blade row environment has to account for the three-dimensionality as well as the unsteadiness of the flow. With the recent development of high performance vector-parallel supercomputers and with the improved and more efficient numerical methods time-accurate flow simulations in turbomachinery stages can be performed with reasonable spatial and temporal resolutions and computational costs. The very brief innovation cycles in the computer industry indicate the future availability of inexpensive high-performance computing resources for daily design processes. Therefore computer codes for the simulation of unsteady flow in turbomachinery will certainly become a demanded tool to increase turbine and compressor efficiency and also to reduce dynamic blade loads.

The scope of this paper is on the three-dimensional highly unsteady flow conditions behind the first stator, behind the rotor, in the passage of the second stator, and behind the second stator of a 1.5 stage axial flow turbine. The numerical results at various locations throughout the computational domain are presented, compared to experimental values and discussed. The simulations allow to take a close look even at spaces where it is impossible to get reasonable experimental data whereas the experiments are especially essential to verify the unsteady flow predictions. The results will on one hand provide a better understanding of unsteady flow phenomena but on the other hand they may help to find ways for further improvement of time accurate numerical methods.

2   Experimental Investigations

The experimental studies to this test case have been carried out in a 1.5 stage axial flow air turbine which is operated at the Institut für Strahlantriebe und Turboarbeitsmaschinen of RWTH Aachen, Germany. Details of the test rig and the evaluation of the data can be found in Walraevens and Gallus [14] and Walraevens et al. [15]. For both stators the well-known Traupel profile is used. Profile geometry, number of blades and stagger are identical for the first and the second stator. A modified VKI profile is used for the rotor. The tip clearance is 0.4 mm. All blades of the three blade rows are untwisted. The stator vanes are stacked in the trailing edge, rotor blades in the center of gravity. A cross section of the turbine with mid-span velocity triangles and definitions of the flow angles is shown in Fig. 1. The design point of the turbine is at a rotational speed of 3500 rpm. In the test runs the shaft speed variation was less than 0.2 percent and the total temperature at turbine inlet was maintained in the range of 308 K +/-0.5 K by cooling the supplying air at the compressor outlet. Mach number at inlet was adjusted to Ma=0.11 with an accuracy of about 0.5 percent.

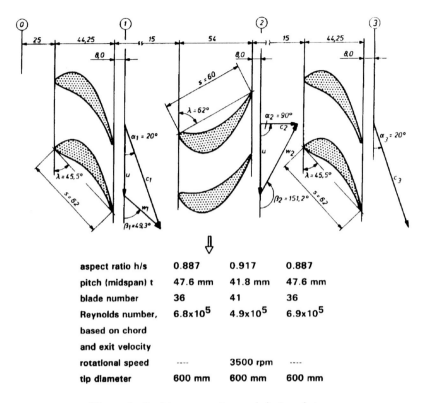

aspect ratio h/s	0.887	0.917	0.887
pitch (midspan) t	47.6 mm	41.8 mm	47.6 mm
blade number	36	41	36
Reynolds number, based on chord and exit velocity	6.8×10^5	4.9×10^5	6.9×10^5
rotational speed	----	3500 rpm	----
tip diameter	600 mm	600 mm	600 mm

Figure1. Turbine geometry and design data

3   Numerical Approach

3.1   Flow Solver ITSM3D

The equations solved are the fully three-dimensional, unsteady, Favre-aver-aged Navier-Stokes equations. They are written for a cylindrical coordinate system that rotates at constant angular velocity [11]. The fluid is assumed to behave as an ideal gas with a constant ratio of specific heat capacities. A modified algebraic Baldwin-Lomax model is used to describe the effects of turbulence. The solution method is a cell-vertex central-difference finite volume scheme and is based on the work of Jameson et al. [9]. An explicit five-stage Runge-Kutta time stepping scheme is used.

In cases of unsteady simulations in which the stator blade count is differ-ent from the rotor blade count, a time-inclining method for three dimensions based on the work of Giles [5] is used in order to model the exact ratio of the blade counts in a single passage calculation. In this approach, time-transformations are applied to both the stator and the rotor domains and different time steps are used in these domains. In this way simple periodic-ity conditions can be applied at the boundaries in pitchwise direction in the transformed space although these boundaries are not periodic in the physical domain. Multiple blade passages can be used to overcome the stabilty limitation of the time-inclination method for those cases in which the difference in the blade counts of the stage is so large that in the time-transformed space the principle of causality would be violated. With the use of multiple blade passages the amount of time inclination necessary for modelling the pitch ratio can be reduced to the stable range. Even then the reduction in computational time is usually at least one order of magnitude less than the time that would be required without time inclination.

At the inlet and exit boundaries as well as at the stator/rotor interfaces in the case of steady-state flow simulations, a non-reflecting post-correction method based on the work of Giles [4] is applied to prevent spurious reflections from waves that leave the computational domain. Solid surfaces are assumed adiabatic and the no-slip condition is applied. Periodicity in pitchwise direction is ensured through the use of dummy cells that keep copies of the periodic values such that the points on these boundaries can be treated like interior points.

Block-structured H-type grids in a multi-block topology allow modelling of complex geometries, e. g. blade tip gaps or computational domains consisting of multiple blade passages. The fourth-order artificial dissipation terms are applied continuously across all inter-block boundaries of the computational domain. For unsteady flow simulations the grids at the sliding interfaces between stationary and rotating blade rows are overlapped by one grid cell. An interpolation procedure consistent with the second order spatial accuracy of the numerical scheme is used to interchange the flow variables during every time step of the integration procedure. As the rotor grid moves relative to the stator, the rotation of the rotor is integrated in time in order to track the position of the grid blocks for a time-resolved coupling at the interface regions.

For steady-state calculations a full multigrid method, local time stepping and implicit residual smoothing can be used to accelerate convergence to a large extent [12]. In the case of unsteady calculations an implicit time-consistent multigrid scheme based on the work of He [8] and an implicit residual averaging method for global time steps can be used to efficiently accelerate the solution process. Recently, a fully implicit time-accurate dual time-stepping method (see Jameson [10]) that solves the governing equations via an explicit time-integration in a pseudo time has been implemented. With this method, all acceleration techniques that apply to steady-state simulations can be used to reduce the number of iterations in the pseudo-time of the implicit method. The message passing interface (MPI) was used to parallelize the solver in an ad hoc manner. The grid block based parallelization takes advantage of the multi-block structure of the solver.

3.2   Flow Simulations and Computational Performance

Two sets of computations have been carried out in order to account for the two different operating conditions which were used in the experiments. Each set consisted of simulations with two different grid densities and efficiency studies of two distinct acceleration techniques for unsteady flow simulations: implicit dual-time stepping with time-accurate multigrid and a pure explicit time-consistent multigrid algorithm. The coarse grid discretization consisted of a total of 293,523 nodes, i.e. roughly 100,000 nodes per blade row, and the tip clearance gap was modelled with 2925 grid points. For the fine grid simulations the computational domain was discretized with 2,116,941 nodes, i.e. compared to the coarse grid the number of grid points was increased by a factor of about 2 in each spatial direction (e.g. $137 \times 73 \times 65$ nodes in the second stator. Here the number of nodes in the rotor tip gap amounted to 31,185. For the fine grid simulation the dimensionless wall distance was $y^+ < 7$ for the two stators and $y^+ < 5$ for the rotor. A three-dimensional view of the coarse grid on the hub and the blade surfaces is shown in Fig. 2. Results

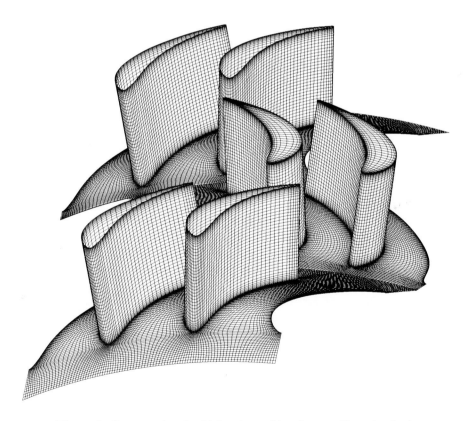

Figure2. Computational grid for the turbine (coarse discretization)

of preceding steady-state simulations were used as initial conditions for the unsteady simulations. It was found that after seven blade passing periods the transient disturbances resulting from these – for unsteady simulations – inconsistent initial conditions had diminished sufficiently. So all the results shown below are extracted from the flow field during the eighth or later blade passing period after the start of the unsteady simulation.

The coarse grid simulations were carried out on a 333 MHz single processor DEC Alpha workstation. With the explicit time-consistent multigrid method each blade passing period took about 10:52 hours of CPU time, i. e. 88 μs/(time step × node). The implicit dual-time-stepping method using three level full multigrid cycles for the pseudo-time integration needed about 22:40 hours per period (124 μs/(pseudo time step × node)). Also the memory requirement was higher for the dual-time stepping method than with the pure explicit algorithm (91 MB vs. 64 MB, 32 bit per word).

The parallel version of the code was used for the fine grid simulations which were carried out on the NEC SX-4 vector-parallel supercomputer at the High-Performance Computing Center (HLRS) of Stuttgart University. Using 4 of the 32 vector processors, each blade passing period took about 7:20 hours in real time with the dual-time stepping method and a five level multigrid cycle for each explicit iteration in the pseudo time (5.8 μs/(pseudo time step × node)). For each period 100 implicit time steps have been used. Here the memory requirement was 1.34 GB (64 bit per word). The concurrent processor performance was more than 1.1 GFlop/s with a parallel speed-up greater than 3 for the pure calculation and going down to 0.91 GFlops/s during the last blade passing period due to the large amount of i/o operations. This relatively poor performance of only about 15 % of the peak performance of 2 GFlop/s per processor is mainly due to the grid topology which allowed an average vector length of 66 only of the possible 256. The vectorization factor of the solver, however, is greater than 94 %. With the fine discretization, the explicit multigrid method proved to be not a quarter as efficient as the dual-time stepping method. The simulations with the explicit algorithm were cancelled as it turned out that more than 7,500 iterations per period would be required in order to get the calculation stable.

An example of the influence of the different grid densities on the numerical results is shown in Fig. 3. It is plotted the instantaneous entropy distribution in the second stator at mid-span at identical stator/rotor positions. The left figure shows the result for the coarse grid simulation whereas the fine grid result is depicted on the right. Looking at the shape of the contours it becomes obvious, that a lot of details are missing in the coarse grid results which are captured by the fine grid. Detail A shows the differences in the rotor wake/boundary layer interaction and wake convection behaviour. Remarkable are the different shapes and locations of the local extrem values in the two results. The extrem value in the coarse grid simulation is located at about 25 % of the blade chord whereas the corresponding extremum of the fine grid simulation is at about 35 % of the chord. This means, that the two simulations

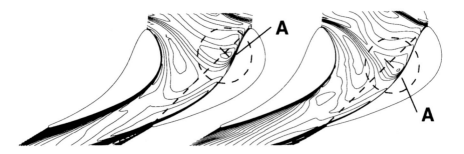

Figure3. Instantaneous entropy distribution in the second stator at mid-span at identical rotor/stator positions (left: coarse grid simulation, right: fine grid simulation)

show a noticable phase shift in the time-dependent behaviour and appearance of phenomena associated with this quantity. Another simulation with an even finer grid would be necessary in order to prove that the fine grid results are already reasonably grid independent. All the results presented below are taken from the fine grid simulations.

Such fine grid simulations of unsteady multistage turbomachinery flow can only be performed with reasonable turnaround time by using high performance computers like the NEC SX-4. However, even on this machine it is necessary to provide a simulation code that is highly vectorized and effectively parallelized in order to take advantage of the system's ressources.

3.3   Visualization by Virtual Reality Techniques

The computed results are very large datasets, covering flow variables given in three spatial dimensions and in the time domain. The following sections describe the computed behaviour of the flow in comparison to the experimental results evaluated at RWTH Aachen by means of two-dimensional cuts at different locations in the machine, given at different points in time. Following such a strategy also in the analysis process itself is very time consuming and requires a distinctive ability of spatial imagination.

With support of the visualization team of HLRS it was possible to analyze the flow features in the presented test case in the Virtual Environments Lab of HLRS where direct three-dimensional interaction is possible by means of stereo projection and magnetical tracking of head and arm movement of the observer (Fig. 4). It should be remarked that it was necessary to reduce the number of nodes in the dataset from 2.1 million per blade passage to approximately 0.2 million in order to enable the storing of the complete unsteady dataset in the memory of the visualization system.

The animation of the turbine flow field in the Virtual Environments Lab proved to be a powerful tool for analyzing and understanding of complex

Figure4. Virtual Reality visualization: observer walking through the blade passage of the second stator towards a cutting plane showing secondary velocity vectors (rotor passage vortex is easily to identify). Colour distribution on the blades corresponds to the entropy distribution

unsteady flow fields by means of this new technology. Once the preparation for such turbomachinery test cases in the visualization software is done, the required amount of time for analyzing the flow field can be considerably reduced. Some smaller flow effects that might have been overlooked by use of traditional methods were easily detected in the Virtual Environment. Fig. 5 gives another glimpse of the possibilities offered there.

4   Results and Discussion

All presented figures of cross flow sections are rear views as seen from downstream. The pitchwise flow angle α starts at circumferential direction and its counterclockwise rotation is positive, see Fig. 1. Spanwise flow angles γ have positive values when directing to the casing. Thus a steady three-dimensional flow vector is given as

$$\boldsymbol{c}_{\text{loc}} = f(c, \alpha, \gamma)_{\text{loc}} \tag{1}$$

and a three-dimensional time-dependent flow vector as

$$\boldsymbol{c}(t)_{\text{loc}} = f(c(t), \alpha(t), \gamma(t))_{\text{loc}} \tag{2}$$

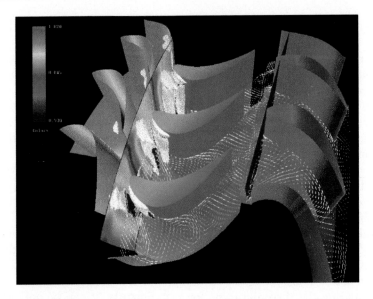

Figure5. Static pressure distribution on the solid surfaces, total pressure distribution in cross-flow sections with corresponding colour key in the top left corner, surface of constant total pressure 1.004 (normalized with total inlet pressure) and secondary velocity vector distribution at mid-span (difference to time-mean velocity)

A secondary flow vector is the difference vector between the local flow vector and an averaged flow vector. The latter is calculated using the total local velocity $|c|$, the radially averaged yaw angle $\bar{\alpha}^r$ and the circumferentially averaged pitch angle $\bar{\gamma}^\varphi$:

$$c_{\text{sec}} = c_{\text{loc}} - c_{\text{avg}} \tag{3}$$

with

$$c_{\text{avg}} = f(|c|, \bar{\alpha}^r, \bar{\gamma}^\varphi) \tag{4}$$

4.1   Flow behind the first stator

As mentioned in the introduction, the unsteady effects with the time scales of interest to this investigation start to develop at the exit of the first stator due to the periodic interaction with the moving rotor blades. The following two sections describe some of the effects.

Averaged flow quantities. A proper way to check the quality of the results in order to decide whether or not a thorough analysis of the unsteady results is reasonable is to start with the steady-state and time-mean flow fields respectively. The steady-state flow field served as initial condition for the unsteady simulation and the time-mean flow field can be computed from the unsteady results. So, this data is available without much of an additional effort.

Taking the circumferential average of these data not only reduces the remaining number of spatial dimensions to 2 but also allows easy comparison to experimental data obtained by pneumatic probe measurements.

The four diagrams in Fig. 6 show the radial distributions of the circumferentially averaged absolute total pressure, absolute total temperature, static pressure and pitchwise flow angle α in a plane located 8 mm downstream of the trailing edge of the first stator. The three data sets in each of the diagrams correspondent to the steady-state solution (blue), the time-averaged unsteady solution (red) and the experimental results (symbols), respectively. To account for the different atmospheric conditions of the test runs at this plane of measurement and at the inlet plane where the boundary conditions were taken and for the sake of an easier qualitative comparison, the average value of the pressure of the experimental data has been shifted slightly to match the average of the unsteady results. The flow angle distribution has been left untouched.

Comparing the three data sets for each quantity, it can be noticed that the time-averaged results of the unsteady simulation show a slightly better agreement with the experiment than do the steady-state results. The biggest differences are detected in the total pressure and the total temperature profiles. The steady-state solution does not show the distinct characteristics near the endwalls as do the unsteady results and the experiments. Also the region of a relatively constant flow angle of about 20° between 20% and 70% span is somewhat underpredicted by the steady-state results. These differencies are due to the unsteady interaction of the stator exit flow with the rotor blades' potential which cannot be covered by a steady-state simulation.

In the next section it is shown that the potential effects influence the flow already far upstream of the rotor blade's leading edge.

Unsteady total pressure. A quite remarkable phenomenon can be observed in the axial gap between the first stator and the rotor: As the rotor blades move past the stator exit flow they actually energize the fluid to a certain extent, i.e. the absolute total pressure is increased to a level which is higher than the total inlet pressure. This effect is caused by an interaction of the blades' potential and an associated displacement of fluid from the stator exit flow. So the rotor first pumps in some energy into the fluid before it actually extracts the energy, which happens further inside the passage. A snapshot of the 3D flow field which tries to visualize this effect is shown in Fig. 5. The iso-value of the total pressure surfaces is slightly above the total inlet pressure, such that the size of these iso-surfaces visualizes the approximate extend of this fluid energization. This figure also shows that these high total pressure regions are divided into two parts by the stator wakes. In spite of the energization, the low energy regions of the wakes prevent these two parts to fuse to one "big bubble". Nevertheless the rotor also energizes the

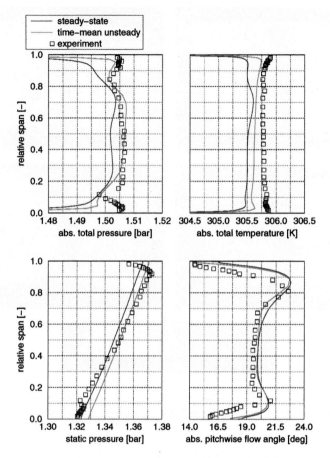

Figure6. Radial distributions of circumferentially averaged flow quantities in the axial gap between the first stator and the rotor

wake to a certain extent and practically smoothes the nonuniform stator exit flow field at a certain instant in time during the blade passing period. This is shown in the diagram of Fig. 7 by means of the time-history of the total pressure distribution in a cross flow section in the axial gap between the first stator and the rotor. Time increases in clockwise direction.

The passing of the rotor blades can be observed in the plots as a red to dark red region which moves from right to left with time increasing. The dark red regions also indicate that region in which the total pressure is higher than the total inlet pressure. The above mentioned energization becomes also obvious, as the dark blue low energy region of the wake becomes brighter and the gradients flatten until the dominating colour inside the wake is a bright cyan.

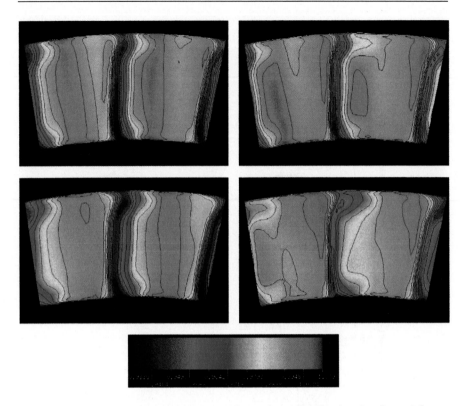

Figure7. Time-dependent absolute total pressure distribution in the axial gap between the first stator and the rotor (time increasing in clockwise direction)

4.2   Flow behind the rotor

The flow leaving the passage of the rotor is much more complex than the exit flow of the first stator as it also contains the remainders of the flow structures generated in and downstream of the first stator in addition to the flow phenomena which have developed during the flow through the rotor passage.

Averaged flow quantities. The diagrams in Fig. 8 depict the comparison of the radial distributions of circumferentially averaged flow variables of the steady-state results, the time-averaged unsteady flow field, and the experimentally obtained data in a plane between rotor and second stator. The plotted quantities are respectively absolute total pressure and Mach number as well as relative total temperature and flow angle. The characteristics of the total pressure distribution has not changed very much compared to the upstream stator/rotor interface region. However, the absolute level is about

200 mbar lower than at the exit of stator 1 due to the work that has been taken out of the fluid by the rotor blades. Also the difference between the predicted results are now much more obvious as the steady-state simulation does not model the unsteady interaction effects. This is most clearly to be seen in the flow angle distribution. The experiments show quite strong and distinctive secondary flow effects close to the endwalls which are not fully re-solved by the simulations due to the deficiencies of the algebraic turbulence model. The discrepancies between the two simulations close to the hub are due to the fact that in the steady-state model the hub rotates at this position whereas in the model for the unsteady simulation and in the real turbine this part of the hub already belongs to the non-rotating part of the machine.

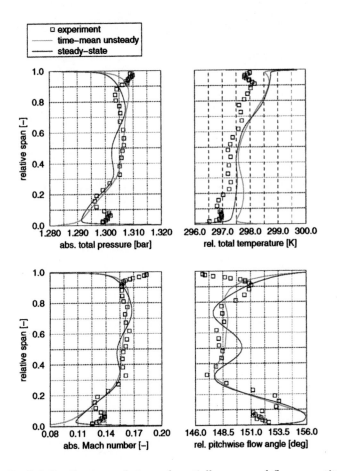

Figure8. Radial distributions of circumferentially averaged flow quantities in the axial gap between the rotor and the second stator

Unsteady secondary flow field. Second stator inlet flow is equivalent with rotor exit flow in the absolute frame. To understand the unsteady flow behaviour in and behind the second stator it is therefore necessary to discuss the results at the rotor exit in frame of reference of the second stator, i. e. in the absolute frame.

The time-dependent secondary flow field in the axial gap between the rotor and the second stator is shown in Fig. 9 for eight different rotor/stator positions. A key for the numbers used to mark flow phenomena is given in Table 1.

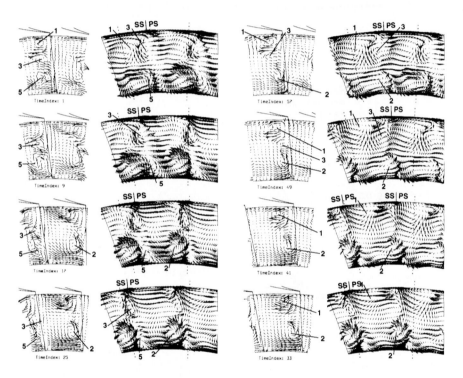

Figure9. Time-dependent secondary flow field at rotor exit in the absolute frame (left: experiment [15], right: simulation)

The arrows represent the components of the secondary flow vector viewed from the downstream direction which is given by the design angle at outlet of the blade row. This is valid for all following figures showing secondary flow vectors. Also, the description of the distinct flow features is – if not noted otherwise – relative to the domain of interest of the experiments. For easier orientation, this domain of interest is also shown in the numerical results, where its approximate boundaries are indicated with dashed lines.

No.	Description
1	Casing passage vortex
2	Hub passage vortex
3	Trailing edge vortex
4	Tip clearance vortex
5	Influence due to first stator
6.1	Rotor casing passage vortex
6.2	Rotor hub passage vortex
6.3	Rotor trailing edge vortex
7	Combi vortex (second stator)

Table1. Reference of secondary flow figures

Close to the hub a distinctive flow from pressure side to suction side, forming the lower part of the hub passage vortex, can be observed. At approximately 75 % span flow in the opposite direction from suction to pressure side forms the lower side of the casing passage vortex. Behind the trailing edge slightly above midspan the upper and lower trailing edge vortices develop from the shear layers in the wake some distance behind the cascade. The mechanism of the formation of the trailing edge vortices is illustrated in the sketch in Fig. 10. Below it will be shown that especially the upper trailing edge vortex plays an important role in the interaction between rotor and second stator.

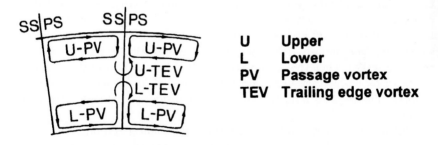

Figure10. Development of trailing edge vortices

Except for the time indices TI 1, TI 9, and TI 17 the casing passage vortex (1) and hub passage vortex (2) are the dominating flow features (Fig. 9). The flow field shows biggest differences between TI 1 and TI 33. The latter leaves an overall balanced impression of a typical blade exit flow containing the distinctive passage vortices. On the other hand at TI 1 a flow distortion due to the first stator (5) appears in the area of the hub passage vortex. The formerly rotational sense in the counterclockwise direction is disturbed and at

TI 17 only a diagonal inward directed slanted structure is left. At TI 1 another vortex (3) that also rotates in counterclockwise direction can be detected on the left of the rotor wake at approximately 70 % span. Its upper part seems to go together with the lower part of the casing passage vortex. Location and rotational sense conclude that this structure is the upper trailing edge vortex of the just passing rotor blade. This vortex can be observed until TI 25. The extension of the trailing edge of the corresponding blade can be recognized in form of the effects of the wake on the flow. Nearly all flow vectors directing from suction to pressure side undergo a strong turning radially upwards forced by the high pressures induced on the pressure side of the blade. Note that this cross flow section is located 8 mm downstream of the trailing edge of the rotor. Hence, at this location, there are already strong mixing processes between the wake and the main flow taking place. Comparing the experiments with the simulation, it can be stated that all the major flow phenomena and their locations are in reasonably good agreement except for the casing passage vortex which in the experiments is found to be more distinct than in the simulation. As was already indicated in the previous section by the circumferentially and time-averaged flow variables, the numerical results do not resolve the very fine details of the endwall flow as they are driven mainly by the unsteady boundary layer behaviour and turbulent effects that are not modelled adequately in the solution method.

4.3   Unsteady flow within the passage of the second stator

Fig. 11 depicts the instantaneous entropy distribution at mid-span. It illustrates the complexity of the stator/rotor/stator interaction process in this machine. Looking closely at this figure one can observe how the wakes of the first stator are cut off and convected through the rotor passage, where their shapes are continuously deforming until they interact, mix up, or join with the rotor wakes. Then the combination of the two wakes enter the second stator passage, where they are again being chopped, deformed, convected and so forth. The result is a highly complex flow inside the passage of the second stator.

The following paragraphs discuss the experimental and numerical results in some selected cutting planes within the passage of the second stator.

The time-dependent secondary velocity vectors at plane 14, which is located a short distance downstream of the inlet of the passage are shown in Fig. 12. Comparing this secondary flow with the secondary flow at rotor exit (Fig. 9), all vortices that have been found at the rotor exit are detectable in plane 14 as well. Starting at TI 1 and moving with time the first full vortex structure recognizable in both the experimental and numerical results is found at TI 17 at about 30 % span. Counterclockwise rotational sense and location point out that it is the rotor hub passage vortex (6.2). At about 85 % span, a strong cross-flow from the right to the left can be seen. TI 25 and TI 33 show this cross-flow as the lower part of the clockwise rotating casing

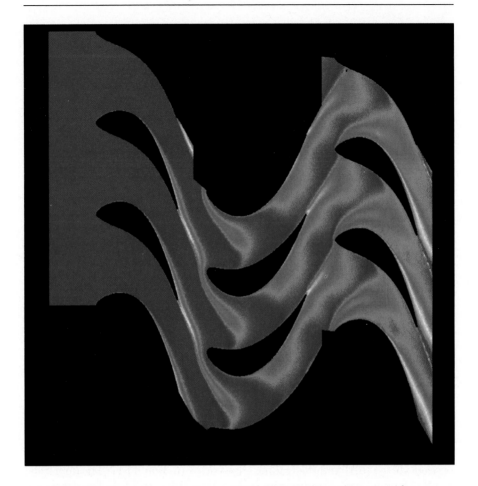

Figure11. Instantaneous entropy distribution in the turbine at mid-span

passage vortex of the rotor (6.1). During the circumferential movement from
TI 17 to TI 33 a remarkable change in the radial position of 6.1 can be noticed. Moving further on with time both vortices have partly been chopped
by the stator vane at TI 41, at TI 57 they are not longer detectable from the
experimental results, whereas the simulation shows that this vortex is pushed
against the stator blade suction side, where it takes as long as until TI 9 till
it is completely dissolved and the cycle starts over again. The trailing edge
vortex (6.3) is not as distinctive as in Fig. 9 but careful observation shows
its presence all the time between TI 1 and TI 41. The simulation shows quite
a good agreement in the motion and the strength of the upper trailing edge
vortex. From TI 17 to TI 33 another vortex structure can be recognized from
the prediction in the lower right corner next to the rotor hub passage vortex.
Its rotational sense and location identify it as the lower trailing edge vortex.

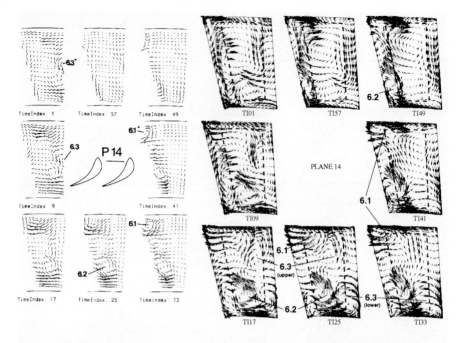

Figure12. Time-dependent secondary flow within the passage of the second stator close to inlet – plane 14 (∗ – chopped vortex, left: experiment [15], right: simulation)

Figure 13 presents time-dependent secondary flow in the outlet of the passage of the second stator (plane 0). The rotor vortex system consisting of 6.1, 6.2 and 6.3 is still detectable and appears clearly with the rotor casing passage vortex (6.1) and the trailing edge vortex (6.3) at TI 17. The numerical results show a dominating vortex (6.3) a bit earlier at TI 9. The rotor hub passage vortex seems just to appear bottom right at about 15 % span at TI 17. When the rotor has moved 12.5 % of its pitch, all three vortices can be seen on the left hand side of figure TI 25. Bottom right in this figure of the experimental results, the stator hub passage vortex can be identified due to its clockwise rotational sense and radial position close to the hub. The simulation predicts its appearance somewhat later. It is clearly recognizable at TI 41. The circumferential position is not, as one would expect, close to the suction side. Unsteady interaction between rotor hub passage vortex (6.2) and stator hub passage vortex (2) has removed the latter from its usual position.

The following figures (Figs. 14 to 16) show selected flow quantities for azimuthal cutting planes. Plotted is the perturbation of the absolute Mach number at 73 % span and the pitchwise flow angle at midspan as well as the unsteady radial flow angle at 73 % span. The perturbation is calculated as the difference between unsteady and time-averaged values for each point, e.g. $Ma' = Ma_{uns} - Ma_{avg}$. In these figures the darker shaded areas correspond

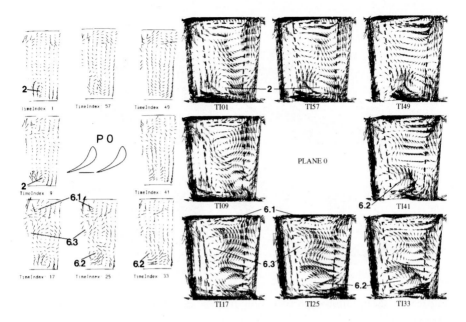

Figure 13. Time-dependent secondary flow at the exit of the passage of the second stator – plane 0 (left: experiment [15], right: simulation)

to values smaller than the time-averaged values. The predicted results are plotted to the right hand side of the corresponding experimental results. The solid line in the plots of the numerical results indicates the measured region.

The low Mach number regions show the path of low energy material (associated with the rotor wake) within the stator passage. Fig. 14 shows top left at TI 49 a just incoming rotor wake. Another dark area can be seen further downstream. It determines the location of the wake which entered the stator passage one blade passing period earlier. At TI 1 three of those zones are detectable: top right, top left and at passage exit when referring to the common domain of interest in the experiments and calculations. Following the time indices the movement of this wake fluid in the stator passage can be traced. So the top right area needs about 1.75 blade passing periods between entering and leaving the stator passage. A very good agreement between the measured and predicted values of this time-dependent behaviour can be stated for the shape of the contours as well as for the magnitude.

Figs. 15 depicts the perturbation of the pitchwise flow angle α' at midspan and thus corresponds to the motion of the low energy fluid as just discussed for the Mach number. In areas of low Mach number perturbations this yaw angle perturbation is negative as well and shows negative incidence, corresponding with a decreased loading of the stator blade row.

Little change with time shows the spanwise flow angle at 73 % span, see Fig. 16. Only in the first quarter of the stator passage (streamwise) the rotor

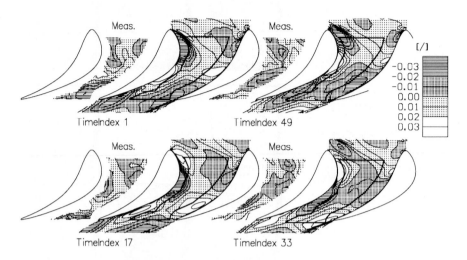

Figure14. Mach number perturbation at 73 % span (left: experiment [15], right: simulation)

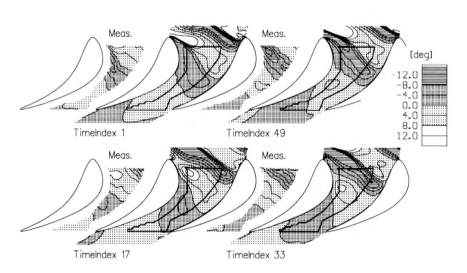

Figure15. Perturbation of pitchwise flow angle α at mid-span (left: experiment [15], right: simulation)

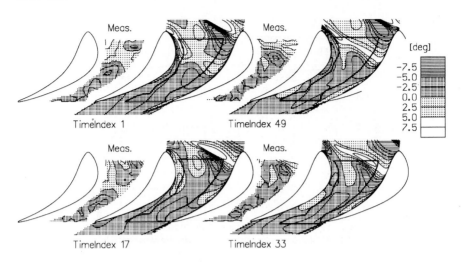

Figure16. Time-dependent radial flow angle γ at 73 % span (left: experiment [15], right: simulation)

influence is clearly detectable. The agreement between the experiments and the simulation can be stated to be excellent. Please note that the quantity compared here – unlike the perturbations discussed above – is the flow angle itself and not its fluctuation. This is remarkable, because good agreement in the fluctuations does not necessarily come along with a good agreement of the quantity itself.

4.4   Flow behind the second stator

Averaged flow quantities. From the inlet of the computational domain to the exit the flow has now followed the curvature of three blade passages, has encountered obstructions such as the solid surfaces of the blades or some of the many vortex structures and other flow phenomena. The diagrams in Fig. 17 once again take a look at the circumferentially averaged flow field of the steady-state and time-averaged unsteady results in comparison to the experiment. Depicted are the radial distributions of the absolute pitchwise flow angle and the Mach number in a plane behind the second stator. Although the flow angle shows an offset of almost 1.5° between simulation and experiment, the characteristics of the distribution in the main flow region between 15 % and 85 % of the span are still in reasonable agreement.

The steady-state result somewhat overpredicts the spanwise flow angle fluctuation whereas the characteristics of the distribution as obtained by the unsteady simulation are closer to the experimental results.

Unsteady secondary flow field. Time-dependent secondary flow behind the second stator is shown in Fig. 18 at eight different rotor/stator positions.

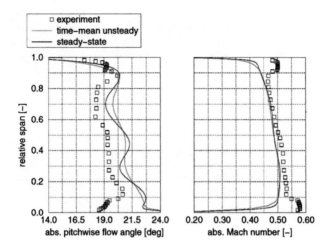

Figure17. Radial distributions of circumferentially averaged flow quantities at the exit plane of the computational domain

The plane of measurements is located 8 mm behind stator outlet in the axial direction. In the experiments at TI 1 several vortex structures can be distinguished. The origin of each vortex can be revealed by taking into account the rotational sense of each vortex, its location, and its time-dependent behaviour. The vortex (6.1) close to casing and suction side of the stator blade rotates in the clockwise direction whereas the weak vortex structure (1) on the right hand side rotates counterclockwise. This is the rotational sense of the stator casing vortex but the location (casing, pressure side) does not fit. Observing the top right corner of TI 33, TI 41, ... TI 1, it can be seen that a structure rotating counterclockwise (as the casing stator passage vortex) appears. It is distinctive at the beginning (TI 33) and diminishing with rotor movement until the weak vortex structure already mentioned appears (TI 1). At TI 9 the stretched vortex (6.1) has disappeared and been replaced by the casing passage vortex (1) of the second stator.

Considering the structure of the rotor exit flow in the absolute frame, the radial inward directing and stretched looking vortex (6.1) must be the rotor casing passage vortex. At TI 33, at the same location, this vortex has the same structure and rotational sense as its counterpart behind the rotor (see Fig. 9). Its sudden appearance at TI 33, the change of its shape with time followed by complete disappearance points clear to a rotor vortex chopped by the stator vanes.

A similar but more complex vortex system (2, 6.2, 6.3) can be seen bottom left at TI 1, filling nearly half the figure. It obviously consists of three different vortices, where the one located bottom left (6.2) shows only a bit more than half of the usual circular shape. Looking at the rotational sense it is found that the two vortices on top of each other (6.3, 6.2) do have the same rotational

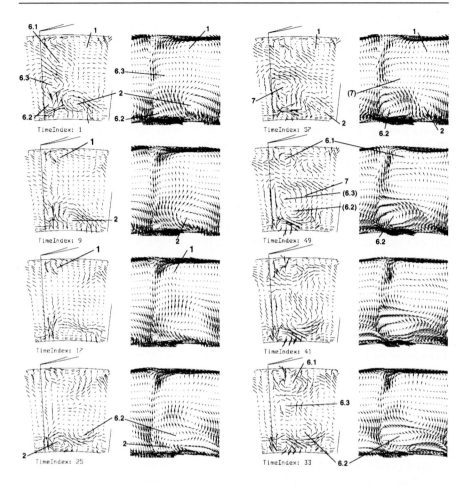

Figure18. Time-dependent secondary flow field behind the second stator (left: experiment [15], right: simulation)

sense (counterclockwise). The third vortex (2) rotates clockwise. Moving with the rotor to TI 9 this structure becomes very weak but is still detectable. Later on at TI 25 the hub passage vortex (2) is clearly to recognize close to the suction side. Following the way from TI 1 to 25 it is found that structure (2) has moved from pressure to suction side and thus must be the hub passage vortex of the second stator.

Bottom in the right third of the figure at TI 25 a new vortex structure rotating clockwise seems to appear. Comparing this with TI 33 the small hub passage vortex has been removed completely by the sudden appearance of a large vortex structure (6.2) rotating in the opposite direction. The sudden appearance and the rotational sense lead to the conclusion that this vortex is originated in the rotor and identical with the rotor hub passage vortex.

Left of the center of the figure (TI 33) a vortex (6.3) which is also rotating counterclockwise can be seen. Rotational sense, location and the observations within the passage of the second stator indicate that this is the upper trailing edge vortex coming from the rotor exit. It is also detectable that there is some transport of material from the lower vortex (6.2) to the upper vortex (6.3). The amplification of two vortices leads to the huge vortex (7) which can be seen at TI 49 filling more than half the area representing this figure. TI 57 shows bottom right a diagonally inward directed new vortex structure (2) which is barely detectable at TI 49. It causes an indentation in the vortex structure (7). This disturbance together with the diminishing rotor hub passage vortex leads to the disintegration of structure (7) as observable at TI 1. Measurements and simulation show a reasonable agreement in the overall structure of the vortex systems and their time-dependency. Discrepancies can be observed in the locations and relative strength of the vortices.

5   Conclusions

Unsteady stator/rotor/stator interaction in a 1.5 stage axial flow turbine has been investigated. Three-dimensional Navier-Stokes simulations which include tip clearance modelling and blade row interaction with the real blade counts of the three blade rows have been carried out. Results of the time-dependent secondary flow fields and other flow properties have been presented in this paper for several cutting planes throughout the domain of the turbine. Discussion of the results leads to the following conclusions:

- High performance supercomputers together with an efficiently vectorized and parallelized numerical method allow unsteady multi-blade row flow simulation with reasonable spatial resolution in an acceptable turnaround time.
- ITSM3D is able to predict most of the unsteady phenomena found in the experiments.
- For the fine grid simulation the implicit multigrid method proved to be much more computationally efficient than the explicit multigrid method.
- A grid dependent phase shift is found in the numerical results. This is an important behaviour which significantly influences the time-accuracy of unsteady multi-blade row calculations.
- Further work is necessary to prove grid independence for unsteady flow simulations.
- Overall agreement between numerical and experimental results for time-dependent quantities is promising and encourages further investigations in order to perform a thorough code validation for such a complex three-dimensional unsteady internal flow.
- Especially in the near endwall region the deficiencies of the turbulence model are obvious.

- An unsteady virtual reality visualization has been successfully performed for this test case at the Virtual Environments Lab of HLRS in Stuttgart.
- Rotor tip clearance flow effects were found to be small and not significant for the second stator flow.
- Rotor exit flow shows influence of the exit flow of the first stator at several rotor/stator positions.
- Passage vortices have been found to be the dominating flow features.
- All vortices leaving the rotor passage strongly influence the flow within and behind the second stator.

Improving the knowledge on unsteady flow physics and the loss production mechanisms in turbomachines will finally help to develop methods for designing more efficient blades.

6   Acknowledgements

The experimental data were provided by the Institut für Strahlantriebe und Turboarbeitsmaschinen of RWTH Aachen. The development of the numerical code was funded by the Deutsche Forschungsgemeinschaft (DFG). The computations were made possible by the Steering-Committee of HLRS. The Virtual Reality visualization was intensively supported by the visualization group of HLRS. The help of all these institutions is gratefully acknowledged. The authors especially like to thank Ralf Walraevens for lots of valuable discussions and his help in interpreting the results.

References

1. Dawes, W. N.: A Numerical Study of the Interaction of a Transonic Compressor Rotor Overtip Leakage Vortex with the Following Stator Blade Row. ASME 94-GT-156 (1994)
2. Eulitz, F., Engel, K., Gebing, H.: Numerical Investigation of the Clocking Effects in a Multistage Turbine. ASME 96-GT-026 (1996)
3. Gallus, H.E., Zeschky, J. and Hah, C.: Endwall and Unsteady Flow Phenomena in an Axial Turbine Stage. ASME 94-GT-143 (1994)
4. Giles, M. B.: Non-Reflecting Boundary Conditions for the Euler Equations. Tech. Rep. TR-88-1. MIT CFD Laboratory (1988)
5. Giles, M. B.: UNSFLO: A Numerical Method for the Calculation of Unsteady Flow in Turbomachinery. GTL Rep. No. 205. MIT Gas Turbine Laboratory (1991)
6. Hah, C., Copenhaver, W.W. and Puterbauch, S.L.: Unsteady Aerodynamic Flow phenomena in a Transonic Compressor Stage. AIAA-93-1868 (1993)
7. Hall, E. J.: Aerodynamic modelling of Multistage Compressor Flowfields – Part1: Analysis of Rotor/Stator/Rotor Aerodynamic Interaction. ASME 97-GT-344 (1997)
8. He, L.: Time-Marching Calculations of Unsteady Flows, Blade Row Interaction and Flutter. VKI-LS 1996-05 (1996)

9. Jameson, A., Schmidt, W., Turkel, E.: Numerical Solutions of the Euler Equations by Finite Volume Methods Using Runge Kutta Time-Stepping Schemes. AIAA 81-1259 (1981)

10. Jameson, A.: Time Dependent Calcuations Using Multigrid, with Applications to Unsteady Flows Past Airfoils and Wings. AIAA-91-1596 (1991)

11. Jung, A. R., Mayer, J. F., Stetter, H.: Simulation of 3D-Unsteady Stator/Rotor Interaction in Turbomachinery Stages of Arbitrary Pitch Ratio. ASME 96-GT-69 (1996)

12. Merz, R., Krückels, J., Mayer, J. F., Stetter, H.: Calculation of Three-Dimensional Viscous Transonic Turbine Stage Flow Including Tip Clearance Effects. ASME 95-GT-76 (1995)

13. Valkov, T. and Tan, C.S.: Control of the Unsteady Flow in a Stator Blade Row Interacting with Upstream Moving Wakes. ASME 93-GT-23 (1993)

14. Walraevens, R. E., Gallus, H. E.: Stator-Rotor-Stator Interaction in an Axial Flow Turbine and its Influence on Loss Mechanisms. AGARD-CP-571 (1996) 39/1–39/14

15. Walraevens, R. E., Gallus, H. E., Jung, A. R., Mayer, J. F., Stetter, H.: Experimental and Computational Study of the Unsteady Flow in a 1.5 Stage Axial Turbine with Emphasis on the Secondary Flow in the Second Stator, ASME Paper 98-GT-254 (1998).

Navier-Stokes-Calculations of the Flow around a Helicopter Fuselage

A. Fischer, S.Wagner

Institut für Aerodynamik und Gasdynamik, Unversität Stuttgart
70550 Stuttgart, Germany

Abstract. The purpose of this paper is to briefly describe the BRITE/EURAM HELIFUSE project in its aims and phases, and to present the activities of the Institute for Aerodynamics and Gas Dynamics, Stuttgart University, as contractor of this project during the period 4/97 to 4/98. The project aims at evaluation and improvement of State-of-the-Art Navier-Stokes solvers for prediction of helicopter fuselage drag. The effect of grid refinement is investigated, and some steps in improving the NSFLEX code used at IAG are presented.

1 Introduction

The fuselage of a helicopter is a major source of aerodynamic drag of a helicopter in forward flight. The interest of the helicopter industry in modern methods of drag prediction of the fuselage is therefore significant, but hitherto unsatisfied. A high effort in wind tunnel testing is still required, which makes progress in fuselage design expensive and time-consuming.

The EC-funded BRITE/EURAM research programme HELIFUSE involves partners from from 3 helicopter manufacturers (AGUSTA, EUROCOPTER, GKN-WHL), a Software company (SIMULOG), 2 University institutes (IAG in Stuttgart and DTU at Lyngby) and 3 National Research Institutes (DLR, CIRA and Onera).

The aim of the research programme is to compare capabilities of different State-of-the-Art Navier-Stokes solvers for prediction of helicopter fuselage drag under steady flow condition.

The codes are to be evaluated for their capability to predict global drag data for simplified geometries.

The IAG takes part in the research programme using the NSFLEX Navier-Stokes-Code, which, initially developed in the industry, was modernised and adapted for high performance supercomputing by T. Michl at IAG [1].

2 The NSFLEX Code

NSFLEX is a a structured, multiblock finite volume Euler and Navier-Stokes solver for two- and threedimensional steady, viscous and compressible flow problems. Space discretization is done by higher order upwind schemes. Several different inviscid flux calculations can alternatively be used (Mod. Steger

& Warming by Eberle [6], flux vector splitting and fluxblending by Eberle, van Leer flux vector splitting).

An implicit backward Euler time integration scheme with local timestepping is used. The resulting nonlinear system is solved using Newton subiterations and Gauss-Seidel-Relaxation. Alternatively, a lower-upper-symmetric-Gauss-Seidel (LUSGS) after Jameson and Yoon scheme was introduced for speedup, using the algorithm implemented by Wehr [4].

Viscous fluxes are calculated explicitly by a thin layer approximation. Flow conditions can be prescribed as laminar, turbulent or with a given location of transition.

A simplified Baldwin & Lomax [5] turbulence model is implemented.

3   Definition of Test Cases

After conduction an extensive series of wind tunnel experiments on a 1/4-scale model of a Dauphin-Grand-Vitesse (DGV) helicopter fuselage at ONERA's F1 pressurized wind tunnel [3], four test cases using two different fuselage geometries at varying Mach- and Reynolds numbers were defined.

testcase	geometry	Ma_∞	Re
TC1	C1	0.89	$60 \cdot 10^6$
TC2	C1	0.235	$30 \cdot 10^6$
TC3	C1	0.232	$60 \cdot 10^6$
TC4	C2	0.235	$30 \cdot 10^6$

In the first phase, calculations have been conducted on the 4 test cases without knowledge of the experimental results. The second phase, which is currently underway, deals with improvement of the codes in terms of solver efficiency and accuracy. The third and last phase will consist of test case calculations to validate the improved Navier-Stokes-codes.

4   Grid Dependency Study

The high requirements for the computational grids were met by using commercial grid generation software, like GridPro [7] and IGG [8], with additional support using in-house grid modification tools, e. g. for boundary layer grid clustering and smoothing.

Test Cases

- simplified helicopter fuselage without rotors or fins
- two different fuselage geometries C_1, C_2
- symmetric flow conditions
- Mach numbers between 0.08 and 0.235
- Reynolds numbers between 30 and 60 million
- wind tunnel measurement on a quarter scale model
- calculation simulates measurement conditions

C_1-Fuselage Geometry

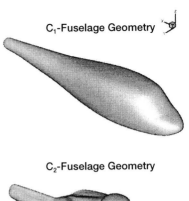

C_2-Fuselage Geometry

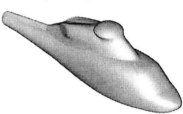

Fig. 1. Test cases and fuselage geometry

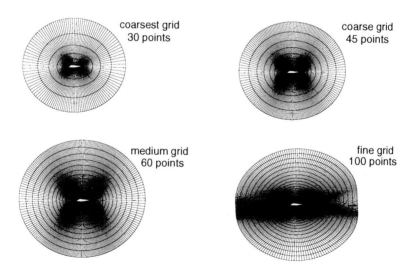

coarsest grid
30 points

coarse grid
45 points

medium grid
60 points

fine grid
100 points

Fig. 2. Grid in symmetry plane

A three-block H-O-H grid topology was chosen in order to avoid grid singularities near the sensitive areas around nose and rear, where the aerodynamic
properties have strong gradients.

In order to investigate the effect of grid differences on numerical results, a
grid refinement study has been carried out. For the study, the influence of
total number of grid points, boundary layer grid density and far field distance
has been analysed using the flow conditions of TC2, but different grids.

The process of grid generation for the refinement study exposed weaknesses
of the GridPro-Software concerning accuracy of the generated surface grids,
resulting in a slightly different surface geometry for the different generated
grids, which is one cause of the discrepancies between the results on different grids. The effect of the computational grid on the numerical results is
significant. Even though the overall pressure and skin friction distributions
may look reasonable, the total force coefficients derived from surface force
integration still vary by a large factor, which makes the applicability of the
code for relatively coarse grids appear questionable.

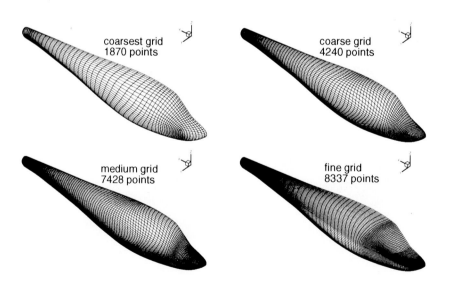

Fig. 3. Surface grid

The size and shape of rear separation areas are strongly affected by surface grid density. The wake area decreases with decreasing grid resolution, leading to underpredicted pressure drag. The position of the separation line also has a noticable effect on the upstream pressure distribution, leading to even more change in global forces.

The accuracy problem of force coefficients arises not only from the solution quality of the field data itself, but also from the difficulty of force integration. Since the absolute value of the force coefficients c_d and c_l are comparatively small, a small *absolute* error in the pressure- and skin friction distribution can produce a very high *relative* error in the force coefficients. A study on this problem has shown that, for the helicopter test case, a systematic error of only 1% in surface pressure coefficients can change the outcome of the integrated forces by up to 20%. From this point of view, the requirements of accuracy of the field data are very high in order to predict total forces at reasonable accuracy.

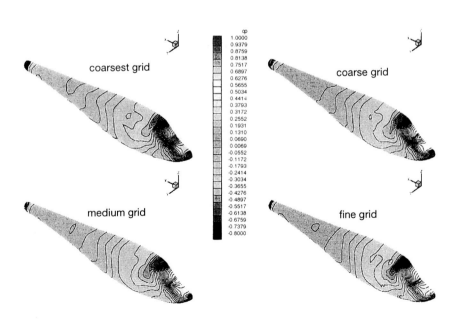

Fig. 4. Surface pressure distribution

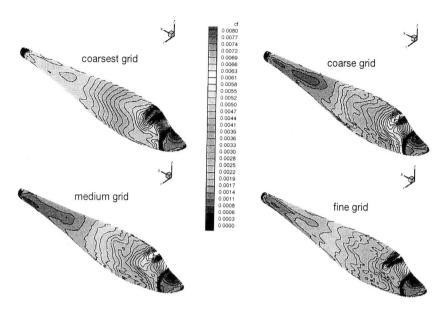

Fig. 5. Skin friction distribution

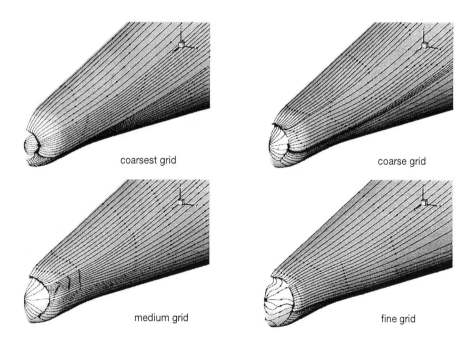

Fig. 6. Tail separation area and streamlines

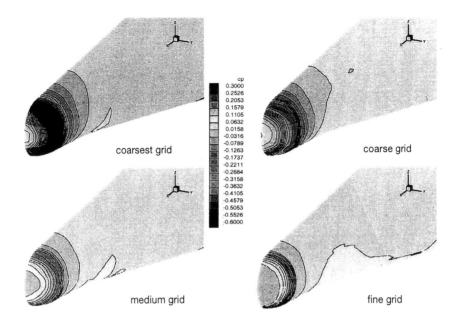

Fig. 7. Change in pressure distribution due to changing separation area

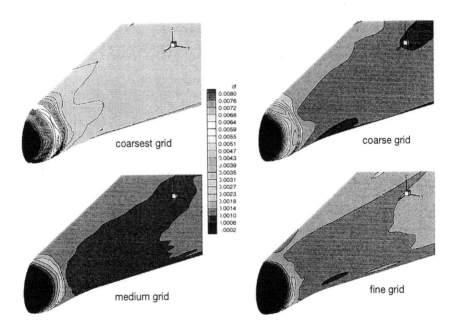

Fig. 8. Change in skin friction due to changing separation area

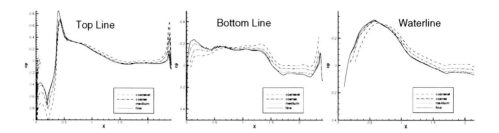

Fig. 9. Pressure distributions along selected lines

5   Computations on Common Grid

In order to separate grid influence from Navier-Stokes solver influence, computations of test case 2 on a common grid provided by DLR have been performed. The comparison of tail separation lines of the common grid calculation and the results gained from processing video sequences taken during wind tunnel testing show that the separation line is predicted very well, despite the use of the relatively simple Baldwin & Lomax turbulence model.

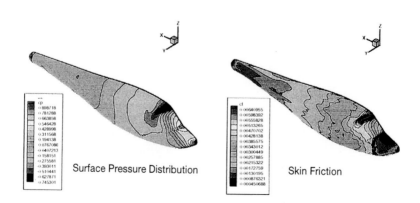

Fig. 10. Pressure distribution and skin friction for test case 2 on common grid

6   Higher Order Metrics

The order of a numerical scheme is a significant measure of quality for the code. In finite volume codes, second order schemes are in common use today. However, the higher order of the schemes is usually restricted only to the computational space, combined with a first order transformation (metrics) of the physical into the computational space. This transformation contains derivatives of the computational space coordinates ξ, η, ζ with respect to the physical coordinates x, y, z, forming a matrix of 9 elements altogether. For the standard 1st order transformation, these coefficients are formed by building the coefficients of the inverse transformation matrix (containing x_ξ, x_η etc.) and then inverting the matrix to obtain ξ_x, η_x...

The derivatives of the inverse transformation matrix are usually formed by first order finite differences.

In an attempt to obtain better solution quality with a higher order transformation, two different higher order metrics methods have been implemented. At this stage, only a two-dimensional version exists.

The first version is based on a cubic spline method, which can produce derivatives of up to 4th order. The grid is used to build up parametric two-dimensional splines along the grid line, resulting in locally defined polynomial functions for the grid geometry. The derivatives of these funktions are known mathematically exact.

The second version uses a 4th order central finite difference scheme to determine the metrics components. The high order can be maintained on the surface wall by switching to non-symmetric finite difference schemes.

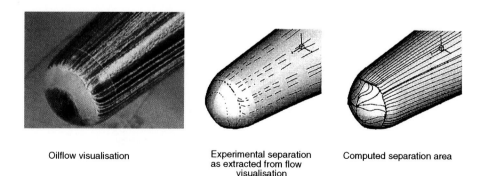

Oilflow visualisation   Experimental separation   Computed separation area
                             as extracted from flow
                             visualisation

Fig. 11. Comparison of computed and experimental separation

The flow around a NACA 0012 airfoil at subsonic speed and zero lift was used as a test case. For this test, the 2-dimensional unsteady Euler-code of H. Pomin, IAG, has been used. This solver is in its inviscid parts and flux computations very similar to the NSFLEX-code.

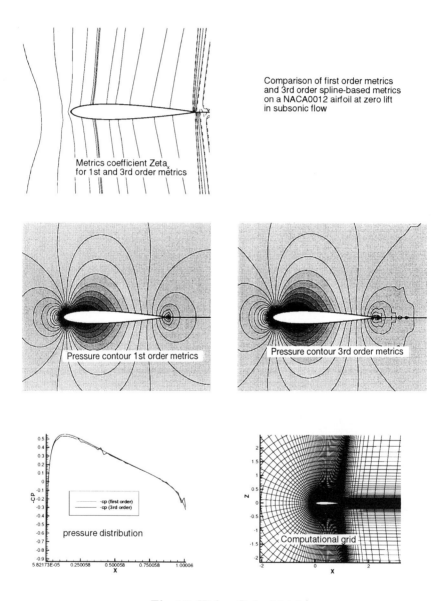

Fig. 12. Higher Order Metrics

The grid used for this test calculations is not particularly regular, nevertheless, the first order metrics computations show a smooth solution of good quality. However, the higher order (in this case 3rd order) metrics computation shows strong wiggles in the pressure distributions. Even though the difference in metrics terms are extremely small (as can be seen by the first picture in figure 12, the effect on the solution of the flow case is significant. The higher order metrics components are obviously stressing small grid irregularities in such a way that they become visible in the flowcase solution. With this early, disappointing result, an expansion to three-dimensional test cases has been postponed.

7   Computational Requirements

All the test calculations for the HELIFUSE project have been conducted on the HLRS NEC-SX4-Platform. Even though a parallel version of the NS-FLEX solver is available, only single cpu runs have been made so far. Since the parallel concept of NSFLEX requires a computational domain decomposition on multiblock level, reasonable parallelisation can hardly be made using the prescribed three-block H-O-H topology.

Since code convergence rates strongly depend on flow conditions like Mach- and Reynolds-numbers, it is difficult to predict computation time. The following short table gives an idea of memory and cpu time requirement for a $Mach = 0.235$ and $Re = 60000000$ test case.

Grid points	Memory	CPU time
200000	100 MB	6 hrs
470000	244 MB	12 hrs
850000	438 MB	20 hrs

With the large grid points involved, the code is assumed to reach a relatively high vectorisation efficiency, and therefore a high MFLOP rate. The measurement of precise numbers for cpu speed have been postponed to the third phase of HELIFUSE (Validation of improved codes) and will therefore not be included in this report. The number of iterations for convergence to reasonable stability is only weakly dependend on the total number of grid points, as long as $200000 < n_{grid} < 1000000$. About 20000 Iterations are necessary to completely smooth variations in the global force coefficients.

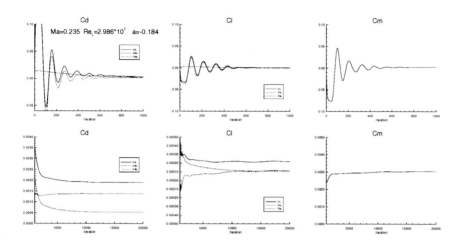

Fig. 13. Convergence history for test case 4

8   Conclusions

The grid dependency study has shown a noticable effect of grid point numbers and grid quality on the solution. A state of *weak* grid effect in terms of field data can only be optained for grids with more than 400000 points. For reasonable accuracy concerning global coefficients, the number of grid points has to be even larger.

The problem of force integration persists. With the small absolute values of these coefficients, integration using surface/field data boosts relative errors.

Higher order metrics terms haven't yet shown satisfactory results. It has to be tested if higher order metrics can be useful when being combined with a similarly based grid generation algorithm. In the long run, a higher order geometry representation might be capable of replacing the established grid principle.

Acknowledgements

The HELIFUSE project is funded by the European Union within the BRITE/ EURAM III framework, Area 3A Aeronautics of the Industrial an Material Technologies Programme.

References

1. T. MICHL Effiziente Euler- und Navier-Stokes-Löser für den Einsatz auf Vektor-Hochleistungsrechnern und massiv-parallelen Systemen. Dissertation, Institut für Aerodynamik und Gasdynamik 1995
2. M.COSTES, R.COLLERCANDY, N.KROLL, H.FRHR. VON GEYR, P. RENZONI, M. AMATO A. KOKKALIS, A. ROCCETO, C. SERR, E. LARRY, A. FILIPPONE, D. WEHR, Navier-Stokes Calculations of Helicopter Fuselage Flowfield and Loads. Proceedings of the 54th Annual Forum of the American Helicopter Society, Washington D.C., 1998 1998
3. J. GATARD, M. COSTES, N. KROLL, P. RENZONI, A. KOKKALIS, A. ROCHETTO, C. SERR E. LARREY, A. FILIPPONE, D. WEHR, High Reynolds Number Helicopter Fuselage Test in the ONERA-F1-Pressurized Wind Tunnel. 23rd European Rotorcraft Forum, Dresden, 1997 1998
4. D. WEHR Untersuchungen zum Wirbeltransport bei der Simulation der instationären Umströmung von Mehrblattrotoren mittels der Eulergleichungen. Institut für Aerodynamik und Gasdynamik 1998
5. B.S. BALDWIN, H. LOMAX Thin Layer Approximations and Algebraic Model for Separated Turbulent Flow Report AIAA 78-0257 1978
6. A. EBERLE Enhanced Numerical Inviscid and Viscous FLuxes for Cell Centered Finite Volume Schemes MBB-LKE-S-PUB-140 1991
7. PROGRAM DEVELOPMENT CORP. Gridpro-The CFD Link to Design, Software reference manual 1995
8. NUMECA INTERNATIONAL IGG - Interactive Geometry Modeller and Grid Generator, User Manual Version 3.4

Parallel multilevel algorithms for solving the incompressible Navier-Stokes equations.

Christian Becker, Hubertus Oswald and Stefan Turek

Institut für Angewandte Mathematik, Universität Heidelberg,
Im Neuenheimer Feld 294, 69120 Heidelberg, Germany

Abstract. This paper presents results of a numerical study for unsteady three–dimensional, incompressible flow. A finite element multigrid method is used in combination with an operator splitting technique and upwind discretization for the convective term. A nonconforming element pair, living on hexahedrons, which is of order $O(h^2/h)$ for velocity and pressure, is used for the spatial discretization. The second order fractional–step–θ–scheme is employed for the time discretization.

For this approach we present the parallel implementation of a multigrid code for MIMD computers with message passing and distributed memory. Multiplicative multigrid methods as stand–alone iterations are considered. We present a very efficient implementation of Gauß-Seidel resp. SOR smoothers, which have the same amount of communication as a Jacobi smoother.

As well we present measured MFLOP for Blas 1 and Lin routines (as SAXPY) for different vector length. The measured performance are between 20 MFLOP for large vectorlength and 450 MFLOP for short vectorlength.

1 Introduction

We consider parallel numerical solution techniques for the nonstationary incompressible Navier–Stokes equations. After discretizing these equations, we have to solve many algebraic systems. For this we use parallel multilevel algorithm. We will discuss additive and multiplicative preconditioner and full multigrid. The parallelization uses the grid decomposition: The decomposition of the algebraic quantities is arranged according to the structure of the discretization. The grouping of gridpoints in subdomains automatically leads to a block structuring of the system matrix.

Multiplicative multigrid methods as stand–alone iterations are considered. The various components of a multigrid algorithm have very different potential for parallelization: The grid transfer operations are local, therefore they can be easily parallelized in the same way as the matrix-vector multiplication. The same holds true for the defect computation. The most difficult problem is in the parallelization of

  - the sequential loops over all elements in the smoothing process,
  - the solution of the coarse grid problem.

Unfortunately all efficient smoothers possess a high degree of recursiveness. This particularly concerns the common Gauß-Seidel and the robust ILU-type smoothers. Both methods can be realized in an efficient parallel code only to the expense of high communication load which is acceptable only on systems with extremly fast communication performance. Hence, a sequential multigrid algorithm and its parallelized counterpart usually differ only in the smoothing process employed.

A solution of this problem is breaking of recursivness by blocking. Here, the global loops over all elements are broken into local ones over the elements belonging to the same processors resulting in a reduced communication overhead similar to that of a global matrix-vector multiplication. This strategy generally leads to a very satisfactory parallel efficiency but also unevitably to a reduction in the numerical performance of the overall multigrid algorithm. Fortunately, practical experience with this strategy has shown that the losses in the numerical efficiency by using simplified block smoothers are relatively small and usually acceptable. This is due to the fact that the smoothers are only supposed to well reduce the high frequency components which does not depend so much on the long-distance flow of information. We use point Jacobi and Gauß–Seidel resp. SOR as smoothers.

2   Numerical Solution Method

The problem under consideration is mathematically described by the incompressible nonstationary Navier–Stokes equations,

$$\mathbf{u}_t - \nu \Delta \mathbf{u} + (\mathbf{u} \cdot \nabla)\mathbf{u} + \nabla p = \mathbf{f} \quad , \quad \nabla \cdot \mathbf{u} = 0 \quad \text{in } \Omega \times (0, T) \,,$$
$$\mathbf{u} = \mathbf{g} \quad \text{on } \partial\Omega \quad , \quad \mathbf{u}_{|t=0} = \mathbf{u}_0 \,,$$

where $\{\mathbf{u}, p\}$ is the unknown velocity $\mathbf{u} = (u_1, u_2, u_3)^T$ and p the pressure of an incompressible flow in Ω with given right hand side $\mathbf{f} = (f_1, f_2, f_3)^T$ and boundary data $\mathbf{g} = (g_1, g_2, g_3)^T$.

In setting up a finite element model of the Navier–Stokes problem we start from the variational formulation of the problem:
Find $\mathbf{u}$ and p, with $\mathbf{u} \in \mathbf{H} \subset \mathbf{H}_0^1$ and $p \in L^2(\Omega)$, such that

$$(\mathbf{u}_t, \varphi) + a(\mathbf{u}, \varphi) + n(\mathbf{u}, \mathbf{u}, \varphi) + b(p, \varphi) = (\mathbf{f}, \varphi) \,, \qquad \forall \varphi \in \mathbf{H} \subset \mathbf{H}^1 \,,$$
$$b(\chi, \mathbf{u}) = 0 \,, \qquad \forall \chi \in L^2 \,,$$

with the notation

$$a(\mathbf{u}, \mathbf{v}) = \nu(\nabla\mathbf{u}, \nabla\mathbf{v}) \,, \quad n(\mathbf{u}, \mathbf{v}, \mathbf{w}) = (\mathbf{u} \cdot \nabla\mathbf{v}, \mathbf{w}) \,, \quad b(p, \mathbf{v}) = -(p, \nabla \cdot \mathbf{v}) \,.$$

Let $\mathbf{T}_h$ be a regular decomposition of the domain $\Omega \subset \mathbf{R}^3$ into hexaeders $T \in \mathbf{T}_h$, where the mesh parameter h represents the maximum diameter of the elements $T \in \mathbf{T}_h$. We use a nonconforming finite element method with a so–called *rotated trilinear ansatz* for the velocity and constant one for the pressure (see [6], [4]). The rotated trilinear finite element functions on element T are given by the space

$$\hat{Q}_1(T) := \{q \circ \psi_T^{-1} \mid q \in span\langle 1, x, y, z, x^2 - y^2, y^2 - z^2 \rangle\}.$$

The degrees of freedom are determined via the functional $\{F_\Gamma(\cdot), \Gamma \in \partial \mathbf{T}_h\}$ (m denotes the center of the areas of each element, $\partial \mathbf{T}_h$ denotes the set of all edges Γ of the elements $T \in \mathbf{T}_h$):

$$F_\Gamma(v) := v(m_\Gamma).$$

The discrete spaces are then defined as:

$$L_h := \{q_h \in L_0^2(\Omega) | q_{h|T} = const., \forall T \in \mathbf{T}_h\},$$

$$\mathbf{H}_h := V_h \times V_h \times V_h,$$

with

$$V_h := \left\{ \begin{array}{l} v_h \in L^2(\Omega) \mid v_{h|T} \in \hat{Q}_1(T), \forall T \in \mathbf{T}_h, \ v_h \text{ continuos w.r.t. the func-} \\ \text{tional } F_{\Gamma_{ij}}(\cdot), \forall \text{faces } \Gamma_{ij}, \text{ and } F_{\Gamma_{i0}}(v_h) = 0, \forall \text{faces } \Gamma_{i0} \end{array} \right\}.$$

The degrees of freedom are the mean value of the pressure for each element and the value for the velocity on each midpoint of the face. Then we have for each element 6 values for the velocity and 1 for the pressure. The discrete bilinear forms $a_h(\cdot, \cdot)$, $n_h(\cdot, \cdot)$ and $b_h(\cdot, \cdot)$ (with corresponding Matrices A_h, N_h, B_h and mass matrix M_h) are defined elementwise, because $\mathbf{H}_h \not\subset \mathbf{H}_0^1(\Omega)$ and therefore $\mathbf{H}_h$ is a nonconforming ansatz space.

It can be shown, that the LBB–condition is fulfilled for this element pair ([6] and [8]), so stability is guarenteed, and that there is h^2/h approximation property.

It is well known that in the case of high Reynolds numbers a central discretization leads to numerical instabilities and oszillations. So we use a different discretization for the convection term, a so called upwind discretization ([10]).

For the time discretization we use the *fractional–step–θ–scheme* ([5]).

Choosing $\theta \in (0, 1)$, $\theta' = 1 - 2\theta$, and $\alpha \in [0.5, 1]$, $\beta = 1 - \alpha$, $\tilde{k} = \alpha\theta k = \beta\theta'k$: the time step $t_n \to t_{n+1}$ is split into three substeps as follows. Here, we assume for simplicity that the forces $\mathbf{f}$ are homogeneous, otherwise see ([12]).

$$[M_h + \tilde{k}S_h(\mathbf{u}^{n+\theta})]\mathbf{u}^{n+\theta} + kB_h p^{n+\theta} = [M_h - \beta\theta k S_h(\mathbf{u}^n)]\mathbf{u}^n$$
$$B_h^T \mathbf{u}^{n+\theta} = 0,$$
$$[M_h + \tilde{k}S_h(\mathbf{u}^{n+1-\theta})]\mathbf{u}^{n+1-\theta} + kB_h p^{n+1-\theta} = [M_h - \alpha\theta' k S_h(\mathbf{u}^{n+\theta})]\mathbf{u}^{n+\theta}$$
$$B_h^T \mathbf{u}^{n+1-\theta} = 0,$$
$$[M_h + \tilde{k}S_h(\mathbf{u}^{n+1})]\mathbf{u}^{n+1} + kB_h p^{n+1} = [M_h - \beta\theta k S_h(\mathbf{u}^{n+1-\theta})]\mathbf{u}^{n+1-\theta}$$
$$B_h^T \mathbf{u}^{n+1} = 0,$$

where we use the abbreviation $S_h(x^m) = A_h + N_h(x^m)$. For the special choice $\theta = 1 - \sqrt{2}/2$ this scheme is of second order and strongly A-stable. For $\alpha = (1 - 2\theta)/(1 - \theta), \beta = \theta/(1 - \theta)$ the coefficient matrices are the same in all substeps. Therefore we think that this scheme is able to combine the advantages of the implicit Euler and Crank–Nicolson–scheme, without more additional numerical amount comparing with three Crank–Nicolson steps.

To avoid solving a saddle-point like problem with strongly indefinite coefficient matrices we use a so called *discrete projection scheme* proposed by Turek (see [11]). This scheme reads as follows:

1. Start with $\mathbf{u}^0 = \mathbf{u}_0$ and $p^0 \approx p(0)$.
2. For $n > 0$ and $\{\mathbf{u}^{n-1}, p^{n-1}\}$ given, determine $\tilde{\mathbf{u}}^n$:

$$S_h(\tilde{\mathbf{u}}^n)\tilde{\mathbf{u}}^n = f_h - kB_h p^{n-1}. \tag{1}$$

3a. Projection step with condensed matrix $P_h = B_h^T M_h^{-1} B_h$:

$$P_h q = \frac{1}{k} B_h^T \tilde{\mathbf{u}}^n. \tag{2}$$

3b. Determine $\{\mathbf{u}^{n+1}, p^{n+1}\}$:

$$p^n = p^{n-1} + q,$$

$$\mathbf{u}^n = \tilde{\mathbf{u}}^n - kM_h^{-1}B_h q.$$

In the fully nonstationary case our practical experiences show that the splitting technique leads to much more robust and efficient methods than fully coupled approaches. Additionally, this scheme can also be applied on general meshes and allows a rigorous error analysis based on variational arguments.

3   Grid Generation and Partitioning

The basis for our parallelization approach are blockstructured grids (see Figure 1). They are constructed in the following way: We start with a nonoverlapping decomposition of the domain Ω into hexaeders M_i, $i = 1, \cdots, N_m$. Now, the finite element mesh for each finer level can be constructed in parallel on the macroelements by dividing each element of the previous coarser grid level into 8 finer elements. Since within this refinement process we bisect the edges of the coarser grid, the separately defined meshes are well matched on adjoining macroelements.

An important issue in domain decomposition is choosing the subdomains. For simple tensor-product grids the procedure is straightforward. For unstructured grids or blockstructured grids it becomes a question of grid partitioning. When applying domain decomposition to parallel computing, there is the goal

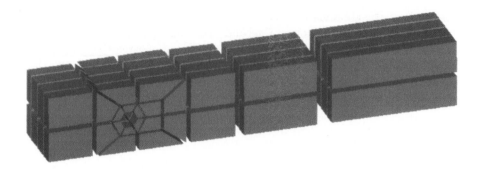

Fig. 1. decomposition of Ω into macroelements M_i

of decomposing the grid into p pieces each roughly the same size while minimizing the size of the borders between subdomains, and hence decreasing the
communication needed between processors. In addition, ideally the amount
of work and storage requirements for each processor should be roughly similar; achieving this referred to as load balancing. To solve this problem we use
partitioning tools (PARTY (University of Paderborn) or METIS (University
of Minnesota)). This tools are using advanced graph partitioning algorithms.
We map a cluster of coarse grid elements, which we call a macroelement, to
one processor P_i (see Figure 2).

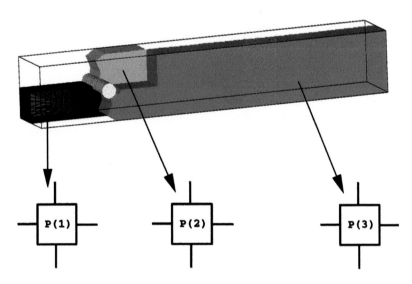

Fig. 2. mapping of macroelements M_i to processors P_i

3.1   Parallel Smoother

The smoothers we used are block Jacobi schemes iterations with different inner solvers. As inner solver we use either damped point Jacobi,

$$x^{m+1} = x^m - \omega D^{-1}(Ax^m - b),$$

or Gauß-Seidel resp. SOR,

$$x^{m+1} = x^m - \omega(D - \omega E)^{-1}(Ax^m - b),$$

or ILU,

$$x^{m+1} = x^m - \omega A_{\text{ILU}}^{-1}(Ax^m - b),$$

with the notation A=D-E-F. Applying one step of point Jacobi requires exactly one exchange over the interface nodes for calculating the consistent defect $Ax^m - b$. There is no change to the sequential version, therefore we get the same result applying point Jacobi smoother.

In each smoothing step of the block Jacobi scheme we update the vector $x^{old} \to x^{new}$. We split up this procedure into several tasks according to the macroelements. Each macroelement task T_i updates its own vector x_k^{old}, $k \in I(M_i)$. The common unknowns of two macroelements $k \in I(M_i) \cap I(M_j)$ have different values $x_k^{T_i}$ and $x_k^{T_j}$, therefore one local communication sweep exchanges these values and the common new values are calculated:

$$x_i^{new} := \frac{1}{2}(x_k^{T_i} + x_k^{T_j}) \quad \forall k \in I(M_i) \cap I(M_j). \tag{3}$$

The advantage of the nonconforming finite elements is that each unknown x_k is at most related to two elements. Compared to conforming finite elements the communication is much more easier.

The next table demonstrates the convergence behavior of full multigrid with block Jacobi scheme as smoother. The used configuration is:

– **PDE:** The Helmholtz equation,

$$-\Delta u + u = x^2 + y^2 + z^2 - 6 \quad \text{in } \Omega,$$
$$u = x^2 + y^2 + z^2 \quad \text{on } \partial\Omega,$$

  with Dirichlet boundary conditions.
– **Domain:** Unit square with 262144 elements on the finest level and with different aspect ratios (1:5, 1:50, 1:500) locally in the macroelement. This means that elements close to the boundary are stretched in y-direction.
– **Discretization:** 'Rotated' trilinear finite elements.
– **Calculations:** For this problem we compare the number of iterations of the parallel block smoothers with the sequential version.

Iteration Count for 10^{-10} Reduction in Error for Full Multigrid (2 Pre- and Post-Smoothing steps):

Procs	Aspect Ratio	Par. Multigrid			Seq. Multigrid		
		Jacobi	SOR	ILU	Jacobi	SOR	ILU
8	1:5	34	21	5	34	9	5
8	1:50	>100	>100	6	>100	>100	6
8	1:500	>100	>100	6	>100	>100	6
16	1:5	34	21	5	34	9	5
16	1:50	>100	>100	6	>100	>100	6
16	1:500	>100	>100	6	>100	>100	6
32	1:5	34	22	6	34	9	5
32	1:50	>100	>100	6	>100	>100	6
32	1:500	>100	>100	6	>100	>100	6
64	1:5	34	22	6	34	9	5
64	1:50	>100	>100	6	>100	>100	6
64	1:500	>100	>100	7	>100	>100	6

Iteration Count for 10^{-10} Reduction in Error for Full Multigrid for different number of smoothing steps (ILU)

Procs	Aspect Ratio	Smoothing Steps	Par. Multigrid	Seq. Multigrid
16	1:5	2	6	5
16	1:50	2	7	6
16	1:500	2	9	8
16	1:5	3	5	5
16	1:50	3	6	6
16	1:500	3	9	8
16	1:5	4	5	5
16	1:50	4	6	6
16	1:500	4	8	8

3.2   Parallel Efficiency

From Figures 3-5 we can draw the following conclusions:

- Figure 3 shows a lost of parallel efficiency for the full multigrid by global communication. It means if we increase the number of processors the costs for global communication increases proportional.
- From Figure 4 and 5 we can draw the conclusion that we have to take the number of grid levels as high as possible in order to receive good parallel efficiency.

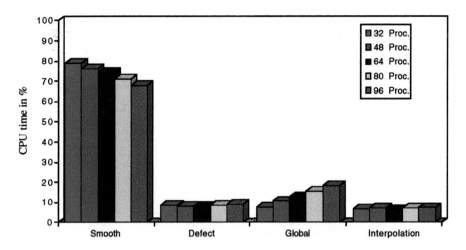

Fig. 3. CPU time in percent for different multigrid components

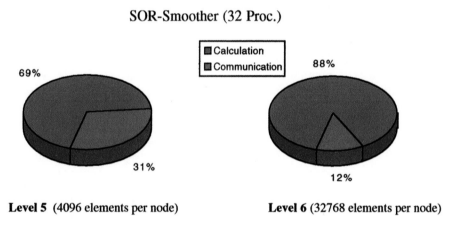

SOR-Smoother (32 Proc.)

Level 5 (4096 elements per node)   **Level 6** (32768 elements per node)

Fig. 4. Parallel efficiency of smoother

4   Numerical Results

In this section we consider the 1995–DFG Benchmark problem 'Flow around a Cylinder'. To facilitate the comparison of these solution approaches, a set of benchmark problems has been defined and all participants of the Priority Research Program working on incompressible flows have been invited to submit their solutions. The paper [7] presents the results of these computations contributed by altogether 17 research groups, 10 from the Priority Research

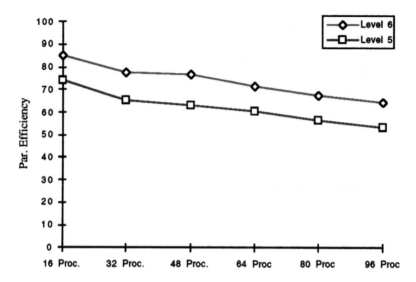

Fig. 5. Parallel efficiency of multigrid algorithm

Program and 7 from outside. The major purpose of the benchmark was to establish whether constructive conclusions can be drawn from a comparison of these results so that the solutions can be improved.

We give a brief summary of the definition of the test case for the benchmark computations in the 3D case, including precise definitions of the quantities which have to be computed and also some additional instructions which were given to the participants. The complete information containing all definitions and results can be found in [7]. An incompressible Newtonian fluid is considered for which the conservation equations of mass and momentum are

$$\frac{\partial U_i}{\partial x_i} = 0 \quad , \quad \rho \frac{\partial U_i}{\partial t} + \rho \frac{\partial}{\partial x_j}(U_j U_i) = \rho \nu \frac{\partial}{\partial x_j}\left(\frac{\partial U_i}{\partial x_j} + \frac{\partial U_j}{\partial x_i}\right) - \frac{\partial P}{\partial x_i}. \quad (4)$$

The notations are time t, cartesian coordinates $(x_1, x_2, x_3) = (x, y, z)$, pressure P and velocity components $(U_1, U_2, U_3) = (U, V, W)$. The kinematic viscosity is defined as $\nu = 10^{-3}\,\mathrm{m}^2/\mathrm{s}$, and the fluid density is $\rho = 1.0\,\mathrm{kg/m}^3$.

For the test case the flow around a cylinder with circular cross–sections is considered. The problem configurations and boundary conditions are illustrated in Fig. 6. We concentrate on the periodically unsteady test case with steady inflow. The relevant input data are:

- no slip condition at the upper and lower walls and the cylinder
- parabolic inflow (left side) with a maximum velocity of $u_{max} = 1.5$
- natural boundary conditions at the "outflow" (right side)
- viscosity parameter $1/\nu = 1,000$, resulting Reynolds number $Re = 100$

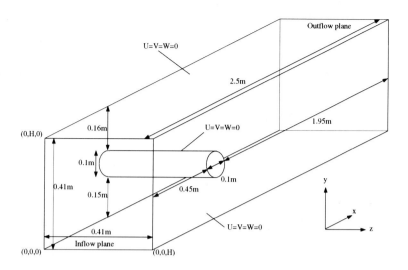

Fig. 6. Configuration and boundary conditions for flow around a cylinder.

– upwind discretization of the convective terms (*adaptive upwinding*)
– Crank–Nicolson time discretization of the temporal derivatives
– calculation performed for $T = [0, 1]$, started with a fully developed solution

The main goal of our benchmark computation was to achieve a reliable reference solution in the described 3D test case. Therefore we will describe the convergence history in terms of drag and lift coefficients.

Some definitions are introduced to specify the drag and lift coefficients which have to be computed. The height and width of the channel is $H = 0.41\,\mathrm{m}$, and the diameter of the cylinder is $D = 0.1\,\mathrm{m}$. The characteristic velocity is $\overline{U}(t) = 4U(0, H/2, H/2, t)/9$, and the Reynolds number is defined by $Re = \overline{U}D/\nu$. The drag and lift forces are

$$F_D = \int_S \left(\rho\nu\frac{\partial v_t}{\partial n}n_y - Pn_x\right)dS \quad , \quad F_L = -\int_S \left(\rho\nu\frac{\partial v_t}{\partial n}n_x + Pn_y\right)dS\,, \quad (5)$$

with the following notations: surface of cylinder S, normal vector n on S with x-component n_x and y-component n_y, tangential velocity v_t on S and tangent vector $t = (n_y, -n_x, 0)$. The drag and lift coefficients are

$$c_D = \frac{2F_w}{\rho\overline{U}^2DH} \quad , \quad c_L = \frac{2F_a}{\rho\overline{U}^2DH}\,. \quad (6)$$

Figure 7 shows the coarse mesh and the refined mesh on level 2. The refined levels have been created via recursively connecting opposite midpoints. All calculations have been done on the levels 3–5. Table 1 shows the corresponding geometrical information and degrees of freedom.

level	vertices	elements	faces	total unknowns
1	1485	1184	3,836	12,692
2	10,642	9,472	29,552	98,128
3	80,388	75,776	231,872	771,392
4	624,520	606,208	1,836,800	6,116,608
5	4,922,640	4,849,664	14,621,696	48,714,752

Table 1. Geometrical information and degrees of freedom for various levels

Table 2 shows the computational time for one Macro time step (one Fractional-θ-step) on SP2 and Cray T3E with a different number of processors:

Computer	Num. Procs	Time
SP2	64	~ 29 min
Cray T3E	128	~ 19 min
Cray T3E	256	~ 12 min

Table 2. Computational time for one macro time-step

In table 3 we present the calculated drag and lift coefficients for various level of refinement. We distinguish between the two methods of calculating the coefficients.

level	c_D	c_L
3	3.37923	0.00193477
4	3.29405	-0.00614614
5	3.29263	-0.00841249

Table 3. Drag and Lift coefficients

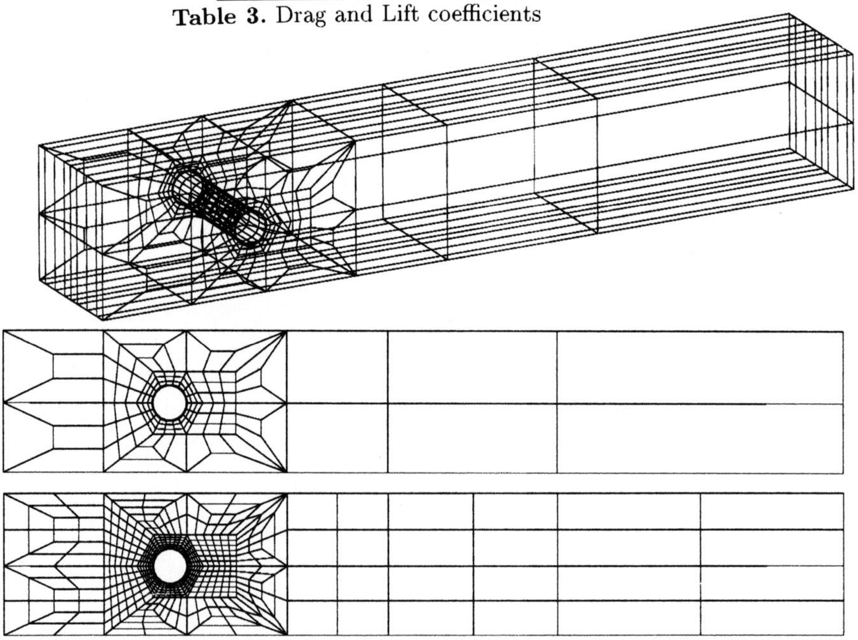

Fig. 7. Coarse mesh and refined meshes (level 2 and level 3)

5   Computational Results

We examine the following main components as part of some basic iteration:

5.1   Linear combination of two vectors:

1. (Standard) linear combination DAXPY: $\boxed{x(i) = \alpha x(i) + y(i)}$

The DAXPY subroutine for the linear combination (with fixed α!) is (mostly) part of machine–optimized libraries and therefore a good - since 'simple' - candidate for testing the quality of such Numerical Linear Algebra packages. While for short vector lengths a high percentage of the possible PEAK performance can be expected, the results for long vectors - which are not completely in the cache - give more realistic performance rates for iterative schemes. Additionally, DAXPY can be viewed as test for matrix-vector multiplication, i.e. for banded matrices with constant coefficients. For such matrices, the MV routine is often based on a sequence of DAXPY-calls.

2. (Variable) linear combination DAXPYV: $\boxed{x(i) = \alpha(i)x(i) + y(i)}$

In contrast to the standard DAXPY subroutine, the scaling factor α is a vector, too. This subroutine is a necessary component for banded matrix-vector multiplications with arbitrary coefficients as matrix entries.

3. (Indexed) linear combination DAXPYI: $\boxed{x(i) = \alpha(j(i))x(i) + y(i)}$

In contrast to the previous subroutines, the scaling factor α is a vector with components which depend from index i via an *index vector* $j(i)$. This subroutine is a typical test for *sparse matrices* which store only the non-vanishing matrix elements together with linked lists or index arrays.

For vectors with length N, all resulting MFLOP rates are measured via $2 \times N/time$.

5.2   Matrix-vector multiplication (MV):

In our tests, we examine more carefully the following five variants which all are typical in the context of iterative schemes with sparse matrices. We prescribe a typical 9–point stencil ("discretized Poisson operator") as test matrix. Consequently, the storage cost and hence the measure for the resulting MFLOP rate is identical for all following techniques, namely $20 \times N/time$.

1. Sparse MV: SMV

The *sparse MV* technique is the standard technique in Finite Element codes (and others), also well known as 'compact storage' technique or similar: the matrix (plus index arrays or lists) is stored as long array containing the "nonzero elements" only. While this approach can be applied for arbitrary meshes and numberings of the unknowns, no explicit advantage of the linewise numbering can be exploited. We expect a massive loss of performance with respect to the possible PEAK rates since - at least for larger problems - no 'caching in' and 'pipelining' can be exploited such that the higher cost of memory access will dominate the resulting MFLOP rates. The results should be similar as those for the previous DAXPYI subroutine.

2. Banded MV: BMV

A 'natural' way to improve the *sparse MV* is to exploit that the matrix is a banded matrix with 9 bands only. Hence, the matrix–vector multiplication is rewritten such that now "band after band" are applied. In fact, each "band multiplication" is performed analogously to the DAXPY, resp., the DAXPYV operation (modulo the "variable" multiplication factors!), and should therefore lead to similar results. The obvious advantage of this *banded MV* approach is that these tasks can be performed on the basis of BLAS1-like routines which may exploit the vectorization facilities of many processors (particularly on vector computers!). However, for 'long' vector lengths the improvements can be absolutely disappointing: For the recent workstation/PC chip technology, the processor cache dominates the resulting efficiency!

3. Banded blocked MV: BBMVA, BBMVL, BBMVC

The final step towards highly efficient components is to rearrange the matrix–vector multiplication in a "blockwise" sense: for a certain set of unknowns, a corresponding part of the matrix is treated such that cache-optimized and fully vectorized operations can be performed. This procedure is called "BLAS 2+"-style since in fact certain techniques for dense matrices which are based on routines from the BLAS2, resp., BLAS3 library, have now been developed for such sparse banded matrices. The exact procedure has to be carefully developed in dependence of the underlying FEM discretization, and a more detailed description can be found in [3].

While version BBMVA has to be applied in the case of arbitrary matrix coefficients, BBMVL and BBMVC are modified version which can be used under certain circumstances only (see [3] for the technical details). For example, PDE's with constant coefficients as the Poisson operator, but on a mesh which is adapted in one special direction, allow the use of BBMVL: This is the case of the Pressure–Poisson problem in flow simulations (see [12]) on boundary adapted meshes! Additionally, version BBMVC may be applied for PDE's with constant coefficients on meshes with equidistant mesh distribution in each (local) direction separately which is often the case in the interior domain where the solution is mostly smooth!

4. Tridiagonal MV: TMV

A careful examination of the resulting matrix stencils which are obtained on logical tensor product meshes for almost arbitrary Finite Element basis functions, one can see that the complete matrix consists of many tridiagonal submatrices and generalized banded matrices. Therefore, one very important component in the treatment of sparse banded matrices is - beside the already introduced DAXPYV routines - the multiplication with a tridiagonal matrix. Particularly the *banded blocked MV* operations can be reduced among others to the frequent use of such *tridiagonal MV* routines. The measured MFLOP rates are based on the prescription $8 \times N/time$. We examine following aspects:

- We expect on workstation/PC platforms 'bad' performance results for the *sparse MV* and the *banded MV*. However, is it possible to improve these results via the *banded blocked MV* techniques which are explicitly based on the fact that the matrices come from FEM discretizations? Do the cache-intensive 'BLAS 2+' techniques work fine for long vectors.
- These new *banded blocked MV* are based on DAXPYV and TMV routines which have to be compiled with FORTRAN compilers. Is it nevertheless possible to achieve 'optimal' rates in comparison to other machine-optimized routines from the BLAS or ESSL?

5.3   Inversion of tridiagonal matrices: TRSA, TRSL

Beside the DAXPYV and tridiagonal matrix-vector multiplication routines (TMV), another essential tool is the inversion of tridiagonal matrices, or better: the solution of linear system with tridiagonal matrix. This task can be reduced to routines which are typically implemented in Numerical Linear Algebra libraries as LAPACK, ESSL or PERFLIB. Analogously to the previous *banded blocked MV* routines we perform two versions (see [3]) which are for arbitrary coefficients (TRSA) or for some special cases (TRSL). However, both subroutines explicitly exploit the fact that the 'complete' tridiagonal is in fact split into multiple 'smaller' tridiagonal submatrices if a FEM discretization is performed.

Since this tridiagonal preconditioning is an important component in the robust multigrid solution process for anisotropic problems, the resulting performance rates are of great importance for us. However, beside the MFLOP rates which are expected to be 'small' due to the internal divisions, the total CPU time is more important to compare with the corresponding cost of the matrix-vector multiplication. Additionally, these measurements are a good test for the quality of the implemented Numerical Linear Algebra libraries. The measured MFLOP rates for the 'inversion process' are based on the prescription $7 \times N/time$.

5.4   linpack test: GE

Gaussian Elimination (GE) is presented to demonstrate the (potentially) high performance on the given processors (often several hundreds of MFLOP!). However, one should look at the corresponding total CPU times! The measured MFLOP are for a dense matrix (analogously to the standard *linpack* test!). In all cases, we attempt to use "optimal" compiler options and machine-optimized libraries as the BLAS, ESSL or PERFLIB. Only in the case of the PENTIUM II we had to perform the Gaussian Elimination with the FORTRAN-sources exclusively which might explain the worse rates.

5.5   Results

The first example shows typical results for some of the discussed components on different computers. The second one demonstrates specific hardware-dependent 'problems' with DAXPY as prototypical example for the other components. Both examples provide realistic performance results in numerical simulations: for different computer architectures and various implementation approaches. More information about the complete 'PERFTEST' set for realistic performance rates and source codes can be obtained from:

> `http://gaia.iwr.uni-heidelberg.de/~featflow`

In the following table, N denotes the vector length which is quite typical in the context of discretized partial differential equations: '4K' corresponds to 4,225 unknowns, while '64K', resp., '256K', correspond to 66,049, resp., 263,169 unknowns. As indicated above, for the linpack test (GE) we prescribe a dense matrix and the corresponding problem size for GE is 289, 1,089 resp., 2,304 unknowns. We provide the typically MFLOP rates, only in the case of DAXPY we show the maximum as well as the minimum (in brackets) values.

Computer	N	$\frac{2N}{T}$ DAXPY	SMV	BMV	BBMVA	BBMVL	BBMVC	GE
IBM RS6000	4K	420(330)	54	154	154	196	240	365
(166 Mhz)	64K	100 (92)	49	71	140	206	234	374
'SP2'	256K	100 (90)	50	71	143	189	240	374
DEC Alpha	4K	390(220)	34	46	81	158	223	309
(433 Mhz)	64K	60 (20)	22	42	63	117	189	409
'CRAY T3E'	256K	60 (20)	22	42	67	110	196	454
SUN U450	4K	165 (3)	35	102	100	99	127	246
(250 Mhz)	64K	123 (3)	15	21	35	85	119	249
	256K	30 (3)	14	17	36	72	99	282
INTEL PII	4K	43 (25)	20	28	24	56	60	34
(233 Mhz)	64K	21 (19)	11	14	20	37	47	27
	256K	19 (17)	–	–	–	–	–	–

(Header spans: $\frac{2N}{T}$ over DAXPY; $\frac{20N}{T}$ over SMV, BMV, BBMVA, BBMVL, BBMVC.)

The results for DAXPY and for the *sparse MV* (SMV) deteriorate massively as explained before, particularly for long vectors. Analogously, the *banded MV* (BMV) does not lead to significant improvements.

The realistic performance for iterative solvers based on such (standard) techniques is far away from the (linpack) PEAK rates. The results are 'quasi-optimal' since the best-available F77 compiler options have been applied. It should be a necessary test for everyone, particularly for those who work in F90, C++ or JAVA, to measure the efficiency of the MV routines!

Moreover, the typical performance result for numerical simulation tools based on these standard techniques (DAXPY, sparse MV, banded MV) is between 10 – 60 MFLOP only. The following examples will even show that

*for the SUN ULTRA450 only 3(!) MFLOP, and for the 'number cruncher'
CRAY T3E also 20 MFLOP only, can be realistic for 'larger problems': this
is about 2 MFLOP higher than a PC with PENTIUM II processor for about
1,500 DM!*

In contrast, the results for the linpack test (GE) and the 'blocked' matrix-
vector routines (BBMV's) show that computers as the IBM SP2, the CRAY
T3E and the SUN ULTRA450 have the potential to be 'number crunchers'.
However, one has to work hard to reach the range of hundreds of MFLOP in
iterative solvers. In particular, our hierarchical solver ScaRC in combination
with the so-called 'BLAS 2+' style for (sparse) matrix-vector operations gives
very promising results. These will be even improved by more careful implementations which will include optimized versions of the introduced DAXPYV
and *tridiagonal MV* routines. It might be desirable to convince the computer
vendors to incorporate these routines into machine-optimized libraries!

Another result in the table is that some of the DAXPY results show large
differences between the minimum and maximum MFLOP rates. Here, we do
not address the small variations of 1 – 10 % but the 'large' discrepancies as
from 165 down to 3 MFLOP or from 60 to 20 MFLOP: These differences are
due to the different position of both vectors to each other!

Many oscillations, as for instance 330, resp., 420 MFLOP on the IBM, or
analogously 130, resp., 165 MFLOP on the SUN, can be simply eliminated by
using <u>even</u> differences between vectors only. Moreover, it might be well-known
to hardware specialists that certain cache architectures lead to performance
losses w.r.t. the positioning of vectors.

Nevertheless, for us as numerical software developers it was very surprising
to detect the massive degradation of compute power: For instance for all SUN
ULTRA models, we could find configurations in which the SUN ULTRA450
decreases down to **3 MFLOP (!)** only, and this for **all** vector lengths (see
also [2]). The following figure shows the periodic behaviour (for the length of
1 MByte which is the size of the LEVEL2-cache!) of the DAXPY MFLOP
rates. Analogous effects can also be detected for the ALPHA DEC Chip which
is used in PC's and workstations.

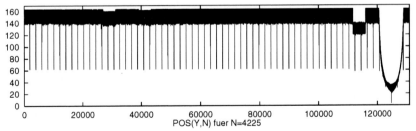

Similar results - without this 'dramatic' loss - can be detected on the
CRAY T3E (Stuttgart) for long vectors: Beside the rather modest 60 MFLOP
(this a 900 MFLOP computer!), certain differences in the positions of the
vectors leads to **20 MFLOP (!)** only, about the quality of Home-PC's!

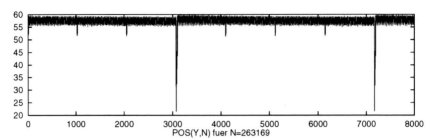

One might discuss the relevance of this 'failure' (see [2]) which seems be well-known to 'hardware specialists', but most of the numerical simulation software is written by mathematicians, physicists, engineers, etc! Typical software developers should be provided with such information since many of these 'failures' can be eliminated through the memory management which is self-developed in most codes! Otherwise it seems to be a 'computational time bomb' in numerical simulations!

6   Conclusions

We have presented an efficient algorithm for solving the nonstationary incompressible Navier-Stokes equations, which uses multilevel preconditioner or full multigrid to solve the linear systems of equations. The parallel full multigrid algorithm has nearly the same convergence properties as the sequential one. To achieve the best efficiency for the parallel algorithm one has to take as many grid levels as possible because each processor has a large number of unknowns on the finest grid level which leads to a good relation between communication and arithmetical work.

Our computational examples have shown that there is a large gap between the highly polished linpack rates of recently several hundreds of MFLOP as typical representant for 'direct solvers', and the realistic results for 'iterative solvers'. The out-of-cache performance for DAXPY-like iterations or for the standard *sparse MV* matrix-vector multiplication is much smaller, often less than 5 % of the possible performance.

References

1. Altieri, M., Becker, Chr., Kilian, S., Oswald, H., Turek, S., Wallis, J.: Some basic concepts of FEAST, Proc. 14th GAMM Seminar 'Concepts of Numerical Software', Kiel, Januar 1998, to appear in *NNFM*, Vieweg, 1998
2. Altieri, M., Becker, Chr., Turek, S.: Konsequenzen eines numerischen 'Elch Tests' für Prozessor–Architektur und Computersimulation, to appear
3. Becker, Chr.: FEAST - The realization of Finite Element software for high-performance applications, Thesis, to appear
4. Crouzeix, M., Raviart, P.A.: *Conforming and non–conforming finite element methods for solving the stationary Stokes equations*, R.A.I.R.O. **R–3**, 77–104 (1973)

5. Müller, S., Prohl, A., Rannacher, R., Turek, S.: *Implicit time–discretization of the nonstationary incompressible Navier–Stokes equations*, Proc. 10th GAMM–Seminar, Kiel, January 14–16, 1994 (G. Wittum, W.Hackbusch, eds), Vieweg

6. Rannacher, R., Turek, S.: *A simple nonconforming quadrilateral Stokes element*, Numer. Meth. Part. Diff. Equ., 8, 97–111 (1992)

7. Schäfer, M., Turek, S.: *Benchmark Computations of Laminar Flow around a Cylinder*, In E. H. Hirschel, editor, *Notes on Numerical Fluid Mechanics*, pages 547–566, Wiesbaden, 1996, Vieweg

8. Schreiber, P.: *Eine nichtkonforme Finite–Elemente–Methode zur Lösung der inkompressiblen 3–D Navier–Stokes Gleichungen*, Thesis Heidelberg 1996

9. Smith, B., Bjorstad, P., Gropp, W.: *Domain decomposition: parallel multilevel methods for elliptic partial differential equation*, Cambridge University Press 1996

10. Tobiska, L., Schieweck, F.: A nonconforming finite element method of upstream type applied to the stationary Navier-Stokes equation, MMAN, 23, 627-647 (1989)

11. Turek, S.: *On discrete projection methods for the incompressible Navier–Stokes equations: An algorithmical approach*, Preprint 94–70 SFB 359, Heidelberg 1994

12. Turek, S.: Efficient Solvers for Incompressible Flow Problems: An Algorithmic Approach in View of Computational Aspects, LNCSE 2, Springer-Verlag, 1998

A Parallel Software-Platform for Solving Problems of Partial Differential Equations using Unstructured Grids and Adaptive Multigrid Methods

Peter Bastian, Klaus Birken, Klaus Johannsen, Stefan Lang, Volker Reichenberger, Christian Wieners, Gabriel Wittum, and Christian Wrobel

Universität Stuttgart, Institut für Computeranwendungen III, Pfaffenwaldring 27, D-70569 Stuttgart, Germany

Abstract. The goal of this work is the development of a parallel software-platform for solving partial differential equation problems. State-of-the-art numerical methods have been developed and implemented for the efficient and comfortable solution of real-world application problems. Emphasis is laid on the following topics: distributed unstructured grids, adaptive grid refinement, derefinement/coarsening, robust parallel multigrid methods, various FE and FV discretizations, dynamic load balancing, mapping and grid partitioning. Some important application examples will be presented including structural mechanics, two-phase flow in porous media, Navier-Stokes problems (CFD) and density-driven groundwater flow.

1   Introduction

Over the past two decades, very efficient techniques for the numerical solution of partial differential equations have been developed. Most notably these are:

- use of unstructured meshes for the approximation of complex geometries;
- adaptive local grid refinement in order to minimize the number of degrees of freedom required for a certain accuracy;
- robust multigrid methods for the fast solution of systems of linear equations;
- parallelization of these algorithms on MIMD type machines.

Up to now, these innovative techniques have been implemented mostly in university research codes [2,3,8,13] and only very few commercial codes use them, *e.g.* [14]. The reason for this is twofold. First, the construction of fast and robust iterative solvers is still a problem. Multigrid methods have been applied very successfully in the field of computational fluid dynamics [10,12, 16] but the application to problems from nonlinear structural mechanics or multiphase–flow in porous media is still in its infancy.

The second reason is that the integration of all the above–mentioned techniques in a single code requires a major coding effort of the order of several tens of man–years. Moreover, the structure of existing codes is often not suited to incorporate all these methods since they require a strong interaction between mesh generator, error estimator, solver and load balancer.

The software package *UG* (shorthand for *U*nstructured *G*rids) has been designed to overcome these problems by providing reusable software tools that simplify the implementation of parallel adaptive multigrid methods on unstructured meshes for complex engineering applications. The heart of *UG* is its unstructured grid data structure. It allows one to create meshes consisting of triangular, quadrilateral, tetrahedral, pyramidal, hexahedral and prism elements in two and three space dimensions. The mesh data structure is hierarchical and elements can be refined and removed locally.

The geometric data structure is complemented by the algebraic data structure used to represent sparse matrices and vectors. The degrees of freedom can be associated with nodes, edges, faces and elements of the mesh, thus also allowing the implementation of nonconforming, mixed or higher–order finite element discretizations. A large number of linear algebra subroutines, iterative kernels and multigrid components is available. For standard situations, like conforming finite elements, the user does not have to write a single line of code in order to use the multigrid method (even for *systems* of partial differential equations). The implementation of discretization schemes is simplified by a large collection of routines providing shape functions and their derivatives, quadrature formulas, finite volume constructions etc.

UG is intended primarily to be a tool to explore new discretization schemes, solvers and error estimators. A powerful graphical user interface can help to reduce development time significantly. *UG* has a built–in shell with command interpreter and allows the user to open any number of windows on his screen. Meshes, contour lines, color plots and vector plots can be displayed in two and three dimensions. Hidden line removal in 3D efficiently uses the hierarchical data representation.

A further great advantage of *UG* is its support for parallelism. The experiences from a first parallel version described in [3] have led to a new programming model *DDD* that can be used for the parallelization of applications with graph–like data structures as described in [6]. *DDD* is the basis of the parallel *UG* version but can also be used independently of it. *UG* will allow a very smooth transition from sequential to parallel computation.

The computational and networking infrastructure at HLRS in Stuttgart has been used for two major goals in the course of the corresponding project:

- During the final development phase of the parallel *UG* software package it was necessary to test functionality and performance of the parallel code on real-world configurations. Especially the Cray T3E with 512 processors at HLRS/Stuttgart provided valuable testing scenarios with high processor numbers and large main memory.
- Due to the hierarchical approach of *UG*'s software design, it was possible to develop and test a variety of applications on a small number of processors of a smaller (and cheaper!) parallel platform (*e.g.*, the Intel Paragon

at RUS/Stuttgart) or even on a single workstation using the sequential build of the code. After that phase, performance tests and – most important – real-world application problems require powerful high-performance platforms, as those provided by HLRS.

The remainder of this paper is organized as follows. The next section gives a rough overview of the parallel software platform developed in the corresponding project. In the third section exemplary applications are presented in order to show the power of this approach. Quality and efficiency of the parallel applications are demonstrated by performance figures. The paper ends with a short conclusion.

2   Parallel Software Architecture

A large software system like *UG* is usually described at a number of different levels of abstraction. In this section, we move through this hierarchy from top to bottom. *UG* knows three design levels which are called *architectural design*, *subsystem design* and *component design*.

At least on the architecture and subsystem level, *UG* is a modular design and the information hiding principle is used extensively. All state information is distributed among the subsystems. *UG* is implemented mostly in the ANSI C programming language, some parts have been implemented in C++.

2.1   Architecture Design

The highest level of abstraction in *UG* is the architecture design level. Its decomposition is motivated as follows:

UG Library
:   The *UG* library is *completely independent* of the partial differential equation to be solved. It provides the geometric and algebraic data structures and a huge number of mesh manipulation options, numerical algorithms, visualization techniques and the user interface.

Problem Class Libraries
:   This part provides discretization, error estimator and, if required, non–standard solvers for a particular set of partial differential equations.

Applications
:   The application finally provides the domain description, boundary conditions and coefficient functions in order to complete the problem description. A simulation run is typically controlled by a script file that is interpreted by *UG*'s user interface.

2.2 UG Library Subsystem Design

Each of the building blocks of the architectural design is decomposed into several subsystems. We now give an informal specification of the services provided by each subsystem.

USER INTERFACE

The user interface provides the user with a "shell–like" command language. All operations of the *UG* library can usually be executed either via a command typed into the shell or by calling a C function within the code. A scripting language is available to control complex simulation runs. Multiple graphics windows can be opened to visualize simulation results. In two space dimensions the mesh can be manipulated interactively. The user interface is based on the portable device interface described below.

GRAPHICS

The graphics subsystem provides some elementary visualization methods like mesh plots, contour plots, color plots or vector fields. In three dimensions planar cuts and hidden line removal have been implemented. The advantages of an integrated graphics package are that no intermediate data files have to be written and also that information like matrix structure and entries can be displayed easily.

NUMERICS

The numerics subsystem provides numerical algorithms in a modular form ranging from basic linear algebra (level 1 and 2) up to methods for the solution of nonlinear time–dependent partial differential equations. In addition, it provides support for the discretization process, *e.g.*, quadrature rules.

DOMAIN MANAGER

The purpose of the domain manager is to provide functionality for the description of general two– and three–dimensional domains as well as functions on the surface (boundary conditions) and the interior (coefficients) of a domain. The general approach is that a d–dimensional domain Ω is described by its boundary $\partial\Omega$ which is a $d-1$–dimensional hypersurface. This is very natural in the context of partial differential equations since boundary conditions have to be provided anyway. The standard way of describing the boundary is through local maps $f_i : \mathbb{R}^{d-1} \to \mathbb{R}^d$ with $i = 1 \ldots n$ and n the number of patches. Another approach consists of decomposing the boundary in a number of patches where each patch is given by a simplicial surface mesh. In that case, no easy mapping f_i exists for a patch. The domain interface is also used to access CAD data.

GRID MANAGER

The grid manager subsystem provides the unstructured mesh and sparse matrix data structures together with functionality for their manipulation.

This includes the generation of two– and three–dimensional simplicial triangulations. The complete grid manager functionality has been parallelized based on the *DDD* library described below. Complicated multigrid structures can reside in a distributed manner in the memories of a parallel supercomputer platform and can be redistributed efficiently.

DEVICE MANAGER

The device manager provides a default device called "screen" that allows at least basic character input/output. Optionally, the screen device also has interactive graphics capabilities. The screen device has been implemented for the standard C library, X11, remote X11 (uses socket communication and an X11 capable daemon on a remote machine), and Apple Macintosh. Write-only graphical output is available in postscript and a portable binary format ("metafile").

LOW

This subsystem provides some basic functionality like memory management, a simple database tool and portable file input/output. Furthermore, some debugging tools are included.

LOAD BALANCER

The load balancer subsystem is intended to solve graph partitioning and scheduling problems that arise when topological and numerical data must be mapped to processors in a parallel environment. The current implementation uses CHACO [9,11] for that purpose.

DYNAMIC DISTRIBUTED DATA (DDD)

The *DDD* subsystem implements an innovative parallel programming model that is especially suited for managing distributed, graph–like data structures. Distributed data objects can be created, deleted and transferred between processes easily. Communication among distributed objects is supported in a flexible and efficient way.

PARALLEL PROCESSOR INTERFACE (PPIF)

PPIF is a portable message passing interface used by *DDD*. It has been implemented for PVM, MPI, PARIX, NX and the T3D/T3E. PPIF has very little overhead when used with fast native communication (*e.g.*, shared memory get/put on the Cray T3E).

2.3   Hierarchical Structure and Component Design

The various subsystems are ordered in a hierarchical structure, *e.g.*, the Grid Manager subsystem relies on the *DDD* subsystem, which again relies on the Parallel Processing Interface. Due to this hierarchy of implementation levels, the resulting program code with about 360.000 lines is still suited for maintenance; further development is possible, sequential and parallel version use the identical program code.

Each subsystem itself consists of a variety of components. A detailed description of this component design level is skipped here due to space limitations (refer to [4] for a detailed explanation).

3   Exemplary Applications

This section describes some exemplary *UG* applications, each accompagnied by numerical and visualized results computed on HLRS platforms.

3.1   Finite Element Applications

For a wide range of applications it is necessary to choose an appropriate discretization for the given problem in order to represent the inherent characteristics of the continuous problem in its approximation. Therefore, in *UG* a general finite element library is realized. It supports various different discretizations, such as linear and quadratic conforming elements, Crouzieux-Raviart elements, Raviart-Thomas elements, BDM-elements, Taylor-Hood elements and Morley elements. For this purpose, degrees of freedom can be associated to nodes, edges, faces and elements. Furthermore, in different parts of the computational domain different models can be chosen, and for nonmatching grids they can be coupled by the introduction of additional Lagrange multipliers via the Mortar finite element method.

The list of provided finite elements can be easily extended: essentially, the assembling of the local stiffness matrices and a local interpolation for every element must be implemented for every discretization, then all other tools of the *UG*-library can be applied. The parallel linear algebra model analysed in [15] guarantees that the parallel solvers provided by *UG* can be applied to all all finite elements.

Table 1. Parallel multigrid performance for Morley elements.

level	6	7	8	9
number of unknowns	66049	263169	1050625	4198401
number of inverse iterations	3	3	4	4
time for linear solver (sec.)	0.99	3.65	14.6	62.3
first eigenvalue	1068.18	1071.48	1072.35	1072.59

The parallel performance on the Cray T3E at HLRS/Stuttgart is demonstrated by three examples. For the first example, we consider the eigenvalue computation of a clamped plate. In our test case, we consider the unit square $\Omega = (0,1)^2$ and the Poisson ratio $\nu = 1/3$. The problem is discretized with Morley elements, where pointwise values of u are associated to the element corners, and the normal derivative of u across the edges is associated to the edge midpoints; locally this defines a piecewise quadratic function. The total computation time for the first eigenvalue on the finest level was 7:28 min. on 128 processors, including the setup phase and the uniform mesh refinement, see Table 1 for more details.

In the next example, the application to a rotating geometry is demonstrated, where the coupling at the interface is realized by Mortar elements. For the resulting saddle point problem, the multigrid method discussed in [7] requires a local solution at the interface. Therefore, we use a load balancing scheme where all elements at the interface are collected on one processor, *cf.* Table 2.

Table 2. Parallel multigrid performance for Mortar finite elements on 128 processors (right) and load balancing on 32 processors (left).

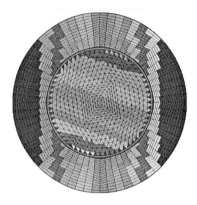

level	elements	conv. rate	time per V-cycle
6	32768	0.22	5.0 sec.
7	131072	0.18	10.3 sec.
8	524288	0.18	21.1 sec.
9	2097152	0.18	57.2 sec.

Finally, we give an example for a simulation of Prandtl-Reuß-plasticity without hardening, realized via a return mapping function. Here, additional data in the elements must be stored for the material history, and the evaluation of the material behaviour is a time consuming task within the total algorithm. Due to the nonsmooth character of this physical model, in particular in 3D a fine resolution of the plastic zone is required for a correct prediction of the resulting deformation after a complete loading cycle, *cf.* Table 3.

3.2   Incompressible Flow and Navier-Stokes Equations

Computational Fluid Dynamics has long been recognized as one of the most prominent examples for grand challenge problems. A problem class for the simulation of incompressible flow modelled by the Navier-Stokes equations has been implemented with *UG* and is a core part of the distribution. The discretization scheme uses 'colocated' variables based on dual finite volumes which are implemented in a fully coupled manner. The discretization is consistently stabilized by either a second or fourth order pressure term, both entering the equation of continuity. An upwind discretization is realized by a skewed upwind approach with an additional physical advection correction. In

Table 3. Parallel performance for Prandtl-Reuß-plasticity in 2D and 3D.

space dimension	2D	3D
elements	262144	202752
nb. of procs	256	96
unknowns	526338	692955
loading cycles	30	18
total time	15:35 min.	21:21 min.
Newton steps	161	55
nonlin. red.	0.000001	0.001
multigrid cycle	1757	223

contrast to many other accurate upwind schemes, this method does not need information from neighbour elements during the element assembly procedure, which is advantageous for unstructured grids and parallelization.

Table 4. Laminar flow around a cylinder: parallel execution times.

processors	elements	t_{lin}	t/it_{lin}	t_{total}
4	6912	60.47	1.63	277
32	52296	102.07	1.76	386
256	442368	158.83	2.06	560

The nonlinear stationary system is solved by a fixed point iteration and the linearized systems are solved either by a geometrical multigrid method or by Krylov subspace methods like BiCGSTAB or GMRES with the multigrid method as a preconditioner. Different smoothers can be employed for the multigrid method, like the incomplete LU factorization with β modification in the example shown below.

Figure 1 shows pressure iso-surfaces and the velocity for the calculation of a laminar flow around a cylinder at a Reynolds number of 20. Parallel performance results can be found in Table 4. A BiCGSTAB solver with a linear multi-grid preconditioner and an ILU_β smoother was employed for the solution of the linear systems within the quasi-Newton nonlinear solver, which itself was used within a nested iteration scheme. t_{lin} denotes the total time spent for solving the linear problem, t/it_{lin} is the time for one multigrid cycle and t_{total} the total solution time on all levels. Almost 1.8 million degrees of freedom were used for the computation on 256 processors. As expected, the multigrid solver scales very nicely and the total solution time only increased by a factor of 2 for a problem with 64 times the size of the initial problem.

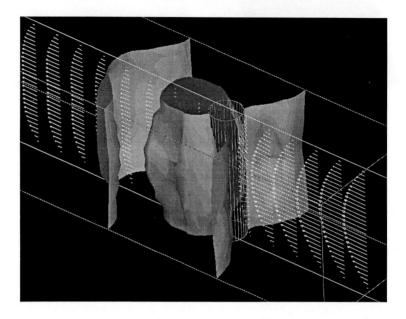

Fig. 1. Flow around a cylinder: Visualization of the result (bottom) and load balancing (top) for 32 processors.

3.3   Two–phase Flow in Porous Media

The flow of two immiscible fluids in a porous medium is described by two coupled highly non–linear time–dependent partial differential equations, see [1] for an introduction. These equations play an important role in oil reservoir simulation, the development of effective in–situ remediation techniques and the security assessment of underground waste repositories. Due to the hyperbolic/parabolic character of the equations, strong heterogeneities and high non–linearity, they pose a challenging problem for multigrid solution.

A problem class has been developed that solves the two–phase flow equations in a fully implicit / fully–coupled manner using either phase pressure–saturation or a global pressure–saturation formulation [5]. A finite volume and a control–volume–finite–element discretization with first–order upwinding have been implemented. Entry pressure effects at porous medium discon-

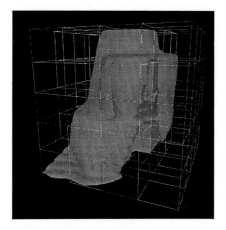 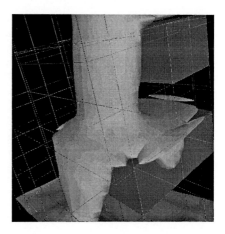

Fig. 2. 3D DNAPL infiltration into a heterogeneous porous medium. 10% saturation isosurface after 800 s shown left and 38% saturation after 1000 s right.

tinuities are handled by incorporating appropriate interface conditions. Both discretizations support all element types in two and three dimensions. Time discretization is fully implicit, resulting in a large set of nonlinear algebraic equations per time step. The nonlinear equations are then solved iteratively by a Newton–Multigrid technique. A line search method is used to achieve global convergence. Several multigrid techniques have been implemented in *UG* to handle coefficient jumps induced by saturation fronts and absolute permeability variations. These jumps are in general *not* aligned with coarse grid lines. In the simulations below, a multigrid method with truncated restriction, point–block ILU smoother and a V-cycle has been used.

Figure 2 shows saturation iso–surfaces for a three–dimensional DNAPL (dense non–aqueous phase liquid, a fluid with density higher than water and immiscible with it) infiltration into a heterogeneous porous medium. Two blocks of low permeability have been inserted into the reservoir. Entry pressure effects prevent the DNAPL from infiltrating the low permeability lenses. The performance data for this problem is shown in Table 5. In the table, MESH denotes the number of hexahedral elements (number of unknowns is twice this number), EXECT the total execution time in seconds, NLIT the number of Newton iterations for all time steps on the finest mesh, AVG the average number of multigrid cycles (within BiCGSTAB) per Newton iteration and Tit is the time for *one* multigrid cycle. Nested iteration is used to obtain good initial guesses on the fine mesh. The example shows that good parallel *and* overall efficiencies are obtained for large scale problems.

Table 5. Parallel performance of the T3E for a 3D computation on a hexahedral mesh with increasing number of elements and processors (scaled computation). 50 time steps of 20 [s] have been computed. A V–cycle multigrid algorithm with ILU smoother with two pre and two post–smoothing step is used as a preconditioner in BiCGSTAB.

T3E	MESH	EXECT	NLIT	AVG	Tit
1	5120	4187	218	1.6	2.10
4	40960	11589	243	2.5	4.69
32	327680	13214	264	3.5	4.76
256	2621440	14719	255	4.3	4.82

3.4 Density–driven Flow in Porous Media

In many cases, groundwater flow in porous media involves the transport of solutes that affect liquid density. If density variations exceed 20%, which occurs near salt domes or bedded salt formations, flow and transport are strongly coupled. The primary coupling arises in the equations through the body–force term of the fluid equation and the advection term of the transport equation. A second coupling arises from the velocity–dependent hydrodynamic dispersion in the transport equation. These couplings cause nonlinearities in the equations that preclude analytical solutions and are a challenge for numerical simulations.

Density–driven flow problems can be described by two nonlinear, coupled, time–dependent differential equations, a continuity equation for the fluid and a continuity equation for the solute transport. The fluid continuity equation is written in terms of pressure, assuming that Darcy's law is valid. Both equations are discretized on vertex-centered finite volumes using different constructions for the control volumes. In cases of dominant convection, an aligned finite volume method, where the finite volumes are aligned to a given velocity, is preferable to the standard finite volume method. Furthermore, a consistent velocity approximation of terms involved in the fluid velocity calculation is implemented. The transient equations are solved with a fully implicit time-stepping scheme with time step control. The nonlinear equations are solved in a fully coupled mode using an approximative Newton multigrid method where the linearized system is solved with a linear multigrid method.

Figure 3 shows the flow around a saltdome (on the bottom of the domain), which consists of four layers with different permeabilities. The top picture illustrates the grid and its distribution on 128 processors. The middle and bottom pictures show the velocity and salt distribution at time $t = 10a$, respectively. The parallel performance of the computations carried out on the Cray T3E is depicted in Table 6. The toplevel of the multigrid varies between grid level 2 and 4 and is scaled to the number of processors used. For performance reasons, the coarse grid is agglomerated on one dedicated processor to avoid communications during the solution of the small coarse

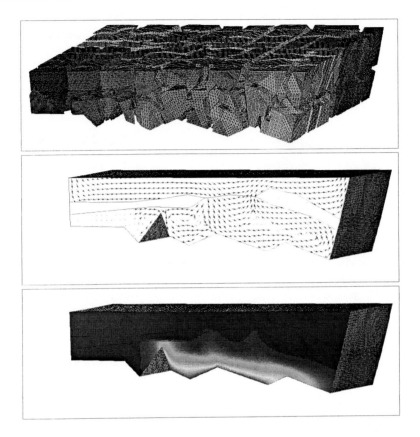

Fig. 3. Density–driven flow around a saltdome. From top to bottom: the mesh and its distribution on 128 processors, velocity field ($t = 10a$) and salt mass fraction ($t = 10a$).

grid problem. Therefore, the performance measure E_{par} shows the relative efficiency in comparison with the optimal balanced computation on 32 processors. Towards both a lower or a higher processor count efficieny degrades in the same amount. In the 4-processor case this is an effect of the coarse grid agglomeration, while the performance loss on 256 processors is mainly due to the degradation of the solver's convergence rate.

Figure 4 shows a parallel adaptive computation of the same problem after 8 time steps with parallel grid adaption (refinement and coarsening) and load balancing. The multigrid has 6 adaptive grid levels. The left upper picture illustrates the grid adaption. Colored (yellow, green and red elements) exists on the highest grid level, white elements reside on lower grid levels. The load balancer was a cheap and simple coordinate based method (Recursive

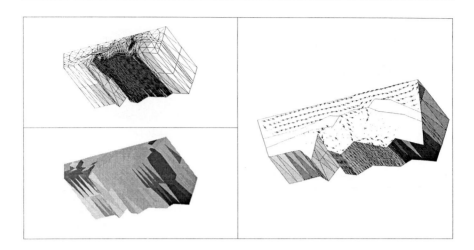

Fig. 4. Parallel adaptive computation on 32 T3E processors: adapted multigrid (left upper), load balancing (left lower) and velocity field of the solution (right picture).

Table 6. Density–driven flow around a saltdome: parallel performance on the Cray T3E at HLRS/Stuttgart.

processors	top-level	tetrahedra	nodes	time-steps	execution time[sec]	E_{par}
4	2	138944	26429	23	50534	0.77
32	3	1111552	198089	23	38728	1.00
256	4	8892416	1532881	23	50115	0.77

Inertial Bisection). The coloring of the left lower picture shows the multigrid partitions on the different processors. Finally, on the right picture the velocity field is shown.

4   Conclusions

This paper described the basic ideas and the software design structure of the *UG* package. Several exemplary applications have been shown together with numerical results on high-performance computing platforms at HLRS in Stuttgart. The resulting performance shows that it is practical and for many application problems even necessary to combine the computational power and main memory sizes of parallel computers with state-of-the-art numerical techniques for the solution of partial differential equations.

The layered, hierarchical approach of the *UG* software design leads to the following advantages:

 – The resulting software is portable on a wide range of platforms.

- For new applications based on *UG* there is only minimal effort for parallelization.
- Using the *UG* approach, high-performance computing platforms can be exploited efficiently for a wide spectrum of different application areas.

References

1. K. Aziz and A. Settari. *Petroleum Reservoir Simulation.* Elsevier, 1979.
2. R. Bank, *PLTMG Users Guide Version 7.0*, SIAM, 1994.
3. P. Bastian, *Parallele adaptive Mehrgitterverfahren*, Teubner Skripten zur Numerik, Teubner-Verlag, 1996.
4. P. Bastian, K. Birken, K. Johannsen, S. Lang, N. Neuss, H. Rentz-Reichert, and C. Wieners. UG – a flexible software toolbox for solving partial differential equations. *Computation and Visualization in Science*, (1), 1997.
5. P. Bastian and R. Helmig. *Efficient Fully-Coupled Solution Techniques for Two-Phase Flow in Porous Media.* Advances in Water Resources Research, 1997 (submitted).
6. K. Birken. An efficient programming model for parallel and adaptive CFD-algorithms. In *Proceedings of Parallel CFD Conference 1994*, Kyoto, Japan, 1995. Elsevier Science.
7. D. Braess, W. Dahmen, and C. Wieners, *A multigrid algorithm for the mortar finite element method.* submitted.
8. P. Deuflhard, P. Leinen, and H. Yserentant, *Concepts of an adaptive hierarchical finite element code*, IMPACT of Computing in Science and Engineering, 1 (1989), pp. 3–35.
9. Hendrickson and R. Leland, *The chaco user's guide version 1.0*, Tech. Rep. SAND93-2339, Sandia National Laboratory, October 1993.
10. E. H. Hirschel, ed., *Flow Simulation with High-Performance Computers II*, Vieweg Verlag, Braunschweig, 1996.
11. S. Lang, *Lastverteilung für paralle adaptive Mehrgitterberechnungen*, Master's thesis, Universität Erlangen-Nürnberg, IMMD III, 1994.
12. D. J. Mavripilis, *Three–dimensional Multigrid Reynolds–averaged Navier–Stokes solver for unstructured meshes*, AIAA Journal, 33 (1995).
13. L. C. McInnes and B. Smith, *PetSc2.0: A case study of using MPI to develop numerical software libraries*, in Proc. of the MPI Developers Conference, Notre Dame, IN, 1995.
14. M. Raw, *A coupled algebraic multigrid solver for the 3D Navier–Stokes equations*, in Proc. of the 10th GAMM Seminar Kiel, Notes on Numerical Fluid Mechanics, G. W. W. Hackbusch, ed., vol. 49, Vieweg–Verlag, 1995.
15. C. Wieners, *Parallel linear algebra and the application to multigrid methods*, in NNFM, vol. 56, W. Hackbusch and G. Wittum, eds., Viewig Verlag, 1999. in preparation.
16. G. Wittum, *Multigrid methods for Stokes- and Navier-Stokes equations*, Numer. Math., 54 (1989), pp. 543–563.

Reactive Flows

Prof. Dr. Dietmar Kröner
Institut für Angewandte Mathematik, Albert-Ludwigs-Universität Freiburg
Hermann-Herder-Str. 10, 79104 Freiburg

Design and optimization of industrial processes and equipments have been based on pure empirical and experimental experience for many years. Now, because of the enormous improvement of hardware resources like parallel computers and algorithmical tools, we are able to study complex multidimensional industrial processes by simulation, and to develop a new platform for the fundamental understanding of problems with high complexity and for the optimal design of industrial systems. The response time for realistic simulations is now of an acceptable order, such that extensive parameter studies can be performed. The fascinating progress in hardware resources and algorithmical tools require further research for combining both. E. g. the dynamical load balancing is still an area which has to be improved.

This means that beside the classical theoretical and experimental subjects a new one "scientific computing" has been established and becomes more and more important in research applications as well as in scientific education.

In the following, two outstanding projects in the area of reactive flows will be presented.

The most ambitious challenge in the area of reactive flows is the simulation of the turbulent combustion the first project in this section. For a direct numerical simulation 10^6 gridpoints are considered as a reasonable minimum with 100 unknowns per grid point. The time scales vary between 10^{-8} s up to 1s. This means that 10^5 time step iterations and 10^8 unknowns are necessary. On the basis of these requirements message passing codes have been developed and used for the investigations of flames with decaying turbulence. The numerical results which have been obtained on the CRAY T3E are in good qualitative agreement with experimental observations.

The second project concerns the furnace simulation in 3-D. The CPU-time for this problem on the NEC SX-4 could be reduced to a couple of hours and the results turned out to be accurate enough to enable the virtual optimization of combustion equipments.

The numerical codes which have been used are based on finite-difference schemes up to sixth-order and conservation finite volume formulations on structured grids. Beside direct numerical simulation also standard k-ε-models or differential Reynolds stress models are used.

Detailed Simulations of Turbulent Flames Using Parallel Supercomputers

Marc Lange and Jürgen Warnatz

Universität Heidelberg, Interdisziplinäres Zentrum für Wissenschaftliches Rechnen
Im Neuenheimer Feld 368, D-69120 Heidelberg, Germany
E-mail: marc.lange@iwr.uni-heidelberg.de

Abstract. Direct numerical simulations (DNS) have become one of the most effective tools to investigate turbulent combustion. To further improve our knowledge about the fundamental interaction processes between turbulent transport and chemical reactions using DNS, it is necessary to include detailed chemical reaction schemes. This leads to an enormous demand of computational power, which can only be provided by the fastest supercomputers available. Therefore, we developed a code for the direct simulation of chemically reacting flows on massively parallel computers. We utilize this code to investigate the interaction of $H_2/O_2/N_2$ flames with decaying turbulence.

1 Introduction

Turbulent reactive flows are of outstanding importance in a broad range of technical applications. At present, about 90% of our worldwide energy support (e.g., in traffic, electrical power generation, heating) is provided by combustion processes [1]. In the last twenty years, numerical simulation has become an essential tool for the investigation of turbulent combustion. The most widely used approach is based on Favre-averaged balance equations which rely on turbulent transport and turbulent combustion models. Today, due to our lack of understanding of the fundamental processes apparent in turbulent combustion, these models are often a very weak point of codes using this approach [2,3].

Direct numerical simulations, i.e. the solution of the time-dependent compressible Navier-Stokes equations for reacting flows given in Sect. 2, can provide comprehensive information about the basic interaction mechanisms of turbulent transport and chemical reactions. To reach this goal, it is necessary to include detailed chemical reaction mechanisms and multicomponent transport models leading to enormous computational costs, as will be shown in Sect. 3.

2 Governing Equations

Chemically reacting flows are described by a set of coupled partial differential equations expressing the conservation of total mass, chemical species masses, momentum and energy [4]. Using the summation convention, these equations can be written in the form

$$\frac{\partial \rho}{\partial t} + \frac{\partial(\rho u_j)}{\partial x_j} = 0, \tag{1}$$

$$\frac{\partial(\rho Y_\alpha)}{\partial t} + \frac{\partial(\rho Y_\alpha u_j)}{\partial x_j} = -\frac{\partial(\rho Y_\alpha V_{D\alpha,j})}{\partial x_j} + W_\alpha \dot{\omega}_\alpha \quad \text{with } \alpha = 1 \dots N_s, \tag{2}$$

$$\frac{\partial(\rho u_i)}{\partial t} + \frac{\partial(\rho u_i u_j)}{\partial x_j} = \frac{\partial \tau_{ij}}{\partial x_j} - \frac{\partial p}{\partial x_i}, \tag{3}$$

$$\frac{\partial e_t}{\partial t} + \frac{\partial((e_t + p)u_j)}{\partial x_j} = \frac{\partial(u_j \tau_{kj})}{\partial x_k} - \frac{\partial q_j}{\partial x_j}, \tag{4}$$

where ρ is the density and u_i the velocity component in ith coordinate direction. Y_α, $\boldsymbol{V}_{D\alpha}$ and W_α are the mass fraction, diffusion velocity and molar mass of the species α. $\boldsymbol{\tau}$ denotes the stress tensor and p the pressure, $\boldsymbol{q}$ is the heat flux and e_t is the total energy given by

$$e_t = \rho \left(\frac{u_i u_i}{2} + \sum_{\alpha=1}^{N_s} h_\alpha Y_\alpha \right) - p, \tag{5}$$

where h_α is the specific enthalpy of the species α. The term $\dot{\omega}_\alpha$ is the chemical production rate of the species α, which is given as the sum over the formation rate equations for all N_r elementary reactions,

$$\dot{\omega}_\alpha = \sum_{\lambda=1}^{N_r} k_\lambda \left(\nu_{\alpha\lambda}^{(p)} - \nu_{\alpha\lambda}^{(r)} \right) \prod_{\alpha=1}^{N_s} c_\alpha^{\nu_{\alpha\lambda}^{(r)}}, \tag{6}$$

where $\nu_{\alpha\lambda}^{(r)}$ and $\nu_{\alpha\lambda}^{(p)}$ denote the stoichiometric coefficients of reactants and products respectively and c_α is the concentration of the species α. The rate coefficient k_λ of an elementary reaction is given by a modified Arrhenius law

$$k_\lambda = A_\lambda T^{b_\lambda} \exp\left(-\frac{E_{a\lambda}}{RT} \right) . \tag{7}$$

The parameters A_λ and b_λ of the pre-exponential factor and the activation energy $E_{a\lambda}$ in (7) are determined by a comparison with experimental data [5]. Multicomponent diffusion velocities are computed using standard methods described in [6,7], thermodynamical properties are computed using fifth-order fits of experimental measurements [1,5]. The state equation used for the closure of the set of equations is the ideal gas law

$$p = \frac{\rho}{\overline{W}} RT \tag{8}$$

with R being the gas constant and $\overline{W}$ the mean molar mass of the mixture.

3   Computational Requirements

We will now give an estimate for the requirements of a three-dimensional DNS of a reactive flow, i.e. the computation of the time dependent solution of the above system of equations resolving all physical and chemical length- and time-scales. In addition to the variables needed for the computation of non-reacting flows, the mass fractions of N_s chemical species have to be considered. The number of species N_s varies typically between nine for a $H_2/O_2/N_2$ system and several hundreds in the case of higher hydrocarbons.

For the spatial discretization, length scales between $100\,\mu m$ for a typical flame front and at least $1\,cm$ for the length of the computational domain have to be considered. When dealing with homogeneous turbulence, the Kolmogorov scale must be resolved everywhere in the computational domain and the number of grid points needed scales as the third power of the turbulent Reynolds number Re_Λ (14). About 100 grid points along each direction and thus a total number of 10^6 grid points may be considered as a reasonable minimum.

The characteristic time scales associated with combustion processes vary between $10^{-8}\,s$ for some important intermediate radicals (e.g. HO_2) and $1\,s$ for slowly produced pollutants like NO [8]. The resulting stiffness of the fully coupled system of partial differential equations leads to very small maximum time steps for the temporal integration. In typical cases of interest time steps required for a stable explicit integration are of the order of $10\,ns$. A significant increase of the time step can be gained by using implicit methods at the expense of much higher computational costs per time step. But even then, the achievable time step is severely limited by the very short time scales associated with turbulence and chemistry [9]. For an investigation of flames interacting with turbulence the integration should generally be continued at least up to the large-eddy turnover time t_Λ (13), which is for typical cases in the order of a millisecond. Summing up the minimum demands for a full DNS of turbulent hydrocarbon combustion, we get about 100 variables at 10^6 grid points and an integration over a millisecond with time steps of about $10\,ns$, in other words 10^5 iterations with 10^8 unknowns.

These requirements explain why no such computation has been carried out up to now. For a statistic use of DNS, which is needed for the enhancement of turbulence models, a large number of such simulations is necessary, leading to an extreme demand of computational power that cannot be provided by today's supercomputers. The use of massively parallel computers (MPPs) however will allow detailed three-dimensional DNS of turbulent combustion processes in the very near future.

4   Numerical Solution Technique

We have developed a portable code for the direct simulation of reactive flows on parallel computers with distributed memory using message-passing communication [10–12]. Detailed models are utilized for the computation of the thermodynamical properties, the viscosity and the molecular and thermal diffusion velocities. At the moment we restrict ourselves to the simulation of two-dimensional flow fields. As turbulence is an inherently three-dimensional phenomenon, some of its aspects cannot be reproduced precisely with such simulations [13]. On the other hand, many authors have shown that the use of reduced chemistry models often leads to large errors in the obtained solution [14]. We consider the inclusion of detailed chemical reaction schemes to be at least as important for the investigation of turbulent flames as an extension to three dimensions.

The spatial discretization is performed using a finite-difference scheme with sixth-order central-dervatives, avoiding numerical dissipation and leading to very high accuracy. Depending on the boundary conditions lower order schemes are used at the outermost grid points. The integration in time is carried out using a fourth-order fully explicit Runge-Kutta method. The time step of the integration is controlled by three independent conditions: a Courant-Friedrichs-Lewy (CFL) stability criterion, a Fourier stability criterion for the diffusion terms and an accuracy control obtained through time-step-doubling.

The fully explicit formulation leads to a parallelization strategy, which is based on a regular two-dimensional domain decomposition of the physical space, projected onto a corresponding two-dimensional processor topology. For a given computational grid and number of processors it is tried to minimize the length of the subdomain boundaries and thus the amount of communication. After this initial decomposition, each processor node controls a rectangular subdomain of the global computational domain. In addition to the grid points belonging to a nodes subdomain a three points wide peripheral surrounding is stored on each node. Using the given values at the grid points of this surrounding region an integration step on the subdomain is carried out independently from the other nodes. After each integration step the new inner boundary values of the subdomain are sent to and the new values of the surrounding region are received from the neighbouring nodes via message-passing communication. In order to achieve a high portability between various MPP-architectures, the modules dealing with communication are seperated from the flow solver. These modules have been adapted to various vendor-specific message-passing libraries as well as to PVM and are currently ported to MPI. The code has been successfully used on Intel Paragon, Parsytec GC/PowerPlus, workstation clusters using PVM3, IBM SP2, Cray T3D and Cray T3E systems [10,12].

5   Performance of the Parallel Code

Figure 1 shows the parallel speedups $S_p(N) = T_1(N)/T_p(N)$, i.e. the ratio between the computing time on one processor and the computing time using p

p	Cray T3E	Parsytec	Paragon
1	100.0	100.0	100.0
2	–	–	95.9
4	94.6	89.1	90.2
8	–	81.8	79.4
16	83.5	75.4	71.3
32	–	66.6	60.3
64	73.2	56.5	50.9
96	–	46.5	–
112	–	–	40.8
128	59.0	–	38.0
256	47.8	–	–

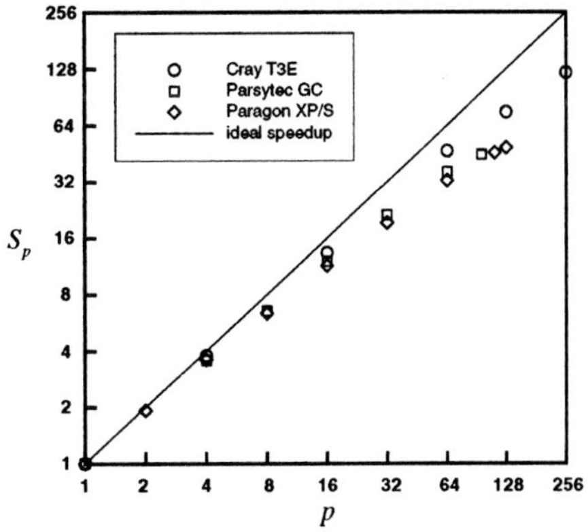

Fig. 1. Efficiency in percent (left) and speedup (right) versus the number of processors p measured on different MPP-systems

processors for a given problem of constant size N, measured on the following systems: a Cray T3E-600 using PVM as message passing library (240^2), a Parsytec GC/PowerPlus with Parix (168^2), and an Intel Paragon XP/S using NX (112^2). The number of grid points used is given in the parentheses as a measure for the problem size. The table on the left of Fig. 1 lists the corresponding efficiencies $E_p = S_p/p$. The test case investigated here was the computation of a given number of CFL-controlled time steps on a fixed grid using the same reaction mechanism with 9 species which was used for the simulations presented in Sect. 6. Due to the limited amount of memory per node, only a relative low number of grid points of up to 240^2 on the T3E could be used in the one-processor reference-computations of this test case, whereas for the simulations of turbulent flames, as presented in the Sect. 6, up to 512^2 grid points have been used. Therefore, a better indication for the performance of memory intensive real world applications may be given by a scaled benchmark, where the problem size is proportionally increased with the number of processors [15]. In this case a scaled speedup can be defined as

$$S_p^S(N) = p \cdot \frac{T_1(N)}{T_p(pN)} \ . \tag{9}$$

For a full-size computation with 512^2 grid points, directly corresponding to the simulations presented in Sect. 6, a scaled efficiency

$$E_p^S(N) = \frac{S_p^S(N)}{p} \tag{10}$$

of

$$E_{256}^S(32^2) = 76.8\,\% \tag{11}$$

is achieved on 256 processors of a Cray T3E-900. The Cray performance analysis tool PAT has been used to determine MFlop/s rates for this test

Table 1. Average MFlop/s per processor (512^2 grid points, 256 processors)

System	Stream Buffers	Tab. of $D_{\alpha\beta}$	MFlop/s per PE
T3E-900	on	no	85.1
T3E-900	on	yes	69.5
T3E-600	off	yes	49.5

case. Table 1 lists the mean values of MFlop/s per processor for three computations. A tabulation of the binary diffusion coefficients $D_{\alpha\beta}$ reduces the computation time by 10.2 % although the MFlop/s rate decreases compared to the case in which the coefficients are newly computed at each grid point. The increase of the clock speed by 50 % in combination with the use of the stream buffers leads to a 40.4 % higher performance on the Cray T3E-900 compared with the T3E-600. The used compiler options for the Cray F90 Compiler (version 3.02) are "-O2,aggress,pipeline1,unroll2".

The achieved high efficieny and performance ratio for full size simulations clearly show that the code is capable of making effective use of large configurations of the Cray T3E, which can be regarded as todays most powerful generally available supercomputer [16].

6   Examples of Results

We use the described parallel DNS-code to investigate the interaction of premixed [17] and non-premixed [18] $H_2/O_2/N_2$ flames interacting with decaying turbulence. For these calculations a detailed reaction mechanism using 9 species and 37 chemical reactions, described by a set of Arrhenius parameters, is employed [19]. For the initialization of a two-dimensional computation, profiles of a one-dimensional calculation of a corresponding laminar flame are uniformly copied in the y-direction. The resulting two-dimensional laminar flame is then superimposed on a turbulent velocity field.

The initiation of this turbulent velocity field is performed in the associated Fourier space. The distribution of turbulent energy E as a function of the wave number k is given by a von Kármán relation with a Pao correction for the near-dissipation scales,

$$E(k) = A \frac{\left(\overline{u'^2}\right)^{5/2}}{\epsilon} \frac{(k/k_e)^4}{[1 + (k/k_e)^2]^{17/6}} \exp\left(-\frac{3}{2}\alpha(k/k_d)^{4/3}\right), \qquad (12)$$

where A and α are model parameters, ϵ is the dissipation, u' is the turbulent velocity fluctuation and k_e and k_d are the wave numbers associated with the maxima of the turbulent kinetic energy and the dissipation. The phases of the turbulent velocities in the Fourier space are considered to be uncorrelated and are thus computed through random number generation. An inverse FFT gives the values of the turbulent velocities in the physical space.

After this initialization the temporal evolution of the flame interacting with the turbulence field is computed. Periodicity is assumed in the y-direction, while both x-boundaries are handled using non-reflecting boundary-conditions with pressure relaxation based on characteristic waves relations [20,21].

An example of such a computation is given in Fig. 2, where the temperature, the heat released by chemical reactions and the mass fractions of OH and H_2O_2 are shown after an interaction of the initially plane premixed stoichiometric hydrogen-air flame with the turbulence for one large-eddy turnover time, which is defined as

$$t_\Lambda = \frac{\Lambda}{u_0'}, \tag{13}$$

where Λ is the integral length-scale and u_0' is the r.m.s velocity fluctuation. For the (initially) homogeneous isotropic turbulence in this simulation we choose $u_0' = 2\,\mathrm{ms}^{-1}$ and $\Lambda = 1.5\,\mathrm{mm}$ giving a turbulent Reynolds number of

$$Re_\Lambda = \frac{u_0'\Lambda}{\nu} \approx 180 \ . \tag{14}$$

The flame is deformed by the interaction with turbulent eddies. While the distribution of H_2O_2 is very similar to that of the local heat release rate $\dot{\Omega}$, the maximum of the OH concentration is located well behind the flame front and is increased in regions curved towards the burnt side of the flame. The relation of hydroxil mass fraction and local heat release is important, because the OH concentration can be very well measured via laser-induced fluorescence imaging (LIF) and has often been used as a tracer for the zone with the highest reaction intensity [22]. Figure 2 shows that in this case the hydroxil radical concentration may be used for a rough approximation of the flame zone, whereas our simulations show that OH is an extremely bad tracer for the heat release in the case of turbulent diffusion flames [18].

Figure 3 shows a detail of the temporal evolution from $t_i = 1.20\,\mathrm{ms}$ up to $t_i = 1.45\,\mathrm{ms} \approx 1.9\,t_\Lambda$ of the same flame as shown in Fig. 2. As already can be seen in Fig. 2, the flame front gets stretched and curved by the interaction with the turbulence leading to an increase of flame surface. At the same time a surface reduction by the concurring process of mutual flame annihilation which results from the interaction of different flame elements because of their proximity and competition for unburnt gas occurs [23]. This leads to a less wrinkled flame front as can be seen at $y \approx 5\,\mathrm{mm}$ in Fig. 3, where the flame cusp is regressed by mutual annihilation.

In addition to the flattening of the flame front the process of mutual annihilation plays an important role in the formation of isolated pockets, which is shown in the region around $y = 10\,\mathrm{mm}$ in Fig. 3. The thermodiffusive and reactive layers of the flame elements on both sides of the channel connecting

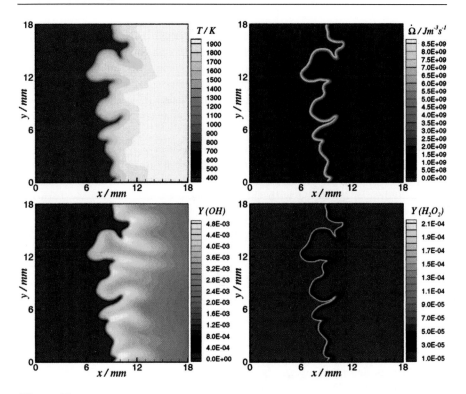

Fig. 2. Temperature, local heat release rate, OH- and H_2O_2-mass-fraction in a turbulent premixed hydrogen-air flame ($t_i = 0.75\,\mathrm{ms} = t_A$)

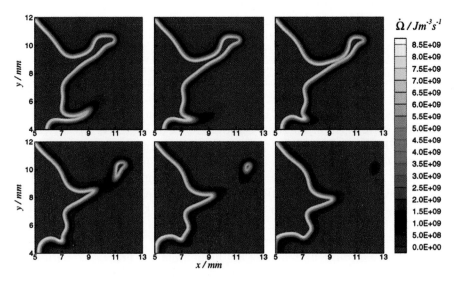

Fig. 3. Formation of an isolated pocket of fresh gas in a turbulent premixed flame ($t_i = 1.20\,\mathrm{ms} + N \cdot 0.05\,\mathrm{ms}$ with $N = 0, \ldots, 5$)

the fuel with the fresh gas later enclosed in the pocket merge followed by the pinching off of a droplet shaped pocket from the flame cusp. The burnout of the pocket starts with its downstream cusp rounding out the pocket and ends with mutual flame annihilation in a near cylindrical geometry. These results are in good qualitative agreement with experimental observations of pocket formation processes [24,25].

7   Conclusion

A parallel code for the direct numerical simulation of turbulent reactive flows has been developed, which employs detailed models for chemical and molecular transport processes in order to allow accurate simulations of the interaction between turbulence and chemical reactions. This code has been successfully used on several MPP architectures including the Cray T3E exhibiting high parallel efficiencies and performance ratios. Simulation results of a turbulent premixed hydrogen-air flame interacting with a turbulent velocity field have been presented. The analysis of direct numerical simulation results like these will help to improve our understanding of turbulent combustion. For example a flame normal analysis of the type of flame discussed in Sect. 6 has been performed, in which cross flame section profiles are compared with those of corresponding laminar flames [17]. This type of analysis can be used to validate and improve flamelet models, which are one of the most important concepts in turbulent combustion modeling [2,26].

References

1. Warnatz, J., Maas, U., Dibble, R.W.: Combustion. Springer-Verlag, New York (1996)
2. Bray, K.N.C.: The Challenge of Turbulent Combustion. Proc. 26th Symp. (Int.) on Combustion, The Combustion Institute, Pittsburgh (1996) 1–26
3. Poinsot, T.: Using Direct Numerical Simulations to Understand Premixed Turbulent Combustion. Proc. 26th Symp. (Int.) on Combustion, The Combustion Institute, Pittsburgh (1996) 219–232
4. Bird, R.B., Stewart, W.E. , Lightfoot, E.N.: Transport Phenomena. John Wiley & Sons, New York (1960)
5. Warnatz, J., Riedel, U., Schmidt, R.: Different Levels of Air Dissociation Chemistry and Its Coupling with Flow Models, Advances in Hypersonics (Bertin, J.J., Periaux, J., Ballmann, J., Eds.), Birkhäuser, Boston (1992) 67–103
6. Kee, R.J., Dixon-Lewis, G., Warnatz, J., Coltrin, M.E., Miller, J.A.: A Fortran Computer Code for the Evaluation of Gas-Phase Multicomponent Transport Properties. Sandia Report SAND86-8246 (1986)
7. Hirschfelder, J.O., Curtiss, C.F. , Bird, R.B.: Molecular Theory of Gases and Liquids. John Wiley & Sons, New York (1954)
8. Maas, U., Pope, S.B.: Symplifying Chemical Kinetics: Intrinsic Low Dimensional Manifolds in Composition Space. Combustion and Flame **88** (1992) 239–264

9. Choi, H., Moin, P.: Effects of the Computational Time-Step on Numerical Solutions of Turbulent Flow, J. Comput. Phys. **113** (1994) 1–4

10. Thévenin, D., Behrendt, F., Maas, U., Przywara, B., Warnatz, J.: Development of a Parallel Direct Simulation Code to Investigate Reactive Flows. Computers and Fluids. Vol. **25**, 5 (1996) 485–496

11. Lange, M. , Warnatz, J.: Direct Numerical Simulation of Chemically Reacting Flows. Supercomputer 1997 (Meuer, H.-W., Ed.), K.G.Saur-Verlag, München (1997) 145–156

12. Lange, M., Thévenin, D., Riedel, U. , Warnatz, J.: Direct Numerical Simulation of Turbulent Reactive Flows Using Massively Parallel Computers. Parallel Computing: Fundamentals, Applications and New Directions (D'Hollander, E., Joubert, G., Peters, F. , Trottenberg, U., Eds.), Elsevier Science, Amsterdam (1998)

13. Lesieur, M.: Turbulence in Fluids. Kluwer Academic, Dordrecht (1997)

14. Sloane, T. M., Ronney, P. D.: Comparison of Ignition Phenomena Modelled with Detailed and Simple Chemistry. Proc. Fourth International Conference on Numerical Combustion. SIAM, Saint Petersburg, Florida (1991)

15. Flatt, H.P., Kennedy, K.: Performance of Parallel Processors. Parallel Computing **12** (1989) 1–20

16. Dongarra, J.J., Meuer, H.-W., Strohmeier, E.: TOP500 Supercomputer Sites. University of Tennessee Computer Science Technical Report CS-97-377 (1997)

17. Lange, M., Riedel, U., Warnatz, J.: Parallel DNS of Turbulent Flames with Detailed Reaction Schemes. AIAA Paper 98-2979 (1998)

18. Lange, M., Riedel, U., Warnatz, J.: Direct Numerical Simulation of Turbulent Flames Using Detailed Chemistry, Verbrennung und Feuerungen, VDI-Berichte 1313 (1997) 431–436

19. Maas, U., Warnatz, J.: Ignition Processes in Hydrogen-Oxygen Mixtures. Combustion and Flame **74** (1988) 53–69

20. Poinsot, T., Lele, S.: Boundary Conditions for Direct Simulations of Compressible Viscous Flows. J. Comput. Phys. **101** (1992) 104–129

21. Baum, M., Poinsot, T., Thévenin, D.: Accurate Boundary Conditions for Multicomponent Reactive Flows. J. Comput. Phys. **116** (1995) 247–261

22. Seitzman, J.M., Üngüt, A., Paul, P.H., Hanson, R.K.: Imaging and Characterization of OH Structures in a Turbulent Nonpremixed Flame. Proc. 23rd Symp. (Int.) on Combustion, The Combustion Institute, Pittsburgh (1990) 637–644

23. Echekki, T., Chen, J.H., Gran, I.R.: The Mechanism of Mutual Flame Annihilation of Stoichiometric Premixed Methane-Air Flames. Proc. 26th Symp. (Int.) on Combustion, The Combustion Institute, Pittsburgh (1996) 855–864

24. Nguyen, Q.-V., Paul, P.H.: The Time Evolution of a Vortex-Flame Interaction Observed via Planar Imaging of CH and OH. Proc. 26th Symp. (Int.) on Combustion, The Combustion Institute, Pittsburgh (1996) 357–364

25. Baillot, F., Bourhela, A.: Burning Velocity of Pockets from a Vibrating Flame Experiment. Combust. Sci. and Tech. **126** (1997) 201–224

26. Peters, N.: Laminar Flamelet Concepts in Turbulent Combustion. Proc. 21st Symp. (Int.) on Combustion, The Combustion Institute, Pittsburgh (1986) 1231–1250

Towards a reliable and efficient furnace simulation tool for coal fired utility boilers

Benedetto Risio, Uwe Schnell, Klaus R.G. Hein

Institute of Process Engineering and Power Plant Technology (IVD)
University of Stuttgart, Pfaffenwaldring 23, D-70550 Stuttgart, Germany
Fax: 0049-711-685 3491, E-mail: risio@ivd.uni-stuttgart.de

Abstract. A validation exercise is presented with the objective of demonstrating that using a mature furnace simulation tool on high end supercomputers enables the reliable prediction of coal-fired utility boiler performance within short time frames. The tool used in the present investigation is the in-house developed 3D-furnace simulation code AIOLOS. To prove the predictive capabilities of AIOLOS the code is applied to the numerical simulation of three different industrial furnaces differing in the firing concepts, sizes and fuels. The discretizations range from 100,000 to 2,000,000 computed cells. Numerical predictions of AIOLOS are validated with measurements of temperature, wall heat fluxes, carbon in fly ash, and species concentrations provided by the industrial partners ENEL, Saarberg and RWE. The comparison of measured and calculated values showed that predictions with AIOLOS are accurate enough to enable the virtual optimization of combustion equipment in large scale utility furnaces. Furthermore, the vector and parallel performance of AIOLOS on the parallel vector computer NEC SX-4/32 has been assessed. The performance results showed that for the above mentioned calculations the runtime can be reduced to a couple of hours being short enough for industrial purposes.

1 Introduction

Design and optimization of industrial scale, coal fired furnaces has been based on pure empirical and experimental approaches for a long time. Nevertheless, in the past years the additional utilization of 3D-furnace simulation models for this purpose is more and more observed in industry (Antifora et al., 1997). Since the reliability of numerical predictions is a key aspect in the industrial use of numerical results it is necessary to verify the validity of numerical results for a great variety of different furnaces and firing concepts at full scale. In order to prove the reliability of the in-house developed 3D-furnace simulation code AIOLOS a validation exercise for three different furnaces is presented comparing numerical predictions with full scale measurements provided by the industrial partners ENEL, Saarberg and RWE. The Fusina Unit 2 furnace of ENEL and the Bexbach Unit 1 furnace of Saarberg are tangential firing systems producing an electrical output of 170 MW and 750 MW, respectively. The Niederaussem Unit B furnace of RWE is a top-fired system with an electrical output of 150 MW.

Since the response time of such simulations must be sufficiently short to be of industrial interest the code is optimized for parallel execution on the parallel vector computer NEC SX-4/32 installed at the High Performance Computing Centre in Stuttgart. Thus reliable predictions can be achieved within industrially relevant time frames.

The remainder of the paper is broken into four sections. Section 2 introduces the furnace simulation code AIOLOS. Section 3 presents the validation of the code against full scale measurements, while results of the computational performance on the NEC SX-4 are presented and discussed in section 4. Finally, section 5 summarizes the work and states conclusions based on the accomplished work.

2 The 3D-furnace simulation code AIOLOS

The 3D-furnace simulation code AIOLOS for quasi-stationary, weakly compressible, turbulent reacting flows is an in-house development of IVD tailored for the numerical simulation of industrial scale furnaces. It allows the description of fluid and particle motion, turbulence, combustion chemistry and heat transfer as well as the complex interaction between these processes which is illustrated in Fig. 1. The code is based on a conservative finite-volume formulation using a collocated, structured grid arrangement. To avoid odd-even oscillations due to the collocated grid the pressure weighted interpolation method of Rhie and Chow (1983) is used. The coupling between velocity and pressure is achieved by the well-known SIMPLEC-method of van Doormal and Raithby (1984). Turbulence closure can be done by a standard k-ε-model or a differential Reynolds stress model (Schneider et al., 1995). In order to reduce numerical diffusion higher-order differencing schemes like QUICK and MLU (Noll, 1992) are implemented for the calculation of the convective fluxes.

Coal combustion is described in a first step by two heterogeneous reactions for pyrolysis and char combustion (Schnell et al., 1995). The subsequent combustion of the volatiles and the products of char burnout is described with a global reaction scheme including two gas phase reactions for the combustion of CO and a light hydrocarbon (Schnell et al., 1995). By assuming a no-slip condition between particles and the surrounding fluid, the motion of the two-phase flow is described with an Eulerian approach. The modelling of fuel nitrogen conversion is in close connection with the coal combustion model. It assumes that fuel nitrogen is released from the coal in two separate stages: Pyrolysis and char burnout. During the first step, the pyrolysis, fuel nitrogen is released only in form of hydrogen cyanide (HCN). The fate of HCN and its successors is strongly dependent on the local conditions, particularly on local stoichiometry and temperature. Following de Soete (see de Soete, 1974), the intermediate nitrogen containing species, e.g. NCO, NH_i, N can be lumped together and the intermediate steps can be considered as fast in the presence of OH radicals. This approach leads to two competing global reaction pathways (see Schnell, 1991): Oxidation of HCN forming NO, and the reduction of NO by HCN yielding N_2. Additionally, the fixation of atmospheric nitrogen is modelled with the well-known Zeldovich mechanism.

Radiative heat transfer, which is the predominant mechanism in coal fired industrial furnaces, can be considered either by a Discrete Ordinates method (Fiveland, 1984), a Discrete Transfer model (Lockwood and Shah, 1981), or a six flux model (De Marco and Lockwood, 1975).

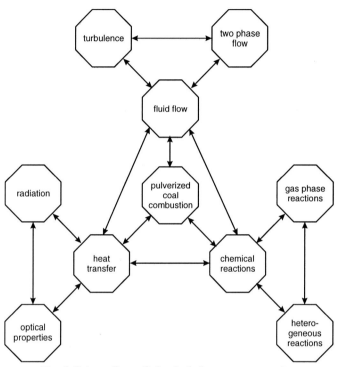

Fig. 1: Interactions of physical phenomena occuring in coal combustion systems

In total, the different submodels form a system of strongly coupled differential equations. Each of these equations can be expressed in form of a general transport equation:

$$\frac{\partial}{\partial x_j}(\rho u_j \phi) = \frac{\partial}{\partial x_j}\left(\Gamma_\phi \frac{\partial \phi}{\partial x_j}\right) + S_\phi \qquad (1)$$

where ϕ and u_j denote Favre-averaged quantities. The terms in equation (1) describe the local change of ϕ due to convective, diffusive and source term contributions under steady state conditions. For example the momentum balance reads:

$$\frac{\partial}{\partial x_j}(\rho U_j U_i) = \frac{\partial}{\partial x_j}\left[\mu\left(\frac{\partial U_i}{\partial x_j}+\frac{\partial U_j}{\partial x_i}\right)\right] - \frac{\partial}{\partial x_j}(\rho u_i u_j) - \frac{\partial p}{\partial x_i} + \rho g_i \qquad (2)$$

where U_i denotes the average velocity under certain assumptions for the turbulent Reynolds-stresses $\rho u_i u_j$. The coupling between the different submodels (see figure 1) is illustrated by the presence of the density ρ in equations (1) and (2). The density is calculated by the ideal gas law using the species concentrations determined in the reaction model as well as the enthalpy and temperature determined in the heat transfer model.

Furthermore, a domain decomposition technique supporting non-matching grids is used (Risio et al., 1997) enabling an individual discretization of the physical space concerning the choice of the applied physical models, numerical methods, grid resolutions, and co-ordinate systems.

3 Validation at full scale

The reliability of numerical predictions is a key aspect in the industrial use of numerical results for the optimization and development of new combustion equipment. It is therefore necessary to verify the validity of numerical results for a great variety of different furnaces and firing concepts at full scale. The purpose of the validation exercise described in the following paragraphs is therefore to assess the predictive capabilities of AIOLOS by comparing predictions and measurements for the numerical simulation of three different furnaces of different firing concepts, sizes and fuels. The Fusina Unit 2 furnace of ENEL and the Bexbach Unit 1 furnace of Saarberg are tangential firing systems burning bituminous coal with an electrical output of 170 MW and 750 MW, respectively. The Niederaussem Unit B furnace of RWE is a top-fired system burning brown coal with an electrical output of 150 MW.

The authors want to stress that the purpose of the present validation exercise is not to achieve the best fit of measurements by adjusting any model parameters or boundary values. Model parameters and boundary values are chosen and fixed according to the experience of the authors being involved in the mathematical modelling of full scale furnaces for several years. This procedure reflects best the usual situation of an engineer who has to perform the calculation of a furnace before measured values are available.

3.1 Validation at the Fusina Unit 2 furnace of ENEL

The Fusina Unit 2 furnace is a tangential firing system with 16 burners on 4 elevations and an electrical output of 170 MW. The size of the furnace is 35 m in height and a cross section of about 8 x 12 m. Low NO_x emissions are achieved by an air staging technique, realized with a special arrangement of the nozzles in the main windbox and the installation of separate overfire air (OFA) nozzles about 5 m above the main windbox. The OFA nozzles can be moved in the vertical plane (tilt angle: $\pm\ 30°$) and in the horizontal plane (yaw angle: $\pm\ 15°$). The physical space is discretized using grids of different fineness: A coarse grid with approximately

100,000 computed cells (figure 2, left), a medium grid of approximately 500,000 cells (not shown), and a fine grid of approximately 1,000,000 computed cells (figure 2, right). The fine grid is obtained by doubling the resolution of the coarse grid in each direction. Furthermore the fine grid comprises the second path of the boiler in order to eliminate the uncertainties when modelling the NO_x formation, since the measurements were taken at the air heater inlet.

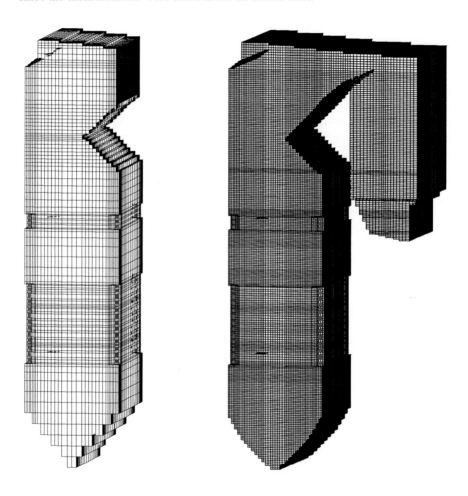

Fig. 2: Coarse discretization (100,000 cells, left) and fine discretization including second path (1,000,000 cells, right)

The ENEL report "Thermal and emissions characterization of ENEL's Fusina Units 1 and 2" contains comprehensive measurements of wall heat fluxes, carbon in fly ash values and NO_x concentrations for a series of 36 tests together with the corresponding operational settings during these tests. The report is part of the "Survey of information on NO_x emissions from boilers" of the "Full boiler performance modelling"-group of the EC-funded project "Performance prediction in advanced coal fired boilers", Contract No. JOF-CT95-0005. These trials comprise the combustion of two test coals with different characteristics: A South African coal with a higher ash content and a lower reactivity as well as a blend of American coals with lower ash content and higher reactivity. For each test, the coal and air distribution is given in terms of damper positions. A particle size distribution is given for a 200, 100, and 50 mesh. Global parameters like the total heat absorbed by the furnace are also available. One quantity that is missing, is the amount of total incoming air. This quantity is calculated by using the measured O_2 concentration in the flue gases at the economizer outlet together with the total coal flow and the coal ultimate analysis to determine the amount of incoming air under the assumption that all combustible matter must be oxidized at the economizer outlet. Although this calculation bears some uncertainties which could be estimated to a few percent of the incoming air, it has the advantage that it includes the amount of false air entering the furnace.

Absorbed heat fluxes in the combustion chamber of Fusina Unit 2 have been monitored by an extensive number of "chordal thermocouples" which measure the metal temperature of a water wall tube about 1 mm from the outer tube surface. The resulting absorbed heat flux can be iteratively calculated, if the thermal resistance of the water side of the tube is known. The comparison of measured and calculated wall heat fluxes is very difficult due to the highly transient situation in the furnace. This is caused by the introduction of a sootblowing cycle in order to get rid of the intrinsic instability due to ash deposition on the furnace walls. Furthermore, the calculation of accurate time averages is a difficult task under these conditions. Therefore, for the assessment of model validity concerning the prediction of wall heat fluxes, six test cases were selected which have nearly the same operating conditions. They only differ in respect to the amount of OFA and the application of the sootblowing cycle. This selection is done under the viewpoint of minimizing the computational effort and the possibility of showing the influence of the varying conditions at the furnace walls due to the sootblowing cycle. The following tests were selected:

Test No. 16   no OFA / American coal / sootblower operation
Test No. 32A   no OFA / American coal / dirty walls
Test No. 32B   no OFA / American coal / clean walls

Test No. 18   200t/h OFA / American coal / sootblower operation
Test No. 31A   200t/h OFA / American coal / dirty walls
Test No. 31B   200t/h OFA / American coal / clean walls

The calculations are performed using different discretizations and differencing schemes together with a fixed wall temperature of 670°C and a constant wall emissivity of 0.65. Figure 3 shows a comparison between measured and calculated wall heat fluxes over the furnace height for the American coal with no OFA (top) and with 200 t/h OFA (bottom). For clarity without introducing a significant loss in information, only the mean measured and calculated values on each elevation are depicted.

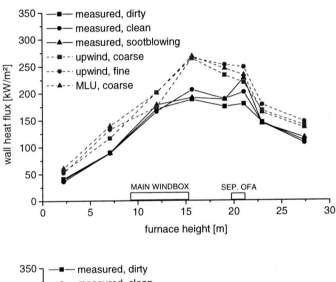

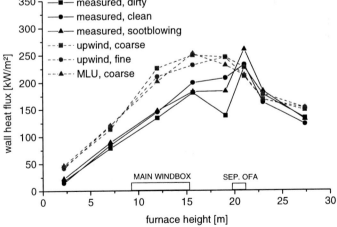

Fig. 3: Measured and calculated wall heat fluxes over furnace height; No OFA (top) and 200 t/h OFA (bottom)

In general the calculated values are always higher than the measured values, although the total heat absorbed by the furnace corresponds exactly to the value specified in the ENEL report. However the general trend of the measurements is maintained in the calculations. Figure 3 shows that the application of a finer grid resolution as well as higher order differencing schemes hardly affects the calculated wall heat fluxes. This explains the success of much simpler engineering models in calculating these quantities. The observed discrepancies may be attributed to the uncertainties of the present validation: Reaction kinetics of the particular coals are unknown; coal and air maldistribution compared to the settings in the model can significantly affect the numerical results (damper settings are not very reliable); ash deposition on the furnace walls together with a non-homogeneous cleaning of the furnace walls may result in strong spatial variations of the wall emissivity and thermal resistance.

The carbon in fly ash is measured by an isokinetic solid sampling at the air heater outlet. In order to assess model validity, five test cases were selected with those operating conditions having the greatest influence on the carbon in fly ash. The selected test cases were:

Test No. 4   no OFA / South African coal
Test No. 9   200 t/h OFA / South African coal / no tilt
Test No. 12   200 t/h OFA / South African coal / tilt angle +30°

together with the test cases of the previous investigation burning American coal. In order to account for coal fineness three representative particle sizes 50, 75, and 100 μm are considered in the present calculations. The mass fraction of the particular size is calculated assuming a Rosin-Rammler distribution determined from the sieving experiments using a 200, 100, and 50 mesh. Table 1 shows a comparison between measured and calculated values.

Table 1: Comparison of measured and calculated carbon in fly ash values for different coals and operational settings

	South African Coal			American Coal	
OFA	no	200 t/h	tilt 30°	no	200 t/h
upwind, coarse	3.5 %	13.3 %	-	2.3 %	14.5 %
MLU, coarse	4.4 %	10.4 %	12.9 %	3.2 %	10.1 %
upwind, fine	5.0 %	13.1 %	-	3.7 %	14.0 %
MLU, fine	4.6 %	10.7 %	15.0 %	3.4 %	9.8 %
measured	6.9 %	10.9 %	14.5 %	5.4 %	7.0 %

Since the reliability of the measurements is estimated to ± 1.5 % by comparing measurements of tests with the same operational settings, the calculations are in good agreement with the experimental results. The major trends as well as the absolute values are reproduced by the calculations. Table 1 reveals the importance of the utilization of a higher order differencing scheme (MLU), in order to obtain more accurate solutions. For staged tests the utilization of the finer grid does not improve the results very much compared to the application of a higher order differencing scheme.

The NO_x concentration is measured from a grid sampling at the air heater outlet (21 points per duct). The same tests as for carbon in fly ash are chosen to evaluate model validity. Since the best results of carbon in fly ash regarding accuracy are only available on the fine grid using MLU as differencing scheme, these calculations are used for the prediction of NO_x formation in a post-processing step. Table 2 shows a comparison between measured and calculated values.

Table 2: Comparison of measured and calculated NO_x concentrations [mg/Nm³, 6% O_2] for different coals and operational settings

	South African Coal			**American Coal**	
OFA	no	200 t/h	tilt 30°	no	200 t/h
MLU, fine	956	592	588	820	480
measured	958	412	333	742	313

The comparison reveals that the calculation is able to reproduce the major trends but fails to predict the absolute values. While for unstaged conditions the difference between measured and calculated values is around 1-10 % the staged tests show a deviation of up to 40 %. This could be attributed to the simplicity of the model and the uncertainties regarding the reaction rates of the two competing global reactions where a variety of rate expressions can be found in literature depending on the particular combustion characteristics. Although this explanation is convincing, it should be kept in mind that there are also uncertainties regarding the reaction kinetics of the utilized coals. Differences between the burnout history calculated in the model and that occuring during the tests may not influence the carbon in fly ash at the end of the furnace but will have strong influence on the NO_x formation due to the strong dependence on local stoichiometry and temperature.

3.2 Validation at the Bexbach Unit 1 furnace of Saarberg

The Bexbach Unit 1 furnace is a tangential firing system with an electrical output of 750 MW. The system is fired with a bituminous coal fed by 16 burners on four elevations. The size of the furnace is 76 m in height with a cross section of approximately 18 m squared. Large furnaces equipped with pulverized coal burners are typically composed of two pulverized coal nozzles, an intermediate air nozzle, and two oil burners (see figure 4).

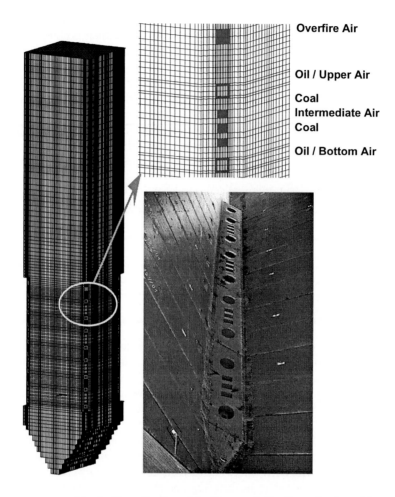

Fig. 4: Discretization of the furnace (left), discretization of the burners (top, right), and burner row (bottom, right)

During pulverized coal operation the secondary air is admitted via the intermediate air nozzles and the oil burners. For NO_x reduction purposes overfire air nozzles are arranged above the four burner levels. Figure 4 shows the discretization of the furnace with approximately 770,000 cells as well as details of the burner discretization and a picture of the whole burner row in one corner. A comparison between calculated and measured mean path temperatures available from LSE (Lehrstuhl für Systemtheorie in der Elektrotechnik, Universität des Saarlandes) is shown in Figure 5. The mean path temperatures are measured with acoustic pyrometry which uses the travel time of an acoustic signal between sender and receiver to determine a mean temperature along the acoustic path, see Spliethoff (1996) for more details. The location of the acoustic paths at an elevation of 71m from the bottom of the ash hopper are illustrated in figure 5. Apart from some exceptions (e.g. paths 10 and 16), the comparison shown in figure 5 reveals a good agreement between measured and calculated values within the accuracy of the measurements which is estimated to 50 K (paths 8 and 11 were out of service).

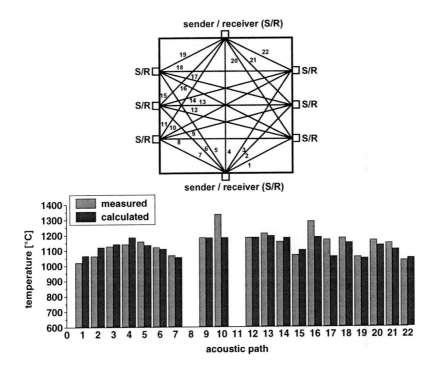

Fig. 5: Location of the acoustic paths at an elevation of 71m (top) and a comparison between measured and calculated mean path temperatures (bottom)

3.3 Validation at the Niederaussem Unit B furnace of RWE

The 150 MW$_e$ utility boiler unit B in power station Niederaußem produces a steam mass flow of 490 tons/h. The unit is top-fired and built in L-shape. In the vertical part of the furnace with a height of 40 m and a cross section of 9 x 15 m tube walls form the evaporator. The furnace of the utility unit is equipped with 6 swirl burners. To operate the vessel with nominal power 5 burners are in use. Each burner consists of an external and an internal pipe. The secondary air is supplied by an air receiver and swirl vanes into the external pipe. The primary flow in the internal pipe is not swirled. The utility boiler is discretized using two subgrids: One discretizing the furnace and the other covering a part of the second path. This leads to approximately 2,000,000 computed cells achieving a coherent fine resolution of the physical space (see Fig. 6).

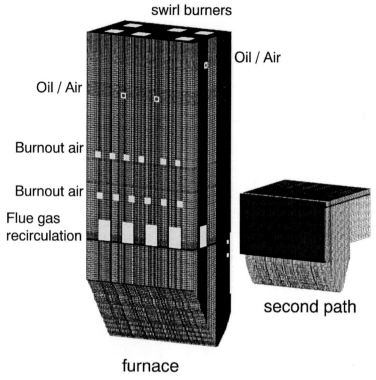

Fig. 6: Discretization of the utility unit B furnace with 2,000,000 cells

The tests at the utility unit were performed at a single burner while the four remaining burners were operated under normal conditions to avoid impairments on the electric power production of the utility unit. The priorities of the tests were set on the adjustment of the momentum ratio for an optimized operation of the particular burner. Temperature measurements were performed 8 m and 4 m below the burner mouth in the flame with a suction pyrometer. The measurement points were located in 7 steps from the middle of the flame radially to the corner. The probes on the two levels (8 m and 4 m) have an angle of about 90° to each other to get a three-dimensional temperature profile in the flame. The gas composition in the flame was determined by taking gas samples from the furnace and analyzing them.

Basic measurements at the utility unit showed that the momentum ratio of secondary to primary flow under custom operating conditions was less than 0.3. This lead to a long non-swirling diffusion flame shown by the temperature distribution in the furnace. The ignition and main combustion was delayed to the lower part of the furnace. Due to the reduced residence time in the furnace the burnout was decreased and the CO emissions were increased. Due to the location of the main combustion zone in the lower furnace part a sufficient zone with a reducing gas composition could not occur. The reduction of already formed NO_x was inhibited. The tests at the utility unit demonstrated that the flame suddenly changed from a long diffusion to a swirling flame when enlarging the momentum ratio to 1.3 by increasing the secondary flow rate. An even temperature and oxygen profile which is typical for the farfield of a swirl flame was formed.

The main air and fuel flows have been determined during the measuring campaign. However, the determination of all flows in a utility unit is difficult. The unknown quantities were recovered from globally measured flows or taken from data sheets of former investigations. Furthermore, the experiments could not be performed at the same day because of the duration of the tests. This may cause a change in the characteristics of the utilized coal. Since a reliable reconstruction of two different sets of coal characteristics is not possible it was decided not to change these parameters in order not to falsify the effects predicted in the calculations.

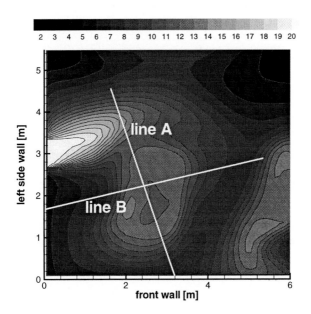

**Fig. 7: Predicted oxygen distribution [Vol-%] for the original
settings at a distance of 4 m from the burner mouth**

Numerical results are compared with in-furnace measurements of temperature and oxygen concentrations performed perpendicular to the burner axis at two different distances from the burner mouth: 8 m and 4 m. For the distance 4 m from the burner mouth only measurements of the original settings with a momentum ratio of 0.3 are available. Figure 7 shows the oxygen distribution in a horizontal slice, zooming the region where the measurements were taken. The crossing point of line

A and line B is the burner axis. A comparison between calculated and measured values of oxygen and temperature at this level is shown in Fig. 8 and 9. The measurements were taken along line B.

Taking into account all the above mentioned uncertainties in specifying the boundary conditions the agreement between measured and calculated profiles can be judged as sufficient. The shape of the profiles as well as the peak level is reproduced by the calculations. Nevertheless, a parallel shift of the profiles of approximately 0.5 m can be observed which is mainly attributed to the lack of knowledge regarding the correct mass flows of the neighbouring burners. These values are specified using the coal dispatcher settings together with the measured coal and air mass flows of the investigated burner.

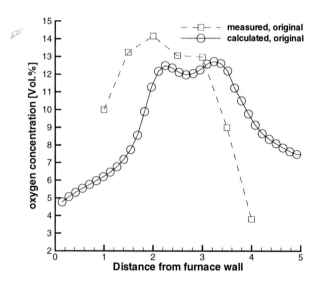

Fig. 8: Comparison between measured and calculated oxygen concentrations [Vol-%] for the original settings at a distance of 4 m from the burner mouth

A further comparison between calculated and measured values of oxygen concentration and temperature measured along line A at the distance 8 m is made. Figures 10 and 11 show the results for the original and the optimized settings. Again for the original settings a parallel shift of the profiles can be observed together with a slight underprediction of the oxygen peak level. For the optimized settings (momentum ratio: 1.3) the calculations are not able to capture the discontinuity in the centre of the oxygen profile. Nevertheless, the basically different flow and flame characteristics of the original and the optimized burner settings are well reproduced in the calculations which is the most important result of this validation exercise.

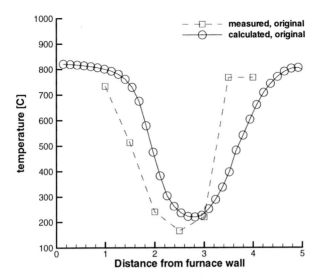

Fig. 9: Comparison between measured and calculated temperatures [°C] for the original settings at a distance of 4 m from the burner mouth

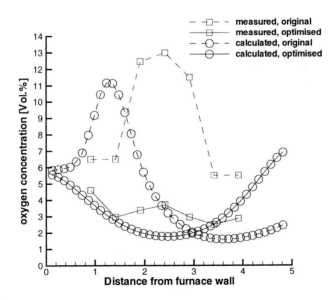

Fig. 10: Comparison between measured and calculated oxygen concentrations [Vol-%] for the original and optimized settings at a distance of 8 m from the burner mouth

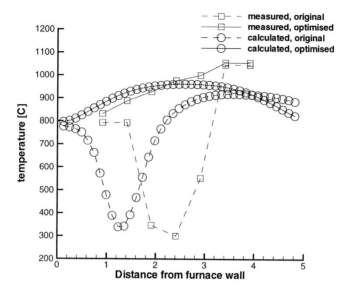

Fig. 11: Comparison between measured and calculated
temperatures [°C] for the original and optimized settings at a
distance of 8 m from the burner mouth

4 Performance statistics on the NEC SX-4

Besides accuracy, investigated in the previous section, computational economy is an important demand for the industrial use of a 3D-furnace simulation code, allowing to obtain solutions of acceptable accuracy within short time periods and at low financial costs. A possibility of reaching this goal is the use of high end parallel computing power available at big computing centres like HWW (Höchstleistungsrechner für Wissenschaft und Wirtschaft Betriebs GmbH) in Stuttgart. HWW offers computing time on high end parallel computers for science and industry with an excellent cost to performance ratio.

In order to exploit the possibilities of parallel execution AIOLOS has successfully been parallelized in the past with two different strategies: a domain decomposition method using MPI (Message Passing Interface) as the message passing environment (see Lepper, 1995 and Lepper et al., 1996) and a data parallel approach using either Microtasking or HPF (High Performance Fortran, see Risio et al., 1996). These investigations were performed either on distributed memory massively parallel computers (MPPs) or pure shared memory vector computers (PVPs), showing acceptable parallel efficiencies for both approaches. The architecture used in the present paper is a single node NEC SX-4/32 with an

aggregate peak-performance of 64 GFLOP/s and a shared main memory of 8 GB SSRAM (Synchronous Static RAM). For the evaluation of the efficiency of AIOLOS two main aspects have to be considered:
- the vector performance of the code on a single processor and
- the parallel performance of the code on an increasing number of processors.

4.1 Vector performance of AIOLOS

Running the four grids of the Fusina and Niederaussem simulations on a single vector processor leads to the results summarized in Table 3. The results are obtained using the hardware performance monitor of the NEC SX-4.

Table 3: Single processor performance of AIOLOS

	Fusina Unit 1	Fusina Unit 1	Fusina Unit 1	Niederaussem Unit B
cells	100,000	500,000	1,000,000	2,000,000
execution time [s/iteration]	0.48 (0.48)	2.16 (2.13)	5.31 (5.13)	11.17 (-)
processor speed [MFLOP/s]	437 (571)	440 (572)	443 (572)	443 (-)

The degree of vectorization of AIOLOS is greater than 99.7 % depending on the problem size. This is due to the reconstruction of the code several years ago. The degree of vectorization is hereby defined as the ratio between the time spent in the vector unit and the total user time. Table 3 shows execution times and processor speed for the default data size of 4 byte and the double precision data size of 8 byte (values in brackets). The values reveal that AIOLOS achieves a maximum processor speed of 572 MFLOP/s on a single processor using the 8 byte data size. This is approximately 60 % of the maximum sustained performance of 1 GFLOP/s obtained by benchmark calculations. The processor speed is slower at the 4 byte data size but this does hardly affect the execution time for the problem (see table 3). Since the usage of the 8 byte data size doubles the required memory without reducing the execution time the 4 byte data size is used in the following.

4.2 Parallel performance of AIOLOS

A comparison between the different parallel programming models (Microtasking and message passing using MPI as the message passing environment) is done for the discretization of the Bexbach Unit 1 furnace with a total number of 770,000 computed cells. The timings are taken using the hardware performance monitor of the SX-4 as well as measurements of the elapsed time. Since the measurements are taken in non-dedicated mode of the machine, each calculation is done several times under weak load conditions to guarantee the reliability of the results. For the same reason only up to 16 processors are accessible to non-privileged users.

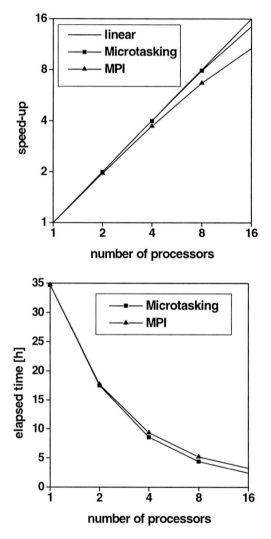

Fig. 12: Elapsed time until convergence (bottom) and speed-up (top) on a varying number of processors using Microtasking and MPI

Figure 12 shows the corresponding execution times until convergence as well as the obtained speed-up. The speed-up which can be used as a measure for the parallel efficiency is defined as the ratio between the execution time on the actual number of processors and the execution time on a single processor. The results depicted in figure 12 show an acceptable performance for both programming models. The computing time of almost 35 h on a single processor can be reduced significantly to a few hours in both cases. Nevertheless, Microtasking saves up to 0.7 h of computing time above 4 processors leading to a 25% reduction of the overall computing costs on 16 processors. Since load balancing problems are very unlikely for this problem size and number of processors, the superiority of Microtasking is mainly attributed to the direct access to the memory instead of performing memory to memory copies via message passing calls for communication. This is not only more costly but also rises the probability for memory access conflicts leading to an additional reduction of the speed-up. Figure 13 shows the total time consumed by access conflicts on the memory banks for both programming models. While the conflict time remains nearly constant for Microtasking when increasing the number of processors, MPI wastes an increasing amount of computing time compared to Microtasking in memory access conflicts.

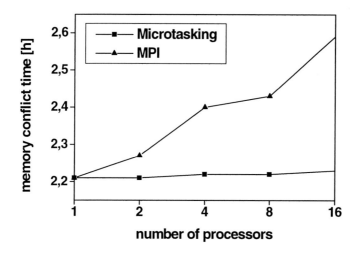

**Fig. 13: Time spent in memory access conflicts until convergence
for Microtasking and MPI on a varying number of processors**

Figure 14 shows the speed-up on a varying number of processors for the three grids of the Fusina Unit 1 simulations using the upwind differencing scheme and the Microtasking programming model. The corresponding execution times are listed in table 4. The execution times are measured as before. The results indicate a nearly linear scaling of the fine grid (1,000,000 cells) and the medium grid (500,000 cells) when increasing the number of processors. For the coarse grid (100,000 cells) the parallel efficiency is much lower resulting in a sub-linear scaling. The reason for this behaviour is the numer of computed cells since it directly influences the loop length in the code. While the fine grid, after dividing the loops by the number of processors, still achieves a sufficiently long loop length to keep the processors busy, the small size of the coarse grid leads to a lack of computational load when rising the number of processors over a certain limit, e.g. 4. The same arguments are valid for the medium grid.

Table 4: Execution times until convergence on a varying number of processors for different discretizations

		processors				
		1	2	4	8	16
100,000 cells	[h:min]	0:40	0:21	0:11	0:07	0:06
500,000 cells	[h:min]	6:42	3:22	1:41	0:52	0:31
1,000,000 cells	[h:min]	22:07	11:20	5:41	2:53	1:36

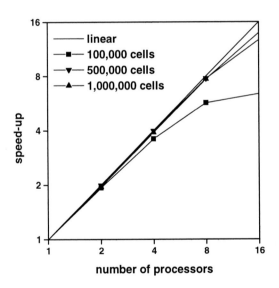

Figure 14: Speed-up on a varying number of processors for discretizations of different fineness

This investigation reveals two main characteristics of the code:
-   There is a certain number of processors where the parallel performance deteriorates and it becomes senseless to further increase the number of processors.

- When increasing the number of calculated cells (e.g. by increasing the size of the problem) this performance limit is pushed towards a higher number of processors which is the prerequisite for scalability.

Although these limits are important to judge the suitability of the code for this particular platform the results in table 4, showing the execution time until convergence, indicate that from a practical point of view this limit is not reached. Examining the execution times under the assumption that it is sufficiently fast to obtain a solution from scratch within less than 3 hours, the fine grid could be executed on a maximum of 8 processors, the medium grid on a maximum of 4 processors and the coarse grid is already fast enough on a single processor. This is always below the scalability limit.

5 CONCLUSIONS

A validation exercise has been presented illustrating the problems of full scale validation. Numerical simulations were performed for three furnaces differing in the firing concept, size and utilized fuel. Numerical results were compared with full scale measurements provided by the industrial partners ENEL, Saarberg and RWE. The comparison revealed a good agreement between measured and calculated values of temperature, oxygen and carbon in fly ash as well as a good representation of the general trend of the variation of the wall heat fluxes over the furnace height. The comparison between measured and calculated NO_x concentrations showed an acceptable representation of the major trends but a failure in reproducing the absolute values. Due to the simplicity of the model and the uncertainties mentioned before, further validation effort will be necessary to prove the reliability of NO_x predictions in industrial furnaces. For the time being the correct reproduction of the major trends is very promising.

Furthermore, the performance of the furnace simulation tool AIOLOS has been assessed on the parallel vector computer NEC SX-4/32. The results showed that AIOLOS achieves a single processor speed equivalent to 60 % of the maximum sustained performance delivered by the system. A comparison of the Microtasking and the message passing programming model showed a superiority of the Microtasking model on this particular platform. Finally, it can be stated that using AIOLOS on the NEC SX-4 enabled accurate predictions of several relevant quantities concerning the performance of industrial scale, coal fired utility boilers. The response time amounted to a few hours which is short enough for boiler manufacturers as well as energy suppliers to take advantage of such predictions.

ACKNOWLEDGEMENTS

The financial support of the European Community within the project "Performance prediction in advanced coal fired boilers", Contract No. JOF-CT95-0005 is gratefully acknowledged.

REFERENCES

Antifora, A., Coelho, L.M.R., Hepburn, P.W., Hesselmann, G., Irons, R, Martins Neves, L.F., Pasini, S., Perrini, A., Sala, M., Schnell, U., Spliethoff, H. (1997): Integration Numerical Modelling and Test Rig Data into the Coal-Over-Coal Reburn Process at Vado Ligure Unit 4 (320 MW$_e$). *Int. Joint Power Generation Conference*, Denver, USA.

De Marco, A.G., Lockwood, F.C. (1975): A New Flux Model for the Calculation of Radiation in Furnaces. *La rivista dei combustibili*, Vol. 29, No. 5-6, pp. 184-196.

De Soete (1974): Overall Reaction Rates of NO and N_2 Formation from Fuel Nitrogen. *15th Symp. (Int.) on Combustion*, Combustion Institute, pp. 1093-1102.

Fiveland, W. A. (1984): Discrete-Ordinates Solutions of the Radiative Transport Equation for Rectangular Enclosures. *Journal of Heat Transfer*, Vol. 106, pp. 699-706.

Lepper, J. (1995): Parallel Computation of Turbulent Reactive Flows in Utility Boilers. *Parallel CFD 95*, Pasadena (USA), pp. 129-136.

Lepper, J., Schnell, U., Hein, K.R.G. (1996): Numerical Simulation of Large-Scale Combustion Processes on Distributed Memory Parallel Computers Using MPI. *Parallel CFD 96*, Capri (Italy), pp. 416-423.

Lockwood, F.C., Shah, N.G. (1981): A New Radiation Solution Method for Incorporation in General Combustion Prediction Procedures, *18th Symposium (International) on Combustion*, The Combustion Institute, Pittsburgh (USA), pp. 1405-1414.

Noll, B. (1992): Evaluation of a Bounded High-Resolution Scheme for Combustor Flow Computation. *AIAA Journal*, Vol.. 30, No. 1, pp. 64-69.

Rhie, C.M., Chow, W.L. (1983): Numerical Study of Turbulent Flow Past an Airfoil with Trailing Edge Separation. *AIAA Journal*, Vol. 21, No. 11, pp. 1525-1532.

Risio, B., Schnell, U., Hein, K.R.G. (1996): HPF-Implementation of a 3D-Combustion Code on Parallel Computer Architectures Using Fine Grain Parallelism. *Parallel CFD 96*, Capri (Italy), pp. 124-130.

Risio, B., Förtsch, D., Schnell., U., Hein, K.R.G. (1997): Prediction of Pulverized Coal-Fired Utility Boiler Performance on Individually Discretized Non-Matching Grids, *4th Int. Conf. on Technologies and Combustion for a Clean Environment*, Lisbon (Portugal).

Schneider, R., Risio, B., Schnell, U., Hein, K.R.G. (1995): Application of a Differential Reynolds-Stress Turbulence Models to the Numerical Simulation of Coal-Fired Utility Boilers. *3rd International Symposium on Coal Combustion*, Beijing (China), pp. 336-343.

Schnell, U. (1991): Berechnung der Stickoxidemissionen von Kohlen-staubfeuerungen. *VDI-Fortschritt-Bericht Reihe 6*, No. 250, VDI-Verlag Düsseldorf.

Schnell, U., Schneider, R., Magel, H.-C., Risio, B., Lepper, J., Hein, K.R.G. (1995): Numerical Simulation of Advanced Coal-Fired Combustion Systems with In-Furnace NO_x Control Technologies, *3rd Int. Conf. Comb. Tech.*, Lisbon (Portugal).

Spliethoff, H. (1996): Untersuchungen und Entwicklungen schallpyrometrischer Temperaturmeßverfahren an zwei Kohlenstaubfeuerungen, VGB Kraftwerkstechnik 76, Heft 7

Van Doormal, J.P., Raithby, G.D. (1984): Enhancements of the SIMPLE Method for Predicting Incompressible Fluid Flows. *Numer. Heat Transfer*, Vol. 7, pp. 147-163.

Engineering and Computer-Science

Prof. Dr. Wolfgang Nagel, Institut für Wissenschaftliches Rechnen
Technische Universität Dresden
Zellescher Weg 12-14, D-01069 Dresden

Prof. Dr. Christoph Zenger, Institut für Informatik, FORTWIHR,
Technische Universität München
Arcisstr. 21, D-80333 München

In this chapter articles from various fields are collected, spanning from computer-science and image-processing to engineering applications from electrical engineering and structural mechanics.

Computer Science plays an important role in scientific computing as a supplier of methods, data structures and tools for the efficient implementation of parallel algorithms. And we hope that more and more computer-scientists cooperate with scientists from the diverse application-areas of HPC in projects to improve the quality of the programs especially under software-engineering aspects. On the otherhand, computer-scientists do not use high performance computers to a large extent as a research tool. This fact is reflected in the rather small number of computer-scince projects at the HLRS. Even these few projects usually originate in another area of research, but they were collected here because computer science or methodological aspects seem to be predominant.

Moreover, visualization, which usually is considered as a computer-science discipline and is a very important tool in scientific computing, often does not appear as a constitutive part of a project, because the post processing part is usually executed on a workstation at the home institute and is therefore not part of the HLRS project itself.

The situation that computer-science projects play only a minor role may change in the future because typical research areas of computer science like data mining, combinatorial optimization, the control of large distributed systems etc. are getting more and more complex and yield very challenging HPSC- problems of great economical importance.

Electrical engineering is not a traditional field for supercomputer usage. Thus, the working groups in this field are still in a startup phase concerning the effective use of High Performance Computing. While in the past high-end workstations were sufficient in most cases to do the necessary computations in an appropriate time frame, now the problems get more and more complex, taking weeks or even months of CPU time on a single processor. Therefore, some research groups took significant effort to improve their codes and to adapt them to the requirements of parallel architectures.

The contribution from electrical engineering in this chapter deals with parallel computing of electromagnetic fields based on integral equations. The analysis of runtimes and the optimization steps in the diverse phases of the program show that, beyond strongly required competences in the algorithmic and methodological field, tools for a detailed performance analysis, complemented by a qualified knowledge of the underlying computer architecture, are an absolute necessity to get performance results expected on parallel architectures.

Parallel Computation of Electromagnetic Fields Based on Integral Equations

Ulrich Jakobus

Institut für Hochfrequenztechnik, University of Stuttgart, Pfaffenwaldring 47,
D-70550 Stuttgart, Germany

Abstract. This paper addresses the analysis of electromagnetic radiation and scattering problems in parallel using the method of moments (MoM) as implemented in the computer code FEKO. The parallelisation of all steps of the solution process including geometry setup, parallel computation of the matrix elements using a distributed storage scheme, solution of the system of linear equations, and near- and far-field calculations is discussed and some results concerning the achieved scalability are presented.

1 Introduction

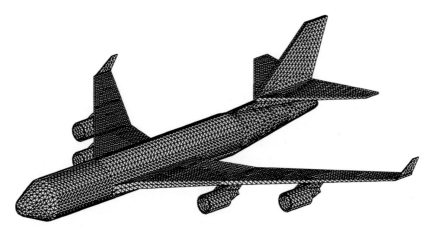

Fig. 1. Example for an electromagnetic scatterer with discretised surface.

We aim at solving electromagnetic radiation and scattering problems. Typical examples in the area of antennas include the analysis and optimisation of mobile communication antennas, where the influence of the human operator can be taken into account, or the investigation of different antenna configurations on cars, ships, air planes, or similar structures. In the area of EMC (*electromagnetic compatibility*) the numerical techniques can be applied in order to determine radiation from interference sources, the coupling of electromagnetic fields into cables, or for example also shielding factors of enclosures with slots. The prediction of the scattered electromagnetic fields is also of importance for radar applications, e.g. we are able to compute the RCS (*radar cross section*) of the aircraft depicted in Fig. 1.

There do exist a variety of different numerical techniques for the computation of electromagnetic fields. The popular ones, which can be applied to arbitrary configurations concerning the geometrical shape and the material properties (metallic, dielectric), include FDTD (*finite difference time domain*), FIT (*finite integration technique*), FEM (*finite element method*), TLM (*transmission line matrix method*), and the MoM (*method of moments*). For our applications as described above we have implemented the MoM in the computer code FEKO mainly because the treatment of open problems (radiation to infinity) is exact and because for 3–dimensional problems only a 2–dim. discretisation of surfaces is required in general. This usually helps reducing the number of unknowns, however, the resulting matrix is dense since there is a coupling between all the elements through radiation.

In Sect. 2 the sequential solution process is described while Sect. 3 concentrates on the parallelisation of the different phases of the solution process. This parallelisation is based on the message passing standard MPI. Some performance results for the CRAY T3E and the Intel Paragon, which is used as development platform, are presented in Sect. 4

2   Description of the Solution Process

In this paper we concentrate on the parallelisation of the MoM based computer code FEKO. Only a very limited description of the MoM covering only some aspects which are important for an understanding of the parallelisation is given in the following. The interested readers can find more details in [1–4].

Consider the problem in Fig. 1, where for instance the radiation pattern of an antenna mounted on the fuselage shall be determined. According to the simplified flow chart in Fig. 2 the first phase of the MoM solution is the geometry setup which includes reading the input data from a file, performing the triangulation of surfaces, and searching for edges between triangular patches. This information is required in order to construct basis functions.

The size of the triangular surface patches must be small as compared to the wavelength $\lambda = \frac{c}{f}$ with the velocity of light c and the frequency f. Thus the number of elements N will scale with f^2 for 2–dim. surfaces. Memory requirement for the matrix (see below) increases proportional to f^4, and the CPU–time of the MoM scales with $f^{4\ldots6}$. This is the reason why we need high–performance computing to solve electrically large scattering problems where the geometrical dimensions are in the range of a few wavelengths or above. To reduce this cost, we are developing hybrid techniques (e.g. [4,5]), but it is still desirable to have MoM–based results for validation purposes.

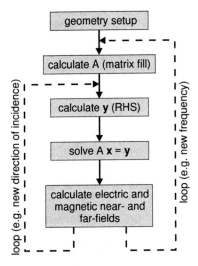

Fig. 2. Simplified structure of the MoM–part of FEKO.

Once the structure has been discretised, the unknown surface currents (equivalent currents in the case of dielectric bodies) are expressed as super-position of basis functions f_n with unknown coefficients. The application of certain boundary conditions for the electromagnetic fields on the scatter-ers' surfaces leads to a coupled set of integral equations, which can then be transformed into a system of linear equations $A \cdot x = y$ for the unknown ex-pansion coefficients by applying suitable weighting functions w_m (Galerkin procedure). Since we support different basis functions (e.g. for metallic wires, metallic surfaces, connections between metallic wires and surfaces, dielectric surfaces, ...), the matrix A consists of 7×7 different sub–matrices A_{ji} as shown in Fig. 3. The elements of these sub–matrices are based on different integral equations involving e.g. 2– or 4–dimensional numerical integrations. For a parallelisation it is important to note that the CPU–time required to compute the elements of different sub–matrices may differ by a factor of 10 or even more. Special techniques are required (see below in Sect. 3.2) to achieve load balancing.

After the elements of the matrix A have been computed the right–hand side (RHS) vector y is constructed, see Fig. 2. Now the system of linear equations $A \cdot x = y$ can be solved for the unknown expansion coefficients x. In principle, different iterative techniques such as the Krylov subspace methods can be used, but since frequently the solution is required for multiple right–hand sides y (see loop indicated by a dashed arrow in Fig. 2), an LU–decomposition with subsequent back–substitution is preferred (but see comment below in Sect. 3.3).

Once the solution vector x is known, the electric near– and far–fields can be computed by an integral over the discretised surfaces.

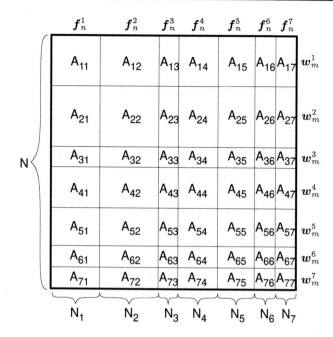

Fig. 3. Matrix A consisting of 7×7 sub–matrices A_{ij} of different size.

3   Parallelisation of the Various Phases of the Solution Process

3.1   Geometry Setup

This phase of setting up the geometry has not been parallelised yet, but we perform a preprocessing of the geometry (triangulation of surfaces, search for common edges, etc.) sequentially on a PC or workstation and write the resulting data to a file which can be read later by the parallel process. Also some acceleration techniques such as spatial decomposition have been implemented to speed up this phase.

3.2   Matrix Fill

The $N \times N$ matrix A is dense and requires a distributed storage scheme. 16 Byte are used for one complex matrix element a_{mn}, thus for an electrically large structure with typically up to $N = 30000 \ldots 50000$ basis functions a total memory requirement of about $10 \ldots 40$ GByte results. Assuming that at most 110 MByte are available for the matrix on each node of the CRAY T3E, we have to use at least 100 nodes for such large scale problems.

The parallel computation of the matrix elements a_{mn} with $m, n = 1 \ldots N$ is not a trivial task for several reasons:

- One might compute the elements a_{mn} just by looping over the indices m and n. However, there do exist efficient fill techniques for some of the sub–matrices (A_{11}, A_{22}, A_{44} and A_{55}). Some common integrals are computed which are associated with the triangular patches, and these integrals contribute then to up to 9 different matrix elements (3 in a row). This results in a CPU–time reduction by a factor of 3...3.5 for the sequential version. For the parallel version, it is advantageous to keep these 9 matrix elements on the same node so that the contributions by the common integrals can be added locally.
- Many problems such as the aircraft in Fig. 1 have some kind of geometrical symmetry. Even if the exciting field is not symmetrical leading to an unsymmetrical solution of the surface currents or the scattered field, we can still exploit symmetry properties in order to reduce CPU–time and memory. However, we then have to make use of symmetry relations between single matrix elements and these should preferably be located on the same node in order to avoid communication.
- It was already mentioned above that the CPU–time required to compute the single matrix elements a_{mn} differs over a wide range for the different sub–matrices (e.g. 4–dimensional integration for metallic surfaces in the sub–matrix A_{11}, 2–dim. integration for metallic wires in the sub–matrix A_{22}). But also for one sub–matrix there are variations in the required CPU–time due to the application of adaptive integration schemes. In some cases integrals become singular and the singularity must be extracted and integrated analytically.

Owing to these constraints, the final strategy for the distributed storage and the parallel computation of the matrix A is the following. A one–dimensional block cyclic row distribution scheme with a block size N_B in the range $1 \leq N_B \leq \lceil \frac{N}{p} \rceil$ with p denoting the number of nodes is selected. This storage scheme ensures that all matrix elements of one row are located on the same node, which is important for the efficient fill techniques and for the exploitation of possible symmetries. Small block sizes N_B support the load balancing since then on average every node has some elements a_{mn} of the different sub–matrices A_{ji}. However, experience has shown that larger block sizes N_B are better for the performance of the efficient fill techniques and especially also for the performance of the matrix solve phase (see Sect. 3.3 below). We therefore use larger block–sizes and achieve the load balancing through a special mapping function which is introduced in order to exchange rows of the matrix A and elements of the vector y based on the estimated time required to compute the different rows of A.

The following example of three wire antennas mounted on an aircraft similar to the model shown in Fig. 1 but at a lower frequency (less number of triangular patches) shall demonstrate the parallelisation of the matrix fill process. The sizes of the sub-matrices in Fig. 3 are $N_1 = 1850$, $N_2 = 33$, $N_3 = 20$, and $N_4 = N_5 = N_6 = N_7 = 0$ leading to $N = 1903$. This is a rather small example for high–performance computing, but it suffices to demonstrate the achieved load balance. Because of symmetry relations only 975 rows of the matrix out of 1903 must be computed. We have used 6 nodes on an Intel Paragon, thus the block size may vary in the range $1 \leq N_B \leq \lceil \frac{975}{6} \rceil = 163$. From the statements above, we expect a good load balancing for small block sizes. The black bar in Fig. 4 represents the run–time for the matrix fill on the 6 nodes with a block size $N_B = 1$. The run–times vary between 391.4 and 402.4 seconds, the run–time difference is less than 3%. However, the efficient fill techniques cannot perform optimally, the grey bar below the black bar shows the result for the maximum block size of $N_B = 163$. The run–times are much shorter now, but the node 5 requires significantly longer than the others since it contains more elements of the sub–matrices A_{2i} and A_{3i} with $i = 1 \ldots 3$ in this case. Only by introducing a special mapping function in order to exchange rows of the matrix, we can benefit from the reduced run–time by the efficient fill techniques and at the same time achieve a satisfactory load balance (dotted bar in Fig. 4).

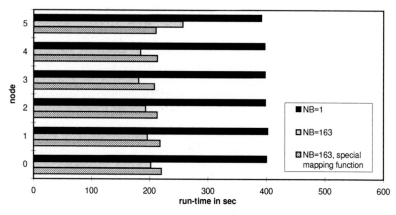

Fig. 4. Run–time of the matrix fill phase on the different nodes using different block–sizes N_B and an optional mapping function (Intel Paragon with $p = 6$ nodes).

3.3   Matrix Solve

In the limit of very large problem sizes N the phase of solving the dense system of linear equations $A \cdot x = y$ dominates the whole solution time of the conventional MoM (but not of the hybrid techniques).

Currently we use the ScaLAPACK [7] library which provides subroutines for the parallel LU–decomposition and subsequent back–substitution of dense matrices. The choice of ScaLAPACK was motivated by available performance results for the CRAY T3E, see Fig. 5 for an example. However, these results are based on a two–dimensional process grid (e.g. 4×8 for 32 nodes), and for our one–dimensional block–cyclic row–distribution scheme for the matrix (see reason above) the performance seems to be worse, as revealed by investigations with the VAMPIR tool. We observed also a strong dependency of the required CPU–time on the block size N_B, see example in Fig. 6.

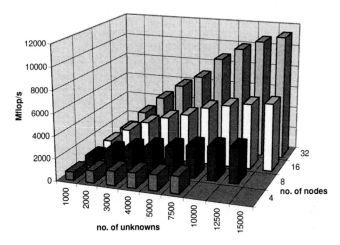

Fig. 5. Performance of the LU factorisation on the CRAY T3E using ScaLAPACK (data from [6]).

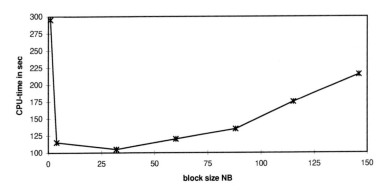

Fig. 6. CPU–time for the LU–decomposition and back substitution on the CRAY T3E for $N = 4656$ unknowns on $p = 32$ nodes as a function of the block size N_B.

Currently we investigate PLAPACK [8] as an alternative to the LU decomposition in ScaLAPACK and the PIM package [9]. PIM offers iterative techniques such as CG, BiCG, BiCGStab, QMR, or GMRES. Convergence studies with a sequential version of FEKO using PIM have shown that one can achieve a reasonable convergence for structures which are based on a

Fredholm integral equation of the second kind (sub-matrices A_{66}, A_{67}, A_{76}, A_{77} in Fig. 3). However, for the treatment of metallic structures as the aircraft in Fig. 1 the underlying electrical field integral equation represents a Fredholm integral equation of the first kind and the convergence is rather poor. Sophisticated preconditioning techniques as proposed in e.g. [10–12] must be applied. These are currently investigated.

3.4 Computation of Near– and Far–Fields

For specific problems with a special Green's function (e.g. for the analysis of mobile telephones radiating close to a simplified head model) this phase of the solution process might dominate the whole solution time. When we started parallelising the FEKO code, we first implemented the near– and far–field computation in parallel using a master/server–concept with a dynamic load balancing scheme. One node acts as master and distributes the tasks of computing the near– or far–field at the different observation points or in the different observation directions, respectively, to the $p - 1$ remaining server nodes. Results have already been reported in the literature [13,14].

4 Examples

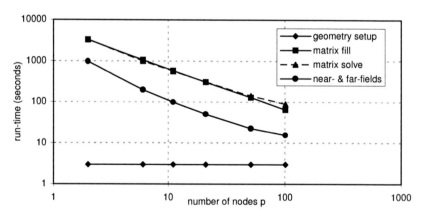

Fig. 7. Run–time of the various phases of the parallelised MoM solution for the analysis of antennas on an aircraft on the Intel Paragon ($N = 1903$).

For the simplified aircraft model introduced in Sect. 3.2 with $N = 1903$ basis functions, the load balancing of the matrix fill phase has been demonstrated in Fig. 4 using $p = 6$ nodes on the Intel Paragon. For the same example the scaling of the different phases of the solution process as a function of the number of nodes between 2 and 100 is depicted in Fig. 7. Besides the obvious fact that the geometry setup phase has not been parallelised, we observe very reasonable scaling properties of the other phases of the solution process. It is interesting to note that the computation of near- and far-fields seems to have a superlinear speedup. The reason for this is the master/server concept, e.g. for $p = 2$ nodes only $p - 1 = 1$ nodes are computing the field. Doubling the nodes to $p = 4$ leads to $p - 1 = 3$ computing processes, hence doubling the number of nodes seems to reduce the required CPU–time by a factor of 3. For a small number of nodes (e.g. a workstation cluster) we can start the master and a server process on the same workstation, so that all CPUs are busy. For a large number of nodes, the master node is also busy collecting the results from the server nodes and distributing new tasks.

Table 1. Wall clock times for the analysis of a scattering problem on the CRAY T3E with $N = 15864$ basis functions.

phase	64 nodes	128 nodes	ratio
geometry setup	8.12 sec	7.56 sec	1.074
matrix fill	390.23 sec	195.91 sec	1.992
matrix solve	1174.48 sec	616.86 sec	1.904
near– & far–fields	39.85 sec	20.66 sec	1.929
total solution time	1616.14 sec	844.77 sec	1.913

Table 1 lists the required wall clock times for a larger example consisting of $N = 15864$ basis functions on the CRAY T3E. Due to the main memory requirement of 3.75 GByte for the matrix and additional 6.4 MByte for other arrays (geometrical data etc.) we have executed FEKO using 64 nodes. In order to demonstrate the scaling properties another run was made with 128 nodes. The last column in Table 1 gives the ratio of the required run–times.

5   Conclusions

The parallelisation of the MoM based computer code FEKO has been presented. We have put special emphasis on optimising the matrix fill phase by exploiting efficient fill techniques and also possible symmetries of a structure. This is possible only by using a one–dimensional block cyclic row distribution scheme for the matrix. However, for an LU decomposition of a dense matrix as supported by the ScaLAPACK or PLAPACK packages, this distribution scheme doesn't seem to be very suitable. Therefore, current investigations concentrate on using iterative techniques with preconditioning schemes. We also consider the out–of–core solution as an option when not enough main memory is available.

FEKO has also been extended by using different Green's functions or by a coupling with asymptotic high frequency techniques, and the parallelisation of these parts is in progress as well.

References

1. R. F. Harrington, *Field Computation by Moment Methods*. Macmillan Company, New York, 1968.

2. U. Jakobus and F. M. Landstorfer, "Erweiterte Momentenmethode zur Berechnung komplizierter elektromagnetischer Streuprobleme," in *Kleinheubacher Berichte 1994*, vol. 37, pp. 19–28, Oct. 1993.

3. U. Jakobus, *Erweiterte Momentenmethode zur Behandlung kompliziert aufgebauter und elektrisch großer elektromagnetischer Streuprobleme*. Fortschrittberichte, Reihe 21, Nr. 171, VDI–Verlag Düsseldorf, 1995. Dissertationsschrift.

4. U. Jakobus and F. M. Landstorfer, "Improved PO–MM hybrid formulation for scattering from three–dimensional perfectly conducting bodies of arbitrary shape," *IEEE Transactions on Antennas and Propagation*, vol. 43, pp. 162–169, Feb. 1995.

5. U. Jakobus and F. M. Landstorfer, "A combination of current– and ray–based techniques for the efficient analysis of electrically large scattering problems," in *Conference Proceedings of the 13th Annual Review of Progress in Applied Computational Electromagnetics, Monterey*, pp. 748–755, Mar. 1997.

6. L. S. Blackford and R. C. Whaley, "ScaLAPACK evaluation and performance at the DoD MSRCs," tech. rep., Department of Computer Science, University of Tennessee, Knoxville, 1998.

7. L. S. Blackford, J. Choi, A. Cleary, E. D'Azevedo, J. Demmel, I. Dhillon, J. Dongarra, S. Hammarling, G. Henry, A. Petitet, K. Stanley, D. Walker, and R. C. Whaley, *ScaLAPACK User's Guide*, 1997. URL http://www.netlib.org/scalapack/scalapack-home.html.

8. R. A. van de Geijn, *Using PLAPACK: Parallel Linear Algebra Package*. The MIT Press, Cambridge, Massachusetts, 1997.

9. R. D. da Cunha and T. Hopkins, *PIM 2.2: The Parallel Iterative Methods package for Systems of Linear Equations User's Guide (Fortran 77 version)*, 1997. URL http://www.mat.ufrgs.br/pim-e.html.

10. J. Shen, T. Hybler, and A. Kost, "Preconditioned iterative solvers for complex and unsymmetric systems of equations resulting from the hybrid FE–BE method," *IEEE Transactions on Magnetics*, vol. 33, pp. 1764–1767, Mar. 1997.

11. G. Bürger, H.-D. Brüns, and H. Singer, "Advanced method of moments based on iterative equation system solver," in *IEEE 1997 International Symposium on Electromagnetic Compatibility, Austin, Texas*, pp. 236–241, Aug. 1997.

12. J. Rahola, "Iterative solution of dense linear systems in electromagnetic scattering calculations," in *Conference Proceedings of the 14th Annual Review of Progress in Computational Electromagnetics, Monterey*, vol. II, pp. 1126–1133, Mar. 1998.

13. U. Jakobus, I. Sulzer, and F. M. Landstorfer, "Parallel implementation of the hybrid MoM/Green's function technique on a cluster of workstations," in *ICAP'97, IEE 10th International Conference on Antennas and Propagation, Edinburgh, Conf. Publication Number 436*, vol. 1, pp. 182–185, Apr. 1997.

14. U. Jakobus, "Parallel computation of the electromagnetic field of hand–held mobile telephones radiating close to the human head," in *Parallel Computing '97 (ParCo97), Bonn*, Sept. 1997.

Numerical Simulation of Mechanical Behaviour of Dynamically Stressed Fencing Mask

Hermann Finckh

Institut für Textil- und Verfahrenstechnik Denkendorf, Germany
Director: Prof. Dr.-Ing. G. Egbers

1.   Summary

Development and improvement of protective clothing has always been a challenging task. New materials and innovative production processes lead to safer and more comfortable products. Because of the large number of influence parameters, optimization by experiments is time-consuming and presents numerous difficulties. Parameter studies can be conduced using computer simulation contribute substantially to development time reduction and product innovations.

The explicit variant of Finite-Element-Method (FEM) for realistic simulation of mechanical properties of knitted fabrics was applied within the scope of an AIF- and DFG-project. With this method, it was possible for the first itme, to model the complex three-dimensional volume contact situations between clasping threads and account for surface friction. The simulation of the penetrating test for a wire fabric of a fencing mask illustrate the efficency of this novel method and the potential for applying the method in the field of protective clothing.

2.   Introduction

Apart from experimental studies of protective clothing behavior, simulation using the Finite Element Method (FEM) is worth consideration. FEM is appropriate für solving strength problems of all kinds related to plastic and elastic coverings. The main advantage of FEM is that once model parameter are verified, simulations regarding material, geometry and boundary conditions may be easily conducted. The calculation results are reproducible at any time.

The results from the AIF-project [1] as well as the findings of the current DFG-project [2] show that the mechanical behaviour of stressed fabrics – in consideration of complex contact situations at the crossing points of the stitches – can successfully be simulated only with the explicit FEM. The explicit Finte Element (FE) program LS-DYNA3D proved to be the appropriate instrument for the simulations. This program, for example, is used for the simulation of crash situations in automobile industry. It can allow numerous complex contact situations at the same time. The explicite FE-program can be used to represent the properties of textile fabrics very similar to real fabric. Here the threads are represented as three-dimensional bars or volume elements. No restrictions on contact processes at the crossing points are implemented, resulting in freely mobile threads. All deformations consider frictional processes and form closures.

Knitted fabrics under stress display considerable crossing points displacement. Thread displacements, elongation of the yarn, and yarn compression at crossing points influence fabric deformation. In the following the simulation of a tensile test of a right-left (rl) fabric composed of a monofilament polyester, 32 dtex yarn count. The draping process of the same knitted fabric over a solid of complex geometry is also presented.

Since 1987 ITV-Denkendorf has been conducting penetrating tests for textile fencing clothing. The Institute is a member of the standardization committee for sports- and leisure equipment in the field of fencing-clothing. The standardization activities show that penetrating tests in connection with fencing clothing are complex and difficult tasks. This is the reason why the fencing mask was subject to FE-simulations based on results of the DFG-project.

3.   Simulation of the penetrating test for fencing masks

In the following a specific area of application of these FE-simulations – the area of protective clothing – shall be discussed in more detail.

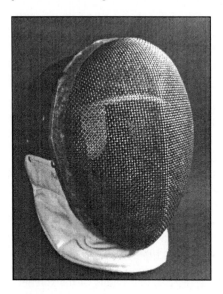
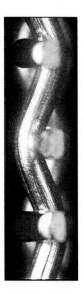

Fig. 1: Fencing mask   Fig. 2: Wire fabric of fencing mask

The filed of area clothing research can benefit from application of FE-simulation. Fencing masks **(fig. 1)** are composed of formed, plain wire fabric **(fig. 2)**. The fencing mask must meet several requirements to be considered protective. The mask must resist the impact stresses of a dynamic heavy weapon strike, be lightweight, and allow good visibility through the fabric.

The mask must be cabable of resisting penetration by a broken blade under wordt case scenario conditions. eapon strick impact speeds range from six to 12 m/s, depending on the weapon [4]. To avoid brakage of wires and guarantee safety, fencing masks must be optimized by means of an expensive, time-consuming testing regime. Application of numerical simulation in this testing phase of development can be very helpful.

The penetrating test for textile fencing clothing is carried out by means of a sample, 38 mm cross-section, fixed in circular form. This sample size is also used for the wire fabric. The geometry of the test spike is well defined. Test spike dimensions correspond to a broken weapon in the upper third (**fig. 3 a, b**). For testing the wire, fabric is laid between the plates of a clamping device and fixed with four screws using a dynamometric key (**fig. 4 a, b**). In the existing impact testing stand, the test spike may be acccelerated to 6 m/s over heigh of fall. **Fig. 5 a, b** illustrate the results from a penetrating test with this test spike.

Fig. 3 a: Impact body   **Fig. 3 b: Test spike**

Fig. 4 a, b: Clamping device for impact tests

Fig. 5 a: Wire fabric after impact test   **Fig. 5 b: Damaged wire**

Impact model

A completely parameter-related generation of the whole impact model is possible
by a developed program. The following parameters are interactively requested to
form the model: wire thickness, number of warp- and weft yarns, fabric density, and
model fineness . The following model data have been taken as a benchmark: the
wire fabric is formed by plain weave with a warp- and weft yarn density of 17.4
units per 100 mm. The wire thickness is 1 mm. The impact event „penetrating of
the wire fabric with a special testing solid" is a three-dimensional process which
requires a three-dimensional FE-model consisting of cube-shaped volume elements
in the impact area. The wire fabric of the following calculations is composed of
13.392 volume- and 8.961 bar elements. The geometry of the clamping device (**fig.
4**) and the test spike (**fig. 3**) are precisely represent by 3.516 plate elements, which
have an appropriate thickness. The complete model designed in this way for the
penetrating test is shown in **fig. 6** and **7**.

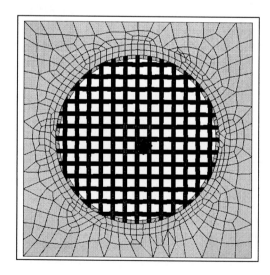

Fig. 6 :   Complete Finite Element model for impact simulation, Top view

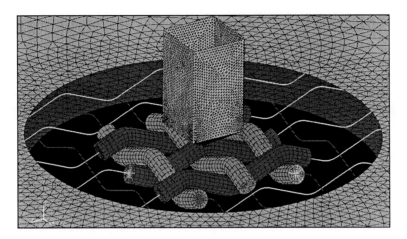

Fig. 7 :   **Impact model with wire fabric consisting of cube-shaped volume elements in the impact area and beam elements outside.**

Material

There exist strict guidelines regarding wire properties. With respect to tensile test according to DIN 50145 the stainless steel wire X6 Cr NiTi 1810 must fulfill the specified limiting values for the upper limit of elasticity, tensile strength and breaking elongation. For the calculations the following characteristic factory data were available:

Diameter of wire sample	Tensile yield strength 0.2%	Tensile strength	Breaking elongation
1,0 + 0,03 mm	794-855 GPa	871-908 GPa	21,1 %

The simulations were conducted with a Young's Modulus of 200 GPa, a Poisson's Ratio of 0.3 and with the elasto-plastic material definition.

Boundary conditions for the impact simulation

The following impact conditions were assumed: The test spike of 5 kg weight is rotated at an angle of 45° in regard to the wires and hits the wire fabric with an impact speed of 5 m/s right between the stitches. The test spike is braked through the impact action.

The following calculations differ with respect to the fact that on one hand the wire fabric is loosely fixed in the clamping device. On the other hand a vertically oriented force of 1000 N is applied to the upper plate, so that the wire fabric is clamped between the plates before the impact occurs. The calculations were carried out on the high-performance computer NEC-SX4 of the University of Stuttgart taking about 20 hours each time, as there was no parallel processor version of LS-DYNA 940 available at that time.

3.1 Impact simulation with wire fabric freely movable between plates

Fig. 8 a: State of deformation after 1.45 ms impact time (wire fabric 7.2 mm deformed)

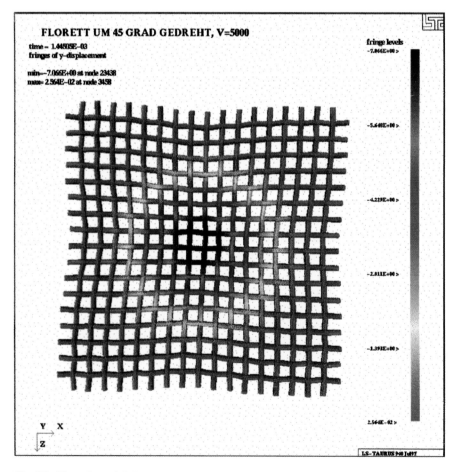

Fig. 8 b: Top view of deformation of wire fabric, fringes show y-displacement in mm

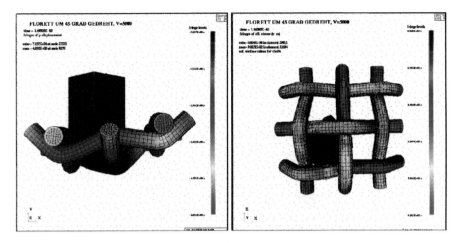

Fig. 8 c, d: State of deformation in the impact area, view from side and bottom

3.2. Impact simulation with wire fabric clamped between plates

Fig. 9 a: State of deformation after 0.55 ms impact time

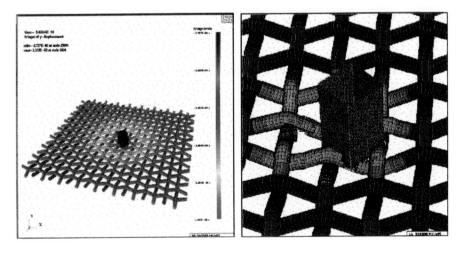

Fig. 9 b,c : Vertical deformation after 0,55 ms, y-displacement in mm (max. 2,73)

**Fig. 9d: Material failure in the impact area after 0.55 ms impact time, fringes show
stress v. mises (max. 870 Gpa)**

Simulation results

If penetrating tests are carried out based on the use of plain wire fabric, then there
is a considerable influence of the fixing force onto the impact behaviour of the
wire fabric. As it could be expected also impact place and position of the test spike
show a certain influence.

By means of the models you are able to investigate parameters such as height of
fall, impact direction, test spike weight, orientation and geometry, impact place
and wire material. Calculation expenditure is considerable, however, for the
investigation of the impact processes all imaginable combinations of the
parameters mentioned above are possible. The advantage can be recognized in so
far, as for example the impact process of the test spike falling down at a certain
angle can be carried through only with difficulties or even not at all.

With regard to the standardization of the fencing mask test, the test of the
semifinished plain wire fabric cannot be recommended because of considerable
influence through clamping; and, in addition, it is difficult to evaluate the
influence of the deformation process with regard to the conditions at the wire
fabric.

The manufacturers of fencing masks were highly interested in parameter studies (wire gauge, wire strength, mass, speed, place and fall direction of impact solid). The simulated forming process of the plain wire fabric to the fencing mask [6] was of high interest, too, as it proved to be problematic in the production process.

Conclusion

With the explicit variant of the Finite-Element-Method (FEM) it is possible to model the complex three-dimensional volume contact situations between clasping threads and account for surface friction.

The penetrating test for a wire fabric of a fencing mask can be simulated under consideration of elasto-plastic material definition, material failure and friction. With the model you are able to investigate parameters like heigh of fall, impact direction, test spike weight, orientation and geometry, impact place and wire material. However calculation time is considerable.

The simulations of the penetrating test showed a high influence of the clamping condition. Therefore for standardization the testing of fencing masks, the penetrating test at the face part of the fencing mask is more appropriate as at the flat wire fabric. Usually protective clothing is stressed by high speed impact processes. As the described numerical method is mostly suitable for dynamically processes, this method can be very useful for research and development tasks in the field of protective clothing.

Literature

[1]   AIF-Forschungsvorhaben: Modellierung der Maschenstruktur als Grundlage für die Berechenbarkeit der Eigenschaften von Maschenwaren (AIF Nr. 9687)

[2]   DFG-Forschungsvorhaben: Untersuchung und Modellierung der Kontaktstelle zweier Fadensysteme unter statischen und dynamischen Bedingungen (DFG-29/34)

[3]   Finckh, Hermann: Simulation der mechanischen Eigenschaften von Maschenwaren, 14. CAD-FEM USERS' MEETING 1996, Bad Aibling

[4]   Institut für Biomechanik der deutschen Sporthochschule Köln Untersuchungsbericht 1984: Dynamische Parameter beim Stoß mit dem Florett

[5]   Finckh, Hermann: Berechnung des Impactverhaltens von Fechtmasken 15. CAD-FEM USERS' MEETING 1997, Fulda

Acknowledgement

We would like to thank *Deutsche Forschungsgemeinschaft* (DFG-29/34) and *Forschungskuratorium Gesamtextil* (AIF Nr. 9687) for their financial support, and also many thanks to the computing centre of Stuttgart university and HLRS for the permission of using its high-performance computer NEC-SX4.

Parallel SPH on Cray T3E and NEC SX-4 using DTS[*]

T. Bubeck[1], M. Hipp[1], S. Hüttemann[1], S. Kunze[2], M. Ritt[1],
W. Rosenstiel[1], H. Ruder[2], and R. Speith[2]

[1] Wilhelm-Schickard-Institut für Informatik, Universität Tübingen
[2] Institut für Astronomie und Astrophysik, Universität Tübingen

Abstract. In this paper we report on the results of a joint effort of astrophysicists and computer scientists to develop and implement a parallel program that enables us to solve large systems of hydrodynamic equations and covers a wide range of applications in astrophysics. We introduce the *Distributed Threads System* (DTS) as an environment for the development of portable parallel applications. The numerical method *Smoothed Particle Hydrodynamics* (SPH) is used to simulate the viscous spreading of an accretion disk around a massive compact object as an astrophysical test problem. The SPH code was parallelized using DTS and successfully ported to systems of different architecture. The use of a parallel SPH code on supercomputers enables us to treat astrophysical systems that were not accessible before. The achieved speedup proves the efficiency of DTS as a parallel programming environment. The physical results show the consistency and accuracy of the SPH method.

1 Introduction

The numerical simulation of large physical systems is still a great challenge even for modern computers. Especially in astrophysics, where laboratory experiments are not available, computer simulations are often the only way to gain new insights, by verifying, improving, or excluding theoretical models based on observational data. In problems involving fluids, which are the major problems in astrophysics, usually large systems of coupled differential equations have to be solved. One suitable method is *Smoothed Particle Hydrodynamics* (SPH). In this study, SPH is used to simulate a gaseous disk around a compact star. Due to the nature of the problem, hardware and CPU time requirements are high and super-computing is a necessity. Usually, physicists are more involved in their physical problems than in parallel programming. Therefore, the parallel programming environment *Distributed Threads System* (DTS), developed and implemented by computer scientists, is a great help for physicists as it provides the means of easily porting their simulation codes to different parallel architectures and effectively uses all parallel features.

[*] This project is funded by the DFG within SFB 382: Verfahren und Algorithmen zur Simulation physikalischer Prozesse auf Höchstleistungsrechnern (Methods and algorithms to simulate physical processes on supercomputers).

In section 2 we give the motivation for using DTS and present some of its implementation details. We also describe the experiences made when porting DTS to the NEC SX-4. Section 3 reviews some fundamentals of SPH. In section 4 the parallelization of SPH is detailed. Finally, we present the results of this study in section 5 and give a conclusion in section 6.

2   Distributed Threads System

Rapidly changing parallel architectures and programming interfaces make it difficult to achieve on-the-edge performance for parallel applications. Either the code has to be adapted with much effort to the native programming model for every new architecture, or it is based upon a portable parallel programming interface, trading code reuse for efficiency. Because we are working on long term research projects, portability was one of our major goals.

Of course, there are already standardized and widespread interfaces like MPI [11] or PVM [7], which provide a portable basis for parallel programming. But the main disadvantage of the message passing systems is their low level approach: It is difficult to concentrate on core parallelization and resulting programs are often erroneous and hard to debug. Another goal in this context was the separation of tasks: Physicists should be able to concentrate on solving their problems, while computer science is to make the physicist's job as easy as possible.

Therefore, we decided to suggest DTS as a portable parallel programming environment. It includes a parallelizing compiler [14], a parallel runtime system [2,3] as well as evaluation tools [4]. The runtime system is based on a thread interface, which has been extended to distributed memory architectures. The thread interface was chosen because it is a well known programming interface and a suitable target for our parallelizing compiler. It provides enough abstraction from simple message passing to concentrate on parallel algorithms, which, in the present study, are mainly regular data-parallel or irregular control-flow-parallel (divide-and-conquer algorithms).

From the user's perspective, in most cases programming in DTS does not differ from programming with conventional threads. The current implementation provides a pure functional progamming model, which proved to be sufficient for our current needs. For algorithms with stronger data dependencies, an extension allowing for direct thread-to-thread communication via distributed shared memory methods is planned in the near future.

2.1   Implementation of DTS

The implementation of DTS comes in two flavors, a completely distributed managed version and one with a centralized manager process. Although the central manager becomes a bottleneck on large numbers of processors, it proved to be more efficient for small and medium processor numbers. Therefore, we used the centralized approach on the NEC SX-4.

Figure 1 shows the major steps in executing a thread in DTS. On one node, called the root node, a central manager administers and controls the creation and distribution of threads to other nodes in the virtual machine. Every client node runs a client manager, waiting for threads to be executed. If a new thread is created, the caller asks the central manager for an executor, and sends it the job. The results are directly passed back to the caller. The choice of a suitable machine for executing the thread (load balancing), sending the parameters to the executor, and collecting them after execution, as well as error recovery is done transparently by the different managers.

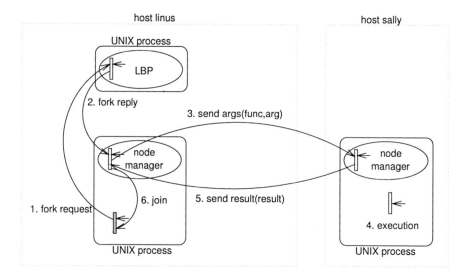

Fig. 1. Remote thread execution in DTS.

2.2 Porting DTS to the NEC SX-4

The DTS system is based upon threads and the message passing library PVM. Porting usually involves translating the machine independent thread interface layer of DTS into native thread calls only.

As the NEC SX-4 is a shared memory system, there was no need to use any kind of message passing. Therefore, we decided to eliminate the message passing layer completely. The PVM library was replaced by a version containing only empty function stubs, and the runtime system was modified to pass thread calls of DTS directly to the underlying thread layer. Actually, DTS has been reduced to a pure threads package. Measurements have shown, that the extra overhead of the DTS system using only threads is about 2%.

To realize the thread functionality, we chose to use the native implementation of POSIX threads. Since we already did a port of the DTS threads interface to another POSIX threads implementation, only minor changes concerning some missing functions which are optional in the POSIX standard, were required. Most problems we had to cope with had their origin in the POSIX-threads implementation of the NEC SX-4 itself[1] and were fixed by NEC.

Currently we are working towards a port for DTS to the Cray T3E. Additionally, the SPH code is parallelized using the native Cray SHMEM interface to serve as a base for quantifying the efficiency of DTS (see section 4).

3 Smoothed Particle Hydrodynamics

3.1 Basics

Smoothed Particle Hydrodynamics is a grid-free Lagrangian particle method for solving a system of hydrodynamic equations for compressible and viscous fluids. It was first introduced independently by Gingold & Monaghan [8] and Lucy [10]. SPH is especially suited for problems with high density contrasts and free boundaries. Rather than being solved on a grid, the equations are solved at the positions of the so-called particles, each of them representing a continuum with a certain mass, density, temperature, etc. and moving with the flow according to the equations of motion.

In contrast to most other flavors of SPH, here the viscous stress tensor is implemented to describe the physical viscosity correctly according to the Navier-Stokes equations. Usually only artificial viscosity is used, which is needed for the treatment of shocks, but vanishes in the continuum limit.

3.2 The Hydrodynamic Equations

The motion of the fluid is described by the Navier-Stokes equation, here in Lagrangian formulation:

$$\frac{dv_\alpha}{dt} = -\frac{1}{\varrho}p_{,\alpha} + \frac{1}{\varrho}t^{\text{visc}}_{\alpha\beta,\beta} + f_\alpha \quad , \tag{1}$$

with f being the gravitational force of the central object and the viscous stress tensor

$$t^{\text{visc}}_{\alpha\beta} = \eta\left(v_{\alpha,\beta} + v_{\beta,\alpha} - \tfrac{2}{3}\delta_{\alpha\beta}\,v_{\gamma,\gamma}\right) + \zeta\,\delta_{\alpha\beta}\,v_{\gamma,\gamma} \quad . \tag{2}$$

---

[1] First experiences have shown that the implementation was not POSIX conform, because a `pthread_detach` was required *after* joining the thread to free up internal thread administration structures. Without doing so the total number of executable fork/join-pairs was reduced to 512.

(Here all spatial derivatives $\partial/\partial x_\alpha$ are represented by $,_\alpha$ and Einstein's summing convention holds). The coefficients of shear and bulk viscosity, η and ζ, are positive scalars and independent of the velocity [9]. The term in parentheses is the shear, denoted by $\sigma_{\alpha\beta}$. Although the treatment of bulk viscosity is no principal problem we assume $\zeta = 0$. Furthermore, the kinematic viscosity coefficient $\nu = \eta/\varrho$ is assumed to be constant.

3.3 SPH Approximations

The purpose of the SPH method is to transform a system of coupled partial differential equations into a system of coupled ordinary differential equations, which can be solved by a standard integration algorithm.

The transformation is achieved by two steps of approximations. First, any variables are replaced according to the convolution

$$f(\mathbf{r}) \longrightarrow \int f(\mathbf{r}')\, W(|\mathbf{r} - \mathbf{r}'|, h)\, dV' \tag{3}$$

with an appropriate kernel W.

Secondly, the convolution integral is evaluated only at the positions of the particles, hence transformed to a sum:

$$f(\mathbf{r}_i) \approx f_i = \sum_j \frac{f(\mathbf{r}_j)}{n_j} W(|\mathbf{r}_i - \mathbf{r}_j|, h) \tag{4}$$

(n_j: Particle density at the point $\mathbf{r}_j$).

The spatial derivatives can now be transferred onto the kernel by partial integration:

$$\nabla f(\mathbf{r}_i) \approx \sum_j \frac{f(\mathbf{r}_j) + \tilde{f}(\mathbf{r}_i)}{n_j} \nabla W(|\mathbf{r}_i - \mathbf{r}_j|, h) \quad . \tag{5}$$

Since the derivatives of the kernel are known analytically, we now have the desired system of ordinary differential equations that can be integrated numerically.

3.4 SPH Formulation of the Equations

As an example, the application of the smoothing discretization scheme to the viscous part of the Navier-Stokes equation (1) yields

$$\left(\frac{dv_\alpha}{dt}\right)_i^{\text{visc}} = \left(\frac{1}{\varrho} t_{\alpha\beta,\beta}\right)_i \tag{6}$$

$$= \sum_j m_j \left(\frac{\nu_j}{\varrho_i}(\sigma_{\alpha\beta})_j + \frac{\nu_i}{\varrho_j}(\sigma_{\alpha\beta})_i\right)(W_{,\beta})_{ij}$$

with the particle form of the shear $\sigma_{\alpha\beta}$

$$(\sigma_{\alpha\beta})_i = (V_{\alpha\beta})_i + (V_{\beta\alpha})_i - \tfrac{2}{3}\delta_{\alpha\beta}(V_{\gamma\gamma})_i \quad , \tag{7}$$

where $(V_{\alpha\beta})_i$ is the particle representation of the velocity gradient $v_{\alpha,\beta}$

$$(V_{\alpha\beta})_i = (v_{\alpha,\beta})_i = \sum_j \frac{m_j}{\varrho_j}\left((v_\alpha)_j - (v_\alpha)_i\right)(W_{,\beta})_{ij} \quad . \tag{8}$$

All other equations (continuity equation, energy equation, state equation) can be formulated in SPH in a similar way.

4   Parallelizing SPH with DTS

First, we will describe our SPH implementation on NEC SX-4 using DTS. Second, we will discuss SPH codes for machines with distributed memory.

There are several papers on parallel SPH for machines such as Cray T3D, CM-5 or Intel Paragon [13,6]. The method introduced in [5] is compared with our parallel SPH code for machines with distributed memory in section 4.3.

4.1   Shared Memory Machines

The basic idea is to find data structures to allow independent parallel threads and to avoid critical sections as much as possible. There are two main problems involved with a SPH algorithm. First, the nearest neighbor search and second, the evaluation of the list of neighbors to calculate the physical quantities for each particle.

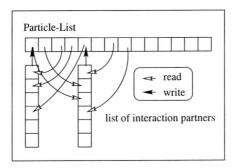

Fig. 2. Data structure of parallel SPH for shared memory machines (the list of particles and the corresponding list of interaction partners).

Concerning the nearest neighbor search, using the linked list algorithm of [1] we were able to develop a parallel algorithm with a parallel efficiency of at least 90% on NEC SX-4 using 20 CPUs (see figure 3). The search for nearest neighbors is divided into a sequential and a parallel part. In the sequential part the particles are projected on a grid which is used to build the linked list. This is an algorithm of order $O(N)$, where N is the number of particles. Since the linked list is only read in the process of finding the interaction partner for each particle, the nearest neighbor search can be done in parallel.

For the evaluation of physical quantities every particle has a complete list of all its neighbors (figure 2). To compute a physical quantity for a certain particle, the information stored in the neighbor list is read only. Thus, a given physical quantity can be evaluated in parallel for each particle. By storing a complete list of all neighbors per particle, the physical symmetry relations between the particles cannot be exploited by the algorithm. This makes the parallel code at most two times slower than an optimized sequential code (see section 5.6).

4.2   SPH on the NEC SX-4 using DTS

The SPH code was implemented on the NEC SX-4 using DTS. The usage of DTS makes it possible to run the same SPH code both on the NEC SX-4 and on other machines[2], just by recompiling with `dtscc`. The parallel SPH code was used for benchmarking, using different numbers of CPUs. The results prove the high quality of the parallelization features of the NEC SX-4.

Figure 3 shows the speedup and the parallel efficiency of the parallel SPH code on the NEC SX-4. For 10 000 particles the parallel efficiency decreases

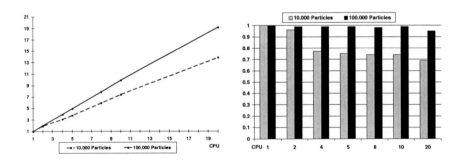

Fig. 3. *Left:* speedup of parallel SPH. *Right:* parallel efficiency on NEC SX-4.

from 90% on two CPUs to 60% on 20 CPUs. For 100 000 particles the parallel efficency is more than 90% for all 20 CPUs.

---

[2] e.g. Ross Hyper Sparc, Sun MP, SGI Onyx2

4.3   Parallel SPH Codes on Distributed Memory Architectures

Besides the DTS SPH code for shared memory machines, there are a few implementations for SPH on parallel machines. Three of them developed especially for machines with distributed memory are the PTreeSPH [5], a port for the MEMSY architecture developed in Erlangen [12], and our own implementation for the Cray T3E. All of them handle the communication in a different way.

The PTreeSPH code is based on MPI and, therefore, is portable to nearly every platform. A general disadvantage of MPI is a loss in performance due to the complex communication protocol. Thus, good domain decomposition and, even more important, smart communication are crucial. The solution was to build a so-called *Locally Essential Particle List* (LEPL). In a synchronous preprocessing step, all nodes check which of their particles interact with particles from a neighbor domain and put them into the LEPL. Further communication is necessary only for those particles. Domains are separated in equally sized parts with an *orthogonal recursive bisection tree*.

On the MEMSY architecture, communication is possible only between neighbor nodes in the squared processor plane. The N particles are combined with every other particle to $N \times N$ interaction pairs. This set of pairs is divided by the number of nodes and distributed over the plane. Figure 4 shows an example. Every node computes a partial sum over its particle pairs. The total sums are computed by sending the partial sums of each node line step by step to the diagonal node of the plane. From there the total sum is sent back to all nodes in the same node line and column. We tested a simple port

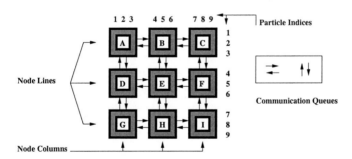

Fig. 4. Example for the distribution of 9 particles 1-9 over 9 nodes A-I. For example node B computes interaction between particles 1-3 and 4-6.

of this implementation on the T3E by simulating the communication queues between two neighbor nodes. It shows that the main disadvantage is that the algorithm to check whether two particles interact scales with $O(N^2)$, where N is the particle number.

4.4   Parallel SPH on Cray T3E

Since DTS has not yet been ported to the Cray T3E, we decided to implement SPH using the Cray T3E SHMEM library, which provides functions oriented at the Cray T3E hardware capabilities. The main reason was to get an optimal implementation by using all possible features the Cray T3E offers, which can serve as a reference implementation for quantifying the efficiency of a later DTS port. Another reason was that we already had a shared memory implementation. A message passing based version would have required a major redesign. The SHMEM library allowed us to reuse as much as possible of the original code.

An essential idea was to use two different domain decompositions depending on the type of computation:

1. All computations without neighbor interaction are done on an equally sized subset on every node. The subset is selected by splitting the particle field into n parts for n nodes. A node also operates as a *relay* node for its subset. Information about a specific particle can always be found on its *relay* node.
2. For computations with neighbor interaction all particles are sorted according to their positions into a grid with equally sized cells. These cells are assigned to nodes in a way that every node holds the same number of particles.

The load balancing is good in both cases, because the computation takes about the same time for every particle except the neighbor search.

The neighbor search uses the grid from the second domain decomposition. The problem here is, that it is not known *a priori* how many comparisons are necessary to find the nearest neighbors of every particle. Hence we added the possibility that one node helps another to find its neighbors. In this step the ability of the Cray T3E to read and write remote memory asynchronously is used. The neighbor indices are stored in a list for later reuse.

Both the neighbor list and two lists similar to the LEPL described in the PTreeSPH section are built simultaneously. Because there are two domain decompositions we also need two lists, a *get* list and a *put* list. The *get* list holds the indices of particles which are not assigned to a node by one of the two domain decompositions but are neighbors of a particle in the second domain decomposition. The *put* list holds the list of particles which are assigned to a node by the second domain decomposition, but not by the first.

It is not possible to decide which node needs which particle positions because of the neighbor search. So we decided to distribute the positions of all particles to all nodes using a broadcast.

To compute a physical quantity which is independent of neighbor interaction, no communication is needed. Every node does this work on its *relay* particles.

The first evaluated quantity with neighbor interaction is the kernel. We can compute it with no further communication, because we still have distributed the particle position. To distribute the computed kernel every node first uses the *put* list to send the kernel back to the *relay* node and then uses the *get* list to get the kernel of all other necessary particles. The same is done for the mass density and all other physical quantities.

The final steps are the computation of the gravitational force and the integration timestep itself. This again requires no neighbor interaction and every node does it on its *relay* particles.

For most physical quantities an array is allocated with enough space to theoretically hold every particle on a single node. On the Cray T3E with 128MB local memory, this currently limits the maximum number of particles to about 750 000 for the 2D case when using double precision floating point. For single precision the maximum number of particles doubles.

5   Simulations and Results

5.1   The Test Problem

The test problem is a thin accretion disk around a compact central mass M. 'Thin' means the size of the disk perpendicular to the disk plane can be neglected. The following approximations are made: $v_z \approx 0$, $z^2 \ll x^2, y^2$.

All variables are integrated over the height of the disk, e.g. the surface density is given by $\Sigma = \int \varrho dz$. The motion of the gas in the disk is described by the Navier-Stokes equation (1), as pointed out in section 3. With the approximations made above, in 2 D form the equation reads

$$\Sigma \frac{dv_\alpha}{dt} = -p_{,\alpha} + t^{\text{visc}}_{\alpha\beta,\beta} \qquad (\alpha, \beta = 1, 2).\tag{9}$$

In order to obtain an analytic solution, we transform to polar coordinates (r, φ) and assume rotational symmetry. Furthermore, pressure forces are neglected, and $v_r \ll v_\varphi$ is assumed. With the constant viscosity coefficient ν and the initial density profile

$$\Sigma_0 = \frac{m}{2\pi r_0} \delta(r - r_0)\tag{10}$$

we get the following analytic solution for the surface density:

$$\Sigma(r, t) = \frac{m}{\pi r_0^2 \tau} \left(\frac{r}{r_0}\right)^{-\frac{1}{4}} e^{-\frac{r_0^2 + r^2}{r_0^2 \tau}} I_{\frac{1}{4}}\left(\frac{2r}{r_0 \tau}\right),\tag{11}$$

Here m denotes the mass of the disk, $I_{\frac{1}{4}}$ is the modified Bessel function to the base $\frac{1}{4}$, and $\tau = 12\nu t/r_0^2$ is the dimensionless 'viscous time'.

Now we have the analytic radial density profile of the disk, which can be compared with the results of the simulations.

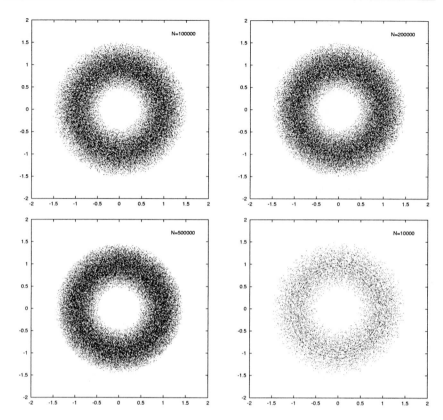

Fig. 5. Positions of particles at $\tau = 0.09$. Upper left: 100 000 particles, upper right: 200 000 particles, lower left: 500 000 particles, lower right: for comparison: simulation with 10 000 particles with a serial code on a workstation. Note the lack of spiral-like structures in the 200 000 and 500 000 particle simulations.

5.2   Simulations of the Test Problem

Numerical simulations of the test problem were performed both on workstations and on the NEC SX-4 at the HLRS. The SPH forms of the 2 D cartesian hydrodynamic equations were used, neglecting pressure forces. The physical parameters for all simulations were ($\odot$ denotes solar units): mass of central object $M = 1M_\odot$, total mass of the disk $m = 10^{-10}M_\odot$, initial radial distance of the disk from the center $r_0 = 1R_\odot$, and the coefficient of viscosity: $\nu = 3 \cdot 10^{-8}R_\odot^2/s$.

Initial particle distribution were produced, according to the density profile at viscous time $\tau = 0.018$, but with the individual particles being placed stochastically on Kepler orbits.

Simulations with 100 000, 200 000, and 500 000 particles were made, using the parallel queues NP2GB8CPU and NP4GB16CPU. Since most people

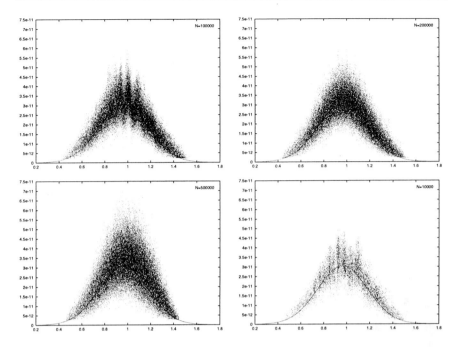

Fig. 6. Surface density of particles at $\tau = 0.09$, only radial coordinate plotted. Arrangement as in figure 5. Underlying is the analytic solution. Note the mean deviation from the analytic value does not decrease with particle number, because the mean number of interaction partners for each particle is the same in all simulations.

seem to use the NEC SX-4 in single processor mode, the jobs started quickly, once submitted to the parallel queues. Output files were produced at viscous times 0.036, 0.054, 0.072, 0.090, and 0.126.

In figures 5 and 6 we show the positions of the particles and the radially plotted surface density $\Sigma(r)$ at viscous time 0.09. Furthermore, the analytic solution of the surface density is shown in figure 6. Also shown are the results of a simulation with 10 000 particles that was carried out on a SGI workstation with a 100MHz R4000 processor (figures 5 and 6 lower right corner). For clarity, from the HLRS simulations only 50 000 randomly chosen particles are plotted.

5.3   Physical and Numerical Accuracy

We know from earlier simulations that the most important numerical parameter is the number of interaction partners per particle. In this implementation of SPH the smoothing length, which corresponds to the interaction radius of a particle, is kept constant throughout a simulation. In order to give each particle the same average number of interaction partners in all simulations,

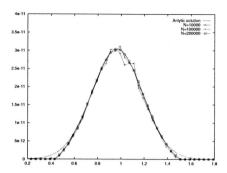

Fig. 7. Averaged radial surface density distribution of the particles. The simulation with 10 000 particles shows some deviation from the analytic value, whereas the simulations with more particles are practically identical.

the smoothing length was scaled with the inverse square root of the total particle number.

With this setup we expect the accuracy to be very similar for all simulations. This can be seen in the distribution of the surface densities in figure 6. The deviation from the mean value is very similar in the simulations with 10 000, 100 000, and 200 000 particles. All these simulations have been carried out with the same error tolerance of the time integrator. In the simulation with 500 000 particles a higher error was tolerated, obviously too high, since the deviation in the surface density distribution is clearly too large. This is not to be considered as a failure, because we also wanted to determine the numerical parameter 'accuracy of integrator'.

Although there is a large scatter about the analytical value of the surface density, the *mean* density is conserved to very high accuracy in the simulations. This can be seen in figure 7, where the surface density of the particles is averaged in 50 bins between radial coordinates 0.05 and 2.05. (Because of the insufficient integrator accuracy the simulation with 500 000 particles is excluded.) The results from the NEC simulations are practically identical, whereas the simulation with only 10 000 particles shows some deviation from the analytical value. This is mainly due to the spiral structures, which are of mainly numerical origin. This can be seen from the fact that they are strongest for smallest particle number and not present at all in the simulations with 200 000 and 500 000 particles.

5.4   Speedup of SPH on Cray T3E

We measured the speedup of SPH simulations of the test problem (section 5.1) with 10 000 and 100 000 particles. The speedup is quite satisfactory, see figure 8. One can also see that there is a problem in the SHMEM communication when the number of nodes is not a power of two (here with 96 and 384 nodes).

The 100 000 particle simulation has a higher efficiency. This is because in the nearest neighbor search, the computation cost rise faster than the communication cost with increasing particle number. Since the computation has a higher parallel efficiency, the total efficiency is better for more particles.

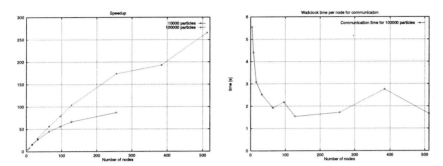

Fig. 8. Speedup for the T3E implementation with 10 000 and 100 000 and time for communication for 100 000 particles. No values were measured for 10000 particles on 384 and 512 nodes. The communication time is the time for internode data transfers and synchronization including data preprocessing necessary for communication.

5.5   Comparison of Parallel SPH Methods for the Cray T3E

The PTreeSPH implementation reaches a maximum speedup of 27 at 64 nodes for 256 000 particles while our SPH implementation gains a speedup of 260 for 512 nodes with only 100 000 particles. We expect even better results for higher particle numbers. The ported version of the MEMSY code cannot keep up with this result. On top of higher total computation time, test runs showed that the queued communication is quite expensive. In a test simulation with 20 000 particles the contribution of the communication to the total computation time rised from 17% on 4 nodes to 76% on 256 nodes.

5.6   Vectorization and F77 solution on NEC SX-4

Apart from good speedup and scalability, it is of course also desirable to achieve a considerable runtime improvement compared to an optimized sequential code. Further runtime improvement can be reached by vectorization of the code. In figure 9 we present a comparison of the runtimes of SPH simulations of the same test problem with different codes. From this, and from figure 3 one can see that already using as less as 2 CPUs on the NEC SX-4 a runtime improvement compared to the optimal sequential SPH code can be achieved. As the speedup is excellent, very good runtime improvements can be obtained using more CPUs.

PISA—Parallel Image Segmentation Algorithms*

Alina Lindner (Moga), Andreas Bieniek, and Hans Burkhardt

Albert-Ludwigs-Universität Freiburg
Institut für Informatik, Am Flughafen 17, D-79110 Freiburg

Abstract. Parallelisation of the watershed segmentation method is studied in this paper. Starting with a successful parallel watershed design solution, extensive tests on various parallel machines are presented to prove its portability and performance. Next, the watershed algorithm has been re-formulated as a modified connected component problem. Consequently, we present a scalable parallel implementation of the connected component problem, which is the key for the future improving of the parallel design for the watershed algorithm.

1 Introduction

Segmentation is a process of partitioning an image into disjoint regions such that each region is homogeneous, according to a certain uniformity criterion, and no union of any two adjacent regions is homogeneous. The problem has been broadly investigated by scientists using both classical and fuzzy based reasoning techniques. Different algorithms can be found in the literature seeking for either feature homogeneity (region growing) or to detect dissimilarities (edge detection) [12,15,23].

Segmentation plays a crucial role in image processing, in particular for coding, edge detection, object recognition, automatic measurements, and analysis. Additionally, in most of the applications, segmentation is expected to complete in real time. However, this goal is difficult to achieve for large images and image sequences, for which the complexity of serial segmentation is usually high. Therefore, fast scalable parallel algorithms are entailed.

The emphasis in this project is on designing high level portable MIMD parallel algorithms to execute efficiently and exhibit scalability, independent of the image content. Our work is dedicated to parallelising a recent segmentation technique named watershed transformation [5,17–19]. As a segmentation method, watershed transformation is often found successfully incorporated into image analysis systems in various domains, e.g., in industry and biomedicine (segmentation of electrophoresis gels, a moving heart, 3D holographic images, road traffic analysis) [19].

Starting with a successful parallel design solution of the watershed algorithm [6,22], further tests on different parallel machines have been performed to evaluate its portability and performance.

In our efforts to find a new parallel algorithm for the watershed problem displaying concurrency, locality, modularity, data independence, and resilience to increasing number of processors, special attention is concentrated on elaborating robust

---

* We acknowledge the High Performance Computing Center Stuttgart for granting us the use of the Cray T3E parallel computer, as well as all firms through which the results included in this report were made possible.

and less error prone sequential techniques with minimal memory costs, reduced software engineering cost, for implementation and testing, and simple data structures. Consequently, the classical watershed algorithm has been reformulated as a connected component problem [6]. The latter algorithm is simpler and faster than the classical method based on hierarchical queues [5].

Therefore, an efficient parallel connected component operator is the key for further improvements of the parallel watershed algorithm, as well as for the parallelisation of other problem classes.

The rest of the paper is organised as follows. In Section 2, the parallel watershed algorithm based on hierarchical queues is described in more detail. Relevant timings and speedup of the algorithm running on various parallel systems are also incorporated toward comparison of the performance. A new approach of the algorithm based on the connected component problem along with preliminary results follow in Section 3. Finally, conclusions and highlights of the future work are comprised in Section 4.

2   A Parallel Watershed Algorithm based on Ordered Queues and Connected Components

The classical watershed algorithm [5,19] regards the gradient of an image as a topographical relief, in which flooding starting from the regional minima is simulated. The algorithm starts by detecting and labeling initial seeds, e.g. minima of the gradient. Minima pixels are then sorted according to their grey-level and stored in a hierarchical queue. The latter consists of N FIFO queues, one queue for each grey-level h existing in the image. Flooding is then performed in the increasing order of the grey-level. A pixel removed from the queue, assigns its label to each unlabeled neighbour, which is, in turn, inserted in the FIFO queue allocated to its grey-level. However, because the classical algorithm implements a global and highly data dependent operation, its parallelisation is not straightforward.

An efficient parallel implementation of the watershed algorithm has been extensively presented in [22], with results collected from a Cray T3D parallel computer. In order to prove the portability of the design solution on different massively parallel computers and hence, of its performance, the algorithm has been tested on several parallel machines. Before presenting the results, a short description of the algorithm follows in the next subsection.

2.1   Description of the algorithm

From the brief description of the sequential watershed algorithm above, one can observe that watershed transformation performs recursively and the overall data access pattern is global. Global operations are generally tackled in MIMD implementations in a *divide-and-conquer* fashion. The solution in [22] resembles the parallel connected component design in [1,10,13]. For this purpose the image domain is divided into sub-domains (blocks or slices) and intermediate labeling, as in the sequential case, is performed within each sub-domain. The boundary connectivity information between sub-images is locally stored in a graph [1] or in an equivalence table [10,13]. More specifically, labels on each side of a common boundary

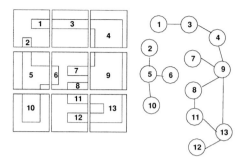

Fig. 1. Boundary connectivity graph of a distributed binary image

between adjacent sub-images and pertaining to the same component are retained as belonging to the same equivalence class (see Fig. 1). Final labels correspond to the connected components of the global boundary connectivity graph obtained by combining all the local graphs (see Fig. 1, where two connected components result).

Unlike in the case of binary images, for the watershed transformation, the grey-levels of two neighbouring pixels do not suffice to retrieve the boundary connectivity information. A solution results from the property that flooding is ruled by a two-dimensional ordering relation. Thus, a pixel p gets a label from an immediate neighbour q of lowest grey-level, if any. On plateaus surrounded by pixels of lower grey-level, the lower distance given by the length of the shortest path, completely included in the plateau, to a lower border of the plateau (see also [17]) imposes the propagation order. Details upon the parallel computation of the lower distance on plateaus can be found in [6,22]. Once established this predecessor-successor flooding relation between pixels, the boundary connectivity information can be easily recovered. Thus, if a pixel has its predecessor in an adjacent sub-domain, they definitely pertain to the same component. After the boundary connectivity graph has been set up in every processor, global connected components are computed in $log_2 P$ steps on P processors, regardless of the data complexity.

2.2   Experimental Results

The above described algorithm has been implemented on top of *Message Passing Interface* (MPI) [11] and tested on six different parallel computers: Comparex/Hitachi, Hewlett-Packard X-Class, Hewlett-Packard Hyper-Class (Beta version), SGI/ Origin 2000, SGI/Cray T3E, and IBM/PWR2. Due to the fact that the implementation has been built on top of MPI, the code has been easily ported on all machines. The running time T for various images is tabulated in Table. 1 and the relative speedup $SP(P) = \frac{T(1)}{T(P)}$ is illustrated in logarithmic scale in Fig. 2. The result of the transformation is shown in Fig. 6 for two example images.

Although the optimisation flags used for each machine in part are not totally identical (O3 assisted by different machine specific flags), one can observe that the highly ascendent relative speedup is preserved, irrespective of the underlying parallel platform. For each of the four images, in part, the speedup curves grow close to each other until a certain number of processors, after which they diverge. For the image *Cermet* this threshold is reached at 8 CPU's, point from where the curve for the SGI/Origin 2000 drops down. Next, at 16 CPU's, the performance on

Machine	Image \ P	1	2	4	8	16	32	64
Comparex/Hitachi	Cermet(256 × 256)	0.601	0.315	0.171	0.105	0.072	0.053	0.046
	Peppers(512 × 512)	2.397	1.333	0.671	0.356	0.208	0.126	0.087
	Lenna (512 × 512)	2.382	1.308	0.629	0.359	0.214	0.132	0.099
	People (1024 × 1024)	9.596	5.491	3.064	1.504	0.727	0.412	0.249
HP/X-Class	Cermet(256 × 256)	0.238	0.129	0.074	0.054	0.039	0.048	
	Peppers(512 × 512)	0.912	0.481	0.257	0.146	0.118	0.089	
	Lenna (512 × 512)	0.931	0.475	0.253	0.151	0.109	0.092	
	People (1024 × 1024)	4.28	2.42	1.21	0.610	0.360	0.241	
HP/Hyper-Class	Cermet(256 × 256)	0.185	0.100	0.056	0.033	0.021		
	Peppers(512 × 512)	0.680	0.392	0.203	0.109	0.067		
	Lenna (512 × 512)	0.700	0.384	0.197	0.114	0.071		
	People (1024 × 1024)	3.259	1.919	0.950	0.462	0.234		
SGI/Origin 2000	Cermet(256 × 256)	0.113	0.057	0.037	0.025	0.028	0.047	
	Peppers(512 × 512)	0.404	0.253	0.142	0.089	0.068	0.089	
	Lenna (512 × 512)	0.411	0.245	0.129	0.086	0.065	0.065	
	People (1024 × 1024)	1.563	0.973	0.631	0.361	0.226	0.180	
SGI/Cray T3E	Cermet(256 × 256)	0.180	0.098	0.056	0.035	0.022	0.012	0.010
	Peppers(512 × 512)	0.686	0.405	0.210	0.110	0.066	0.040	0.026
	Lenna (512 × 512)	0.726	0.421	0.221	0.119	0.070	0.041	0.028
	People (1024 × 1024)	2.885	1.772	1.024	0.506	0.257	0.148	0.084
IBM/PWR2	Cermet(256 × 256)	0.154	0.084	0.047	0.028	0.020	0.037	0.027
	Peppers(512 × 512)	0.608	0.370	0.197	0.103	0.063	0.037	0.027
	Lenna (512 × 512)	0.606	0.357	0.183	0.102	0.062	0.038	0.028
	People (1024 × 1024)	2.578	1.629	1.008	0.505	0.235	0.129	0.077

Table 1. Execution times of watershed algorithm (in seconds)

the IBM/PWR2, HP/X-Class saturates. Still increasing relative speedup, until 64 CPU's, remains for Comparex/Hitachi and SGI/Cray T3E.

A more uniform behaviour is observed for the other three images, excepting the downward slope for image *Lenna*, between 16 CPU's and 32 CPU's on the SGI/Origin 2000.

Naturally, better performance is obtained for larger images, like *Peppers* and *Lenna* of size 512 × 512, or *People* 1024 × 1024. However, globally, the algorithm proves to be extremely portable, issuing a very good performance on each parallel machine.

3   A Parallel Connected Component Algorithm

In the previous sections, we have shown that the watershed algorithm can be regarded as a connected component operator, where the notion of connectivity between two neighbouring pixels is defined by the predecessor-successor flooding relation [6,7,21,22]. Therefore, in the first phase of the project, our research is focused on finding efficient parallel algorithms for the connected component problem. The connected component operator can be additionally regarded as a foundation for the efficient parallelisation of various other problems.

A good survey on sequential and parallel connected component algorithms for different computation models is given in [1]. In most sequential connected component algorithms, two passes are performed: first, a raster scan through the image to set up equivalences between neigbouring pixels, and second, to replace each label with the representative of its equivalence class [1,10,14,16,24]. Equivalences are usually solved with the help of a lookup table. Alternatively, the image connected

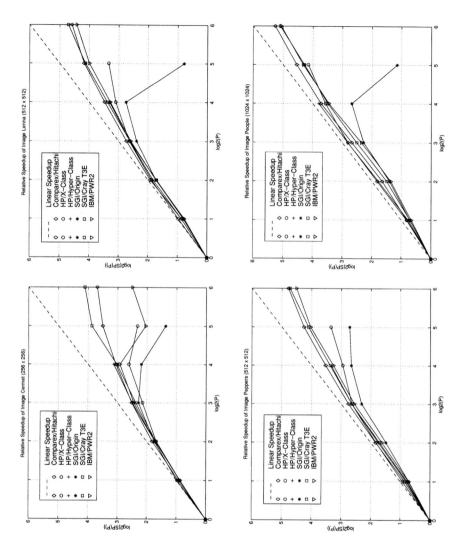

Fig. 2. Relative speedup of the watershed algorithm on different machines and with different images

component problem can be transformed into the equivalent graph connected component problem. An example of such an equivalent graph is shown in Fig. 1.

Several *divide-and-conquer* algorithms for the parallel connected component on MIMD machines exist in the literature. In most cases the image domain is divided into sub-domains and the local connected component problem is first solved with a sequential algorithm. Global connected components are then computed by applying a global merge-and-split operation on the boundary data of the sub-images.

A global boundary connected graph can be constructed by combining all the local graphs, as described in Section 2. Alternatively, a global equivalence table can be built by combining the local tables of all sub-domains. These solutions are not optimal, because, in the worst-case, the size of the graph or table increases with the number of processors. The size of the connectivity graph can be bounded to the perimeter of the merged sub-domains, if the boundary information is updated with the help of a separate graph at each merging step, as shown in [2–4]. In [9,10], the boundaries are updated with the help of a separate and therefore small equivalence table at every merging step.

Nevertheless, due to the fact that the sequential connected component operation is relatively fast, it is essential that the overhead of the merge-and-split operation is kept as small as possible. Otherwise, the scalability of the algorithm is compromised.

3.1   Outline of the parallel algorithm

The outline of the parallel algorithm follows next: first, a fast sequential connected component algorithm, which uses the image of labels to solve equivalences [7,8,20], is performed independently within each sub-domain. After the sequential algorithm, the label of every pixel refers to the representative of the component the pixel pertains at, within the local sub-image. A global representative denotes a representative of a connected component which extends across the boundaries of a sub-domain.

At the next step, the boundary data structure for each sub-domain is packed. The boundary data structure is organised in such a way, that a graph type connected component algorithm works directly on the communicated data. For each pixel in the image boundary, its label, grey-value, and a relative offset to a replacement pixel within the boundary data structure are stored, as shown in Fig. 3. The use of

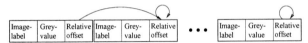

Fig. 3. Data structure to store border information of sub-images

relative offsets has the advantage that the references between border pixels are still valid after a communication step, as long as all references are within the communicated data structure. The packing operation moves all global representatives into the boundary data structure. This is done by linking the old representative, and therefore the whole component, to the new representative within the border data structure. Then a resolve phase is performed on the boundary data, by following and short-cutting all references to the root. The effect is that all border pixels refer to a representative within the border data structure, which is shown in Fig. 4a. The representatives of the grey shaded connected components are marked with black squares. Global representatives within the image point to a new representative in the border stripes, as shown by an arrow.

At the next step, the boundary data is merged recursively until the whole image is encompassed. At each merging step, neighbouring edges of adjacent sub-images are merged. A new data packet, which consists of the combined edges except the merged ones, is created. The merging algorithm resembles the sequential connected component algorithm on the neighbouring edges, but, for the sake of communication, references (relative offsets) within the edge data structures are used (Fig. 4b). The key idea of the presented merging algorithm is that, after linking neighbouring pixels which belong to the same equivalence class, all global representatives are

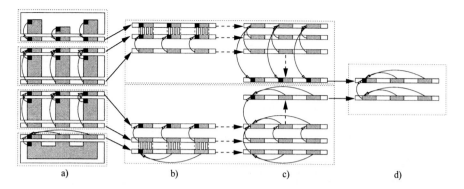

Fig. 4. An example of the divide-and-conquer phase of the parallel connected component algorithm for a stripe-wise distributed image.

moved to the new boundary data. A resolve phase guarantees that all new border pixels refer to a representative within the new border data structure (Fig. 4c). Following the merging process shown in Fig. 4, the representatives of the local sub-images in Fig. 4a are pointing to a single representative in Fig. 4d.

At the next step, the final labels of the last merging step are distributed in the reverse order of the merging process. For this purpose, the label of each border pixel is updated with the label of the final representative. Then, the stored and updated data of the corresponding merging step is sent back to its source. Finally, all pixels in the sub-images are re-labelled, replacing the representative with the global representative.

3.2   Experimental results

Fig. 5 shows the speedup of the algorithm compared to the unchanged sequential algorithm for 512×512 and 1024×1024 images. There is no significant difference in speedup (see Fig. 5a,b) for the different images we tested. In Fig. 5c and Fig. 5d stripe-wise decomposition of the image is compared with block-wise decomposition. The results show that the speedup for block-wise decomposition is significantly better than for stripe-wise. Additionally, redundant merging, which redundantly performs the merging steps on all processors, is compared with non-redundant merging [6]. The results show that performing the merging process redundantly, a slightly better speedup can be observed. The reason is that the split phase can be done within the local memory at the expense of sending much more data in the merging phase. This can lead to network saturation, which is visible for 1024×1024 stripe-wise distributed images in Fig. 5d. Performing the merging operation using a butterfly communication graph or a deBruijn graph makes little difference on a Cray T3E.

4   Conclusions and Future Work

The results in Section 2 show the portability and scalability of a parallel watershed segmentation algorithm. In Section 3, we propose a new, scalable connected com-

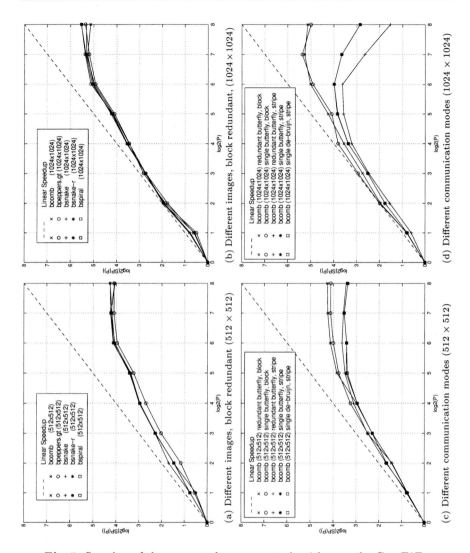

Fig. 5. Speedup of the connected component algorithm on the CrayT3E

ponent algorithm, which can be seen as a foundation for the efficient parallelisation of the watershed transformation, as well as of various other problems in the field of image processing. Therefore, our future work is focused onto extending the parallel connected component algorithm for watersheds.

Further on, analysing the drawbacks of the watershed algorithm, namely, over-segmentation, remedies based on multiscale pyramid algorithms have been investigated and implemented. This part, is still under development and therefore, results will be published later. However, the problem of multi-resolution watersheds opens an extremely challenging topic for parallel computation.

Fig. 6. Example images lenna and peppers with result of the watershed transformation.

References

1. H. M. Alnuweiri and V. K. Prasanna. Parallel architectures and algorithms for image component labeling. *IEEE Trans. on Pattern Analysis and Machine Intelligence*, 14(10):1014–1034, October 1992.

2. D. A. Bader and J. JáJá. Parallel algorithms for image histogramming and connected components with an experimental study. *Journal of Parallel and Distributed Computing*, 35(2):173–190, June 1996.

3. D. A. Bader, J. JáJá, D. Harwood, and L. S. Davis. Parallel algorithms for image enhancement and segmentation by region growing with an experimental study. *Journal of Supercomputing*, 10(2):141–168, 1996.

4. K. P. Belkhale and P. Banerjee. Parallel algorithms for geometric connected component labeling on a hypercube multiprocessor. *IEEE Transactions on Computers*, 41(6):699–709, June 1992.

5. S. Beucher and F. Meyer. The morphological approach to segmentation: The watershed transformation. In E.R. Dougherty, editor, *Mathematical Morphology in Image Processing*, pages 433–481, N.Y., 1993. Marcel Dekker Inc.

6. A. Bieniek, H. Burkhardt, H. Marschner, M. Nöelle, and G. Schreiber. A parallel watershed algorithm. In *Proceedings of 10th Scandinavian Conference on Image Analysis*, pages 237–244, Lappeenranta, Finland, June 1997.
7. A. Bieniek and A. Moga. A connected component approach to the watershed segmentation. In *Mathematical Morphology and its Applications to Image and Signal Processing*, volume 12 of *Computational Imaging and Vision*, pages 215–222. Kluwer Academic Publishers, 1998.
8. A. Choudhary and R. Thakur. Connected component labeling on coarse grain parallel computers: an experimental study. *Journal of Parallel and Distributed Computing*, 20(1):78–83, January 1994.
9. H. Embrechts. *MIMD Divide-and-Conquer algorithms for geometric operations on binary images*. PhD thesis, Department of Computer Science, Katholieke Universiteit Leuven, Belgium, March 1994.
10. H. Embrechts, D. Roose, and P. Wambacq. Component labelling on a MIMD multiprocessor. *CVGIP: Image Understanding*, 57(2):155–165, March 1993.
11. Message Passing Interface Forum. MPI: A message-passing interface standard. Technical report, University of Tennessee, Knoxville, Tennessee, June 1995. Version 1.1.
12. R.M. Haralick and L.G.Shapiro. Image segmentation technique. *Computer Vision, Graphics, and Image Processing*, 29:100–132, 1985.
13. T. Johansson. *Image Analysis Algorithms on General Purpose Parallel Architectures*. Ph.D. thesis, Centre for Image Analysis, University of Uppsala, Uppsala, 1994.
14. T. Johansson and E. Bengtsson. A new parallel MIMD connected component labeling algorithm. In *PARLE: Parallel Architectures and Languages Europe*, pages 801–804. LNCS, Springer-Verlag, 1994.
15. T. Kanade. Survey, region segmentation: Signal vs semantics. *CVGIP*, 13(4):279–297, August 1980.
16. R. Lumia, L. Shapiro, and O. Zuniga. A New Connected Components Algorithm for Virtual Memory Computers. *Computer Vision, Graphics, and Image Processing*, 22(2):287–300, 1983.
17. F. Meyer. Integrals, gradients and watershed lines. In *Proceedings of Workshop on Mathematical Morphology and its Applications to Signal Processing*, pages 70–75, Barcelona, Spain, May 1993.
18. F. Meyer. Topographic distance and watershed lines. *Signal Processing*, 38(1):113–125, July 1994.
19. F. Meyer and S. Beucher. Morphological segmentation. *Journal of Visual Communication and Image Representation*, 1(1):21–46, September 1990.
20. R. Miller and Q. F. Stout. *Parallel Algorithms for Regular Architectures: Meshes and Pyramids*. MIT Press, Cambridge Massachusetts, London England, 1996.
21. A. Moga. *Parallel Watershed Algorithms for Image Segmentation*. PhD thesis, Tampere University of Technology, Tampere, Finland, February 1997.
22. A.N. Moga and M. Gabbouj. Parallel image component labeling with watershed transformation. *IEEE Transactions on Pattern Analysis and Machine Intelligence*, 19(5):441–450, May 1997.
23. N.R. Pal and S.K. Pal. A review on image segmentation techniques. *Pattern Recognition*, 26(9):1277–1294, 1993.
24. A. Rosenfeld and J. L. Pfaltz. Sequential operations in digital picture processing. *Journal of the ACM*, 13(4):471–494, October 1966.

Interactive Parallel Visualization of Large Scale Computer Simulations in Physics

Roland Niemeier, Paul Benölken, Ulrich Lang

Institute of Computer Applications II and Computing Center
University of Stuttgart

Abstract. The project "Interactive Parallel Visualization in the Framework of the Sonderforschungsbereich 382" (IPV 382) is concerned with the development of visualization and steering tools for large scale applications in physics with simulations running on parallel computers.

Typical examples are online visualizations of molecular dynamic simulations with up to about one billion of atoms. For the visualization of the information contained in these huge data sets direct volume visualization proved to be an appropriate tool.

1 Introduction

Computer simulations on high performance computers reached new fields with the rise of massiv parallel computers. In molecular dynamic simulations the maximum number of interacting atoms in one simulation has raised from one million of molecules to about one billion of molecules in only three years. This makes more realisitic simulations possible, i.e. the simulation of three-dimensional cracks in different materials. These simulations will most likely become an important instrument for material sciences.

An urgent problem that has shown up during the last years is to extract the important information from these large scale simulations. The way still used by most of the phycisists running large scale computer simulations is to store huge data sets for each time step, transfer the information as complete as possible to their workstation and trying to visualize some aspects of the information on their local work stations. This "classical" approach leads to a slow processing of information and to ineffective long runs of the computer simulations.

Interactive visualization and computational steering of large scale computer simulations provide appropriate methods for extracting important information without transfering unimportant information contained in gigabytes of data to hard disks and networks and avoiding long scarcely controlled runs, that may just produce difficult to understand core dumps. For example, in one of our case studies we simulated a cubic cristal with one missing half plane. During the run the controlled total kinetic energy converged. The simulation however aborted with overflow. The overflow would not have been expected without the online visualization and would have lead to a cumbersome investigation of the problem. The attached visualization however gave us insight to see the strong oscillations that finally tore the cube into two parts, shortly before the overflow appeared.

In the development of our prototypes we applied direct volume rendering as an appropriate tool for the visualization of large three-dimensional scalar fields. The progress in software algorithms allows to run the visualization even on small work stations and personal computers. Some aspects of these algorithms that are relevant for our tools will be discussed below.

The following two sections will describe our approach to build a flexible and extensible tool for the interactive visualization and computational steering of large scale computer simulations. The fourth section will show some results followed by a summary and the discussion of some problems we experienced with our prototypes. In the last section we will give an outlook to our further research.

2   The direct volume visualization tool VolRend

Direct volume rendering is a flexible technique for visualizing scalar fields with widespread applicability in scientific visualization. It is very useful in cases where surfaces are artifical or noisy but it is use has been limited to a number of factors, especially:

- computational expensive rendering
- lack of hardware support
- missing comfortable user interfaces

Direct volume rendering is computational expensive because ray tracing can not be aborted at the first nontransparent voxel encountered as it is the case for surface rendering. All nontransparent voxels may contribute to the image. Table one shows requirements on memory and performance for realtime direct volume rendering assuming storage of 1 B(yte)/voxel, 30 Instruction/voxel and a frame rate of 30 pictures per second.

Table 1. memory and performance requirements for real time direct volume rendering, assuming 1B/voxel, 30 instructions/voxel and a frame rate of 30 pictures/s

#voxels	memory	instructions/s
128^3	2 MB	2 Ginstr/s
256^3	16 MB	15 Ginstr/s
512^3	128 MB	115 Ginstr/s
1024^3	1 GB	1 Tinstr/s

During the last decade a lot of software algorithms as well as hardware based methods have appeared to accelerate direct volume rendering [1]. Among the fastest approaches are software algorithms based on a shear-warp factorization of the viewing matrix [2]. Shear-warp factorizations have the property that rows of voxels in the volume are aligned with rows of pixels in the intermediage image. In the volpack library [3] this fact is used to contruct a scanline-based algorithm that traverses the volume and the intermediate image in synchrony, taking advantage of the spatial coherence present in both.

Based on these algorithms we developed the flexible and extensible tool VolRend to harness the power of direct volume rendering. Especially appreciated from our project partners of the SFB 382 is the possibility for interactive assignment of colors and opacities. Meanwhile it is not only in use on different platforms of our project partners, but also in other areas like i.e. medicine.

A web page is maintained, from where the tool and more information can be obtained [4].

Figure 1 shows a direct volume rendering example. The image is from a study of a low excited hydrogen atom in external electric and magnetic fields and shows the probabilities of presence of the electron. A typical advantage compared to surface rendering is that here the contour (red) as well as high values inside (blue) are displayed.

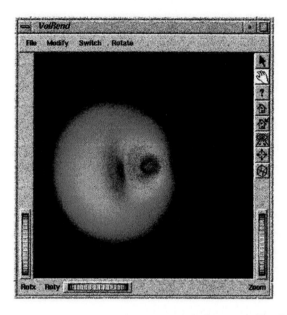

Fig. 1. A direct volume rendering example from atomic physics

3   Extensions for the interactive visualization and for computational steering

As previously stated the possibilities of interactive visualization and computational steering have become important issues for simulations running on parallel computers. We integrated into Vol-Rend the ability to connect to a running computer simulations and to exchange information with them. The connections are established using TCP/IP sockets. Typically the simulation acts as a server and the visualization as a client. The visualization client sends a token to the simulation indicating the specific current request.

Typical requests can be:

- send all data from a threedimensional scalar array
- resample data on a grid and send
- only send data of the array that fulfill specified features
- do the visualization on the parallel computer and send the picture
- start to store specific results on hard disc during the next timesteps
- stop to store specific results on hard disc
- change current run-time parameters
- change initial parameters and restart
- terminate the computer simulation

With a project partner from the Institute for Applied and Theoretical Physics (Itap) of the university of Stuttgart, we developed a prototype where the simulation is build from the IMD package (IMD - Itap Molecular Dynamics). Details about this package, including performance on different parallel computers, is available online [5] or can be found in [6]

If not receiving byte values, the visualization client has to take care for the order of the data type received. If this order (little endian or big endian) is not the same on both connected machines a byte swap must be done. The adaptation of VolRend for the IMD package, named VolIMD, can also act as a server for the socket-socket connection. One of the specific features is a switch between the kinectic and the potential energy distribution. Another possibility for the visualization of data from two-dimensional simulation has been included. Interactive visualization were carried out with the IMD running on the Cray T3E, the Nec SX4 and the Intel Paragon XP/S-5 at the computing center of the university of Stuttgart.

4   Results

Figure 2 shows an example from an online visualization of data from a molecular dynamic simulation where shear forces have been applied to a cubic cristal. The image results from a direct volume rendering of the kinetic energy distribution. Direct volume rendering enables here to display fractured shock waves (green color) and shock emitters at the corners (red color).

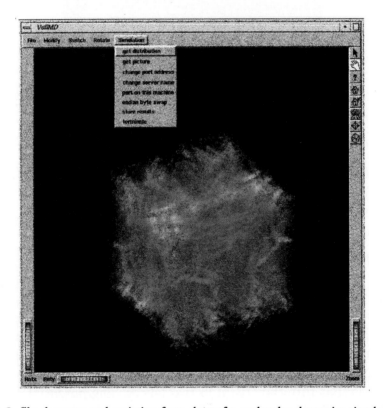

Fig. 2. Shock waves and emission from data of a molecular dynamics simulation

Figure 3 shows the cristal at a later time, when the shear forces already caused strong deformations and cracks at the surface.

The development of this interactive visualization tool helped the physicists to study for the first time realistic molecular dynamic simulation in three dimensions. Even if some effects are already known from previous studies of two-dimensional simula-

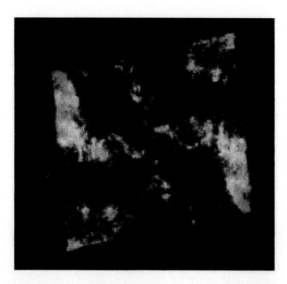

Fig. 3. Kinetic energy distribution of a deformed cube

tions, like that the shock emitters are in the corner even if the shear forces are attached to two opposed faces, three-dimensional simulations are essential for more realistic studies enabling quantitative evaluation of characteristics of specific materials.

Figure 4 shows the potential energy distribution of a completed crack. High potential energy values, that is almost free and free molecules, are shown with a red color in the crack. Here the simulation has been carried out starting with a missing half plane in the middle and periodic boundary conditions. As previous mentioned a minimum configuration closing the gap was assumed. The online visualization however showed us strong oscillations that tore the cristal in two pieces. The potential energy distribution for this image was the last we received before an overflow in the simulation program appeared.

With project partners from the Institute of Computer Applications I (ICA I) of the university of Stuttgart we adapted our tool VolRend to become the visualization counterpart for their online simulation of granular media. Figure 5 is an early example of the first three-dimensional visualization of density instabilities. Because of the unphysical agglomeration of the density at one face

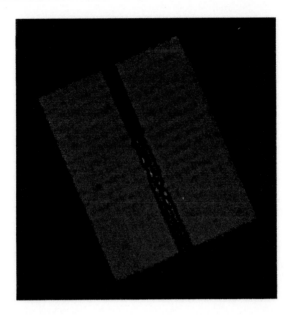

Fig. 4. Potential energy distribution of a cracked cube

of the cube (right side of the image), the physicist detected here an error of missing periodic boundary conditions in the program.

5 Summary and Criticism

For large data sets from volumetric data direct volume rendering is an appropriate rendering method. Interactive parallel visualization of data from running computer simulations proved to be an important instrument for insight and for computational steering. We experienced however a lot of problems especially from the security aspects and its management for some parallel machines. Thus the visualization tool can not run simply as a client for the TCP/IP socket-socket connections with machines behind the firewall of the HWW (Höchstleistungrechenzentrum für Wirtschaft und Wissenschaft). Signals can only be sent from an additional program running behind the firewall. Thus permanent checks for visualization requests in an internal loop of the simulation program proved to be adequate for handling this problem. Even if running the visualization as the server with a dedicated port only

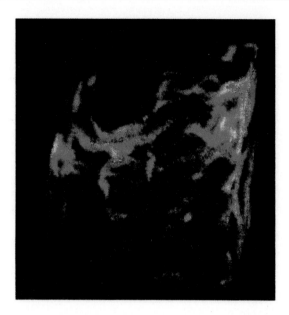

Fig. 5. Density instabilities from data of Monte Carlo Simulation

on the work station side, the firewall problems of delivering data only to specially registered machines is still augmented because for these machines the port access has to be registered and controlled. More and easier facilities for this as well as for adding new users and machines to projects are desired.

6   Outlook

Feature extraction from huge data sets is an important problem for large scale computer simulations. In our further development we will integrate the possibility of direct volume rendering with other rendering methods. Thus an aim is to first start from an overview of the volume with direct volume rendering, selecting then more specific details of interest and changing the rendering method. Thus a few atoms are more appropriate displayed using spheres. An important aspects of this integration is the possibility to use it in a virtual immersive environment. An integration into the collaborative visualisation tool COVISE (COllaborative VIsualization and Simulation Environment) [7] with its immersive abilites will be carried out as one of the next steps.

Acknowledgements

We wish to thank our project partners from the SFB 382 for the close and helpful cooperation. Especially for the data to the images in this paper, provided by Peter Faßbinder and Wolfgang Schweizer from the Institute of Theoretical Astrophysics of the University of Tübingen, Jörg Stadler from the Institute of Theoretical and Applied Physics and by Matthias Müller from the Institute of Computer Applications I.

References

1. A. Kaufman (organizer). Advances in Volume Visualization, SIGGRAPH '97 course notes 32, Los Angeles (1997).
2. P. G. Lacroute, M. Levoy. Fast Volume Rendering using a Shear-Warp Factorization of the Viewing Transformation, Computer Graphics Proceedings, SIGGRAPH '94, Orlando (1994), pp. 451-458.
3. http://graphics.stanford.edu:80/software/volpack (April 1998).
4. http://www.hlrs.de/people/niemeier/volrend/volrend.html (April 1998).
5. http://www.itap.physik.uni-stuttgart.de/ joerg/imd.html (April 1998).
6. http://www.uni-tuebingen.de/uni/opx/reports.html online report Nr. 82 (April 1998).
7. http://www.hlrs.de/structure/organisation/vis/covise/ (April 1998).

Construction of Large Permutation Representations for Matrix Groups

Michael Weller*

Institute for Experimental Mathematics, University of Essen, Germany

Abstract. This article describes the general computational tools for a new proof of the existence of the large sporadic simple Janko group J_4 [10] given by Cooperman, Lempken, Michler and the author [7] which is independent of Norton [12] and Benson [1].

Its basic step requires a generalization of the Cooperman, Finkelstein, Tselman and York algorithm [6] transforming a matrix group into a permutation group.

An efficient implementation of this algorithm on high performance parallel computers is described. Another general algorithm is given for the construction of representatives of the double cosets of the stabilizer of this permutation representation. It is then used to compute a base and strong generating set for the permutation group. In particular, we obtain an algorithm for computing the group order of a large matrix subgroup of $GL_n(q)$, provided we are given enough computational means.

It is applied to the subgroup $G = \langle x, y \rangle < GL_{1333}(11)$ corresponding to Lempken's construction of J_4 [11].

1 Introduction

Given finitely many matrices of a matrix group of reasonable size, it is almost impossible to determine the order of the subgroup U of $GL_n(q)$ generated by these matrices or to decide if another matrix of $GL_n(q)$ is an element of U.

These questions are easy to answer if one knows a permutation representation and a base and strong generating set for the group. This paper deals with the construction of such a base and strong generating set in the situation of a really huge matrix group, where the term huge does not necessarily refer to the dimension of the matrices but to the order of the group generated.

The main result can be summarized in the following theorem:

Theorem 1. *Let G be a finite group given by means of a matrix representation Γ. Let H be a subgroup of G given by means of generating matrices in Γ. Let ω_0 be a proper FH-submodule of $\Gamma|_H$ which is not invariant under G.*

Then there is an algorithm to construct the stabilizer $\widehat{H} := \mathrm{Stab}_G(\omega_0) \geq H$, a full set of double coset representatives of $\widehat{H}\backslash G/\widehat{H}$ and a base and strong generating set based on the permutation action of G on the cosets of $\widehat{H}$ (which coincides with the operation of G on the set of G-images).

---

* The work on this paper has been supported by the DFG research project *"Algorithmic Number Theory and Algebra"*

To improve the efficiency of the computations it is beneficial if the matrices of Γ are of small dimension. Thus Γ will usually be an irreducible representation over a field of small characteristic. If it is not irreducible, it can be reduced using the Meat-Axe described in [13] or [14].

For the same reasons, the FH-submodule should be the smallest irreducible constituent of $\Gamma|_H$.

To reduce the degree of the resulting permutation representation and the length of the orbits which are to be calculated, H should be a maximal subgroup. Ideally, H should be the largest maximal subgroup.

Finally, if $H \neq \widehat{H}$, the algorithm will find the missing generators of $\widehat{H}$ but all previous results must be recomputed. Thus, especially for large examples, it is helpful if $H = \widehat{H}$. The algorithm will prove this equality, hence it suffices to have a well estimated guess for the generators of $\widehat{H}$. One does not need to have a set of generators which is proven to generate $\widehat{H}$ in a strictly theoretical way.

The algorithm mentioned in theorem 1 is explicitly described as algorithm 3 in sections 2f. The implementation uses special hashing techniques which are described in subsection 2.2.

Concerning notation and terminology the reader is referred to Butler's book [3]. In particular he should be familiar with the definitions and results on base and strong generating sets. In addition, the following non standard notation is used:

Ech($\mathcal{W}$) The first vector of the echelonized basis of the subspace $\mathcal{W}$.

F_q The field with q elements.

$\mathcal{G}$ We use caligraphic letters to mark matrices. Usually $\mathcal{G}$ will be the matrix related to an abstract group element or permutation g.

$S[i]$ With a finite set S and a non negative integer i this notation implies that a fixed, computable bijection between S and $\{1, \ldots, |S|\}$ is known and that $S[i]$ is the image in S of i under it.

Often S is an array or vector. In this case $S[i]$ refers to its i-th entry.

2   Conversion of matrices to permutations

2.1   Basic principle

Matrices operate on F_q^n and its subspaces in a natural way. It is possible to investigate the operation of the group on a set Ω of arbitrary vectors or subspaces, but usually a permutation of smallest degree $|\Omega|$ is most interesting.

The smallest degree is achieved if Ω consists of a single orbit of a vector or subspace ω_0 and $\mathrm{Stab}_G(\omega_0)$ is a maximal subgroup (the largest subgroup yields the smallest degree). The mapping $\iota : \omega_0^G \to G/\mathrm{Stab}_G(\omega_0)$ defined by

$\omega_0^g \mapsto \mathrm{Stab}_G(\omega_0)g$ defines a one-to-one correspondence between elements of Ω and the cosets of the stabilizer.

With the notation of theorem 1 any subspace or F-span of a vector stabilized by $\mathrm{Stab}_G(\omega_0)$ is an invariant submodule of $F\mathrm{Stab}_G(\omega_0)$. This is the motivation to investigate the specific permutation operation of theorem 1 and the reason for the choice of ω_0. This and the following sections discuss the construction of the permutation representation of a G generated by matrices $\mathcal{G}_i$ on $\Omega = \omega_0^G$.

Remark 2. To check faithfulness of the resulting permutation representation note that the matrices actually yield a faithful permutation representation on the power set of the set F_q^n.

The algorithms construct full matrix stabilizers in this permutation representation. Therefore, if the operation on ω_0^G is not faithful, non identity matrices which stabilize ω_0^G pointwise will necessarily occur in the strong generating set. It is then possible to find a vector or vector space which is not stabilized by these and can be used to extend the base and the operation domain.

Algorithm 3. *The task to find the permutations corresponding to matrices $\mathcal{G}_i$ is performed by the following steps.*

1. *Construct ω_0^G. To do this, apply each matrix $\mathcal{G}_i$ on ω_0. Apply them to each new element of ω_0^G constructed, until the set of images becomes stationary. This set is ω_0^G.*
2. *Count and index the elements of ω_0^G.*
3. *For each matrix $\mathcal{G}_i$ and each $j \in \{1, \ldots, |\omega_0^G|\}$ find the number $g_i[j]$ of the image $\omega_0^G[j]^{\mathcal{G}_i}$ in ω_0^G. Arranged in a one dimensional array the images $j \mapsto g_i[j]$ are the permutation of $\{1, \ldots, |\omega_0^G|\}$ corresponding to $\mathcal{G}_i$.*

Unfortunately the size of the interesting examples makes such an approach impossible. For instance, in section 5 it is $|\omega_0^G| = 173\,067\,389$.

The computational problems start in step 1: Each newly constructed $\omega \in \omega_0^G$ must be compared to up to $|\omega_0^G|$ other elements to check if it is really a new element. Also, one must not underestimate the storage implications of step 1. Although a vector or basis of a subspace of F_q^n can typically be stored in a few hundred bytes of memory, $|\omega_0^G|$ of these occur.

Once this problem is solved, indexing and counting the elements becomes trivial as the computational solution of step 1 usually includes a solution for this.

Step 3 simply reintroduces the problems of step 1. When the image of a certain element of ω_0^G under $\mathcal{G}_i$ is constructed, it must be compared to up to $|\omega_0^G|$ other elements to determine its index number.

Remark 4. Application of algorithm 3 in any non trivial situation requires the ability to store $|\omega_0^G|$ vectors or bases of spaces efficiently for large values of $|\omega_0^G|$ while allowing to

- retrieve the vector or basis $\omega_0^G[i]$, given any integer i in $1, \ldots, |\omega_0^G|$.
- find i, s.t. $\omega_0^G[i] = \omega$ or prove that $\omega \notin \omega_0^G$, given a vector or basis ω.

In Computer Science this kind of problem is often solved with *hash functions*. It is the major accomplishment of Cooperman, Finkelstein, Tselman and York [6] to introduce this approach into Computational Group Theory:

2.2   Hashing

Consider a function $f : \omega_0^G \to 1, \ldots, N$. By no means we require f to be an bijection or even injection. Still, simple arguments show that a function f with evenly distributed return values will only have $\frac{|\omega_0^G|}{2N}$ elements in ω_0^G with a non unique return value.

Remark 5. Such a hash function allows to allocate an N dimensional array (with N a small multiple of the expected $|\omega_0^G|$) and store an element ω_0^g of ω_0^G in table position $f(\omega_0^g)$. If that position is empty, we may claim that ω_0^g was not computed before, even without a single comparison with any element of ω_0^G.

Figure 1 shows this generic situation. In addition, the elements of ω_0^G are

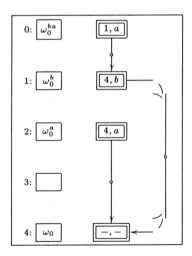

Fig. 1. Generic hash table layout.

not stored in the table directly, Instead, a reference to another hash entry and the generator applied to it to reach the new element of ω_0^G is recorded.

Thus, for each element of ω_0^G (actually for each entry in the N-dimensional hash table) only the double outlined data must be stored. The vertices leading from one element of ω_0^G to another form linked lists or a tree with the *root* or *starting point* ω_0.

Remark 6. As f is not injective, different ω_0^g and ω_0^h may have the same hash value. To resolve this *hash collision*, if the destination of ω_0^h is already occupied by ω_0^g, one retrieves the element ω_0^g from the table by following the vertices in figure 1. After an explicit check that $\omega_0^g \neq \omega_0^h$, one tries hash position $1 + (f(\omega_0^h) + p - 1 \bmod N)$ (and following positions in p steps) for p prime to N to find a free location. The relative primality of p ensures that a free place is found if $N \geq |\omega_0^G|$.

Of course, the equality of $\omega_0^g = \omega_0^h$ has to be proven often, especially when proving completeness of ω_0^G. This indeed is, where most of the computation resources go.

However, hash collisions are fairly rare and when there is a collision, only few elements have the same hash value. Also, in the examples only 20% – 28% of the hash values were not unique, although $N = 2^{24}$ was only two times the expected $|\omega_0^G|$.

The hash table does also ease step 2 of algorithm 3. Once computed, the hash table may contain holes like position 3 in figure 1. It is a straightforward procedure to loop over the hash table and build an array of size ω_0^G which maps i to the i-th non empty hash entry. As the array entries are sorted, an inverse mapping is easily evaluated using a binary search.

2.3   The hash function

The quality of the hash function is important for the efficiency of the hash table. A high quality hash function has perfectly even distributed result values. With a function like $x \mapsto 1$ every search would degenerate to a linear search. Fortunately, simple but sensible straightforward hash functions seem to be sufficient.

It is easy to assign a hash value to a vector space if one has a basis by taking certain entries of the basis vectors to build the hash value. However, the basis is not unique and the hash function must be well defined. To achieve uniqueness it suffices to construct the echelonized basis with Gaussian elimination.

A simple hash function is

$$f(\mathcal{W}) := \sum_{i=m+1}^{m+k} \text{Ech}(\mathcal{W})[i] \cdot q^{m+k-i} \qquad (1)$$

where m shouldn't be less than the dimension of $\mathcal{W}$ (the first vector entries are usually eliminated to 0). Choose k big enough to ensure hash values $> N$ (s.t. it covers the whole range of $1, \ldots, N$ when reduced modulo N).

In addition, this implicitly requires some embedding of the field elements into the integers. For prime fields the canonical embedding is well suited. For other fields just interpreting the internal machine realization as an integer or using a logarithm will do.

However, in section 5 actually the following variation of equation 1 with $m = 48$ and $k = 7$ is used:

$$
f_{11}(\mathcal{W}) := \begin{cases} 3 + \sum_{i=1}^{22} 11^{22-i} \text{Ech}(\mathcal{W})[i] & \text{if } f(\mathcal{W}) + 3\text{Ech}(\mathcal{W})[1] \equiv 3 \\[2ex] f(\mathcal{W}) + 3\text{Ech}(\mathcal{W})[1] & \text{otherwise.} \end{cases} \tag{2}
$$

Remark 7. All computations are done modulo 2^{32}. $\text{Ech}(\mathcal{W})[1]$ is involved to make it more likely that different $\langle \mathcal{C} \rangle$-orbit elements receive different hash values (reconsider this after reading section 2.4).

During the computations the hash value 3 was returned by definition (1) much too often. All points in double cosets in Mx_2M and Mx_4M had this hash value.

This, of course, was due to the structure of G and the matrices, especially of $\mathcal{C}$.

It would have been better if the basis entries used in equation 1 were chosen from more different vector entry cycles under operation of $\mathcal{C}$ from the beginning.

Its modification, definition (2), fixes this mistake. Care was taken that only the hash values we need to cure were affected. Theoretically, the choice of cycle representants as defined in section 2.4 might have been affected for all cycles whose representant has hash value 3 or less. Fortunately these small hash values occurred not very often, hence it was easy to explicitly check that the already computed parts of the hash table were not affected by the modification.

Only the entries of the first columns of the basis' are used as only these were calculated in the already implemented cycle representant search. Still, definition (2) turned out to be a very good source of hash values for these two double cosets.

Remark 8. When operating on vectors echelonization is not required. Nevertheless a similar hash function can be used on vectors.

Remark 9. Of course, the hash function is applied often (especially when a suborbit representative is searched in 2.4). So the question comes up, if the continuous Gaussian elimination has large effects on the execution times and takes a major part of the computations. And indeed, usually Gaussian elimination is almost as slow as matrix multiplication as both are $O(n^3)$ algorithms.

However, this is not the usual square situation. Assuming an m-dimensional subspace (which coincides nicely with the use of m in (1)), m is much smaller than n as it is usually the dimension of the smallest invariant subspace. Thus, closer inspection yields $O(m^2 \cdot n)$ for Gaussian elimination and $O(m \cdot n^2)$ for vector space × matrix multiplication.

This indicates that the Gaussian elimination is of no significant impact to the efficiency of the algorithm at all. Table 1 shows a few run times supporting this observation.

2.4   Reducing the size of the hash table

The storage problem was already dealt with. Still, in the $173\,067\,389$ degree examples, each hash entry needs 4 bytes. Constructing such a 660MB table will usually need a workstation with about 768MB of main memory or more. This is possible today, but too close to the current hardware limits to feel comfortable and to apply the results to larger examples.

Hence a small, well known, subgroup of G is introduced. One must know the number of its elements and how each of them operates on an element of ω_0^G. It is not necessary that the orbits of this subgroup on ω_0^G are all of the same or out of a very small set of lengths, but it simplifies the implementation.

Remark 10. In interesting examples it is difficult to find generators of such a small subgroup. But one may choose an element c of large order and use $\langle c \rangle$. Such an element is found easily by building random products in G without any knowledge on the group structure.

Then only a representative of every $\langle c \rangle$-orbit is stored in the hash table. Figure 2 shows this situation for a group $G := \langle a, b \rangle$: Each vertex in the hash table records on which element (which power of c applied) of the preceding suborbit the group generator a or b was applied. To improve efficiency, it records which power to apply to reach the representative of the resulting orbit as well. This increases the size of the hash entries (6 bytes in the examples) but reduces the size of the table by $o(c)$ for fix point free operation and $o(c)$ a prime.

Definition 11. It was not yet explained how to choose representatives of the suborbits. The implementation of the hash function f actually provides results in a larger range than $1, \ldots, N$ which are then reduced modulo N.

The element with the smallest, non reduced, hash value is called *the representative*. If this value is not unique in the suborbit, the entry with the lexicographically smallest subspace basis or vector is *the representative*.

Remark 12. The element c is used most often. As an improvement over [6] a basis transformation of the underlying vector space is made to achieve a form of $\mathcal{C}$ which makes its application faster.

Transformation of $\mathcal{C}$ to rational canonical form can always be done, and as $o(\mathcal{C})$ is typically much smaller than the dimension one will at least divide

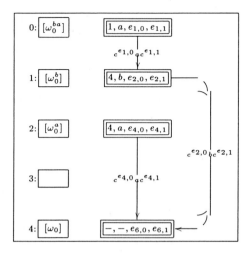

Fig. 2. Compressed hash table layout.

$\mathcal{C}$ in many small — often sparse — blocks which already speeds up matrix multiplication.

In a special purpose implementation like this, multiplication with $\mathcal{C}$ can be replaced by a specific subroutine. In section 5, $\mathcal{C}$ simply rotates every 23 basis vectors and does a very simple operation on the remaining 22 vectors.

3   Finding a base and a strong generating set

The construction of the permutations as described above already requires generating matrices for G as well as for a certain subgroup which has a proper invariant subspace (which will become the first base point). However, we may not assume that this subgroup is already the whole stabilizer. (Except when it is known that it is a maximal subgroup and the representation of G is irreducible.)

This proof is achieved with 3.1 and is constructive. If the subgroup is not the complete stabilizer, the algorithm provides an additional generator to enlarge the conjectured stabilizer.

Thus, given any subspace and starting with the trivial subgroup it calculates generators of the stabilizer. Unfortunately, the algorithm might construct too many generators and the arbitrary base point might not be a good choice as well. Also, starting with such a trivial guess, many unsuccessful applications of 3.1 are required until the stabilizer is found. Even worse, the algorithm is recursive. Therefore, even more unsuccessful applications of it are required in the deeper recursion levels.

Because of this, it is better if a good guess is already known and just has to be proven correct.

The following variation of the Schreier-Sims method is well known and already used in many places. For the sake of shortness no proofs or intermediate steps are given. Only the tests which must be run to check the stabilizer for completeness are included.

3.1   The Double Coset Trick

As a first ingredient the hash table or Schreier-vector must be constructed according to the conjectured point stabilizer H of ω_0 with algorithm 13.

Note that the element c as used in section 2.4 is applied in the inner loops. It must therefore be chosen out of H which make it impossible to use an element of largest order in G.

As a result the suborbits of ω_0^G under operation of H are obtained. It is straightforward to see that these correspond to the $S\backslash G/H$ double cosets of G where S is the stabilizer of ω_0.

Algorithm 13. *Construct Ω with respect to H by the following steps:*

1. *Start with $\Omega := \{\omega_1\} := \{\omega_0\}$ and $i := 1$.*
2. *Construct ω_i^H building the trees of vertices as described in Figures 1 & 2 with starting points ω_i.*
3. *Find and store a new orbit element ω^g as the starting point of a new (now i-th) H-suborbit where g is a generator of G not in H and ω is any of the known orbit elements. If a new ω^g was found, increase i, set $\omega_i := \omega^g$ and go to step 2.*
4. *Otherwise, Ω is closed under operation of G.*

This avoids continuous application of generators of G outside of H once a new starting point is found. Nevertheless, we record the words g_{ω_i} with $\omega_i = \omega_0^{g_{\omega_i}}$ which are of vital interest later.

Remark 14. One is able to determine the index number i of the double coset containing an arbitrary orbit element ω by looking it up in the hash table and following the vertices down to ω_i. This ability is the major computational ingredient used for [15].

Of course, one can also use this to sort out a certain double coset and study the permutation operation of H on this, smaller H-set. This is used to ease the computations required to prove theorem 24.

Algorithm 15 is quoted from Gollan [9], section 2.3. It proves that a proposed set of elements generates a whole stabilizer or finds an element missing from the set of generators. Previous versions are due to Brownie, Cannon and Havas [4], and originally Sims.

Algorithm 15 (Double Coset Trick). *Let* $\{\gamma_1, \ldots, \gamma_r\}$ *be the starting points of the* ω_0^G-*suborbits under operation of* H. *Using the hash table, find elements* $x_i \in G$ *(as words in the generators) with* $\omega_0^{x_i} = \gamma_i$.

By induction, a base and strong generating set for H *is known and it is possible to perform efficient computations in* H. *Use this to find generators* y_{ij} *with* $\mathrm{Stab}_H(\gamma_i) = \langle y_{i1}, \ldots, y_{ik_i}\rangle$.

To prove that $S = H$, *check the following conditions:*

1. $y_{ij}^{x_i^{-1}} \in H$ $\forall i, j$. *This membership problem is easily solved in* H *with the membership test described as Algorithm 3 in Chapter 10 of [3].*
2. *For each element* t *of the known orbits, check that each group generator* g_i *maps* t *into a known coset of* $\mathrm{Stab}_G(\omega_0)$. *Note that it does not suffice to find* $\omega_0 t g_i = \omega_0 t'$ *in the hash table. Using the base and strong generating set it must be checked that* $t g_i t'^{-1} \in H$ *(otherwise it is a new generator for* $\mathrm{Stab}_G(\omega_0)$).

Remark 16. For an orbit element ω, let $g_\omega \in G$ be a word in the group generators s.t. $\omega_0^{g_\omega} = \omega$. (We can find such an element following the vertices in Figures 1 or 2, resp.)

Then, for each generator $g_i \notin H$, define $K = H \cap H^{g_i^{-1}}$. It suffices to apply check 2 only to the orbit elements ω where the last generator in word g_ω is outside K.

Generators $g_i \in H$ do not need to be checked at all.

If the base and strong generating set is constructed inductively using 3.1, it is very likely that K is another point stabilizer in the stabilizer chain, hence generators for it are part of the set of strong generators.

3.2   Efficient calculation with permutations

Once 3 is performed we have permutations operating on $|\omega_0^G|$ points which are usually represented as an array of the $|\omega_0^G|$ images. However, in the examples such a permutation requires about 660MB storage. Such a permutation can be handled on today's computers, but not conveniently (usually one needs to handle several at once), and one might want to be able to address even larger problems. Of course, due to the arrangement of the compressed hash table the generator c introduced in section 2.4 has a nice permutation representation (like $(1, \ldots, o(c))(o(c) + 1, \ldots, 2o(c)) \ldots$ assuming fix point free operation) which can be implemented directly.

Remark 17. The most time consuming part in 3 is step 3 where all the images of the permutation are computed. However, almost all of them are never used again in 3.1 or one of the other algorithms.

Thus, a kind of lazy permutation construction seems to be most sensible. One simply does not perform step 3 of 3! Instead, whenever the image of a certain point under a permutation is needed, the space/vector corresponding to this point of Ω is constructed using the hash table, the matrix corresponding to the permutation is applied and the space/vector is translated back to the number of the corresponding point of Ω.

Note that this procedure needs much more time than just looking up the image in a permutation. However, on the other hand it is only applied for very few permutation points. Hence, much more time is saved skipping step 3 than needed here.

Remark 18. In addition, only the matrices and spaces/vectors ω_i (which do not use a significant amount of memory in comparison) and one hash table must be stored. Actually, one needs a hash table for each base point and the corresponding stabilizer in the stabilizer chain. But their size reduces dramatically in each step. The size of the first hash table is also dramatically reduced with the techniques from section 2.4.

To underline this remark, in the example, the size of an ordinary permutation is 660MB. The reduced hash table of ω_0^G needs 73MB. Together with matrices of all strong generators and further hash tables for the other base points, this information does not exceed 120MB.

Remark 19. From a theoretical point of view, this means that we actually view the matrices of $GL(n, q)$ as permutations of F_q^n.

The order or equality of permutations can be checked on the matrices as well which involves much less data. However, as mentioned already, the operation on ω_0^G may not be faithful in which case other orbits on F_q^n can be added to achieve a faithful permutation representation.

Even then, if one is interested in the non faithful operation on the cosets of S, this trick may be applied. However, one may not check equality or orders on the matrices then. In this case they are just preimages of the canonical epimorphism to G/S.

As already mentioned, there are many uses for the permutation representation to calculate within the group G. However, there are two which are very interesting to find out more about the structure of G and which can be adopted to be used more efficiently in our special situation:

Remark 20. Another application is the ability to count fix points of a given group element in this permutation representation. Of course, one can decide to generate the whole permutation and just count the fix points, but the following simplifications are possible:

1. To determine if a point of Ω is fixed, it is not required to locate it in the hash table by calculating the hash value of the result and evaluate the word of generators give by following the corresponding vertices. It suffices to check the vector/space immediately. In the latter case, a single basis vector mapped outside the space already proves that it is no fix point.

2. Starting with a root or very short vertex list all entries with a vertex list running through this point can be checked by a recursive procedure. This reduces the amount of computations required significantly by optimal use of intermediate results. A recursive implementation is not critical here as the tree was build breadth first and is relatively shallow.

4 Parallel Implementation

Because of the size of the examples a parallel implementation was required. A simple master-slave model seemed to be most sensible. A single master process maintains the hash table and instructs slave processes to do the actual matrix calculations. As of now, only a single master maintains the hash table. A hash table distributed on several masters might allow to handle even larger examples, but the necessarily resulting overhead is not worth being added for the size of problems we are currently handling.

Algorithm 21 (Parallel Implementation). *Figure 3 illustrates the data*

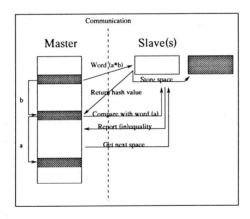

Fig. 3. Data flow between master and slave.

flow between master and slave. The main steps are as follows:

1. *The master selects a new point in the hash table whose images under G need to be checked. If there is no such point left, the program terminates.*
2. *The master sends the corresponding word and index i of the start point ω_i to a free slave. The slave knows all the group generators and starting points ω_i. Hence, it can calculate the corresponding vector/subspace, keep it in a buffer on the slave and compute its hash value.*
3. *The master looks the value up in the hash table. If the slot is empty, the entry is added to the hash table and the master goes to step 6.*

4. *If the corresponding slot is already occupied, the master sends the group generators leading to this, maybe different, element back to the same slave. Using the temporary buffer, the slave determines if this is the same entry than the one previously computed or not.*
5. *If not, the master looks at the next secondary slot in the hash table to store this entry and proceeds with step 3.*
6. *The master asks the slave for another image of the original point in step 2 and continues there if there is one. If the slave indicates that all images under the group generators have been processed, the master starts again at step 1.*

Further status information like original hash value and flags, if the slave has some group generators left which still need to be applied, or if any new entries were found under the images of this point (useful for optimizations) is exchanged to ease processing.

Remark 22. Of course, the master handles several slaves at once. In addition, in some examples the actual linear algebra operations are very fast, s.t. it seemed necessary to send more than one request in one message to a slave which in turn reports several results back in one message.

Remark 23. The master maintains two maps with one bit for each hash table entry which are initialized to zero for all but the starting points.

One contains set bits for all points whose images still must be investigated. Every new point is marked in the second bitmap. When the first is exhausted, they are exchanged to ensure a breadth first search. This is already due to [6].

The first implementation used in section 5 had a bug, swapping those bitmaps whenever the program was restarted (the program had to make check points every 4h – 10h due to the job management on the machines used). After the bug was fixed, no points with a depth higher than 4 were build.

In the example more than 99% of all points have a depth of 7 or less, more than 60% a depth of 4 or less. The maximal depth is 13. The majority of points (54%) has a depth of 4. Because of this only slightly suboptimal result and the CPU time already spent at this point none of the already constructed entries were discarded.

5   A new existence proof for Janko's group J_4

Table 1 shows run times of certain subroutines. All were found using an IBM RS/6000 workstation 590. The actual application is a subgroup of $GL_{1333}(11)$ operating on 45-dimensional vector spaces. Lempken's construction of such matrices is described in [11]. He kindly gave us direct access to these matrices, s.t. it was not necessary to repeat their construction. The results of the computations are summarized in the next theorem:

45-dimensional F_{11}^{1333}-subspace$\times\mathcal{C}$	$57.6 \cdot 10^{-6}$s
random 45-dimensional F_{11}^{1333}-subspace echelon	$0.4 \cdot 10^{-3}$s
very sparse 45-dimensional F_{11}^{1333}-subspace echelon	$< 10^{-4}$s
45-dimensional F_{11}^{1333}-subspace$\times\mathcal{Y}$ (fast)	0.213s
(but requires a 100MB table made in	5.22s)
45-dimensional F_{11}^{1333}-subspace$\times\mathcal{X}$ (slow)	5.02s

Table 1. Run times for the vector arithmetic.

Theorem 24. Let $G = \langle x, y \rangle \leq \mathrm{GL}_{1333}(11)$ and $M = \langle x^3, y, (x^{14})^t \rangle$ with $t = (x^{14}y^5)^2$ as defined in [11]. Then the following assertions hold:

1. Let $V_{|M} = \mathcal{W} \oplus \mathcal{S}$ be the restriction of the simple KG-module $V = K^{1333}$ to the subgroup M of G. Then G operates on the set $\{\mathcal{W}g | g \in G\}$ and the trivial coset of $\mathrm{Stab}_G(\mathcal{W})$ corresponds to the subspace $\mathcal{W}$ of $V_{|M}$, and $\mathcal{W}$ has a 45-dimensional basis consisting of the first 45 canonical basis vectors of $V = K^{1333}$.

2. $G = \bigcup\limits_{i=1}^{7} M x_i M$ with x_i as defined in table 2.

Name	Representative	Order $|Mx_iM|$
x_1	1	1
x_2	$x^{14}c^{12}$	15 180
x_3	$x_6 y^2 c^{16} y c^{13} y c^4 y c^{10} y c^{18} x c^{21}$	28 336
x_4	$x_3 c^3 x^{-1} c^{11}$	3 400 320
x_5	$x_6 x c$	32 643 072
x_6	$x c^{12} x c^3 x c^2$	54 405 120
x_7	$x_5 x c^9 x c^{16} x^2 c^{16}$	82 575 360

where $c := (x^{14})^t y^4 (x^{14})^t y^{-1}(x^{14})^t$ has order 23 with $t := (x^{14}y^5)^2$ of order 5.

Table 2. Double cosets of G.

3. The sequence $B = [b_1, b_2, \ldots, b_7]$ of points defined in table 3 is a base for G. Furthermore, the words s_i, $1 \leq i \leq 11$ given in table 4 form a set of strong generators for G with respect to the base B. The set stabilizers are $G_0 = \langle s_1, s_2 \rangle$, $G_1 = \langle s_2, s_3 \rangle$, $G_2 = \langle s_4, s_5 \rangle$, $G_3 = \langle s_6, s_7, s_8, s_9, s_{12}, s_{14} \rangle$, $G_4 = \langle s_{10}, s_{11}, s_{12}, s_{13}, s_{14} \rangle$, $G_5 = \langle s_{12}, s_{13}, s_{14} \rangle$, $G_6 = \langle s_{14} \rangle$ and $G_7 = \{1\}$.

4. $|G : M| = 173\,067\,389$

Base point	Length of orbit $\lvert b_i \cdot G_{i-1}\rvert$	Element of	Coset representative
b_1	173 067 389	Mx_1M	$\mathcal{W} \cdot 1$
b_2	15 180	Mx_2M	$\mathcal{W} \cdot x_2c^{14}yc^5yc^2$
b_3	4 032	Mx_2M	$\mathcal{W} \cdot x_2c^{14}yc^5yc^7$
b_4	256	Mx_2M	$\mathcal{W} \cdot x_2c^{14}yc^5yc^3$
b_5	4	Mx_2M	$\mathcal{W} \cdot x_2c^{14}yc^5yc^6$
b_6	4	Mx_2M	$\mathcal{W} \cdot x_2c^{14}yc^5yc^4$
b_7	2	Mx_2M	$\mathcal{W} \cdot x_2c^{14}yc^5yc^5$

Table 3. A base of G.

Name	Generator	Order	Stabilized base points
s_1	x	42	none
s_2	y	10	b_1
s_3	c	23	b_1
s_4	$c^{19}yc^6yc^{18}(c^{11}yc^{12})^{-1}$	14	b_1, b_2
s_5	$c^{19}yc^{12}yc^{13}(c^{13}yc^{11})^{-1}$	8	b_1, b_2
s_6	$s_5^2s_4^3s_5s_4(s_4s_5s_4s_5^2)^{-1}$	4	b_1, b_2, b_3
s_7	$s_4s_5s_4^2s_4^4(s_5^2s_4s_5s_4)^{-1}$	4	b_1, b_2, b_3
s_8	$s_4^2s_5^4(s_4s_5^4s_4)^{-1}s_4^2s_5s_5^2s_4^4(s_4^2s_5s_4^2)^{-1}$	2	b_1, b_2, b_3
s_9	$s_4s_5s_4^7(s_4s_5)^{-1}$	2	b_1, b_2, b_3
s_{10}	$s_7s_{14}s_7^{-1}$	2	b_1, b_2, b_3, b_4 (and b_7)
s_{11}	$s_9s_6(s_6s_9)^{-1}$	2	b_1, b_2, b_3, b_4 (and b_6)
s_{12}	$\gamma s_4^4s_5^2s_4^2(s_5^2s_4s_5^2s_4s_5^2)^{-1}\gamma^2$	2	b_1, b_2, b_3, b_4, b_5
s_{13}	$s_8s_6(s_6s_8)^{-1}$	2	b_1, b_2, b_3, b_4, b_5
s_{14}	$\gamma s_7^2(s_8s_9)^2$	2	$b_1, b_2, b_3, b_4, b_5, b_6$

where $\gamma := s_4s_5^2s_4^2s_5^2(s_4^4s_5^2s_4)^{-1}$ has order 4 and stabilizes base points b_1, b_2 and b_3.

Table 4. Strong generators of G.

5. $|G| = 2^{21} \cdot 3^3 \cdot 5 \cdot 7 \cdot 11^3 \cdot 23 \cdot 29 \cdot 31 \cdot 37 \cdot 43$
6. If Ω denotes the index set of the cosets Mg_i of M in G and $Mg_1 = M$, then G induces a faithful permutation representation with stabilizer $\mathrm{Stab}_G(1) = M$ on $\Omega = \{1, 2, \ldots, 173\,067\,389\}$.

Proof. All proofs are performed by explicit computer calculations using the previously described algorithms. In more detail: **(1)** Building random products in the matrices $\mathcal{X}$ and $\mathcal{Y}$ for a short time c in table 2 is found. It is used to apply remark 10.

A 45-dimensional vector space which is invariant under M is constructed by splitting the module $\langle \mathcal{Y}, \mathcal{C} \rangle$ into $1288 \oplus 45$ with the MeatAxe[13,14]. It turns out that the first 45 canonical base vectors of F_{11}^{1333} are a basis of it.

This is, of course, due to Lempken's construction. It is checked that it is invariant under all generators of M.

(2) The orders of many random products in y and c (see table 2) were checked to make it very probably that $\langle y, c \rangle = M$. By definition, $\langle y, c \rangle < M$ and [7, Proposition 1.3] calculates the order of the matrix group M independently of this paper. In the end, explicit machine computations proved $|\langle y, c \rangle| \geq |M|$.

As proposed in remark 12 the matrix C is transformed to rational canonical form which has 57 23-dimensional blocks $\mathcal{A}$ and one 22-dimensional block $\mathcal{B}$:

$$\mathcal{A} = \begin{pmatrix} 0 & 1 & & 0 \\ \vdots & \ddots & \ddots & \\ 0 & & 0 & 1 \\ 1 & 0 & \ldots & 0 \end{pmatrix}, \quad \mathcal{B} = \begin{pmatrix} 1 & & & 0 \\ & \ddots & & \\ 0 & & & 1 \\ -1 & \ldots & & -1 \end{pmatrix}.$$

A special subroutine performs this simple operation directly on the vector entries. The operation also almost maintains an already existing echelon form. Hence, the echelonization routine tries to take advantage of this. Table 1 shows how this succeeds.

Standard techniques as described in [8] are used to speed up the remaining multiplications with the emphasis on $\mathcal{Y}$. Huge tables on each slave are initialized at the start of the program and are used to speed it up. They store linear combinations of every two consecutive rows of $\mathcal{Y}$. The choice of two is a compromise based on the available memory on the slaves. The multiplication with $\mathcal{X}$ is not optimized, as it is only used when the start of a new double coset is searched.

Repeated application of algorithm 13 constructs the orbits of $\mathcal{W}$ with respect to M and yields the given double coset representatives.

(3) As algorithm 15 is recursive, many tedious small steps are required for a complete construction of a base and strong generating set. To perform these, several implementations of long known algorithms applicable in this specific environment are required, albeit the actual size of the smaller problems is not challenging.

However, M induces a permutation representation of degree 15 180 on the smallest non trivial double coset. Fortunately MAGMA [2] is able to handle permutation groups of this degree, at least in most aspects (it failed constructing all conjugacy classes, for example). MAGMA constructed a base and strong generating set of this group. However, repeated application of 3.1 is required to check it also holds for the matrices. Certainly the permutation group is a homomorphic image of M, hence it suffices to show that the orders coincide. This, however, MAGMA could not accomplish with the $GL_{1333}(11)$ matrices on the machines available. Fortunately, [7, Proposition 1.3] proves the order (and structure) of the matrix group independently from this paper.

Unfortunately the lengths of the words for the strong generators produced by MAGMA makes it impossible to use them immediately. Hence, a modified version of the orbit generating program is used to print any pair of group elements mapping ω_2 to the same element. Each quotient of these is an element of the stabilizer. MAGMA allows to check easily if a given set of those already generates the stabilizer using the 15 180-representation. After reordering the base points tables 3 and 4 are found. The equation $\sum_{i=2}^{7} |b_i G_{i-1}| = |M|$ shows that a base and strong generating set of M is constructed.

The conditions of algorithm 15 need to be checked to prove that a base and strong generating set for G was constructed. **These calculations are not finished as of this writing.** It has not yet been shown that the operation of x does not move a point out of the known double cosets. Remark 26 explains the missing calculations. Closure under y was proven indirectly with Lemma 25.

The remaining statements **(4)**, **(5)** and **(6)** are direct consequences of the tables and algorithm 15. □

Lemma 25. *The double cosets in table 2 are closed under operation of M.*

Proof. As many different points of the double cosets as given in table 2 were constructed, hence lower bounds of the lengths are proven. The same tool used for the base construction is then used to find words in M stabilizing the starting point. With MAGMA it is easy to check the index of the subgroup generated in M, hence an upper bound is established.

Table 5 lists the generators y_{ij} of the double coset stabilizers in M. Coincidence of subgroup index and double coset length was checked in all cases.

Note that the generators y_{ij} are those required for step 1 of algorithm 15.

□

Remark 26. It is important that remark 16 can be applied to speed up the check in step 2 of algorithm 15. Unfortunately, K does not show up in the stabilizer chain. Using the knowledge gained from the computations done so far, it would now be possible to conjecture a better suited generating system for G but then all expensive results got so far are lost.

The subspace $W \cdot \widetilde{x}$ with $\widetilde{x} := x_7 c^4 y c^{11} y c^8 y c^{21} y c^{17} y c^{19} y$ of order 43 is the only non-trivial fix point of c. The existence of exactly two fix points was also predicted assuming $G \cong J_4$.

Using not yet proven results in [15] all words are transformed into matrices in $GL_{112}(2)$. There it is possible to express x as a word in $\widetilde{x}$ and y with algorithms described here in less than one week of sequential CPU time. Of course, as nothing is proven at this point this is no proof yet. However, the resulting relation expressing $\mathcal{X}$ in matrices $\widetilde{\mathcal{X}}$ and $\mathcal{Y}$ can be checked easily on the large matrices. Then, all results made using $\mathcal{X}$ can be interpreted for $G = \langle \widetilde{x}, y \rangle = \langle x, y \rangle$.

Name	Generator	Order	Stabilizes
y_{11}	y	10	$\mathcal{W} \cdot x_1$
y_{12}	c	23	$\mathcal{W} \cdot x_1$
y_{21}	s_4	14	$\mathcal{W} \cdot x_2$
y_{22}	s_5	8	$\mathcal{W} \cdot x_2$
y_{31}	$cyc^9yc^{15}(c^{10}yc^7)^{-1}$	12	$\mathcal{W} \cdot x_3$
y_{32}	$c^2yc^{16}yc^5(c^8yc^{10})^{-1}c^2yc^3yc^{17}(y^2c^{15})^{-1}$	8	$\mathcal{W} \cdot x_3$
y_{41}	$c^9yc^2yc(c^{19}yc^{12}yc^8)^{-1}c^{22}yc^{21}yc^4yc^{11}(c^2ycyc^2)^{-1}$	12	$\mathcal{W} \cdot x_4$
y_{42}	$c^4ycyc^{11}yc(c^3yc^8yc^{14})^{-1}$	12	$\mathcal{W} \cdot x_4$
y_{51}	$c^{10}yc^6yc^5yc^2(yc^4yc^{13})^{-1}$	4	$\mathcal{W} \cdot x_5$
y_{52}	$c^6yc^6yc^{10}yc^{15}(c^2yc^2)^{-1}$	6	$\mathcal{W} \cdot x_5$
y_{53}	$c^6yc^{11}yc^{12}yc^{10}(c^3yc^{17}ycyc^{16})^{-1}$	4	$\mathcal{W} \cdot x_5$
y_{61}	$c^2yc^{22}yc^{17}yc^4(c^9yc^{21}yc^8yc^{22})^{-1}$	4	$\mathcal{W} \cdot x_6$
y_{62}	$c^8yc^{16}yc^{22}yc^{19}(c^4yc^{10}yc^{15}yc^{12})^{-1}$	12	$\mathcal{W} \cdot x_6$
y_{71}	$c^{19}yc^1yc^{13}yc^2(y^5yc^9yc^{15}yc^{14})^{-1}$	11	$\mathcal{W} \cdot x_7$
y_{72}	$c^5yc^3yc^{12}yc^4(c^{13}yc^7yc^{20}yc^2)^{-1}$	12	$\mathcal{W} \cdot x_7$

Note that $y_{51}' = y_{51}y_{53}$ with order 4 and $y_{52}' = y_{52}$ is a better generating set for the stabilizer of $\mathcal{W} \cdot x_5$ in M.

Table 5. Generators of double coset stabilizers in M.

Then we have $c \in K := M \cap M^{\tilde{x}}$. Hence only one 23rd of the tests in step 2 needs to be performed.

Remark 27. The major restrictions of the applicability are due to memory constraints. The current implementation assumes that a single master holds the whole hash table which should be about twice the expected number of $\langle c \rangle$-suborbits.

The size of the hash entries depends on the size of the hash table and the order of c, as it needs to store a pointer into the table, index of a generator, two exponents of c and a few flag bits. In the examples 6 bytes per hash entry sufficed.

Thus, with a gigabyte of memory on the master and c as in the examples, it is possible to compute orbits with up to 4 billion entries while still having memory left for the programs and operating system.

However, computation time is another limiting factor which is mainly controlled by the dimension of the matrix representation and the underlying field. The calculations required more than 67 000 hours of CPU time which is probably more than the common mathematician is able or willing to invest.

However, as pointed out in [8], the times vary greatly depending on the base field and the amount of available memory on the computing slaves.

6   Used computer resources

The actual computation was broken into many small runs. At the beginning of each of the seven double coset enumerations small sequential runs of a few hours were performed to find a new starting point. Then the program was run again on few processors (typically 8) once or twice until enough new orbit points were found to keep many processors busy.

At the start and end of the calculations the 100Mbyte large hash table must be retrieved and stored to disk. To ensure consistency of the table the program waits until all slaves have ceased their computations when stopping. Vice versa, at the beginning of each run, matrices must be broadcasted and tables of linear combinations calculated. This causes several minutes of overhead at the start and end of each run. In order to minimize this overhead, each run was configured to be as long as the batch system allowed.

At the Cornell Theory Center 10h jobs were used, whereas the Computer Center of Karlsruhe University allowed only for a maximum running time of 4 hours. The program was designed to stop 20 minutes early to allow the slaves to finish their current job and the intermediate results to be saved prior to the batch system killing the job. Early versions of the program tried to use Unix signals to make the program stop when desired by the batch system. However, especially with the changes in AIX and POE over the time we did the computations (they began in Cornell at the 21st February 1997), it was not possible to use any Unix signaling.

The program was run on up to 128 nodes (127 slaves). However, it is difficult to allocate 128 nodes simultaneously on a batch system. It turned out to be more efficient to use only 64 nodes. These perform only half as good, but are scheduled more often than 128 node jobs, hence the overall computation proceeds faster. Therefore, almost only 64 node jobs were issued.

Table 6 lists the number of jobs run and the amount of CPU time × nodes we used.

Unfortunately some of the invested computation time was lost. Often the SP/2 crashed during the calculations. Most of the time, this was due to problems with the underlying network file system or when the switch or scheduling system crashed and connection to some of the nodes was lost. Sometimes it was not possible to find the exact cause.

In all, we ran 64 successful runs at Cornell (28 137h) and 383 (84 006h) at Karlsruhe. Those missing from table 6 went wrong due to programming or usage errors. 36 runs (4 509h) were discarded because it turned out the hash function in use was not efficient enough for the computations to be continued. A new one was implemented in a way which did not effect the other double cosets.

Double coset	Cornell Theory Center		University of Karlsruhe	
	Jobs	CPU-time	Jobs	CPU-time
1	–*	–*		
6†	39	19 652h		
5†	10	4 887h	11	4 907h
7	2	1 150h	100	21 181h
3			22	4 686h
2			2	4h
4			108	25 064h
	51	25 689h	243	55 842h

* calculation of this double coset is trivial.
† during this time the Cornell Theory Center was undergoing several reorganizations and we also moved the job several times between the Cornell Theory Center and the University of Karlsruhe. These lines might therefore be incomplete. It should also be noted that the performance of the computing nodes changed over the time. It is therefore not possible to directly compare these run times.
The jobs are listed chronologically as they were found.

Table 6. Number of jobs and cpu time used.

However, the majority of the lost computation time (104 jobs or 23 656h) is due to a wrong construction of the 4th double coset. During the first try the program did not stop finding new points in this double coset despite contradictions within the computations themselves and resulting mistakes within the mathematical context. A second run of the very same program starting with the already existing 6 other double cosets produced a proper result.

The occurence of further bugs in the program is very unlikely. Nevertheless the exact order of the points found depends highly on the timing, i.e. a bug does not need to show up in every run. Still, it seems very unlikely that such a broken program could be run 294 times in a row producing very sensible results.

One should note that the main memory of the machine will already produce 10 1-bit errors due to the refresh cycles during the computations. The programs are very memory access bound, hence the actual number of bit errors is several magnitudes larger, although we were not able to find an explicit estimate in the technical publications. Still, ECC checking should correct most of these and securely detect the others.

However, not all parts of the machine (caches, CPU, memory busses, I/O devices) are protected as welwell as the main memory. During other projects we already learned about broken disk devices returning wrong data without any error indication. As a consequence, we will take this into account for our upcoming projects and perform excessive check summing and even more consistency tests as the current implementation in the future.

7   Documentation of the Results

It is astonishing how simple computations in G become with the hash tables and strong generators. All this data occupies only 120MB of memory. Thus it seems important that these tables are stored in a central place and preserved for future reference. This database might also include explicit permutations which occupy 660MB and are expensive to construct, but are of great use in some situations.

It is intended to publish all intermediate results and tables as a part of the DFG research program *"Elektronische Publikationen im Literatur- und Informationsangebot wissenschaftlicher Bibliotheken"* in digital, directly machine usable form, possibly at the Göttinger Digitalisierungs Zentrum. In the mean time, these data can be requested from the author in urgent cases.

This digital publication will also include all the programs used. All are implemented for calculation in $GL_{1333}(11)$ operating on 45-dimensional subspaces and $GL_{112}(2)$ on vectors. Most important there is:

1. the program generating the orbit of a subgroup. It can be used in parallel and sequential environments. The calculation can be stopped after a given time or in response to external events and continued later. With user interaction the program is also able to construct the orbit in a way reflecting the double coset structure.

   The parallelization was done using Gene D. Cooperman's TOP-C package [5]. It consist of the required framework and manages the tasks. Unfortunately it is mostly designed for and tested on shared memory machines which could not be used for these examples.

   Hence, in conjunction with its author TOP-C was slightly enhanced to be of use in this specific application.
2. a utility counting the hash table entries, building an index table for the used entries and compressing the hash table by removing unused entries.
3. a program using the compressed table to construct vectors and subspaces corresponding to hash entries, apply generators or other matrices to them and inspect the result (this includes locating it in the hash table). This program is also able to construct the matrices used in [15].
4. a variation of the last program which transforms matrices to explicit permutations on all points or a certain double coset (if possible). Again, parallel versions using TOP-C exist.

8   Acknowledgments

The author thanks Gene D. Cooperman, Holger Gollan, Wolfgang Lempken, Gerhard O. Michler, Reiner Staszewski for the helpful and constructive comments given in continuous private communication while working on this subject.

A substantial part of the high performance computations was conducted using the resources of the Cornell Theory Center, which receives major funding from the National Science Foundation and New York State with additional support from the Research Resources at the National Institutes of Health, IBM Cooperation and members of the Corporate Research Institute. The total computing time on all the involved nodes was 28 137 CPU-h. The author owes special thanks to Professor J. Guckenheimer and Dr. A. Hoisie for their support.

The author also would like to thank the Computer Center of Karlsruhe University for providing 84 006 CPU-h on their supercomputer IBM RS/6000 SP with 256 nodes. This help was necessary to complete the above mentioned computations. The author is very grateful to Professor W. Schönauer for his assistance.

Finally, small parallel test runs were done at the 32 node IBM SP/2 of the GMD, St. Augustin, Germany for debugging purposes.

References

1. D. J. Benson. *The Simple Group J_4*. PhD thesis, Trinity College, Cambridge, August 1980.
2. W. Bosma and J. Cannon. *Handbook of* MAGMA *functions*. Department of Pure Mathematics, University of Sydney, 1994.
3. G. Butler. *Fundamental Algorithms for Permutation Groups*, volume 559 of *Lecture Notes in Comput. Sci.* Springer-Verlag, Berlin, Heidelberg, New York, 1991.
4. J. Cannon and G. Havas. Algorithms for groups. *Australian Computer Journal*, 24(2):51–60, 1992.
5. G. Cooperman. TOP-C: a Task-Oriented Parallel C interface. In 5th *International Symposium on High Performance Distributed Computing (*HPDC-5*)*, pages 141–150. IEEE Press, 1996.
6. G. Cooperman, L. Finkelstein, M. Tselman, and B. York. Constructing permutation representations for matrix groups. *J. Symbolic Comput.*, 1997.
7. G. Cooperman, W. Lempken, M. Weller, and G. O. Michler. A new existence proof of Janko's simple group J_4. Preprint, 1997.
8. P. Fleischmann, G. O. Michler, P. Roelse, J. Rosenboom, R. Staszewski, C. Wagner, and M. Weller. *Linear Algebra over Small Finite Fields on Parallel Machines*, volume 23 of *Vorlesungen aus dem Fachbereich Mathematik*. University of Essen, 1995.

9. H. W. Gollan. A new existence proof for Ly, the sporadic simple group of R. Lyons. Preprint 30, Institut für Experimentelle Mathematik, University of Essen, Ellernstraße 29, 45326 Essen, Germany, 1995.

10. Z. Janko. A new finite simple group of order 86,775,571,046,077,562,880 which possesses M_{24} and the full covering group of M_{22} as subgroups. *J. Algebra*, 42:564–596, 1976.

11. W. Lempken. Constructing J_4 in GL(1333, 11). *Comm. Algebra*, 21:4311–3251, 1993.

12. S. Norton. The construction of J_4. In B. Cooperstein and G. Mason, editors, *Proc. Santa Cruz Conference on Finite Groups*, pages 271–277. Amer. Math. Soc., 1980.

13. R. Parker. The computer calculation of modular characters (the Meat-Axe). In M. Atkinson, editor, *Computational Group Theory*, pages 267–274, London, New York, 1984. (Durham, 1982), Academic Press.

14. M. Ringe. *The C MeatAxe.* Lehrstuhl D für Mathematik, RWTH, Aachen, 1992.

15. M. Weller and G. O. Michler. A new computer construction of the irreducible 112-dimensional 2-modular representation of Janko's group J_4. In preparation, 1997.

Lecture Notes in Computational Science and Engineering

Series Editor:
M. Griebel, D.E. Keyes, R.M. Nieminen, D. Roose, T. Schlick.

This series covers monographs, lecture course material, and high-quality proceedings on topics from all subspecialties described by the term "computational science and engineering". This includes theoretical aspects of scientific computing such as mathematical modeling, optimization methods, discretization techniques, multiscale approaches, fast solution algorithms, parallelization, and visualization methods as well as the application of these approaches throughout the disciplines of biology, chemistry, physics, engineering, earth sciences, and economics.

Spectral Elements
for Transport-Dominated
Equations

Volume 1
D. Funaro
Spectral Elements for Transport-Dominated Equations
1997. X, 211 pp. 97 figs., 12 tabs.
Softcover DM 78,-
ISBN 3-540-62649-2

Volume 2
H.P. Langtangen
Computational Partial Differential Equations
Numerical Methods and
Diffpack Programming
1999. XXIV, 658 pp.,
with CD-ROM.
Hardcover
ISBN 3-540-65274-4

Volume 3
W. Hackbusch,
G. Wittum (Eds.)
Multigrid Methods V
Proceedings of the Fifth
European Multigrid
Conference held in Stuttgart,
Germany, October 1-4, 1996
1998. VIII, 334 pp.
Softcover DM 129,-
ISBN 3-540-63133-X

Volume 4
P. Deuflhard, J. Hermans,
B. Leimkuhler, A. Mark,
S. Reich, R.D. Skeel (Eds.)
Computational Molecular Dynamics: Challenges, Methods, Ideas
Proceedings of the 2nd
International Symposium
on Algorithms for Macro-
molecular Modelling,
Berlin, May 21-24, 1997
1998. XI, 489 pp.
Softcover DM 149,-
ISBN 3-540-63242-5

Volume 5
D. Kröner, M. Ohlberger,
C. Rohde (Eds.)
An Introduction to Recent Developments in Theory and Numerics for Conservation Laws
Proceedings of the Inter-
national School on Theory
and Numerics for Conser-
vation Laws, Freiburg/
Littenweiler,
October 20-24, 1997
1998. VIII, 284 pp
Softcover DM 129,-
ISBN 3-540-65081-4

Please order from
Springer-Verlag Berlin
Fax: + 49 / 30 / 8 27 87- 301
e-mail: orders@springer.de
or through your bookseller

■ ■ ■ ■ ■ ■ ■ ■ ■ ■

Springer

Springer-Verlag, P. O. Box 14 02 01, D-14302 Berlin, Germany.

Gha.

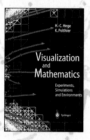

C.W. Ueberhuber
Numerical Computation 1
Methods, Software, and Analysis
1997. XVI, 474 pp. 157 figs.
Softcover DM 68,-
ISBN 3-540-62058-3

A modern, two-volume introduction to numerical computation, which strongly emphasizes software aspects. It can serve as a textbook for courses on numerical analysis, particularly for engineers. The book can also be used as a reference book and it includes an extensive bibliography. The author is a well-known specialist in numerical analysis who was involved in the creation of the software package QUADPACK.

See also:

C.W. Ueberhuber
Numerical Computation 2
Methods, Software, and Analysis
1997. XVI, 495 pp. 73 figs.
Softcover DM 68,-
ISBN 3-540-62057-5

Computing and Visualization in Science
Managing Editor:
G. Wittum

This journal publishes papers presenting new methods and new areas of applications where these techniques make the solution of complex problems faster, more reliable or even possible at all. Making full use of the potential of electronic publishing, the journal offers additional electronic material via Internet.

Subscription information for 1999:

Volume 2, 4 issues each
DM 480,-

ISSN 1432-9360 (print)   Title No. 791
ISSN 1433-0369 (electronic)

Please order from
Springer-Verlag Berlin
Books: Fax: + 49 / 30 / 8 27 87- 301
e-mail: orders@springer.de
Journals: Fax: + 49 / 30 / 8 27 87- 448
e-mail: subscriptions@springer.de
or through your bookseller

Springer

Printing: Mercedesdruck, Berlin
Binding: Buchbinderei Lüderitz & Bauer, Berlin